Selves: Drama in Perspective

Selves:
Drama in Perspective

edited by
IRVING DEER *AND* HARRIET A. DEER
University of South Florida

HARCOURT BRACE JOVANOVICH, INC.
New York   Chicago   San Francisco   Atlanta

© 1975 by Harcourt Brace Jovanovich, Inc.

All rights reserved. No part of this publication may be reproduced or transmitted in any form or by any means, electronic or mechanical, including photocopy, recording, or any information storage and retrieval system, without permission in writing from the publisher.

ISBN: 0-15-579633-X

Library of Congress Catalog Card Number: 74-28820

Printed in the United States of America

COVER: Set and lighting design by Jo Mielziner.

To Our Parents:

Ethel Godinger Deer
James Smith Hall
Martha Andrews Hall

Preface

Selves: Drama in Perspective has two principal functions: one, to focus on past and present concepts of western drama and, two, to show how drama reveals the individual's perennial search for self-fulfillment. These functions are not only interrelated but vitally interdependent; for when they present their concepts of drama, playwrights generally reveal their attitudes toward the search for self-fulfillment. Those playwrights who consider the self subordinate to the design of the universe tend to subordinate character to plot, as Sophocles does in *Oedipus the King;* while those who consider the self superior usually make character at least as important if not more important than plot, as Ibsen does in *A Doll's House.* Similarly, playwrights who see diminishing order in the universe generally create characters who, like the protagonist in Strindberg's *Miss Julie,* are in danger of losing their sense of themselves and their place in the world. Playwrights who see no immanent order in the universe or society—only an arbitrary one imposed by human beings—tend to write extremely subjective plays wherein the characters try to create order through their own imaginations, as is demonstrated in Giraudoux's *Madwoman of Chaillot* and Bullins's *A Son, Come Home.*

To the extent that it fulfills these principal functions, this anthology can be used in two ways: one to study different literary approaches to the search for self-knowledge and, two, to analyze changes in the forms of drama, that is, transformations in the idea of drama itself. Using the book in the first way involves an examination of the themes and ideas expressed in the plays. Using it in the second way requires scrutiny of the elements of the plays—their form and structure, the kinds of plots, characters, dialogue, and spectacle they include.

In addition to its special concern with the theme of self-realization and the ways in which writers have treated this theme, the collection offers several other distinctive features. A section of the Introduction, for example, is devoted to a discussion of fundamentals in the actual presentation of a play—sets, costumes, placement of characters and so on—and to an analysis of how those fundamentals can be used to express a play's main conflicts and meanings. This discussion attempts to make it clear that a play is both literature and theater, both a literary expression and a living spectacle. An understanding of this principle, often lacking in those who have not seen performances of the plays they have read, can make the reading of a play a vital experience that engages all our faculties and stretches not merely our minds but our imaginations as well.

Another feature of the volume is the inclusion of a film script and the story on which the script was based. These paired selections allow the reader to see how the theme of self-realization has been handled in two other media, and, more generally, to begin to examine the relationship between literature and film. Since most of the plays in this collection have been the basis for a film, we hope that such an examination will include their adaptations as well; and, thus, a filmography has been provided at the end of the book.

Yet another special feature of the book is the aid it offers the reader who is interested in writing about plays and films. For, along with an appendix that presents basic questions a student should ask in developing a theme subject, the book also includes critical analyses of the selections that can serve as models for themes. In addition, each of these analyses is followed by a list of discussion and theme questions.

We hope that the special features of this collection will help students and teachers to enjoy the plays more than they otherwise might. Ultimately, however, the value of the collection will rest on the interest aroused by the selections themselves. We believe that, like us, the reader will find that they have both literary appeal and value in understanding society and ourselves.

Irving Deer
Harriet A. Deer

Contents

Preface	vii
Introduction	
I. The Selections	1
II. Key Elements of Drama	7
III. Dramatic Presentation and Meaning	16
Sophocles	
OEDIPUS THE KING	22
Translated by Bernard Knox	
DISCUSSION	57
Theme and Discussion Questions	60
William Shakespeare	
OTHELLO	62
Edited by G. B. Harrison	
DISCUSSION	155
Theme and Discussion Questions	158
Henrik Ibsen	
A DOLL'S HOUSE	160
Translated by Rolf Fjelde	
DISCUSSION	220
Theme and Discussion Questions	222

August Strindberg
MISS JULIE — 224
   Miss Julie, A Foreword — 255
Translated by Elizabeth Sprigge
   DISCUSSION — 266
   Theme and Discussion Questions — 268

Jean Giraudoux
THE MADWOMAN OF CHAILLOT — 270
Adapted by Maurice Valency
   DISCUSSION — 330
   Theme and Discussion Questions — 332

Arthur Miller
DEATH OF A SALESMAN — 334
   DISCUSSION — 414
   Theme and Discussion Questions — 417

Ed Bullins
A SON, COME HOME — 418
   DISCUSSION — 432
   Theme and Discussion Questions — 434

Stephen Crane
"THE BRIDE COMES TO YELLOW SKY" — 435

James Agee
THE BRIDE COMES TO YELLOW SKY (a film script) — 446
   Glossary of Film Terms — 448
   DISCUSSION — 478
   Theme and Discussion Questions — 481

APPENDIXES
   Approaches to Writing about Drama and Film — 485
   Filmography — 491

Selves: Drama in Perspective

Introduction

I. THE SELECTIONS

One of the most probing and important questions a human being can ask is: "Who am I?" Of course, that question can be asked on many different levels. For example, "What's My Line," the well-known television program, has for years had "mystery guests" whose names the panelists try to guess. They are concerned simply with a factual answer. The characters in great drama, on the other hand, usually mean a great deal more when they pose this question. The answer they seek is often factual, psychological, social, and even religious all at the same time. For in creating characters who are seeking an answer to this question, playwrights have sought to explore the ultimate mystery of existence itself; to help us discover the answers to yet another question: "What is mankind?"

Among the great plays that focus on this search for identity is Sophocles' *Oedipus the King*. This Greek play is literally based on Oedipus' struggles with the question, "Who am I?" At the beginning of the play, Oedipus thinks he knows who he is; but as the play progresses, he begins to question that knowledge and, in doing so, to explore what he means to Thebes, the community he rules. At first, he thinks he is its savior: by solving the riddle of the Sphinx, he rescued his community from the plague that was destroying it; and once he became king, he ruled well. But now, having been told by Tiresias that he is the cause of a new plague that is attacking Thebes, Oedipus must discover whether he is the savior of his community or its destroyer.

In order to do that, he must find out who he is—first, in terms of parentage. Is he really the son of the king of Corinth, or is he the son of Laius and Jocasta, the Theban woman he has married? Second, he must learn who he is psychologically. He has believed himself to be superior to other men, both intellectually and morally; but under the stress of Tiresias' accusations, his reason is beginning to break down. Oedipus frequently loses his temper, leaps to unwarranted conclusions about Creon and Tiresias, and fluctuates almost senselessly between feelings of joy and despair. Moreover, he discovers in himself an underlying sense of guilt, for which he can find no explanation. Finally, he must learn who he is morally and religiously. Despite the fact that many Thebans consider him "the best of men," the gods are apparently punishing him more severely than they punish lesser men; and he is unable to make sense of a universe in which the best men are punished the most. Is the universe merely chaotic and arbitrary, without meaning and purpose, or is he, perhaps, guilty of such heinous crimes that his punishment is deserved? If he is unwittingly guilty of having murdered his father and married his mother, he must learn how he can face the consequences of such enormous guilt. In sum, before he can truly know who he is—whether he is, in the final analysis, creative or destructive, just or unjust, brave or cowardly, good or evil—he must discover his capacity for living a significant life in the face of the knowledge of his origins, of what he has done, and of how he fits into the universe.

As we watch Oedipus' struggle, we become aware that a man's sense of his identity is deeply dependent not only on his knowledge of himself but on his perception of his relationship to his society and to the universe. This last concern has often been thought of as moral and religious or, since the nineteenth century, as being related to the laws of nature. Oedipus' struggle to discover who he is in each of these ways suggests that a person's identity rests on what seem to be irreconcilable contradictions in his character. He learns, for example, that he is governed by passion as much as by reason; that, although capable of brutality, he is also capable of great love; that, although afraid of the truth, he also wants to discover it; that, although not a god, he is capable of living with dignity; that, although corrupt, he wants to expiate his sins.

By the end of the play, both Oedipus and his community have arrived at the same evaluation of his character; the people have come to see him as a limited but noble human being, and he has learned that not even a king is omniscient. Moreover, both Oedipus and the community have learned to recognize and respect the infinite power of the gods.

Shakespeare's *Othello* also shows the intense struggle and deep suffering an individual may experience when he lacks self-knowledge. Othello, like Oedipus, is a man who acts rashly because he is unaware of the contradictions within himself. He does not, for example, recognize that there are conflicts between his military and domestic values, and between the pagan traditions he was born into and the Christian traditions he has adopted. Inexperienced in love, he is unaware of his capacity for jealousy, a jealousy that Iago can arouse to frenzy because Othello misunderstands the familiarity common between Venetian men and women and is, moreover, unsure whether, as a foreigner of another race, he is fully accepted by either Venetian society or his own wife. Othello is overtaken by disaster because he cannot discover the conflicts and contradictions within himself quickly enough to control his rash acts.

In Henrik Ibsen's *A Doll's House,* the implications of the struggle between a husband and wife, the use of the family as a metaphor for nature and the universe, are far less important and overt than in Shakespeare's *Othello.* The family still serves as a metaphor for society; if it is an institution in which fulfillment is impossible, so is society in general such an institution. The predicament in which Ibsen's protagonist Nora finds herself is caused not only by her husband but by the values of their society. Those values demand that she play a role subordinate to that of her husband and his egotistical desires for success, rather than be a person in her own right. Only when she discovers that she has been blind to her true status, that she has gone along with society's demand that she be a doll in her husband's house, is she able to assert herself and to begin the struggle for self-fulfillment. In this play, Ibsen sees such fulfillment as something the individual alone can achieve—if such achievement is at all possible—not as something an external agency, such as a god or nature, makes possible. For Ibsen, society is intrinsically hostile to the individual; therefore, man must somehow fulfill himself in isolation from society.

This concept, which grew out of the nineteenth century Romantic idea that the isolated individual is more important than the individual as a member of the community, is extremely different from what Sophocles and Shakespeare meant by self-fulfillment. The problem with this more modern view is that, eventually, the writer must in some way show that the individual and society can be reconciled. How this will ever be possible for Nora, given the fact that Ibsen sees her society as being essentially hostile to her desire for independent status and self-fulfillment, is not among the main concerns of *A Doll's House.* There is a hint at the end of the play that such reconciliation is possible, that Nora may be able to return to Torvald, but that possibility is clearly shown as being very remote. Ibsen's personal struggle as a playwright—to find some way of believing that, although the individual alone can achieve self-fulfillment, there must also be some way for him to act in society—was one of his main concerns throughout his career. Although dealing with this problem at length is beyond the scope of this collection, mention of it here does give us an indication of how the emphasis on individuality in the last hundred years seems to have led dramatists into an impasse, and it hints at some of the reasons why the struggle for self-fulfillment is so perplexing today. If modern man is confronting a society —indeed, an entire world—that is his absolute enemy, how can he ever use any of the traditional means of handling the problem of gaining self-fulfillment? For Oedipus and Othello, only society and nature are the enemy; and, in the end, a reconciliation is not only possible but essential for self-fulfillment. For Ibsen, that reconciliation is almost impossible. How, then, can self-fulfillment be achieved?

The principal character in Strindberg's *Miss Julie* also finds herself the victim of the external world. Although she wants to know who she is, socially and emotionally, everything around her seems to conspire against her quest for self-knowledge. The time of the play is Midsummer's Eve. The scent of lilacs, the warmth of the night, the flush of revelry—all lead to the moment of her seduction by her father's valet. And once she allows herself to be seduced, her illusions about her status in the world are shattered. She is not a grand lady, her wealth does not earn her respect, and she is not exempt from common passion.

Faced with all this, Julie attempts to build up new illusions. Perhaps, she thinks, Jean the valet is noble. She soon sees, however, that he is totally self-seeking and materialistic. Perhaps, then, she can furnish enough money so that they can have a wonderful future together running a Swiss hotel. But that illusion, too, vanishes, for Jean makes Julie understand that she will be only a servant in the hotel, and that the household will also include her servant girl, Christine, who is in love with Jean. Unable to manufacture any more illusions to shield herself from Jean's brutality and cowardice, Julie can no longer act in the world, so she attempts to turn inward to search for her identity. When she does, she discovers that she has no real identity, only a collection of false images she has presented to the world.

The next play in this collection, Jean Giraudoux's *The Madwoman of Chaillot,* also deals with the individual's adjustment to society, though in a less intense and more humorous way. The world of Giraudoux's play is a world run by faceless, inhuman, mechanical people dedicated only to their greed for gold. For the sake of profit, they manipulate everything and everyone, from the stock market to the beggars on the street. Love, truth, and beauty have no appeal to them; none is a means to profit. These values have all but disappeared from the face of the earth, remaining only in the dreams and fantasies of the Madwoman and her friends.

Giraudoux's play is a sign of the growing recognition among writers since the Second World War that realism is only one of many alternative forms of drama. If, as Miss Julie discovered, people spend all their time trying to manipulate one another, if external reality has little or no room for meaningful action, for love, or for beauty, all that remains for one to turn to is internal reality, the realm of dream and fantasy. It is an especially paradoxical occurrence of our time that many of our best writers and intellects are beginning to accept the truth embodied in fiction and fantasy as more valid than the manipulated truths evidenced everywhere in the real, external world. This is not to say that we can all improve our lives by simply retreating into dreams. Giraudoux clearly conveys the idea that it is up to us to apply whatever lessons we draw from the play. He advocates no course of action, suggesting only that, whatever we do, we must be human about it. If we are to have meaningful selves, if we are to be anything more than interchangeable parts in a society conceived as an industrial machine, we must, he shows us, assert the element of humanity above all else and in the face of any obstacle.

Retreating into ourselves in the manner of Miss Julie and the Madwoman does us no good unless it helps us to return to the world and lead better lives. Thus, the dream world of Willy Loman in Arthur Miller's *Death of a Salesman* is a futile and destructive one. Willy's dreams are a means of escaping from life rather than affirming it. There is something terribly wrong in his business-oriented world; his dreams of success are based on a set of outmoded notions that Miller labels "the American dream." The pathos of Willy's predicament is that he genuinely believes that his worth as a human being rests solely on his capacity to hold his job. Faced with joblessness, he retreats into daydreams of the past. He remembers the struggles to pay the grocery bills, but he invents for himself a past career of fabulous success. And even here, Willy cannot see the contradictions between his beliefs and the facts.

In the most recent play in this collection, Ed Bullins' *A Son, Come Home,* a retreat into the self is a way of dealing with a world where even language seems to deny the individual his right to be himself. Bullins explores the problem of a young black man who can never express his feelings to his mother because the conventions of family relationships and polite conversation deny the propriety of doing so. As the son tries to communicate with his mother, he comes to understand that perhaps there is greater integrity and self-fulfillment in silence than in the dishonest language conventions of civilized discourse. But the price for silence is very great. If the son cannot talk about the past, he cannot really explore it and put it into perspective. He cannot, therefore, ever come to a full recognition of who and what he is. In order to maintain his uniqueness, then, the son must sacrifice having a full sense of his own identity.

Bullins' recognition that people can achieve full identity only if the conventions of the world permit them to express themselves is a theme of many other works of American literature. Among these is Stephen Crane's short story "The Bride Comes to Yellow Sky," which was written in 1899 and adapted for film by James Agee in 1952; both versions are included in this volume. Broadly comic in tone, they present two figures of the old West who, as young men, found their identities in the codes of gunfighting and violence, but who now face a world in which gunfighting is no longer acceptable. One of these men finds ways of modifying his codes and his identity to fit the onrush of civilization; the other insists on maintaining the old ways and is driven into isolation. Through these characters, Crane explores the problem of identifying oneself with vanishing codes and social structures. And if discussions of it in the works of contemporary artists are a measure, this problem has become a common one in today's changeable and complex world.

We can see, then, from even this preliminary survey of the plays in this collection, that man's quest to know himself has always been one of his most important and challenging pursuits. We need hardly dwell on the implications of the search for identity to recognize how significant it still is today. In the last decade, our society has been wracked by internal dissension unequalled at least since the Civil War. Ethnic minorities, the young, women, and the poor have maintained that society denies them a full identity. They rebel against what seems to them a society that catalogues, classifies, and stereotypes them, that pays no attention to their values or even punishes them for having such values, that seems to them willing to literally destroy humanity in the service of abstractions. Whatever we may feel as individuals about any of the specific issues that torment modern society, through imaginative participation in the struggles of the men and women represented in these plays, we may come to a better understanding of ourselves and our place in the world.

II. KEY ELEMENTS OF DRAMA

All drama is the expression of conflict—that is, of one force acting against another. Whether the forces involved in a play are external or internal, concrete or abstract, their opposition creates the possibility for a wide range of complex responses. What problems the conflict suggests depend on the kinds of characters involved, their motives, the social situation (family, economy, larger society) in which the characters find themselves, and on their general moral assumptions about themselves and the rest of the world.

Thus, in order to analyze and understand even the simplest play, it is helpful to focus on certain basic aspects of the dramatic conflict: the *plot*—that is, both what happens and how it happens as well; the *action*—what the characters want to achieve and how their behavior helps or hinders them in achieving these goals; and the *theme*—what kind of statement the playwright is making. Each of these aspects is a major element of drama, a factor that must be understood and analyzed if the reader is to gain an active appreciation of the conflict. For, in any good play, anything that happens is expressed through conflict rather than presented as mere information. Therefore, we should be able to see the conflict underlying any detail in a play and, if we examine it carefully, this should lead us to the discovery of the main conflict of the play.

The reader who has learned to recognize and analyze these major elements can experience a much deeper and livelier participation in a play than he otherwise would. He can pick out details, anticipate action, feel with the characters as they fight through their internal or external struggles and, in short, become a creative partner to the playwright as the play unfolds. The following explanations of dramatic elements can help you to become such a creative participant. After each description, you will find questions designed to help you discover for yourselves the particular ways in which each playwright uses these elements.

Character

We come to know the characters in a drama in three ways: by what they do, by what they say about themselves, and by what others say about them. For example, we know Strindberg's Miss Julie, not only through what she says about herself, but also through the cynical evaluations of her made by Jean and Christine. More important, we know Julie through what she does—her orders to "abort her bitch," her treatment of Jean and Christine, and her willingness to be seduced. Without what we learn from Julie herself, from the criticisms of Jean and Christine, and from our own evaluation of her behavior, we might not understand Julie's conflict between freedom and tradition, passion and supremacy, comradery and aristocracy.

Questions to Help You Analyze Character:

1. What does the character say about himself?
2. What do others say about him?
3. What does the character do and say to support or contradict what he says about himself?
4. What do other characters do and say to support or contradict what they say about him?
5. To what extent do statements made by the character show an understanding of his personal predicament and the general conditions—physical, social, and moral—of the world in which he lives?
6. How favorably does the character appraise himself at the beginning of the play? At the end of it? What does his change of attitude (or lack of change) tell us about how well he has faced the problems that confronted him?
7. Does the character seem to be realistic—that is, capable of both good and evil, of many dimensions and contradictory desires—or is he a "flat" character, capable of only one kind of action or response?

8. Does the character share the attitudes and values of other characters in the play, or are his attitudes and values unique to him? If his attitudes and values are unique, how do we come to understand what they are? How do his values affect his actions?

Plot

In common parlance, when someone asks about the plot of a play or film, we assume that they are asking us to tell them the story. In the most general sense, plot is "what happens." However, according to Aristotle, whose definition is the basis for the modern concept of plot, it is more than simply "what happens": it is the "arrangement of incidents" in a play. In other words, the plot of a play includes not only *what* happens but also *how* it happens, the way the playwright *orders* the events that take place.

Aristotle used Sophocles' *Oedipus the King* to explain this definition, and today, this ancient play remains a good illustration of what he meant. Sophocles arranges the incidents of the play to highlight Oedipus' struggle to know who he is, not his struggle to avoid his fate. Instead of showing him first as a respected ruler, the playwright could have started at several other points in the history of Oedipus—with his birth, with the prophecy that he would kill his father and marry his mother, with the riddle of the Sphinx, with his marriage to Jocasta—and each different starting point would have produced a different drama. If, for example, Sophocles had started with Oedipus' encounter with Laius, we might have had a story about how violence begets violence. We would have focused our attention primarily on how the killing of Laius caused Oedipus' later problems. As Sophocles handles the killing of Laius, however, it is merely one incident contributing to Oedipus' predicament, no more important than the prophecy or Oedipus' own blindness to his irrational nature. If Sophocles had started with Oedipus' encounter with the oracle, we would have had a story about how the gods pursue man even when man seems most fortunate. Our attention would focus on Oedipus' struggle to avoid his fate, not on his attempt to confront it.

Playwrights sometimes include plot incidents, not only to explain what happens, but also to help us understand the nature of their central characters. We may, perhaps, understand this most easily by looking at *Othello*. Shakespeare could have arranged his story so that it went quickly from the marriage to the brawl on Cypress. But if he had done so, we would not have been able to witness Othello's behavior before the night watch and the Senate or Desdemona's defense of her marriage, and we would miss the entire point that, potentially, Othello and Desdemona are exceptionally noble and creative human beings.

Finally, a playwright sometimes treats the plot incidents unconventionally in order to show the significance of those incidents for a particular character. For example, many of the incidents in *Death of a Salesman* seem to materialize from Willy's memory and represent Willy's personal interpretation of the past. Miller presents the events that way to show that, literal reality notwithstanding, Willy believes that his sons are capable of greatness, that only money stands between them and "magnificence." Because we see Willy's perspective, we can recognize his capacity for love as well as for folly; we can see his suicide as an act of generosity as well as an escape from futility.

Questions to Help You Analyze Plot:

1. From what you learn of the total story involved in the play, what other incidents might the playwright have used as an opening? How would each of these different openings have influenced the meaning of later events and the theme of the play?
2. How is the actual initial incident a clue to the conflicts and attitudes later stressed in the play?
3. How does each incident in the beginning and the middle of the play serve to create a need for further action?
4. What choices do the characters make in each incident? How do these choices force the characters to take further action? In what specific ways do the choices of the characters serve either to complicate or to simplify their situations?
5. Which incidents in the play seem to exist in the "real" world, and which seem to be projections of the characters' minds? Do details of the "projected" scenes conflict with details of the "real" scenes? If so, what can you tell about the way a character helps to create his own difficulties? What can you learn about how a character feels toward the world he lives in? What can you tell about why he has difficulty in solving his problems?

6. In some plays, the action rises to a climax, or crisis, in which the final action is determined, and then drops to a dénouement, in which the consequences of the hero's actions become apparent. Do all the plays in this collection follow this pattern? Look particularly at *Death of a Salesman* and *A Son, Come Home*. If they vary in structure, how do they differ, and what does the variation tell you about whether or not the major conflict is resolved?

Action

Aristotle defined drama as "the imitation of an action." Though what he meant by that phrase has been the subject of controversy, most subsequent critics and playwrights have agreed that action is the very heart of drama. Action can be usefully defined both as what a character is trying to achieve or avoid and as the central movement that holds a play together.

Aristotle was always careful to describe the action of a play in terms of an infinitive—to marry, to discover the identity of, to revenge, and so on—and the infinitive remains the appropriate verb form for several reasons: first, if you think of action in terms of an infinitive, you emphasize what the character wants to do in the future, the motive that gives the play its forward thrust. Oedipus wants to know his past, not merely out of curiosity, but so that he can act in the future; the past matters to him primarily as it provides a base for future action. Ed Bullins' protagonist in *A Son, Come Home* also wants a better understanding of the past so that he can cope with the future.

Second, if the reader thinks of action as an infinitive, he is more likely to see the way the characters of a play relate to each other and fit together to form a unified drama. In *Death of a Salesman,* for example, almost everyone in the play wants "to succeed," but they have very limited definitions of success. Willy, Biff, and Happy all want to succeed financially; Linda wants to be a successful wife and, secondarily, a successful mother; Howard wants to be an organizational success; and Charlie, a successful friend. Every scene in the play shows one of the characters in pursuit of some form of success. By looking both at what they want to do and what keeps them from achieving their goals—what keeps them from replacing the infinitive with the past tense, if you will—we can understand the structure of the play, what gives it its coherence, unity, and forward progression.

Third, and equally important, by thinking of the action of a play as an infinitive that the characters are trying to act out, we can more easily understand what the playwright is contending are the means and problems involved in achieving the characters' particular goal. For example, by watching the characters in Miller's play try to succeed, we discover some of the ways in which people define and pursue success, and some of the hazards of each approach.

Questions to Help You Analyze Action:

1. What are the goals of the characters in the play?
2. What keeps each character from achieving his goal?
3. What do these barriers tell us about how each character defines his goals?
4. What single major goal are most of the characters trying to achieve?
5. How does our interpretation of the action change as we watch the characters try to achieve their goals?
6. How do the words of the characters—their thoughts, the images they use, and the "philosophical" or apparently nondramatic speeches—contribute to the action?
7. How does each scene help to move the central characters closer to or farther away from their goals?

Dialogue

The dialogue in a play is, simply, the words spoken by the characters. Usually in the form of a give-and-take between two characters, dramatic dialogue can also include a speech by one character to many, a soliloquy (like Hamlet's "to be or not to be" speech), a line delivered from offstage, a shout by a character who is having a nightmare, or any other utterances assigned to the characters by the playwright. The words in most plays can be considered a form of action, as effective in helping a character to achieve his goals as a duel or a fight would be. This view of words is not unrealistic, since in most societies people fight much more often with words than with pistols, knives, or fists.

If words are a form of physical action, like other physical actions in a good play, they should be motivated—that is, they should be caused by some kind of pressure on the character who speaks them. A line of dramatic dialogue should never be a statement that is entirely unrelated to the action, no matter how irrelevant it may seem; each line of dialogue should represent a response to a need felt by the character who speaks it.

Questions to Help You Analyze Dialogue:

1. When one character talks about himself to others
   a) What facts about himself does he stress? What facts does he ignore or underplay?
   b) Does he seem to be learning anything about himself?
   c) How does he adjust his conversation to take into account the person to whom he is speaking?
   d) What does his failure to adjust either to those to whom he is speaking or to their responses to his dialogue tell you about a particular character?
2. When one character talks about another character
   a) Do his descriptions agree with what we have seen and heard from other sources?
   b) Do his descriptions suggest concealed dislike toward or unexpressed attraction for the other character? If so, is the speaker aware of his true feelings?
   c) Do his descriptions reveal insight into others that is concealed from the rest of the characters?
3. When characters conflict openly with each other in an exchange of dialogue
   a) Do they express the real conflict between them, or are they fighting about something only indirectly related to the real conflict?
   b) Do all of the characters involved recognize the real conflict? What words does each use that show his understanding of the conflict?
4. When a character talks about past events
   a) Does his account accurately reflect what you have seen on stage? If not, how does it vary?
   b) Does his account of unseen events confirm or contradict what other characters say about the same events? In what ways?

    c) What kinds of images and emotional language does he use in describing these events? What does his language tell you about how he feels about the past?
    d) Does he find private meanings in them—that is, meanings that are not apparent to the other characters? If so, why do these private meanings seem justified, or unjustified, by the action? What do the excesses of the character tell you about how he faces or avoids conflicts?
5. When a character "philosophizes" about the larger implications of a conflict in which he is engaged
    a) Is the character learning something new about the meaning of this conflict?
    b) Is the dialogue a way for the character to think over his situation before taking further action, or is it simply a way to give information to the audience?
    c) Is the audience learning something new, even if the character is not?
    d) Do the conclusions the character reaches help him to act purposefully, or do they plunge him into even deeper difficulties? Or both?
6. When two characters seem to be "playing games" with each other through dialogue
    a) Are both characters playing the same game?
    b) Is the primary purpose of the playful dialogue what it appears to be, or is there some deeper purpose? (For example, when Julie and Jean exchange polite witticisms throughout the first act of *Miss Julie,* is the exchange merely a harmless display of wits, or is each character trying to dominate the other in some deeper sense?
7. Sometimes a character will use words that mean little to those around him. He will talk to himself and often appear to be in a dream.
    a) Why does a particular character talk only to himself?
    b) Why does the language a character uses have full meaning only to him?
    c) By retreating into dream states, does the character confront or avoid his problems? What words and images does he use that reveal how he deals with conflict in these private or dreamlike moments?

Theme

The theme of a play is the fundamental idea that emerges from the combination of conflicts and actions presented in the drama. It is the universal statement implied by the events of the play, not simply its subject. All of the plays in this collection deal with the general subject of "self." Yet each play makes a different statement about the problem of dealing with or achieving a sense of self.

A theme of a good play is, at the same time, both particular and universal, concrete and abstract. Though it is revealed through the circumstances of particular imaginary or fictionalized characters, it has general significance for actual human beings as well. A great play, such as *Oedipus the King* or *Othello,* usually offers several themes, all of which are related and can be supported by the details of the drama. From the perspective of this collection, a good statement of the theme of *Oedipus the King* would be: A man knows himself only when he knows the evil he is capable of as well as the good. From another perspective, one could define the theme as: Man is capable of greatness in the face of disaster. For *Othello,* one might say: A man who is estranged from his own culture cannot know himself. From another perspective, it would be equally valid to say that *Othello* is based on the theme that "innocence is a mortal sin." Each of these themes can be pinned to the actions of the play from which it is derived. A theme is, then, a general statement that comes out of the play's conflict and is qualified by the dramatic elements, which are themselves expressions of the play's conflict.

Questions to Help You Analyze Theme:

1. How does the plot express the theme?
2. How does the choice of characters express the theme?
3. How does the spectacle of the play support the theme?
4. How does the emotional interaction among the characters express the theme?
5. How do specific incidents in the play contribute to the theme?
6. How do recurrent images in the dialogue express the theme?
7. How is the theme qualified by the unrealistic qualities of the characters and scenes?

III. DRAMATIC PRESENTATION AND MEANING

Since most of what we come to know about the conflicts of the characters in a play we learn through their spoken words, drama is generally thought of as the expression of conflict through dialogue. Readers of drama are thus likely to forget that, along with their emphasis on language, most plays are meant to include certain production details and physical actions. These elements of a play, described collectively by Aristotle as spectacle, are generally only suggested by the playwright, rather than described in detail. Thus, the reader of a play must develop his own sense of how it looks onstage. For the reader of this collection, developing such a sense of production will probably be most difficult in regard to *Oedipus the King* and *Othello*, examples of the ancient Greek and Elizabethan periods respectively.

To the modern reader, the Greek play seems a very austere kind of drama. The characters talk in highly stylized ways; a chorus sings formal songs; and there is no physical violence enacted on stage. For its original audiences, however, Greek drama must have been a very exciting visual experience. Seated in a huge amphitheater, the audience at a performance of a tragedy in ancient Greece watched lead actors who, according to the best authorities on the subject, wore elaborate masks, crowns, and elevated shoes—giving the audience the impression that they were superhuman in comparison with the chorus, who were merely common men. (This visual impression matches the Greek playwright's vision of the tragic hero. Oedipus, for example, is a mortal, but he is the "best of mortals.") And between episodes of the play, the chorus, which represented the community, danced as well as sang their responses to the action. This was a particularly important visual element for a Greek audience, because the Greek hero suffered not only for himself but for the community as well.

We do not know what scenery, if any, accompanied most Greek drama, but we do know from his script that Sophocles intended that palace doors be part of the set for *Oedipus the King*. The doors to Oedipus' palace take on intense meaning as the play progresses; for each time Oedipus goes beyond them into his palace, a new disaster ensues. Thus, by the time he disappears behind these doors after Jocasta's death, we know that yet another catastrophe is about to occur; his retreats into the palace have become a signal. Because of it, though horrifying and grotesque, Oedipus' bloody reentrance is not totally unexpected. Significantly, at the end of the play, Oedipus leaves the stage not through the palace doors but through the entrance used by the chorus and other mere mortals. He now knows that he is one of them and must join the world from which they come. As suggested by *Oedipus the King,* Greek drama typically uses a limited number of visual devices, but it uses them with great selectivity and meaning.

Elizabethan drama has also often been regarded as visually unexciting; and, as in the case of Greek drama, this impression is, for the most part, erroneous. Though the Elizabethan playwright could not depend upon the use of a great deal of scenery, he could expect that many other devices would aid his descriptions of character, mood, and locale. For example, the platform stage of most Elizabethan theaters, including the Globe theater we associate with Shakespeare, permitted an extraordinarily rapid flow of characters back and forth. This gave the playwright an opportunity to present simultaneous but isolated actions—for instance, Othello watching from a distance while Cassio talks to Bianca—and, with an expressively painted backdrop curtain, the stage could suggest nearly any locale. Only occasionally does Shakespeare feel called on to ask his audience to use their imaginations, as when, in *Henry V,* he asks for indulgence because he is trying to present an entire fleet embarking for and landing in France, and two encamped armies preparing for the Battle of Agincourt. Ordinarily, however, Shakespeare found the resources of his stage sufficient.

Magnificent costumes were another visual device of the Elizabethan production, the nobility often being not only its central characters but the suppliers of its wardrobes as well. In addition to seeing clothes suitable for the queen and her court, the Elizabethan audience was also treated to some ingenious, if rudimentary, lighting effects. Records of the Globe theater show numerous expenditures for lanterns and the lenses then used to magnify lantern light. Many of these lighting devices were no doubt pressed into service for the opening and closing scenes of *Othello,* in which Shakespeare makes much use of light and dark imagery.

And in all his major plays, Shakespeare is also highly aware of the visual interest created when numerous characters appear onstage at the same time, especially for ritualistic occasions. Think, for example, of the spectacle of Othello confronting the massed group of the Venetian nightwatch and, later in the same act, of the formal, dignified effect of his plea for his defense before the assembled Venetian Senate. In both cases—the disorder of the watch and the hastily assembled Senate—Othello's measured and considered language serves to heighten and contradict the disorder of the Venetians. Even the scene in which Othello is roused from his wedding bed is visually spectacular and expressive of the profound disorder that is lying in wait for him. Indeed, all of the socially ordered occasions in the play are soon disrupted. A soldiers' friendly drinking party is torn apart by Cassio's swordfight. The dinner with the Venetian ambassadors falls apart when Othello fights with Desdemona. And the kiss Othello gives Desdemona at the end of the play, a prelude to death rather than love, is the climactic visual rupture of ceremony.

When readers of this collection proceed from Othello to Ibsen's *A Doll's House,* they will encounter theatrical conventions that seem to defy the concept of spectacle. By the late-nineteenth century, contemporary theater no longer attempted the grandeur it achieved in ancient Greece and Elizabethan England. The apron stage had been supplanted by the "picture frame" stage, which separates the audience sharply from the action and scales the action down to "room size"; and the protagonists were not royalty but reflections of the average man. Much like the viewers' own living rooms, the stage of Ibsen's day seemed to invite calm observation rather than excited participation.

And yet, spectacle is an integral part of Ibsen's day. Many of the contradictions related to Nora, for instance, are visually rather than verbally expressed. She enters and hides a sack of macaroons; then she plays a game with her children. Because her physical actions contrast sharply with her descriptions of her efforts to save Torvald, we realize that Nora herself does not know whether she is a woman or a doll. The contradictions she feels are illustrated by her dancing of a tarantella to please her husband. Torvald thinks of the dance as frothy entertainment; but Nora pursues it with frenzy and passion, using it to express the turmoil she feels. When Torvald suddenly stops the dance, we immediately sense the frustration, the waste of passion and intensity, the inhibition of self-expression that characterize her life with him. Even the setting of the play—a living room—suggests the contradictions of Nora's life. The room is conventionally Victorian, heavy, overstuffed, and pompous. Yet, within this setting Nora is expected to act like a gay doll, a carefree and empty-headed decoration. It is small wonder that the contradictions she finds in her situation begin to weigh on her. Even her physical world contradicts her basic desires.

Ibsen's drama does contain some elements of spectacle. Yet, even to some of his contemporaries, it seemed pallid and restrictive. Thus, in his preface to *Miss Julie,* Strindberg makes a plea for a loosening of what he conceives to be the restrictions of realism. He contends that plays that merely duplicate the surface of reality only point out the artificiality of the stage. His rejection of canvas doors and stage make-up are directed at this point. Strindberg wants a theater that suggests rather than duplicates reality. For *Miss Julie,* he describes a setting that is only part of a kitchen; the rest of the room seems to flow offstage. Beyond the windows are lilacs, and the sound of fiddles can be heard from the barn. Through the use of incomplete lines and extended vistas, Strindberg is trying to suggest that his stage set is only a corner of the larger world referred to throughout the play. This world includes aristocrats and peasants, dirt and perfume, degradation and surface nobility, and all the pressures at work on Miss Julie. Strindberg brings some of those pressures onstage when the peasants dance while Jean seduces Julie. He suggests the pressure of aristocracy through the servant's bell that will summon Jean to his master, and through the boots Jean cleans. Most spectacularly, when Jean butchers the bird onstage, Strindberg suggests the cruel primitivism of which Julie is a part but from which she hides. Strindberg's concept of theater suggests not so much the surface reality of the world as its underlying psychological and moral reality. All of the physical and visual details in *Miss Julie* point toward this kind of symbolic reality.

Strindberg's desire to present the meanings hidden by the surfaces of the world is shared by other playwrights represented in this collection. In *Death of a Salesman,* for example, Arthur Miller uses the visual dimensions of the play to reveal the past as well as the present. The Loman house is merely a skeleton—an outline of Willy's life. Physical objects keep pushing Willy into the past—a football, tennis sneakers, silk stockings, his car. His actions are often the measure of his dislocation. He arrives home from a sales trip at noon; he plants a garden at night. Lights and sounds suggest the offstage world. Lights, car noises, and the scream of a siren symbolize Willy's suicide. The cemetary is suggested merely by a pattern of leaves projected onstage, in contrast to the tall buildings projected around his home. Places are sketched in only by furniture; a hotel room is a bed and bureau; a restaurant is simply tables; and the office is only desks. Even the sketchiness of these sets suggests their shallowness, the kinds of inadequate values they represent. Miller is trying to show visually as well as through language how insubstantial are the beliefs on which Willy has erected his identity.

Giraudoux leaves behind the demand for surface reality almost entirely in *The Madwoman of Chaillot*. He travels from sidewalk cafés inexplicably inhabited by robotlike businessmen and poetic flower girls to an equally unlikely basement in Paris that opens unexpectedly into a sewer. Nothing in the play—the assemblage of characters, their clothes, or their dwellings—makes literal sense. Yet, since these are only exaggerated physical outlines of the world, we wonder how those outlines hang together. When we put all the mad costumes, sets, and characters together, however, we discover the outlines of a world that bears an uncomfortable resemblance to our own.

The play in this collection that is the least concerned with literal reality is Ed Bullins' *A Son, Come Home*. In this one-act play, Bullins uses no sets at all; the only stage furnishings are two chairs, and two of the four characters pantomime throughout the play. Yet the play is exceptionally visual. The actions of the mimers suggest houses, streets, rooms from coast to coast. Although they do work on "bare boards," they evoke a wide range of visual responses in the minds of the audience. Through Bullins we discover that spectacle and a sense of what is real may rest more in the minds of the viewers than in their eyes, and that spectacle may be created effectively, even by a few gestures or movements.

From this description of the visual elements of the plays in this collection, we can see that play readers interested in spectacle should ask a number of basic questions about any play they read:

1) Who is onstage?
2) What actions are implied by the lines the characters are speaking?
3) What are they doing onstage while others are talking?
4) In what major social ceremonies do the characters participate, and how well do they fulfill the requirements of the ceremonies?
5) How realistic are the costumes and settings? Why are they realistic or unrealistic?

6) What has the setting to do with the conflict the hero undergoes?
7) What is the importance of the objects a character uses?

As a reader becomes more skilled in reading plays and more experienced in seeing them, other questions will become apparent. And considering even just these basic questions, the beginning reader of plays will gain some idea of the visual excitement of drama.

Oedipus the King: Production directed by Tyrone Guthrie, at Stratford (Ontario) Festival (1955), starring Douglas Campbell, with costumes and masks by Tanya Moiseiwitsch. Photograph courtesy of Piper Studio Ltd., Toronto.

SOPHOCLES

Oedipus the King

Sophocles, who was born about 496 B.C. in a suburb of Athens and died about 405 B.C., lived during the period called the Golden Age of Greece, a time in which Athens became a major political and cultural force in the Western world. As a young man he wanted to be an actor but, hampered by a weak voice, turned instead to playwriting. During subsequent years, Sophocles wrote over one hundred plays and was first-prize winner in the annual Athenian drama contest at least eighteen times. His greatest surviving drama, *Oedipus the King*, became the prototype for tragic drama throughout the Western world; the discussion of the tragic form in Aristotle's *Poetics*, probably the most influential work of literary criticism ever written, is based on this Sophoclean play. Oedipus has for centuries remained a major tragic figure in literature because he encompasses so many of the contradictories in actual human experience: reason and passion, knowledge and mystery, pride and humility, good intentions and evil results. He is the best of men and the worst of men; the most limited and yet, in the face of those limitations, the most heroic. Thus he embodies not merely our sense of human frailty but our sense of human potential as well.

OEDIPUS THE KING Copyright © 1959, by Bernard M. W. Knox. Reprinted by permission of Washington Square Press, a division of Simon & Schuster, Inc.

CHARACTERS

Oedipus, *King of Thebes*
A **Priest** *of Zeus*
Creon, *brother of Jocasta*
A **Chorus** *of Theban citizens*
Tiresias, *a blind prophet*
Jocasta, *the queen, wife of Oedipus*
A **Messenger** *from Corinth*
A **Shepherd**
A **Messenger** *from inside the palace*
Antigone ⎫
Ismene ⎭ *daughters of Oedipus and Jocasta*

The background is the front wall of a building, with a double door in the center. Steps lead down from the door to stage level. In front of the steps, in the center, a square stone altar.

(Enter, from the side, a procession of priests and citizens. They carry olive branches which have tufts of wool tied on them. They lay these branches on the altar, then sit on the ground in front of it. The door opens. Enter Oedipus.*)*

Oedipus. My sons! Newest generation of this ancient city of Thebes! Why are you here? Why are you seated there at the altar, with these branches of supplication?
 The city is filled with the smoke of burning incense, with hymns to the healing god, with laments for the dead. I did not think it right, my children, to hear reports of this from others. Here I am, myself, world-famous Oedipus.
 You, old man, speak up—you are the man to speak for the others. In what mood are you sitting there—in fear or resignation? You may count on me; I am ready to do anything to help. I would be insensitive to pain, if I felt no pity for my people seated here.
 Priest. Oedipus, ruler of Thebes, you see us here at your altar, men of all ages—some not yet strong enough to fly far from the nest, others heavy with age, priests, of Zeus in my case, and these are picked men from the city's youth. The rest of the Thebans, carrying boughs like us, are sitting in the market place, at the two temples of Athena, and at the prophetic fire of Apollo near the river Ismenus.
 You can see for yourself—the city is like a ship rolling dangerously; it has lost the power to right itself and raise its head up out of the waves of death. Thebes is dying. There is a blight on the crops of the land, on the ranging herds of cattle, on the still-born labor of our women. The fever-god swoops down on us, hateful plague, he hounds the city and empties the

houses of Thebes. The black god of death is made rich with wailing and funeral laments.

It is not because we regard you as equal to the gods that we sit here in supplication, these children and I; in our judgment you are first of men, both in the normal crises of human life and in relations with the gods.

You came to us once and liberated our city, you freed us from the tribute which we paid that cruel singer, the Sphinx. You did this with no extra knowledge you got from us, you had no training for the task, but, so it is said and we believe, it was with divine support that you restored our city to life. And now, Oedipus, power to whom all men turn, we beg you, all of us here, in supplication—find some relief for us! Perhaps you have heard some divine voice, or have knowledge from some human source. You are a man of experience, the kind whose plans result in effective action. Noblest of men, we beg you, save the city. You must take thought for your reputation. Thebes now calls you its savior because of the energy you displayed once before. Let us not remember your reign as a time when we stood upright only to fall again. Set us firmly on our feet. You brought us good fortune then, with favorable signs from heaven—be now the equal of the man you were. You are king; if you are to rule Thebes, you must have an inhabited city, not a desert waste. A walled city or a ship abandoned, without men living together inside it, is nothing at all.

OEDIPUS. My children, I am filled with pity. I knew what you were longing for when you came here. I know only too well that you are all sick—but sick though you may be, there is not one of you as sick as I. *Your* pain torments each one of you, alone, by himself—but my spirit within me mourns for the city, and myself, and all of you. You see then, I was no dreamer you awoke from sleep. I have wept many tears, as you must know, and in my ceaseless reflection I have followed many paths of thought. My search has found one way to treat our disease—and I have acted already. I have sent Creon, my brother-in-law, to the prophetic oracle of Apollo, to find out by what action or speech, if any, I may rescue Thebes. I am anxious now when I count the days since he left; I wonder what he is doing. He has been away longer than one would expect, longer than he should be. But when he comes, at that moment I would be a vile object if I did not do whatever the god prescribes.

PRIEST. Just as you say these words, these men have signaled to me to announce Creon's arrival.

(*Enter* CREON, *from side.*)

OEDIPUS (*turns to the altar*). O King Apollo! May Creon bring us good fortune and rescue, bright as the expression I see on his face.

PRIEST. I guess that his news is joyful. For on his head is a crown of laurel in bloom.

OEDIPUS. No more guessing—soon we shall know. For he is near enough to hear us now.

(*Raising his voice*) Lord Creon, what statement do you bring us from the god Apollo?

CREON. Good news. For, as I see it, even things hard to bear, if they should turn out right in the end, would be good fortune.

OEDIPUS. What exactly did the god say? *Your* words inspire neither confidence nor fear.

CREON. If you wish to hear my report in the presence of these people (*points to priests*) I am ready. Or shall we go inside?

OEDIPUS. Speak out, before all of us. The sorrows of my people here mean more to me than any fear I may have for my own life.

CREON. Very well. Here is what I was told by the god Apollo. He ordered us, in clear terms, to drive out the thing that defiles this land, which we, he says, have fed and cherished. We must not let it grow so far that it is beyond cure.

OEDIPUS. What is the nature of our misfortune? How are we to rid ourselves of it—by what rites?

CREON. Banishment—or repaying blood with blood. We must atone for a murder which brings this plague-storm on the city.

OEDIPUS. Whose murder? Who is the man whose death Apollo lays to our charge?

CREON. The ruler of this land, my lord, was called Laius. That was before *you* took the helm of state.

OEDIPUS. I know—at least I have heard so. I never saw the man.

CREON. It is to *his* death that Apollo's command clearly refers. We must punish those who killed him—whoever they may be.

OEDIPUS. But where on earth are they? The track of this ancient guilt is hard to detect; how shall we find it now?

CREON. Here in Thebes, Apollo said. What is searched for can be caught. What is neglected escapes.

OEDIPUS. Where did Laius meet his death? In his palace, in the countryside, or on some foreign soil?

CREON. He left Thebes to consult the oracle, so he announced. But he never returned to his home.

OEDIPUS. And no messenger came back? No fellow traveler who saw what happened?

CREON. No, they were all killed—except for one, who ran away in terror. But he could give no clear account of what he saw—except one thing.

OEDIPUS. And what was that? One thing might be the clue to knowledge of many more—if we could get even a slight basis for hope.

CREON. Laius was killed, he said, not by one man, but by a strong and numerous band of robbers.

OEDIPUS. But how could a *robber* reach such a pitch of daring—to kill a king? Unless there had been words—and money—passed between him and someone here in Thebes.

CREON.   We thought of that, too. But the death of Laius left us helpless and leaderless in our trouble—

OEDIPUS.   Trouble? What kind of trouble could be big enough to prevent a full investigation? Your *king* has been killed.

CREON.   The Sphinx with her riddling songs forced us to give up the mystery and think about more urgent matters.

OEDIPUS.   But I will begin afresh. I will bring it all to light. You have done well, Creon, and Apollo has, too, to show this solicitude for the murdered man. Now you will have *me* on your side, as is only right. I shall be the defender of Thebes, and Apollo's champion, too. I shall rid us of this pollution, not for the sake of a distant relative, but for my own sake. For whoever killed Laius might decide to raise his hand against me. So, acting on behalf of Laius, I benefit myself, too.

(*To priests*) Quickly, my children, as fast as you can, stand up from the steps and take these branches of supplication off the altar.

(*To guards*) One of you summon the people of Thebes here.

I shall leave nothing undone. With God's help we shall prove fortunate —or fall.

PRIEST.   My sons, stand up. (*The priests rise.*) King Oedipus has volunteered to do what we came to ask. May Apollo, who sent the message from his oracle, come as our savior, and put an end to the plague.

(*The priests take the olive branches off the altar and exeunt to side.* OEDIPUS *goes back through the palace doors. Enter, from side, the* CHORUS. *They are fifteen dancers, representing old men. They stand for the people of Thebes, whom* OEDIPUS *has just summoned. They chant in unison the following lines, which, in the original Greek, make great use of solemn, traditional formulas of prayer to the gods.*)

CHORUS.   Sweet message of Zeus! You have come from Apollo's golden temple to splendid Thebes, bringing us news. My fearful heart is stretched on the rack and shudders in terror.

Hail Apollo, Lord of Delos, healer! I worship and revere you. What new form of atonement will you demand? Or will it be some ancient ceremony, repeated often as the seasons come round? Tell me, daughter of golden Hope, immortal Voice of Apollo.

First I call upon you, immortal Athena, daughter of Zeus. And on your sister Artemis, the protector of this land, who sits in glory on her throne in the market place. And I call on far-shooting Apollo, the archer. Trinity of Defenders against Death, appear to me! If ever in time past, when destruction threatened our city, you kept the flame of pain out of our borders, come now also.

There is no way to count the pains we suffer. All our people are sick.

There is no sword of thought which will protect us. The fruits of our famous land do not ripen. Our women cannot ease their labor pains by giving birth. One after another you can see our people speed like winged birds, faster than irresistible fire, to the shore of evening, to death. The city is dying, the deaths cannot be counted. The children lie unburied, unmourned, spreading death. Wives and gray-haired mothers come from all over the city, wailing they come to the altar steps to pray for release from pain and sorrow. The hymn to the Healer flashes out, and with it, accompanied by flutes, the mourning for the dead. Golden daughter of Zeus, Athena, send help and bring us joy.

I pray that the raging War-god, who now without shield and armor hems me in with shouting and burns me, I pray that he may turn back and leave the borders of this land. Let him go to the great sea gulf of the Western ocean or north to the Thracian coasts which give no shelter from the sea. For now, what the night spares, he comes for by day.

Father Zeus, you that in majesty govern the blazing lightning, destroy him beneath your thunderbolt!

Apollo, king and protector! I pray for the arrows from your golden bow—let them be ranged on my side to help me. And with them the flaming torches of Artemis, with which she speeds along the Eastern mountains. And I invoke the god with the golden headdress, who gave this land his name, wine-faced Dionysus, who runs with the maddened girls—let him come to my side, shining with his blazing pine-torch, to fight the god who is without honor among all other gods.

(*The* CHORUS *stays on stage. Enter* OEDIPUS, *from the palace doors. He addresses the* CHORUS—*the people of Thebes.*)

OEDIPUS. You are praying. As for your prayers, if you are willing to hear and accept what I say now and so treat the disease, you will find rescue and relief from distress. I shall make a proclamation, speaking as one who has no connection with this affair, nor with the murder. Even if I had been here at the time, I could not have followed the track very far without some clue. As it is, I became a Theban citizen with you after it happened. So I now proclaim to all of you, citizens of Thebes: whoever among you knows by whose hand Laius son of Labdacus was killed, I order him to reveal the whole truth to me.

If he is afraid to speak up, I order him to speak even against himself, and so escape the indictment, for he will suffer no unpleasant consequence except exile; he can leave Thebes unharmed.

(*Silence while* OEDIPUS *waits for a reply.*)

Secondly, if anyone knows the identity of the murderer, and that he is a foreigner, from another land, let him speak up. I shall make it profitable for him, and he will have my gratitude, too.

(*Pause.*)

But if you keep silent—if someone among you refuses my offer, shielding some relative or friend, or himself—now, listen to what I intend to do in that case. That man, whoever he may be, I banish from this land where I sit on the throne and hold the power; no one shall take him in or speak to him. He is forbidden communion in prayers or offerings to the gods, or in holy water. Everyone is to expel him from their homes as if he were himself the source of infection which Apollo's oracle has just made known to me. That is how I fulfill my obligations as an ally to the god and to the murdered man. As for the murderer himself, I call down a curse on him, whether that unknown figure be one man or one among many. May he drag out an evil death-in-life in misery. And further, I pronounce a curse on myself if the murderer should, with my knowledge, share my house; in that case may I be subject to all the curses I have just called down on these people here. I order you all to obey these commands in full for my sake, for Apollo's sake, and for the sake of this land, withering away in famine, abandoned by heaven.

Even if this action had not been urged by the god, it was not proper for you to have left the matter unsolved—the death of a good man and a king. You should have investigated it. But now I am in command. I hold the office he once held, the wife who once was his is now mine, the mother of my children. Laius and I would be closely connected by children from the same wife, if his line had not met with disaster. But chance swooped down on his life. So I shall fight for him, as if he were my own father. I shall shrink from nothing in my search to find the murderer of Laius, of the royal line of Thebes, stretching back through Labdacus, Polydorus and Cadmus, to ancient Agenor. On those who do not co-operate with these measures I call down this curse in the gods' name: let no crop grow out of the earth for them, their wives bear no children. Rather let them be destroyed by the present plague, or something even worse. But to you people of Thebes who approve of my action I say this: May justice be our ally and all the gods be with us forever!

CHORUS. (*One member of the* CHORUS *speaks for them all.*) You have put me under a curse, King, and under the threat of that curse I shall make my statement. I did not kill Laius and I am not in a position to say who did. This search to find the murderer should have been undertaken by Apollo who sent the message which began it.

OEDIPUS. What you say is just. But to compel the gods to act against their will—no man could do that.

CHORUS LEADER. Then let me make a second suggestion.

OEDIPUS. And a third, if you like—speak up.

CHORUS LEADER. The man who sees most eye to eye with Lord Apollo is Tiresias and from him you might learn most clearly the truth for which you are searching.

OEDIPUS. I did not leave *that* undone either. I have already sent for him, at Creon's suggestion. I have sent for him twice, in fact, and have been wondering for some time why he is not yet here.

CHORUS LEADER. Apart from what he will say, there is nothing but old, faint rumors.

OEDIPUS. What were they? I want to examine every single word.

CHORUS LEADER. Laius was killed, so they say, by some travelers.

OEDIPUS. I heard that, too. Where is the man who saw it?

CHORUS LEADER. If he has any trace of fear in him, he won't stand firm when he hears the curses you have called down on him.

OEDIPUS. If he didn't shrink from the action he won't be frightened by a word.

CHORUS LEADER. But here comes the one who will convict him. These men are bringing the holy prophet of the gods, the only man in whom truth is inborn.

(*Enter* TIRESIAS, *from the side. He has a boy to lead him, and is accompanied by guards.*)

OEDIPUS. Tiresias, you who understand all things—those which can be taught and those which may not be mentioned, things in the heavens and things which walk the earth! You cannot see, but you understand the city's distress, the disease from which it is suffering. You, my lord, are our shield against it, our savior, the only one we have. You may not have heard the news from the messengers. We sent to Apollo and he sent us back this answer: relief from this disease would come to us only if we discovered the identity of the murderers of Laius and then either killed them or banished them from Thebes. Do not begrudge us your knowledge—any voice from the birds or any other way of prophecy you have. Save yourself and this city, save me, from all the infection caused by the dead man. We are in your hands. And the noblest of labors is for a man to help his fellow men with all he has and can do.

TIRESIAS. Wisdom is a dreadful thing when it brings no profit to its possessor. I knew all this well, but forgot. Otherwise I would never have come here.

OEDIPUS. What is the matter? Why this despairing mood?

TIRESIAS. Dismiss me, send me home. That will be the easiest way for both of us to bear our burden.

OEDIPUS. What you propose is unlawful—and unfriendly to this city which raised you. You are withholding information.

TIRESIAS. I do not see that your talking is to the point. And I don't want the same thing to happen to me.

OEDIPUS. If you know something, in God's name, do not turn your back on us. All of us here, on our knees, beseech you.

TIRESIAS. You are all ignorant. I will never reveal my dreadful secrets, or rather, yours.

OEDIPUS. What do you say? You know something? And will not speak? You intend to betray us, do you, and wreck the state?

TIRESIAS. I will not cause pain to myself or to you. Why do you question me? It is useless. You will get nothing from me.

OEDIPUS. You scoundrel! You would enrage a lifeless stone. Will nothing move you? Speak out and make an end of it.

TIRESIAS. You blame my temper, but you are not aware of one *you* live with.

OEDIPUS (*to* CHORUS). Who could control his anger listening to talk like this—these insults to Thebes?

TIRESIAS. What is to come will come, even if I shroud it in silence.

OEDIPUS. What is to come, *that* is what you are bound to tell *me*.

TIRESIAS. I will say no more. Do what you like—rage at me in the wildest anger you can muster.

OEDIPUS. I will. I am angry enough to speak out. I understand it all. Listen to me, I think that *you* helped to plan the murder of Laius—yes, and short of actually raising your hand against him you did it. If you weren't blind, I'd say that you alone struck him down.

TIRESIAS. Is that what you say? I charge you now to carry out the articles of the proclamation you made. From now on do not presume to speak to me or to any of these people. *You* are the murderer, *you* are the unholy defilement of this land.

OEDIPUS. Have you no shame? To start up such a story! Do you think you will get away with this?

TIRESIAS. Yes. The truth with all its strength is in me.

OEDIPUS. Who taught you this lesson? You didn't learn it from your prophet's trade.

TIRESIAS. *You* did. I was unwilling to speak but you drove me to it.

OEDIPUS. What was it you said? I want to understand it clearly.

TIRESIAS. Didn't you understand it the first time? Aren't you just trying to trip me up?

OEDIPUS. No, I did not grasp it fully. Repeat your statement.

TIRESIAS. I say that you are the murderer you are searching for.

OEDIPUS. Do you think you can say that twice and not pay for it?

TIRESIAS. Shall I say something more, to make you angrier still?

OEDIPUS. Say what you like. It will all be meaningless.

TIRESIAS. I say that without knowing it you are living in shameful intimacy with your nearest and dearest. You do not see the evil in which you live.

OEDIPUS. Do you think you can go on like this with impunity forever?

TIRESIAS. Yes, if the truth has power.

OEDIPUS. It has, except for you. You have no power or truth. You are blind, your ears and mind as well as eyes.

TIRESIAS. You are a pitiful figure. These reproaches you fling at me, all these people here will fling them at you—and before very long.

OEDIPUS (*contemptuously*). You live your life in one continuous night of darkness. Neither I nor any other man that can see would do you any harm.

TIRESIAS. It is not destiny that I should fall through you. Apollo is enough for that. It is *his* concern.

OEDIPUS. Was it Creon, or you, that invented this story?

TIRESIAS. It is not Creon who harms you—you harm yourself.

OEDIPUS. Wealth, absolute power, skill surpassing skill in the competition of life—what envy is your reward! For the sake of this power which Thebes entrusted to me—I did not ask for it—to win this power faithful Creon, my friend from the beginning, sneaks up on me treacherously, longing to drive me out. He sets this intriguing magician on me, a lying quack, keen sighted for what he can make, but blind in prophecy.

(*To* TIRESIAS) Tell me, when were you a true prophet? When the Sphinx chanted her riddle here, did *you* come forward to speak the word that would liberate the people of this town? That riddle was not for anyone who came along to answer—it called for prophetic insight. But you didn't come forward, you offered no answer told you by the birds or the gods. No. *I* came, know-nothing Oedipus. *I* stopped the Sphinx. I answered the riddle with my own intelligence—the birds had nothing to teach me. And now you try to drive me out, you think you will stand beside Creon's throne. I tell you, you will pay in tears for this witch-hunting—you and Creon, the man that organized this conspiracy. If you weren't an old man, you would already have realized, in suffering, what your schemes lead to.

CHORUS LEADER. If we may make a suggestion—both his words and yours, Oedipus, seem to have been spoken in anger. This sort of talk is not what we need—what we must think of is how to solve the problem set by the god's oracle.

TIRESIAS. King though you are, you must treat me as your equal in one respect—the right to reply. That is a power which belongs to me, too. I am not your servant, but Apollo's. I am not inscribed on the records as a dependent of Creon, with no right to speak in person. I can speak, and here is what I have to say. You have mocked at my blindness, but you, who have eyes, cannot see the evil in which you stand; you cannot see where you are living, nor with whom you share your house. Do you even know who your parents are? Without knowing it, you are the enemy of your own flesh and blood, the dead below and the living here above. The double-edged curse of your mother and father, moving on dread feet, shall one day drive you from this land. You see straight now but then you will see darkness. You will scream aloud on that day; there is no place which shall not hear you, no part of Mount Cithaeron here which will not ring in echo, on that day when you know the truth about your wedding, that evil harbor into which you sailed before a fair wind.

There is a multitude of other horrors which you do not even suspect, and they will equate you to yourself and to your own children. There! Now smear me and Creon with your accusations. There is no man alive whose ruin will be more pitiful than yours.

OEDIPUS. Enough! I won't listen to this sort of talk from you. Damn you! My curse on you! Get out of here, quickly. Away from this house, back to where you came from!

TIRESIAS. I would never have come here if you had not summoned me.

OEDIPUS. I didn't know that you were going to speak like a fool—or it would have been a long time before I summoned you to my palace.

TIRESIAS. I am what I am—a fool to you, so it seems, but the parents who brought you into the world thought me sensible enough. (TIRESIAS *turns to go.*)

OEDIPUS. Whom do you mean? Wait! Who is my father?

TIRESIAS. This present day will give you birth and death.

OEDIPUS. Everything you say is the same—riddles, obscurities.

TIRESIAS. Aren't you the best man alive at guessing riddles?

OEDIPUS. Insult me, go on—but that, you will find, is what makes me great.

TIRESIAS. Yet that good fortune was your destruction.

OEDIPUS. What does that matter, if I saved Thebes?

TIRESIAS. I will go, then. Boy, lead me away.

OEDIPUS. Yes, take him away. While you're here you are a hindrance, a nuisance; once out of the way you won't annoy me any more.

TIRESIAS. I am going. But first I will say what I came here to say. I have no fear of you. You cannot destroy me. Listen to me now. The man you are trying to find, with your threatening proclamations, the murderer of Laius, that man is here in Thebes. He is apparently an immigrant of foreign birth, but he will be revealed as a native-born Theban. He will take no pleasure in that revelation. Blind instead of seeing, beggar instead of rich, he will make his way to foreign soil, feeling his way with a stick. He will be revealed as a brother and father of the children with whom he now lives, the son and husband of the woman who gave him birth, the murderer and marriage-partner of his father. Go think this out. And if you find that I am wrong, then say I have no skill in prophecy.

(*Exit* TIRESIAS *led by boy to side.* OEDIPUS *goes back into the palace.*)

CHORUS. Who is the man denounced by the prophetic voice from Delphi's cliffs—the man whose bloodstained hands committed a nameless crime? Now is the time for him to run, faster than storm-swift horses. In full armor Apollo son of Zeus leaps upon him, with the fire of the lightning. And in the murderer's track follow dreadful unfailing spirits of vengeance.

The word of Apollo has blazed out from snowy Parnassus for all to see. Track down the unknown murderer by every means. He roams under cover of the wild forest, among caves and rocks, like a wild bull, wretched, cut off from mankind, his feet in pain. He turns his back on the prophecies delivered at the world's center, but they, alive forever, hover round him.

The wise prophet's words have brought me terror and confusion. I cannot agree with him, nor speak against him. I do not know what to say. I waver in hope and fear; I cannot see forward or back. What cause for quarrel was there between Oedipus and Laius? I never heard of one in time past; I know of none now.

I see no reason to attack the great fame of Oedipus in order to avenge the mysterious murder of Laius.

Zeus and Apollo, it is true, understand and know in full the events of man's life. But whether a mere man knows the truth—whether a human prophet knows more than I do—who is to be a fair judge of that? It is true that one man may be wiser than another. But I, for my part, will never join those who blame Oedipus, until I see these charges proved. We all saw how the Sphinx came against him—there his wisdom was proved. In that hour of danger he was the joy of Thebes. Remembering that day, my heart will never judge him guilty of evil action.

(*Enter* CREON, *from side.*)

CREON. Fellow citizens of Thebes, I am here in an angry mood. I hear that King Oedipus brings terrible charges against me. If, in the present dangerous situation, he thinks that I have injured him in any way, by word or deed, let me not live out the rest of my days with such a reputation. The damage done to me by such a report is no simple thing—it is the worst there is—to be called a traitor in the city, by all of you, by my friends.

CHORUS LEADER. This attack on you must have been forced out of him by anger; he lost control of himself.

CREON. Who told him that *I* advised Tiresias to make these false statements?

CHORUS LEADER. That's what was said—but I don't know what the intention was.

CREON. Were his eyes and mind unclouded when he made this charge against me?
CHORUS LEADER. I don't know. It is no use asking *me* about the actions of those who rule Thebes. Here is Oedipus. Look, he is coming out of the palace.

(*Enter* OEDIPUS, *from door.*)

OEDIPUS (*to* CREON). You! What are you doing here? Do you have the face to come to my palace—you who are convicted as my murderer, exposed as a robber attempting to steal my throne? In God's name, tell me, what did you take me for when you made this plot—a coward? Or a fool? Did you think I wouldn't notice this conspiracy of yours creeeping up on me in the dark? That once I saw it, I wouldn't defend myself? Don't you see that your plan is foolish—to hunt for a crown without numbers or friends behind you? A crown is won by numbers and money.
CREON. I have a suggestion. You in your turn listen to a reply as long as your speech, and, after you have heard me, *then* judge me.
OEDIPUS. You are a clever speaker, but I am a slow learner—from *you*. I have found you an enemy and a burden to me.
CREON. Just one thing, just listen to what I say.
OEDIPUS. Just one thing, don't try to tell me you are not a traitor.
CREON. Listen, if you think stubbornness deprived of intelligence is a worth-while possession, you are out of your mind.
OEDIPUS. Listen, if you think you can injure a close relative and then not pay for it, you are out of your mind.
CREON. All right, that's fair. But at least explain to me what I am supposed to have done.
OEDIPUS. Did you or did you not persuade me that I ought to send for that "holy" prophet?
CREON. Yes, I did, and I am still of the same mind.
OEDIPUS. Well then, how long is it since Laius . . . (*Pause.*)
CREON. Did what? I don't follow your drift.
OEDIPUS. Disappeared, vanished, violently murdered?
CREON. Many years ago; it is a long count back in time.
OEDIPUS. And at that time, was this prophet at his trade?
CREON. Yes, wise as he is now, and honored then as now.
OEDIPUS. Did he mention my name at that time?
CREON. No, at least not in my presence.
OEDIPUS. You investigated the murder of Laius, didn't you?
CREON. We did what we could, of course. But we learned nothing.
OEDIPUS. How was it that this wise prophet did not say all this *then*?

CREON. I don't know. And when I don't understand, *I* keep silent.

OEDIPUS. Here's something you *do* know, and could say, too, if you were a loyal man.

CREON. What do you mean? If I know, I will not refuse to answer.

OEDIPUS. Just this. If he had not come to an agreement with you, Tiresias would never have called the murder of Laius *my* work.

CREON. If that's what he says—you are the one to know. Now I claim my rights from you—answer my questions as I did yours just now.

OEDIPUS. Ask your questions. I shall not be proved a murderer.

CREON. You are married to my sister, are you not?

OEDIPUS. The answer to that question is yes.

CREON. And you rule Thebes jointly and equally with her?

OEDIPUS. She gets from me whatever she wants.

CREON. And I am on an equal basis with the two of you, isn't that right?

OEDIPUS. Yes, it is, and that fact shows what a disloyal friend you are.

CREON. No, not if you look at it rationally, as I am explaining it to you. Consider this point first—do you think anyone would prefer to be supreme ruler and live in fear rather than to sleep soundly at night and still have the same power as the king? I am not the man to long for royalty rather than royal power, and anyone who has any sense agrees with me. As it is now, I have everything I want from you, and nothing to fear; but if I were king, I would have to do many things I have no mind to. How could the throne seem more desirable to me than power and authority which bring me no trouble? I can see clearly—all I want is what is pleasant and profitable at the same time. As it is now, I am greeted by all, everyone salutes me, all those who want something from you play up to me—that's the key to success for them. What makes you think I would give up all this and accept what you have? No, a mind which sees things clearly, as I do, would never turn traitor. I have never been tempted by such an idea, and I would never have put up with anyone who took such action.

You can test the truth of what I say. Go to Delphi and ask for the text of the oracle, to see if I gave you an accurate report. One thing more. If you find that I conspired with the prophet Tiresias, then condemn me to death, not by a single vote, but by a double, yours and mine both. But do not accuse me in isolation, on private, baseless fancy. It is not justice to make the mistake of taking bad men for good, or good for bad. To reject a good friend is the equivalent of throwing away one's own dear life—that's my opinion. Given time you will realize all this without fail: time alone reveals the just man—the unjust you can recognize in one short day.

CHORUS LEADER. That is good advice, my lord, for anyone who wants to avoid mistakes. Quick decisions are not the safest.

OEDIPUS. When a plotter moves against me in speed and secrecy, then

I too must be quick to counterplot. If I take my time and wait, then his cause is won, and mine lost.

CREON. What do you want then? Surely you don't mean to banish me from Thebes?

OEDIPUS. Not at all. Death is what I want for you, not exile.

CREON. You give a clear example of what it is to feel hate and envy.

OEDIPUS. You don't believe me, eh? You won't give way?

CREON. No, for I can see you don't know what you are doing.

OEDIPUS. Looking after my own interests.

CREON. And what about mine?

OEDIPUS. You are a born traitor.

CREON. And you don't understand anything.

OEDIPUS. Whether I do or not—I am in power here.

CREON. Not if you rule badly.

OEDIPUS (to CHORUS). Listen to him, Thebes, my city.

CREON. My city, too, not yours alone.

CHORUS LEADER. Stop, my lords. Here comes Jocasta from the house, in the nick of time. With her help, you must compose this quarrel between you.

(Enter JOCASTA, from door.)

JOCASTA. Have you no sense, God help you, raising your voices in strife like this? Have you no sense of shame? The land is plague-stricken and you pursue private quarrels. (*To* OEDIPUS) You go into the house, and you, too, Creon, inside. Don't make so much trouble over some small annoyance.

CREON. Sister, your husband, Oedipus, claims the right to inflict dreadful punishments on me. He will choose between banishing me from my fatherland and killing me.

OEDIPUS. Exactly, Jocasta, I caught him in a treacherous plot against my life.

CREON. May I never enjoy life, but perish under a curse, if I have done to you any of the things you charge me with.

JOCASTA. In God's name, Oedipus, believe what he says. Show respect for the oath he swore by the gods—do it for my sake and the sake of these people here.

CHORUS. Listen to her, King Oedipus. Think over your decision, take her advice, I beg you.

OEDIPUS. What concession do you want me to make?

CHORUS. Creon was no fool before, and now his oath increases his stature. Respect him.

OEDIPUS. Do you know what you are asking?

CHORUS. Yes, I know.
OEDIPUS. Tell me what it means, then.
CHORUS. This man is your friend—he has sworn an oath—don't throw him out dishonored on the strength of hearsay alone.
OEDIPUS. Understand this. If that is what you are after, you want me to be killed or banished from this land.
CHORUS. No. By the sun, foremost of all the gods! May I perish miserably abandoned by man and God, if any such thought is in my mind. My heart is racked with pain for the dying land of Thebes—must you add new sorrows of your own making to those we already have?
OEDIPUS. Well then, let him go—even if it *does* lead to my death or inglorious banishment. It is *your* piteous speech that rouses my compassion—not what *he* says. As for him, I shall hate him, wherever he goes.
CREON. You show your sulky temper in giving way, just as you did in your ferocious anger. Natures like yours are hardest to bear for their owners—and justly so.
OEDIPUS. Get out, will you? Out!
CREON. I am going. I found you ignorant—but these men think I am right.

(*Exit* CREON *to side.*)

CHORUS (*to* JOCASTA). Lady, why don't you get him into the house quickly?
JOCASTA. I will—when I have found out what happened here.
CHORUS. There was some ignorant talk based on hearsay and some hurt caused by injustice.
JOCASTA. On both sides?
CHORUS. Yes.
JOCASTA. And what did they say?
CHORUS. Enough, that is enough, it seems to me. I speak in the interests of the whole country. Let this matter lie where they left it.
OEDIPUS. You see where your good intentions have brought you. This is the result of turning aside and blunting the edge of my anger.
CHORUS. My king, I said it before, more than once—listen to me. I would be exposed as a madman, useless, brainless, if I were to turn my back on you. You found Thebes laboring in a sea of trouble, you righted her and set her on a fair course. All I wish now is that you should guide us as well as you did then.
JOCASTA. In God's name, explain to me, my lord—what was it made you so angry?
OEDIPUS. I will tell you. I have more respect for you than for these people here. Creon and his conspiracy against me, that's what made me angry.

JOCASTA. Tell me clearly, what was the quarrel between you?
OEDIPUS. He says that *I* am the murderer of Laius.
JOCASTA. On what evidence? His own knowledge, or hearsay?
OEDIPUS. Oh, he keeps his own lips clear of responsibility—he sent a swindling prophet in to speak for him.
JOCASTA. A prophet? In that case, rid your mind of your fear, and listen to me. I can teach you something. There is no human being born that is endowed with prophetic power. I can prove it to you—and in a few words.

A prophecy came to Laius once—I won't say from Apollo himself, but from his priests. It said that Laius was fated to die by the hand of his son, a son to be born to him and to me. Well, Laius, so the story goes, was killed by foreign robbers at a place where three highways meet. As for the son—three days after his birth Laius fastened his ankles together and had him cast away on the pathless mountains.

So, in this case, Apollo did not make the son kill his father or Laius die by his own son's hand, as he had feared. Yet these were the definite statements of the prophetic voices. Don't pay any attention to prophecies. If God seeks or needs anything, he will easily make it clear to us himself.

OEDIPUS. Jocasta, something I heard you say has disturbed me to the soul, unhinged my mind.
JOCASTA. What do you mean? What was it that alarmed you so?
OEDIPUS. I thought I heard you say that Laius was killed at a place where three highways meet.
JOCASTA. Yes, that's what the story was—and still is.
OEDIPUS. Where is the place where this thing happened?
JOCASTA. The country is called Phocis: two roads, one from Delphi and one from Daulia, come together and form one.
OEDIPUS. When did it happen? How long ago?
JOCASTA. We heard the news here in Thebes just before you appeared and became King.
OEDIPUS. O God, what have you planned to do to me?
JOCASTA. What is it, Oedipus, which haunts your spirit so?
OEDIPUS. No questions, not yet. Laius—tell me what he looked like, how old he was.
JOCASTA. He was a big man—his hair had just begun to turn white. And he had more or less the same build as you.
OEDIPUS. O God! I think I have just called down on myself a dreadful curse—not knowing what I did.
JOCASTA. What do you mean? To look at you makes me shudder, my lord.
OEDIPUS. I am dreadfully afraid the blind prophet could see. But tell me one more thing that will throw light on this.
JOCASTA. I am afraid. But ask your question; I will answer if I can.

OEDIPUS. Was Laius poorly attended, or did he have a big bodyguard, like a king?

JOCASTA. There were five men in his party. One of them was a herald. And there was one wagon—Laius was riding in it.

OEDIPUS. Oh, it is all clear as daylight now. Who was it told you all this at the time?

JOCASTA. A slave from the royal household. He was the only one who came back.

OEDIPUS. Is he by any chance in the palace now?

JOCASTA. No, he is not. When he came back and saw you ruling in place of Laius, he seized my hand and begged me to send him to work in the country, to the pastures, to the flocks, as far away as I could—out of sight of Thebes. And I sent him. Though he was a slave he deserved this favor from me—and much more.

OEDIPUS. Can I get him back here, in haste?

JOCASTA. It can be done. But why are you so intent on this?

OEDIPUS. I am afraid, Jocasta, that I have said too much—that's why I want to see this man.

JOCASTA. Well, he shall come. But I have a right, it seems to me, to know what it is that torments you so.

OEDIPUS. So you shall. Since I am so full of dreadful expectation, I shall hold nothing back from you. Who else should I speak to, who means more to me than you, in this time of trouble?

My father was Polybus, a Dorian, and my mother Merope, of Corinth. I was regarded as the greatest man in that city until something happened to me quite by chance, a strange thing, but not worth all the attention I paid it. A man at the banquet table, who had had too much to drink, told me, over his wine, that I was not the true son of my father. I was furious, but, hard though it was, I controlled my feelings, for that day at least. On the next day I went to my parents and questioned them. They were enraged against the man who had so taunted me. So I took comfort from their attitude, but still the thing tormented me—for the story spread far and wide. Without telling my parents, I set off on a journey to the oracle of Apollo, at Delphi. Apollo sent me away with my question unanswered but he foretold a dreadful, calamitous future for me—to lie with my mother and beget children men's eyes would not bear the sight of—and to be the killer of the father that gave me life.

When I heard that, I ran away. From that point on I measured the distance to the land of Corinth by the stars. I was running to a place where I would never see that shameful prophecy come true. On my way I came to the place in which you say this king, Laius, met his death.

I will tell you the truth, all of it. As I journeyed on I came near to this triple crossroad and there I was met by a herald and a man riding on a horse-drawn wagon, just as you described it. The driver, and the old man himself, tried to push me off the road. In anger I struck the driver as he tried to crowd me off. When the old man saw me coming past the wheels he aimed at my head with a two-pronged goad, and hit me. I paid him back in full, with interest: in no time at all he was hit by the stick I held in my hand and rolled backwards from the center of the wagon. I killed the whole lot of them.

Now, if this stranger had anything to do with Laius—is there a more unhappy man alive than I? Who could be more hateful to the gods than I am? No foreigner or citizen may take me into his house, no one can talk to me—everyone must expel me from his home. And the man who called down these curses on me was I myself, no one else. With these hands that killed him I defile the dead man's marriage bed. How can I deny that I am vile, utterly unclean? I must be banished from Thebes, and then I may not even see my own parents or set foot on my own fatherland—or else I am doomed to marry my own mother and kill my father Polybus, who brought me up and gave me life. I am the victim of some harsh divinity; what other explanation can there be?

Let it not happen, not that, I beg you, holy majesty of God, may I never see that day! May I disappear from among men without trace before I see such a stain of misfortune come upon me!

CHORUS LEADER. My lord, this makes us tremble. But do not despair—you have still to hear the story from the eyewitness.

OEDIPUS. That's right. That's my hope now, such as it is—to wait for the shepherd.

JOCASTA. Why all this urgency about his coming?

OEDIPUS. I'll tell you. If it turns out that he tells the same story as you —then I, at least, will be cleared of responsibility.

JOCASTA. What was so important in what you heard from me?

OEDIPUS. You said his story was that *several* robbers killed Laius. Well, if he speaks of the same number as you—then I am not the killer. For one could never be equal to many. But if he speaks of one man alone—then clearly the balance tips towards me as the killer.

JOCASTA. You can be sure that his account was made public just as I told it to you; he cannot go back on it, the whole city heard it, not I alone. But, my lord, even if he should depart from his former account in some particular, he still would never make the death of Laius what it was supposed to be—for Apollo said clearly that Laius was to be killed by my son. But that poor infant never killed Laius; it met his own death first. So much for prophecy. For all it can say, I would not, from now on, so much as look to right or left.

OEDIPUS. Yes, I agree. But all the same, the shepherd—send someone to fetch him. Do it at once.

JOCASTA. I shall send immediately. And now let us go in. I would not do anything except what pleases you.

(*Exeunt* OEDIPUS *and* JOCASTA *through doors.*)

CHORUS (*chanting in unison*).
May Destiny be with me always;
Let me observe reverence and purity
In word and deed.
Laws that stand above have been established—
Born in the upper air on high;
Their only father in heaven;
No mortal nature, no man gave them birth.
They never forget, or sleep.
In them God is great, and He does not grow old.

The despot is the child of violent pride,
Pride that vainly stuffs itself
With food unseasonable, unfit,
Climbs to the highest rim
And then plunges sheer down into defeat
Where its feet are of no use.
Yet I pray to God to spare that vigor
Which benefits the state.
God is my protector, on Him I shall never cease to call.

The man who goes his way
Overbearing in word and deed,
Who fears no justice,
Honors no temples of the gods—
May an evil destiny seize him
And punish his ill-starred pride.
How shall such a man defend his life
Against God's arrows?
If such deeds as this are honored,
Why should we join the sacred dance and worship?

I shall go no more in reverence to Delphi,
The holy center of the earth,
Nor to any temple in the world,
Unless these prophecies come true,
For all men to point at in wonder.
O Zeus, King of heaven, ruler of all,
If you deserve this name,

Do not let your everlasting power be deceived,
Do not forget.
The old prophecies about Laius are failing,
Men reject them now.
Apollo is without honor everywhere.
The gods are defeated.

(*Enter* JOCASTA, *with branches of olive.*)

JOCASTA (*to* CHORUS). Lords of Thebes, it occurred to me to come to the temples of the gods bearing in my hands these branches and offerings of incense. For Oedipus is distracted with sorrows of all kinds. He does not act like a man in control of his reason, judging the present by the past—he is at the mercy of anyone who speaks to him, especially one who speaks of terrors. I have given him advice, but it does no good. (*Facing the altar*) So I come to you, Lord Apollo, for you are closest to hand. I come in supplication with these emblems of prayer. Deliver us, make us free and clear of defilement. We are all afraid, like passengers on a ship who see their pilot crazed with fear.

(*Enter from side* CORINTHIAN MESSENGER.)

CORINTHIAN MESSENGER (*to* CHORUS). Strangers, can one of you tell me—where is the palace of King Oedipus? Better still, if you know, where is the king himself?

CHORUS LEADER. This is his palace, and he is inside, stranger. This lady is his queen, his wife and mother of his children.

CORINTHIAN MESSENGER. Greetings to the noble wife of Oedipus! May you and all your family be blessed forever.

JOCASTA. The same blessings on you, stranger, for your kind words. But tell us what you want. Why have you come? Have you some news for us?

CORINTHIAN MESSENGER. Good news for your house and your husband, lady.

JOCASTA. What news? Who sent you?

CORINTHIAN MESSENGER. I come from Corinth. My message will bring you joy—no doubt of that—but sorrow, too.

JOCASTA. What is it? How can it work both ways?

CORINTHIAN MESSENGER. The people of Corinth will make Oedipus their king, so I heard there.

JOCASTA. What? Is old Polybus no longer on the throne?

CORINTHIAN MESSENGER. No. He is dead and in his grave.

JOCASTA. What did you say? Polybus is dead? Dead?

CORINTHIAN MESSENGER. Condemn me to death if I am not telling the truth.

JOCASTA (*to servant*). You there, go in quickly and tell your master.

O prophecies of the gods, where are you now? Polybus was the man Oedipus feared he might kill—and so avoided him all this time. And now he's dead—a natural death, and not by the hand of Oedipus.

(*Enter* OEDIPUS, *from doors.*)

OEDIPUS. Jocasta, why did you send for me to come out here?

JOCASTA. Listen to what this man says, and see what has become of the holy prophecies of the gods.

OEDIPUS. Who is he? What does he have to say to me?

JOCASTA. He's from Corinth. He came to tell you that your father Polybus is dead and gone.

OEDIPUS. Is this true? Tell me yourself.

CORINTHIAN MESSENGER. If that's what you want to hear first, here it is, a plain statement: Polybus is dead and gone.

OEDIPUS. How? Killed by a traitor, or wasted by disease?

CORINTHIAN MESSENGER. He was old. It did not take much to put him to sleep.

OEDIPUS. By disease, then—that's how he died?

CORINTHIAN MESSENGER. Yes, that, and the length of years he had lived.

OEDIPUS. So! Why then, Jocasta, should we study Apollo's oracle, or gaze at the birds screaming over our heads—those prophets who announced that I would kill my father? He's dead, buried, below ground. And here I am in Thebes—I did not put hand to sword.

Perhaps he died from longing to see me again. That way, it could be said that I was the cause of his death. But there he lies, dead, taking with him all these prophecies I feared—they are worth nothing!

JOCASTA. Is that not what I told you?

OEDIPUS. It is. But I was led astray by fear.

JOCASTA. Now rid your heart of fear forever.

OEDIPUS. No, I must still fear—and who would not?—a marriage with my mother.

JOCASTA. Fear? Why should man fear? His life is governed by the operations of chance. Nothing can be clearly foreseen. The best way to live is by hit and miss, as best you can. Don't be afraid that you may marry your mother. Many a man before you, in dreams, has shared his mother's bed. But to live at ease one must attach no importance to such things.

OEDIPUS. All that you have said would be fine—if my mother were not still alive. But she is, and no matter how good a case you make, I am still a prey to fear.

JOCASTA. But you father's death—that much at least is a great blessing.

OEDIPUS. Yes, I see that. But my mother, as long as she is alive, fills me with fear.

CORINTHIAN MESSENGER. Who is this woman that inspires such fear in you?

OEDIPUS. Merope, old man, the wife of Polybus.

CORINTHIAN MESSENGER. And what is there about her which frightens you?

OEDIPUS. A dreadful prophecy sent by the gods.

CORINTHIAN MESSENGER. Can you tell me what it is? Or is it forbidden for others to know?

OEDIPUS. Yes, I can tell you. Apollo once announced that I am destined to mate with my mother, and shed my father's blood with my own hand. That is why for so many years I have lived far away from Corinth. It has turned out well—but still, there's nothing sweeter than the sight of one's parents.

CORINTHIAN MESSENGER. Is that it? It was in fear of this that you banished yourself from Corinth?

OEDIPUS. Yes. I did not want to be my father's murderer.

CORINTHIAN MESSENGER. My lord, I do not know why I have not already released you from that fear. I came here to bring you good news.

OEDIPUS. If you can do that, you will be handsomely rewarded.

CORINTHIAN MESSENGER. Yes, that was why I came, to bring you home to Corinth, and be rewarded for it.

OEDIPUS. I will never go to the city where my parents live.

CORINTHIAN MESSENGER. My son, it is clear that you don't know what you are doing.

OEDIPUS. What do you mean, old man? In God's name, explain yourself.

CORINTHIAN MESSENGER. You don't know what you are doing, if you are afraid to come home because of *them*.

OEDIPUS. I am afraid that Apollo's prophecy may come true.

CORINTHIAN MESSENGER. That you will be stained with guilt through your parents?

OEDIPUS. Yes, that's it, old man, that's the fear which pursues me always.

CORINTHIAN MESSENGER. In reality, you have nothing to fear.

OEDIPUS. Nothing? How, if I am the son of Polybus and Merope?

CORINTHIAN MESSENGER. Because Polybus was not related to you in any way.

OEDIPUS. What do you mean? Was Polybus not my father?

CORINTHIAN MESSENGER. No more than I am—he was as much your father as I.

OEDIPUS. How can my father be on the same level as you who are nothing to me?

CORINTHIAN MESSENGER. Because he was no more your father than I am.
OEDIPUS. Then why did he call me his son?
CORINTHIAN MESSENGER. He took you from my hands—I gave you to him.
OEDIPUS. Took me from your hands? Then how could he love me so much?
CORINTHIAN MESSENGER. He had been childless, that was why he loved you.
OEDIPUS. *You* gave me to him? Did you . . . buy me? or find me somewhere?
CORINTHIAN MESSENGER. I found you in the shady valleys of Mount Cithaeron.
OEDIPUS. What were you doing there?
CORINTHIAN MESSENGER. Watching over my flocks on the mountainside.
OEDIPUS. A shepherd, were you? A wandering day laborer?
CORINTHIAN MESSENGER. Yes, but at that moment I was your savior.
OEDIPUS. When you picked me up, was I in pain?
CORINTHIAN MESSENGER. Your ankles would bear witness on that point.
OEDIPUS. Oh, why do you speak of that old affliction?
CORINTHIAN MESSENGER. You had your ankles pinned together, and I freed you.
OEDIPUS. It is a dreadful mark of shame I have borne since childhood.
CORINTHIAN MESSENGER. From that misfortune comes the name which you still bear.[1]
OEDIPUS. In God's name, who did it? My mother, or my father? Speak.
CORINTHIAN MESSENGER. I don't know. The one who gave you to me is the man to ask, not me.
OEDIPUS. You got me from someone else—you did not find me yourself?
CORINTHIAN MESSENGER. No. Another shepherd gave you to me.
OEDIPUS. Who was he? Do you know? Could you describe him?
CORINTHIAN MESSENGER. I think he belonged to the household of Laius.
OEDIPUS. You mean the man who was once king of this country?
CORINTHIAN MESSENGER. Yes. He was one of the shepherds of Laius.
OEDIPUS. Is he still alive? Can I talk to him?
CORINTHIAN MESSENGER (*to* CHORUS). You people who live here would know that better than I.

---

[1] His name, Oedipus, means, in Greek, "swollen foot." [Translator's note.]

OEDIPUS (*to* CHORUS). Is there any one of you people here who knows this shepherd he mentioned? Has anyone seen him in the fields, or here in Thebes?

CHORUS LEADER. I think it is the same man from the fields you wanted to see before. But the queen here, Jocasta, could tell you that.

OEDIPUS. Jocasta, do you remember the man we sent for just now? Is *that* the man he is talking about?

JOCASTA. Why ask who he means? Don't pay any attention to him. Don't even think about what he said—it makes no sense.

OEDIPUS. What? With a clue like this? Give up the search? Fail to solve the mystery of my birth? Never!

JOCASTA. In God's name, if you place any value on your life, don't pursue the search. It is enough that *I* am sick to death.

OEDIPUS. *You* have nothing to be afraid of. Even if my mother turns out to be a slave, and I a slave for three generations back, *your* noble birth will not be called in question.

JOCASTA. Take my advice, I beg you—do not go on with it.

OEDIPUS. Nothing will move me. I *will* find out the whole truth.

JOCASTA. It is good advice I am giving you—I am thinking of you.

OEDIPUS. That "good advice" of yours is trying my patience.

JOCASTA. Ill-fated man. May you never find out who you are!

OEDIPUS (*to attendants*). One of you go and get that shepherd, bring him here. We will leave *her* to pride herself on her royal birth.

JOCASTA. Unfortunate! That is the only name I can you by now. I shall not call your name again—ever! (*Exit* JOCASTA *to palace.*)

(*A long silence.*)

CHORUS. Why has the queen gone, Oedipus, why has she rushed away in such wild grief? I am afraid that from this silence evil will burst out.

OEDIPUS. Burst out what will! I shall know my origin, mean though it be. Jocasta perhaps—she is proud, *like* a woman—feels shame at the low circumstances of my birth. But I count myself the son of Good Chance, the giver of success—I shall not be dishonored. Chance is my mother. My brothers are the months which have made me sometimes small and sometimes great. Such is my lineage and I shall not betray it. I will not give up the search for the truth about my birth. (*Exit* OEDIPUS *to palace.*)

CHORUS (*chanting in unison*).
If I am a true prophet
And see clear in my mind,
Tomorrow at the full moon
Oedipus will honor Mount Cithaeron
As his nurse and mother.
Mount Cithaeron—our king's Theban birthplace!

We shall celebrate it in dance and song—
A place loved by our king.
Lord Apollo, may this find favor in your sight.

Who was it, Oedipus my son, who bore you?
Which of the nymphs that live so long
Was the bride of Pan the mountain god?
Was your mother the bride of Apollo himself?
He loves the upland pastures.
Or was Hermes your father?
Perhaps Dionysus who lives on the mountain peaks
Received you as a welcome gift
From one of the nymphs of Helicon,
His companions in sport.

(*Enter from side the* SHEPHERD, *accompanied by two guards.*)
(*Enter* OEDIPUS, *from doors.*)

OEDIPUS. I never met the man, but, if I may make a guess, I think this man I see is the shepherd we have been looking for all this time. His age corresponds to that of the Corinthian here, and, in any case, the men bringing him are my servants, I recognize them.

(*To* CHORUS LEADER) You have seen the shepherd before, you should know better than I.

CHORUS LEADER. Yes, I recognize him. He was in the household of Laius—a devoted servant, and a shepherd.

OEDIPUS. I question you first—you, the stranger from Corinth. Is this the man you spoke of?

CORINTHIAN MESSENGER. This is the man.

OEDIPUS (*to* SHEPHERD). You, old man, come here. Look me in the face. Answer my questions. Were you a servant of Laius once?

SHEPHERD. I was. A slave. Not bought, though. I was born and reared in the palace.

OEDIPUS. What was your work? How did you earn your living?

SHEPHERD. For most of my life I have followed where the sheep flocks went.

OEDIPUS. And where did you graze your sheep most of the time?

SHEPHERD. Well, there was Mount Cithaeron, and all the country round it.

OEDIPUS. Do you know this man here? Did you ever see him before?

SHEPHERD. Which man do you mean? What could he be doing there?

OEDIPUS. This one, here. Did you ever come across him?

SHEPHERD. I can't say, right away. Give me time. I don't remember.

CORINTHIAN MESSENGER. No wonder he doesn't remember, master.

He forgets, but I'll remind him, and make it clear. I am sure he knows very well how the two of us grazed our flocks on Cithaeron—he had two and I only one—we were together three whole summers, from spring until the rising of Arcturus in the fall. When winter came I used to herd my sheep back to their winter huts, and he took his back to the farms belonging to Laius. Do you remember any of this? Isn't that what happened?

SHEPHERD. What you say is true, but it was a long time ago.

CORINTHIAN MESSENGER. Well, then, tell me this. Do you remember giving me a child, a boy, for me to bring up as my own?

SHEPHERD. What are you talking about? Why do you ask that question?

CORINTHIAN MESSENGER. Oedipus here, my good man, Oedipus and that child are one and the same.

SHEPHERD. Damn you! Shut your mouth. Keep quiet!

OEDIPUS. Old man, don't you correct *him*. It is you and your tongue that need correction.

SHEPHERD. What have I done wrong, noble master?

OEDIPUS. You refuse to answer his question about the child.

SHEPHERD. That's because he does not know what he's talking about—he is just wasting your time.

OEDIPUS. If you won't speak willingly, we shall see if pain can make your speak.

(*The guards seize the* SHEPHERD.)

SHEPHERD. In God's name, don't! Don't torture me. I am an old man.

OEDIPUS. One of you twist his arms behind his back, quickly!

SHEPHERD. Oh, God, what for? What more do you want to know?

OEDIPUS. Did you give him the child he asked about?

SHEPHERD. Yes, I did. And I wish I had died that day.

OEDIPUS. You will die now, if you don't give an honest answer.

SHEPHERD. And if I speak, I shall be even worse off.

OEDIPUS (*to guards*). What? More delay?

SHEPHERD. No! No! I said it before—I gave him the child.

OEDIPUS. Where did *you* get it? Was it yours? Or did it belong to someone else?

SHEPHERD. It wasn't mine. Someone gave it to me.

OEDIPUS. Which of these Thebans here? From whose house did it come?

SHEPHERD. In God's name, master, don't ask any more questions.

OEDIPUS. You are a dead man if I have to ask you again.

SHEPHERD. It was a child born in the house of Laius.

OEDIPUS. Was it a slave? Or a member of the royal family?

SHEPHERD. Oh, God, here comes the dreadful truth. And I must speak.

OEDIPUS. And I must hear it. But hear it I will.

SHEPHERD. It was the son of Laius, so I was told. But the lady inside there, your wife, she is the one to tell you.
OEDIPUS. Did *she* give it to you?
SHEPHERD. Yes, my lord, she did.
OEDIPUS. For what purpose?
SHEPHERD. To destroy it.
OEDIPUS. Her own child?
SHEPHERD. She was afraid of dreadful prophecies.
OEDIPUS. What were they?
SHEPHERD. The child would kill its parents, that was the story.
OEDIPUS. Then why did you give it to this old man here?
SHEPHERD. In pity, master. I thought he would take it away to a foreign country—to the place he came from. If you are the man he says you are, you were born the most unfortunate of men.
OEDIPUS. O God! It has all come true. Light, let this be the last time I see you. I stand revealed—born in shame, married in shame, an unnatural murderer. (*Exit* OEDIPUS *into palace.*)

(*Exeunt others at sides.*)

CHORUS.
O generations of mortal men,
I add up the total of your lives
And find it equal to nothing.
What man wins more happiness
Than a mere appearance which quickly fades away?
With your example before me,
Your life, your destiny, miserable Oedipus,
      I call no man happy.

Oedipus outranged all others
And won complete prosperity and happiness.
He destroyed the Sphinx, that maiden
With curved claws and riddling songs,
And rose up like a towered wall against death—
Oedipus, savior of our city.
From that time on you were called King,
You were honored above all men,
Ruling over great Thebes.

And now—is there a man whose story is more pitiful?
His life is lived in merciless calamity and pain—
A complete reversal from his happy state.
O Oedipus, famous king,
You whom the same great harbor sheltered

As child and father both,
How could the furrows which your father plowed
Bear *you* in silence for so long?

Time, which sees all things, has found you out;
It sits in judgment on the unnatural marriage
Which was both begetter and begot.
    O son of Laius,
I wish I had never seen you.
I weep, like a man wailing for the dead.
    This is the truth:
You returned me to life once
And now you have closed my eyes in darkness.

 (*Enter, from the palace, a* MESSENGER.)

 MESSENGER. Citizens of Thebes, you who are most honored in this city! What dreadful things you will see and hear! What a cry of sorrow you will raise, if, as true Thebans, you have any feeling for the royal house. Not even the great rivers of Ister and Phasis could wash this house clean of the horrors it hides within. And it will soon expose them to the light of day—horrors deliberately willed, not involuntary. Those calamities we inflict on ourselves are those which cause the most pain.
 CHORUS LEADER. The horrors we knew about before were burden enough. What other dreadful news do you bring?
 MESSENGER. Here is the thing quickest for me to say and you to hear. Jocasta, our queen, is dead.
 CHORUS LEADER. Poor lady. From what cause?
 MESSENGER. By her own hand. You are spared the worst of what has happened—you were not there to see it. But as far as my memory serves, you shall hear the full story of that unhappy woman's sufferings.
 She came in through the door in a fury of passion and rushed straight towards her marriage bed, tearing at her hair with both hands. Into her bedroom she went, and slammed the doors behind her. She was calling the name of Laius, so long dead, remembering the child she bore to him so long ago—the child by whose hand Laius was to die, and leave her, its mother, to bear monstrous children to her own son. She wailed in mourning for her marriage, in which she had borne double offspring, a husband from her husband and children from her child. And after that—but I do not know exactly how she died. For Oedipus came bursting in, shouting, and so we could not watch Jocasta's suffering to the end; all of us looked at him as he ran to and fro. He rushed from one of us to the other, asking us to give him a sword, to tell him where he could find his wife—no, not his wife, but his mother, his mother and the mother of his children.

It must have been some supernatural being that showed the raving man where she was; it was not one of us. As if led by a guide he threw himself against the doors of her room with a terrible cry; he bent the bolts out of their sockets, and so forced his way into the room. And there we saw Jocasta, hanging, her neck caught in a swinging noose of rope. When Oedipus saw her he gave a deep dreadful cry of sorrow and loosened the rope round her neck. And when the poor woman was lying on the ground—then we saw the most dreadful sight of all. He ripped out the golden pins with which her clothes were fastened, raised them high above his head, and speared the pupils of his eyes. "You will not see," he said, "the horrors I have suffered and done. Be dark forever now—eyes that saw those you should never have seen, and failed to recognize those you longed to see." Murmuring words like these he raised his hands and struck his eyes again, and again. And each time the wounded eyes sent a stream of blood down his chin, no oozing flow but a dark shower of it, thick as a hailstorm.

These are the sorrows which have burst out and overwhelmed them both, man and wife alike. The wealth and happiness they once had was real while it lasted, but now—weeping, destruction, death, shame—name any shape of evil you will, they have them all.

CHORUS. And Oedipus—poor wretched Oedipus—has he now some rest from pain?

MESSENGER. He is shouting, "Open the doors, someone: show me to all the people of Thebes, my father's killer, my mother's"—I cannot repeat his unholy words. He speaks of banishing himself from Thebes, says he will not remain in his house under the curse which he himself pronounced. But he has no strength: he needs someone to guide his steps. The pain is more than he can bear.

But he will show you himself. The bolts of this door are opening. Now you will see a spectacle that even his enemies would pity.

(*Enter* OEDIPUS *from door, blind.*)

CHORUS. O suffering dreadful for mankind to see, most dreadful of all I ever saw. What madness came over you? What unearthly spirit, leaping farther than the mind can conceive, swooped down on your destiny? I pity you. I have many questions to ask you, much I wish to know; my eyes are drawn towards you—but I cannot bear to look. You fill me with horror.

OEDIPUS. Where am I going? Pity me! Where does my voice range to through the air? O spirit, what a leap you made!

CHORUS. To a point of dread, too far from men's ears and eyes.

OEDIPUS. Darkness, dark cloud all around me, enclosing me, unspeakable darkness, irresistible—you came to me on a wind that seemed favorable. Ah, I feel the stab of these sharp pains, and with it the memory of my sorrow.

CHORUS. In such torment it is no wonder that your pain and mourning should be double.

OEDIPUS. My friend! You are by my side still, you alone. You still stay by me, looking after the blind man. I know you are there. I am in the dark, but I can distinguish your voice clearly.

CHORUS. You have done a dreadful thing. How could you bring yourself to put out the light of your eyes? What superhuman power urged you on?

OEDIPUS. It was Apollo, friends, Apollo, who brought to fulfillment all my sufferings. But the hand that struck my eyes was mine and mine alone. What use had I for eyes? Nothing I could see would bring me joy.

CHORUS. It was just as you say.

OEDIPUS. What was there for me to look at, to speak to, to love? What joyful word can I expect to hear, my friends? Take me away, out of this country, quickly, take me away. I am lost, accursed, and hated by the gods beyond all other men.

CHORUS. I am moved to pity by your misfortunes and your understanding of them, too. I wish I had never known you!

OEDIPUS. A curse on the man who freed my feet from the cruel bonds on the mountain, who saved me and rescued me from death. He will get no thanks from me. I might have died then and there; but now I am a source of grief for myself and all who love me.

CHORUS. I wish it had turned out that way, too.

OEDIPUS. I would never have become my father's killer, never have been known to all men as my own mother's husband. Now I am godforsaken, the son of an accursed marriage, my own father's successor in the marriage bed. If there is any evil worse than the worst that a man can suffer—Oedipus has drawn it for his lot.

CHORUS. I cannot say you made the right decision. You would have been better dead than blind.

OEDIPUS. What I have done was the best thing to do. Don't read me any more lessons, don't give me any more advice. With what eyes could I have faced my father in the house of the dead, or my poor mother? I have done things to them both for which hanging is too small a punishment.

Do you think I longed to look at my children, born the way they were? No, not with these eyes of mine, never! Not this town either, its walls, its holy temples of the gods. From all of this I am cut off, I, the most nobly raised in Thebes, cut off by own act. It was I who proclaimed that everyone should expel the impious man—the man the gods have now revealed as unholy—and the son of Laius. After I had exposed my own guilt—and what a guilt!—do you think I could have looked at my fellow citizens with steady eyes?

No, no! If there had been some way to block the source of hearing, I

SOPHOCLES 53

would not have held back: I would have isolated my wretched body completely, so as to see and hear nothing at all. If my mind could be put beyond reach of my miseries—that would be my pleasure.

O Cithaeron, why did you receive me? Why did you not take and kill me on the spot, so that I should never reveal my origin to mankind?

O Polybus, and Corinth, and the ancient house I thought was my father's—what a handsome heir you raised up in me, how rotten beneath the surface! For now I am exposed—evil and born in evil.

O three roads in the deep valley, you oak wood and you narrow pass where the three roads meet, you who soaked up my father's blood, spilled by my hand—do you remember me? Do you remember what I did there, and what I did when I came here?

O marriage, marriage! You gave me birth, and then bred up seed from the one you brought into the world. You made an incestuous breed of father, brother, son—bride, wife, mother—all the most shameful things known to man.

But I must not speak of things that should never have been done. Quickly, in God's name, hide me somewhere outside Thebes, kill me, throw me into the sea, where you will never see me again.

Come close to me. I am a man of sorrow, but take courage and touch me. Do not be afraid; do what I ask. The evil is mine; no one but me can bear its weight.

(*Enter* CREON, *from side, with attendants.*)

CHORUS LEADER.   Here is Creon. He will listen to your request. Decision and action are up to him, now that he has taken your place as the sole ruler of Thebes.

OEDIPUS.   What shall I say to him? What justification, what grounds for trust can I present? In everything I did to him before, I have been proved wrong.

CREON.   I have not come to mock you, Oedipus, nor to reproach you for the wrong you did.

(*To attendants*) If you have no respect for the feelings of human beings, at least show reverence for the sunlight which nourishes all men. Do not leave him there in full view, an object of dread and horror which appalls the holy rain and the daylight. Get him into the palace as fast as you can.

(*The attendants move over to* OEDIPUS, *and stand by him until the end of the scene.*)

Only his family should see the family shame; this public spectacle is indecent.

OEDIPUS.   In God's name—since you have exceeded my hopes and come in so generous a spirit to one so low—do something for me. I ask it in your interest, not mine.

CREON. What is it you are so anxious to have me do?

OEDIPUS. Banish me from this country as fast as you can—to a place where no man can see me or speak to me.

CREON. You can be sure I would have done so already, but first I wanted to ask the god Apollo what should be done.

OEDIPUS. But his command was clear, every word of it; death for the unholy man, the father-killer.

CREON. That is what the oracle said. But all the same, in our situation, it is better to inquire what should be done.

OEDIPUS. Will you consult Apollo about anyone as miserable as I?

CREON. Yes, and this time, I take it, you will believe what the god says.

OEDIPUS. Yes. I command you—and beg you—the woman in the palace, see to her burial. She is your sister, you are the man to do this. As for me, do not condemn this city of my fathers to shelter me within its walls, but let me live on the mountain, on Cithaeron, forever linked with my name, the mountain which my mother and father while they still lived chose as my burial place. Let me die there where they tried to kill me.

And yet I know this—no disease or anything else will destroy me. Otherwise I would never have been saved from death in the first place. I was saved—for some strange and dreadful end.

Well, let my destiny go where it will. As for my children, do not concern yourself about the boys, Creon. They are men; and will always find a way to live, wherever they may be. But my two poor helpless girls, who were always at my table, who shared the same food I ate—take care of them for me.

What I wish for most is this. Let me touch them with these hands, as I weep for my sorrows. Please, my lord! Grant my prayer, generous man! If I could hold them I would think I had them with me, as I did when I could see.

(ANTIGONE *and* ISMENE *are led in from the door by a nurse.*)

What's that? I hear something. Oh, God. It is my daughters, weeping. Creon took pity on me, and sent them to me, my dearest ones, my children. Am I right?

CREON. Yes, you are. I did this for you knowing the joy you always took in them, the joy you feel now.

OEDIPUS. Bless you for it! May you be rewarded for sending them. May God watch over you better than He did over me.

Children, where are you? Come here, come to these hands of mine, your brother's hands, the hands that intervened to make your father's once bright eyes so dim. Blind and thoughtless, I became your father, and your mother was my mother, too. I weep for you—see you I cannot—when I think of your future, the bitter life you will lead, the way men will treat you. What gatherings will you go to, what festivals, without returning home in tears, instead of taking part in the ceremonies?

And when you come to the age of marriage, who will take the risk, my daughters, and shoulder the burden of reproach which will be directed at my children—and yours? No reproach is missing. Your father killed his father. He sowed the field from which he himself had sprung, and begot you, his children, at the source of his own being. These are the reproaches you will hear. And who will marry you? There is no one who will do so, children; your destiny is clear—to waste away unmarried, childless.

Creon, you are the only father they have now, for we who brought them into the world are both of us destroyed. Do not abandon them to wander husbandless in poverty: they are your own flesh and blood. Do not make them equal to me and my miserable state, but pity them. They are children, they have no protector but you. Promise me this, noble Creon, touch me with your hand to confirm your promise.

And you, children—if you were old enough to understand, I would have much advice to give you. But as it is, I will tell you what to pray for. Pray that you may find a place where you are allowed to live, and for a life happier than your father's.

CREON. You have wept long enough. Now go inside the house.
OEDIPUS. I must obey, though it gives me no pleasure.
CREON. Yes, everything is good in its proper place and time.
OEDIPUS. I will go in then, but on one condition.
CREON. Tell me what it is. I am listening.
OEDIPUS. You must send me into exile—away from Thebes.
CREON. What you ask for is a gift only Apollo can grant.
OEDIPUS. But I am hateful to the gods above all men.
CREON. In that case, they will grant your request at once.
OEDIPUS. You consent, then?
CREON. It is not my habit to say what I don't mean.
OEDIPUS. Then take me away from here at once.
CREON. Come then, but let go of the children.
OEDIPUS. No, don't take them away from me.
CREON. Don't try to be master in everything. What you once won and held did not stay with you all your life long.

CHORUS.[2] Citizens who dwell in Thebes, look at Oedipus here, who knew the answer to the famous riddle and was a power in the land. On his good fortune all the citizens gazed with envy. Into what a stormy sea of

---

[2] The translator, sharing the opinion of many authorities, believed the following speech to be an addition to the play made by a later producer, but included the lines for those who wished to use them.

dreadful trouble he has come now. Therefore we must call no man happy while he waits to see his last day, not until he has passed the border of life and death without suffering pain.

DISCUSSION

Oedipus the King is the quintessential classical expression of man's quest for self-knowledge. If we can learn to see it with the imagination it asks us to use, we can come to understand something significant about both the nature of drama and the meaning of the Greek admonition "know thyself."

This is not to say that the play is some kind of dramatized lecture or sermon on self-knowledge. Far from it. The play is filled with contradictions that continue to perplex scholars and philosophers. If we take it to mean one thing, we find evidence that it also means the opposite. If Oedipus is objectively guilty of the heinous crimes of having killed his father and married his mother, he is subjectively innocent of both crimes, having done them unwittingly. If Oedipus' nobility comes from his resolve to know the truth and from his faith in his ability to discover it, so does his final degradation. If there is order in the universe, as the play implies, why is so noble and innocent a man as Oedipus punished so harshly? How can it be just to punish him for doing what he was fated to do; for what, in other words, he could not avoid doing? How can the play be considered a "great" drama, or even dramatic at all, if Oedipus is fated, rather than free, to act and make choices for which he is responsible? How can he be called "heroic" if he is a mere puppet of the gods?

These and a great many other puzzling contradictions confront anyone who delves very deeply into the play. How, then, can we say that the play presents a "philosophy" or, for that matter, that it takes any position? Is it for religious faith and against faith in reason? Why, then, is Oedipus shown at his most noble as well as his most ignoble when he is asserting his reasoning ability against all others, including the gods? Is the play for religion or against it? For reason or against it? For action or against it? For heroism or against it?

There are a number of ways in which someone bent on ferreting out the "philosophy" of the play could try to resolve its apparent contradictions. One could, for example, decide that the play is about what the Greeks called *sophrosyne,* that is, modesty, balance, and restraint, or simply knowing one's limitations. If this is true, one might argue that Sophocles is both for and against everything: for a balanced view of faith, reason, and action—

against any extremism. However, if Sophocles is out to illustrate the virtue of modesty and balance, it is unfortunate that Creon, the play's most perfect example of these qualities, is a pallid creature next to the high-spirited and bold sinner Oedipus.

What, then, do we make of the play's contradictions? Do they tell us anything of the play's meaning? Or, perhaps, do they tell us that it has no meaning in the usual sense of that term? Do they tell us something about why the play is considered a great play? Something, at least, about the nature of drama? What, if anything, is it they do tell us?

Perhaps one thing the play does is to show us that merely being told about human experience is not enough; we must experience life's complexities for ourselves, at least through imaginative participation in art and literature, in order to understand feelingly the difficulties men have in facing and resolving contradictions. Oedipus believes in his ability to solve riddles logically, but he cannot solve the riddle of his own life until he is totally immersed, emotionally as well as logically, in making sense of it. At first he thinks he is above involvement in life. Despite the words he and the Chorus say to the contrary, at the beginning of the play Oedipus acts as though he were a god, the final judge of the one who caused the plague, the dispenser of justice and retribution. But here again we soon see, as he does, that the opposite of what he had thought to be the whole truth is also true: once the hunter, he becomes the hunted; once the measurer and reasoner, he becomes the measured; once a public man who spoke to his citizens as if they were children, he becomes a private citizen who must be led like a child; once the greatest of men, he becomes the lowest.

Almost everything that Oedipus does seems to involve a struggle. Yet he constantly tries to do a great deal: to end the plague, to find the murderer of Laius, to find out who he is, and so on. Perhaps fated to kill his father and marry his mother, he is certainly not fated to know that he has done these things. The knowledge that he has fulfilled the prophecy is something he learns through doggedness and dedication to the truth, no matter what the cost to himself. Although he is at times rash and impetuous, we admire him for his honesty and drive. The other characters are afraid of the truth; Tiresias, Jocasta, Creon, and the Chorus all quail from it. Some of them try to stop Oedipus from seeking it, but he will not be turned away from its pursuit.

Could it be that Sophocles is showing us that what gives our lives true meaning is how we act, not what restrictions are placed on us? We are all born and, some day, we all must die. One could say that we are fated to die. What counts, however, is how we act while we live. Will we act heroically or basely? Can we turn the given conditions of our existence to creative advantage, or will we merely bemoan our fate? We are all both fated and free, subjects and objects, living and dying, reasoners and feelers, good and evil, and an endless number of other contradictories. Do we accept one aspect of what we are and reject its opposite? To some of us who are mathematically oriented, pure reason seems to tell us that negatives and positives do not mix. But life shows us that they do and must. If we are to act at all, we must often ignore the contradictions that reason imposes. Perhaps it is one function of drama to show us that action is possible despite the struggle and suffering that it entails. In Sophoclean drama, at least, man can know the truth. The prophecy holds: there is pattern and meaning in the universe. Each man is not his own creator of purpose and meaning in a universe of chance, as Jocasta implies at one point. Difficult and contradictory as the idea may seem, especially in our age of reason and science, in Sophocles man can learn to come into harmony with himself, his society, and his gods. Beast and angel, subject and object, living and dying, he can nevertheless act, and with grandeur. And, chaotic and purposeless as his life may seem, he can, if he recognizes the contradictions of which life is made, have a beginning, a middle, and an end—a purpose and design that brings him into harmony with the mysterious design of things he can know but cannot reason. Just as the tragedy of Oedipus is that he hides from the truth—the truth about his own nature as well as the nature of things—the grandeur of the play comes from his having the capacity and the will to eventually learn the truth about both. Learning to see only when he becomes blind, he shows us our own capacities in the face of limitations, our capacities to know the truth about ourselves and the world and to act heroically in the full knowledge of that truth.

Among the things that we can learn from the play, then, are the following:

1) Man's search for true self-realization is fraught with great difficulty.
2) This search is difficult because man is a creature of infinite complexities and contradictions; human experience can be seen from so many different and contradictory perspectives that the wiser a man gets, the more he may be unable to act.
3) Self-realization is the ability to act in a way that takes into account the totality of what a man is, not merely one or a few of his aspects.
4) Drama is a medium that imaginatively presents man's struggle to act in the face of a full knowledge of the contradictories that would seem to prevent him from acting.
5) Drama implies that action is possible even in the face of the greatest obstacles.
6) Greek drama implies that there is order in the universe, and that it is possible for heroic men to come into harmony with it.

THEME AND DISCUSSION QUESTIONS

1. Modern audiences, accustomed to the theatrical tradition of realism, find it difficult to understand or appreciate Greek drama's use of a chorus. How integral a part of *Oedipus the King* is the chorus? Does it function as a character involved in the conflict, or merely as an observer who is detached from the events happening around him?
2. *Oedipus the King* was presented by Sophocles at an annual ceremony that was both a civic and a religious celebration. In what ways is the play concerned with human beings, both as citizens and as religious beings?
3. Sophocles wrote *Oedipus the King* at a time when the old religions were under attack by advocates of the new, more scientific philosophies. The Sophists, for example, were advocating that man and not God should be the measure of all things. In what ways is that particular issue central to this play? If Sophocles was in some way trying to convince the Greeks to hold onto the religious values they were threatening to reject, why is he so emphatic about the harshness of the gods, about what almost appears to be their arbitrariness?
4. One of the central issues modern audiences see raised by the play is the question of how free Oedipus is to act. If he is fated to kill his father and marry his mother, why should he be punished at all? If Oedipus is not free to act, can the play be considered one of the greatest plays ever written?
5. At the very beginning of the play the chorus calls Oedipus "the best of men," although his violent temper has already led him to kill his father and will surface again in his scenes with Creon and Tiresias. Is Oedipus basically a good man? In what ways is he a better person than Creon? Than Tiresias?
6. It is relatively simple to see Oedipus' external struggles with others: he fights with Creon and Tiresias and he even fights against Jocasta's appeals that he discontinue his search for his identity. What indications are there of an internal struggle in Oedipus? Is he, despite his determination to find out who he is, also afraid of finding out?
7. At one point the chorus calls Oedipus the "paradigm of men." In what ways does he stand for humanity?
8. In its last remarks, the chorus says, in effect, that we should not count a man happy until he is dead. Does this make the play merely a cynical statement?
9. Sophocles wrote three Oedipus plays: *Oedipus the King, Antigone,* and *Oedipus at Colonus.* The first deals with Oedipus' discovery of his identity, the second, with what happens to his children after his death, and the third, his exile and death. The fact that they were originally staged years

apart suggests that Sophocles at least thought each was an independent play. What evidence do you find in the play to support or refute that conclusion?

Othello: Production directed by John Dexter, at National Theatre, London (1964); starring Laurence Olivier, Maggie Smith, and Frank Finlay. Photograph, by Angus McBean, courtesy of the Harvard Theatre Collection.

WILLIAM SHAKESPEARE

Othello

Though the plays of William Shakespeare are generally accepted as among the greatest ever written, the facts of his life are the subject of seemingly endless controversy. Most authorities agree, however, that Shakespeare was born in 1564 in the English borough of Stratford-upon-Avon and that he was the son of a town official and a woman from a respected landowning family. The elder Shakespeare, by trade a glover, apparently lost his fortune before his son was old enough to enter a university; thus, William Shakespeare never received an advanced education. In his late teens he married a woman named Anne Hathaway and, fairly soon after their marriage, left Stratford for London. Little is known about Shakespeare's activities during the next seven or eight years; but, by the time he was twenty-eight, he was associated with the Globe Theatre as both an actor and a playwright. Eventually, he became a co-owner of the Globe and gave up acting in favor of a greater commitment to playwriting. Shakespeare retired from the theater about 1610 and returned to Stratford, where, having bought himself a coat of arms and one of the finest houses in town, he lived with his wife until his death, in April, 1616. He is buried beneath the chancel of the parish church at Stratford.

OTHELLO from *Shakespeare: The Complete Works* edited by G. B. Harrison, copyright, 1948, 1952, by Harcourt Brace Jovanovich, Inc. and reprinted with their permission.

CHARACTERS

DUKE OF VENICE
BRABANTIO, *a Senator*
OTHER SENATORS
GRATIANO, *brother to Brabantio*
LODOVICO, *kinsman to Brabantio*
OTHELLO, *a noble Moor in the service of the Venetian state*
CASSIO, *his lieutenant*
IAGO, *his ancient*
MONTANO, *Othello's predecessor in the government of Cyprus*
RODERIGO, *a Venetian gentleman*
CLOWN, *servant to Othello*
DESDEMONA, *daughter to Brabantio and wife to Othello*
EMILIA, *wife to Iago*
BIANCA, *mistress to Cassio*
SAILOR, MESSENGER, HERALD, OFFICERS, GENTLEMEN, MUSICIANS, *and* ATTENDANTS

SCENE. *Venice; a seaport in Cyprus.*

ACT I

SCENE I. *Venice. A street.*

Enter RODERIGO *and* IAGO.

RODERIGO.   Tush, never tell me. I take it much unkindly
That thou, Iago, who hast had my purse
As if the strings were thine, shouldst know of this.
    IAGO.   'Sblood, but you will not hear me.
If ever I did dream of such a matter,   5
Abhor me.
    RODERIGO.   Thou told'st me thou didst hold him in thy hate.
    IAGO.   Despise me if I do not. Three great ones of the city,
In personal suit to make me his Lieutenant,
Off-capped to him. And, by the faith of man,   10
I know my price, I am worth no worse a place.
But he, as loving his own pride and purposes,
Evades them, with a bombast circumstance
Horribly stuffed with epithets of war.

And, in conclusion, 15
Nonsuits° my mediators, for, "Certes," says he,
"I have already chose my officer."
And what was he?
Forsooth, a great arithmetician,°
One Michael Cassio, a Florentine, 20
A fellow almost damned in a fair wife,°
That never set a squadron in the field,
Nor the division of a battle knows
More than a spinster, unless the bookish theoric,
Wherein the toged° Consuls can propose 25
As masterly as he—mere prattle without practice
Is all his soldiership. But he, sir, had the election.
And I, of whom his eyes had seen the proof
At Rhodes, at Cyprus, and on other grounds
Christian and heathen, must be beleed° and calmed 30
By debtor and creditor. This countercaster,°
He, in good time,° must his Lieutenant be,
And I—God bless the mark!—his Moorship's Ancient.°
    RODERIGO. By Heaven, I rather would have been his hangman.
    IAGO. Why, there's no remedy. 'Tis the course of service, 35
Preferment goes by letter and affection,
And not by old gradation,° where each second
Stood heir to the first. Now, sir, be judge yourself
Whether I in any just term am affined°
To love the Moor.
    RODERIGO. I would not follow him, then. 40
    IAGO. Oh, sir, content you,
I follow him to serve my turn upon him.
We cannot all be masters, nor all masters
Cannot be truly followed. You shall mark

---

16. Nonsuits: rejects the petition of. **19. arithmetician:** Contemporary books on military tactics are full of elaborate diagrams and numerals to explain military formations. Cassio is a student of such books. **21. almost . . . wife:** A much-disputed phrase. There is an Italian proverb, "You have married a fair wife? You are damned." If Iago has this in mind, he means by *almost* that Cassio is about to marry. **25. toged:** wearing a toga. **30. beleed:** placed on the lee (or unfavorable) side. **31. countercaster:** calculator (repeating the idea of arithmetician). Counters were used in making calculations. **32. in . . . time:** A phrase expressing indignation. **33. Ancient:** ensign, the third officer in the company of which Othello is Captain and Cassio Lieutenant. **36–37. Preferment . . . gradation:** promotion comes through private recommendation and favoritism and not by order of seniority. **39. affined:** tied by affection.

Many a duteous and knee-crooking knave 45
That doting on his own obsequious bondage
Wears out his time, much like his master's ass,
For naught but provender, and when he's old, cashiered.
Whip me such honest knaves. Others there are
Who, trimmed in forms and visages of duty, 50
Keep yet their hearts attending on themselves,
And throwing but shows of service on their lords
Do well thrive by them, and when they have lined their coats
Do themselves homage. These fellows have some soul,
And such a one do I profess myself. For, sir, 55
It is as sure as you are Roderigo,
Were I the Moor, I would not be Iago.
In following him, I follow but myself.
Heaven is my judge, not I for love and duty,
But seeming so, for my peculiar° end. 60
For when my outward action doth demonstrate
The native act and figure of my heart
In compliment extern, 'tis not long after
But I will wear my heart upon my sleeve
For daws to peck at. I am not what I am. 65
 RODERIGO. What a full fortune does the thick-lips owe°
If he can carry 't thus!°
 IAGO.   Call up her father,
Rouse him. Make after him, poison his delight,
Proclaim him in the streets. Incense her kinsmen,
And though he in a fertile climate dwell, 70
Plague him with flies. Though that his joy be joy,
Yet throw such changes of vexation on 't
As it may lose some color.
 RODERIGO. Here is her father's house, I'll call aloud.
 IAGO. Do, with like timorous° accent and dire yell 75
As when, by night and negligence, the fire
Is spied in populous cities.
 RODERIGO. What ho, Brabantio! Signior Brabantio, ho!
 IAGO. Awake! What ho, Brabantio! Thieves! Thieves! Thieves!
Look to your house, your daughter and your bags!° 80
Thieves! Thieves!

 (BRABANTIO *appears above, at a window.*)

 BRABANTIO. What is the reason of this terrible summons?
What is the matter there?

60. **peculiar**: particular, personal. 66. **owe**: own. 67. **carry't thus**: i.e., bring off this marriage. 75. **timorous**: terrifying. 80. **bags**: moneybags.

RODERIGO. Signior, is all your family within?
IAGO. Are your doors locked?
BRABANTIO. Why, wherefore ask you this? 85
IAGO. 'Zounds, sir, you're robbed. For shame, put on your gown,
Your heart is burst, you have lost half your soul.
Even now, now, very now, an old black ram
Is tupping your white ewe. Arise, arise,
Awake the snorting° citizens with the bell, 90
Or else the Devil° will make a grandsire of you.
Arise, I say.
BRABANTIO. What, have you lost your wits?
RODERIGO. Most reverend signior, do you know my voice?
BRABANTIO. Not I. What are you?
RODERIGO. My name is Roderigo.
BRABANTIO. The worser welcome. 95
I have charged thee not to haunt about my doors.
In honest plainness thou hast heard me say
My daughter is not for thee, and now, in madness,
Being full of supper and distempering draughts,
Upon malicious bravery° dost thou come 100
To start° my quiet.
RODERIGO. Sir, sir, sir—
BRABANTIO. But thou must needs be sure
My spirit and my place have in them power
To make this bitter to thee.
RODERIGO. Patience, good sir.
BRABANTIO. What tell'st thou me of robbing? This is Venice, 105
My house is not a grange.°
RODERIGO. Most grave Brabantio,
In simple and pure soul I come to you.
IAGO. 'Zounds, sir, you are one of those that will not serve God if the Devil bid you. Because we come to do you service and you think we are ruffians, you'll have your daughter covered with a Barbary° horse, 110
you'll have your nephews° neigh to you, you'll have coursers for cousins,° and jennets° for germans.°
BRABANTIO. What profane wretch art thou?
IAGO. I am one, sir, that comes to tell you your daughter and the Moor are now making the beast with two backs. 115
BRABANTIO. Thou art a villain.
IAGO. You are—a Senator.

90. **snorting:** snoring. 91. **Devil:** The Devil in old pictures and woodcuts was represented as black. 100. **bravery:** defiance. 101. **start:** startle. 106. **grange:** lonely farm. 110. **Barbary:** Moorish. 111. **nephews:** grandsons. **cousins:** near relations. 112. **jennets:** Moorish ponies. **germans:** kinsmen.

WILLIAM SHAKESPEARE   67

BRABANTIO. This thou shalt answer. I know thee, Roderigo.
RODERIGO. Sir, I will answer anything. But I beseech you
If 't be your pleasure and most wise consent,
As partly I find it is, that your fair daughter, 120
At this odd-even° and dull watch o' the night,
Transported with no worse nor better guard
But with a knave of common hire, a gondolier,
To the gross clasps of a lascivious Moor—
If this be known to you, and your allowance,° 125
We then have done you bold and saucy wrongs.
But if you know not this, my manners tell me
We have your wrong rebuke. Do not believe
That from the sense of all civility
I thus would play and trifle with your reverence. 130
Your daughter, if you have not given her leave,
I say again, hath made a gross revolt,
Tying her duty, beauty, wit, and fortunes
In an extravagant° and wheeling° stranger
Of here and everywhere. Straight satisfy yourself. 135
If she be in her chamber or your house,
Let loose on me the justice of the state
For thus deluding you.
    BRABANTIO.   Strike on the tinder,° ho!
Give me a taper!° Call up all my people!
This accident is not unlike my dream. 140
Belief of it oppresses me already.
Light, I say! Light!

   (*Exit above.*)

    IAGO.   Farewell, for I must leave you.
It seems not meet, nor wholesome to my place,°
To be produced—as if I stay I shall— 145
Against the Moor. For I do know the state,
However this may gall him with some check,
Cannot with safety cast° him. For he's embarked
With such loud reason to the Cyprus wars,
Which even now stand in act, that, for their souls, 150
Another of his fathom they have none
To lead their business. In which regard,
Though I do hate him as I do Hell pains,

121. **odd-even**: about midnight.   125. **your allowance**: by your permission.
134. **extravagant**: vagabond.   **wheeling**: wandering.   138. **tinder**: the primitive method of making fire, used before the invention of matches.   139. **taper**: candle.
144. **place**: i.e., as Othello's officer.   148. **cast**: dismiss from service.

68   OTHELLO

Yet for necessity of present life
I must show out a flag and sign of love, 155
Which is indeed but sign. That you shall surely find him,
Lead to the Sagittary° the raisèd search,
And there will I be with him. So farewell. (*Exit.*)

(*Enter, below,* Brabantio, *in his nightgown, and* Servants *with torches.*)

Brabantio. It is too true an evil. Gone she is,
And what's to come of my despisèd time 160
Is naught but bitterness. Now, Roderigo,
Where didst thou see her? Oh, unhappy girl!
With the Moor, say'st thou? Who would be a father!
How didst thou know 'twas she? Oh, she deceives me
Past thought! What said she to you? Get more tapers. 165
Raise all my kindred. Are they married, think you?

Roderigo. Truly, I think they are.

Brabantio. Oh Heaven! How got she out? Oh, treason of the blood!
Fathers, from hence trust not your daughters' minds
By what you see them act. Are there not charms° 170
By which the property° of youth and maidhood
May be abused?° Have you not read, Roderigo,
Of some such thing?

Roderigo. Yes, sir, I have indeed.

Brabantio. Call up my brother. Oh, would you had had her!
Some one way, some another. Do you know 175
Where we may apprehend her and the Moor?

Roderigo. I think I can discover him, if you please
To get good guard and go along with me.

Brabantio. Pray you, lead on. At every house I'll call,
I may command° at most. Get weapons, ho! 180
And raise some special officers of night.
On, good Roderigo, I'll deserve your pains.°

(*Exeunt.*)

SCENE II. *Another street.*

Enter Othello, Iago, *and* Attendants *with torches.*

---

157. **Sagittary:** presumably some building in Venice, not identified, used as a meeting place for the Council.   170. **charms:** magic spells.   171. **property:** nature.   172. **abused:** deceived.   180. **command:** find supporters.   182. **deserve . . . pains:** reward your labor.

WILLIAM SHAKESPEARE

IAGO. Though in the trade of war I have slain men,
Yet do I hold it very stuff o' the conscience
To do no contrivèd murder. I lack iniquity
Sometimes to do me service. Nine or ten times
I had thought to have yerked him here under the ribs.   5
　　　OTHELLO. 'Tis better as it is.
　　　IAGO.　　　　　　　　Nay, but he prated
And spoke such scurvy and provoking terms
Against your honor
That, with the little godliness I have,
I did full hard forbear him. But I pray you, sir,   10
Are you fast married? Be assured of this,
That the Magnifico is much beloved,
And hath in his effect a voice potential
As double as° the Duke's. He will divorce you,
Or put upon you what restraint and grievance   15
The law, with all his might to enforce it on,
Will give him cable.
　　　OTHELLO.　　Let him do his spite.
My services which I have done the signiory°
Shall outtongue his complaints. 'Tis yet to know—
Which, when I know that boasting is an honor,   20
I shall promulgate—I fetch my life and being
From men of royal siege, and my demerits°
May speak unbonneted to as proud a fortune
As this that I have reached. For know, Iago,
But that I love the gentle Desdemona,   25
I would not my unhousèd° free condition
Put into circumscription and confine
For the sea's worth. But look! What lights come yond?
　　　IAGO. Those are the raisèd father and his friends.
You were best go in.
　　　OTHELLO.　　Not I, I must be found.   30
My parts, my title, and my perfect° soul
Shall manifest me rightly. Is it they?
　　　IAGO. By Janus, I think no.

(*Enter* CASSIO, *and certain* OFFICERS *with torches.*)

　　　OTHELLO. The servants of the Duke, and my Lieutenant.
The goodness of the night upon you, friends!   35
What is the news?

13–14. **potential . . . as:** twice as powerful as.　18. **signiory:** state of Venice.
22. **demerits:** deserts.　26. **unhousèd:** unmarried.　31. **perfect:** ready.

CASSIO.   The Duke does greet you, General
And he requires your haste-posthaste appearance,
Even on the instant.
    OTHELLO.   What is the matter, think you?
    CASSIO. Something from Cyprus, as I may divine.
It is a business of some heat. The galleys   40
Have sent a dozen sequent messengers
This very night at one another's heels,
And many of the consuls, raised and met,
Are at the Duke's already. You have been hotly called for
When, being not at your lodging to be found,   45
The Senate hath sent about three several° quests
To search you out.
    OTHELLO.   'Tis well I am found by you.
I will but spend a word here in the house
And go with you. (*Exit.*)
    CASSIO.   Ancient, what makes he here?
    IAGO. Faith, he tonight hath boarded a land carrack.°   50
If it prove lawful prize, he's made forever.
    CASSIO. I do not understand.
    IAGO.   He's married.
    CASSIO.   To who?

(*Re-enter* OTHELLO.)

    IAGO. Marry, to—Come, Captain, will you go?
    OTHELLO.   Have with you.
    CASSIO. Here comes another troop to seek for you.
    IAGO. It is Brabantio. General, be advised,   55
He comes to bad intent.
    (*Enter* BRABANTIO, RODERIGO, *and* OFFICERS *with torches and weapons.*)
    OTHELLO.   Holloa! Stand there!
    RODERIGO. Signior, it is the Moor.
    BRABANTIO.   Down with him, thief!

(*They draw on both sides.*)

    IAGO. You, Roderigo! Come, sir, I am for you.
    OTHELLO. Keep up° your bright swords, for the dew will rust them.
Good signior, you shall more command with years   60
Than with your weapons.

46. **several:** separate.   50. **carrack:** the largest type of Spanish merchant ship.
59. **Keep up:** sheathe.

BRABANTIO. O thou foul thief, where hast thou stowed my daughter?
Damned as thou art, thou hast enchanted her.
For I'll refer me to all things of sense
If she in chains of magic were not bound, 65
Whether a maid so tender, fair, and happy,
So opposite to marriage that she shunned
The wealthy curlèd darlings of our nation,
Would ever have, to incur a general mock,
Run from her guardage° to the sooty bosom 70
Of such a thing as thou, to fear, not to delight.
Judge me the world if 'tis not gross in sense
That thou hast practiced on her with foul charms,
Abused her delicate youth with drugs or minerals
That weaken motion.° I'll have 't disputed on,° 75
'Tis probable, and palpable to thinking.
I therefore apprehend and do attach° thee
For an abuser of the world, a practicer
Of arts inhibited and out of warrant.°
Lay hold upon him. If he do resist, 80
Subdue him at his peril.
    OTHELLO.   Hold your hands,
Both you of my inclining and the rest.
Were it my cue to fight, I should have known it
Without a prompter. Where will you that I go
To answer this your charge?
    BRABANTIO.   To prison, till fit time 85
Of law and course of direct session
Call thee to answer.
    OTHELLO.   What if I do obey?
How may the Duke be therewith satisfied,
Whose messengers are here about my side
Upon some present business of the state 90
To bring me to him?
    FIRST OFFICER.   'Tis true, most worthy signior.
The Duke's in Council, and your noble self
I am sure is sent for.
    BRABANTIO.   How! The Duke in Council!
In this time of the night! Bring him away.
Mine's not an idle cause. The Duke himself, 95
Or any of my brothers of the state,
Cannot but feel this wrong as 'twere their own.

70. **guardage:** guardianship.   75. **motion:** sense.   **disputed on:** argued in the courts of law.   77. **attach:** arrest.   79. **inhibited . . . warrant:** forbidden and illegal acts; i.e., magic and witchcraft.

For if such actions may have passage free,
Bondslaves and pagans shall our statesmen be.

(*Exeunt.*)

SCENE III. *A council chamber.*

The DUKE *and* SENATORS *sitting at a table,* OFFICERS *attending.*

DUKE.   There is no composition° in these news°
That gives them credit.
   FIRST SENATOR.   Indeed they are disproportioned.
My letters say a hundred and seven galleys.
   DUKE.   And mine, a hundred and forty.
   SECOND SENATOR.   And mine, two hundred.
But though they jump not on a just account°—   5
As in these cases, where the aim reports,°
'Tis oft with difference—yet do they all confirm
A Turkish fleet, and bearing up to Cyprus.
   DUKE.   Nay, it is possible enough to judgment.
I do not so secure me in the error,°   10
But the main article° I do approve
In fearful° sense.
   SAILOR (*within*).   What ho! What ho! What ho!
   FIRST OFFICER.   A messenger from the galleys.

(*Enter* SAILOR.)

   DUKE.   Now, what's the business
   SAILOR.   The Turkish preparation makes for Rhodes.
So was I bid report here to the state.   15
By Signior Angelo.
   DUKE.   How say you by this change?
   FIRST SENATOR.   This cannot be,
By no assay of reason. 'Tis a pageant
To keep us in false gaze. When we consider
The importancy of Cyprus to the Turk,   20
And let ourselves again but understand
That as it more concerns the Turk than Rhodes,
So may he with more facile question bear it,°

1. composition: agreement. **news:** reports. **5. jump . . . account:** do not agree with an exact estimate. **6. aim reports:** i.e., intelligence reports of an enemy's intention often differ in the details. **10. I . . . error:** I do not consider myself free from danger, because the reports may not all be accurate. **11. main article:** general report. **12. fearful:** to be feared. **23. with . . . it:** take it more easily.

For that it stands not in such warlike brace
But altogether lacks the abilities 25
That Rhodes is dressed in—if we make thought of this,
We must not think the Turk is so unskillful
To leave that latest which concerns him first,
Neglecting an attempt of ease and gain
To wake and wage a danger profitless. 30
    DUKE. Nay, in all confidence, he's not for Rhodes.
    FIRST OFFICER. Here is more news.

(Enter a MESSENGER.*)*

    MESSENGER. The Ottomites,° Reverend and Gracious,
Steering with due course toward the isle of Rhodes,
Have there injointed° them with an after-fleet.° 35
    FIRST SENATOR. Aye, so I thought. How many, as you guess?
    MESSENGER. Of thirty sail. And now they do restem°
Their backward course, bearing with frank appearance
Their purposes toward Cyprus. Signior Montano,
Your trusty and most valiant servitor, 40
With his free duty recommends° you thus,
And prays you to believe him.
    DUKE. 'Tis certain then for Cyprus.
Marcus Luccicos, is not he in town?
    FIRST SENATOR. He's now in Florence. 45
    DUKE. Write from us to him, post-posthaste dispatch.
    FIRST SENATOR. Here comes Brabantio and the valiant Moor.

(Enter BRABANTIO, OTHELLO, IAGO, RODERIGO, *and* OFFICERS.*)*

    DUKE. Valiant Othello, we must straight employ you
Against the general enemy Ottoman.
(To BRABANTIO*)* I did not see you. Welcome, gentle signior, 50
We lacked your counsel and your help tonight.
    BRABANTIO. So did I yours. Good your Grace, pardon me,
Neither my place nor aught I heard of business
Hath raised me from my bed, nor doth the general care
Take hold on me. For my particular° grief 55
Is of so floodgate and o'erbearing nature
That it engluts and swallows other sorrows,
And it is still itself.
    DUKE. Why, what's the matter?
    BRABANTIO. My daughter! Oh, my daughter!

---

33. **Ottomites**: Turks.   35. **injointed**: joined. **after-fleet**: second fleet.   37. **restem**: steer again.   41. **recommends**: advises.   55. **particular**: personal.

ALL.   Dead?
BRABANTIO.   Aye, to me.
She is abused, stol'n from me and corrupted   60
By spells and medicines bought of mountebanks.
For nature so preposterously to err,
Being not deficient, blind, or lame of sense,
Sans witchcraft could not.
   DUKE.   Whoe'er he be that in this foul proceeding   65
Hath thus beguiled your daughter of herself
And you of her, the bloody book of law
You shall yourself read in the bitter letter
After your own sense—yea, though our proper° son
Stood in your action.
   BRABANTIO.   Humbly I thank your Grace.   70
Here is the man, this Moor, whom now, it seems,
Your special mandate for the state affairs
Hath hither brought.
   ALL.   We are very sorry for 't.
   DUKE (to OTHELLO).   What in your own part can you say to this?
   BRABANTIO.   Nothing but this is so.   75
   OTHELLO.   Most potent, grave, and reverend signiors,
My very noble and approved good masters,
That I have ta'en away this old man's daughter,
It is most true—true, I have married her.
The very head and front of my offending   80
Hath this extent, no more. Rude am I in my speech,
And little blest with the soft phrase of peace.
For since these arms of mine had seven years' pith
Till now some nine moons wasted, they have used
Their dearest action in the tented field.   85
And little of this great world can I speak,
More than pertains to feats of broil and battle,
And therefore little shall I grace my cause
In speaking for myself. Yet, by your gracious patience,
I will a round unvarnished tale deliver   90
Of my whole course of love—what drugs, what charms,
What conjuration and what mighty magic—
For such proceeding I am charged withal—
I won his daughter.
   BRABANTIO.   A maiden never bold,
Of spirit so still and quiet that her motion   95
Blushed at herself, and she—in spite of nature,

69. proper: own.

WILLIAM SHAKESPEARE   75

Of years, of country, credit,° everything—
To fall in love with what she feared to look on!
It is a judgment maimed and most imperfect
That will confess perfection so could err 100
Against all rules of nature, and must be driven
To find out practices of cunning Hell
Why this should be. I therefore vouch again
That with some mixtures powerful o'er the blood,
Or with some dram conjured to this effect, 105
He wrought upon her.
    DUKE.   To vouch this is no proof
Without more certain and more overt test
Than these thin habits and poor likelihoods
Of modern seeming do prefer against him.
    FIRST SENATOR.   But, Othello, speak. 110
Did you by indirect and forcèd courses
Subdue and poison this young maid's affections?
Or came it by request, and such fair question
As soul to soul affordeth?
    OTHELLO.   I do beseech you
Send for the lady to the Sagittary, 115
And let her speak of me before her father.
If you do find me foul in her report,
The trust, the office I do hold of you,
Not only take away, but let your sentence
Even fall upon my life.
    DUKE.   Fetch Desdemona hither. 120
    OTHELLO.   Ancient, conduct them, you best know the place.

(*Exeunt* IAGO *and* ATTENDANTS.)

And till she come, as truly as to Heaven
I do confess the vices of my blood,
So justly to your grave ears I'll present
How I did thrive in this fair lady's love 125
And she in mine.
    DUKE.   Say it, Othello.
    OTHELLO.   Her father loved me, oft invited me,
Still questioned me the story of my life
From year to year, the battles, sieges, fortunes,
That I have passed. 130
I ran it through, even from my boyish days
To the very moment that he bade me tell it.

97. credit: reputation.

Wherein I spake of most disastrous chances,
Of moving accidents by flood and field,
Of hairbreadth 'scapes i' the imminent deadly breach, 135
Of being taken by the insolent foe
And sold to slavery, of my redemption thence,
And portance in my travels' history.
Wherein of antres° vast and deserts idle,
Rough quarries, rocks, and hills whose heads touch heaven, 140
It was my hint to speak—such was the process.
And of the cannibals that each other eat,
The anthropophagi,° and men whose heads
Do grow beneath their shoulders. This to hear
Would Desdemona seriously incline. 145
But still the house affairs would draw her thence,
Which ever as she could with haste dispatch,
She'd come again, and with a greedy ear
Devour up my discourse. Which I observing,
Took once a pliant hour and found good means 150
To draw from her a prayer of earnest heart
That I would all my pilgrimage dilate,
Whereof by parcels she had something heard,
But not intentively. I did consent,
And often did beguile her of her tears 155
When I did speak of some distressful stroke
That my youth suffered. My story being done,
She gave me for my pains a world of sighs.
She swore, in faith, 'twas strange, 'twas passing strange,
'Twas pitiful, 'twas wondrous pitiful. 160
She wished she had not heard it, yet she wished
That Heaven had made her° such a man. She thanked me,
And bade me, if I had a friend that loved her,
I should but teach him how to tell my story
And that would woo her. Upon this hint I spake. 165
She loved me for the dangers I had passed,
And I loved her that she did pity them.
This only is the witchcraft I have used.
Here comes the lady, let her witness it.

(*Enter* DESDEMONA, IAGO, *and* ATTENDANTS.)

   DUKE. I think this tale would win my daughter too. 170
Good Brabantio,
Take up this mangled matter at the best.°

139. **antres:** caves. 143. **anthropophagi:** cannibals. 162. **her:** for her. 172.
Take . . . best: make the best settlement you can of this confused business.

WILLIAM SHAKESPEARE   77

Men do their broken weapons rather use
Than their bare hands.
    BRABANTIO.   I pray you hear her speak.
If she confess that she was half the wooer, 175
Destruction on my head if my bad blame
Light on the man! Come hither, gentle mistress.
Do you perceive in all this noble company
Where most you owe obedience?
    DESDEMONA.   My noble Father,
I do perceive here a divided duty. 180
To you I am bound for life and education,
My life and education both do learn me
How to respect you, you are the lord of duty,
I am hitherto your daughter. But here's my husband,
And so much duty as my mother showed 185
To you, preferring you before her father
So much I challenge that I may profess
Due to the Moor my lord.
    BRABANTIO.   God be with you! I have done.
Please it your Grace, on to the state affairs.
I had rather to adopt a child than get° it. 190
Come hither, Moor.
I here do give thee that with all my heart
Which, but thou hast already, with all my heart
I would keep from thee. For your sake, jewel,
I am glad at soul I have no other child, 195
For thy escape would teach me tyranny,
To hang clogs on them. I have done, my lord.
    DUKE. Let me speak like yourself, and lay a sentence°
Which, as a grise° or step, may help these lovers
Into your favor. 200
When remedies are past, the griefs are ended
By seeing the worst, which late on hopes depended.
To mourn a mischief that is past and gone
Is the next way to draw new mischief on.
What cannot be preserved when fortune takes, 205
Patience her injury a mockery makes.
The robbed that smiles steals something from the thief.
He robs himself that spends a bootless grief.
    BRABANTIO. So let the Turk of Cyprus us beguile,
We lose it not so long as we can smile. 210
He bears the sentence well that nothing bears

190. get: beget.   **198. sentence:** proverbial saying.   **199. grise:** degree.

But the free comfort which from thence he hears.
But he bears both the sentence and the sorrow
That, to pay grief, must of poor patience borrow.
These sentences, to sugar or to gall, 215
Being strong on both sides, are equivocal.
But words are words. I never yet did hear
That the bruised heart was piercèd through the ear.
I humbly beseech you, proceed to the affairs of state.

DUKE. The Turk with a most mighty preparation makes for 220 Cyprus. Othello, the fortitude of the place is best known to you, and though we have there a substitute° of most allowed sufficiency, yet opinion, a sovereign mistress of effects, throws a more safer voice on you. You must therefore be content to slubber° the gloss of your new fortunes with this more stubborn and boisterous expedition. 225

OTHELLO. The tyrant custom, most grave Senators,
Hath made the flinty and steel couch of war
My thrice-driven bed of down. I do agnize°
A natural and prompt alacrity
I find in hardness, and do undertake 230
These present wars against the Ottomites.
Most humbly therefore bending to your state,
I crave fit disposition for my wife,
Due reference of place and exhibition,°
With such accommodation and besort° 235
As levels with her breeding.

DUKE.   If you please,
Be 't at her father's.

BRABANTIO.   I'll not have it so.
OTHELLO. Nor I.
DESDEMONA.   Nor I. I would not there reside,
To put my father in impatient thoughts
By being in his eye. Most gracious Duke, 240
To my unfolding lend your prosperous° ear,
And let me find a charter in your voice
To assist my simpleness.

DUKE. What would you, Desdemona?
DESDEMONA. That I did love the Moor to live with him, 245
My downright violence and storm of fortunes
May trumpet to the world. My heart's subdued
Even to the very quality° of my lord.
I saw Othello's visage in his mind,

---

222. substitute: deputy commander. **224. slubber:** tarnish. **228. agnize:** confess. **234. exhibition:** allowance. **235. besort:** attendants. **241. prosperous:** favorable. **248. quality:** profession.

And to his honors and his valiant parts 250
Did I my soul and fortunes consecrate.
So that, dear lords, if I be left behind,
A moth of peace, and he go to the war,
The rites for which I love him are bereft me,
And I a heavy interim shall support 255
By his dear absence. Let me go with him.
　　OTHELLO.　Let her have your voices.
Vouch with me, Heaven, I therefore beg it not
To please the palate of my appetite,
Nor to comply with heat—the young affects 260
In me defunct°—and proper satisfaction,
But to be free and bounteous to her mind.°
And Heaven defend your good souls, that you think
I will your serious and great business scant
For she is with me. No, when light-winged toys 265
Of feathered Cupid seel° with wanton dullness
My speculative and officed instruments,°
That my disports° corrupt and taint my business,
Let housewives make a skillet of my helm,
And all indign° and base adversities 270
Make head against my estimation!°
　　DUKE.　Be it as you shall privately determine,
Either for her stay or going. The affair cries haste,
And speed must answer 't. You must hence tonight.
　　DESDEMONA.　Tonight, my lord?
　　DUKE.　　　　　　　　　This night.
　　OTHELLO.　　　　　　　　　　　With all my heart. 275
　　DUKE.　At nine i' the morning here we'll meet again.
Othello, leave some officer behind,
And he shall our commission bring to you,
With such things else of quality and respect
As doth import you.
　　OTHELLO.　　So please your Grace, my Ancient, 280
A man he is of honesty and trust.
To his conveyance I assign my wife,
With what else needful your good grace shall think
To be sent after me.
　　DUKE.　　　　Let it be so.

260–61. **young . . . defunct:** in me the passion of youth is dead.　262. **to . . . mind:** Othello repeats Desdemona's claim that this is a marriage of minds.　266. **seel:** close up.　267. **speculative . . . instruments:** powers of sight and action; i.e., my efficiency as your general.　268. **disports:** amusements.　270. **indign:** unworthy.　271. **estimation:** reputation.

Good night to everyone. (*To* BRABANTIO) And, noble signior, 285
If virtue no delighted beauty lack,
Your son-in-law is far more fair than black.
    FIRST SENATOR.   Adieu, brave Moor. Use Desdemona well.
    BRABANTIO.   Look to her, Moor, if thou hast eyes to see.
She has deceived her father, and may thee. 290

    (*Exeunt* DUKE, SENATORS, OFFICERS, *etc.*)

    OTHELLO.   My life upon her faith! Honest Iago,
My Desdemona must I leave to thee.
I prithee, let thy wife attend on her,
And bring them after in the best advantage.
Come, Desdemona, I have but an hour 295
Of love, of worldly matters and direction,
To spend with thee. We must obey the time.

    (*Exeunt* OTHELLO *and* DESDEMONA.)

    RODERIGO.   Iago!
    IAGO.   What say'st thou, noble heart?
    RODERIGO.   What will I do, thinkest thou? 300
    IAGO.   Why, go to bed and sleep.
    RODERIGO.   I will incontinently° drown myself.
    IAGO.   If thou dost, I shall never love thee after. Why, thou silly gentleman!
    RODERIGO.   It is silliness to live when to live is torment, and then 305
have we a prescription to die when death is our physician.
    IAGO.   Oh, villainous! I have looked upon the world for four times seven years, and since I could distinguish betwixt a benefit and an injury I never found man that knew how to love himself. Ere I would say I would drown myself for the love of a guinea hen, I would change my human- 310
ity with a baboon.
    RODERIGO.   What should I do? I confess it is my shame to be so found, but it is not in my virtue to amend it.
    IAGO.   Virtue! A fig! 'Tis in ourselves that we are thus or thus. Our bodies are gardens, to the which our wills are gardeners. So that if we 315
will plant nettles or sow lettuce, set hyssop and weed up thyme, supply it with one gender of herbs or distract it with many, either to have it sterile with idleness or manured with industry—why, the power and corrigible° authority of this lies in our wills. If the balance of our lives had not one scale of reason to poise another of sensuality, the blood and baseness of our 320
natures would conduct us to most preposterous conclusions. But we have reason to cool our raging motions, our carnal stings, our unbitted lusts, whereof

302. incontinently: immediately.   **318. corrigible:** correcting, directing.

I take this that you call love to be a sect or scion.°

RODERIGO.   It cannot be.

IAGO.   It is merely a lust of the blood and a permission of the will. Come, be a man. Drown thyself! Drown cats and blind puppies. I have professed me thy friend, and I confess me knit to thy deserving with cables of perdurable toughness. I could never better stead thee than now. Put money in thy purse, follow thou the wars, defeat thy favor with an usurped beard°— I say put money in thy purse. It cannot be that Desdemona should long continue her love to the Moor—put money in thy purse—nor he his to her. It was a violent commencement, and thou shalt see an answerable sequestration°—put but money in thy purse. These Moors and changeable in their wills.—Fill thy purse with money. The food that to him now is as luscious as locusts shall be to him shortly as bitter as coloquintida. She must change for youth. When she is sated with his body, she will find the error of her choice. She must have change, she must—therefore put money in thy purse. If thou wilt needs damn thyself, do it a more delicate way than drowning. Make all the money thou canst. If sanctimony and a frail vow betwixt an erring° barbarian and a supersubtle Venetian be not too hard for my wits and all the tribe of Hell, thou shalt enjoy her— therefore make money. A pox of drowning thyself! It is clean out of the way. Seek thou rather to be hanged in compassing thy joy than to be drowned and go without her.

RODERIGO.   Wilt thou be fast to my hopes if I depend on the issue?

IAGO.   Thou art sure of me. Go, make money. I have told thee often, and I retell thee again and again, I hate the Moor. My cause is hearted,° thine hath no less reason. Let us be conjunctive in our revenge against him. If thou canst cuckold him thou dost thyself a pleasure, me a sport. There are many events in the womb of time, which will be delivered. Traverse, go, provide thy money. We will have more of this tomorrow. Adieu.

RODERIGO.   Where shall we meet i' the morning?

IAGO.   At my lodging.

RODERIGO.   I'll be with thee betimes.

IAGO.   Go to, farewell. Do you hear, Roderigo?

RODERIGO.   What say you?

IAGO.   No more of drowning, do you hear?

RODERIGO.   I am changed. I'll go sell all my land. (*Exit.*)

IAGO.   Thus do I ever make my fool my purse,
For I mine own gained knowledge should profane

---

323. **sect or scion**: Both words mean a slip taken from a tree and planted to produce a new growth.   329. **defeat . . . beard**: disguise your face by growing a beard.   332–33. **answerable sequestration**: corresponding separation; i.e., reaction.   339. **Make . . . canst**: turn all you can into ready cash.   340. **erring**: vagabond.   347. **hearted**: heartfelt.

82   OTHELLO

If I would time expend with such a snipe
But for my sport and profit. I hate the Moor,
And it is thought abroad that 'twixt my sheets
He has done my office. I know not if 't be true, 365
But I for mere suspicion in that kind
Will do as if for surety. He holds me well,
The better shall my purpose work on him.
Cassio's a proper° man. Let me see now,
To get his place, and to plume up my will 370
In double knavery—How, how?—Let's see.—
After some time, to abuse Othello's ear
That he is too familiar with his wife.
He hath a person and a smooth dispose
To be suspected,° framed to make women false. 375
The Moor is of a free and open nature
That thinks men honest that but seem to be so,
And will as tenderly be led by the nose
As asses are.
I have 't. It is engendered. Hell and night 380
Must bring this monstrous birth to the world's light. (*Exit.*)

ACT II

SCENE I. *A seaport in Cyprus. An open place near the wharf.*
Enter MONTANO *and two* GENTLEMEN.

MONTANO. What from the cape can you discern at sea?
FIRST GENTLEMAN. Nothing at all. It is a high-wrought flood.
I cannot 'twixt the heaven and the main
Descry a sail.
MONTANO. Methinks the wind hath spoke aloud at land, 5
A fuller blast ne'er shook our battlements.
If it hath ruffianed so upon the sea,
What ribs of oak, when mountains melt on them,
Can hold the mortise? What shall we hear of this?
SECOND GENTLEMAN. A segregation° of the Turkish fleet. 10
For do but stand upon the foaming shore,
The chidden billow seems to pelt the clouds,
The wind-shaked surge, with high and monstrous mane,
Seems to cast water on the burning Bear,
And quench the guards of the ever-fixèd Pole. 15
I never did like molestation view

369. **proper**: handsome. 374–75. **He . . . suspected**: an easy way with him that is naturally suspected.
Act II, Sc. i: 10. **segregation**: separation.

On the enchafèd flood.
    MONTANO.   If that the Turkish fleet
Be not ensheltered and embayed, they are drowned.
It is impossible to bear it out.

    (*Enter a* THIRD GENTLEMAN.)

    THIRD GENTLEMAN.   News, lads! Our wars are done.   20
The desperate tempest hath so banged the Turks
That their designment halts. A noble ship of Venice
Hath seen a grievous wreck and sufferance°
On most part of their fleet.
    MONTANO.   How! Is this true?
    THIRD GENTLEMAN.   The ship is here put in,   25
A Veronesa. Michael Cassio,
Lieutenant to the warlike Moor Othello,
Is come on shore, the Moor himself at sea,
And is in full commission here for Cyprus.
    MONTANO.   I am glad on 't. 'Tis a worthy governor.   30
    THIRD GENTLEMAN.   But this same Cassio, though he speak of comfort
Touching the Turkish loss, yet he looks sadly
And prays the Moor be safe, for they were parted
With foul and violent tempest.
    MONTANO.   Pray Heavens he be,
For I have served him, and the man commands   35
Like a full soldier. Let's to the seaside, ho!
As well to see the vessel that's come in
As to throw out our eyes for brave Othello,
Even till we make the main and the aerial blue
An indistinct regard.
    THIRD GENTLEMAN.   Come, let's do so.   40
For every minute is expectancy
Of more arrivance.

    (*Enter* CASSIO.)

    CASSIO.   Thanks, you the valiant of this warlike isle
That so approve the Moor! Oh, let the heavens
Give him defense against the elements,   45
For I have lost him on a dangerous sea.
    MONTANO.   Is he well shipped?
    CASSIO.   His bark is stoutly timbered, and his pilot
Of very expert and approved allowance.
Therefore my hopes, not surfeited to death,   50
Stand in bold cure.

23. sufferance: damage.

(*A cry within:* "*A sail, a sail, a sail!*" *Enter a* FOURTH GENTLEMAN.)

CASSIO. What noise?
FOURTH GENTLEMAN. The town is empty. On the brow o' the sea
Stand ranks of people, and they cry "A sail!"
CASSIO. My hopes do shape him for the governor. 55

(*Guns heard.*)

SECOND GENTLEMAN. They do discharge their shot of courtesy.
Our friends, at least.
CASSIO. I pray you, sir, go forth,
And give us truth who 'tis that is arrived.
SECOND GENTLEMAN. I shall. (*Exit.*)
MONTANO. But, good Lieutenant, is your General wived? 60
CASSIO. Most fortunately. He hath achieved a maid
That paragons description and wild fame,
One that excels the quirks of blazoning pens
And in the essential vesture of creation
Does tire the ingener.°

(*Re-enter* SECOND GENTLEMAN.)

How now! Who has put in? 65
SECOND GENTLEMAN. 'Tis one Iago, Ancient to the General.
CASSIO. He has had most favorable and happy speed.
Tempests themselves, high seas, and howling winds,
The guttered rocks, and congregated sands,
Traitors ensteeped to clog the guiltless keel, 70
As having sense of beauty, do omit
Their mortal nature, letting go safely by
The divine Desdemona.
MONTANO. What is she?
CASSIO. She that I spake of, our great Captain's captain,
Left in the conduct of the bold Iago, 75
Whose footing here anticipates our thoughts
A sennight's speed. Great Jove, Othello guard,
And swell his sail with thine own powerful breath,
That he may bless this bay with his tall ship,
Make love's quick pants in Desdemona's arms, 80
Give renewed fire to our extinct spirits,
And bring all Cyprus comfort.

(*Enter* DESDEMONA, EMILIA, IAGO, RODERIGO, *and* ATTENDANTS.)

63–65. One . . . ingener: one that is too good for the fancy phrases (*quirks*) of painting pens (i.e., poets) and in her absolute perfection wearies the artist (i.e., the painter). (Cassio is full of gallant phrases and behavior, in contrast to Iago's bluntness.) **ingener:** inventor.

WILLIAM SHAKESPEARE 85

                              Oh, behold,
The riches of the ship is come on shore!
Ye men of Cyprus, let her have your knees.
Hail to thee, lady! And the grace of Heaven,   85
Before, behind thee, and on every hand,
Enwheel thee round!
     DESDEMONA.   I thank you, valiant Cassio.
What tidings can you tell me of my lord?
     CASSIO.   He is not yet arrived, nor know I aught
But that he's well and will be shortly here.   90
     DESDEMONA.   Oh, but I fear—How lost you company?
     CASSIO.   The great contention of the sea and skies
Parted our fellowship.—But hark! A sail.

     (*A cry within: "A sail, a sail!" Guns heard.*)

     SECOND GENTLEMAN.   They give their greeting to the citadel.
This likewise is a friend.
     CASSIO.   See for the news.   95

     (*Exit* GENTLEMAN.)

Good Ancient, you are welcome. (*To* EMILIA) Welcome, mistress.
Let it not gall your patience, good Iago,
That I extend my manners. 'Tis my breeding
That gives me this bold show of courtesy. (*Kissing her.*)
     IAGO.   Sir, would she give you so much of her lips   100
As of her tongue she oft bestows on me,
You'd have enough.
     DESDEMONA.   Alas, she has no speech.
     IAGO.   In faith, too much,
I find it still when I have list° to sleep.
Marry, before your ladyship, I grant,   105
She puts her tongue a little in her heart
And chides with thinking.
     EMILIA.   You have little cause to say so.
     IAGO.   Come on, come on. You are pictures° out of doors,
Bells° in your parlors, wildcats in your kitchens,   110
Saints in your injuries,° devils being offended,
Players in your housewifery, and housewives in your beds.
     DESDEMONA.   Oh, fie upon thee, slanderer!
     IAGO.   Nay, it is true, or else I am a Turk.
You rise to play, and go to bed to work.   115

---

104. list: desire.   **109. pictures:** i.e., painted and dumb.   **110. Bells:** i.e., ever clacking.   **111. Saints . . . injuries:** saints when you hurt anyone else.

EMILIA. You shall not write my praise.
IAGO. No, let me not.
DESDEMONA. What wouldst thou write of me if thou shouldst praise me?
IAGO. O gentle lady, do not put me to 't,
For I am nothing if not critical.
DESDEMONA. Come on, assay.°—There's one gone to the harbor? 120
IAGO. Aye, madam.
DESDEMONA. I am not merry, but I do beguile
The thing I am by seeming otherwise.
Come, how wouldst thou praise me?
IAGO. I am about it, but indeed my invention 125
Comes from my pate as birdlime does from frieze°—
It plucks out brains and all. But my Muse labors,
And thus she is delivered.
If she be fair and wise, fairness and wit,
The one's for use, the other useth it. 130
DESDEMONA. Well praised! How if she be black and witty?
IAGO. If she be black, and thereto have a wit,
She'll find a white° that shall her blackness fit.
DESDEMONA. Worse and worse.
EMILIA. How if fair and foolish? 135
IAGO. She never yet was foolish that was fair,
For even her folly helped her to an heir.
DESDEMONA. These are old fond paradoxes to make fools laugh i' the alehouse. What miserable praise hast thou for her that's foul and foolish?
IAGO. There's none so foul, and foolish thereunto, 140
But does foul pranks which fair and wise ones do.
DESDEMONA. Oh, heavy ignorance! Thou praisest the worst best. But what praise couldst thou bestow on a deserving woman indeed, one that in the authority of her merit did justly put on the vouch of very malice itself?° 145
IAGO. She that was ever fair and never proud,
Had tongue at will° and yet was never loud,
Never lacked gold and yet went never gay,
Fled from her wish and yet said "Now I may."
She that, being angered, her revenge being nigh, 150
Bade her wrong stay and her displeasure fly.
She that in wisdom never was so frail
To change the cod's head for the salmon's tail.°

120. assay: try.   125–26. my . . . frieze: my literary effort (*invention*) is as hard to pull out of my head as frieze (cloth with a nap) stuck to birdlime.   133. white: with a pun on *wight* (l. 156), man, person.   143–45. one . . . itself: one so deserving that even malice would declare her good.   147. tongue . . . will: a ready flow of words.   153. To . . . tail: to prefer the tail end of a good thing to the head of a poor thing.

She could think and ne'er disclose her mind,
See suitors following and not look behind.   155
She was a wight, if ever such wight were—
  DESDEMONA. To do what?
  IAGO. To suckle fools and chronicle small beer.°
  DESDEMONA. Oh, most lame and impotent conclusion! Do not learn
of him, Emilia, though he be thy husband. How say you, Cassio? Is   160
he not a most profane and liberal° counselor?
  CASSIO. He speaks home, madam. You may relish him more in the
soldier than in the scholar.
  IAGO (*aside*). He takes her by the palm. Aye, well said, whisper. With
as little a web as this will I ensnare as great a fly as Cassio. Aye, smile 165
upon her, do, I will gyve thee in thine own courtship. You say true, 'tis so
indeed. If such tricks as these strip you out of your Lieutenantry, it had
been better you had not kissed your three fingers° so oft, which now
again you are most apt to play the sir° in. Very good, well kissed! An excellent
courtesy! 'Tis so indeed. Yet again your fingers to your lips?   170
Would they were clyster pipes° for your sake! (*Trumpet within.*) The Moor!
I know the trumpet.
  CASSIO. 'Tis truly so.
  DESDEMONA. Let's meet him and receive him.
  CASSIO. Lo where he comes!   175

(*Enter* OTHELLO *and* ATTENDANTS.)

  OTHELLO. O my fair warrior!°
  DESDEMONA.   My dear Othello!
  OTHELLO. It gives me wonder great as my content
To see you here before me. O my soul's joy!
If after every tempest come such calms,
May the winds blow till they have wakened death!   180
And let the laboring bark climb hills of seas
Olympus-high, and duck again as low
As Hell's from Heaven! If it were now to die,
'Twere now to be most happy, for I fear
My soul hath her content so absolute   185
That not another comfort like to this
Succeeds in unknown fate.
  DESDEMONA.   The Heavens forbid
But that our loves and comforts should increase,
Even as our days do grow!

---

158. chronicle . . . beer: write a whole history about trifles (*small beer* thin drink).
161. liberal: gross.   **168. kissed . . . fingers:** a gesture of gallantry.   **169. play
. . . sir:** act the fine gentleman.   **171. clyster pipes:** an enema syringe.   **176.
warrior:** because she is a soldier's wife.

OTHELLO. Amen to that, sweet powers!
I cannot speak enough of this content.
It stops me here,° it is too much of joy.
And this, and this, the greatest discords be (*Kissing her*)
That e'er our hearts shall make!
    IAGO (*aside*). Oh, you are well tuned now,
But I'll set down the pegs° that make this music,
As honest as I am.
    OTHELLO. Come, let us to the castle.
News, friends. Our wars are done, the Turks are drowned.
How does my old acquaintance of this isle?
Honey, you shall be well desired in Cyprus,
I have found great love amongst them. O my sweet,
I prattle out of fashion, and I dote
In mine own comforts. I prithee, good Iago,
Go to the bay and disembark my coffers.°
Bring thou the master° to the citadel.
He is a good one, and his worthiness
Does challenge much respect. Come, Desdemona,
Once more well met at Cyprus.

    (*Exeunt all but* IAGO *and* RODERIGO.)

    IAGO. Do thou meet me presently at the harbor. Come hither. If thou beest valiant—as they say base men being in love have then a nobility in their natures more than is native to them—list me. The Lieutenant tonight watches on the court of guard. First, I must tell thee this. Desdemona is directly in love with him.
    RODERIGO. With him! Why, 'tis not possible.
    IAGO. Lay thy finger thus,° and let thy soul be instructed. Mark me with what violence she first loved the Moor, but for bragging and telling her fantastical lies. And will she love him still for prating? Let not thy discreet heart think it. Her eye must be fed, and what delight shall she have to look on the Devil? When the blood is made dull with the act of sport, there should be, again to inflame it and to give satiety a fresh appetite, loveliness in favor,° sympathy in years, manners, and beauties, all which the Moor is defective in. Now, for want of these required conveniences, her delicate tenderness will find itself abused, begin to heave the gorge, disrelish and abhor the Moor. Very nature will instruct her in it and compel her to some second choice. Now, sir, this granted—as it is a most pregnant and unforced position°—who stands so eminently in the degree of this fortune

---

191. here: i.e., in the heart.   194. set . . . pegs: i.e., make you sing in a different key. A stringed instrument was tuned by the pegs.   202. coffers: trunks.   203. master: captain of the ship.   213. thus: i.e., on the lips.   219. favor: face.   223–24. pregnant . . . position: very significant and probable argument.

as Cassio does? A knave very voluble, no further conscionable° than 225
in putting on the mere form of civil and humane seeming° for the better
compassing of his salt° and most hidden loose affection? Why, none, why,
none. A slipper° and subtle knave, a finder-out of occasions, that has an
eye can stamp and counterfeit advantages,° though true advantage never
present itself. A devilish knave! Besides, the knave is handsome, young, 230
and hath all those requisites in him that folly and green minds look after. A
pestilent complete knave, and the woman hath found him already.

RODERIGO. I cannot believe that in her. She's full of most blest
condition.°

IAGO. Blest fig's-end!° The wine she drinks is made of grapes. If 235
she had been blest, she would never have loved the Moor. Blest pudding!
Didst thou not see her paddle with the palm of his hand? Didst not mark that?

RODERIGO. Yes, that I did, but that was just courtesy.

IAGO. Lechery, by this hand, an index and obscure prologue to the
history of lust and foul thoughts. They met so near with their lips that 240
their breaths embraced together. Villainous thoughts, Roderigo! When these
mutualities so marshal the way, hard at hand comes the master and main exercise, the incorporate° conclusion. Pish! But, sir, be you ruled by me. I
have brought you from Venice. Watch you tonight. For the command, I'll
lay't upon you. Cassio knows you not. I'll not be far from you. Do you 245
find some occasion to anger Cassio, either by speaking too loud, or tainting°
his discipline, or from what other curse you please which the time shall more
favorably minister.

RODERIGO. Well.

IAGO. Sir, he is rash and very sudden in choler,° and haply may 250
strike at you. Provoke him, that he may, for even out of that will I cause these
of Cyprus to mutiny, whose qualification shall come into no true taste again
but by the displanting of Cassio. So shall you have a shorter journey
to your desires by the means I shall then have to prefer° them, and the
impediment most profitably removed without the which there were 255
no expectation of our prosperity.

RODERIGO. I will do this, if I can bring it to any opportunity.

IAGO. I warrant thee. Meet me by and by at the citadel. I must
fetch his necessaries ashore. Farewell.

RODERIGO. Adieu. (*Exit.*) 260

IAGO. That Cassio loves her, I do well believe it.
That she loves him, 'tis apt and of great credit.
The Moor, howbeit that I endure him not,
Is of a constant, loving, noble nature,

---

225. no . . . conscionable: who has no more conscience. **226. humane seeming:** courteous appearance. **227. salt:** lecherous. **228. slipper:** slippery. **229. stamp . . . advantages:** forge false opportunities. **234. condition:** disposition. **235. fig's-end:** nonsense. **243. incorporate:** bodily. **246. tainting:** disparaging. **250. choler:** anger. **254. prefer:** promote.

And I dare think he'll prove to Desdemona 265
A most dear husband. Now, I do love her too,
Not out of absolute lust, though peradventure
I stand accountant for as great a sin.
But partly led to diet° my revenge
For that I do suspect the lusty Moor 270
Hath leaped into my seat. The thought whereof
Doth like a poisonous mineral gnaw my inwards.
And nothing can or shall content my soul
Till I am evened with him, wife for wife.
At least into a jealousy so strong
Or failing so, yet that I put the Moor 275
That judgment cannot cure. Which thing to do,
If this poor trash of Venice, whom I trash
For his quick hunting,° stand the putting-on,
I'll have our Michael Cassio on the hip,
Abuse him to the Moor in the rank garb°— 280
For I fear Cassio with my nightcap too—
Make the Moor thank me, love me, and reward me
For making him egregiously an ass
And practicing upon his peace and quiet 285
Even to madness. 'Tis here, but yet confused.
Knavery's plain face is never seen till used. (*Exit.*)

SCENE II. *A street.*

Enter a HERALD *with a proclamation,* PEOPLE *following.*

HERALD. It is Othello's pleasure, our noble and valiant General, that upon certain tidings now arrived, importing the mere perdition° of the Turkish fleet, every man put himself into triumph°—some to dance, some to make bonfires, each man to what sport and revels his addiction leads him. For, besides these beneficial news, it is the celebration of his nuptial. 5 So much was his pleasure should be proclaimed. All offices° are open, and there is full liberty of feasting from this present hour of five till the bell have told eleven. Heaven bless the isle of Cyprus and our noble General Othello!

(*Exeunt.*)

SCENE III. *A hall in the castle.*

Enter OTHELLO, DESDEMONA, CASSIO, *and* ATTENDANTS.

269. **diet:** feed. 278–79. **trash . . . hunting:** hold back from outrunning the pack. 281. **rank garb:** gross manner; i.e., by accusing him of being Desdemona's lover.
    Sc. ii. 2. **mere perdition:** absolute destruction. 3. **triumph:** celebrate. 6. **offices:** the kitchen and buttery—i.e., free food and drink for all.

OTHELLO. Good Michael, look you to the guard tonight.
Let's teach ourselves that honorable stop,
Not to outsport discretion.
    CASSIO. Iago hath direction what to do,
But notwithstanding with my personal eye 5
Will I look to 't.
    OTHELLO. Iago is most honest.
Michael, good night. Tomorrow with your earliest
Let me have speech with you. Come, my dear love,
The purchase made, the fruits are to ensue—
That profit's yet to come 'tween me and you. 10
Good night.

    (*Exeunt* OTHELLO, DESDEMONA, *and* ATTENDANTS. *Enter* IAGO.)

    CASSIO. Welcome, Iago. We must to the watch.
    IAGO. Not this hour, Lieutenant, 'tis not yet ten o' the clock. Our General cast° us thus early for the love of his Desdemona, who let us not therefore blame. He hath not yet made wanton the night with her, and 15 she is sport for Jove.
    CASSIO. She's a most exquisite lady.
    IAGO. And, I'll warrant her, full of game
    CASSIO. Indeed she's a most fresh and delicate creature.
    IAGO. What an eye she has! Methinks it sounds a parley to provo- 20 cation.
    CASSIO. An inviting eye, and yet methinks right modest.
    IAGO. And when she speaks, is it not an alarum to love?
    CASSIO. She is indeed perfection.
    IAGO. Well, happiness to their sheets! Come, Lieutenant, I have a 25 stoup of wine, and here without are a brace of Cyprus gallants that would fain have a measure to the health of black Othello.
    CASSIO. Not tonight, good Iago. I have very poor and unhappy brains for drinking. I could well wish courtesy would invent some other custom of entertainment. 30
    IAGO. Oh, they are our friends. But one cup—I'll drink for you.
    CASSIO. I have drunk but one cup tonight, and that was craftily qualified too, and behold what innovation it makes here. I am unfortunate in the infirmity, and dare not task my weakness with any more.
    IAGO. What, man! 'Tis a night of revels. The gallants desire it. 35
    CASSIO. Where are they?
    IAGO. Here at the door. I pray you call them in.
    CASSIO. I'll do 't, but it dislikes me. (*Exit.*)
    IAGO. If I can fasten but one cup upon him,

14. **cast:** dismissed.

With that which he hath drunk tonight already 40
He'll be as full of quarrel and offense
As my young mistress' dog. Now my sick fool Roderigo,
Whom love hath turned almost the wrong side out,
To Desdemona hath tonight caroused
Potations pottle-deep, and he's to watch. 45
Three lads of Cyprus, noble swelling spirits
That hold their honors in a wary distance,°
The very elements° of this warlike isle,
Have I tonight flustered with flowing cups,
And they watch too. Now, 'mongst this flock of drunkards, 50
Am I to put our Cassio in some action
That may offend the isle. But here they come.
If consequence do but approve my dream,
My boat sails freely, both with wind and stream.

(*Re-enter* CASSIO, *with him* MONTANO *and* GENTLEMEN, SERVANTS *following with wine.*)

CASSIO. 'Fore God, they have given me a rouse already. 55
MONTANO. Good faith, a little one—not past a pint, as I am a soldier.
IAGO. Some wine, ho! (*Sings*)
　　　　"And let me the cannikin clink, clink,
　　　　And let me the cannikin clink.
　　　　A soldier's a man, 60
　　　　A life's but a span.°
　　　　Why, then let a soldier drink."
Some wine, boys!
CASSIO. 'Fore God, an excellent song.
IAGO. I learned it in England, where indeed they are most potent 65
in potting.° Your Dane, your German, and your swag-bellied Hollander—
Drink, ho!—are nothing to your English.
CASSIO. Is your Englishman so expert in his drinking?
IAGO. Why, he drinks you with facility your Dane dead drunk, he
sweats not to overthrow your Almain, he gives your Hollander a vomit° 70
ere the next pottle can be filled.
CASSIO. To the health of our General!
MONTANO. I am for it, Lieutenant, and I'll do you justice.
IAGO. O sweet England! (*Sings*)
　　　　"King Stephen was a worthy peer, 75
　　　　His breeches cost him but a crown.

47. **hold . . . distance:** "have a chip on their shoulders." 48. **very elements:** typical specimens. 61. **span:** lit., the measure between the thumb and little finger of the outstretched hand; about 9 inches. 66. **potting:** drinking. 70. **gives . . . vomit:** drinks as much as will make a Dutchman throw up.

WILLIAM SHAKESPEARE 93

>   He held them sixpence all too dear,
>   With that he called the tailor lown.°
>
>   "He was a wight of high renown,
>   And thou art but of low degree.   80
>   'Tis pride that pulls the country down.
>   Then take thine auld cloak about thee."

Some wine, ho!

CASSIO. Why, this is a more exquisite song than the other.

IAGO. Will you hear 't again?   85

CASSIO. No, for I hold him to be unworthy of his place that does those things. Well, God's above all, and there be souls must be saved and there be souls must not be saved.

IAGO. It's true, good Lieutenant.

CASSIO. For mine own part—no offense to the General, nor any   90
man of quality—I hope to be saved.

IAGO. And so do I too, Lieutenant.

CASSIO. Aye, but, by your leave, not before me. The Lieutenant is to be saved before the Ancient. Let's have no more of this, let's to our affairs. God forgive us our sins! Gentlemen, let's look to our business.   95
Do not think, gentlemen, I am drunk. This is my Ancient, this is my right hand and this is my left. I am not drunk now, I can stand well enough and speak well enough.

ALL. Excellent well.

CASSIO. Why, very well, then, you must not think then that I am   100
drunk. (*Exit.*)

MONTANO. To the platform, masters. Come, let's set the watch.

IAGO. You see this fellow that is gone before.
He is a soldier fit to stand by Caesar
And give direction. And do but see his vice.   105
'Tis to his virtue a just equinox,
The one as long as the other. 'Tis pity of him.
I fear the trust Othello puts him in
On some odd time of his infirmity
Will shake this island.

MONTANO.   But is he often thus?   110

IAGO. 'Tis evermore the prologue to his sleep.
He'll watch the horologe a double set,°
If drink rock not his cradle.

MONTANO.   It were well
The General were put in mind of it.
Perhaps he sees it not, or his good nature   115

---

78. lown: lout.   **112. watch . . . set:** stay awake the clock twice round.

Prizes the virtue that appears in Cassio
And looks not on his evils. Is not this true?

(*Enter* RODERIGO.)

IAGO (*aside to him*). How now, Roderigo! I pray you, after the Lieutenant. Go.

(*Exit* RODERIGO.)

MONTANO. And 'tis great pity that the noble Moor 120
Should hazard such a place as his own second
With one of an ingraft infirmity.
It were an honest action to say
So to the Moor.
    IAGO. Not I, for this fair island.
I do love Cassio well, and would do much 125
To cure him of this evil—But, hark! What noise?

(*A cry within:* "*Help! Help!*" *Re-enter* CASSIO, *driving in* RODERIGO.)

CASSIO. 'Zounds! You rogue! You rascal!
MONTANO. What's the matter, Lieutenant?
CASSIO. A knave teach me my duty!
But I'll beat the knave into a wicker bottle.
    RODERIGO. Beat me! 130
    CASSIO. Dost thou prate, rogue? (*Striking* RODERIGO.)
    MONTANO. Nay, good Lieutenant, (*staying him*)
I pray you, sir, hold your hand.
    CASSIO. Let me go, sir,
Or I'll knock you o'er the mazzard.
    MONTANO. Come, come, you're drunk.
    CASSIO. Drunk!

(*They fight.*)

IAGO (*aside to* RODERIGO). Away, I say. Go out and cry a mutiny. 135

(*Exit* RODERIGO.)

Nay, good Lieutenant! God's will, gentlemen!
Help, ho!—Lieutenant—sir—Montano—sir—
Help, masters!—Here's a goodly watch indeed!

(*A bell rings.*)

Who's that that rings the bell?—Diablo, ho!
The town will rise. God's will, Lieutenant, hold— 140
You will be shamed forever.

(*Re-enter* OTHELLO *and* ATTENDANTS.)

OTHELLO. What is the matter here?
MONTANO. 'Zounds, I bleed still, I am hurt to the death. (*Faints.*)
OTHELLO. Hold, for your lives!
IAGO. Hold, ho! Lieutenant—sir—Montano—gentlemen—
Have you forgot all sense of place and duty? 145
Hold! The General speaks to you. Hold, hold, for shame!
OTHELLO. Why, how now, ho! From whence ariseth this?
Are we turned Turks, and to ourselves do that
Which Heaven hath forbid the Ottomites?
For Christian shame, put by this barbarous brawl. 150
He that stirs next to carve for his own rage
Holds his soul light, he dies upon his motion.
Silence that dreadful bell. It frights the isle
From her propriety. What is the matter, masters?
Honest Iago, that look'st dead with grieving, 155
Speak, who began this? On thy love, I charge thee.
IAGO. I do not know. Friends all but now, even now,
In quarter and in terms like bride and groom
Devesting them for bed. And then, but now,
As if some planet had unwitted men, 160
Swords out, and tilting one at other's breast
In opposition bloody. I cannot speak
Any beginning to this peevish odds,
And would in action glorious I had lost
Those legs that brought me to a part of it! 165
OTHELLO. How comes it, Michael, you are thus forgot?°
CASSIO. I pray you, pardon me, I cannot speak.
OTHELLO. Worthy Montano, you were wont be civil.
The gravity and stillness of your youth
The world hath noted, and your name is great 170
In mouths of wisest censure.° What's the matter
That you unlace your reputation thus,
And spend your rich opinion° for the name
Of a night brawler? Give me answer to it.
MONTANO. Worthy Othello, I am hurt to danger. 175
Your officer, Iago, can inform you—
While I spare speech, which something now offends me—
Of all that I do know. Nor know I aught
By me that's said or done amiss this night,
Unless self-charity° be sometimes a vice, 180

---

166. are . . . forgot: have so forgotten yourself. **171. censure:** judgment.
173. opinion: reputation. **180. self-charity:** love for oneself.

96   OTHELLO

And to defend ourselves it be a sin
When violence assails us.
    OTHELLO.   Now, by Heaven,
My blood begins my safer guides to rule,
And passion, having my best judgment collied,°
Assays to lead the way. If I once stir,   185
Or do but lift this arm, the best of you
Shall sink in my rebuke. Give me to know
How this foul rout began, who set it on,
And he that is approved° in this offense,
Though he had twinned with me, both at a birth,   190
Shall lose me. What! In a town of war,
Yet wild, the people's hearts brimful of fear,
To manage private and domestic quarrel,
In night, and on the court and guard of safety!
'Tis monstrous. Iago, who began 't?   195
    MONTANO.   If partially affined, or leagued in office,
Thou dost deliver more or less than truth,
Thou art no soldier.
    IAGO.   Touch me not so near.
I had rather have this tongue cut from my mouth
Than it should do offense to Michael Cassio.   200
Yet I persuade myself to speak the truth
Shall nothing wrong him. Thus it is, General.
Montano and myself being in speech,
There comes a fellow crying out for help,
And Cassio following him with determined sword   205
To execute upon him. Sir, this gentleman
Steps in to Cassio and entreats his pause.
Myself the crying fellow did pursue,
Lest by his clamor—as it so fell out—
The town might fall in fright. He, swift of foot,   210
Outran my purpose, and I returned the rather
For that I heard the clink and fall of swords,
And Cassio high in oath, which till tonight
I ne'er might say before. When I came back—
For this was brief—I found them close together,   215
At blow and thrust, even as again they were
When you yourself did part them.
More of this matter cannot I report.
But men are men, the best sometimes forget
Though Cassio did some little wrong to him,   220

184. collied: darkened. **189. approved:** proved guilty.

As men in rage strike those that wish them best,
Yet surely Cassio, I believe, received
From him that fled some strange indignity,
Which patience could not pass.
  OTHELLO.   I know, Iago,
Thy honesty and love doth mince this matter,   225
Making it light to Cassio. Cassio, I love thee,
But never more be officer of mine.

  (*Re-enter* DESDEMONA, *attended*.)

Look, if my gentle love be not raised up!
I'll make thee an example.
  DESDEMONA.   What's the matter?
  OTHELLO. All's well now, sweeting. Come away to 230
bed. (*To* MONTANO, *who is led off*)
Sir, for your hurts, myself will be your surgeon.
Lead him off.
Iago, look with care about the town,
And silence those whom this vile brawl distracted.
Come, Desdemona. 'Tis the soldiers' life   235
To have their balmy slumbers waked with strife.

  (*Exeunt all but* IAGO *and* CASSIO.)

  IAGO. What, are you hurt, Lieutenant?
  CASSIO. Aye, past all surgery.
  IAGO. Marry, Heaven forbid!
  CASSIO. Reputation, reputation, reputation! Oh, I have lost my 240
reputation! I have lost the immortal part of myself, and what remains is
bestial. My reputation, Iago, my reputation!
  IAGO. As I am an honest man, I thought you had received some bodily
wound. There is more sense in that than in reputation. Reputation is an idle
and most false imposition, oft got without merit and lost without 245
deserving. You have lost no reputation at all unless you repute yourself
such a loser. What, man! There are ways to recover the General again. You
are but now cast in his mood,° a punishment more in policy° than in malice
—even so as one would beat his offenseless dog to affright an imperious
lion.° Sue to him again and he's yours.   250
  CASSIO. I will rather sue to be despised than to deceive so good a
commander with so slight, so drunken, and so indiscreet an officer. Drunk?
And speak parrot?° And squabble? Swagger? Swear? And discourse fustian

---

248. **cast . . . mood**: dismissed because he is in a bad mood. **in policy**: i.e., because he must appear to be angry before the Cypriots. **249–50. even . . . lion**: a proverb meaning that when the lion sees the dog beaten, he will know what is coming to him. **253. speak parrot**: babble.

with one's own shadow? O thou invisible spirit of wine, if thou has no name to be known by, let us call thee devil! 255

IAGO. What was he that you followed with your sword? What had he done to you?

CASSIO. I know not.

IAGO. Is 't possible?

CASSIO. I remember a mass of things, but nothing distinctly—a 260 quarrel, but nothing wherefore. Oh God, that men should put an enemy in their mouths to steal away their brains! That we should, with joy, pleasance, revel, and applause, transform ourselves into beasts!

IAGO. Why, but you are now well enough. How came you thus recovered? 265

CASSIO. It hath pleased the devil drunkenness to give place to the devil wrath. One unperfectness shows me another, to make me frankly despise myself.

IAGO. Come, you are too severe a moraler. As the time, the place, and the condition of this country stands, I could heartily wish this had not 270 befallen. But since it is as it is, mend it for your own good.

CASSIO. I will ask him for my place again, he shall tell me I am a drunkard! Had I as many mouths as Hydra, such an answer would stop them all. To be now a sensible man, by and by a fool, and presently a beast! Oh, strange! Every inordinate cup is unblest, and the ingredient is a 275 devil.

IAGO. Come, come, good wine is a good familiar creature, if it be well used. Exclaim no more against it. And, good Lieutenant, I think you think I love you.

CASSIO. I have well approved it, sir. I drunk! 280

IAGO. You or any man living may be drunk at some time, man. I'll tell you what you shall do. Our General's wife is now the General. I may say so in this respect, for that he hath devoted and given up himself to the contemplation, mark, and denotement of her parts and graces. Confess yourself freely to her, importune her help to put you in your place 285 again. She is of so free, so kind, so apt, so blessed a disposition, she holds it a vice in her goodness not to do more than she is requested. This broken joint between you and her husband entreat her to splinter° and, my fortunes against any lay° worth naming, this crack of your love shall grow stronger than it was before. 290

CASSIO. You advise me well.

IAGO. I protest, in the sincerity of love and honest kindness.

CASSIO. I think it freely, and betimes in the morning I will beseech the virtuous Desdemona to undertake for me. I am desperate of my fortunes if they check me here. 295

288. splinter: put in splints. **289. lay:** bet.

IAGO. You are in the right. Good night, Lieutenant, I must to the watch.

CASSIO. Good night, honest Iago. (*Exit.*)

IAGO. And what's he then that says I play the villain?
When this advice is free I give and honest,   300
Probal° to thinking, and indeed the course
To win the Moor again? For 'tis most easy
The inclining Desdemona to subdue
In any honest suit. She's framed as fruitful
As the free elements. And then for her   305
To win the Moor, were 't to renounce his baptism,
All seals and symbols of redeemèd sin,
His soul is so enfettered to her love
That she may make, unmake, do what she list,
Even as her appetite shall play the god   310
With his weak function.° How am I then a villain
To counsel Cassio to this parallel course,
Directly to his good? Divinity of Hell!
When devils will the blackest sins put on,
They do suggest at first with heavenly shows,   315
As I do now. For whiles this honest fool
Plies Desdemona to repair his fortunes,
And she for him pleads strongly to the Moor,
I'll pour this pestilence into his ear,
That she repeals° him for her body's lust.   320
And by how much she strives to do him good,
She shall undo her credit with the Moor.
So will I turn her virtue into pitch,
And out of her own goodness make the net
That shall enmesh them all.

(*Enter* RODERIGO.)

How now, Roderigo!   325

RODERIGO. I do follow here in the chase, not like a hound that hunts but one that fills up the cry. My money is almost spent, I have been tonight exceedingly well cudgeled, and I think the issue will be I shall have so much experience for my pains and so, with no money at all and a little more wit, return again to Venice.   330

IAGO. How poor are they that have not patience!
What wound did ever heal but by degrees?
Thou know'st we work by wit and not by witchcraft,
And wit depends on dilatory Time.

301. **Probal**: probable.   310. **function**: intelligence.   320. **repeals**: calls back.

Does't not go well? Cassio hath beaten thee, 335
And thou by that small hurt hast cashiered Cassio.
Though other things grow fair against the sun,
Yet fruits that blossom first will first be ripe.
Content thyself awhile. By the mass, 'tis morning.
Pleasure and action make the hours seem short. 340
Retire thee, go where thou art billeted.
Away, I say. Thou shalt know more hereafter.
Nay, get thee gone.

(*Exit* RODERIGO.)

     Two things are to be done:
My wife must move for Cassio to her mistress,
I'll set her on, 345
Myself the while to draw the Moor apart
And bring him jump when he may Cassio find
Soliciting his wife. Aye, that's the way.
Dull not device by coldness and delay. (*Exit.*)

ACT III

SCENE I. *Before the castle.*

Enter CASSIO *and some* MUSICIANS.

CASSIO. Masters, play here, I will content your pains°—
Something that's brief, and bid "Good morrow, General."°

(*Music. Enter* CLOWN.)

CLOWN. Why, masters, have your instruments been in Naples, that they speak i' the nose thus?
FIRST MUSICIAN. How, sir, how? 5
CLOWN. Are these, I pray you, wind instruments?
FIRST MUSICIAN. Aye, marry are they, sir.
CLOWN. Oh, thereby hangs a tail.
FIRST MUSICIAN. Whereby hangs a tale, sir?
CLOWN. Marry, sir, by many a wind instrument that I know. 10
But, masters, here's money for you. And the General so likes your music that he desires you, for love's sake, to make no more noise with it.
FIRST MUSICIAN. Well, sir, we will not.

---

1. content . . . pains: reward your labor. 2. bid . . . General: It was a common custom to play or sing a song beneath the bedroom window of a distinguished guest or of a newly wedded couple on the morning after their wedding night.

WILLIAM SHAKESPEARE   101

CLOWN. If you have any music that may not be heard, to 't again.
But, as they say, to hear music the General does not greatly care.   15
FIRST MUSICIAN. We have none such, sir.
CLOWN. Then put up your pipes in your bag, for I'll away. Go, vanish into air, away!

(*Exeunt* MUSICIANS.)

CASSIO. Dost thou hear, my honest friend?
CLOWN. No, I hear not your honest friend, I hear you.   20
CASSIO. Prithee keep up thy quillets.° There's a poor piece of gold for thee. If the gentlewoman that attends the General's wife be stirring, tell her there's one Cassio entreats her a little favor of speech. Wilt thou do this?
CLOWN. She is stirring, sir. If she will stir hither, I shall seem to notify unto her.   25
CASSIO. Do, good my friend.

(*Exit* CLOWN. *Enter* IAGO.)

                                        In happy time, Iago.
IAGO. You have not been abed, then?
CASSIO. Why, no, the day had broke
Before we parted. I have made bold, Iago,
To send in to your wife. My suit to her   30
Is that she will to virtuous Desdemona
Procure me some access.
IAGO.   I'll send her to you presently,
And I'll devise a mean to draw the Moor
Out of the way, that your convérse and business
May be more free.   35
CASSIO. I humbly thank you for 't.

(*Exit* IAGO.)

                                      I never knew
A Florentine more kind and honest.

(*Enter* EMILIA.)

EMILIA. Good morrow, good Lieutenant. I am sorry
For your displeasure, but all will sure be well.
The General and his wife are talking of it,   40
And she speaks for you stoutly. The Moor replies
That he you hurt is of great fame in Cyprus
And great affinity,° and that in wholesome wisdom
He might not but refuse you. But he protests he loves you,

---

21. keep . . . quillets: put away your wisecracks.   **43. affinity:** kindred.

And needs no other suitor but his likings 45
To take the safest occasion by the front
To bring you in again.
    CASSIO.   Yet I beseech you
If you think fit, or that it may be done,
Give me advantage of some brief discourse
With Desdemona alone.
    EMILIA.   Pray you, come in. 50
I will bestow you where you shall have time
To speak your bosom freely.
    CASSIO.   I am much bound to you.

(*Exeunt.*)

SCENE II. *A room in the castle.*

Enter OTHELLO, IAGO, *and* GENTLEMEN.

    OTHELLO.   These letters give, Iago, to the pilot,
And by him do my duties to the Senate.
That done, I will be walking on the works.
Repair there to me.
    IAGO.   Well, my good lord, I'll do 't.
    OTHELLO.   This fortification, gentlemen, shall we see 't? 5
    GENTLEMEN.   We'll wait upon your lordship.

(*Exeunt.*)

SCENE III. *The garden of the castle.*

Enter DESDEMONA, CASSIO, *and* EMILIA.

    DESDEMONA.   Be thou assured, good Cassio, I will do
All my abilities in thy behalf.
    EMILIA.   Good madam, do. I warrant it grieves my husband
As if the case were his.
    DESDEMONA.   Oh, that's an honest fellow. Do not doubt, Cassio, 5
But I will have my lord and you again
As friendly as you were.
    CASSIO.   Bounteous madam,
Whatever shall become of Michael Cassio,
He's never anything but your true servant.
    DESDEMONA.   I know 't. I thank you. You do love my lord. 10
You have known him long, and be you well assured

He shall in strangeness stand no farther off
Than in a politic distance.°
    CASSIO.   Aye, but, lady,
That policy may either last so long,
Or feed upon such nice and waterish diet,   15
Or breed itself so out of circumstance,
That, I being absent and my place supplied,
My General will forget my love and service.
    DESDEMONA.   Do not doubt° that. Before Emilia here
I give thee warrant of thy place.° Assure thee,   20
If I do vow a friendship, I'll perform it
To the last article. My lord shall never rest.
I'll watch him tame and talk him out of patience,
His bed shall seem a school, his board a shrift.°
I'll intermingle every thing he does   25
With Cassio's suit. Therefore be merry, Cassio,
For thy solicitor shall rather die
Than give thy cause away.

    (*Enter* OTHELLO *and* IAGO, *at a distance.*)

    EMILIA.   Madam, here comes my lord.
    CASSIO.   Madam, I'll take my leave.   30
    DESDEMONA.   Nay, stay and hear me speak.
    CASSIO.   Madam, not now. I am very ill at ease,
Unfit for mine own purposes.
    DESDEMONA.   Well, do your discretion.

    (*Exit* CASSIO.)

    IAGO.   Ha! I like not that.   35
    OTHELLO.   What dost thou say?
    IAGO.   Nothing, my lord. Or if—I know not what.
    OTHELLO.   Was not that Cassio parted from my wife?
    IAGO.   Cassio, my lord! No, sure, I cannot think it,
That he would steal away so guilty-like,   40
Seeing you coming.
    OTHELLO.   I do believe 'twas he.
    DESDEMONA.   How now, my lord!
I have been talking with a suitor here,
A man that languishes in your displeasure.
    OTHELLO.   Who is 't you mean?   45

12–13. He . . . distance: i.e., his apparent coldness to you shall only be so much as his official position demands for reasons of policy.   **19. doubt:** fear.   **20. give . . . place:** guarantee that you will be restored to your position.   **24. shrift:** place of confession and absolution.

DESDEMONA.   Why, your Lieutenant, Cassio. Good my lord,
If I have any grace or power to move you,
His present reconciliation take.°
For if he be not one that truly loves you,
That errs in ignorance and not in cunning,   50
I have no judgment in an honest face.
I prithee call him back.
        OTHELLO.   Went he hence now?
        DESDEMONA.   Aye, sooth, so humbled
That he hath left part of his grief with me,
To suffer with him. Good love, call him back.   55
        OTHELLO.   Not now, sweet Desdemona, some other time.
        DESDEMONA.   But shall 't be shortly?
        OTHELLO.   The sooner, sweet, for you.
        DESDEMONA.   Shall 't be tonight at supper?
        OTHELLO.   No, not tonight.
        DESDEMONA.   Tomorrow dinner then?
        OTHELLO.   I shall not dine at home.
I meet the captains at the citadel.   60
        DESDEMONA.   Why, then tomorrow night or Tuesday morn,
On Tuesday noon, or night, on Wednesday morn.
I prithee name the time, but let it not
Exceed three days. In faith, he's penitent,
And yet his trespass, in our common reason—   65
Save that, they say, the wars must make examples
Out of their best—is not almost° a fault
To incur a private check.° When shall he come?
Tell me, Othello. I wonder in my soul
What you would ask me that I should deny,   70
Or stand so mammering° on. What! Michael Cassio,
That came a-wooing with you, and so many a time
When I have spoke of you dispraisingly
Hath ta'en your part—to have so much to do
To bring him in! Trust me, I could do much—   75
        OTHELLO.   Prithee, no more. Let him come when he will.
I will deny thee nothing.
        DESDEMONA.   Why, this is not a boon.
'Tis as I should entreat you wear your gloves,
Or feed on nourishing dishes, or keep you warm,
Or sue to you to do a peculiar profit   80
To your own person. Nay, when I have a suit

48. His . . . take: accept his immediate apology and forgive him.   67. almost: hardly.   68. check: rebuke.   71. mammering: hesitating.

Wherein I mean to touch your love indeed,
It shall be full of poise and difficult weight,
And fearful to be granted.
  OTHELLO.   I will deny thee nothing.
Whereon I do beseech thee grant me this,   85
To leave me but a little to myself.
  DESDEMONA. Shall I deny you? No. Farewell, my lord.
  OTHELLO. Farewell, my Desdemona. I'll come to thee straight.
  DESDEMONA. Emilia, come. Be as your fancies teach you.
Whate'er you be, I am obedient.   90

  (*Exeunt* DESDEMONA *and* EMILIA.)

  OTHELLO. Excellent wretch! Perdition catch my soul
But I do love thee! And when I love thee not,
Chaos is come again.
  IAGO. My noble lord—
  OTHELLO.   What dost thou say, Iago?
  IAGO. Did Michael Cassio, when you wooed my lady,   95
Know of your love?
  OTHELLO. He did, from first to last. Why dost thou ask?
  IAGO. But for a satisfaction of my thought,
No further harm.
  OTHELLO. Why of thy thought, Iago?
  IAGO. I did not think he had been acquainted with her.   100
  OTHELLO. Oh yes, and went between us very oft.
  IAGO. Indeed!
  OTHELLO. Indeed! Aye, indeed. Discern'st thou aught in that?
Is he not honest?
  IAGO.   Honest, my lord!
  OTHELLO.   Honest! Aye, honest.
  IAGO. My lord, for aught I know.   105
  OTHELLO. What dost thou think?
  IAGO.   Think, my lord!
  OTHELLO. Think, my lord! By Heaven, he echoes me
As if there were some monster in his thought
Too hideous to be shown. Thou dost mean something.
I heard thee say even now thou likedst not that   110
When Cassio left my wife. What didst not like?
And when I told thee he was of my counsel
In my whole course of wooing, thou criedst "Indeed!"
And didst contract and purse thy brow together
As if thou then hadst shut up in thy brain   115
Some horrible conceit. If thou dost love me,
Show me thy thought.
  IAGO. My lord, you know I love you.

OTHELLO.   I think thou dost,
And for I know thou'rt full of love and honesty
And weigh'st thy words before thou givest them breath,   120
Therefore these stops of thine fright me the more.
For such things in a false disloyal knave
Are tricks of custom, but in a man that's just
They're close delations,° working from the heart,
That passion cannot rule.
        IAGO.   For Michael Cassio,   125
I dare be sworn I think that he is honest.
        OTHELLO. I think so too.
        IAGO.   Men should be what they seem,
Or those that be not, would they might seem none!°
        OTHELLO. Certain, men should be what they seem.
        IAGO. Why, then I think Cassio's an honest man.   130
        OTHELLO. Nay, yet there's more in this.
I prithee speak to me as to thy thinkings,
As thou dost ruminate, and give thy worst of thoughts
The worst of words.
        IAGO.   Good my lord, pardon me.
Though I am bound to every act of duty,   135
I am not bound to that all slaves are free to.
Utter my thoughts? Why, say they are vile and false,
As where's that palace whereinto foul things
Sometimes intrude not? Who has a breast so pure
But some uncleanly apprehensions   140
Keep leets° and law days, and in session sit
With meditations lawful?
        OTHELLO. Thou dost conspire against thy friend, Iago,
If thou but think'st him wronged and makest his ear
A stranger to thy thoughts.
        IAGO.   I do beseech you—   145
Though I perchance am vicious in my guess,
As, I confess, it is my nature's plague
To spy into abuses, and oft my jealousy°
Shapes faults that are not—that your wisdom yet,
From one that so imperfectly conceits,°   150
Would take no notice, nor build yourself a trouble
Out of his scattering and unsure observance.°
It were not for your quiet nor your good,

---

124. close delations: concealed accusations. **128. seem none:** i.e., not seem to be honest men. **141. leets:** courts. **148. jealousy:** suspicion. **150. conceits:** conceives. **152. observance:** observation.

Nor for my manhood, honesty, or wisdom,
To let you know my thoughts.
    OTHELLO.   What dost thou mean?   155
    IAGO.   Good name in man and woman, dear my lord,
Is the immediate jewel of their souls.
Who steals my purse steals trash—'tis something, nothing,
'Twas mine, 'tis his, and has been slave to thousands—
But he that filches from me my good name   160
Robs me of that which not enriches him
And makes me poor indeed.
    OTHELLO.   By Heaven, I'll know thy thoughts.
    IAGO.   You cannot if my heart were in your hand,
Nor shall not whilst 'tis in my custody.   165
    OTHELLO.   Ha!
    IAGO.   Oh, beware, my lord, of jealousy.
It is the green-eyed monster which doth mock
The meat it feeds on. That cuckold lives in bliss
Who, certain of his fate, loves not his wronger.°
But, oh, what damnèd minutes tells he o'er   170
Who dotes, yet doubts, suspects, yet strongly loves!
    OTHELLO.   Oh, misery!
    IAGO.   Poor and content is rich, and rich enough,
But riches fineless° is as poor as winter
To him that ever fears he shall be poor.   175
Good Heaven, the souls of all my tribe defend
From jealousy!
    OTHELLO. Why, why is this?
Think'st thou I'd make a life of jealousy,
To follow still the changes of the moon
With fresh suspicions? No, to be once in doubt   180
Is once to be resolved.° Exchange me for a goat
When I shall turn the business of my soul
To such exsufflicate and blown surmises,
Matching thy inference.° 'Tis not to make me jealous
To say my wife is fair, feeds well, loves company,   185
Is free of speech, sings, plays, and dances well.
Where virtue is, these are more virtuous.
Nor from mine own weak merits will I draw

168–69. **That . . . wronger:** i.e., the cuckold who hates his wife and knows her falseness is not tormented by suspicious jealousy. 174. **fineless:** limitless. 180–81. **to . . . resolved:** whenever I find myself in doubt I at once seek out the truth. 182–84. **When . . . inference:** when I shall allow that which concerns me most dearly to be influenced by such trifling suggestions as yours. **exsufflicate:** blown up like a bubble.

The smallest fear or doubt of her revolt,
For she had eyes, and chose me. No, Iago, 190
I'll see before I doubt, when I doubt, prove,
And on the proof, there is no more but this—
Away at once with love or jealousy!
    IAGO. I am glad of it, for now I shall have reason
To show the love and duty that I bear you 195
With franker spirit. Therefore, as I am bound,
Receive it from me. I speak not yet of proof.
Look to your wife. Observe her well with Cassio.
Wear your eye thus, not jealous nor secure.
I would not have your free and noble nature 200
Out of self-bounty° be abused, look to 't.
I know our country disposition well.
In Venice° they do let Heaven see the pranks
They dare not show their husbands. Their best conscience
Is not to leave 't undone, but keep 't unknown. 205
    OTHELLO. Dost thou say so?
    IAGO. She did deceive her father, marrying you,
And when she seemed to shake and fear your looks,
She loved them most.
    OTHELLO.   And so she did.
    IAGO.   Why, go to, then.
She that so young could give out such a seeming 210
To seel° her father's eyes up close as oak—
He thought 'twas witchcraft—but I am much to blame.
I humbly do beseech you of your pardon
For too much loving you.
    OTHELLO.   I am bound to thee forever.
    IAGO. I see this hath a little dashed your spirits. 215
    OTHELLO. Not a jot, not a jot.
    IAGO.   I' faith, I fear it has.
I hope you will consider what is spoke
Comes from my love, but I do see you're moved.
I am to pray you not to strain my speech
To grosser issues nor to larger reach 220
Than to suspicion.
    OTHELLO. I will not.
    IAGO.   Should you do so, my lord,
My speech should fall into such vile success
As my thoughts aim not at. Cassio's my worthy friend.—

---

201. self-bounty: natural goodness. **203. In Venice:** Venice was notorious for its loose women; the Venetian courtesans were among the sights of Europe and were much commented upon by travelers. **211. seel:** blind.

My lord, I see you're moved.
  OTHELLO.   No, not much moved.   225
I do not think but Desdemona's honest.°
  IAGO. Long live she so! And long live you to think so!
  OTHELLO. And yet, how nature erring from itself—
  IAGO. Aye, there's the point. As—to be bold with you—
Not to affect° many proposed matches   230
Of her own clime, complexion, and degree,
Whereto we see in all things nature tends°—
Foh! One may smell in such a will most rank,°
Foul disproportion, thoughts unnatural.
But pardon me. I do not in position   235
Distinctly speak of her, though I may fear
Her will, recoiling to her better judgment,
May fall to match° you with her country forms,°
And happily° repent.
  OTHELLO. Farewell, farewell.
If more thou dost perceive, let me know more.   240
Set on thy wife to observe. Leave me, Iago.
  IAGO (*going*). My lord, I take my leave.
  OTHELLO. Why did I marry? This honest creature doubtless
Sees and knows more, much more, than he unfolds.
  IAGO (*returning*). My lord, I would I might entreat your   245
  honor
To scan this thing no further. Leave it to time.
Though it be fit that Cassio have his place,
For sure he fills it up with great ability,
Yet if you please to hold him off awhile,
You shall by that perceive him and his means.   250
Note if your lady strain his entertainment°
With any strong or vehement importunity—
Much will be seen in that. In the meantime,
Let me be thought too busy in my fears—
As worthy cause I have to fear I am—   255
And hold her free, I do beseech your Honor.
  OTHELLO. Fear not my government.°
  IAGO. I once more take my leave. (*Exit*.)
  OTHELLO. This fellow's of exceeding honesty,

226. honest: When applied to Desdemona, "honest" means "chaste," but applied to Iago it has the modern meaning of "open and sincere." **230. affect:** be inclined to. **232. in . . . tends:** i.e., a woman naturally marries a man of her own country, color, and rank. **233. will . . . rank:** desire most lustful. **238. match:** compare. **country forms:** the appearance of her countrymen; i.e., white men. **239. happily:** haply, by chance. **251. strain . . . entertainment:** urge you to receive him. **257. government:** self-control.

And knows all qualities, with a learned spirit, 260
Of human dealings. If I do prove her haggard,
Though that her jesses were my dear heartstrings,
I'd whistle her off and let her down the wind
To prey at fortune.° Haply, for I am black
And have not those soft parts of conversation 265
That chamberers° have, or for I am declined
Into the vale of years—yet that's not much—
She's gone, I am abused, and my relief
Must be to loathe her. Oh, curse of marriage,
That we can call these delicate creatures ours, 270
And not their appetites! I had rather be a toad
And live upon the vapor of a dungeon
Than keep a corner in the thing I love
For others' uses. Yet, 'tis the plague of great ones,
Prerogatived are they less than the base. 275
'Tis destiny unshunnable, like death.
Even then this forkèd plague° is fated to us
When we do quicken.° Desdemona comes.

(Re-enter DESDEMONA and EMILIA.)

If she be false, oh, then Heaven mocks itself!
I'll not believe 't.
    DESDEMONA. How now, my dear Othello! 280
Your dinner, and the generous° islanders
By you invited, do attend your presence.
    OTHELLO.   I am to blame.
    DESDEMONA.   Why do you speak so faintly?
Are you not well?
    OTHELLO. I have a pain upon my forehead here. 285
    DESDEMONA. Faith, that's with watching,° 'twill away again.
Let me but bind it hard, within this hour
It will be well.
    OTHELLO. Your napkin° is too little,

(He puts the handkerchief from him, and she drops it.)

Let it alone. Come, I'll go in with you.
    DESDEMONA. I am very sorry that you are not well. 290

261–64. If . . . fortune: Othello keeps up the imagery of falconry throughout.
He means: If I find that she is wild, I'll whistle her off the game and let her go
where she will, for she's not worth keeping. haggard: a wild hawk. jesses: the
straps attached to a hawk's legs. 266. chamberers: playboys. 277. forkèd
plague: i.e., to be a cuckold. 278. quicken: stir in our mother's womb. 281.
generous: noble, of gentle blood. 286. watching: lack of sleep. 288. napkin:
handkerchief.

WILLIAM SHAKESPEARE   111

(*Exeunt* OTHELLO *and* DESDEMONA.)

EMILIA. I am glad I have found this napkin.
This was her first remembrance from the Moor.
My wayward° husband hath a hundred times
Wooed me to steal it, but she so loves the token,
For he conjured° her she should ever keep it,   295
That she reserves it evermore about her
To kiss and talk to. I'll have the work ta'en out,°
And give 't Iago. What he will do with it
Heaven knows, not I.
I nothing but to please his fantasy.°   300

(*Re-enter* IAGO.)

IAGO. How now! What do you here alone?
EMILIA. Do not you chide, I have a thing for you.
IAGO. A thing for me? It is a common thing—
EMILIA. Ha!
IAGO. To have a foolish wife.   305
EMILIA. Oh, is that all? What will you give me now
For that same handkerchief?
IAGO.   What handkerchief?
EMILIA. What handkerchief!
Why, that the Moor first gave to Desdemona,
That which so often you did bid me steal.   310
IAGO. Hast stol'n it from her?
EMILIA. No, faith, she let it drop by negligence,
And, to the advantage, I being here took 't up.
Look, here it is.
IAGO.   A good wench. Give it me.
EMILIA. What will you do with 't, that you have been so earnest   315
To have me filch it?
IAGO (*snatching it*). Why, what's that to you?
EMILIA. If 't be not for some purpose of import,
Give 't me again. Poor lady, she'll run mad
When she shall lack it.   320
IAGO. Be not acknown on 't,° I have use for it.
Go, leave me.

(*Exit* EMILIA.)

I will in Cassio's lodging lose this napkin,
And let him find it. Trifles light as air

---

293. **wayward**: unaccountable. 295. **conjured**: begged with an oath. 297. **work ... out**: pattern copied. 300. **fantasy**: whim. 321. **Be ... 't**: know nothing about it.

112   OTHELLO

Are to the jealous confirmations strong 325
As proofs of Holy Writ. This may do something.
The Moor already changes with my poison.
Dangerous conceits are in their natures poisons,
Which at the first are scarce found to distaste,
But with a little act upon the blood 330
Burn like the mines of sulphur. I did say so.°
Look where he comes!

(*Re-enter* OTHELLO.)

                    Not poppy,° nor mandragora,°
Nor all the drowsy syrups of the world,
Shall ever medicine thee to that sweet sleep
Which thou owedst° yesterday,
    OTHELLO.   Ha! Ha! False to me? 335
    IAGO.   Why, how now, General! No more of that.
    OTHELLO.   Avaunt! Be gone! Thou hast set me on the rack.
I swear 'tis better to be much abused
Than but to know 't a little.
    IAGO.   How now, my lord!
    OTHELLO.   What sense had I of her stol'n hours of lust? 340
I saw 't not, thought it not, it harmed not me.
I slept the next night well, was free and merry.
I found not Cassio's kisses on her lips.
He that is robbed, not wanting° what is stol'n,
Let him not know 't and he's not robbed at all. 345
    IAGO.   I am sorry to hear this.
    OTHELLO.   I had been happy if the general camp,
Pioners° and all, had tasted her sweet body,
So I had nothing known. Oh, now forever
Farewell the tranquil mind! Farewell content! 350
Farewell the pluméd troop and the big wars
That make ambition virtue! Oh, farewell,
Farewell the neighing steed and the shrill trump,
The spirit-stirring drum, the ear-piercing fife,
The royal banner and all quality, 355
Pride, pomp, and circumstance of glorious war!
And, O you mortal engines, whose rude throats
The immortal Jove's dread clamors counterfeit,
Farewell! Othello's occupation's gone!

---

331. I . . . so: As Iago says this, Othello is seen approaching, with all the signs of his agitation outwardly visible.   **332. poppy:** opium. **mandragora:** called also mandrake, a root used as a drug to bring sleep.   **335. owedst:** owned.   **344. wanting:** missing.   **348. Pioners:** pioneers, the lowest type of soldier.

WILLIAM SHAKESPEARE   113

IAGO. Is 't possible, my lord? 360
OTHELLO. Villain, be sure thou prove my love a whore,
Be sure of it, give me the ocular proof.
Or by the worth of man's eternal soul,
Thou hadst been better have been born a dog
Than answer my waked wrath!
IAGO. Is 't come to this? 365
OTHELLO. Make me to see 't, or at the least so prove it
That the probation° bear no hinge nor loop
To hang a doubt on, or woe upon thy life!
IAGO. My noble lord—
OTHELLO. If thou dost slander her and torture me, 370
Never pray more, abandon all remorse.°
On horror's head horrors accumulate,
Do deeds to make Heaven weep, all earth amazed,
For nothing canst thou to damnation add
Greater than that.
IAGO. Oh, grace! Oh, Heaven defend me! 375
Are you a man? Have you a soul or sense?
God be wi' you, take mine office. O wretched fool,
That livest to make thine honesty a vice!
O monstrous world! Take note, take note, O world,
To be direct and honest is not safe. 380
I thank you for this profit, and from hence
I'll love no friend, sith° love breeds such offense.
OTHELLO. Nay, stay. Thou shouldst be honest.
IAGO. I should be wise, for honesty's a fool,
And loses that it works for.
OTHELLO. By the world, 385
I think my wife be honest, and think she is not.
I think that thou art just, and think thou art not.
I'll have some proof. Her name, that was as fresh
As Dian's° visage, is now begrimed and black
As mine own face. If there be cords, or knives, 390
Poison, or fire, or suffocating streams,
I'll not endure it. Would I were satisfied!
IAGO. I see, sir, you are eaten up with passion.
I do repent me that I put it to you.
You would be satisfied?
OTHELLO. Would! Nay, I will. 395
IAGO. And may, but, how? How satisfied, my lord?

367. **probation:** proof. 371. **remorse:** pity. 382. **sith:** since. 389. **Dian:** Diana, goddess of chastity.

114 OTHELLO

Would you, the supervisor,° grossly gape on?
Behold her topped?
    OTHELLO.   Death and damnation! Oh!
    IAGO.   It were a tedious difficulty, I think,
To bring them to that prospect. Damn them then,   400
If ever mortal eyes do see them bolster°
More than their own! What then? How then?
What shall I say? Where's satisfaction?
It is impossible you should see this,
Were they as prime° as goats, as hot as monkeys,   405
As salt° as wolves in pride,° and fools as gross
As ignorance made drunk. But yet I say
If imputation° and strong circumstances,
Which lead directly to the door of truth,
Will give you satisfaction, you may have 't.   410
    OTHELLO.   Give me a living reason she's disloyal.
    IAGO.   I do not like the office.
But sith I am entered in this cause so far,
Pricked to 't by foolish honesty and love,
I will go on. I lay with Cassio lately,   415
And being troubled with a raging tooth,
I could not sleep.
There are a kind of men so loose of soul
That in their sleeps will mutter their affairs.
One of this kind is Cassio.   420
In sleep I heard him say "Sweet Desdemona,
Let us be wary, let us hide our loves."
And then, sir, would he gripe° and wring my hand,
Cry "O sweet creature!" and then kiss me hard,
As if he plucked up kisses by the roots   425
That grew upon my lips. Then laid his leg
Over my thigh, and sighed and kissed, and then
Cried "Cursed fate that gave thee to the Moor!"
    OTHELLO.   Oh, monstrous! Monstrous!
    IAGO.   Nay, this was but his dream.
    OTHELLO.   But this denoted a foregone conclusion.   430
'Tis a shrewd doubt,° though it be but a dream.
    IAGO.   And this may help to thicken other proofs
That do demónstrate thinly.
    OTHELLO.   I'll tear her all to pieces.

---

397. **supervisor**: looker-on.   401. **bolster**: sleep together.   405. **prime**: lustful.
406. **salt**: eager. **pride**: in heat.   408. **imputation**: probability.   423. **gripe**: grip.
431. **shrewd doubt**: bitter suspicion.

> IAGO.   Nay, but be wise. Yet we see nothing done.
> She may be honest yet. Tell me but this: 435
> Have you not sometimes seen a handkerchief
> Spotted with strawberries in your wife's hand?
>   OTHELLO.   I gave her such a one, 'twas my first gift.
>   IAGO.   I know not that. But such a handkerchief—
> I am sure it was your wife's—did I today   440
> See Cassio wipe his beard with.
>   OTHELLO.   If it be that—
>   IAGO.   If it be that, or any that was hers,
> It speaks against her with the other proofs.
>   OTHELLO.   Oh, that the slave had forty thousand lives!
> One is too poor, too weak, for my revenge.   445
> Now do I see 'tis true. Look here, Iago,
> All my fond love thus do I blow to Heaven—
> 'Tis gone.
> Arise, black Vengeance, from thy hollow cell!
> Yield up, O Love, thy crown and hearted throne   450
> To tyrannous hate! Swell, bosom, with thy fraught,°
> For 'tis of aspics'° tongues!
>   IAGO.   Yet be content.
>   OTHELLO.   Oh, blood, blood, blood!
>   IAGO.   Patience, I say. Your mind perhaps may change.
>   OTHELLO.   Never, Iago. Like to the Pontic Sea,   455
> Whose icy current and compulsive course
> Ne'er feels retiring ebb but keeps due on
> To the Propontic and the Hellespont;
> Even so my bloody thoughts, with violent pace,
> Shall ne'er look back, ne'er ebb to humble love,   460
> Till that capable° and wide revenge
> Swallow them up. Now, by yond marble Heaven,
> In the due reverence of a sacred vow (*Kneels.*)
> I here engage my words.
>   IAGO.   Do not rise yet. (*Kneels.*)
> Witness, you ever burning lights above,   465
> You elements that clip° us round about,
> Witness that here Iago doth give up
> The execution of his wit, hands, heart,
> To wronged Othello's service! Let him command,
> And to obey shall be in me remorse,°   470

---

451. fraught: freight.   **452. aspics':** asps'.   **461. capable:** comprehensive.   **466. clip:** embrace.   **470. remorse:** solemn obligation.

What bloody business ever.

(*They rise.*)

OTHELLO.   I greet thy love,
Not with vain thanks, but with acceptance bounteous,
And will upon the instant put thee to 't.
Within these three days let me hear thee say
That Cassio's not alive. 475
  IAGO.   My friend is dead. 'Tis done at your request.
But let her live.
  OTHELLO.   Damn her, lewd minx! Oh, damn her!
Come, go with me apart. I will withdraw,
To furnish me with some swift means of death 480
For the fair devil. Now art thou my Lieutenant.
  IAGO.   I am your own forever.

(*Exeunt.*)

SCENE IV. *Before the castle.*

Enter DESDEMONA, EMILIA, *and* CLOWN.

DESDEMONA.   Do you know, sirrah, where Lieutenant Cassio lies?
CLOWN.   I dare not say he lies anywhere.
DESDEMONA.   Why, man?
CLOWN.   He's a soldier, and for one to say a soldier lies is stabbing.
DESDEMONA.   Go to. Where lodges he? 5
CLOWN.   To tell you where he lodges is to tell you where I lie.
DESDEMONA.   Can anything be made of this?
CLOWN.   I know not where he lodges, and for me to devise a lodging, and say he lies here or he lies there, were to lie in mine own throat.
DESDEMONA.   Can you inquire him out and be edified by report?° 10
CLOWN.   I will catechize the world for him; that is, make questions and by them answer.
DESDEMONA.   Seek him, bid him come hither. Tell him I have moved my lord on his behalf and hope all will be well.
CLOWN.   To do this is within the compass of man's wit, and there- 15
fore I will attempt the doing it. (*Exit.*)
DESDEMONA.   Where should I lose that handkerchief, Emilia?
EMILIA.   I know not, madam.
DESDEMONA.   Believe me, I had rather have lost my purse
Full of crusados. And, but my noble Moor 20
Is true of mind and made of no such baseness
As jealous creatures are, it were enough

10. **edified . . . report**: enlightened by the information. Desdemona speaks with mock pomposity.

To put him to ill thinking.
EMILIA. Is he not jealous?
DESDEMONA. Who, he? I think the sun where he was born
Drew all such humors from him.
EMILIA. Look where he comes. 25
DESDEMONA. I will not leave him now till Cassio
Be called to him.

(*Enter* OTHELLO.)

How is 't with you, my lord?
OTHELLO. Well, my good lady. (*Aside*) Oh, hardness to dissemble!
How do you, Desdemona?
DESDEMONA. Well, my good lord.
OTHELLO. Give me your hand. This hand is moist,° my lady. 30
DESDEMONA. It yet has felt no age nor known no sorrow.
OTHELLO. This argues fruitfulness and liberal heart.
Hot, hot, and moist—this hand of yours requires
A sequester from liberty, fasting and prayer,
Much castigation, exercise devout. 35
For here's a young and sweating devil here,
That commonly rebels. 'Tis a good hand,
A frank one.
DESDEMONA. You may indeed say so,
For 'twas that hand that gave away my heart.
OTHELLO. A liberal° hand. The hearts of old gave hands, 40
But our new heraldry is hands, not hearts.°
DESDEMONA. I cannot speak of this. Come now, your promise.
OTHELLO. What promise, chuck?°
DESDEMONA. I have sent to bid Cassio come speak with you.
OTHELLO. I have a salt and sorry rheum offends me. 45
Lend me thy handkerchief.
DESDEMONA. Here, my lord.
OTHELLO. That which I gave you.
DESDEMONA. I have it not about me.
OTHELLO. Not?
DESDEMONA. No indeed, my lord.
OTHELLO. That's a fault. That handkerchief
Did an Egyptian to my mother give. 50
She was a charmer, and could almost read
The thoughts of people. She told her while she kept it

---

30. **moist**: a hot moist palm was believed to show desire. 40. **liberal**: overgenerous. 40–41. **The . . . hearts**: once love and deeds went together, but now it is all deeds (i.e., faithlessness) and no love. 43. **chuck**: a term of affection, but not the kind of word with which a person of Othello's dignity would normally address his wife. He is beginning to treat her with contemptuous familiarity.

'Twould make her amiable and subdue my father
Entirely to her love, but if she lost it
Or made a gift of it, my father's eye
Should hold her loathed and his spirits should hunt
After new fancies. She dying gave it me,
And bid me, when my fate would have me wive,
To give it her. I did so. And take heed on 't,
Make it a darling like your precious eye.
To lose 't or give 't away were such perdition
As nothing else could match.
    DESDEMONA.   It 't possible?
    OTHELLO.   'Tis true. There's magic in the web of it.
A sibyl that had numbered in the world
The sun to course two hundred compasses
In her prophetic fury sewed the work.
The worms were hallowed that did breed the silk,
And it was dyed in mummy which the skillful
Conserved° of maidens' hearts.
    DESDEMONA.   Indeed! Is 't true?
    OTHELLO.   Most veritable, therefore look to 't well.
    DESDEMONA.   Then would to God that I had never seen 't.
    OTHELLO.   Ha! Wherefore?
    DESDEMONA.   Why do you speak so startlingly and rash?
    OTHELLO.   Is 't lost? Is 't gone? Speak, is it out o' the way?
    DESDEMONA.   Heaven bless us!
    OTHELLO.   Say you?
    DESDEMONA.   It is not lost, but what an if it were?
    OTHELLO.   How!
    DESDEMONA.   I say it is not lost.
    OTHELLO.   Fetch 't, let me see it.
    DESDEMONA.   Why, so I can, sir, but I will not now.
This is a trick to put me from my suit.
Pray you let Cassio be received again.
    OTHELLO.   Fetch me the handkerchief. My mind misgives.
    DESDEMONA.   Come, come,
You'll never meet a more sufficient man.
    OTHELLO.   The handkerchief!
    DESDEMONA.   I pray talk me of Cassio.
    OTHELLO.   The handkerchief!
    DESDEMONA.   A man that all his time
Hath founded his good fortunes on your love,
Shared dangers with you—

69. Conserved: prepared.

OTHELLO. The handkerchief! 90
DESDEMONA. In sooth, you are to blame.
OTHELLO. Away! (*Exit.*)
EMILIA. Is not this man jealous?
DESDEMONA. I ne'er saw this before.
Sure there's some wonder in this handkerchief. 95
I am most unhappy in the loss of it.
    EMILIA. 'Tis not a year or two shows us a man.°
They are all but stomachs and we all but food.
They eat us hungerly, and when they are full
They belch us. Look you, Cassio and my husband. 100

(*Enter* CASSIO *and* IAGO.)

    IAGO. There is no other way, 'tis she must do 't.
And, lo, the happiness!° Go and impórtune her.
    DESDEMONA. How now, good Cassio! What's the news with you?
    CASSIO. Madam, my former suit. I do beseech you
That by your virtuous means I may again 105
Exist, and be a member of his love
Whom I with all the office of my heart
Entirely honor. I would not be delayed.
If my offense be of such mortal kind
That nor my service past nor present sorrows 110
Nor purposed merit in futurity
Can ransom me into his love again,
But to know so must be my benefit.
So shall I clothe me in a forced content
And shut myself up in some other course 115
To Fortune's alms.
    DESDEMONA. Alas, thrice-gentle Cassio!
My advocation° is not now in tune.
My lord is not my lord, nor should I know him
Were he in favor° as in humor altered.
So help me every spirit sanctified, 120
As I have spoken for you all my best
And stood within the blank° of his displeasure
For my free speech! You must awhile be patient.
What I can do I will, and more I will
Than for myself I dare. Let that suffice you. 125

---

97. 'Tis . . . man: it does not take a couple of years for us to discover the nature of a man; i.e., he soon shows his real nature. **102. And . . . happiness:** what good luck, here she is. **117. advocation:** advocacy. **119. favor:** face. **122. blank:** aim.

IAGO. Is my lord angry?
EMILIA.   He went hence but now,
And certainly in strange unquietness.
   IAGO. Can he be angry? I have seen the cannon
When it hath blown his ranks into the air,
And, like the Devil, from his very arm   130
Puffed his own brother, and can he be angry?
Something of moment then. I will go meet him.
There's matter in 't indeed if he be angry.
   DESDEMONA. I prithee do so.

(*Exit* IAGO.)

                    Something sure of state,
Either from Venice, or some unhatched practice   135
Made demonstrable here in Cyprus to him,
Hath puddled his clear spirit. And in such cases
Men's natures wrangle with inferior things,
Though great ones are their object. 'Tis even so,
For let our finger ache and it indues   140
Our other healthful members even to that sense
Of pain. Nay, we must think men are not gods,
Nor of them look for such observancy
As fits the bridal.° Beshrew me much, Emilia,
I was, unhandsome warrior° as I am,   145
Arraigning his unkindness with my soul,
But now I find I had suborned the witness,°
And he's indicted falsely.
   EMILIA. Pray Heaven it be state matters, as you think,
And no conception nor no jealous toy°   150
Concerning you.
   DESDEMONA. Alas the day, I never gave him cause!
   EMILIA. But jealous souls will not be answered so.
They are not ever jealous for the cause,
But jealous for they are jealous 'Tis a monster   155
Begot upon itself, born on itself.
   DESDEMONA. Heaven keep that monster from Othello's mind!
   EMILIA. Lady, amen.
   DESDEMONA. I will go seek him. Cassio, walk hereabout.
If I do find him fit, I'll move your suit,   160
And seek to effect it to my uttermost.

144. bridal: honeymoon.   **145. unhandsome warrior:** clumsy soldier. Desdemona continually thinks of herself as Othello's companion in arms. Cf. I.iii249 ff.
147. suborned ... witness: corrupted the evidence; i.e., it is my fault, not his.
150. jealous toy: silly suspicion.

CASSIO. I humbly thank your ladyship.

(*Exeunt* DESDEMONA *and* EMILIA. *Enter* BIANCA.)

BIANCA. Save you, friend Cassio!
CASSIO.   What make you from home?
How is it with you, my most fair Bianca?
I' faith, sweet love, I was coming to your house.   165
BIANCA. And I was going to your lodging, Cassio.
What, keep a week away? Seven days and nights?
Eightscore eight hours? And lovers' absent hours,
More tedious than the dial eightscore times?
Oh, weary reckoning!
CASSIO.   Pardon me, Bianca.   170
I have this while with leaden thoughts been pressed,
But I shall in a more continuate time
Strike off this score of absence. Sweet Bianca,

(*Giving her* DESDEMONA's *handkerchief*)

Take me this work out.
BIANCA.   O' Cassio, whence came this?
This is some token from a newer friend.   175
To the felt absence now I feel a cause.
Is 't come to this? Well, well.
CASSIO.   Go to, woman!
Throw your vile guesses in the Devil's teeth,
From whence you have them. You are jealous now
That this is from some mistress, some remembrance.   180
No, by my faith, Bianca.
BIANCA.   Why, whose is it?
CASSIO. I know not, sweet. I found it in my chamber.
I like the work well. Ere it be demanded—
As like enough it will—I'd have it copied.
Take it, and do 't, and leave me for this time.   185
BIANCA. Leave you! Wherefore?
CASSIO. I do attend here on the General,
And think it no addition,° nor my wish,
To have him see me womaned.°
BIANCA.   Why, I pray you?
CASSIO. Not that I love you not.
BIANCA.   But that you do not love me.   190
I pray you bring me on the way a little,
And say if I shall see you soon at night.

188. addition: honor.   **189. womaned**: with a girl.

CASSIO. 'Tis but a little way that I can bring you,
For I attend here. But I'll see you soon.
BIANCA. 'Tis very good, I must be circumstanced.° 195

(*Exeunt.*)

ACT IV

SCENE I. *Cyprus. Before the castle.*

Enter OTHELLO *and* IAGO.

IAGO. Will you think so?
OTHELLO. Think so, Iago!
IAGO. What,
To kiss in private?
OTHELLO. An unauthorized kiss.
IAGO. Or to be naked with her friend in bed
An hour or more, not meaning any harm?
OTHELLO. Naked in bed, Iago, and not mean harm! 5
It is hypocrisy against the Devil.
They that mean virtuously and yet do so,
The Devil their virtue tempts and they tempt Heaven.
IAGO. So they do nothing, 'tis a venial° slip.
But if I give my wife a handkerchief— 10
OTHELLO. What then?
IAGO. Why, then, 'tis hers, my lord, and being hers,
She may, I think, bestow 't on any man.
OTHELLO. She is protectress of her honor too.
May she give that? 15
IAGO. Her honor is an essence that's not seen.
They have it very oft that have it not.
But for the handkerchief—
OTHELLO. By Heaven, I would most gladly have forgot it.
Thou said'st—oh, it comes o'er my memory, 20
As doth the raven o'er the infected house,°
Boding to all—he had my handkerchief.
IAGO. Aye, what of that?
OTHELLO. That's not so good now.
IAGO. What,
If I had said I had seen him do you wrong?
Or heard him say—as knaves be such abroad, 25

195. **circumstanced**: put off.
    Act iv, Sc. 1. 9. **venial**: pardonable.   21. **As . . . house**: i.e., as a bird of prey waits for its victim to die.

Who having, by their own importunate suit,
Or voluntary dotage of some mistress,
Convincèd or supplied° them, cannot choose
But they must blab—
    OTHELLO.   Hath he said anything?
    IAGO. He hath, my lord, but be you well assured,   30
No more, than he'll unswear.
    OTHELLO.   What hath he said?
    IAGO. Faith, that he did—I know not what he did.
    OTHELLO. What? What?
    IAGO. Lie—
    OTHELLO. With her?
    IAGO.   With her, on her, what you will.
    OTHELLO. Lie° with her! Lie on her!—We say lie on her when   35
they belie her.—Lie with her! 'Zounds, that's fulsome!° Handkerchief—
confessions—handkerchief!—To confess, and be hanged for his labor. First
to be hanged, and then to confess. I tremble at it. Nature would not invest
herself in such shadowing passion without some instruction.° It is not
words that shake me thus. Pish! Noses, ears, and lips. Is 't possible?—   40
Confess?—Handkerchief?—Oh, devil! (*Falls in a trance.*)
    IAGO. Work on,
My medicine, work! Thus credulous fools are caught,
And many worthy and chaste dames even thus,
All guiltless, meet reproach. What ho! My lord!   45
My lord, I say! Othello!

    (*Enter* CASSIO.)
                       How now, Cassio!
    CASSIO. What's the matter?
    IAGO. My lord is fall'n into an epilepsy.
This is his second fit, he had one yesterday.
    CASSIO. Rub him about the temples.
    IAGO.   No, forbear,   50
The lethargy° must have his quiet course.
If not, he foams at mouth and by and by
Breaks out to savage madness. Look, he stirs.
Do you withdraw yourself a little while,
He will recover straight. When he is gone,   55
I would on great occasion speak with you.

    (*Exit* CASSIO.)

---

28. Convincèd or supplied: overcome or satisfied their desires. **35–41. Lie . . . devil**: Othello breaks into incoherent muttering before he falls down in a fit. **36. fulsome**: disgusting. **38–39. Nature . . . instruction**: nature would not fill me with such overwhelming emotion unless there was some cause. **51. lethargy**: epileptic fit.

How is it, General? Have you not hurt your head?°
    OTHELLO.   Dost thou mock me?
    IAGO.   I mock you! No, by Heaven.
Would you would bear your fortune like a man!
    OTHELLO.   A hornèd man's a monster and a beast.   60
    IAGO.   There's many a beast, then, in a populous city,
And many a civil monster.
    OTHELLO.   Did he confess it?
    IAGO.   Good sir, be a man.
Think every bearded fellow that's but yoked°
May draw with you.° There's millions now alive   65
That nightly lie in those unproper beds
Which they dare swear peculiar.° Your case is better.
Oh, 'tis the spite of Hell, the Fiend's archmock,
To lip° a wanton in a secure couch°
And to suppose her chaste! No, let me know,   70
And knowing what I am, I know what she shall be.
    OTHELLO.   Oh, thou art wise, 'tis certain.
    IAGO.   Stand you awhile apart,
Confine yourself but in a patient list.°
Whilst you were here o'erwhelmèd with your grief—
A passion most unsuiting such a man—   75
Cassio came hither. I shifted him away,
And laid good 'scuse upon your ecstasy,°
Bade him anon return and here speak with me,
The which he promisèd. Do but encave yourself,
And mark the fleers, the gibes, and notable scorns,   80
That dwell in every region of his face.
For I will make him tell the tale anew,
Where, how, how oft, how long ago, and when
He hath and is again to cope° your wife.
I say but mark his gesture. Marry, patience,   85
Or I shall say you are all in all in spleen,
And nothing of a man.
    OTHELLO.   Dost thou hear, Iago?
I will be found most cunning in my patience,
But—dost thou hear?—most bloody.
    IAGO.   That's not amiss,
But yet keep time in all. Will you withdraw?   90

57. Have . . . head: With brutal cynicism Iago asks whether Othello is suffering from cuckold's headache. **64. yoked:** married. **65. draw . . . you:** be your yoke fellow **66–67. That . . . peculiar:** that lie nightly in beds which they believe are their own but which others have shared. **69. lip:** kiss. **secure couch:** lit., a carefree bed; i.e., a bed which has been used by the wife's lover, but secretly. **73. patient list:** confines of patience. **77. ecstasy:** fit. **84. cope:** encounter.

(OTHELLO *retires.*)

Now will I question Cassio of Bianca,
A housewife° that by selling her desires
Buys herself bread and clothes. It is a creature
That dotes on Cassio, as 'tis the strumpet's plague
To beguile many and be beguiled by one.   95
He, when he hears of her, cannot refrain
From the excess of laughter. Here he comes.

(*Re-enter* CASSIO.)

As he shall smile, Othello shall go mad,
And his unbookish° jealousy must construe
Poor Cassio's smiles, gestures, and light behavior   100
Quite in the wrong. How do you now, Lieutenant?
  CASSIO.   The worser that you give me the addition°
Whose want even kills me.
  IAGO.   Ply Desdemona well, and you are sure on 't.
Now, if this suit lay in Bianca's power,   105
How quickly should you speed!
  CASSIO.   Alas, poor caitiff!°
  OTHELLO.   Look how he laughs already!
  IAGO.   I never knew a woman love man so.
  CASSIO.   Alas, poor rogue! I think, i' faith, she loves me.
  OTHELLO.   Now he denies it faintly and laughs it out. 110
  IAGO.   Do you hear, Cassio?
  OTHELLO.   Now he impórtunes him
To tell it o'er. Go to. Well said, well said.
  IAGO.   She gives it out that you shall marry her.
Do you intend it?
  CASSIO.   Ha, ha, ha!   115
  OTHELLO.   Do you triumph, Roman?° Do you triumph?
  CASSIO.   I marry her! What, a customer! I prithee bear some charity
to my wit. Do not think it so unwholesome. Ha, ha, ha!
  OTHELLO.   So, so, so, so. They laugh that win.
  IAGO.   Faith, the cry goes that you shall marry her.   120
  CASSIO.   Prithee say true.
  IAGO.   I am a very villain else.
  OTHELLO.   Have you scored° me? Well.
  CASSIO.   This is the monkey's own giving out. She is persuaded I

---

92. **housewife**: hussy.   99. **unbookish**: unlearned.   102. **addition**: title (Lieutenant) which he has lost.   106. **caitiff**: wretch.   116. **triumph, Roman**: The word "triumph" suggests "Roman" because the Romans celebrated their victories with triumphs, elaborate shows, and processions.   123. **scored**: marked, as with a blow from a whip.

will marry her out of her own love and flattery, not out of my promise. 125
OTHELLO. Iago beckons me, now he begins the story.
CASSIO. She was here even now. She haunts me in every place. I was the other day talking on the sea bank with certain Venetians, and thither comes the bauble, and, by this hand, she falls me thus about my neck— 130
OTHELLO. Crying "O dear Cassio!" as it were. His gesture imports it.
CASSIO. So hangs and lolls and weeps upon me, so hales and pulls me. Ha, ha, ha!
OTHELLO. Now he tells how she plucked him to my chamber. Oh, I see that nose of yours, but not that dog I shall throw it to. 135
CASSIO. Well, I must leave her company.
IAGO. Before me!° Look where she comes.
CASSIO. 'Tis such another fitchew!° Marry, a perfumed one.

(*Enter* BIANCA.)

What do you mean by this haunting of me?
BIANCA. Let the Devil and his dam haunt you! What did you 140 mean by that same handkerchief you gave me even now? I was a fine fool to take it. I must take out the work? A likely piece of work, that you should find it in your chamber and not know who left it there! This is some minx's token, and I must take out the work? There, give it your hobbyhorse. Wheresoever you had it, I'll take out no work on 't. 145
CASSIO. How now, my sweet Bianca! How now! How now!
OTHELLO. By Heaven, that should be my handkerchief!
BIANCA. An° you'll come to supper tonight, you may. An you will not, come when you are next prepared for. (*Exit.*)
IAGO. After her, after her.
CASSIO. Faith, I must, she'll rail i' the street else. 150
IAGO. Will you sup there?
CASSIO. Faith, I intend so.
IAGO. Well, I may chance to see you, for I would very fain speak with you.
CASSIO. Prithee, come, will you? 155
IAGO. Go to. Say no more.

(*Exit* CASSIO.)

OTHELLO (*advancing*). How shall I murder him, Iago?
IAGO. Did you perceive how he laughed at his vice?
OTHELLO. Oh, Iago!
IAGO. And did you see the handkerchief? 160
OTHELLO. Was that mine?
IAGO. Yours, by this hand. And to see how he prizes the foolish

137. **Before me:** by my soul.   138. **fitchew:** polecat.   148. **An:** if.

woman your wife! She gave it him, and he hath given it his whore.

OTHELLO. I would have him nine years a-killing. A fine woman! A fair woman! A sweet woman! 165

IAGO. Nay, you must forget that.

OTHELLO. Aye, let her rot, and perish, and be damned tonight, for she shall not live. No, my heart is turned to stone, I strike it and it hurts my hand. Oh, the world hath not a sweeter creature. She might lie by an emperor's side, and command him tasks. 170

IAGO. Nay, that's not your way.°

OTHELLO. Hang her! I do but say what she is, so delicate with her needle, an admirable musician—oh, she will sing the savageness out of a bear—of so high and plenteous wit and invention—

IAGO. She's the worse for all this. 175

OTHELLO. Oh, a thousand thousand times. And then, of so gentle a condition!

IAGO. Aye, too gentle.

OTHELLO. Nay, that's certain. But yet the pity of it, Iago! O Iago, the pity of it, Iago! 180

IAGO. If you are so fond over her iniquity, give her patent to offend, for if it touch not you, it comes near nobody.

OTHELLO. I will chop her into messes. Cuckold me!

IAGO. Oh, 'tis foul in her.

OTHELLO. With mine officer! 185

IAGO. That's fouler.

OTHELLO. Get me some poison, Iago, this night. I'll not expostulate with her, lest her body and beauty unprovide my mind again. This night, Iago.

IAGO. Do it not with poison, strangle her in her bed, even the bed she hath contaminated. 190

OTHELLO. Good, good. The justice of it pleases. Very good.

IAGO. And for Cassio, let me be his undertaker.° You shall hear more by midnight.

OTHELLO. Excellent good. (*A trumpet within.*) What trumpet is that same?

IAGO. Something from Venice, sure. 'Tis Lodovico 195 Come from the Duke. And see, your wife is with him.

(*Enter* LODOVICO, DESDEMONA, *and* ATTENDANTS.)

LODOVICO. God save the worthy General!

OTHELLO. With all my heart, sir.

LODOVICO. The Duke and Senators of Venice greet you. (*Gives him a letter.*)

---

171. Nay . . . way: i.e., don't get soft thoughts about her.   192. be . . . undertaker: undertake to manage his business. In Shakespeare's plays the word does *not* mean "mortician."

OTHELLO. I kiss the instrument of their pleasures. (*Opens the letter, and reads.*) 200
DESDEMONA. And what's the news, good Cousin Lodovico?
IAGO. I am very glad to see you, signior. Welcome to Cyprus.
LODOVICO. I thank you. How does Lieutenant Cassio?
IAGO. Lives, sir. 205
DESDEMONA. Cousin, there's fall'n between him and my lord An unkind breach, but you shall make all well.
OTHELLO. Are you sure of that?
DESDEMONA. My lord?
OTHELLO (*reads*). "This fail you not to do, as you will—" 210
LODOVICO. He did not call, he's busy in the paper. Is there division 'twixt my lord and Cassio?
DESDEMONA. A most unhappy one. I would do much To atone° them, for the love I bear to Cassio.
OTHELLO. Fire and brimstone!
DESDEMONA.   My lord?
OTHELLO.   Are you wise?° 215
DESDEMONA. What, is he angry?
LODOVICO.   Maybe the letter moved him, For, as I think, they do command him home, Deputing Cassio in his government.
DESDEMONA. By my troth, I am glad on 't.
OTHELLO.   Indeed!
DESDEMONA.   My lord?
OTHELLO. I am glad to see you mad.
DESDEMONA.   Why, sweet Othello? 220
OTHELLO. Devil! (*Striking her.*)
DESDEMONA. I have not deserved this.
LODOVICO. My lord, this would not be believed in Venice, Though I should swear I saw 't. 'Tis very much. Make her amends, she weeps.
OTHELLO.   O devil, devil! 225
If that the earth could teem with a woman's tears, Each drop she falls would prove a crocodile.° Out of my sight!
DESDEMONA. I will not stay to offend you. (*Going.*)
LODOVICO. Truly, an obedient lady. I do beseech your lordship, call her back. 230

214. **atone**: reconcile. 215. **Are ... wise**: i.e., in saying you bear love to Cassio. 226–27. **If ... crocodile**: If the earth could breed from woman's tears, each tear that she lets fall would become a crocodile. It was believed that the crocodile would cry and sob to attract the sympathetic passer-by, who was then snapped up.

WILLIAM SHAKESPEARE   129

OTHELLO. Mistress!
DESDEMONA. My lord?
OTHELLO. What would you with her, sir?
LODOVICO. Who, I, my lord?
OTHELLO. Aye, you did wish that I would make her turn.
Sir, she can turn and turn, and yet go on 235
And turn again. And she can weep, sir, weep.
And she's obedient, as you say, obedient,
Very obedient. Proceed you in your tears.
Concerning this, sir—oh, well-painted passion!°—
I am commanded home. Get you away. 240
I'll send for you anon. Sir, I obey the mandate,
And will return to Venice. Hence, avaunt!

(*Exit* DESDEMONA.)

Cassio shall have my place. And, sir, tonight,
I do entreat that we may sup together.
You are welcome, sir, to Cyprus. Goats and monkeys! (*Exit.*) 245
    LODOVICO. Is this the noble Moor whom our full Senate
Call all-in-all sufficient? This the nature
Whom passion could not shake? Whose solid virtue
The shot of accident nor dart of chance
Could neither graze nor pierce?
    IAGO. He is much changed. 250
    LODOVICO. Are his wits safe? Is he not light of brain?
    IAGO. He's that he is. I may not breathe my censure°
What he might be. If what he might he is not,
I would to Heaven he were!
    LODOVICO. What, strike his wife!
    IAGO. Faith, that was not so well, yet would I knew 255
That stroke would prove the worst!
    LODOVICO. Is it his use?
Or did the letters work upon his blood,
And new-create this fault?
    IAGO. Alas, alas!
It is not honesty in me to speak
What I have seen and known. You shall observe him, 260
And his own courses will denote him so
That I may save my speech. Do but go after,
And mark how he continues.
    LODOVICO. I am sorry that I am deceived in him.

(*Exeunt.*)

239. **well-painted passion:** cleverly imitated emotion. 252. **censure:** opinion, judgment.

SCENE II. *A room in the castle.*

Enter OTHELLO *and* EMILIA.

OTHELLO. You have seen nothing, then?
EMILIA. Nor ever heard, nor ever did suspect.
OTHELLO. Yes, you have seen Cassio and she together.
EMILIA. But then I saw no harm, and then I heard
Each syllable that breath made up between them. 5
OTHELLO. What, did they never whisper?
EMILIA. Never, my lord.
OTHELLO. Nor send you out o' the way?
EMILIA. Never.
OTHELLO. To fetch her fan, her gloves, her mask, nor nothing?
EMILIA. Never, my lord. 10
OTHELLO. That's strange.
EMILIA. I durst, my lord, to wager she is honest,
Lay down my soul at stake. If you think other,
Remove your thought, it doth abuse your bosom.
If any wretch have put this in your head, 15
Let Heaven requite it with the serpent's curse!
For if she be not honest, chaste, and true,
There's no man happy, the purest of their wives
Is foul as slander.
OTHELLO. Bid her come hither. Go.

(*Exit* EMILIA.)

She says enough. Yet she's a simple bawd 20
That cannot say as much. This is a subtle whore,
A closet lock and key of villainous secrets.
And yet she'll kneel and pray, I have seen her do 't.

(*Enter* DESDEMONA *with* EMILIA.)

DESDEMONA. My lord, what is your will?
OTHELLO. Pray, chuck, come hither.
DESDEMONA. What is your pleasure?
OTHELLO. Let me see your eyes. 25
Look in my face.
DESDEMONA. What horrible fancy's this?
OTHELLO (*to* EMILIA). Some of your function,° mistress.
Leave procreants alone and shut the door,
Cough, or cry hem, if anybody come.

---

27. Some ... function: get about your business; i.e., prostitution. Othello pretends that Emilia is keeper of a brothel and Desdemona one of the women.

Your mystery,° your mystery. Nay, dispatch. 30

    (*Exit* EMILIA.)

    DESDEMONA. Upon my knees, what doth your speech import?
I understand a fury in your words,
But not the words.
    OTHELLO.   Why, what art thou?
    DESDEMONA. Your wife, my lord, your true and loyal wife.
    OTHELLO. Come, swear it, damn thyself, 35
Lest, being like one of Heaven,° the devils themselves
Should fear to seize thee. Therefore be double-damned.
Swear thou art honest.
    DESDEMONA.   Heaven doth truly know it.
    OTHELLO. Heaven truly knows that thou art false as Hell.
    DESDEMONA. To whom, my lord? With whom? How am I false? 40
    OTHELLO. O Desdemona! Away! Away! Away!
    DESDEMONA. Alas the heavy day! Why do you weep?
Am I the motive of these tears, my lord?
If haply you my father do suspect
An instrument of this your calling-back, 45
Lay not your blame on me. If you have lost him,
Why, I have lost him too.
    OTHELLO.   Had it pleased Heaven
To try me with affliction, had they rained
All kinds of sores and shames on my bare head,
Steeped me in poverty to the very lips, 50
Given to captivity me and my utmost hopes,
I should have found in some place of my soul
A drop of patience. But, alas, to make me
A fixèd figure for the time of scorn
To point his slow unmoving finger at! 55
Yet could I bear that too, well, very well.
But there where I have garnered up my heart,
Where either I must live or bear no life,
The fountain from the which my current runs
Or else dries up—to be discarded thence! 60
Or keep it as a cistern for foul toads
To knot and gender in! Turn thy complexion there,
Patience, thou young and rose-lipped cherubin—
Aye, there, look grim as Hell!
    DESDEMONA. I hope my noble lord esteems me honest. 65

    30. mystery: profession.   **36. being . . . Heaven:** because you look like an angel.

OTHELLO. Oh, aye, as summer flies are in the shambles,°
That quicken even with blowing.° O thou weed,
Who art so lovely fair and smell'st so sweet
That the sense aches at thee, would thou hadst ne'er been born!
    DESDEMONA. Alas, what ignorant sin have I committed?   70
    OTHELLO. Was this fair paper,° this most goodly book,
Made to write "whore" upon? What committed!
Committed! O thou public commoner!°
I should make very forges of my cheeks
That would to cinders burn up modesty   75
Did I but speak thy deeds. What committed!
Heaven stops the nose at it, and the moon winks.
The bawdy wind, that kisses all it meets,
Is hushed within the hollow mine of earth
And will not hear it. What committed!   80
Impudent strumpet!
    DESDEMONA. By Heaven, you do me wrong.
    OTHELLO. Are not you a strumpet?
    DESDEMONA.   No, as I am a Christian.
If to preserve this vessel for my lord
From any other foul unlawful touch
Be not to be a strumpet, I am none.   85
    OTHELLO. What, not a whore?
    DESDEMONA.   No, as I shall be saved.
    OTHELLO. Is 't possible?
    DESDEMONA. Oh, Heaven forgive us!
    OTHELLO.   I cry you mercy, then.
I took you for that cunning whore of Venice
That married with Othello. (*Raising his voice*) You, mistress,   90
That have the office opposite to Saint Peter,
And keep the gate of Hell!

    (*Re-enter* EMILIA.)

    You, you, aye, you!
We have done our course, there's money for your pains.
I pray you turn the key, and keep our counsel. (*Exit.*)
    EMILIA. Alas, what does this gentleman conceive?   95
How do you, madam? How do you, my good lady?
    DESDEMONA. Faith, half-asleep.
    EMILIA. Good madam, what's the matter with my lord?
    DESDEMONA. With who?

66. shambles: slaughterhouse. **67. quicken . . . blowing:** come to life as soon as the eggs are laid. **71. fair paper:** i.e., her white body. **73. public commoner:** one who offers herself to all comers.

EMILIA. Why, with my lord, madam.
DESDEMONA. Who is thy lord?
EMILIA. He that is yours, sweet lady.
DESDEMONA. I have none. Do not talk to me, Emilia.
I cannot weep, nor answer have I none
But what should go by water.° Prithee tonight
Lay on my bed my wedding sheets. Remember,
And call thy husband hither.
EMILIA. Here's a change indeed! (*Exit*.)
DESDEMONA. 'Tis meet I should be used so, very meet.
How have I been behaved that he might stick
The small'st opinion on my least misuse?°

(*Re-enter* EMILIA *with* IAGO.)

IAGO. What is your pleasure, madam? How is 't with you?
DESDEMONA. I cannot tell. Those that do teach young babes
Do it with gentle means and easy tasks.
He might have chid me so, for, in good faith,
I am a child to chiding.
IAGO. What's the matter, lady?
EMILIA. Alas, Iago, my lord hath so bewhored her,
Thrown such despite and heavy terms upon her,
As true hearts cannot bear.
DESDEMONA. Am I that name, Iago?
IAGO. What name, fair lady?
DESDEMONA. Such as she says my lord did say I was.
EMILIA. He called her whore. A beggar in his drink
Could not have laid such terms upon his callet.°
IAGO. Why did he so?
DESDEMONA. I do not know. I am sure I am none such.
IAGO. Do not weep, do not weep. Alas the day!
EMILIA. Hath she forsook so many noble matches,
Her father and her country and her friends,
To be called whore? Would it not make one weep?
DESDEMONA. It is my wretched fortune.
IAGO. Beshrew him for 't!
How comes this trick upon him?
DESDEMONA. Nay, Heaven doth know.
EMILIA. I will be hanged if some eternal villain,
Some busy and insinuating rogue,
Some cogging, cozening slave, to get some office,

---

104. go . . . water: be expressed in tears. **109. misuse:** mistake. **121. callet:** moll.

Have not devised this slander. I'll be hanged else.
  IAGO. Fie, there is no such man, it is impossible.
  DESDEMONA. If any such there be, Heaven pardon him!   135
  EMILIA. A halter pardon him! And Hell gnaw his bones!
Why should he call her whore? Who keeps her company?
What place? What time? What form? What likelihood?
The Moor's abused by some most villainous knave,
Some base notorious knave, some scurvy fellow.   140
O Heaven, that such companions° Thou'dst unfold,°
And put in every honest hand a whip
To lash the rascals naked through the world
Even from the east to the west!
  IAGO.   Speak withindoor.°
  EMILIA. Oh, fie upon them! Some such squire he was   145
That turned your wit the seamy side without,
And made you to suspect me with the Moor.
  IAGO. You are a fool. Go to.°
  DESDEMONA.   O good Iago,
What shall I do to win my lord again?
Good friend, go to him, for, by this light of Heaven,   150
I know not how I lost him. Here I kneel.
If e'er my will did trespass 'gainst his love
Either in discourse of thought or actual deed,
Or that mine eyes, mine ears, or any sense
Delighted them in any other form,   155
Or that I do not yet, and ever did,
And ever will, though he do shake me off
To beggarly divorcement, love him dearly,
Comfort forswear me! Unkindness may do much,
And his unkindness may defeat my life,   160
But never taint my love. I cannot say "whore,"
It doth abhor me now I speak the word.
To do the act that might the addition° earn
Not the world's mass of vanity° could make me.
  IAGO. I pray you be content, 'tis but his humor.   165
The business of the state does him offense,
And he does chide with you.
  DESDEMONA.   If 'twere no other—
  IAGO. 'Tis but so, I warrant. (*Trumpets within.*)
Hark how these instruments summon to supper!
The messengers of Venice stay the meat.°   170

141. **companions**: low creatures. **unfold**: bring to light. 144. **Speak withindoor**: don't shout so loud that all the street will hear you. 148. **Go to**: an expression of derision. 163. **addition**: title. 164. **vanity**: i.e., riches. 170. **meat**: serving of supper.

Go in, and weep not, all things shall be well.

(*Exeunt* DESDEMONA *and* EMILIA. *Enter* RODERIGO.)

How now, Roderigo!

RODERIGO. I do not find that thou dealest justly with me.

IAGO. What in the contrary?

RODERIGO. Every day thou daffest me with some device, Iago, and rather, as it seems to me now, keepest from me all conveniency than suppliest me with the least advantage of hope. I will indeed no longer endure it, nor am I yet persuaded to put up in peace what already I have foolishly suffered.

IAGO. Will you hear me, Roderigo?

RODERIGO. Faith, I have heard too much, for your words and performances are no kin together.

IAGO. You charge me most unjustly.

RODERIGO. With naught but truth. I have wasted myself out of my means. The jewels you have had from me to deliver to Desdemona would half have corrupted a votarist.° You have told me she hath received them, and returned me expectations and comforts of sudden respect and acquaintance, but I find none.

IAGO. Well, go to, very well.

RODERIGO. Very well! Go to! I cannot go to, man, nor 'tis not very well. By this hand, I say 'tis very scurvy, and begin to find myself fopped in it.

IAGO. Very well.

RODERIGO. I tell you 'tis not very well. I will make myself known to Desdemona. If she will return me my jewels, I will give over my suit and repent my unlawful solicitation. If not, assure yourself I will seek satisfaction of you.

IAGO. You have said now.°

RODERIGO. Aye, and said nothing but what I protest intendment of doing.

IAGO. Why, now I see there's mettle in thee, and even from this instant do build on thee a better opinion than ever before. Give me thy hand, Roderigo. Thou hast taken against me a most just exception, but yet I protest I have dealt most directly in thy affair.

RODERIGO. It hath not appeared.

IAGO. I grant indeed it hath not appeared, and your suspicion is not without wit and judgment. But, Roderigo, if thou hast that in thee indeed which I have greater reason to believe now than ever—I mean purpose, courage, and valor—this night show it. If thou the next night following

---

186. votarist: nun.   **198. You . . . now:** or in modern slang, "Oh yeah."

enjoy not Desdemona, take me from this world with treachery and 210
devise engines° for my life.
 RODERIGO. Well, what is it? Is it within reason and compass?
 IAGO. Sir, there is especial commission come from Venice to depute Cassio in Othello's place.
 RODERIGO. Is that true? Why, then Othello and Desdemona 215
return again to Venice.
 IAGO. Oh, no. He goes into Mauritania, and takes away with him the fair Desdemona, unless his abode be lingered here by some accident. Wherein none can be so determinate as the removing of Cassio.
 RODERIGO. How do you mean, "removing of" him? 220
 IAGO. Why, by making him uncapable of Othello's place, knocking out his brains.
 RODERIGO. And that you would have me to do?
 IAGO. Aye, if you dare do yourself a profit and a right. He sups tonight with a harlotry,° and thither will I go to him. He knows not yet of his 225
honorable fortune. If you will watch his going thence, which I will fashion to fall out between twelve and one, you may take him at your pleasure. I will be near to second your attempt, and he shall fall between us. Come, stand not amazed at it, but go along with me. I will show you such a necessity in his death that you shall think yourself bound to put it on 230
him. It is now high suppertime, and the night grows to waste. About it.
 RODERIGO. I will hear further reason for this.
 IAGO. And you shall be satisfied.

(*Exeunt.*)

SCENE III. *Another room in the castle.*

Enter OTHELLO, LODOVICO, DESDEMONA, EMILIA, *and* ATTENDANTS.

 LODOVICO. I do beseech you, sir, trouble yourself no further.
 OTHELLO. Oh, pardon me, 'twill do me good to walk.
 LODOVICO. Madam, good night. I humbly thank your ladyship.
 DESDEMONA. Your Honor is most welcome.
 OTHELLO.   Will you walk, sir?
Oh—Desdemona— 5
 DESDEMONA. My lord?
 OTHELLO. Get you to bed on the instant, I will be returned forthwith. Dismiss your attendant there. Look it be done.
 DESDEMONA. I will, my lord.

(*Exeunt* OTHELLO, LODOVICO, *and* ATTENDANTS.)

211. engines: instruments of torture.   **225. harlotry:** harlot.

EMILIA. How goes it now? He looks gentler than he did.
DESDEMONA. He says he will return incontinent.°
He hath commanded me to go to bed,
And bade me to dismiss you.
EMILIA. Dismiss me!
DESDEMONA. It was his bidding, therefore, good Emilia,
Give me my nightly wearing, and adieu.
We must not now displease him.
EMILIA. I would you had never seen him!
DESDEMONA. So would not I. My love doth so approve him
That even his stubbornness, his checks, his frowns—
Prithee, unpin me—have grace and favor in them.
EMILIA. I have laid those sheets you bade me on the bed.
DESDEMONA. All's one. Good faith, how foolish are our minds!
If I do die before thee, prithee shroud me
In one of those same sheets.
EMILIA. Come, come, you talk.
DESDEMONA. My mother had a maid called Barbara.
She was in love, and he she loved proved mad
And did forsake her. She had a song of "willow"°—
An old thing 'twas, but it expressed her fortune,
And she died singing it. That song tonight
Will not go from my mind. I have much to do
But to go hang my head all at one side
And sing it like poor Barbara. Prithee, dispatch.
EMILIA. Shall I go fetch your nightgown?
DESDEMONA. No, unpin me here.
This Lodovico is a proper man.
EMILIA. A very handsome man.
DESDEMONA. He speaks well.
EMILIA. I know a lady in Venice would have walked barefoot to Palestine for a touch of his nether lip.
DESDEMONA (*singing*).
    "The poor soul sat sighing by a sycamore tree,
        Sing all a green willow.
    Her hand on her bosom, her head on her knee,
        Sing willow, willow, willow.
    The fresh streams ran by her, and murmured her moans,
        Sing willow, willow, willow.
    Her salt tears fell from her, and softened the stones—"
Lay by these—(*singing*)
        "Sing willow, willow, willow"

11. **incontinent**: immediately.   27. **willow**: the emblem of the forlorn lover.

Prithee, hie thee, he'll come anon.—(*singing*)
        "Sing all a green willow must be my garland.
        Let nobody blame him, his scorn I approve—" 50
Nay, that's not next. Hark! Who is 't that knocks?
  EMILIA. It's the wind.
  DESDEMONA (*singing*).
        "I called my love false love, but what said he then?
        Sing willow, willow, willow.
        If I court moe° women, you'll couch with moe men." 55
So get thee gone, good night. Mine eyes do itch.
Doth that bode weeping?
  EMILIA.   'Tis neither here nor there.
  DESDEMONA. I have heard it said so. Oh, these men, these men!
Dost thou in conscience think—tell me, Emilia—
That there be women do abuse their husbands 60
In such gross kind?
  EMILIA.   There be some such, no question.
  DESDEMONA. Wouldst thou do such a deed for all the world?
  EMILIA. Why, would not you?
  DESDEMONA.   No, by this heavenly light!
  EMILIA. Nor I neither by this heavenly light. I might do 't as well i' the dark. 65
  DESDEMONA. Wouldst thou do such a deed for all the world?
  EMILIA. The world's a huge thing. It is a great price
For a small vice.
  DESDEMONA. In troth, I think thou wouldst not.
  EMILIA. In troth, I think I should, and undo 't when I had done. 70
Marry, I would not do such a thing for a joint ring,° nor for measures of lawn,° nor for gowns, petticoats, nor caps, nor any petty exhibition;° but for the whole world—why, who would not make her husband a cuckold to make him a monarch? I should venture Purgatory for 't.
  DESDEMONA. Beshrew me if I would do such a wrong 75
For the whole world.
  EMILIA. Why, the wrong is but a wrong i' the world, and having the world for your labor, 'tis a wrong in your own world and you might quickly make it right.
  DESDEMONA. I do not think there is any such woman. 80
  EMILIA. Yes, a dozen, and as many to the vantage as would store the world they played for. But I do think it is their husbands' faults

---

55. **moe**: more. 71–72. **joint ring**: ring made in two pieces, a lover's gift. **measures of lawn**: lengths of finest lawn, or as a modern woman would say, "sheer nylon." **petty exhibition**: small allowance of money.

If wives do fall. Say that they slack their duties
And pour our treasures into foreign laps, 85
Or else break out in peevish jealousies,
Throwing restraint upon us, or say they strike us,
Or scant our former having in despite,°
Why, we have galls,° and though we have some grace,
Yet have we some revenge. Let husbands know 90
Their wives have sense like them. They see and smell
And have their palates both for sweet and sour,
As husbands have. What is it that they do
When they change us for others? Is it sport?
I think it is. And doth affection breed it? 95
I think it doth. Is 't frailty that thus errs?
It is so too. And have not we affections,
Desires for sport, and frailty, as men have?
Then let them use us well. Else let them know
The ills we do, their ills instruct us so. 100

    DESDEMONA.   Good night, good night. Heaven me such uses send,
Not to pick bad from bad, but by bad mend!

    (*Exeunt.*)

ACT V

SCENE I. *Cyprus. A street.*

Enter IAGO *and* RODERIGO.

    IAGO.   Here, stand behind this bulk, straight will he come.
Wear thy good rapier bare, and put it home.
Quick, quick, fear nothing, I'll be at thy elbow.
It makes us, or it mars us. Think on that,
And fix most firm thy resolution. 5

    RODERIGO.   Be near at hand, I may miscarry in 't.

    IAGO.   Here, at thy hand. Be bold, and take thy stand. (*Retires.*)

    RODERIGO.   I have no great devotion to the deed,
And yet he hath given me satisfying reasons.
'Tis but a man gone. Forth, my sword. He dies. 10

    IAGO.   I have rubbed this young quat° almost to the sense,°
And he grows angry. Now, whether he kill Cassio,
Or Cassio him, or each do kill the other,

---

88. **scant . . . despite:** for spite cut down our allowance.   89. **galls:** bile, the cause of bitterness.

    Act V, Sc. i. 11. quat: pimple. **sense:** quick.

Every way makes my gain. Live Roderigo,
He calls me to a restitution large 15
Of gold and jewels that I bobbed from him
As gifts to Desdemona.
It must not be. If Cassio do remain,
He hath a daily beauty in his life
That makes me ugly,° and besides, the Moor 20
May unfold me to him. There stand I in much peril.
No, he must die. Be 't so. I hear him coming.

(*Enter* CASSIO.)

RODERIGO.   I know his gait, 'tis he. Villain, thou diest! (*Makes a pass at* CASSIO.)
CASSIO.   That thrust had been mine enemy indeed
But that my coat is better than thou know'st. 25
I will make proof of thine. (*Draws, and wounds* RODERIGO.)
RODERIGO.   Oh, I am slain!

(IAGO *from behind wounds* CASSIO *in the leg, and exit.*)

CASSIO.   I am maimed for ever. Help, ho! Murder! Murder! (*Falls.*)

(*Enter* OTHELLO.)

OTHELLO.   The voice of Cassio. Iago keeps his word.
RODERIGO.   Oh, villain that I am!
OTHELLO.   It is even so.
CASSIO.   Oh, help, ho! Light! A surgeon! 30
OTHELLO.   'Tis he. O brave Iago, honest and just,
That hast such noble sense of thy friend's wrong!
Thou teachest me. Minion,° your dear lies dead,
And your unblest fate hies. Strumpet, I come!
Forth of my heart those charms, thine eyes, are blotted. 35
Thy bed lust-stained shall with lust's blood be spotted. (*Exit.*)

(*Enter* LODOVICO *and* GRATIANO.)

CASSIO.   What ho! No watch?° No passage?° Murder! Murder!
GRATIANO.   'Tis some mischance, the cry is very direful.
CASSIO.   Oh, help!
LODOVICO.   Hark! 40
RODERIGO.   Oh, wretched villain!
LODOVICO.   Two or three groan. It is a heavy° night.
These may be counterfeits. Let's think 't unsafe

19–20. He ... ugly: by comparison with him I am a poor thing. Iago is conscious of his lack of social graces.   **33. Minion**: darling, in a bad sense.   **37. watch**: police. **No passage**: nobody passing.   **42. heavy**: thick.

WILLIAM SHAKESPEARE   141

To come in to the cry without more help.
    RODERIGO. Nobody come? Then shall I bleed to death.   45
    LODOVICO. Hark!

    (*Re-enter* IAGO, *with a light.*)

    GRATIANO. Here's one comes in his shirt, with light and weapons.
    IAGO. Who's there? Whose noise is this that cries on murder?
    LODOVICO. We do not know.
    IAGO.   Did not you hear a cry?
    CASSIO. Here, here! For Heaven's sake, help me!
    IAGO.   What's the matter?   50
    GRATIANO. This is Othello's Ancient, as I take it.
    LODOVICO. The same indeed, a very valiant fellow.
    IAGO. What are you here that cry so grievously?
    CASSIO. Iago? Oh, I am spoiled, undone by villains! Give me some
help.   55
    IAGO. Oh me, Lieutenant! What villains have done this?
    CASSIO. I think that one of them is hereabout,
And cannot make away.
    IAGO.   Oh, treacherous villains!
(*To* LODOVICO *and* GRATIANO) What are you there?
Come in and give some help.
    RODERIGO.   Oh, help me here!   60
    CASSIO. That's one of them.
    IAGO.   Oh, murderous slave! Oh, villain! (*Stabs*
RODERIGO.)
    RODERIGO. Oh, damned Iago! Oh, inhuman dog!
    IAGO. Kill men i' the dark! Where be these bloody thieves?
How silent is this town! Ho! Murder! Murder!
What may you be? Are you of good or evil?   65
    LODOVICO. As you shall prove us, praise us.
    IAGO. Signior Lodovico?
    LODOVICO. He, sir.
    IAGO. I cry you mercy. Here's Cassio hurt by villains.
    GRATIANO. Cassio!   70
    IAGO. How is 't, brother?
    CASSIO. My leg is cut in two.
    IAGO.   Marry, Heaven forbid!
Light, gentlemen. I'll bind it with my shirt.

    (*Enter* BIANCA.)

    BIANCA. What is the matter, ho? Who is 't that cried?
    IAGO. Who is 't that cried!   75

BIANCA. Oh, my dear Cassio! My sweet Cassio! Oh, Cassio, Cassio, Cassio!
IAGO. Oh, notable strumpet, Cassio, may you suspect
Who they should be that have thus mangled you?
CASSIO. No.
GRATIANO. I am sorry to find you thus. I have been to seek you.
IAGO. Lend me a garter. So. Oh, for a chair,
To bear him easily hence!
BIANCA. Alas, he faints! Oh, Cassio, Cassio, Cassio!
IAGO. Gentlemen all, I do suspect this trash
To be a party in this injury.
Patience awhile, good Cassio. Come, come,
Lend me a light. Know we this face or no?
Alas, my friend and my dear countryman
Roderigo? No—yes, sure. Oh Heaven! Roderigo.
GRATIANO. What, of Venice?
IAGO. Even he, sir. Did you know him?
GRATIANO. Know him! Aye.
IAGO. Signior Gratiano? I cry you gentle pardon.
These bloody accidents must excuse my manners,
That so neglected you.
GRATIANO. I am glad to see you.
IAGO. How do you, Cassio? Oh, a chair, a chair!
GRATIANO. Roderigo!
IAGO. He, he, 'tis he. (*A chair brought in*) Oh, that's well said, the chair.
Some good man bear him carefully from hence.
I'll fetch the General's surgeon. (*To* BIANCA) For you, mistress,
Save you your labor. He that lies slain here, Cassio,
Was my dear friend. What malice was between you?
CASSIO. None in the world, nor do I know the man.
IAGO (*to* BIANCA). What, look you pale? Oh, bear him out o' the air.

(CASSIO *and* RODERIGO *are borne off.*)

Stay you, good gentlemen. Look you pale, mistress?
Do you perceive the gastness of her eye?
Nay, if you stare, we shall hear more anon.
Behold her well, I pray you look upon her.
Do you see, gentlemen? Nay, guiltiness will speak,
Though tongues were out of use.

(*Enter* EMILIA.)

EMILIA. 'Las, what's the matter? What's the matter, husband?
IAGO. Cassio hath here been set on in the dark

WILLIAM SHAKESPEARE 143

By Roderigo, and fellows that are 'scaped.
He's almost slain, and Roderigo dead.
    EMILIA. Alas, good gentlemen! Alas, good Cassio!
    IAGO. This is the fruit of whoring. Prithee, Emilia, 115
Go know of Cassio where he supped tonight.
What, do you shake at that?
    BIANCA. He supped at my house, but I therefore shake not.
    IAGO. Oh, did he so? I charge you, go with me.
    EMILIA. Fie, fie upon thee, strumpet! 120
    BIANCA. I am no strumpet, but of life as honest
As you that thus abuse me.
    EMILIA.   As I! Foh! Fie upon thee!
    IAGO. Kind gentlemen, let's go see poor Cassio dressed.°
Come, mistress, you must tell 's another tale.
Emilia, run you to the citadel, 125
And tell my lord and lady what hath happed!
Will you go on? I pray. (*Aside*) This is the night
That either makes me or fordoes me quite.

(*Exeunt.*)

SCENE II. *A bedchamber in the castle.* DESDEMONA *in bed asleep, a light burning.*

Enter OTHELLO.

    OTHELLO. It is the cause,° it is the cause, my soul.
Let me not name it to you, you chaste stars!
It is the cause. Yet I'll not shed her blood,
Nor scar that whiter skin of hers than snow
And smooth as monumental alabaster. 5
Yet she must die, else she'll betray more men.
Put out the light, and then put out the light.
If I quench thee, thou flaming minister,°
I can again thy former light restore,
Should I repent me. But once put out thy light, 10
Thou cunning'st° pattern of excelling nature,
I know not where is that Promethean heat
That can thy light relume. When I have plucked the rose,

---

123. **dressed**: i.e., his wound dressed.
    Sc. ii. 1. It . . . cause: The meaning of the opening lines of this speech has been much discussed. The *cause* is Desdemona's supposed faithlessness; Othello, at this moment, sees himself as embodied vengeance, the venger of man betrayed by woman. **8. minister**: servant. **11. cunning'st**: most skillfully made.

I cannot give it vital growth again,
It needs must wither. I'll smell it on the tree. (*Kissing her*)
Ah, balmy breath, that dost almost persuade
Justice to break her sword! One more, one more.
Be thus when thou art dead, and I will kill thee,
And love thee after. One more, and this the last.
So sweet was ne'er so fatal. I must weep,
But they are cruel tears. This sorrow's heavenly,
It strikes where it doth love. She wakes.

DESDEMONA. Who's there? Othello?
OTHELLO. Aye, Desdemona.
DESDEMONA. Will you come to bed, my lord?
OTHELLO. Have you prayed tonight, Desdemona?
DESDEMONA. Aye, my lord.
OTHELLO. If you bethink yourself of any crime
Unreconciled as yet to Heaven and grace,
Solicit for it straight.
DESDEMONA. Alas, my lord, what may you mean by that?
OTHELLO. Well, do it, and be brief. I will walk by.
I would not kill thy unprepared spirit.
No, Heaven forfend! I would not kill thy soul.
DESDEMONA. Talk you of killing?
OTHELLO. Aye, I do.
DESDEMONA. Then Heaven have mercy on me!
OTHELLO. Amen, with all my heart!
DESDEMONA. If you say so, I hope you will not kill me.
OTHELLO. Hum!
DESDEMONA. And yet I fear you, for you are fatal then
When your eyes roll so. Why I should fear I know not,
Since guiltiness I know not, but yet I feel I fear.
OTHELLO. Think on thy sins.
DESDEMONA. They are loves I bear to you.
OTHELLO. Aye, and for that thou diest.
DESDEMONA. That death's unnatural that kills for loving.
Alas, why gnaw you so your nether lip?
Some bloody passion shakes your very frame.
These are portents, but yet I hope, I hope,
They do not point on me.
OTHELLO. Peace, and be still!
DESDEMONA. I will so. What's the matter?
OTHELLO. That handkerchief which I so loved and gave thee
Thou gavest to Cassio.
DESDEMONA. No, by my life and soul!

Send for the man, and ask him.
>OTHELLO.   Sweet soul, take heed,

Take heed of perjury, thou art on thy deathbed.
>DESDEMONA.   Aye, but not yet to die.
>OTHELLO.   Yes, presently.°

Therefore confess thee freely of thy sin,   55
For to deny each article with oath
Cannot remove nor choke the strong conception
That I do groan withal. Thou art to die.
>DESDEMONA.   Then Lord have mercy on me!
>OTHELLO.   I say amen.
>DESDEMONA.   And have you mercy too! I never did   60

Offend you in my life, never loved Cassio
But with such general warranty of Heaven
As I might love. I never gave him token.
>OTHELLO. By Heaven, I saw my handkerchief in 's hand.

O perjured woman! Thou dost stone° my heart,   65
And makest me call what I intend to do
A murder, which I thought a sacrifice.
I saw the handkerchief.
>DESDEMONA.   He found it, then,

I never gave it him. Send for him hither.
Let him confess a truth.
>OTHELLO.   He hath confessed.   70
>DESDEMONA.   What, my lord?
>OTHELLO. That he hath used thee.
>DESDEMONA.   How? Unlawfully?
>OTHELLO. Aye.
>DESDEMONA.   He will not say so.
>OTHELLO.   No, his mouth is stopped.

Honest Iago hath ta'en order for 't.   75
>DESDEMONA. Oh, my fear interprets! What, is he dead?
>OTHELLO. Had all his hairs been lives, my great revenge

Had stomach for them all.
>DESDEMONA.   Alas, he is betrayed, and I undone!
>OTHELLO. Out, strumpet! Weep'st thou for him to my face?   80
>DESDEMONA.   Oh, banish me, my lord, but kill me not!
>OTHELLO. Down, strumpet!
>DESDEMONA.   Kill me tomorrow, let me live tonight!
>OTHELLO. Nay, if you strive—
>DESDEMONA.   But half an hour!
>OTHELLO.   Being done, there is no pause.   85

54. presently: at once.   **65. stone:** turn to stone.

DESDEMONA.   But while I say one prayer!
OTHELLO.   It is too late. (*He stifles her.*)
EMILIA (*within*).   My lord, my lord! What ho! My lord, my lord!
OTHELLO.   What noise is this? Not dead? Not yet quite dead?
I that am cruel am yet merciful,
I would not have thee linger in thy pain.   90
So, so.
   EMILIA (*within*).   What ho! My lord, my lord!
   OTHELLO.   Who's there?
   EMILIA (*within*).   Oh, good my lord, I would speak a word with you!
   OTHELLO.   Yes, 'tis Emilia. By and by. She's dead.
'Tis like she comes to speak of Cassio's death.   95
The noise was here. Ha! No more moving?
Still as the grave. Shall she come in? Were 't good?
I think she stirs again. No. What's best to do?
If she come in, she'll sure speak to my wife.
My wife! My wife! My wife! I have no wife.   100
Oh, insupportable! Oh, heavy hour!
Methinks it should be now a huge eclipse
Of sun and moon, and that the affrighted globe
Should yawn at alteration.°
   EMILIA (*within*).   I do beseech you
That I may speak with you, O good my lord!   105
   OTHELLO.   I had forgot thee. Oh, come in, Emilia.
Soft, by and by. Let me the curtains° draw.
Where art thou? (*Unlocks the door.*)

(*Enter* EMILIA.)

                  What's the matter with thee now?
   EMILIA.   Oh, my good lord, yonder 's foul murders done!
   OTHELLO.   What, now?   110
   EMILIA.   But now, my lord.
   OTHELLO.   It is the very error of the moon.
She comes more nearer earth than she was wont
And makes men mad.
   EMILIA.   Cassio, my lord, hath killed a young Venetian   115
Called Roderigo.
   OTHELLO.   Roderigo killed!
And Cassio killed!
   EMILIA.   No, Cassio is not killed.
   OTHELLO.   Not Cassio killed! Then murder's out of tune,

---

104. yawn: gape with wonder at some monstrous change.   **107. curtains:** i.e., of the bed.

And sweet revenge grows harsh.
 DESDEMONA. Oh, falsely, falsely murdered!
 EMILIA.   Alas, what cry is that? 120
 OTHELLO. That! What?
 EMILIA. Out and alas! That was my lady's voice.
Help! Help, ho! Help! O lady, speak again!
Sweet Desdemona! O sweet mistress, speak!
 DESDEMONA. A guiltless death I die. 125
 EMILIA. Oh, who hath done this deed?
 DESDEMONA. Nobody, I myself. Farewell.
Commend me to my kind lord. Oh, farewell! (*Dies.*)
 OTHELLO. Why, how should she be murdered?
 EMILIA. Alas, who knows? 130
 OTHELLO. You heard her say herself it was not I.
 EMILIA. She said so. I must needs report the truth.
 OTHELLO. She's like a liar gone to burning Hell.
'Twas I that killed her.
 EMILIA.   Oh, the more angel she,
And you the blacker devil! 135
 OTHELLO. She turned to folly, and she was a whore.
 EMILIA. Thou dost belie her, and thou art a devil.
 OTHELLO. She was false as water.
 EMILIA.   Thou art rash as fire to say
That she was false. Oh, she was heavenly true!
 OTHELLO. Cassio did top her, ask thy husband else. 140
Oh, I were damned beneath all depth in Hell
But that I did proceed upon just grounds
To this extremity. Thy husband knew it all.
 EMILIA. My husband!
 OTHELLO. Thy husband. 145
 EMILIA. That she was false to wedlock?
 OTHELLO. Aye, with Cassio. Nay, had she been true,
If Heaven would make me such another world
Of one entire and perfect chrysolite,
I'd not have sold her for it. 150
 EMILIA. My husband!
 OTHELLO.   Aye, 'twas he that told me first.
An honest man he is, and hates the slime
That sticks on filthy deeds.
 EMILIA.   My husband!
 OTHELLO. What needs this iteration, woman? I say thy husband.
 EMILIA. Oh, mistress, villainy hath made mocks with love! 155
My husband say that she was false!
 OTHELLO.   He, woman.

I say thy husband. Dost understand the word?
My friend, thy husband, honest, honest Iago.
    EMILIA.   If he say so, may his pernicious soul
Rot half a grain a day! He lies to the heart.   160
She was too fond of her most filthy bargain.
    OTHELLO.   Ha!
    EMILIA.   Do thy worst.
This deed of thine is no more worthy Heaven
Than thou wast worthy her.
    OTHELLO.   Peace, you were best.   165
    EMILIA.   Thou hast not half that power to do me harm
As I have to be hurt. O gull! O dolt!
As ignorant as dirt! Thou hast done a deed—
I care not for thy sword, I'll make thee known,
Though I lost twenty lives. Help! Help, ho! Help!   170
The Moor hath killed my mistress! Murder! Murder!

    (*Enter* MONTANO, GRATIANO, IAGO, *and others.*)

    MONTANO.   What is the matter? How now, General!
    EMILIA.   Oh, are you come, Iago? You have done well,
That men must lay their murders on your neck.
    GRATIANO.   What is the matter?   175
    EMILIA.   Disprove this villain, if thou be'st a man.
He says thou told'st him that his wife was false.
I know thou didst not, thou'rt not such a villain.
Speak, for my heart is full.
    IAGO.   I told him what I thought, and told no more   180
Than what he found himself was apt and true.
    EMILIA.   But did you ever tell him she was false?
    IAGO.   I did.
    EMILIA.   You told a lie, an odious, damnèd lie,
Upon my soul, a lie, a wicked lie!   185
She false with Cassio! Did you say with Cassio?
    IAGO.   With Cassio, mistress. Go to, charm your tongue.°
    EMILIA.   I will not charm my tongue, I am bound to speak.
My mistress here lies murdered in her bed.
    ALL.   Oh, Heavens forfend!   190
    EMILIA.   And your reports have set the murder on.
    OTHELLO.   Nay, stare not, masters. It is true indeed.
    GRATIANO.   'Tis a strange truth.
    MONTANO.   Oh, monstrous act!
    EMILIA.   Villainy, villainy, villainy!

187. **charm . . . tongue:** be silent.

I think upon 't. I think I smell 't. Oh, villainy!   195
I thought so then.° I'll kill myself for grief.
Oh, villainy, villainy!
    IAGO. What, are you mad? I charge you, get you home.
    EMILIA. Good gentlemen, let me have leave to speak.
'Tis proper I obey him, but not now.   200
Perchance, Iago, I will ne'er go home.
    OTHELLO. Oh! Oh! Oh! (*Falling on the bed.*)
    EMILIA.   Nay, lay thee down and roar,
For thou hast killed the sweetest innocent
That e'er did lift up eye.
    OTHELLO (*rising*). Oh, she was foul!
I scarce did know you, Uncle. There lies your niece,   205
Whose breath indeed these hands have newly stopped.
I know this act shows horrible and grim.
    GRATIANO. Poor Desdemona! I am glad thy father's dead.
Thy match was mortal to him, and pure grief
Shore his old thread in twain. Did he live now,   210
This sight would make him do a desperate turn—
Yea, curse his better angel from his side,
And fall to reprobation.°
    OTHELLO. 'Tis pitiful, but yet Iago knows
That she with Cassio hath the act of shame   215
A thousand times committed. Cassio confessed it.
And she did gratify his amorous works
With that recognizance and pledge of love
Which I first gave her, I saw it in his hand.
It was a handkerchief, an antique token   220
My father gave my mother.
    EMILIA. Oh, Heaven! Oh, heavenly powers!
    IAGO. 'Zounds! Hold your peace.
    EMILIA.   'Twill out, 'twill out. I peace!
No, I will speak as liberal as the north.°
Let Heaven and men and devils, let them all,   225
All, all, cry shame against me, yet I'll speak.
    IAGO. Be wise, and get you home.
    EMILIA.   I will not.

(IAGO *offers to stab* EMILIA.)

    GRATIANO.   Fie!
Your sword upon a woman!

---

196. I . . . then: i.e., I suspected this earlier—as for example when Iago took the handkerchief. **213. reprobation:** damnation; i.e., by self-murder. **224. liberal . . . north:** as freely as the north wind, which is loud and bitter.

EMILIA.   O thou dull Moor! That handkerchief thou speak'st of
I found by fortune and did give my husband,   230
For often with a solemn earnestness,
More than indeed belonged to such a trifle,
He begged of me to steal it.
    IAGO.   Villainous whore!
    EMILIA.   She give it Cassio! No, alas, I found it,
And I did give 't my husband.
    IAGO.   Filth, thou liest!   235
    EMILIA.   By Heaven, I do not, I do not, gentlemen.
Oh, murderous coxcomb! What should such a fool
Do with so good a wife?
    OTHELLO.   Are there no stones° in Heaven
But what serve for the thunder? Precious villain!

(*He runs at* IAGO. IAGO, *from behind, stabs* EMILIA, *and exit.*)

    GRATIANO.   The woman falls. Sure, he hath killed his wife.   240
    EMILIA.   Aye, aye. Oh, lay me by my mistress' side.
    GRATIANO.   He's gone, but his wife's killed.
    MONTANO.   'Tis a notorious villain. Take you this weapon,
Which I have here recovered from the Moor.
Come, guard the door without, let him not pass,   245
But kill him rather. I'll after that same villain,
For 'tis a damnèd slave.

(*Exeunt all but* OTHELLO *and* EMILIA.)

    OTHELLO.   I am not valiant neither.
But every puny whipster gets my sword.
But why should honor outlive honesty?
Let it go all.
    EMILIA. What did thy song bode, lady?   250
Hark, canst thou hear me? I will play the swan,
And die in music. (*Singing.*)
                "Willow, willow, willow."
Moor, she was chaste. She loved thee, cruel Moor,
So come my soul to bliss as I speak true.
So speaking as I think, I die, I die. (*Dies.*)   255
    OTHELLO.   I have another weapon in this chamber.
It is a sword of Spain, the ice brook's temper.—
Oh, here it is. Uncle, I must come forth.
    GRATIANO (*within*).   If thou attempt it, it will cost thee dear.
Thou hast no weapon, and perforce must suffer.   260

238. stones: thunderbolts.

OTHELLO. Look in upon me then, and speak with me,
Or, naked° as I am, I will assault thee.

(*Re-enter* GRATIANO.)

GRATIANO. What is the matter?
OTHELLO. Behold, I have a weapon,
A better never did itself sustain
Upon a soldier's thigh. I have seen the day 265
That with this little arm and this good sword
I have made my way through more impediments
Than twenty times your stop. But, oh, vain boast!
Who can control his fate? 'Tis not so now.
Be not afraid, though you do see me weaponed. 270
Here is my journey's end, here is my butt°
And very sea mark of my utmost sail.
Do you go back dismayed? 'Tis a lost fear.
Man but a rush° against Othello's breast,
And he retires. Where should Othello go? 275
Now, how dost thou look now? O ill-starred wench!
Pale as thy smock! When we shall meet at compt,°
This look of thine will hurl my soul from Heaven
And fiends will snatch at it. Cold, cold, my girl!
Even like thy chastity. Oh, cursèd slave! 280
Whip me, ye devils,
From the possession of this heavenly sight!
Blow me about in winds! Roast me in sulphur!
Wash me in steep-down gulfs of liquid fire!
O Desdemona! Desdemona! Dead! 285
Oh! Oh! Oh!

(*Enter* LODOVICO, MONTANO, CASSIO *carried in a chair,
and* OFFICERS *with* IAGO, *prisoner.*)

LODOVICO. Where is this rash and most unfortunate man?
OTHELLO. That's he that was Othello. Here I am.
LODOVICO. Where is that viper? Bring the villain forth.
OTHELLO. I look down toward his feet,° but that's a fable. 290
If that thou be'st a devil, I cannot kill thee. (*Wounds* IAGO.)
LODOVICO. Wrench his sword from him.
IAGO. I bleed, sir, but not killed.
OTHELLO. I am not sorry neither. I'd have thee live,
For, in my sense, 'tis happiness to die.

262. **naked**: unarmed. 271. **butt**: aim. 274. **Man . . . rush**: attack with only a reed. 277. **compt**: account; i.e., the Day of Judgment. 290. **toward . . . feet**: i.e., to see if he has the cloven hoof of a devil.

LODOVICO. O thou Othello, that wert once so good, 295
Fall'n in the practice° of a damnèd slave,
What shall be said to thee?
    OTHELLO.   Why, anything.
An honorable murderer, if you will,
For naught did I in hate, but all in honor.
    LODOVICO. This wretch hath part confessed his villainy. 300
Did you and he consent in Cassio's death?
    OTHELLO. Aye.
    CASSIO. Dear General, I never gave you cause.
    OTHELLO. I do believe it, and I ask your pardon.
Will you, I pray, demand that demidevil 305
Why he hath thus ensnared my soul and body?
    IAGO. Demand me nothing. What you know, you know.
From this time forth I never will speak word.
    LODOVICO. What, not to pray?
    GRATIANO.   Torments will ope your lips.
    OTHELLO. Well, thou dost best. 310
    LODOVICO. Sir, you shall understand what hath befall'n,
Which, as I think, you know not. Here is a letter
Found in the pocket of the slain Roderigo,
And here another. The one of them imports
The death of Cassio to be undertook 315
By Roderigo.
    OTHELLO. Oh, villain!
    CASSIO.   Most heathenish and most gross!
    LODOVICO. Now here's another discontented paper,
Found in his pocket too. And this, it seems,
Roderigo meant to have sent this damnèd villain 320
But that, belike, Iago in the interim
Came in and satisfied him.
    OTHELLO.   Oh, the pernicious caitiff!
How came you, Cassio, by that handkerchief
That was my wife's?
    CASSIO.   I found it in my chamber.
And he himself confessed but even now 325
That there he dropped it for a special purpose
Which wrought to his desire.
    OTHELLO.   O fool! Fool! Fool!
    CASSIO. There is besides in Roderigo's letter
How he upbraids Iago, that he made him
Brave° me upon the watch, whereon it came 330

296. Fall'n . . . practice: destroyed by the plotting.   **330. Brave:** insult.

WILLIAM SHAKESPEARE   153

That I was cast.° And even but now he spake
After long seeming dead, Iago hurt him,
Iago set him on.
    LODOVICO.   You must forsake this room, and go with us.
Your power and your command is taken off,   335
And Cassio rules in Cyprus. For this slave,
If there be any cunning cruelty
That can torment him much and hold him long,°
It shall be his. You shall close prisoner rest
Till that the nature of your fault be known   340
To the Venetian state. Come, bring away.
    OTHELLO.   Soft you, a word or two before you go.
I have done the state some service, and they know 't.
No more of that. I pray you, in your letters,
When you shall these unlucky deeds relate,   345
Speak of me as I am, nothing extenuate,
Nor set down aught in malice. Then must you speak
Of one that loved not wisely but too well,
Of one not easily jealous, but, being wrought,
Perplexed in the extreme, of one whose hand,   350
Like the base Indian, threw a pearl away
Richer than all his tribe—of one whose subdued eyes,
Albeit unusèd to the melting mood,
Drop tears as fast as the Arabian trees
Their medicinal gum. Set you down this,   355
And say besides that in Aleppo once,
Where a malignant and a turbaned Turk
Beat a Venetian and traduced the state,
I took by the throat the circumcisèd dog
And smote him, thus. (*Stabs himself.*)   360
    LODOVICO.   Oh, bloody period!
    GRATIANO.   All that's spoke is marred.
    OTHELLO.   I kissed thee ere I killed thee. No way but this,
Killing myself, to die upon a kiss. (*Falls on the bed, and dies.*)
    CASSIO.   This did I fear, but thought he had no weapon.
For he was great of heart.   365
    LODOVICO (*to* IAGO).   O Spartan° dog,
More fell° than anguish, hunger, or the sea!
Look on the tragic loading of this bed,
This is thy work. The object poisons sight,
Let it be hid.° Gratiano, keep the house,   370

---

331. **cast:** dismissed.   338. **long:** i.e., in dying.   366. **Spartan:** i.e., hardhearted.   367. **fell:** cruel.   370. **Let . . . hid:** At these words the curtains are closed across the inner stage (or chamber, if this scene was acted aloft), concealing all three bodies.

And seize upon the fortunes of the Moor,
For they succeed on you. To you, Lord Governor,
Remains the censure of this hellish villain,
The time, the place, the torture.
Oh, enforce it!
Myself will straight aboard, and to the state
This heavy act with heavy heart relate.

(*Exeunt.*)

DISCUSSION

Othello seems, from one perspective, to be a play about the destruction of a marriage through suspicion and unwarranted jealousy. From another, it seems to deal with the destruction of a naive man by a devious, sophisticated subordinate. And from yet another, the play can be interpreted as the story of the fall of man from grace. In none of these interpretations does the question of individual identity seem predominant. Yet, in an underlying sense, each of these is concerned with who Othello is, how he can learn to know himself, and how his identity is dependent on and defined by the world in which he finds himself.

With its very first mention of Othello, the play raises the question of his identity. For Iago, having roused the old man Brabantio by creating a commotion beneath his window, tells him, in obscene terms, that his daughter, Desdemona, has married "an old black ram." Enraged, Brabantio accuses the black man of having used witchcraft to win her and rushes out to get help from the law. When we see this black man, however, he is quiet, controlled, eloquent, discriminating in his use of force, and far more sophisticated in dealing with the Venetian Senate than are his denouncers. While Iago and Brabantio speak in obscenities and invective in Act I, Othello's language is imaginative and expressive. While Iago invents stories that are cynical and destructive, Othello invents tales that express wonder and create love. Far from being a lecher and a necromancer, in the first act Othello seems the most creative person in Venice.

However, in Act II it becomes apparent that Othello's ease may rest more on ignorance than on virtue. He is naively in love with his young wife, whom he believes to be the perfect embodiment of virtue and beauty. He worships her with an almost religious fervor, and she becomes the source of his values, notwithstanding the fact that she is yet in her teens and knows very little of the world. Othello is also naive about his subordinates; he assumes their loyalty almost as an article of faith. Moreover, he can be rash and excessive when his orders are disobeyed; he dismisses, without investigation his aide, Cassio, when Cassio becomes involved in a drunken brawl. Othello is also superstitious: he believes that there is a love charm woven into the handkerchief he has given Desdemona. How can we reconcile this naiveté and rashness with his surface urbanity and self-assurance?

Some of the answer lies in the complexity and contradictions implicit in Othello's situation. Important as his position as general is to the Venetian state, Othello himself is an outsider in Venetian society. The senators reveal their slight suspicion of him as an outsider, when they agree without hesitation to consider whether he might have won Desdemona by witchcraft. Othello's situation. Important as his position as general is to the Venetian tionships between Venetian men and women. For example, although he has a natural nobility of demeanor, he does not understand Desdemona's taking of Cassio's hand as she talks with him in semi-privacy. To Othello, this casual display of physical familiarity is unsettling; he is from a Muslim society where women are rarely touched by men other than their husbands. But Desdemona is accustomed to the casual hand-kissing and hand-play of the Venetian court. Nor can Othello understand Cassio's treating Desdemona as a revered love object. In fact, Cassio is merely following, in a desultory way, the Italian conventions of courtly love; he is treating Desdemona as an object of courtly admiration, and his effusive speeches to her mean only that he sees her as a distant ideal and as a benefactress who may intercede for him. Othello's lack of understanding of courtly behavior helps him fall prey to Iago's insinuations regarding this exchange between Cassio and Desdemona.

Just as Othello is confused by courtliness, he is unable to cope with any subversion of the military relationship between a general and his subordinates. As a general, he places implicit trust in the word of his officers, his battle experience having taught him this necessity. And, as his remarks to Iago indicate, Othello has had very little experience outside of military life. Thus, he does not understand that Iago's behavior on civil matters may be quite different from his military behavior as Othello's lieutenant. Othello assumes that, since Iago has seemed totally honest as a soldier, he can be relied upon to be honest in all situations.

Perhaps most crucial, Othello is uncertain of his ultimate values. Born a Muslim, he is a convert to Christianity. But the shallowness of his conversion becomes apparent—his conversion is only partial; his insistence on "judging" Desdemona suggests the Muslim's absolute power over his wife, and his inability to find either mercy or forgiveness in his soul indicates how far he is from understanding the central values of the religion he has adopted. Moreover, beneath both his Christian and Muslim façades lies a profoundly primitive superstition that becomes apparent when he talks about the magic of the handkerchief.

None of these uncertainties might have proved fatal, however, were it not for the situation Othello finds on Cyprus; there, he is a general with no war to fight. And as Act I makes clear, Othello defines and expresses himself through his military role. He is expert at handling armed men. He has wooed Desdemona with his soldier–adventurer tales. He holds an advantage over the Venetian senators because they need him to fight a war. When he lands on Cyprus after the storm (Act II, scene i), he calls Desdemona his "fair warrior" and describes his journey to Cyprus almost as a battle to reach her (Act II, scene i). In the absence of battle, Othello is a man without a sense of who he is. Unable to exercise his functions as a soldier, uncertain of the courtly conventions of Venice and his status in civilian society, and without deeply held religious convictions to give him a sense of identity, Othello is thrown back on his love for Desdemona as his only means of defining himself and assuring himself of his worth. Without her, he seems to have neither a literal purpose to his life nor any deeply held set of values. As he says, "Perdition catch my soul . . . but when I love thee not, chaos is come again" (Act III, scene iii). Desdemona becomes a substitute for the only constant identity he has ever known, his military identity. When he becomes convinced of Desdemona's infidelity, he mourns her loss in terms of his military occupation: "Othello's occupation's gone" (Act III, scene iii). And when he finally commits suicide, he describes it as an act of warrior's vengeance.

Othello, much like many modern men, believes that his identity lies in his occupation. But his occupation, though respected, tends to shield him from any real knowledge of himself or of his capacity for corruption. As a general, he is accustomed to relationships based on absolute commands and absolute obedience. Moreover, he is accustomed to making clear-cut decisions and to administering swift and uncomplicated justice. As a general, he depends on objective evidence and external action; emotional, internal problems are of little importance to him. Virtue is equated with service, valor, and competence; evil, with sloth, cowardice, and incompetence. In the military system, objective virtue is rewarded and observable vice is punished, and jealousy concerns mainly matters of professional advancement. So Othello is totally unprepared for an attack on his marriage that calls into question the intangible and subjective qualities of his relationship with Desdemona. Iago, in attacking Othello's marriage, is attacking as well Othello's belief in himself, in his past, and in his security as an alien in a strange country.

Othello's response is tragically predictable. Lacking a clear understanding of Venetian customs and uncertain of his religious convictions, he reverts to his military identity. Desperate for the kind of "objective" evidence and external action he has always known as a soldier, he searches for "proof." But, in asking for proof, he makes a fatal error. He would like proof that Desdemona is faithful; but since fidelity in this instance means an absence of action, he cannot prove that his wife has not been unfaithful, only that she has been. Iago, the subtle reasoner, sees Othello's confusion and manufactures the proof of infidelity. No longer sure of his identity, no longer trusting his intuition, Othello seizes on this "observed" proof as his only security, his only guide to action. From that moment on, Desdemona's death is inevitable. Even as he suffocates his wife, he is affirming himself as the center of his universe. He thinks of himself, not merely as judge and executioner, but as divine: "This sorrow's heavenly" (Act V, scene ii). Even at the moment of death, Othello sees his act as the battle of two selves: a Christian self that he has come to understand too late and a pagan self that has proved treacherous both to him and to Venice. In his final speech, he tells the parable of a Christian slaying a Turk—of one self destroying the other.

Othello is, then, the story of a man who loses his sense of identity and gains a new sense only through great suffering and sacrifice. From this basic plot spring other rich images a thoughtful reader will want to explore: innocence versus knowledge, primitivism versus civilization, Christianity versus paganism. Each of these images adds a different moral and psychological dimension to Othello's story, allowing the play to represent many facets of the experience of alienation.

THEME AND DISCUSSION QUESTIONS

1. How does the fact that Othello is a black man in a white society complicate his marital and occupational roles?
2. What similarities are there between Othello's preoccupation with being a soldier and the ways modern men feel about their jobs?
3. What reasons does Iago give for his hatred of Othello? How believable are they?
4. What evidence is there of the intensity and breadth of Iago's evil nature?
5. What are some of the different kinds of love dealt with in *Othello*? How does their inclusion in the play help to express its meaning? What kind of self-knowledge does Othello acquire by the end of the play?
6. What kind of self-knowledge does Othello acquire by the end of the play?
7. In *Othello,* Shakespeare presents many interesting relationships: some between two men—Othello–Iago, Othello–Cassio, Iago–Roderigo—and some between men and women—Othello–Desdemona, Cassio–Bianca, Iago–Emilia. Compare several of these relationships and explain what their similarities or contrasts help to express in the play.
8. One of the basic aspects of human experience often dramatized by Shakespeare is the contradiction between good intentions and evil results. The evil in the killing of Desdemona by Othello is fairly evident. In what sense can it be said that his intentions were good?
9. Despite the fact that external forces, mainly Iago, fight against Othello, in what way is the play primarily about his internal conflict?

10. There are a great many images of animality and sexuality in the play. Which character interjects most of them? What does the use of such images tell us about the character? How does their use help to express the main conflict and meaning of the play?
11. Othello has often been described as a man whose greatest strengths are also his greatest weaknesses. How just does this description seem to you, and why?

A Doll's House: Production directed by Patrick Garland, at Playhouse Theatre, New York (1971), starring Claire Bloom and Donald Madden. Photograph courtesy of Henry Grossman.

HENRIK IBSEN

A Doll's House

Henrik Ibsen was born in Norway in 1828 and died there in 1906. Much of his artistic career, however, was spent in other countries of western Europe, where, almost single-handedly, he transformed his era's artificial and outdated dramatic tradition into a type of drama capable of expressing contemporary experience. In his half century of playwriting, Ibsen explored a wide range of dramatic forms, creating first epic dramas about Norwegian heroes, then the poetic tragedy and satire of his *Brand* (1866) and *Peer Gynt* (1867); next, such realistic social-problem plays as *A Doll's House* (1879), *Ghosts* (1881), and *An Enemy of the People* (1882); and, eventually, symbolist, expressionistic dramas epitomized by *The Master Builder* (1892) and *John Gabriel Borkmann* (1896). In moving through these dramatic forms, he managed to free himself from eighteenth-century and early-nineteenth-century imitations of Renaissance drama. This, in turn, allowed him to explore the limitations of the dramatist's illusion of objectivity and, ultimately, to develop the kind of drama that stresses the internal struggles of its characters. Although many of the specific "problems" they treat have long since disappeared, Ibsen's realistic social-problem plays, his best-known works during his lifetime, are often revived today as successful productions. In addition, in recent years, many readers have also admired his symbolist dramas, finding in them a strong expression of the conflict many contemporary people often feel between their subjective lives and the claims of the objective world.

A DOLL'S HOUSE   From *Ibsen: Four Major Plays* as translated by Rolf Fjelde. Copyright © 1965 by Rolf Fjelde. Reprinted by arrangement with the New American Library, Inc., New York, New York.

CHARACTERS

Torvald Helmer, *a lawyer*
Nora, *his wife*
Dr. Rank
Mrs. Linde
Nils Krogstad, *a bank clerk*
The Helmers' Three Small Children
Anne-Marie, *their nurse*
Helene, *a maid*
A Delivery Boy

The action takes place in **Helmer**'s *residence.*

ACT ONE

A comfortable room, tastefully but not expensively furnished. A door to the right in the back wall leads to the entryway; another to the left leads to **Helmer**'s *study. Between these doors, a piano. Midway in the left-hand wall a door, and further back a window. Near the window a round table with an armchair and a small sofa. In the right-hand wall, toward the rear, a door, and nearer the foreground a porcelain stove with two armchairs and a rocking chair beside it. Between the stove and the side door, a small table. Engravings on the walls. An etagère with china figures and other small art objects; a small bookcase with richly bound books; the floor carpeted; a fire burning in the stove. It is a winter day.*

A bell rings in the entryway; shortly after we hear the door being unlocked. **Nora** *comes into the room, humming happily to herself; she is wearing street clothes and carries an armload of packages, which she puts down on the table to the right. She has left the hall door open; and through it a* **Delivery Boy** *is seen, holding a Christmas tree and a basket, which he gives to the* **Maid** *who let them in.*

Nora. Hide the tree well, Helene. The children mustn't get a glimpse of it till this evening, after it's trimmed. (*To the* **Delivery Boy**, *taking out her purse.*) How much?

Delivery Boy. Fifty, ma'am.

Nora. There's a crown. No, keep the change. (*The* **Boy** *thanks her and leaves.* **Nora** *shuts the door. She laughs softly to herself while taking off her street things. Drawing a bag of macaroons from her pocket, she eats a couple, then steals over and listens at her husband's study door.*) Yes, he's home. (*Hums again as she moves to the table, right.*)

Helmer (*from the study*). Is that my little lark twittering out there?

Nora (*busy opening some packages*). Yes, it is.

HELMER. Is that my squirrel rummaging around?

NORA. Yes!

HELMER. When did my squirrel get in?

NORA. Just now. (*Putting the macaroon bag in her pocket and wiping her mouth.*) Do come in, Torvald, and see what I've bought.

HELMER. Can't be disturbed. (*After a moment he opens the door and peers in, pen in hand.*) Bought, you say? All that there? Has the little spendthrift been out throwing money around again?

NORA. Oh, but Torvald, this year we really should let ourselves go a bit. It's the first Christmas we haven't had to economize.

HELMER. But you know we can't go squandering.

NORA. Oh yes, Torvald, we can squander a little now. Can't we? Just a tiny, wee bit. Now that you've got a big salary and are going to make piles and piles of money.

HELMER. Yes—starting New Year's. But then it's a full three months till the raise comes through.

NORA. Pooh! We can borrow that long.

HELMER. Nora! (*Goes over and playfully takes her by the ear.*) Are your scatterbrains off again? What if today I borrowed a thousand crowns, and you squandered them over Christmas week, and then on New Year's Eve a roof tile fell on my head, and I lay there—

NORA (*putting her hand on his mouth*). Oh! Don't say such things!

HELMER. Yes, but what if it happened—then what?

NORA. If anything so awful happened, then it just wouldn't matter if I had debts or not.

HELMER. Well, but the people I'd borrowed from?

NORA. Them? Who cares about them! They're strangers.

HELMER. Nora, Nora, how like a woman! No, but seriously, Nora, you know what I think about that. No debts! Never borrow! Something of freedom's lost—and something of beauty, too—from a home that's founded on borrowing and debt. We've made a brave stand up to now, the two of us; and we'll go right on like that the little while we have to.

NORA (*going toward the stove*). Yes, whatever you say, Torvald.

HELMER (*following her*). Now, now, the little lark's wing's mustn't droop. Come on, don't be a sulky squirrel. (*Taking out his wallet.*) Nora, guess what I have here.

NORA (*turning quickly*). Money!

HELMER. There, see. (*Hands her some notes.*) Good grief, I know how costs go up in a house at Christmastime.

NORA. Ten—twenty—thirty—forty. Oh, thank you, Torvald; I can manage no end on this.

HELMER. You really will have to.

NORA. Oh yes, I promise I will! But come here so I can show you everything I bought. And so cheap! Look, new clothes for Ivar here—and a sword. Here a horse and a trumpet for Bob. And a doll and a doll's bed here for Emmy; they're nothing much, but she'll tear them to bits in no time anyway. And here I have dress material and handkerchiefs for the maids. Old Anne-Marie really deserves something more.

HELMER. And what's in that package there?

NORA (*with a cry*). Torvald, no! You can't see that till tonight!

HELMER. I see. But tell me now, you little prodigal, what have you thought of for yourself?

NORA. For myself? Oh, I don't want anything at all.

HELMER. Of course you do. Tell me just what—within reason—you'd most like to have.

NORA. I honestly don't know. Oh, listen, Torvald—

HELMER. Well?

NORA (*fumbling at his coat buttons, without looking at him*). If you want to give me something, then maybe you could—you could—

HELMER. Come on, out with it.

NORA (*hurriedly*). You could give me money, Torvald. No more than you think you can spare; then one of these days I'll buy something with it.

HELMER. But Nora—

NORA. Oh, please, Torvald darling, do that! I beg you, please. Then I could hang the bills in pretty gilt paper on the Christmas tree. Wouldn't that be fun?

HELMER. What are those little birds called that always fly through their fortunes?

NORA. Oh yes, spendthrifts; I know all that. But let's do as I say, Torvald; then I'll have time to decide what I really need most. That's very sensible, isn't it?

HELMER (*smiling*). Yes, very—that is, if you actually hung onto the money I give you, and you actually used it to buy yourself something. But it goes for the house and for all sorts of foolish things, and then I only have to lay out some more.

NORA. Oh, but Torvald—

HELMER. Don't deny it, my dear little Nora. (*Putting his arm around her waist.*) Spendthrifts are sweet, but they use up a frightful amount of money. It's incredible what it costs a man to feed such birds.

NORA. Oh, how can you say that! Really, I save everything I can.

HELMER (*laughing*). Yes, that's the truth. Everything you can. But that's nothing at all.

NORA (*humming, with a smile of quiet satisfaction*). Hm, if you only knew what expenses we larks and squirrels have, Torvald.

HELMER. You're an odd little one. Exactly the way your father was.

You're never at a loss for scaring up money; but the moment you have it, it runs right out through your fingers; you never know what you've done with it. Well, one takes you as you are. It's deep in your blood. Yes, these things are hereditary, Nora.

NORA. Ah, I could wish I'd inherited many of Papa's qualities.

HELMER. And I couldn't wish you anything but just what you are, my sweet little lark. But wait; it seems to me you have a very—what should I call it?—a very suspicious look today—

NORA. I do?

HELMER. You certainly do. Look me straight in the eye.

NORA (*looking at him*). Well?

HELMER (*shaking an admonitory finger*). Surely my sweet tooth hasn't been running riot in town today, has she?

NORA. No. Why do you imagine that?

HELMER. My sweet tooth really didn't make a little detour through the confectioner's?

NORA. No, I assure you, Torvald—

HELMER. Hasn't nibbled some pastry?

NORA. No, not at all.

HELMER. Not even munched a macaroon or two?

NORA. No, Torvald, I assure you, really—

HELMER. There, there now. Of course I'm only joking.

NORA (*going to the table, right*). You know I could never think of going against you.

HELMER. No, I understand that; and you *have* given me your word. (*Going over to her.*) Well, you keep your little Christmas secrets to yourself, Nora darling. I expect they'll come to light this evening, when the tree is lit.

NORA. Did you remember to ask Dr. Rank?

HELMER. No. But there's no need for that; it's assumed he'll be dining with us. All the same, I'll ask him when he stops by here this morning. I've ordered some fine wine. Nora, you can't imagine how I'm looking forward to this evening.

NORA. So am I. And what fun for the children, Torvald!

HELMER. Ah, it's so gratifying to know that one's gotten a safe, secure job, and with a comfortable salary. It's a great satisfaction, isn't it?

NORA. Oh, it's wonderful!

HELMER. Remember last Christmas? Three whole weeks before, you shut yourself in every evening till long after midnight, making flowers for the Christmas tree, and all the other decorations to surprise us. Ugh, that was the dullest time I've ever lived through.

NORA. It wasn't at all dull for me.

HELMER (*smiling*). But the outcome *was* pretty sorry, Nora.

NORA. Oh, don't tease me with that again. How could I help it that the cat came in and tore everything to shreds.

HELMER. No, poor thing, you certainly couldn't. You wanted so much to please us all, and that's what counts. But it's just as well that the hard times are past.

NORA. Yes, it's really wonderful.

HELMER. Now I don't have to sit here alone, boring myself, and you don't have to tire your precious eyes and your fair little delicate hands—

NORA (*clapping her hands*). No, is it really true, Torvald, I don't have to? Oh, how wonderfully lovely to hear! (*Taking his arm.*) Now I'll tell you just how I've thought we should plan things. Right after Christmas— (*The doorbell rings.*) Oh, the bell. (*Straightening the room up a bit.*) Somebody would have to come. What a bore!

HELMER. I'm not at home to visitors, don't forget.

MAID (*from the hall doorway*). Ma'am, a lady to see you—

NORA. All right, let her come in.

MAID (*to* HELMER). And the doctor's just come too.

HELMER. Did he go right to my study?

MAID. Yes, he did.

(HELMER *goes into his room. The* MAID *shows in* MRS. LINDE, *dressed in traveling clothes, and shuts the door after her.*)

MRS. LINDE (*in a dispirited and somewhat hesitant voice*). Hello, Nora.

NORA (*uncertain*). Hello—

MRS. LINDE. You don't recognize me.

NORA. No, I don't know—but wait, I think—(*Exclaiming.*) What! Kristine! Is it really you?

MRS. LINDE. Yes, it's me.

NORA. Kristine! To think I didn't recognize you. But then, how could I? (*More quietly.*) How you've changed, Kristine!

MRS. LINDE. Yes, no doubt I have. In nine—ten long years.

NORA. Is it so long since we met! Yes, it's all of that. Oh, these last eight years have been a happy time, believe me. And so now you've come in to town, too. Made the long trip in the winter. That took courage.

MRS. LINDE. I just got here by ship this morning.

NORA. To enjoy yourself over Christmas, of course. Oh, how lovely! Yes, enjoy ourselves, we'll do that. But take your coat off. You're not still cold? (*Helping her.*) There now, let's get cozy here by the stove. No, the easy chair there! I'll take the rocker here. (*Seizing her hands.*) Yes, now you have your old look again; it was only in that first moment. You're a bit pale, Kristine—and maybe a bit thinner.

Mrs. Linde. And much, much older, Nora.

Nora. Yes, perhaps a bit older; a tiny, tiny bit; not much at all. (*Stopping short; suddenly serious.*)Oh, but thoughtless me, to sit here, chattering away. Sweet, good Kristine, can you forgive me?

Mrs. Linde. What do you mean, Nora?

Nora (*softly*). Poor Kristine, you've become a widow.

Mrs. Linde. Yes, three years ago.

Nora. Oh, I knew it, of course; I read it in the papers. Oh Kristine, you must believe me; I often thought of writing you then, but I kept postponing it, and something always interfered.

Mrs. Linde. Nora dear, I understand completely.

Nora. No, it was awful of me, Kristine. You poor thing, how much you must have gone through. And he left you nothing?

Mrs. Linde. No.

Nora. And no children?

Mrs. Linde. No.

Nora. Nothing at all, then?

Mrs. Linde. Not even a sense of loss to feed on.

Nora (*looking incredulously at her*). But Kristine, how could that be?

Mrs. Linde (*smiling wearily and smoothing her hair*). Oh, sometimes it happens, Nora.

Nora. So completely alone. How terribly hard that must be for you. I have three lovely children. You can't see them now; they're out with the maid. But now you must tell me everything—

Mrs. Linde. No, no, no, tell me about yourself.

Nora. No, you begin. Today I don't want to be selfish. I want to think only of you today. But there *is* something I must tell you. Did you hear of the wonderful luck we had recently?

Mrs. Linde. No, what's that?

Nora. My husband's been made manager in the bank, just think!

Mrs. Linde. Your husband? How marvelous!

Nora. Isn't it? Being a lawyer is such an uncertain living, you know, especially if one won't touch any cases that aren't clean and decent. And of course Torvald would never do that, and I'm with him completely there. Oh, we're simply delighted, believe me! He'll join the bank right after New Year's and start getting a huge salary and lots of commissions. From now on we can live quite differently—just as we want. Oh, Kristine, I feel so light and happy! Won't it be lovely to have stacks of money and not a care in the world?

Mrs. Linde. Well, anyway, it would be lovely to have enough for necessities.

Nora. No, not just for necessities, but stacks and stacks of money!

Mrs. Linde (*smiling*). Nora, Nora, aren't you sensible yet? Back in school you were such a free spender.

Nora (*with a quiet laugh*). Yes, that's what Torvald still says. (*Shaking her finger.*) But "Nora, Nora" isn't as silly as you all think. Really, we've been in no position for me to go squandering. We've had to work, both of us.

Mrs. Linde. You too?

Nora. Yes, at odd jobs—needlework, crocheting, embroidery, and such—(*Casually.*) and other things too. You remember that Torvald left the department when we were married? There was no chance of promotion in his office, and of course he needed to earn more money. But that first year he drove himself terribly. He took on all kinds of extra work that kept him going morning and night. It wore him down, and then he fell deathly ill. The doctors said it was essential for him to travel south.

Mrs. Linde. Yes, didn't you spend a whole year in Italy?

Nora. That's right. It wasn't easy to get away, you know. Ivar had just been born. But of course we had to go. Oh, that was a beautiful trip, and it saved Torvald's life. But it cost a frightful sum, Kristine.

Mrs. Linde. I can well imagine.

Nora. Four thousand, eight hundred crowns it cost. That's really a lot of money.

Mrs. Linde. But it's lucky you had it when you needed it.

Nora. Well, as it was, we got it from Papa.

Mrs. Linde. I see. It was just about the time your father died.

Nora. Yes, just about then. And, you know, I couldn't make that trip out to nurse him. I had to stay here, expecting Ivar any moment, and with my poor sick Torvald to care for. Dearest Papa, I never saw him again, Kristine. Oh, that was the worst time I've known in all my marriage.

Mrs. Linde. I know how you loved him. And then you went off to Italy?

Nora. Yes. We had the means now, and the doctors urged us. So we left a month after.

Mrs. Linde. And your husband came back completely cured?

Nora. Sound as a drum!

Mrs. Linde. But—the doctor?

Nora. Who?

Mrs. Linde. I thought the maid said he was a doctor, the man who came in with me.

Nora. Yes, that was Dr. Rank—but he's not making a sick call. He's our closest friend, and he stops by at least once a day. No, Torvald hasn't had a sick moment since, and the children are fit and strong, and I am, too. (*Jumping up and clapping her hands.*) Oh, dear God, Kristine, what a lovely thing to live and be happy! But how disgusting of me—I'm talking of nothing but my own affairs. (*Sits on a stool close by* Kristine, *arms rest-*

ing across her knees.) Oh, don't be angry with me! Tell me, is it really true that you weren't in love with your husband? Why did you marry him, then?

Mrs. Linde.   My mother was still alive, but bedridden and helpless—and I had two younger brothers to look after. In all conscience, I didn't think I could turn him down.

Nora.   No, you were right there. But was he rich at the time?

Mrs. Linde.   He was very well off, I'd say. But the business was shaky, Nora. When he died, it all fell apart, and nothing was left.

Nora.   And then——?

Mrs. Linde.   Yes, so I had to scrape up a living with a little shop and a little teaching and whatever else I could find. The last three years have been like one endless workday without a rest for me. Now it's over, Nora. My poor mother doesn't need me, for she's passed on. Nor the boys, either; they're working now and can take care of themselves.

Nora.   How free you must feel—

Mrs. Linde.   No—only unspeakably empty. Nothing to live for now. (*Standing up anxiously.*) That's why I couldn't take it any longer out in that desolate hole. Maybe here it'll be easier to find something to do and keep my mind occupied. If I could only be lucky enough to get a steady job, some office work—

Nora.   Oh, but Kristine, that's so dreadfully tiring, and you already look so tired. It would be much better for you if you could go off to a bathing resort.

Mrs. Linde (*going toward the window*).   I have no father to give me travel money, Nora.

Nora (*rising*).   Oh, don't be angry with me.

Mrs. Linde (*going to her*).   Nora dear, don't you be angry with me. The worst of my kind of situation is all the bitterness that's stored away. No one to work for, and yet you're always having to snap up your opportunities. You have to live; and so you grow selfish. When you told me the happy change in your lot, do you know I was delighted less for your sakes than for mine?

Nora.   How so? Oh, I see. You think maybe Torvald could do something for you.

Mrs. Linde.   Yes, that's what I thought.

Nora.   And he will, Kristine! Just leave it to me; I'll bring it up so delicately—find something attractive to humor him with. Oh, I'm so eager to help you.

Mrs. Linde.   How very kind of you, Nora, to be so concerned over me—doubly kind, considering you really know so little of life's burdens yourself.

Nora.   I——? I know so little——?

Mrs. Linde (*smiling*). Well, my heavens—a little needlework and such—Nora, you're just a child.

Nora (*tossing her head and pacing the floor*). You don't have to act so superior.

Mrs. Linde. Oh?

Nora. You're just like the others. You all think I'm incapable of anything serious—

Mrs. Linde. Come now—

Nora. That I've never had to face the raw world.

Mrs. Linde. Nora dear, you've just been telling me all your troubles.

Nora. Hm! Trivia! (*Quietly*). I haven't told you the big thing.

Mrs. Linde. Big thing? What do you mean?

Nora. You look down on me so, Kristine, but you shouldn't. You're proud that you worked so long and hard for your mother.

Mrs. Linde. I don't look down on a soul. But it *is* true: I'm proud—and happy, too—to think it was given to me to make my mother's last days almost free of care.

Nora. And you're also proud thinking of what you've done for your brothers.

Mrs. Linde. I feel I've a right to be.

Nora. I agree. But listen to this, Kristine—I've also got something to be proud and happy for.

Mrs. Linde. I don't doubt it. But whatever do you mean?

Nora. Not so loud. What if Torvald heard! He mustn't, not for anything in the world. Nobody must know, Kristine. No one but you.

Mrs. Linde. But what is it, then?

Nora. Come here. (*Drawing her down beside her on the sofa.*) It's true—I've also got something to be proud and happy for. I'm the one who saved Torvald's life.

Mrs. Linde. Saved—? Saved how?

Nora. I told you about the trip to Italy. Torvald never would have lived if he hadn't gone south—

Mrs. Linde. Of course; your father gave you the means—

Nora (*smiling*). That's what Torvald and all the rest think, but—

Mrs. Linde. But—?

Nora. Papa didn't give us a pin. I was the one who raised the money.

Mrs. Linde. You? The whole amount?

Nora. Four thousand, eight hundred crowns. What do you say to that?

Mrs. Linde. But Nora, how was it possible? Did you win the lottery?

Nora (*disdainfully*). The lottery? Pooh! No art to that.

Mrs. Linde. But where did you get it from then?

Nora (*humming, with a mysterious smile*). Hmm, tra-la-la-la.

Mrs. Linde. Because you couldn't have borrowed it.

NORA. No? Why not?

MRS. LINDE. A wife can't borrow without her husband's consent.

NORA (*tossing her head*). Oh, but a wife with a little business sense, a wife who knows how to manage—

MRS. LINDE. Nora, I simply don't understand—

NORA. You don't have to. Whoever said I *borrowed* the money? I could have gotten it other ways. (*Throwing herself back on the sofa.*) I could have gotten it from some admirer or other. After all, a girl with my ravishing appeal—

MRS. LINDE. You lunatic.

NORA. I'll bet you're eaten up with curiosity, Kristine.

MRS. LINDE. Now listen here, Nora—you haven't done something indiscreet?

NORA (*sitting up again*). Is it indiscreet to save your husband's life?

MRS. LINDE. I think it's indiscreet that without his knowledge you—

NORA. But that's the point: he mustn't know! My Lord, can't you understand? He mustn't ever know the close call he had. It was to *me* the doctors came to say his life was in danger—that nothing could save him but a stay in the south. Didn't I try strategy then! I began talking about how lovely it would be for me to travel abroad like other young wives; I begged and I cried; I told him please to remember my condition, to be kind and indulge me; and then I dropped a hint that he could easily take out a loan. But at that, Kristine, he nearly exploded. He said I was frivolous, and it was his duty as man of the house not to indulge me in whims and fancies—as I think he called them. Aha, I thought, now you'll just have to be saved—and that's when I saw my chance.

MRS. LINDE. And your father never told Torvald the money wasn't from him?

NORA. No, never. Papa died right about then. I'd considered bringing him into my secret and begging him never to tell. But he was too sick at the time—and then, sadly, it didn't matter.

MRS. LINDE. And you've never confided in your husband since?

NORA. For heaven's sake, no! Are you serious? He's so strict on that subject. Besides—Torvald, with all his masculine pride—how painfully humiliating for him if he ever found out he was in debt to me. That would just ruin our relationship. Our beautiful, happy home would never be the same.

MRS. LINDE. Won't you ever tell him?

NORA (*thoughtfully, half smiling*). Yes—maybe sometime, years from now, when I'm no longer so attractive. Don't laugh! I only mean when Torvald loves me less than now, when he stops enjoying my dancing and dressing up and reciting for him. Then it might be wise to have something in reserve—(*Breaking off.*) How ridiculous! That'll never happen—Well,

Kristine, what do you think of my big secret? I'm capable of something too, hm? You can imagine, of course, how this thing hangs over me. It really hasn't been easy meeting the payments on time. In the business world there's what they call quarterly interest and what they call amortization, and these are always so terribly hard to manage. I've had to skimp a little here and there, wherever I could, you know. I could hardly spare anything from my house allowance, because Torvald has to live well. I couldn't let the children go poorly dressed; whatever I got for them, I felt I had to use up completely—the darlings!

MRS. LINDE. Poor Nora, so it had to come out of your own budget, then?

NORA. Yes, of course. But I was the one most responsible, too. Every time Torvald gave me money for new clothes and such, I never used more than half; always bought the simplest, cheapest outfits. It was a godsend that everything looks so well on me that Torvald never noticed. But it did weigh me down at times, Kristine. It *is* such a joy to wear fine things. You understand.

MRS. LINDE. Oh, of course.

NORA. And then I found other ways of making money. Last winter I was lucky enough to get a lot of copying to do. I locked myself in and sat writing every evening till late in the night. Ah, I was tired so often, dead tired. But still it was wonderful fun, sitting and working like that, earning money. It was almost like being a man.

MRS. LINDE. But how much have you paid off this way so far?

NORA. That's hard to say, exactly. These accounts, you know, aren't easy to figure. I only know that I've paid out all I could scrape together. Time and again I haven't known where to turn. (*Smiling.*) Then I'd sit here dreaming of a rich old gentleman who had fallen in love with me—

MRS. LINDE. What! Who is he?

NORA. Oh, really! And that he'd died, and when his will was opened, there in big letters it said, "All my fortune shall be paid over in cash, immediately, to that enchanting Mrs. Nora Helmer."

MRS. LINDE. But Nora dear—who *was* this gentleman?

NORA. Good grief, can't you understand? The old man never existed; that was only something I'd dream up time and again whenever I was at my wits' end for money. But it makes no difference now; the old fossil can go where he pleases for all I care; I don't need him or his will—because now I'm free. (*Jumping up.*) Oh, how lovely to think of that, Kristine! Carefree! To know you're carefree, utterly carefree; to be able to romp and play with the children, and to keep up a beautiful, charming home—everything just the way Torvald likes it! And think, spring is coming, with big blue skies. Maybe we can travel a little then. Maybe I'll see the ocean again. Oh yes, it *is* so marvelous to live and be happy!

(*The front doorbell rings.*)

MRS. LINDE (*rising*).   There's the bell. It's probably best that I go.
NORA.   No, stay. No one's expected. It must be for Torvald.
MAID (*from the hall doorway*).   Excuse me, ma'am—there's a gentleman here to see Mr. Helmer, but I didn't know—since the doctor's with him—
NORA.   Who is the gentleman?
KROGSTAD (*from the doorway*).   It's me, Mrs. Helmer.

(MRS. LINDE *starts and turns away towards the window.*)

NORA (*stepping toward him, tense, her voice a whisper*).   You? What is it? Why do you want to speak to my husband?
KROGSTAD.   Bank business—after a fashion. I have a small job in the investment bank, and I hear now your husband is going to be our chief—
NORA.   In other words, it's—
KROGSTAD.   Just dry business, Mrs. Helmer. Nothing but that.
NORA.   Yes, then please be good enough to step into the study. (*She nods indifferently as she sees him out by the hall door, then returns and begins stirring up the stove.*)
MRS. LINDE.   Nora—who was that man?
NORA.   That was a Mr. Krogstad—a lawyer.
MRS. LINDE.   Then it really was him.
NORA.   Do you know that person?
MRS. LINDE.   I did once—many years ago. For a time he was a law clerk in our town.
NORA.   Yes, he's been that.
MRS. LINDE.   How he's changed.
NORA.   I understand he had a very unhappy marriage.
MRS. LINDE.   He's a widower now.
NORA.   With a number of children. There now, it's burning. (*She closes the stove door and moves the rocker a bit to one side.*)
MRS. LINDE.   They say he has a hand in all kinds of business.
NORA.   Oh? That may be true; I wouldn't know. But let's not think about business. It's so dull.

(DR. RANK *enters from* HELMER'S *study.*)

RANK (*still in the doorway*).   No, no, really—I don't want to intrude, I'd just as soon talk a little while with your wife. (*Shuts the door, then notices* MRS. LINDE.)   Oh, beg pardon, I'm intruding here too.
NORA.   No, not at all. (*Introducing him.*) Dr. Rank, Mrs. Linde.
RANK.   Well now, that's a name much heard in this house. I believe I passed the lady on the stairs as I came.

Mrs. Linde. Yes, I take the stairs very slowly. They're rather hard on me.

Rank. Uh-hm, some touch of internal weakness?

Mrs. Linde. More overexertion, I'd say.

Rank. Nothing else? Then you're probably here in town to rest up in a round of parties?

Mrs. Linde. I'm here to look for work.

Rank. Is that the best cure for overexertion?

Mrs. Linde. One has to live, Doctor.

Rank. Yes, there's a common prejudice to that effect.

Nora. Oh, come on, Dr. Rank—you really do want to live yourself.

Rank. Yes, I really do. Wretched as I am, I'll gladly prolong my torment indefinitely. All my patients feel like that. And it's quite the same, too, with the morally sick. Right at this moment there's one of those moral invalids in there with Helmer—

Mrs. Linde (*softly*). Ah!

Nora. Who do you mean?

Rank. Oh, it's a lawyer, Krogstad, a type you wouldn't know. His character is rotten to the root—but even he began chattering all-importantly about how he had to *live*.

Nora. Oh? What did he want to talk to Torvald about?

Rank. I really don't know. I only heard something about the bank.

Nora. I didn't know that Krog—that this man Krogstad had anything to do with the bank.

Rank. Yes, he's gotten some kind of berth down there. (*To* Mrs. Linde.) I don't know if you also have, in your neck of the woods, a type of person who scuttles about breathlessly, sniffing out hints of moral corruption, and then maneuvers his victim into some sort of key position where he can keep an eye on him. It's the healthy these days that are out in the cold.

Mrs. Linde. All the same, it's the sick who most need to be taken in.

Rank (*with a shrug*). Yes, there we have it. That's the concept that's turning society into a sanatorium.

(Nora, *lost in her thoughts, breaks out into quiet laughter and claps her hands.*)

Rank. Why do you laugh at that? Do you have any real idea of what society is?

Nora. What do I care about dreary old society? I was laughing at something quite different—something terribly funny. Tell me, Doctor—is everyone who works in the bank dependent now on Torvald?

Rank. Is that what you find so terribly funny?

NORA (*smiling and humming*). Never mind, never mind! (*Pacing the floor.*) Yes, that's really immensely amusing: that we—that Torvald has so much power now over all those people. (*Taking the bag out of her pocket.*) Dr. Rank, a little macaroon on that?

RANK. See here, macaroons! I thought they were contraband here.

NORA. Yes, but these are some that Kristine gave me.

MRS. LINDE. What? I—?

NORA. Now, now, don't be afraid. You couldn't possibly know that Torvald had forbidden them. You see, he's worried they'll ruin my teeth. But hmp! Just this once! Isn't that so, Dr. Rank? Help yourself! (*Puts a macaroon in his mouth.*) And you too, Kristine. And I'll also have one, only a little one—or two, at the most. (*Walking about again.*) Now I'm really tremendously happy. Now there's just one last thing in the world that I have an enormous desire to do.

RANK. Well! And what's that?

NORA. It's something I have such a consuming desire to say so Torvald could hear.

RANK. And why can't you say it?

NORA. I don't dare. It's quite shocking.

MRS. LINDE. Shocking?

RANK. Well, then it isn't advisable. But in front of us you certainly can. What do you have such a desire to say so Torvald could hear?

NORA. I have such a huge desire to say—to hell and be damned!

RANK. Are you crazy?

MRS. LINDE. My goodness, Nora!

RANK. Go on, say it. Here he is.

NORA (*hiding the macaroon bag*). Shh, shh, shh!

(HELMER *comes in from his study, hat in hand, overcoat over his arm.*)

NORA (*going toward him*). Well, Torvald dear, are you through with him?

HELMER. Yes, he just left.

NORA. Let me introduce you—this is Kristine, who's arrived here in town.

HELMER. Kristine—? I'm sorry, but I don't know—

NORA. Mrs. Linde, Torvald dear. Mrs. Kristine Linde.

HELMER. Of course. A childhood friend of my wife's, no doubt?

MRS. LINDE. Yes, we knew each other in those days.

NORA. And just think, she made the long trip down here in order to talk with you.

HELMER. What's this?

MRS LINDE. Well, not exactly—

NORA. You see, Kristine is remarkably clever in office work, and so she's terribly eager to come under a capable man's supervision and add more to what she already knows—

Helmer. Very wise, Mrs. Linde.

Nora. And then when she heard that you'd become a bank manager—the story was wired out to the papers—then she came in as fast as she could and—Really, Torvald, for my sake you can do a little something for Kristine, can't you?

Helmer. Yes, it's not at all impossible. Mrs. Linde, I suppose you're a widow?

Mrs. Linde. Yes.

Helmer. Any experience in office work?

Mrs. Linde. Yes, a good deal.

Helmer. Well, it's quite likely that I can make an opening for you—

Nora (*clapping her hands*). You see, you see!

Helmer. You've come at a lucky moment, Mrs. Linde.

Mrs. Linde. Oh, how can I thank you?

Helmer. Not necessary. (*Putting his overcoat on.*) But today you'll have to excuse me—

Rank. Wait, I'll go with you. (*He fetches his coat from the hall and warms it at the stove.*)

Nora. Don't stay out long, dear.

Helmer. An hour; no more.

Nora. Are you going too, Kristine?

Mrs. Linde (*putting on her winter garments*). Yes, I have to see about a room now.

Helmer. Then perhaps we can all walk together.

Nora (*helping her*). What a shame we're so cramped here, but it's quite impossible for us to—

Mrs. Linde. Oh, don't even think of it! Good-bye, Nora dear, and thanks for everything.

Nora. Good-bye for now. Of course you'll be back this evening. And you too, Dr. Rank. What? If you're well enough? Oh, you've got to be! Wrap up tight now.

(*In a ripple of small talk the company moves out into the hall; children's voices are heard outside on the steps.*)

Nora. There they are! There they are! (*She runs to open the door. The children come in with their nurse,* Anne-Marie.) Come in, come in! (*Bends down and kisses them.*) Oh, you darlings—! Look at them, Kristine. Aren't they lovely!

Rank. No loitering in the draft here.

HELMER. Come, Mrs. Linde—this place is unbearable now for anyone but mothers.

(DR. RANK, HELMER, *and* MRS. LINDE *go down the stairs.* ANNE-MARIE *goes into the living room with the children.* NORA *follows, after closing the hall door.*)

NORA. How fresh and strong you look. Oh, such red cheeks you have! Like apples and roses. (*The children interrupt her throughout the following.*) And it was so much fun? That's wonderful. Really? You pulled both Emmy and Bob on the sled? Imagine, all together! Yes, you're a clever boy, Ivar. Oh, let me hold her a bit, Anne-Marie. My sweet little doll baby! (*Takes the smallest from the nurse and dances with her.*) Yes, yes, Mama will dance with Bob as well. What? Did you throw snowballs? Oh, if I'd only been there! No, don't bother, Anne-Marie—I'll undress them myself. Oh yes, let me. It's such fun. Go in and rest; you look half frozen. There's hot coffee waiting for you on the stove. (*The nurse goes into the room to the left.* NORA *takes the children's winter things off, throwing them about, while the children talk to her all at once.*) Is that so? A big dog chased you? But it didn't bite? No, dogs never bite little, lovely doll babies. Don't peek in the packages, Ivar! What is it? Yes, wouldn t you like to know. No, no, it's an ugly something. Well? Shall we play? What shall we play? Hide-and-seek? Yes, let's play hide-and-seek. Bob must hide first. I must? Yes, let me hide first. (*Laughing and shouting, she and the children play in and out of the living room and the adjoining room to the right. At last* NORA *hides under the table. The children come storming in, search, but cannot find her, then hear her muffled laughter, dash over to the table, lift the cloth and find her. Wild shouting. She creeps forward as if to scare them. More shouts. Meanwhile, a knock at the hall door; no one has noticed it. Now the door half opens, and* KROGSTAD *appears. He waits a moment; the game goes on.*)

KROGSTAD. Beg pardon, Mrs. Helmer—

NORA (*with a strangled cry, turning and scrambling to her knees*). Oh! what do you want?

KROGSTAD. Excuse me. The outer door was ajar; it must be someone forgot to shut it—

NORA (*rising*). My husband isn't home, Mr. Krogstad.

KROGSTAD. I know that.

NORA. Yes—then what do you want here?

KROGSTAD. A word with you.

NORA. With—? (*To the children, quietly.*) Go in to Anne-Marie. What? No, the strange man won't hurt Mama. When he's gone, we'll play some more. (*She leads the children into the room to the left and shuts the door after them. Then, tense and nervous:*) You want to speak to me?

KROGSTAD. Yes, I want to.

NORA. Today? But it's not yet the first of the month—

KROGSTAD. No, it's Christmas Eve. It's going to be up to you how merry a Christmas you have.

NORA. What is it you want? Today I absolutely can't—

KROGSTAD. We won't talk about that till later. This is something else. You do have a moment to spare, I suppose?

NORA. Oh yes, of course—I do, except—

KROGSTAD. Good. I was sitting over at Olsen's Restaurant when I saw your husband go down the street—

NORA. Yes?

KROGSTAD. With a lady.

NORA. Yes. So?

KROGSTAD. If you'll pardon my asking: wasn't that lady a Mrs. Linde?

NORA. Yes.

KROGSTAD. Just now come into town?

NORA. Yes, today.

KROGSTAD. She's a good friend of yours?

NORA. Yes, she is. But I don't see—

KROGSTAD. I also knew her once.

NORA. I'm aware of that.

KROGSTAD. Oh? You know all about it. I thought so. Well, then let me ask you short and sweet: is Mrs. Linde getting a job in the bank?

NORA. What makes you think you can cross-examine me, Mr. Krogstad —you, one of my husband's employees? But since you ask, you might as well know—yes, Mrs. Linde's going to be taken on at the bank. And I'm the one who spoke for her, Mr. Krogstad. Now you know.

KROGSTAD. So I guessed right.

NORA (*pacing up and down*). Oh, one does have a tiny bit of influence, I should hope. Just because I am a woman, don't think it means that—When one has a subordinate position, Mr. Krogstad, one really ought to be careful about pushing somebody who—hm—

KROGSTAD. Who has influence?

NORA. That's right.

KROGSTAD (*in a different tone*). Mrs. Helmer, would you be good enough to use your influence on my behalf?

NORA. What? What do you mean?

KROGSTAD. Would you please make sure that I keep my subordinate position in the bank?

NORA. What does that mean? Who's thinking of taking away your position?

KROGSTAD. Oh, don't play the innocent with me. I'm quite aware that your friend would hardly relish the chance of running into me again; and I'm also aware now whom I can thank for being turned out.

NORA. But I promise you—

KROGSTAD. Yes, yes, yes, to the point: there's still time, and I'm advising you to use your influence to prevent it.

NORA. But Mr. Krogstad, I have absolutely no influence.

KROGSTAD. You haven't? I thought you were just saying—

NORA. You shouldn't take me so literally. I! How can you believe that I have any such influence over my husband?

KROGSTAD. Oh, I've known your husband from our student days. I don't think the great bank manager's more steadfast than any other married man.

NORA. You speak insolently about my husband, and I'll show you the door.

KROGSTAD. The lady has spirit.

NORA. I'm not afraid of you any longer. After New Year's, I'll soon be done with the whole business.

KROGSTAD (*restraining himself*). Now listen to me, Mrs. Helmer. If necessary, I'll fight for my little job in the bank as if it were life itself.

NORA. Yes, so it seems.

KROGSTAD. It's not just a matter of income; that's the least of it. It's something else—All right, out with it! Look, this is the thing. You know, just like all the others, of course, that once, a good many years ago, I did something rather rash.

NORA. I've heard rumors to that effect.

KROGSTAD. The case never got into court; but all the same, every door was closed in my face from then on. So I took up those various activities you know about. I had to grab hold somewhere; and I dare say I haven't been among the worst. But now I want to drop all that. My boys are growing up. For their sakes, I'll have to win back as much respect as possible here in town. That job in the bank was like the first rung in my ladder. And now your husband wants to kick me right back down in the mud again.

NORA. But for heaven's sake, Mr. Krogstad, it's simply not in my power to help you.

KROGSTAD. That's because you haven't the will to—but I have the means to make you.

NORA. You certainly won't tell my husband that I owe you money?

KROGSTAD. Hm—what if I told him that?

NORA. That would be shameful of you. (*Nearly in tears.*) This secret —my joy and my pride—that he should learn it in such a crude and disgusting way—learn it from you. You'd expose me to the most horrible unpleasantness—

KROGSTAD. Only unpleasantness?

NORA (*vehemently*). But go on and try. It'll turn out the worse for you, because then my husband will really see what a crook you are, and then you'll *never* be able to hold your job.

KROGSTAD. I asked if it was just domestic unpleasantness you were afraid of?

NORA. If my husband finds out, then of course he'll pay what I owe at once, and then we'd be through with you for good.

KROGSTAD (*a step closer*). Listen, Mrs. Helmer—you've either got a very bad memory, or else no head at all for business. I'd better put you a little more in touch with the facts.

NORA. What do you mean?

KROGSTAD. When your husband was sick, you came to me for a loan of four thousand, eight hundred crowns.

NORA. Where else could I go?

KROGSTAD. I promised to get you that sum—

NORA. And you got it.

KROGSTAD. I promised to get you that sum, on certain conditions. You were so involved in your husband's illness, and so eager to finance your trip, that I guess you didn't think out all the details. It might just be a good idea to remind you. I promised you the money on the strength of a note I drew up.

NORA. Yes, and that I signed.

KROGSTAD. Right. But at the bottom I added some lines for your father to guarantee the loan. He was supposed to sign down there.

NORA. Supposed to? He did sign.

KROGSTAD. I left the date blank. In other words, your father would have dated his signature himself. Do you remember that?

NORA. Yes, I think—

KROGSTAD. Then I gave you the note for you to mail to your father. Isn't that so?

NORA. Yes.

KROGSTAD. And naturally you sent it at once—because only some five, six days later you brought me the note, properly signed. And with that, the money was yours.

NORA. Well, then; I've made my payments regularly, haven't I?

KROGSTAD. More or less. But—getting back to the point—those were hard times for you then, Mrs. Helmer.

NORA. Yes, they were.

KROGSTAD. Your father was very ill, I believe.

NORA. He was near the end.

KROGSTAD. He died soon after?

NORA. Yes.

KROGSTAD. Tell me, Mrs. Helmer, do you happen to recall the date of your father's death? The day of the month, I mean.

NORA. Papa died the twenty-ninth of September.

KROGSTAD. That's quite correct; I've already looked into that. And now we come to a curious thing—(*Taking out a paper.*) which I simply cannot comprehend.

NORA. Curious thing? I don't know—

KROGSTAD. This is the curious thing: that your father co-signed the note for your loan three days after his death.

NORA. How—? I don't understand.

KROGSTAD. Your father died the twenty-ninth of September. But look. Here your father dated his signature October second. Isn't that curious, Mrs. Helmer? (NORA *is silent.*) Can you explain it to me? (NORA *remains silent.*) It's also remarkable that the words "October second" and the year aren't written in your father's hand, but rather in one that I think I know. Well, it's easy to understand. Your father forgot perhaps to date his signature, and then someone or other added it, a bit sloppily, before anyone knew of his death. There's nothing wrong in that. It all comes down to the signature. And there's no question about *that,* Mrs. Helmer. It really *was* your father who signed his own name here, wasn't it?

NORA (*after a short silence, throwing her head back and looking squarely at him*). No, it wasn't. *I* signed Papa's name.

KROGSTAD. Wait, now—are you fully aware that this is a dangerous confession?

NORA. Why? You'll soon get your money.

KROGSTAD. Let me ask you a question—why didn't you send the paper to your father?

NORA. That was impossible. Papa was so sick. If I'd asked him for his signature, I also would have had to tell him what the money was for. But I couldn't tell him, sick as he was, that my husband's life was in danger. That was just impossible.

KROGSTAD. Then it would have been better if you'd given up the trip abroad.

NORA. I couldn't possibly. The trip was to save my husband's life. I couldn't give that up.

KROGSTAD. But didn't you ever consider that this was a fraud against me?

NORA. I couldn't let myself be bothered by that. You weren't any concern of mine. I couldn't stand you, with all those cold complications you made, even though you knew how badly off my husband was.

KROGSTAD. Mrs. Helmer, obviously you haven't the vaguest idea of what you've involved yourself in. But I can tell you this: it was nothing more and nothing worse than I once did—and it wrecked my whole reputation.

NORA. You? Do you expect me to believe that you ever acted bravely to save your wife's life?

KROGSTAD. Laws don't inquire into motives.

NORA. Then they must be very poor laws.

KROGSTAD. Poor or not—if I introduce this paper in court, you'll be judged according to law.

NORA. This I refuse to believe. A daughter hasn't a right to protect her dying father from anxiety and care? A wife hasn't a right to save her husband's life? I don't know much about laws, but I'm sure that somewhere in the books these things are allowed. And you don't know anything about it—you who practice the law? You must be an awful lawyer, Mr. Krogstad.

KROGSTAD. Could be. But business—the kind of business we two are mixed up in—don't you think I know about that? All right. Do what you want now. But I'm telling you *this*: if I get shoved down a second time, you're going to keep me company. (*He bows and goes out through the hall.*)

NORA (*pensive for a moment, then tossing her head*). Oh, really! Trying to frighten me! I'm not so silly as all that. (*Begins gathering up the children's clothes, but soon stops.*) But—? No, but that's impossible! I did it out of love.

THE CHILDREN (*in the doorway, left*). Mama, that strange man's gone out the door.

NORA. Yes, yes, I know it. But don't tell anyone about the strange man. Do you hear? Not even Papa!

THE CHILDREN. No, Mama. But now will you play again?

NORA. No, not now.

THE CHILDREN. Oh, but Mama, you promised.

NORA. Yes, but I can't now. Go inside; I have too much to do. Go in, go in, my sweet darlings. (*She herds them gently back in the room and shuts the door after them. Settling on the sofa, she takes up a piece of embroidery and makes some stitches, but soon stops abruptly.*) No! (*Throws the work aside, rises, goes to the hall door and calls out.*) Helene! Let me have the tree in here. (*Goes to the table, left, opens the table drawer, and stops again.*) No, but that's utterly impossible!

MAID (*with the Christmas tree*). Where should I put it, ma'am?

NORA. There. The middle of the floor.

MAID. Should I bring anything else?

NORA. No, thanks. I have what I need.

(*The* MAID, *who has set the tree down, goes out.*)

NORA (*absorbed in trimming the tree*). Candles here—and flowers here. That terrible creature! Talk, talk, talk! There's nothing to it at all. The tree's going to be lovely. I'll do anything to please you, Torvald. I'll sing for you, dance for you—

(HELMER *comes in from the hall, with a sheaf of papers under his arm.*)

NORA. Oh! You're back so soon?
HELMER. Yes. Has anyone been here?
NORA. Here? No.
HELMER. That's odd. I saw Krogstad leaving the front door.
NORA. So? Oh yes, that's true. Krogstad was here a moment.
HELMER. Nora, I can see by your face that he's been here, begging you to put in a good word for him.
NORA. Yes.
HELMER. And it was supposed to seem like your own idea? You were to hide it from me that he'd been here. He asked you that, too, didn't he?
NORA. Yes, Torvald, but—
HELMER. Nora, Nora, and you could fall for that? Talk with that sort of person and promise him anything? And then in the bargain, tell me an untruth.
NORA. An untruth—?
HELMER. Didn't you say that no one had been here? (*Wagging his finger.*) My little songbird must never do that again. A songbird needs a clean beak to warble with. No false notes. (*Putting his arm about her waist.*) That's the way it should be, isn't it? Yes, I'm sure of it. (*Releasing her.*) And so, enough of that. (*Sitting by the stove.*) Ah, how snug and cozy it is here. (*Leafing among his papers.*)
NORA (*busy with the tree, after a short pause*). Torvald!
HELMER. Yes.
NORA. I'm so much looking forward to the Stenborgs' costume party, day after tomorrow.
HELMER. And I can't wait to see what you'll surprise me with.
NORA. Oh, that stupid business!
HELMER. What?
NORA. I can't find anything that's right. Everything seems so ridiculous, so inane.
HELMER. So my little Nora's come to *that* recognition?
NORA (*going behind his chair, her arms resting on its back*). Are you very busy, Torvald?
HELMER. Oh—
NORA. What papers are those?
HELMER. Bank matters.
NORA. Already?
HELMER. I've gotten full authority from the retiring management to make all necessary changes in personnel and procedure. I'll need Christmas week for that. I want to have everything in order by New Year's.
NORA. So that was the reason this poor Krogstad—

HELMER. Hm.

NORA (*still leaning on the chair and slowly stroking the nape of his neck*). If you weren't so very busy, I would have asked you an enormous favor, Torvald.

HELMER. Let's hear. What is it?

NORA. You know, there isn't anyone who has your good taste—and I want so much to look well at the costume party. Torvald, couldn't you take over and decide what I should be and plan my costume?

HELMER. Ah, is my stubborn little creature calling for a lifeguard?

NORA. Yes, Torvald, I can't get anywhere without your help.

HELMER. All right—I'll think it over. We'll hit on something.

NORA. Oh, how sweet of you. (*Goes to the tree again. Pause.*) Aren't the red flowers pretty—? But tell me, was it really such a crime that this Krogstad committed?

HELMER. Forgery. Do you have any idea what that means?

NORA. Couldn't he have done it out of need?

HELMER. Yes, or thoughtlessness, like so many others. I'm not so heartless that I'd condemn a man categorically for just one mistake.

NORA. No, of course not, Torvald!

HELMER. Plenty of men have redeemed themselves by openly confessing their crimes and taking their punishment.

NORA. Punishment—?

HELMER. But now Krogstad didn't go that way. He got himself out by sharp practices, and that's the real cause of his moral breakdown.

NORA. Do you really think that would—?

HELMER. Just imagine how a man with that sort of guilt in him has to lie and cheat and deceive on all sides, has to wear a mask even with the nearest and dearest he has, even with his own wife and children. And with the children, Nora—that's where it's most horrible.

NORA. Why?

HELMER. Because that kind of atmosphere of lies infects the whole life of a home. Every breath the children take in is filled with the germs of something degenerate.

NORA (*coming closer behind him*). Are you sure of that?

HELMER. Oh, I've seen it often enough as a lawyer. Almost everyone who goes bad early in life has a mother who's a chronic liar.

NORA. Why just—the mother?

HELMER. It's usually the mother's influence that's dominant, but the father's works in the same way, of course. Every lawyer is quite familiar with it. And still this Krogstad's been going home year in, year out, poisoning his own children with lies and pretense; that's why I call him morally lost. (*Reaching his hands out toward her.*) So my sweet little Nora must promise me never to plead his cause. Your hand on it. Come, come, what's this? Give me your hand. There, now. All settled. I can tell you it'd be impossible for me to work alongside of him. I literally feel physically revolted when I'm anywhere near such a person.

NORA (*withdraws her hand and goes to the other side of the Christmas tree*).   How hot it is here! And I've got so much to do.

HELMER (*getting up and gathering his papers*).   Yes, and I have to think about getting some of these read through before dinner. I'll think about your costume, too. And something to hang on the tree in gilt paper, I may even see about that. (*Putting his hand on her head.*) Oh you, my darling little songbird. (*He goes into his study and closes the door after him.*)

NORA (*softly, after a silence*).   Oh, really! it isn't so. It's impossible. It must be impossible.

ANNE-MARIE (*in the doorway, left*).   The children are begging so hard to come in to Mama.

NORA.   No, no, no, don't let them in to me! You stay with them, Anne-Marie.

ANNE-MARIE.   Of course, ma'am. (*Closes the door.*)

NORA (*pale with terror*).   Hurt my children—! Poison my home? (*A moment's pause; then she tosses her head.*) That's not true. Never. Never in all the world.

ACT TWO

Same room. Beside the piano the Christmas tree now stands stripped of ornament, burned-down candle stubs on its ragged branches. NORA's *street clothes lie on the sofa.* NORA, *alone in the room, moves restlessly about; at last she stops at the sofa and picks up her coat.*

NORA (*dropping the coat again*).   Someone's coming! (*Goes toward the door, listens.*) No—there's no one. Of course—nobody's coming today, Christmas Day—or tomorrow, either. But maybe—(*Opens the door and looks out.*) No, nothing in the mailbox. Quite empty. (*Coming forward.*) What nonsense! He won't do anything serious. Nothing terrible could happen. It's impossible. Why, I have three small children.

(ANNE-MARIE, *with a large carton, comes in from the room to the left.*)

ANNE-MARIE.   Well, at last I found the box with the masquerade clothes.

NORA.   Thanks. Put it on the table.

ANNE-MARIE (*does so*).   But they're all pretty much of a mess.

NORA.   Ahh! I'd love to rip them in a million pieces!

ANNE-MARIE.   Oh, mercy, they can be fixed right up. Just a little patience.

NORA. Yes, I'll go get Mrs. Linde to help me.

ANNE-MARIE. Out again now? In this nasty weather? Miss Nora will catch cold—get sick.

NORA. Oh, worse things could happen—How are the children?

ANNE-MARIE. The poor mites are playing with their Christmas presents, but—

NORA. Do they ask for me much?

ANNE-MARIE. They're so used to having Mama around, you know.

NORA. Yes, but Anne-Marie, I *can't* be together with them as much as I was.

ANNE-MARIE. Well, small children get used to anything.

NORA. You think so? Do you think they'd forget their mother if she was gone for good?

ANNE-MARIE. Oh, mercy—gone for good!

NORA. Wait, tell me, Anne-Marie—I've wondered so often—how could you ever have the heart to give your child over to strangers?

ANNE-MARIE. But I had to, you know, to become little Nora's nurse.

NORA. Yes, but how could you *do* it?

ANNE-MARIE. When I could get such a good place? A girl who's poor and who's gotten in trouble is glad enough for that. Because that slippery fish, he didn't do a thing for me, you know.

NORA. But your daughter's surely forgotten you.

ANNE-MARIE. Oh, she certainly has not. She's written to me, both when she was confirmed and when she was married.

NORA (*clasping her about the neck*). You old Anne-Marie, you were a good mother for me when I was little.

ANNE-MARIE. Poor little Nora, with no other mother but me.

NORA. And if the babies didn't have one, then I know that you'd— What silly talk! (*Opening the carton.*) Go in to them. Now I'll have to— Tomorrow you can see how lovely I'll look.

ANNE-MARIE. Oh, there won't be anyone at the party as lovely as Miss Nora. (*She goes off into the room, left.*)

NORA (*begins unpacking the box, but soon throws it aside*). Oh, if I dared to go out. If only nobody would come. If only nothing would happen here while I'm out. What craziness—nobody's coming. Just don't think. This muff—needs a brushing. Beautiful gloves, beautiful gloves. Let it go. Let it go! One, two, three, four, five, six—(*With a cry.*) Oh, there they are! (*Poises to move toward the door, but remains irresolutely standing.* MRS. LINDE *enters from the hall, where she has removed her street clothes.*)

NORA. Oh, it's you, Kristine. There's no one else out there? How good that you've come.

MRS. LINDE. I hear you were up asking for me.

NORA. Yes, I just stopped by. There's something you really can help me with. Let's get settled on the sofa. Look, there's going to be a costume party tomorrow evening at the Stenborgs' right above us, and now Torvald wants me to go as a Neapolitan peasant girl and dance the tarantella that I learned in Capri.

MRS. LINDE. Really, you are giving a whole performance?

NORA. Torvald says yes, I should. See, here's the dress. Torvald had it made for me down there; but now it's all so tattered that I just don't know—

MRS. LINDE. Oh, we'll fix that up in no time. It's nothing more than the trimmings—they're a bit loose here and there. Needle and thread? Good, now we have what we need.

NORA. Oh, how sweet of you!

MRS. LINDE (*sewing*). So you'll be in disguise tomorrow, Nora. You know what? I'll stop by then for a moment and have a look at you all dressed up. But listen, I've absolutely forgotten to thank you for that pleasant evening yesterday.

NORA (*getting up and walking about*). I don't think it was as pleasant as usual yesterday. You should have come to town a bit sooner, Kristine— Yes, Torvald really knows how to give a home elegance and charm.

MRS. LINDE. And you do, too, if you ask me. You're not your father's daughter for nothing. But tell me, is Dr. Rank always so down in the mouth as yesterday?

NORA. No, that was quite an exception. But he goes around critically ill all the time—tuberculosis of the spine, poor man. You know, his father was a disgusting thing who kept mistresses and so on—and that's why the son's been sickly from birth.

MRS. LINDE (*lets her sewing fall to her lap*). But my dearest Nora, how do you know about such things?

NORA (*walking more jauntily*). Hmp! When you've had three children, then you've had a few visits from—women who know something of medicine, and they tell you this and that.

MRS. LINDE (*resumes sewing; a short pause*). Does Dr. Rank come here every day?

NORA. Every blessed day. He's Torvald's best friend from childhood, and *my* good friend, too. Dr. Rank almost belongs to this house.

MRS. LINDE. But tell me—is he quite sincere? I mean, doesn't he rather enjoy flattering people?

NORA. Just the opposite. Why do you think that?

MRS. LINDE. When you introduced us yesterday, he was proclaiming that he'd often heard my name in this house; but later I noticed that your husband hadn't the slightest idea who I really was. So how could Dr. Rank—?

NORA. But it's all true, Kristine. You see, Torvald loves me beyond words, and, as he puts it, he'd like to keep me all to himself. For a long time he'd almost be jealous if I even mentioned any of my old friends back home.

So of course I dropped that. But with Dr. Rank I talk a lot about such things, because he likes hearing about them.

MRS. LINDE. Now listen, Nora; in many ways you're still like a child. I'm a good deal older than you, with a little more experience. I'll tell you something: you ought to put an end to all this with Dr. Rank.

NORA. What should I put an end to?

MRS. LINDE. Both parts of it, I think. Yesterday you said something about a rich admirer who'd provide you with money—

NORA. Yes, one who doesn't exist—worse luck. So?

MRS. LINDE. Is Dr. Rank well off?

NORA. Yes, he is.

MRS. LINDE. With no dependents?

NORA. No, no one. But—

MRS. LINDE. And he's over here every day?

NORA. Yes, I told you that.

MRS. LINDE. How can a man of such refinement be so grasping?

NORA. I don't follow you at all.

MRS. LINDE. Now don't try to hide it, Nora. You think I can't guess who loaned you the forty-eight hundred crowns?

NORA. Are you out of your mind? How could you think of such a thing! A friend of ours, who comes here every single day. What an intolerable situation that would have been!

MRS. LINDE. Then it really wasn't him.

NORA. No, absolutely not. It never even crossed my mind for a moment —And he had nothing to lend in those days; his inheritance came later.

MRS. LINDE. Well, I think that was a stroke of luck for you, Nora dear.

NORA. No, it never would have occurred to me to ask Dr. Rank— Still, I'm quite sure that if I had asked him—

MRS. LINDE. Which you won't, of course.

NORA. No, of course not. I can't see that I'd ever need to. But I'm quite positive that if I talked to Dr. Rank—

MRS. LINDE. Behind your husband's back?

NORA. I've got to clear up this other thing; *that's* also behind his back. I've *got* to clear it all up.

MRS. LINDE. Yes, I was saying that yesterday, but—

NORA (*pacing up and down*). A man handles these problems so much better than a woman—

MRS. LINDE. One's husband does, yes.

NORA. Nonsense. (*Stopping.*) When you pay everything you owe, then you get your note back, right?

MRS. LINDE. Yes, naturally.

NORA. And can rip it into a million pieces and burn it up—that filthy scrap of paper!

MRS. LINDE (*looking hard at her, laying her sewing aside, and rising slowly*). Nora, you're hiding something from me.

NORA. You can see it in my face?

MRS. LINDE. Something's happened to you since yesterday morning. Nora, what is it?

NORA (*hurrying toward her*). Kristine! (*Listening.*) Shh! Torvald's home. Look, go in with the children a while. Torvald can't bear all this snipping and stitching. Let Anne-Marie help you.

MRS. LINDE (*gathering up some of the things*). All right, but I'm not leaving here until we've talked this out. (*She disappears into the room, left, as* TORVALD *enters from the hall.*)

NORA. Oh, how I've been waiting for you, Torvald dear.

HELMER. Was that the dressmaker?

NORA. No, that was Kristine. She's helping me fix up my costume. You know, it's going to be quite attractive.

HELMER. Yes, wasn't that a bright idea I had?

NORA. Brilliant! But then wasn't I good as well to give in to you?

HELMER. Good—because you give in to your husband's judgment? All right, you little goose, I know you didn't mean it like that. But I won't disturb you. You'll want to have a fitting, I suppose.

NORA. And you'll be working?

HELMER. Yes. (*Indicating a bundle of papers.*) See. I've been down to the bank. (*Starts toward his study.*)

NORA. Torvald.

HELMER (*stops*). Yes.

NORA. If your little squirrel begged you, with all her heart and soul, for something—?

HELMER. What's that?

NORA. Then would you do it?

HELMER. First, naturally, I'd have to know what it was.

NORA. Your squirrel would scamper about and do tricks, if you'd only be sweet and give in.

HELMER. Out with it.

NORA. Your lark would be singing high and low in every room—

HELMER. Come on, she does that anyway.

NORA. I'd be a wood nymph and dance for you in the moonlight.

HELMER. Nora—don't tell me it's that same business from this morning?

NORA (*coming closer*). Yes, Torvald, I beg you, please!

HELMER. And you actually have the nerve to drag that up again?

NORA. Yes, yes, you've got to give in to me; you *have* to let Krogstad keep his job in the bank.

HELMER. My dear Nora, I've slated his job for Mrs. Linde.

NORA. That's awfully kind of you. But you could just fire another clerk instead of Krogstad.

HELMER. This is the most incredible stubbornness! Because you go and give an impulsive promise to speak up for him, I'm expected to—

NORA. That's not the reason, Torvald. It's for your own sake. That man does writing for the worst papers; you said it yourself. He could do you any amount of harm. I'm scared to death of him—

HELMER. Ah, I understand. It's the old memories haunting you.

NORA. What do you mean by that?

HELMER. Of course, you're thinking about your father.

NORA. Yes, all right. Just remember how those nasty gossips wrote in the papers about Papa and slandered him so cruelly. I think they'd have had him dismissed if the department hadn't sent you up to investigate, and if you hadn't been so kind and open-minded toward him.

HELMER. My dear Nora, there's a notable difference between your father and me. Your father's official career was hardly above reproach. But mine is; and I hope it'll stay that way as long as I hold my position.

NORA. Oh, who can ever tell what vicious minds can invent? We could be so snug and happy now in our quiet, carefree home—you and I and the children, Torvald! That's why I'm pleading with you so—

HELMER. And just by pleading for him you make it impossible for me to keep him on. It's already known at the bank that I'm firing Krogstad. What if it's rumored around now that the new bank manager was vetoed by his wife—

NORA. Yes, what then—?

HELMER. Oh yes—as long as your little bundle of stubbornness gets her way—! I should go and make myself ridiculous in front of the whole office—give people the idea I can be swayed by all kinds of outside pressure. Oh, you can bet I'd feel the effects of that soon enough! Besides—there's something that rules Krogstad right out at the bank as long as I'm the manager.

NORA. What's that?

HELMER. His moral failings I could maybe overlook if I had to—

NORA. Yes, Torvald, why not?

HELMER. And I hear he's quite efficient on the job. But he was a crony of mine back in my teens—one of those rash friendships that crop up again and again to embarrass you later in life. Well, I might as well say it straight out: we're on a first-name basis. And that tactless fool makes no effort at all to hide it in front of others. Quite the contrary—he thinks that entitles him to take a familiar air around me, and so every other second he comes booming out with his "Yes, Torvald!" and "Sure thing, Torvald!" I tell you, it's been excruciating for me. He's out to make my place in the bank unbearable.

NORA. Torvald, you can't be serious about all this.
HELMER. Oh no? Why not?
NORA. Because these are such petty considerations.
HELMER. What are you saying? Petty? You think I'm petty!
NORA. No, just the opposite, Torvald dear. That's exactly why—
HELMER. Never mind. You call my motives petty; then I might as well be just that. Petty! All right! We'll put a stop to this for good. (*Goes to the hall door and calls.*) Helene!
NORA. What do you want?
HELMER (*searching among his papers*). A decision. (*The* MAID *comes in.*) Look here; take this letter; go out with it at once. Get hold of a messenger and have him deliver it. Quick now. It's already addressed. Wait, here's some money.
MAID. Yes, sir. (*She leaves with the letter.*)
HELMER (*straightening his papers*). There, now, little Miss Willful.
NORA (*breathlessly*). Torvald, what was that letter?
HELMER. Krogstad's notice.
NORA. Call it back, Torvald! There's still time. Oh, Torvald, call it back! Do it for my sake—for your sake, for the children's sake! Do you hear, Torvald; do it! You don't know how this can harm us.
HELMER. Too late.
NORA. Yes, too late.
HELMER. Nora dear, I can forgive you this panic, even though basically you're insulting me. Yes, you are! Or isn't it an insult to think that I should be afraid of a courtroom hack's revenge? But I forgive you anyway, because this shows so beautifully how much you love me. (*Takes her in his arms.*) This is the way it should be, my darling Nora. Whatever comes, you'll see: when it really counts, I have strength and courage enough as a man to take on the whole weight myself.
NORA (*terrified*). What do you mean by that?
HELMER. The whole weight, I said.
NORA (*resolutely*). No, never in all the world.
HELMER. Good. So we'll share it, Nora, as man and wife. That's as it should be. (*Fondling her.*) Are you happy now? There, there, there—not these frightened dove's eyes. It's nothing at all but empty fantasies—Now you should run through your tarantella and practice your tambourine. I'll go to the inner office and shut both doors, so I won't hear a thing; you can make all the noise you like. (*Turning in the doorway.*) And when Rank comes, just tell him where he can find me. (*He nods to her and goes with his papers into the study, closing the door.*)
NORA (*standing as though rooted, dazed with fright, in a whisper*). He really could do it. He will do it. He'll do it in spite of everything. No, not that, never, never! Anything but that! Escape! A way out—(*The doorbell

rings.) Dr. Rank! Anything but that! *Anything*, whatever it is! (*Her hands pass over her face, smoothing it; she pulls herself together, goes over and opens the hall door.* Dr. Rank *stands outside, hanging his fur coat up. During the following scene, it begins getting dark.*)

NORA. Hello, Dr. Rank. I recognized your ring. But you mustn't go in to Torvald yet; I believe he's working.

RANK. And you?

NORA. For you, I always have an hour to spare—you know that. (*He has entered, and she shuts the door after him.*)

RANK. Many thanks. I'll make use of these hours while I can.

NORA. What do you mean by that? While you can?

RANK. Does that disturb you?

NORA. Well, it's such an odd phrase. Is anything going to happen?

RANK. What's going to happen is what I've been expecting so long—but I honestly didn't think it would come so soon.

NORA (*gripping his arm*). What is it you've found out? Dr. Rank, you have to tell me!

RANK (*sitting by the stove*). It's all over with me. There's nothing to be done about it.

NORA (*breathing easier*). Is it you—then—?

RANK. Who else? There's no point in lying to one's self. I'm the most miserable of all my patients, Mrs. Helmer. These past few days I've been auditing my internal accounts. Bankrupt! Within a month I'll probably be laid out and rotting in the churchyard.

NORA. Oh, what a horrible thing to say.

RANK. The thing itself is horrible. But the worst of it is all the other horror before it's over. There's only one final examination left; when I'm finished with that, I'll know about when my disintegration will begin. There's something I want to say. Helmer with his sensitivity has such a sharp distaste for anything ugly. I don't want him near my sickroom.

NORA. Oh, but Dr. Rank—

RANK. I won't have him in there. Under no condition. I'll lock my door to him— As soon as I'm completely sure of the worst, I'll send you my calling card marked with a black cross, and you'll know then the wreck has started to come apart.

NORA. No, today you're completely unreasonable. And I wanted you so much to be in a really good humor.

RANK. With death up my sleeve? And then to suffer this way for somebody else's sins. Is there any justice in that? And in every single family, in some way or another, this inevitable retribution of nature goes on—

NORA (*her hands pressed over her ears*). Oh, stuff! Cheer up! Please—be gay!

RANK. Yes, I'd just as soon laugh at it all. My poor, innocent spine, serving time for my father's gay army days.

NORA (*by the table, left*). He was so infatuated with asparagus tips and *pâté de foie gras,* wasn't that it?

RANK. Yes—and with truffles.

NORA. Truffles, yes. And then with oysters, I suppose?

RANK. Yes, tons of oysters, naturally.

NORA. And then the port and champagne to go with it. It's so sad that all these delectable things have to strike at our bones.

RANK. Especially when they strike at the unhappy bones that never shared in the fun.

NORA. Ah, that's the saddest of all.

RANK (*looks searchingly at her*). Hm.

NORA (*after a moment*). Why did you smile?

RANK. No, it was you who laughed.

NORA. No, it was you who smiled, Dr. Rank!

RANK (*getting up*). You're even a bigger tease than I'd thought.

NORA. I'm full of wild ideas today.

RANK. That's obvious.

NORA (*putting both hands on his shoulders*). Dear, dear Dr. Rank, you'll never die for Torvald and me.

RANK. Oh, that loss you'll easily get over. Those who go away are soon forgotten.

NORA (*looks fearfully at him*). You believe that?

RANK. One makes new connections, and then—

NORA. Who makes new connections?

RANK. Both you and Torvald will when I'm gone. I'd say you're well under way already. What was that Mrs. Linde doing here last evening?

NORA. Oh, come—you can't be jealous of poor Kristine?

RANK. Oh yes, I am. She'll be my successor here in the house. When I'm down under, that woman will probably—

NORA. Shh! Not so loud. She's right in there.

RANK. Today as well. So you see.

NORA. Only to sew on my dress. Good gracious, how unreasonable you are. (*Sitting on the sofa.*) Be nice now, Dr. Rank. Tomorrow you'll see how beautifully I'll dance; and you can imagine then that I'm dancing only for you—yes, and of course for Torvald, too—that's understood. (*Takes various items out of the carton.*) Dr. Rank, sit over here and I'll show you something.

RANK (*sitting*). What's that?

NORA. Look here. Look.

RANK. Silk stockings.

NORA. Flesh-colored. Aren't they lovely? Now it's so dark here, but tomorrow—No, no, no, just look at the feet. Oh well, you might as well look at the rest.

RANK. Hm—

NORA. Why do you look so critical? Don't you believe they'll fit?

RANK. I've never had any chance to form an opinion on that.

NORA (*glancing at him a moment*). Shame on you. (*Hits him lightly on the ear with the stockings.*) That's for you. (*Puts them away again.*)

RANK. And what other splendors am I going to see now?

NORA. Not the least bit more, because you've been naughty. (*She hums a little and rummages among her things.*)

RANK (*after a short silence*). When I sit here together with you like this, completely easy and open, then I don't know—I simply can't imagine—whatever would have become of me if I'd never come into this house.

NORA (*smiling*). Yes, I really think you feel completely at ease with us.

RANK (*more quietly, staring straight ahead*). And then to have to go away from it all—

NORA. Nonsense, you're not going away.

RANK (*his voice unchanged*). —and not even be able to leave some poor show of gratitude behind, scarcely a fleeting regret—no more than a vacant place that anyone can fill.

NORA. And if I asked you now for—? No—

RANK. For what?

NORA. For a great proof of your friendship—

RANK. Yes, yes?

NORA. No, I mean—for an exceptionally big favor—

RANK. Would you really, for once, make me so happy?

NORA. Oh, you haven't the vaguest idea what it is.

RANK. All right, then tell me.

NORA. No, but I can't, Dr. Rank—it's all out of reason. It's advice and help, too—and a favor—

RANK. So much the better. I can't fathom what you're hinting at. Just speak out. Don't you trust me?

NORA. Of course. More than anyone else. You're my best and truest friend, I'm sure. That's why I want to talk to you. All right, then, Dr. Rank: there's something you can help me prevent. You know how deeply, how inexpressibly dearly Torvald loves me; he'd never hesitate a second to give up his life for me.

RANK (*leaning close to her*). Nora—do you think he's the only one—

NORA (*with a slight start*). Who—?

RANK. Who'd gladly give up his life for you.

NORA (*heavily*). I see.

RANK. I swore to myself you should know this before I'm gone. I'll never find a better chance. Yes, Nora, now you know. And also you know now that you can trust me beyond anyone else.

NORA (*rising, natural and calm*). Let me by.

RANK (*making room for her, but still sitting*). Nora—

NORA (*in the hall doorway*). Helene, bring the lamp in. (*Goes over to the stove.*) Ah, dear Dr. Rank, that was really mean of you.

RANK (*getting up*). That I've loved you just as deeply as somebody else? Was *that* mean?

NORA. No, but that you came out and told me. That was quite unnecessary—

RANK. What do you mean? Have you known—?

(*The* MAID *comes in with the lamp, sets it on the table, and goes out again.*)

RANK. Nora—Mrs. Helmer—I'm asking you: have you known about it?

NORA. Oh, how can I tell what I know or don't know? Really, I don't know what to say—Why did you have to be so clumsy, Dr. Rank! Everything was so good.

RANK. Well, in any case, you now have the knowledge that my body and soul are at your command. So won't you speak out?

NORA (*looking at him*). After that?

RANK. Please, just let me know what it is.

NORA. You can't know anything now.

RANK. I have to. You mustn't punish me like this. Give me the chance to do whatever is humanly possible for you.

NORA. Now there's nothing you can do for me. Besides, actually, I don't need any help. You'll see—it's only my fantasies. That's what it is. Of course! (*Sits in the rocker, looks at him, and smiles.*) What a nice one you are, Dr. Rank. Aren't you a little bit ashamed, now that the lamp is here?

RANK. No, not exactly. But perhaps I'd better go—for good?

NORA. No, you certainly can't do that. You must come here just as you always have. You know Torvald can't do without you.

RANK. Yes, but *you*?

NORA. You know how much I enjoy it when you're here.

RANK. That's precisely what threw me off. You're a mystery to me. So many times I've felt you'd almost rather be with me than with Helmer.

NORA. Yes—you see, there are some people that one loves most and other people that one would almost prefer being with.

RANK. Yes, there's something to that.

NORA. When I was back home, of course I loved Papa most. But I always thought it was so much fun when I could sneak down to the maids' quarters, because they never tried to improve me, and it was always so amusing, the way they talked to each other.

RANK. Aha, so it's *their* place that I've filled.

NORA (*jumping up and going to him*). Oh, dear, sweet Dr. Rank, that's not what I meant at all. But you can understand that with Torvald it's just the same as with Papa—

(*The* MAID *enters from the hall.*)

MAID. Ma'am—please! (*She whispers to* NORA *and hands her a calling card.*)

NORA (*glancing at the card*). Ah! (*Slips it into her pocket.*)

RANK. Anything wrong?

NORA. No, no, not at all. It's only some—it's my new dress—

RANK. Really? But—there's your dress.

NORA. Oh, that. But this is another one—I ordered it—Torvald mustn't know—

RANK. Ah, now we have the big secret.

NORA. That's right. Just go in with him—he's back in the inner study. Keep him there as long as—

RANK. Don't worry. He won't get away. (*Goes into the study.*)

NORA (*to the* MAID). And he's standing waiting in the kitchen.

MAID. Yes, he came up by the back stairs.

NORA. But didn't you tell him somebody was here?

MAID. Yes, but that didn't do any good.

NORA. He won't leave?

MAID. No, he won't go till he's talked with you, ma'am.

NORA. Let him come in, then—but quietly. Helene, don't breathe a word about this. It's a surprise for my husband.

MAID. Yes, yes, I understand— (*Goes out.*)

NORA. This horror—it's going to happen. No, no, no, it can't happen, it mustn't. (*She goes and bolts* HELMER's *door. The* MAID *opens the hall door for* KROGSTAD *and shuts it behind him. He is dressed for travel in a fur coat, boots, and a fur cap.*)

NORA (*going toward him*). Talk softly. My husband's home.

KROGSTAD. Well, good for him.

NORA. What do you want?

KROGSTAD. Some information.

NORA. Hurry up, then. What is it?

KROGSTAD. You know, of course, that I got my notice.

NORA. I couldn't prevent it, Mr. Krogstad. I fought for you to the bitter end, but nothing worked.

KROGSTAD. Does your husband's love for you run so thin? He knows everything I can expose you to, and all the same he dares to—

NORA. How can you imagine he knows anything about this?

KROGSTAD. Ah, no—I can't imagine it either, now. It's not at all like my fine Torvald Helmer to have so much guts—

NORA. Mr. Krogstad, I demand respect for my husband!

KROGSTAD. Why, of course—all due respect. But since the lady's keeping it so carefully hidden, may I presume to ask if you're also a bit better informed than yesterday about what you've actually done?

NORA. More than you ever could teach me.

KROGSTAD. Yes, I *am* such an awful lawyer.

NORA. What is it you want from me?

KROGSTAD. Just a glimpse of how you are, Mrs. Helmer. I've been thinking about you all day long. A cashier, a night-court scribbler, a—well, a type like me also has a little of what they call a heart, you know.

NORA. Then show it. Think of my children.

KROGSTAD. Did you or your husband ever think of mine? But never mind. I simply wanted to tell you that you don't need to take this thing too seriously. For the present, I'm not proceeding with any action.

NORA. Oh no, really! Well—I knew that.

KROGSTAD. Everything can be settled in a friendly spirit. It doesn't have to get around town at all; it can stay just among us three.

NORA. My husband may never know anything of this.

KROGSTAD. How can you manage that? Perhaps you can pay me the balance?

NORA. No, not right now.

KROGSTAD. Or you know some way of raising the money in a day or two?

NORA. No way that I'm willing to use.

KROGSTAD. Well, it wouldn't have done you any good, anyway. If you stood in front of me with a fistful of bills, you still couldn't buy your signature back.

NORA. Then tell me what you're going to do with it.

KROGSTAD. I'll just hold onto it—keep it on file. There's no outsider who'll even get wind of it. So if you've been thinking of taking some desperate step—

NORA. I have.

KROGSTAD. Been thinking of running away from home—

NORA. I have!

KROGSTAD. Or even of something worse—

NORA. How could you guess that?

KROGSTAD. You can drop those thoughts.

NORA. How could you guess I was thinking of *that*?

KROGSTAD. Most of us think about *that* at first. I thought about it too, but I discovered I hadn't the courage—

Nora (*lifelessly*). I don't either.
Krogstad (*relieved*). That's true, you haven't the courage? You too?
Nora. I don't have it—I don't have it.
Krogstad. It would be terribly stupid, anyway. After that first storm at home blows out, why, then—I have here in my pocket a letter for your husband—
Nora. Telling everything?
Krogstad. As charitably as possible.
Nora (*quickly*). He mustn't ever get that letter. Tear it up. I'll find some way to get money.
Krogstad. Beg pardon, Mrs. Helmer, but I think I just told you—
Nora. Oh, I don't mean the money I owe you. Let me know how much you want from my husband, and I'll manage it.
Krogstad. I don't want any money from your husband.
Nora. What do you want, then?
Krogstad. I'll tell you what. I want to recoup, Mrs. Helmer; I want to get on in the world—and there's where your husband can help me. For a year and a half I've kept myself clean of anything disreputable—all that time struggling with the worst conditions; but I was satisfied, working my way up step by step. Now I've been written right off, and I'm just not in the mood to come crawling back. I tell you, I want to move on. I want to get back in the bank—in a better position. Your husband can set up a job for me—
Nora. He'll never do that!
Krogstad. He'll do it. I know him. He won't dare breathe a word of protest. And once I'm in there together with him, you just wait and see! Inside of a year, I'll be the manager's right-hand man. It'll be Nils Krogstad, not Torvald Helmer, who runs the bank.
Nora. You'll never see the day!
Krogstad. Maybe you think you can—
Nora. I have the courage now—for *that*.
Krogstad. Oh, you don't scare me. A smart, spoiled lady like you—
Nora. You'll see; you'll see!
Krogstad. Under the ice, maybe? Down in the freezing, coal-black water? There, till you float up in the spring, ugly, unrecognizable, with your hair falling out—
Nora. You don't frighten me.
Krogstad. Nor do you frighten me. One doesn't do these things, Mrs. Helmer. Besides, what good would it be? I'd still have him safe in my pocket.
Nora. Afterwards? When I'm no longer—?
Krogstad. Are you forgetting that *I'll* be in control then over your final reputation? (Nora *stands speechless, staring at him.*) Good; now I've

warned you. Don't do anything stupid. When Helmer's read my letter, I'll be waiting for his reply. And bear in mind that it's your husband himself who's forced me back to my old ways. I'll never forgive him for that. Goodbye, Mrs. Helmer. (*He goes out through the hall.*)

NORA (*goes to the hall door, opens it a crack, and listens*).   He's gone. Didn't leave the letter. Oh no, no, that's impossible too! (*Opening the door more and more.*) What's that? He's standing outside—not going downstairs. He's thinking it over? Maybe he'll—? (*A letter falls in the mailbox; then* KROGSTAD's *footsteps are heard, dying away down a flight of stairs.* NORA *gives a muffled cry and runs over toward the sofa table. A short pause.*) In the mailbox. (*Slips warily over to the hall door.*) It's lying there. Torvald, Torvald—now we're lost!

MRS. LINDE (*entering with the costume from the room, left*).   There now, I can't see anything else to mend. Perhaps you'd like to try—

NORA (*in a hoarse whisper*).   Kristine, come here.

MRS. LINDE (*tossing the dress on the sofa*).   What's wrong? You look upset.

NORA.   Come here. See that letter? *There!* Look—through the glass in the mailbox.

MRS. LINDE.   Yes, yes, I see it.

NORA.   That letter's from Krogstad—

MRS. LINDE.   Nora—it's Krogstad who loaned you the money!

NORA.   Yes, and now Torvald will find out everything.

MRS. LINDE.   Believe me, Nora, it's best for both of you.

NORA.   There's more you don't know. I forged a name.

MRS. LINDE.   But for heaven's sake—?

NORA.   I only want to tell you that, Kristine, so that you can be my witness.

MRS. LINDE.   Witness? Why should I—?

NORA.   If I should go out of my mind—it could easily happen—

MRS. LINDE.   Nora!

NORA.   Or anything else occurred—so I couldn't be present here—

MRS. LINDE.   Nora, Nora, you aren't yourself at all!

NORA.   And someone should try to take on the whole weight, all of the guilt, you follow me—

MRS. LINDE.   Yes, of course, but why do you think—?

NORA.   Then you're the witness that it isn't true, Kristine. I'm very much myself; my mind right now is perfectly clear; and I'm telling you: nobody else has known about this; I alone did everything. Remember that.

MRS. LINDE.   I will. But I don't understand all this.

NORA.   Oh, how could you ever understand it? It's the miracle now that's going to take place.

MRS. LINDE.   The miracle?

NORA.   Yes, the miracle. But it's so awful, Kristine. It mustn't take place, not for anything in the world.

MRS. LINDE.   I'm going right over and talk with Krogstad.

NORA.   Don't go near him; he'll do you some terrible harm!

MRS. LINDE.   There was a time once when he'd gladly have done anything for me.

NORA.   He?

MRS. LINDE.   Where does he live?

NORA.   Oh, how do I know? Yes. (*Searches in her pocket.*) Here's his card. But the letter, the letter—!

HELMER (*from the study, knocking on the door*).   Nora!

NORA (*with a cry of fear*).   Oh! What is it? What do you want?

HELMER.   Now, now, don't be so frightened. We're not coming in. You locked the door—are you trying on the dress?

NORA.   Yes, I'm trying it. I'll look just beautiful, Torvald.

MRS. LINDE (*who has read the card*).   He's living right around the corner.

NORA.   Yes, but what's the use? We're lost. The letter's in the box.

MRS. LINDE.   And your husband has the key?

NORA.   Yes, always.

MRS. LINDE.   Krogstad can ask for his letter back unread; he can find some excuse—

NORA.   But it's just this time that Torvald usually—

MRS. LINDE.   Stall him. Keep him in there. I'll be back as quick as I can. (*She hurries out through the hall entrance.*)

NORA (*goes to* HELMER's *door, opens it, and peers in*).   Torvald!

HELMER (*from the inner study*).   Well—does one dare set foot in one's own living room at last? Come on, Rank, now we'll get a look—(*In the doorway.*) But what's this?

NORA.   What, Torvald dear?

HELMER.   Rank had me expecting some grand masquerade.

RANK (*in the doorway*).   That was my impression, but I must have been wrong.

NORA.   No one can admire me in my splendor—not till tomorrow.

HELMER.   But Nora dear, you look so exhausted. Have you practiced too hard?

NORA.   No, I haven't practiced at all yet.

HELMER.   You know, it's necessary—

NORA.   Oh, it's absolutely necessary, Torvald. But I can't get anywhere without your help. I've forgotten the whole thing completely.

HELMER.   Ah, we'll soon take care of that.

NORA.   Yes, take care of me, Torvald, please! Promise me that? Oh, I'm so nervous. That big party— You must give up everything this evening for me. No business—don't even touch your pen. Yes? Dear Torvald, promise?

HELMER. It's a promise. Tonight I'm totally at your service—you little helpless thing. Hm—but first there's one thing I want to—(*Goes toward the hall door.*)

NORA. What are you looking for?

HELMER. Just to see if there's any mail.

NORA. No, no, don't do that, Torvald!

HELMER. Now what?

NORA. Torvald, please. There isn't any.

HELMER. Let me look, though. (*Starts out.* NORA, *at the piano, srikes the first notes of the tarantella.* HELMER, *at the door, stops.*) Aha!

NORA. I can't dance tomorrow if I don't practice with you.

HELMER (*going over to her*). Nora dear, are you really so frightened?

NORA. Yes, so terribly frightened. Let me practice right now; there's still time before dinner. Oh, sit down and play for me, Torvald. Direct me. Teach me, the way you always have.

HELMER. Gladly, if it's what you want. (*Sits at the piano.*)

NORA (*snatches the tambourine up from the box, then a long, varicolored shawl, which she throws around herself, whereupon she springs forward and cries out*). Play for me now! Now I'll dance!

(HELMER *plays and* NORA *dances.* RANK *stands behind* HELMER *at the piano and looks on.*)

HELMER (*as he plays*). Slower. Slow down.

NORA. Can't change it.

HELMER. Not so violent, Nora!

NORA. Has to be just like this.

HELMER (*stopping*). No, no, that won't do at all.

NORA (*laughing and swinging her tambourine*). Isn't that what I told you?

RANK. Let me play for her.

HELMER (*getting up*). Yes, go on. I can teach her more easily then.

(RANK *sits at the piano and plays;* NORA *dances more and more wildly.* HELMER *has stationed himself by the stove and repeatedly gives her directions; she seems not to hear them; her hair loosens and falls over her shoulders; she does not notice, but goes on dancing.* MRS. LINDE *enters.*)

MRS. LINDE (*standing dumbfounded at the door*). Ah—!

NORA (*still dancing*). See what fun, Kristine!

HELMER. But Nora darling, you dance as if your life were at stake.

NORA. And it is.

HELMER. Rank, stop! This is pure madness. Stop it, I say!

(RANK *breaks off playing, and* NORA *halts abruptly.*)

HELMER (*going over to her*).   I never would have believed it. You've forgotten everything I taught you.

NORA (*throwing away the tambourine*).   You see for yourself.

HELMER.   Well, there's certainly room for instruction here.

NORA.   Yes, you see how important it is. You've got to teach me to the very last minute. Promise me that, Torvald?

HELMER.   You can bet on it.

NORA.   You mustn't, either today or tomorrow, think about anything else but me; you mustn't open any letters—or the mailbox—

HELMER.   Ah, its still the fear of that man—

NORA.   Oh yes, yes, that too.

HELMER.   Nora, it's written all over you—there's already a letter from him out there.

NORA.   I don't know. I guess so. But you mustn't read such things now; there mustn't be anything ugly between us before it's all over.

RANK (*quietly to* HELMER).   You shouldn't deny her.

HELMER (*putting his arm around her*).   The child can have her way. But tomorrow night, after you've danced—

NORA.   Then you'll be free.

MAID (*in the doorway, right*).   Ma'am, dinner is served.

NORA.   We'll be wanting champagne, Helene.

MAID.   Very good, ma'am. (*Goes out.*)

HELMER.   So—a regular banquet, hm?

NORA.   Yes, a banquet—champagne till daybreak! (*Calling out.*) And some macaroons, Helene. Heaps of them—just this once.

HELMER (*taking her hands*).   Now, now, now—no hysterics. Be my own little lark again.

NORA.   Oh, I will soon enough. But go on in—and you, Dr. Rank. Kristine, help me put up my hair.

RANK (*whispering, as they go*).   There's nothing wrong—really wrong, is there?

HELMER.   Oh, of course not. It's nothing more than this childish anxiety I was telling you about. (*They go out, right.*)

NORA.   Well?

MRS. LINDE.   Left town.

NORA.   I could see by your face.

MRS. LINDE.   He'll be home tomorrow evening. I wrote him a note.

NORA.   You shouldn't have. Don't try to stop anything now. After all, it's a wonderful joy, this waiting here for the miracle.

MRS. LINDE.   What is it you're waiting for?

NORA. Oh, you can't understand that. Go in to them, I'll be along in a moment.

(MRS. LINDE *goes into the dining room.* NORA *stands a short while as if composing herself; then she looks at her watch.*)

NORA. Five. Seven hours to midnight. Twenty-four hours to the midnight after, and then the tarantella's done. Seven and twenty-four? Thirty-one hours to live.

HELMER (*in the doorway, right*). What's become of the little lark?

NORA (*going toward him with open arms*). Here's your lark!

ACT THREE

Same scene. The table, with chairs around it, has been moved to the center of the room. A lamp on the table is lit. The hall door stands open. Dance music drifts down from the floor above. MRS. LINDE *sits at the table, absently paging through a book, trying to read, but apparently unable to focus her thoughts. Once or twice she pauses, tensely listening for a sound at the outer entrance.*

MRS. LINDE (*glancing at her watch*). Not yet—and there's hardly any time left. If only he's not—(*Listening again.*) Ah, there he is. (*She goes out in the hall and cautiously opens the outer door. Quiet footsteps are heard on the stairs. She whispers:*) Come in. Nobody's here.

KROGSTAD (*in the doorway*). I found a note from you at home. What's back of all this?

MRS. LINDE. I just *had* to talk to you.

KROGSTAD. Oh? And it just *had* to be here in this house?

MRS. LINDE. At my place it was impossible; my room hasn't a private entrance. Come in; we're all alone. The maid's asleep, and the Helmers are at the dance upstairs.

KROGSTAD (*entering the room*). Well, well, the Helmers are dancing tonight? Really?

MRS. LINDE. Yes, why not?

KROGSTAD. How true—why not?

MRS. LINDE. All right, Krogstad, let's talk.

KROGSTAD. Do we two have anything more to talk about?

MRS. LINDE. We have a great deal to talk about.

KROGSTAD. I wouldn't have thought so.

MRS. LINDE. No, because you've never understood me, really.

KROGSTAD. Was there anything more to understand—except what's all too common in life? A calculating woman throws over a man the moment a better catch comes by.

MRS. LINDE. You think I'm so thoroughly calculating? You think I broke it off lightly?

KROGSTAD. Didn't you?

MRS. LINDE. Nils—is that what you really thought?

KROGSTAD. If you cared, then why did you write me the way you did?

MRS. LINDE. What else could I do? If I had to break off with you, then it was my job as well to root out everything you felt for me.

KROGSTAD (*wringing his hands*). So that was it. And this—all this, simply for money!

MRS. LINDE. Don't forget I had a helpless mother and two small brothers. We couldn't wait for you, Nils; you had such a long road ahead of you then.

KROGSTAD. That may be; but you still hadn't the right to abandon me for somebody else's sake.

MRS. LINDE. Yes—I don't know. So many, many times I've asked myself if I did have that right.

KROGSTAD (*more softly*). When I lost you, it was as if all the solid ground dissolved from under my feet. Look at me; I'm a half-drowned man now, hanging onto a wreck.

MRS. LINDE. Help may be near.

KROGSTAD. It was near—but then you came and blocked it off.

MRS. LINDE. Without my knowing it, Nils. Today for the first time I learned that it's you I'm replacing at the bank.

KROGSTAD. All right—I believe you. But now that you know, will you step aside?

MRS. LINDE. No, because that wouldn't benefit you in the slightest.

KROGSTAD. Not "benefit" me, hm! I'd step aside anyway.

MRS. LINDE. I've learned to be realistic. Life and hard, bitter necessity have taught me that.

KROGSTAD. And life's taught me never to trust fine phrases.

MRS. LINDE. Then life's taught you a very sound thing. But you do have to trust in actions, don't you?

KROGSTAD. What does that mean?

MRS. LINDE. You said you were hanging on like a half-drowned man to a wreck.

KROGSTAD. I've good reason to say that.

MRS. LINDE. I'm also like a half-drowned woman on a wreck. No one to suffer with; no one to care for.

KROGSTAD. You made your choice.

MRS. LINDE. There wasn't any choice then.

KROGSTAD. So—what of it?

Mrs. Linde. Nils, if only we two shipwrecked people could reach across to each other.

Krogstad. What are you saying?

Mrs. Linde. Two on one wreck are at least better off than each on his own.

Krogstad. Kristine!

Mrs. Linde. Why do you think I came into town?

Krogstad. Did you really have some thought of me?

Mrs. Linde. I have to work to go on living. All my born days, as long as I can remember, I've worked, and it's been my best and my only joy. But now I'm completely alone in the world; it frightens me to be so empty and lost. To work for yourself—there's no joy in that. Nils, give me something—someone to work for.

Krogstad. I don't believe all this. It's just some hysterical feminine urge to go out and make a noble sacrifice.

Mrs. Linde. Have you ever found me to be hysterical?

Krogstad. Can you honestly mean this? Tell me—do you know everything about my past?

Mrs. Linde. Yes.

Krogstad. And you know what they think I'm worth around here.

Mrs. Linde. From what you were saying before, it would seem that with me you could have been another person.

Krogstad. I'm positive of that.

Mrs. Linde. Couldn't it happen still?

Krogstad. Kristine—you're saying this in all seriousness? Yes, you are! I can see it in you. And do you really have the courage, then—?

Mrs. Linde. I need to have someone to care for; and your children need a mother. We both need each other. Nils, I have faith that you're good at heart—I'll risk everything together with you.

Krogstad (*gripping her hands*). Kristine, thank you, thank you—Now I know I can win back a place in their eyes. Yes—but I forgot—

Mrs. Linde (*listening*). Shh! The tarantella. Go now! Go on!

Krogstad. Why? What is it?

Mrs. Linde. Hear the dance up there? When that's over, they'll be coming down.

Krogstad. Oh, then I'll go. But—it's all pointless. Of course, you don't know the move I made against the Helmers.

Mrs. Linde. Yes, Nils, I know.

Krogstad. And all the same, you have the courage to—?

Mrs. Linde. I know how far despair can drive a man like you.

Krogstad. Oh, if I only could take it all back.

Mrs. Linde. You easily could—your letter's still lying in the mailbox.

Krogstad. Are you sure of that?

Mrs. Linde. Positive. But—

Krogstad (*looks at her searchingly*). Is that the meaning of it, then? You'll have your friend at any price. Tell me straight out. Is that it?

Mrs. Linde. Nils—anyone who's sold herself for somebody else once isn't going to do it again.

Krogstad. I'll demand my letter back.

Mrs. Linde. No, no.

Krogstad. Yes, of course. I'll stay here till Helmer comes down; I'll tell him to give me my letter again—that it only involves my dismissal—that he shouldn't read it—

Mrs. Linde. No, Nils, don't call the letter back.

Krogstad. But wasn't that exactly why you wrote me to come here?

Mrs. Linde. Yes, in that first panic. But it's been a whole day and night since then, and in that time I've seen such incredible things in this house. Helmer's got to learn everything; this dreadful secret has to be aired; those two have to come to a full understanding; all these lies and evasions can't go on.

Krogstad. Well, then, if you want to chance it. But at least there's one thing I can do, and do right away—

Mrs. Linde (*listening*). Go now, go, quick! The dance is over. We're not safe another second.

Krogstad. I'll wait for you downstairs.

Mrs. Linde. Yes, please do; take me home.

Krogstad. I can't believe it; I've never been so happy. (*He leaves by way of the outer door; the door between the room and the hall stays open.*)

Mrs. Linde (*straightening up a bit and getting together her street clothes*). How different now! How different! Someone to work for, to live for—a home to build. Well, it is worth the try! Oh, if they'd only come! (*Listening.*) Ah, there they are. Bundle up. (*She picks up her hat and coat.* Nora's *and* Helmer's *voices can be heard outside; a key turns in the lock, and* Helmer *brings* Nora *into the hall almost by force. She is wearing the Italian costume with a large black shawl about her; he has on evening dress, with a black domino open over it.*)

Nora (*struggling in the doorway*). No, no, no, not inside! I'm going up again. I don't want to leave so soon.

Helmer. But Nora dear—

Nora. Oh, I beg you, please, Torvald. From the bottom of my heart, please—only an hour more!

Helmer. Not a single minute, Nora darling. You know our agreement. Come on, in we go; you'll catch cold out here. (*In spite of her resistance, he gently draws her into the room.*)

Mrs. Linde. Good evening.

Nora. Kristine!

HELMER. Why, Mrs. Linde—are you here so late?
MRS. LINDE. Yes, I'm sorry, but I did want to see Nora in costume.
NORA. Have you been sitting here, waiting for me?
MRS. LINDE. Yes. I didn't come early enough; you were all upstairs; and then I thought I really couldn't leave without seeing you.
HELMER (*removing* NORA's *shawl*). Yes, take a good look. She's worth looking at, I can tell you that, Mrs. Linde. Isn't she lovely?
MRS. LINDE. Yes, I should say—
HELMER. A dream of loveliness, isn't she? That's what everyone thought at the party, too. But she's horribly stubborn—this sweet little thing. What's to be done with her? Can you imagine, I almost had to use force to pry her away.
NORA. Oh, Torvald, you're going to regret you didn't indulge me, even for just a half hour more.
HELMER. There, you see. She danced her tarantella and got a tumultuous hand—which was well earned, although the performance may have been a bit too naturalistic—I mean it rather overstepped the proprieties of art. But never mind—what's important is, she made a success, an overwhelming success. You think I could let her stay on after that and spoil the effect? Oh no; I took my lovely little Capri girl—my capricious little Capri girl, I should say—took her under my arm; one quick tour of the ballroom, a curtsy to every side, and then—as they say in novels—the beautiful vision disappeared. An exit should always be effective, Mrs. Linde, but that's what I can't get Nora to grasp. Phew, it's hot in here. (*Flings the domino on a chair and opens the door to his room.*) Why's it dark in here? Oh yes, of course. Excuse me. (*He goes in and lights a couple of candles.*)
NORA (*in a sharp, breathless whisper*). So?
MRS. LINDE (*quietly*). I talked with him.
NORA. And—?
MRS. LINDE. Nora—you must tell your husband everything.
NORA (*dully*). I knew it.
MRS. LINDE. You've got nothing to fear from Krogstad, but you have to speak out.
NORA. I won't tell.
MRS. LINDE. Then the letter will.
NORA. Thanks, Kristine. I know now what's to be done. Shh!
HELMER (*reentering*). Well, then, Mrs. Linde—have you admired her?
MRS. LINDE. Yes, and now I'll say good night.
HELMER. Oh, come, so soon? Is this yours, this knitting?
MRS. LINDE. Yes, thanks. I nearly forgot it.
HELMER. Do you knit, then?
MRS. LINDE. Oh yes.

HELMER. You know what? You should embroider instead.

MRS. LINDE. Really? Why?

HELMER. Yes, because it's a lot prettier. See here, one holds the embroidery so, in the left hand, and then one guides the needle with the right —so—in an easy, sweeping curve—right?

MRS. LINDE. Yes, I guess that's—

HELMER. But, on the other hand, knitting—it can never be anything but ugly. Look, see here, the arms tucked in, the knitting needles going up and down—there's something Chinese about it. Ah, that was really a glorious champagne they served.

MRS. LINDE. Yes, good night, Nora, and don't be stubborn anymore.

HELMER. Well put, Mrs. Linde!

MRS. LINDE. Good night, Mr. Helmer.

HELMER (*accompanying her to the door*). Good night, good night. I hope you get home all right. I'd be very happy to—but you don't have far to go. Good night, good night. (*She leaves. He shuts the door after her and returns.*) There, now, at last we got her out the door. She's a deadly bore, that creature.

NORA. Aren't you pretty tired, Torvald?

HELMER. No, not a bit.

NORA. You're not sleepy?

HELMER. Not at all. On the contrary, I'm feeling quite exhilarated. But you? Yes, you really look tired and sleepy.

NORA. Yes, I'm very tired. Soon now I'll sleep.

HELMER. See! You see! I was right all along that we shouldn't stay longer.

NORA. Whatever you do is always right.

HELMER (*kissing her brow*). Now my little lark talks sense. Say, did you notice what a time Rank was having tonight?

NORA. Oh, was he? I didn't get to speak with him.

HELMER. I scarcely did either, but it's a long time since I've seen him in such high spirits. (*Gazes at her a moment, then comes nearer her.*) Hm— it's marvelous, though, to be back home again—to be completely alone with you. Oh, you bewitchingly lovely young woman!

NORA. Torvald, don't look at me like that!

HELMER. Can't I look at my richest treasure? At all that beauty that's mine, mine alone—completely and utterly.

NORA (*moving around to the other side of the table*). You mustn't talk to me that way tonight.

HELMER (*following her*). The tarantella is still in your blood, I can see—and it makes you even more enticing. Listen. The guests are beginning to go. (*Dropping his voice.*) Nora—it'll soon be quiet through this whole house.

NORA. Yes, I hope so.

HELMER. You do, don't you, my love? Do you realize—when I'm out at a party like this with you—do you know why I talk to you so little, and keep such a distance away; just send you a stolen look now and then—you know why I do it? It's because I'm imagining then that you're my secret darling, my secret young bride-to-be, and that no one suspects there's anything between us.

NORA. Yes, yes; oh, yes, I know you're always thinking of me.

HELMER. And then when we leave and I place the shawl over those fine young rounded shoulders—over that wonderful curving neck—then I pretend that you're my young bride, that we're just coming from the wedding, that for the first time I'm bringing you into my house—that for the first time I'm alone with you—completely alone with you, your trembling young beauty! All this evening I've longed for nothing but you. When I saw you turn and sway in the tarantella—my blood was pounding till I couldn't stand it—that's why I brought you down here so early—

NORA. Go away, Torvald! Leave me alone. I don't want all this.

HELMER. What do you mean? Nora, you're teasing me. You will, won't you? Aren't I your husband—?

(*A knock at the outside door.*)

NORA (*startled*). What's that?

HELMER (*going toward the hall*). Who is it?

RANK (*outside*). It's me. May I come in a moment?

HELMER (*with quiet irritation*). Oh, what does he want now? (*Aloud.*) Hold on. (*Goes and opens the door.*) Oh, how nice that you didn't just pass us by!

RANK. I thought I heard your voice, and then I wanted so badly to have a look in. (*Lightly glancing about.*) Ah, me, these old familiar haunts. You have it snug and cozy in here, you two.

HELMER. You seemed to be having it pretty cozy upstairs, too.

RANK. Absolutely. Why shouldn't I? Why not take in everything in life? As much as you can, anyway, and as long as you can. The wine was superb—

HELMER. The champagne especially.

RANK. You noticed that too? It's amazing how much I could guzzle down.

NORA. Torvald also drank a lot of champagne this evening.

RANK. Oh?

NORA. Yes, and that always makes him so entertaining.

RANK. Well, why shouldn't one have a pleasant evening after a well-spent day?

HELMER. Well spent? I'm afraid I can't claim that.

RANK (*slapping him on the back*). But I can, you see!
NORA. Dr. Rank, you must have done some scientific research today.
RANK. Quite so.
HELMER. Come now—little Nora talking about scientific research!
NORA. And can I congratulate you on the results?
RANK. Indeed you may.
NORA. Then they were good?
RANK. The best possible for both doctor and patient—certainty.
NORA (*quickly and searchingly*). Certainty?
RANK. Complete certainty. So don't I owe myself a gay evening afterwards?
NORA. Yes, you're right, Dr. Rank.
HELMER. I'm with you—just so long as you don't have to suffer for it in the morning.
RANK. Well, one never gets something for nothing in life.
NORA. Dr. Rank—are you very fond of masquerade parties?
RANK. Yes, if there's a good array of odd disguises—
NORA. Tell me, what should we two go as at the next masquerade?
HELMER. You little featherhead—already thinking of the next!
RANK. We two? I'll tell you what: you must go as Charmed Life—
HELMER. Yes, but find a costume for *that*!
RANK. Your wife can appear just as she looks every day.
HELMER. That was nicely put. But don't you know what you're going to be?
RANK. Yes, Helmer, I've made up my mind.
HELMER. Well?
RANK. At the next masquerade I'm going to be invisible.
HELMER. That's a funny idea.
RANK. They say there's a hat—black, huge—have you never heard of the hat that makes you invisible? You put it on, and then no one on earth can see you.
HELMER (*suppressing a smile*). Ah, of course.
RANK. But I'm quite forgetting what I came for. Helmer, give me a cigar, one of the dark Havanas.
HELMER. With the greatest pleasure. (*Holds out his case.*)
RANK. Thanks. (*Takes one and cuts off the tip.*)
NORA (*striking a match*). Let me give you a light.
RANK. Thank you. (*She holds the match for him; he lights the cigar.*) And now good-bye.
HELMER. Good-bye, good-bye, old friend.
NORA. Sleep well, Doctor.
RANK. Thanks for that wish.

NORA. Wish me the same.

RANK. You? All right, if you like— Sleep well. And thanks for the light. (*He nods to them both and leaves.*)

HELMER (*his voice subdued*). He's been drinking heavily.

NORA (*absently*). Could be. (HELMER *takes his keys from his pocket and goes out in the hall.*) Torvald—what are you after?

HELMER. Got to empty the mailbox; it's nearly full. There won't be room for the morning papers.

NORA. Are you working tonight?

HELMER. You know I'm not. Why—what's this? Someone's been at the lock.

NORA. At the lock—?

HELMER. Yes, I'm positive. What do you suppose—? I can't imagine one of the maids—? Here's a broken hairpin. Nora, it's yours—

NORA (*quickly*). Then it must be the children—

HELMER. You'd better break them of that. Hm, hm—well, opened it after all. (*Takes the contents out and calls into the kitchen.*) Helene! Helene, would you put out the lamp in the hall. (*He returns to the room, shutting the hall door, then displays the handful of mail.*) Look how it's piled up. (*Sorting through them.*) Now what's this?

NORA (*at the window*). The letter! Oh, Torvald, no!

HELMER. Two calling cards—from Rank.

NORA. From Dr. Rank?

HELMER (*examining them*). "Dr. Rank, Consulting Physician." They were on top. He must have dropped them in as he left.

NORA. Is there anything on them?

HELMER. There's a black cross over the name. See? That's a gruesome notion. He could almost be announcing his own death.

NORA. That's just what he's doing.

HELMER. What! You've heard something? Something he's told you?

NORA. Yes. That when those cards came, he'd be taking his leave of us. He'll shut himself in now and die.

HELMER. Ah, my poor friend! Of course I knew he wouldn't be here much longer. But so soon— And then to hide himself away like a wounded animal.

NORA. If it has to happen, then it's best it happens in silence—don't you think so, Torvald?

HELMER (*pacing up and down*). He'd grown right into our lives. I simply can't imagine him gone. He with his suffering and loneliness—like a dark cloud setting off our sunlit happiness. Well, maybe it's best this way. For him, at least. (*Standing still.*) And maybe for us too, Nora. Now we're thrown back on each other, completely. (*Embracing her.*) Oh you, my darling wife, how can I hold you close enough? You know what, Nora—time and again I've wished you were in some terrible danger, just so I could stake my life and soul and everything, for your sake.

NORA (*tearing herself away, her voice firm and decisive*).   Now you must read your mail, Torvald.

HELMER.   No, no, not tonight. I want to stay with you, dearest.

NORA.   With a dying friend on your mind?

HELMER.   You're right. We've both had a shock. There's ugliness between us—these thoughts of death and corruption. We'll have to get free of them first. Until then—we'll stay apart.

NORA (*clinging about his neck*).   Torvald—good night! Good night!

HELMER (*kissing her on the cheek*).   Good night, little songbird. Sleep well, Nora. I'll be reading my mail now. (*He takes the letters into his room and shuts the door after him.*)

NORA (*with bewildered glances, groping about, seizing* HELMER's *domino, throwing it around her, and speaking in short, hoarse, broken whispers*).   Never see him again. Never, never. (*Putting her shawl over her head.*) Never see the children either—them, too. Never, never. Oh, the freezing black water! The depths—down—Oh, I wish it were over—He has it now; he's reading it—now. Oh no, no, not yet. Torvald, good-bye, you and the children— (*She starts for the hall; as she does,* HELMER *throws open his door and stands with an open letter in his hand.*)

HELMER.   Nora!

NORA (*screams*).   Oh—!

HELMER.   What is this? You know what's in this letter?

NORA.   Yes, I know. Let me go! Let me out!

HELMER (*holding her back*).   Where are you going?

NORA (*struggling to break loose*).   You can't save me, Torvald!

HELMER (*slumping back*).   True! Then it's true what he writes? How horrible! No, no, it's impossible—it can't be true.

NORA.   It *is* true. I've loved you more than all this world.

HELMER.   Ah, none of your slippery tricks.

NORA (*taking one step toward him*).   Torvald—!

HELMER.   What *is* this you've blundered into!

NORA.   Just let me loose. You're not going to suffer for my sake. You're not going to take on my guilt.

HELMER.   No more playacting. (*Locks the hall door.*) You stay right here and give me a reckoning. You understand what you've done? Answer! You understand?

NORA (*looking squarely at him, her face hardening*).   Yes. I'm beginning to understand everything now.

HELMER (*striding about*).   Oh, what an awful awakening! In all these eight years—she who was my pride and joy—a hypocrite, a liar—worse, worse—a criminal! How infinitely disgusting it all is! The shame! (NORA *says nothing and goes on looking straight at him. He stops in front of her.*) I should have suspected something of the kind. I should have known. All your father's flimsy values— Be still! All your father's flimsy values have come out in you. No religion, no morals, no sense of duty— Oh, how I'm punished for letting him off! I did it for your sake, and you repay me like this.

NORA. Yes, like this.

HELMER. Now you've wrecked all my happiness—ruined my whole future. Oh, it's awful to think of. I'm in a cheap little grafter's hands; he can do anything he wants with me, ask for anything, play with me like a puppet—and I can't breathe a word. I'll be swept down miserably into the depths on account of a featherbrained woman.

NORA. When I'm gone from this world, you'll be free.

HELMER. Oh, quit posing. Your father had a mess of those speeches too. What good would that ever do me if you were gone from this world, as you say? Not the slightest. He can still make the whole thing known; and if he does, I could be falsely suspected as your accomplice. They might even think that I was behind it—that I put you up to it. And all that I can thank you for—you that I've coddled the whole of our marriage. Can you see now what you've done to me?

NORA (*icily calm*). Yes.

HELMER. It's so incredible, I just can't grasp it. But we'll have to patch up whatever we can. Take off the shawl. I said, take it off! I've got to appease him somehow or other. The thing has to be hushed up at any cost. And as for you and me, it's got to seem like everything between us is just as it was—to the outside world, that is. You'll go right on living in this house, of course. But you can't be allowed to bring up the children; I don't dare trust you with them— Oh, to have to say this to someone I've loved so much! Well, that's done with. From now on happiness doesn't matter; all that matters is saving the bits and pieces, the appearance— (*The doorbell rings.* HELMER *starts.*) What's that? And so late. Maybe the worst—? You think he'd—? Hide, Nora! Say you're sick. (NORA *remains standing motionless.* HELMER *goes and opens the door.*)

MAID (*half dressed, in the hall*). A letter for Mrs. Helmer.

HELMER. I'll take it. (*Snatches the letter and shuts the door.*) Yes, it's from him. You don't get it; I'm reading it myself.

NORA. Then read it.

HELMER (*by the lamp*). I hardly dare. We may be ruined, you and I. But—I've got to know. (*Rips open the letter, skims through a few lines, glances at an enclosure, then cries out joyfully.*) Nora! (NORA *looks inquiringly at him.*) Nora! Wait—better check it again— Yes, yes, it's true. I'm saved. Nora, I'm saved!

NORA. And I?

HELMER. You too, of course. We're both saved, both of us. Look. He's sent back your note. He says he's sorry and ashamed—that a happy development in his life—oh, who cares what he says! Nora, we're saved! No one can hurt you. Oh, Nora, Nora—but first, this ugliness all has to go. Let me see— (*Takes a look at the note.*) No, I don't want to see it; I want the whole thing to fade like a dream. (*Tears the note and both letters to pieces, throws them into the stove and watches them burn.*) There—now there's nothing left— He wrote that since Christmas Eve you— Oh, they must have been three terrible days for you, Nora.

NORA. I fought a hard fight.

HELMER. And suffered pain and saw no escape but— No, we're not going to dwell on anything unpleasant. We'll just be grateful and keep on repeating: it's over now, it's over! You hear me, Nora? You don't seem to realize—it's over. What's it mean—that frozen look? Oh, poor little Nora, I understand. You can't believe I've forgiven you. But I have, Nora; I swear I have. I know that what you did, you did out of love for me.

NORA. That's true.

HELMER. You loved me the way a wife ought to love her husband. It's simply the means that you couldn't judge. But you think I love you any the less for not knowing how to handle your affairs? No, no—just lean on me: I'll guide you and teach you. I wouldn't be a man if this feminine helplessness didn't make you twice as attractive to me. You mustn't mind those sharp words I said—that was all in the first confusion of thinking my world had collapsed. I've forgiven you, Nora; I swear I've forgiven you.

NORA. My thanks for your forgiveness. (*She goes out through the door, right.*)

HELMER. No, wait— (*Peers in.*) What are you doing in there?

NORA (*inside*). Getting out of my costume.

HELMER (*by the open door*). Yes, do that. Try to calm yourself and collect your thoughts again, my frightened little songbird. You can rest easy now; I've got wide wings to shelter you with. (*Walking about close by the door.*) How snug and nice our home is, Nora. You're safe here; I'll keep you like a hunted dove I've rescued out of a hawk's claws. I'll bring peace to your poor, shuddering heart. Gradually it'll happen, Nora; you'll see. Tomorrow all this will look different to you; then everything will be as it was. I won't have to go on repeating I forgive you; you'll feel it for yourself. How can you imagine I'd ever conceivably want to disown you—or even blame you in any way? Ah, you don't know a man's heart, Nora. For a man there's something indescribably sweet and satisfying in knowing he's forgiven his wife—and forgiven her out of a full and open heart. It's as if she belongs to him in two ways now: in a sense he's given her fresh into the world again, and she's become his wife and his child as well. From now on that's what you'll be to me—you little, bewildered, helpless thing. Don't be afraid of anything, Nora; just open your heart to me, and I'll be conscience and will to you both—(NORA *enters in her regular clothes.*) What's this? Not in bed? You've changed your dress?

NORA. Yes, Torvald, I've changed my dress.

HELMER. But why now, so late?

NORA. Tonight I'm not sleeping.

HELMER. But Nora dear—

NORA (*looking at her watch*). It's still not so very late. Sit down, Torvald; we have a lot to talk over. (*She sits at one side of the table.*)

HELMER. Nora—what is this? That hard expression—

NORA. Sit down. This'll take some time. I have a lot to say.

HELMER (*sitting at the table directly opposite her*). You worry me, Nora. And I don't understand you.

NORA. No, that's exactly it. You don't understand me. And I've never understood you either—until tonight. No, don't interrupt. You can just listen to what I say. We're closing out accounts, Torvald.

HELMER. How do you mean that?

NORA (*after a short pause*). Doesn't anything strike you about our sitting here like this?

HELMER. What's that?

NORA. We've been married now eight years. Doesn't it occur to you that this is the first time we two, you and I, man and wife, have ever talked seriously together?

HELMER. What do you mean—seriously?

NORA. In eight whole years—longer even—right from our first acquaintance, we've never exchanged a serious word on any serious thing.

HELMER. You mean I should constantly go and involve you in problems you couldn't possibly help me with?

NORA. I'm not talking of problems. I'm saying that we've never sat down seriously together and tried to get to the bottom of anything.

HELMER. But dearest, what good would that ever do you?

NORA. That's the point right there: you've never understood me. I've been wronged greatly, Torvald—first by Papa, and then by you.

HELMER. What! By us—the two people who've loved you more than anyone else?

NORA (*shaking her head*). You never loved me. You've thought it fun to be in love with me, that's all.

HELMER. Nora, what a thing to say!

NORA. Yes, it's true now, Torvald. When I lived at home with Papa, he told me all his opinions, so I had the same ones too; or if they were different I hid them, since he wouldn't have cared for that. He used to call me his doll-child, and he played with me the way I played with my dolls. Then I came into your house—

HELMER. How can you speak of our marriage like that?

NORA (*unperturbed*). I mean, then I went from Papa's hands into yours. You arranged everything to your own taste, and so I got the same taste as you—or I pretended to; I can't remember. I guess a little of both, first one, then the other. Now when I look back, it seems as if I'd lived here like a beggar—just from hand to mouth. I've lived by doing tricks for you, Torvald. But that's the way you wanted it. It's a great sin what you and Papa did to me. You're to blame that nothing's become of me.

HELMER. Nora, how unfair and ungrateful you are! Haven't you been happy here?

NORA. No, never. I thought so—but I never have.

HELMER. Not—not happy!

NORA. No, only lighthearted. And you've always been so kind to me. But our home's been nothing but a playpen. I've been your doll-wife here, just as at home I was Papa's doll-child. And in turn the children have been my dolls. I thought it was fun when you played with me, just as they thought it fun when I played with them. That's been our marriage, Torvald.

HELMER. There's some truth in what you're saying—under all the raving exaggeration. But it'll all be different after this. Playtime's over; now for the schooling.

NORA. Whose schooling—mine or the children's?

HELMER. Both yours and the children's, dearest.

NORA. Oh, Torvald, you're not the man to teach me to be a good wife to you.

HELMER. And you can say that?

NORA. And I—how am I equipped to bring up children?

HELMER. Nora!

NORA. Didn't you say a moment ago that that was no job to trust me with?

HELMER. In a flare of temper! Why fasten on that?

NORA. Yes, but you were so very right. I'm not up to the job. There's another job I have to do first. I have to try to educate myself. You can't help me with that. I've got to do it alone. And that's why I'm leaving you now.

HELMER (*jumping up*). What's that?

NORA. I have to stand completely alone, if I'm ever going to discover myself and the world out there. So I can't go on living with you.

HELMER. Nora, Nora!

NORA. I want to leave right away. Kristine should put me up for the night—

HELMER. You're insane! You've no right! I forbid you!

NORA. From here on, there's no use forbidding me anything. I'll take with me whatever is mine. I don't want a thing from you, either now or later.

HELMER. What kind of madness is this!

NORA. Tomorrow I'm going home—I mean, home where I came from. It'll be easier up there to find something to do.

HELMER. Oh, you blind, incompetent child!

NORA. I must learn to be competent, Torvald.

HELMER. Abandon your home, your husband, your children! And you're not even thinking what people will say.

NORA. I can't be concerned about that. I only know how essential this is.

HELMER. Oh, it's outrageous. So you'll run out like this on your most sacred vows.

NORA. What do you think are my most sacred vows?

HELMER. And I have to tell you that! Aren't they your duties to your husband and children?

NORA. I have other duties equally sacred.

HELMER. That isn't true. What duties are they?

NORA. Duties to myself.

HELMER. Before all else, you're a wife and a mother.

NORA. I don't believe in that anymore. I believe that, before all else, I'm a human being, no less than you—or anyway, I ought to try to become one. I know the majority thinks you're right, Torvald, and plenty of books agree with you, too. But I can't go on believing what the majority says, or what's written in books. I have to think over these things myself and try to understand them.

HELMER. Why can't you understand your place in your own home? On a point like that, isn't there one everlasting guide you can turn to? Where's your religion?

NORA. Oh, Torvald, I'm really not sure what religion is.

HELMER. What—?

NORA. I only know what the minister said when I was confirmed. He told me religion was this thing and that. When I get clear and away by myself, I'll go into that problem too. I'll see if what the minister said was right, or, in any case, if it's right for me.

HELMER. A young woman your age shouldn't talk like that. If religion can't move you, I can try to rouse your conscience. You do have some moral feeling? Or, tell me—has that gone too?

NORA. It's not easy to answer that, Torvald. I simply don't know. I'm all confused about these things. I just know I see them so differently from you. I find out, for one thing, that the law's not at all what I'd thought—but I can't get it through my head that the law is fair. A woman hasn't a right to protect her dying father or save her husband's life! I can't believe that.

HELMER. You talk like a child. You don't know anything of the world you live in.

NORA. No, I don't. But now I'll begin to learn for myself. I'll try to discover who's right, the world or I.

HELMER. Nora, you're sick; you've got a fever. I almost think you're out of your head.

NORA. I've never felt more clearheaded and sure in my life.

HELMER. And—clearheaded and sure—you're leaving your husband and children?

NORA. Yes.

HELMER. Then there's only one possible reason.

NORA. What?

HELMER. You no longer love me.

NORA. No. That's exactly it.

HELMER. Nora! You can't be serious!

NORA. Oh, this is so hard, Torvald—you've been so kind to me always. But I can't help it. I don't love you anymore.

HELMER (*struggling for composure*). Are you also clearheaded and sure about that?

NORA. Yes, completely. That's why I can't go on staying here.

HELMER. Can you tell me what I did to lose your love?

NORA. Yes, I can tell you. It was this evening when the miraculous thing didn't come—then I knew you weren't the man I'd imagined.

HELMER. Be more explicit; I don't follow you.

NORA. I've waited now so patiently eight long years—for, my Lord, I know miracles don't come every day. Then this crisis broke over me, and such a certainty filled me: *now* the miraculous event would occur. While Krogstad's letter was lying out there, I never for an instant dreamed that you could give in to his terms. I was so utterly sure you'd say to him: go on, tell your tale to the whole wide world. And when he'd done that—

HELMER. Yes, what then? When I'd delivered my own wife into shame and disgrace—!

NORA. When he'd done that, I was so utterly sure that you'd step forward, take the blame on yourself and say: I am the guilty one.

HELMER. Nora—!

NORA. You're thinking I'd never accept such a sacrifice from you? No, of course not. But what good would my protests be against you? That was the miracle I was waiting for, in terror and hope. And to stave that off, I would have taken my life.

HELMER. I'd gladly work for you day and night, Nora—and take on pain and deprivation. But there's no one who gives up honor for love.

NORA. Millions of women have done just that.

HELMER. Oh, you think and talk like a silly child.

NORA. Perhaps. But you neither think nor talk like the man I could join myself to. When your big fright was over—and it wasn't from any threat against me, only for what might damage you—when all the danger was past, for you it was just as if nothing had happened. I was exactly the same, your little lark, your doll, that you'd have to handle with double care now that I'd turned out so brittle and frail. (*Gets up.*) Torvald—in that instant it dawned on me that for eight years I've been living here with a stranger, and that I'd even conceived three children—oh, I can't stand the thought of it! I could tear myself to bits.

HELMER (*heavily*). I see. There's a gulf that's opened between us—that's clear. Oh, but Nora, can't we bridge it somehow?

NORA. The way I am now, I'm no wife for you.

HELMER. I have the strength to make myself over.

NORA. Maybe—if your doll gets taken away.

HELMER. But to part! To part from you! No, Nora, no—I can't imagine it.

NORA (*going out, right*). All the more reason why it has to be. (*She reenters with her coat and a small overnight bag, which she puts on a chair by the table.*)

HELMER. Nora, Nora, not now! Wait till tomorrow.

NORA. I can't spend the night in a strange man's room.

HELMER. But couldn't we live here like brother and sister—

NORA. You know very well how long that would last. (*Throws her shawl about her.*) Good-bye, Torvald. I won't look in on the children. I know they're in better hands than mine. The way I am now, I'm no use to them.

HELMER. But someday, Nora—someday—?

NORA. How can I tell? I haven't the least idea what'll become of me.

HELMER. But you're my wife, now and wherever you go.

NORA. Listen, Torvald—I've heard that when a wife deserts her husband's house just as I'm doing, then the law frees him from all responsibility. In any case, I'm freeing you from being responsible. Don't feel yourself bound, any more than I will. There has to be absolute freedom for us both. Here, take your ring back. Give me mine.

HELMER. That too?

NORA. That too.

HELMER. There it is.

NORA. Good. Well, now it's all over. I'm putting the keys here. The maids know all about keeping up the house—better than I do. Tomorrow, after I've left town, Kristine will stop by to pack up everything that's mine from home. I'd like those things shipped up to me.

HELMER. Over! All over! Nora, won't you ever think about me?

NORA. I'm sure I'll think of you often, and about the children and the house here.

HELMER. May I write you?
NORA. No—never. You're not to do that.
HELMER. Oh, but let me send you—
NORA. Nothing. Nothing.
HELMER. Or help you if you need it.
NORA. No. I accept nothing from strangers.
HELMER. Nora—can I never be more than a stranger to you?
NORA (*picking up the overnight bag*). Ah, Torvald—it would take the greatest miracle of all—
HELMER. Tell me the greatest miracle!
NORA. You and I both would have to transform ourselves to the point that— Oh, Torvald, I've stopped believing in miracles.
HELMER. But I'll believe. Tell me! Transform ourselves to the point that—?
NORA. That our living together could be a true marriage. (*She goes out down the hall.*)
HELMER (*sinks down on a chair by the door, face buried in his hands*). Nora! Nora! (*Looking about and rising.*) Empty. She's gone. (*A sudden hope leaps in him.*) The greatest miracle—?

(*From below, the sound of a door slamming shut.*)

DISCUSSION

The focus on Women's Liberation in the past few years has no doubt helped to inspire the recent revivals of *A Doll's House*. In the United States, such revivals have included a successful Broadway production, a major film, and a television special. Ibsen, however, might have been dismayed by the topical interest the play has lately received, for he maintained that his play was not about the rights of women but about everyone's right to fulfillment. Like most serious dramatists, he knew that a play based on a specific topical issue—such as, whether to give women the vote—would lose much of its impact once that issue was resolved. Ibsen was concerned with a bigger issue—the permanent, universal problem everyone has in trying to find fulfillment.

Nora is at first a rather flighty, coquettish, romantic young woman, given to playing the game her husband and society want her to play. She is not even aware of the game until her actions threaten its continuation —that is, until she tries to act as an independent person rather than as one of her husband's toys—his doll.

Many playgoers and readers find it hard to believe that Nora is capable of recognizing her doll-like status, rejecting it, and seriously pursuing genuine fulfillment. She does, after all, treat her own children as dolls; she is naive about practical matters, preferring romantic illusions to harsh realities; and she finds satisfaction in petty enjoyments (like her macaroons) and in small talk. Only after her sudden, rude awakening does she realize that she has never had a serious talk with her husband. Never before in all the years of their marriage has she recognized her husband's egotistical pursuit of his own career or his relegation of her to the status of a possession, incapable of independent thought, feeling, or action. With her previous behavior so much against her, it is very difficult to accept her transformation at the end of the play.

How does Ibsen make Nora's change believable? How can we accept the slamming door at the end of the play as anything more than another romantic gesture, a kind of childish defiance of conventional responsibility? Audiences of the first performances of the play in Europe were horrified that Nora could leave her children. Some people have even assumed that Ibsen purposely shows us an irresponsible, flighty young woman who gets carried away by her romantic notions. How can we know whether Ibsen wants us to take Nora seriously?

There is evidence both within and beyond the play that suggests that Nora is indeed to be taken seriously. She does not simply leave her children without having suffered greatly in anticipation of this separation. When she leaves, she knows that the nurse who raised her will continue to care for her children. Even the disappointment of discovering her husband's genuine attitude toward her sacrifice and independent action has been expected. She has been willing to commit suicide if necessary to prevent him from sacrificing his career for her. She has suffered greatly at the prospect of leaving her children and the life she has so adored. Though it horrifies her, she has come to accept the prospect of suicide because she believes, without question, that her husband loves her and will recognize the degree of her suffering and sacrifice on his behalf. When she discovers that he is interested only in the social and legal consequences of her forgery of her father's signature, her whole world collapses. She discovers that what she thought to be reality was only a dream. She sees that her identity as an independent, suffering being is the farthest thing from her husband's consciousness, that he thinks only of himself and of society's conventions. For the first time, she realizes that both her husband and society see her merely as an extension of his ego, not as a person in her own right. Given the immensity of this discovery and the immediate impact it has on her, Nora's final actions should not seem arbitrary to the careful reader or viewer of the play.

Several facts beyond the play also suggest that Nora is to be taken seriously. For example, in July, 1879, a month or so before he finished writing *A Doll's House,* Ibsen wrote a letter to Björnstjerne Björnson in which he asserted that the mission of "we poets" was "to awaken individuals to freedom and independence." It is difficult to imagine that with such thoughts on his mind as he was finishing *A Doll's House* he did not take Nora seriously.

A speech he had given a few months earlier also indicates that Ibsen intended Nora's behavior to exemplify the type of person who could awaken to the need for individual freedom and self-fulfillment. Just after he had begun to work on *A Doll's House,* in January, 1879, he gave an impassioned speech before the Scandinavian Club of Rome, exhorting the club members to reject their traditional treatment of women and the young. He asked the members to vote out the rules that barred women from employment by the club and kept them and the young from voting in club elections. He argued that as impractical and untried as women and the young were considered to be, they had something better than practical wisdom and experience, something they shared "with the true artist," an "instinctive genius which unconsciously hits at the right answer" to the most complex issues. "I fear," said Ibsen, "women, youth and inexperience as little as I fear the true artist. What I do fear is the wordly wisdom of the old." This speech should give us some indication of Ibsen's general concerns and of his significance to us today. Many of the dissenters of the late 1960s could have written it, as could some of today's fighters for the rights of women, students, and other groups who feel that society denies their identity.

THEME AND DISCUSSION QUESTIONS

1. What evidence is there that Nora is afraid to face reality?
2. What indications are there that Nora can be extremely romantic, or even egotistical?
3. In what ways is the tarantella danced in the play symbolic of the general situation depicted by Ibsen? What other symbolic details do you see in the play?
4. What purpose does the Mrs. Linde–Krogstad relationship serve in the play?
5. What evidence is there that Nora's decision to leave is not as sudden as it may at first seem?
6. How does the character of Dr. Rank contribute to the development of the play?
7. In what ways are some of the basic principles of the current Women's Liberation movement evident in *A Doll's House?*
8. Many feminists maintain that the liberation of women will mean the liberation of men as well. What are the ways in which Nora's liberation might also help Torvald?

9. Two opposing interpretations of Nora have been widely proposed: one says that Ibsen idealized her, the other, that he satirized her. What evidence do you see for each interpretation?
10. Can the two opposing interpretations of Nora described above be reconciled? Using specific information from the play, explain why Ibsen might have deliberately provided two such opposing sets of data about her.
11. Nora tells Torvald that there is a chance that she may come back to him in time. How remote is that possibility? How would Nora have to change? How would Torvald have to change?

Miss Julie: Production directed by Leila Blake, at Lyric Theatre, Hammersmith, England (1960); starring Diane Cilento, Pamela Pitchford, and Leon Peers. Photograph, by Angus McBean, courtesy of the Harvard Theatre Collection.

AUGUST STRINDBERG

Miss Julie

August Strindberg, who was born in Stockholm, Sweden, in 1849 and died in 1912, ranks with Ibsen as one of the great innovators of modern drama. A sufferer of melancholia throughout his adult life, Strindberg approached playwriting with an intense awareness of the power of subjective experience. He grasped, perhaps even more willingly than Ibsen, the value of expressionism in portraying the subjective life of any human being. Thus, even his most naturalistic plays, such as *The Father* (1887), are naked articulations of the unspoken thoughts and feelings that the social and theatrical conventions of his day ordinarily kept hidden. At his best—in *Miss Julie* (1888), *Dance of Death* (1901), or the *Ghost Sonata* (1907), for example—Strindberg goes dynamically beyond naturalism, presenting not only the concrete facts of everyday life but the subjective, grotesque vitality that lies beneath them. In so doing, he sets the ground rules demonstrated later in this collection by the plays of Giraudoux and Bullins and followed as well by such contemporary dramatists as Beckett, Ionesco, and Genêt. Just as Ibsen is considered the "father of modern drama," so may Strindberg be rightfully considered its greatest exponent.

MISS JULIE   Reprinted by permission of Collins-Knowlton-Wing, Inc. Copyright © 1955 by Elizabeth Sprigge.

CHARACTERS

Miss Julie, *aged 25*
Jean, *the valet, aged 30*
Kristin, *the cook, aged 35*

Scene. *The large kitchen of a Swedish manor house in a country district in the eighties.*

Midsummer eve.

The kitchen has three doors, two small ones into Jean's *and* Kristin's *bedrooms, and a large, glass-fronted double one, opening on to a court-yard. This is the only way to the rest of the house. Through these glass doors can be seen part of a fountain with a cupid, lilac bushes in flower and the tops of some Lombardy poplars. On one wall are shelves edged with scalloped paper on which are kitchen utensils of copper, iron and tin. To the left is the corner of a large tiled range and part of its chimneyhood, to the right the end of the servants' dinner table with chairs beside it. The stove is decorated with birch boughs, the floor strewn with twigs of juniper. On the end of the table is a large Japanese spice jar full of lilac. There are also an ice-box, a scullery table and a sink. Above the double door hangs a big old-fashioned bell; near it is a speaking-tube. A fiddle can be heard from the dance in the barn near-by.* Kristin *is standing at the stove, frying something in a pan. She wears a light-coloured cotton dress and a big apron.*

(Jean *enters, wearing livery and carrying a pair of large riding-boots with spurs, which he puts in a conspicuous place.*)

Jean. Miss Julie's crazy again to-night, absolutely crazy.

Kristin. Oh, so you're back, are you?

Jean. When I'd taken the Count to the station, I came back and dropped in at the Barn for a dance. And who did I see there but our young lady leading off with the gamekeeper. But the moment she sets eyes on me, up she rushes and invites me to waltz with her. And how she waltzed—I've never seen anything like it! She's crazy.

Kristin. Always has been, but never so bad as this last fortnight since the engagement was broken off.

Jean. Yes, that was a pretty business, to be sure. He's a decent enough chap, too, even if he isn't rich. Oh, but they're choosy! (*Sits down at the end of the table.*) In any case, it's a bit odd that our young—er—lady would rather stay at home with the yokels than go with her father to visit her relations.

Kristin. Perhaps she feels a bit awkward, after that bust-up with her fiancé.

Jean. Maybe. That chap had some guts, though. Do you know the sort of thing that was going on, Kristin? I saw it with my own eyes, though I didn't let on I had.

KRISTIN. You saw them . . . ?

JEAN. Didn't I just! Came across the pair of them one evening in the stable-yard. Miss Julie was doing what she called "training" him. Know what that was? Making him jump over her riding-whip—the way you teach a dog. He did it twice and got a cut each time for his pains, but when it came to the third go, he snatched the whip out of her hand and broke it into smithereens. And then he cleared off.

KRISTIN. What goings on! I never did!

JEAN. Well, that's how it was with that little affair . . . Now, what have you got for me, Kristin? Something tasty?

KRISTIN (*serving from the pan to his plate*). Well, it's just a little bit of kidney I cut off their joint.

JEAN (*smelling it*). Fine! That's my special delice. (*Feels the plate.*) But you might have warmed the plate.

KRISTIN. When you choose to be finicky you're worse than the Count himself. (*Pulls his hair affectionately.*)

JEAN (*crossly*). Stop pulling my hair. You know how sensitive I am.

KRISTIN. There, there! It's only love, you know.

(JEAN *eats.* KRISTIN *brings a bottle of beer.*)

JEAN. Beer on Midsummer Eve? No thanks! I've got something better than that. (*From a drawer in the table brings out a bottle of red wine with a yellow seal.*) Yellow seal, see! Now get me a glass. You use a glass with a stem of course when you're drinking it straight.

KRISTIN (*giving him a wine-glass*). Lord help the woman who gets you for a husband, you old fusser! (*She puts the beer in the ice-box and sets a small saucepan in the stove.*)

JEAN. Nonsense! You'll be glad enough to get a fellow as smart as me. And I don't think it's done you any harm people calling me your fiancé. (*Tastes the wine.*) Good. Very good indeed. But not quite warmed enough. (*Warms the glass in his hand.*) We bought this in Dijon. Four francs the litre without the bottle, and duty on top of that. What are you cooking now? It stinks.

KRISTIN. Some bloody muck Miss Julie wants for Diana.

JEAN. You should be more refined in your speech, Kristin. But why should you spend a holiday cooking for that bitch? Is she sick or what?

KRISTIN. Yes, she's sick. She sneaked out with the pug at the lodge and got in the usual mess. And that, you know, Miss Julie won't have.

JEAN. Miss Julie's too high-and-mighty in some respects, and not enough in others, just like her mother before her. The Countess was more at home in the kitchen and cowsheds than anywhere else, but would she ever go driving with only one horse? She went round with her cuffs filthy, but she had to have the coronet on the cuff-links. Our young lady—to come back to her—hasn't any proper respect for herself or her position. I mean she isn't refined. In the Barn just now she dragged the gamekeeper away from Anna and made him dance with her—no waiting to be asked. We wouldn't do a thing like that. But that's what happens when the gentry try to behave like the common people—they become common . . . Still she's a fine girl. Smashing! What shoulders! And what—er—etcetera!

KRISTIN. Oh come off it! I know what Clara says, and she dresses her.

JEAN. Clara? Pooh, you're all jealous! But I've been out riding with her . . . and as for her dancing!

KRISTIN. Listen, Jean. You will dance with me, won't you, as soon as I'm through.

JEAN. Of course I will.

KRISTIN. Promise?

JEAN. Promise? When I say I'll do a thing I do it. Well, thanks for the supper. It was a real treat. (*Corks the bottle.*)

(JULIE *appears in the doorway, speaking to someone outside.*)

JULIE. I'll be back in a moment. Don't wait. (JEAN *slips the bottle into the drawer and rises respectfully.* JULIE *enters and joins* KRISTIN *at the stove.*) Well, have you made it?

(KRISTIN *signs that* JEAN *is near them.*)

JEAN (*gallantly*). Have you ladies got some secret?

JULIE (*flipping his face with her handkerchief*). You're very inquisitive.

JEAN. What a delicious smell! Violets.

JULIE (*coquettishly*). Impertinence! Are you an expert of scent too? I must say you know how to dance. Now don't look. Go away.

(*The music of a schottische begins.*)

JEAN (*with impudent politeness*). Is it some witches' brew you're cooking on Midsummer Eve? Something to tell your stars by, so you can see your future?

JULIE (*sharply*). If you could see that you'd have good eyes. (*To* KRISTIN.) Put it in a bottle and cork it tight. Come and dance this schottische with me, Jean.

JEAN (*hesitating*). I don't want to be rude, but I've promised to dance this one with Kristin.

JULIE. Well, she can have another, can't you, Kristin? You'll lend me Jean, won't you?

KRISTIN (*bottling*). It's nothing to do with me. When you're so condescending, Miss, it's not his place to say no. Go on, Jean, and thank Miss Julie for the honour.

JEAN. Frankly speaking, Miss, and no offence meant, I wonder if it's wise for you to dance twice running with the same partner, specially as those people are so ready to jump to conclusions.

JULIE (*flaring up*). What did you say? What sort of conclusions? What do you mean?

JEAN (*meekly*). As you choose not to understand, Miss Julie, I'll have to speak more plainly. It looks bad to show a preference for one of your retainers when they're all hoping for the same unusual favour.

JULIE. Show a preference! The very idea! I'm surprised at you. I'm doing the people an honour by attending their ball when I'm mistress of the house, but if I'm really going to dance, I mean to have a partner who can lead and doesn't make me look ridiculous.

JEAN. If those are your orders, Miss, I'm at your service.

JULIE (*gently*). Don't take it as an order. To-night we're all just people enjoying a party. There's no question of class. So now give me your arm. Don't worry, Kristin. I shan't steal your sweetheart.

(JEAN *gives* JULIE *his arm and leads her out.*)

(*Left alone,* KRISTIN *plays her scene in an unhurried, natural way, humming to the tune of the schottische, played on a distant violin. She clears* JEAN'S *place, washes up and puts things away, then takes off her apron, brings out a small mirror from a drawer, props it against the jar of lilac, lights a candle, warms a small pair of tongs and curls her fringe. She goes to the door and listens, then turning back to the table finds* MISS JULIE'S *forgotten handkerchief. She smells it, then meditatively smooths it out and folds it.*)

(Enter JEAN.)

JEAN. She really *is* crazy. What a way to dance! With people standing grinning at her too from behind the doors. What's got into her, Kristin?

KRISTIN. Oh, it's just her time coming on. She's always queer then. Are you going to dance with me now?

JEAN. Then you're not wild with me for cutting that one.

KRISTIN. You know I'm not—for a little thing like that. Besides, I know my place.

JEAN (*putting his arm round her waist*). You're a sensible girl, Kristin, and you'll make a very good wife . . .

(Enter JULIE, *unpleasantly surprised.*)

JULIE (*with forced gaiety*). You're a fine beau—running away from your partner.

JEAN. Not away, Miss Julie, but as you see back to the one I deserted.

JULIE (*changing her tone*). You really can dance, you know. But why are you wearing your livery on a holiday. Take it off at once.

JEAN. Then I must ask you to go away for a moment, Miss. My black coat's here. (*Indicates it hanging on the door to his room.*)

JULIE. Are you so shy of me—just over changing a coat? Go into your room then—or stay here and I'll turn my back.

JEAN. Excuse me then, Miss. (*He goes to his room and is partly visible as he changes his coat.*)

JULIE. Tell me, Kristin, is Jean your fiancé? You seem very intimate.

KRISTIN. My fiancé? Yes, if you like. We call it that.

JULIE. Call it?

KRISTIN. Well, you've had a fiancé yourself, Miss, and . . .

JULIE. But we really were engaged.

KRISTIN. All the same it didn't come to anything.

(JEAN *returns in his black coat.*)

JULIE. Très gentil, Monsieur Jean. Très gentil.

JEAN. Vous voulez plaisanter, Madame.

JULIE. Et vous voulez parler français. Where did you learn it?

JEAN. In Switzerland, when I was sommelier at one of the biggest hotels in Lucerne.

JULIE. You look quite the gentleman in that get-up. Charming. (*Sits at the table.*)

JEAN. Oh, you're just flattering me!

JULIE (*annoyed*). Flattering you?

JEAN. I'm too modest to believe you would pay real compliments to a man like me, so I must take it you are exaggerating—that this is what's known as flattery.

JULIE. Where on earth did you learn to make speeches like that? Perhaps you've been to the theatre a lot.

JEAN. That's right. And travelled a lot too.

JULIE. But you come from this neighbourhood, don't you?

JEAN. Yes, my father was a labourer on the next estate—the District Attorney's place. I often used to see you, Miss Julie, when you were little, though you never noticed me.

JULIE. Did you really?

JEAN. Yes. One time specially I remember . . . but I can't tell you about that.

JULIE. Oh do! Why not? This is just the time.

JEAN. No, I really can't now. Another time perhaps.

JULIE. Another time means never. What harm in now?

JEAN. No harm, but I'd rather not. (*Points to* KRISTIN, *now fast asleep.*) Look at her.

JULIE. She'll make a charming wife, won't she? I wonder if she snores.
JEAN. No, she doesn't, but she talks in her sleep.
JULIE (*cynically*). How do you know she talks in her sleep?
JEAN (*brazenly*). I've heard her.

(*Pause. They look at one another.*)

JULIE. Why don't you sit down?
JEAN. I can't take such a liberty in your presence.
JULIE. Supposing I order you to.
JEAN. I'll obey.
JULIE. Then sit down. No, wait a minute. Will you get me a drink first?
JEAN. I don't know what's in the ice-box. Only beer, I expect.
JULIE. There's no only about it. My taste is so simple I prefer it to wine.

(JEAN *takes a bottle from the ice-box, fetches a glass and plate and serves the beer.*)

JEAN. At your service.
JULIE. Thank you. Won't you have some yourself?
JEAN. I'm not really a beer-drinker, but if it's an order . . .
JULIE. Order? I should have thought it was ordinary manners to keep your partner company.
JEAN. That's a good way of putting it. (*He opens another bottle and fetches a glass.*)
JULIE. Now drink my health. (*He hesitates.*) I believe the man really is shy.

(JEAN *kneels and raises his glass with mock ceremony.*)

JEAN. To the health of my lady!
JULIE. Bravo! Now kiss my shoe and everything will be perfect. (*He hesitates, then boldly takes hold of her foot and lightly kisses it.*) Splendid. You ought to have been an actor.
JEAN (*rising*). We can't go on like this, Miss Julie. Someone might come in and see us.
JULIE. Why would that matter?
JEAN. For the simple reason that they'd talk. And if you knew the way their tongues were wagging out there just now, you . . .
JULIE. What were they saying? Tell me. Sit down.
JEAN (*sitting*). No offense meant, Miss, but . . . well, their language wasn't nice, and they were hinting . . . oh, you know quite well what. You're not a child, and if a lady's seen drinking alone at night with a man—and a servant at that—then . . .

AUGUST STRINDBERG

JULIE. Then what? Besides, we're not alone. Kristin's here.
JEAN. Yes, asleep.
JULIE. I'll wake her up. (*Rises.*) Kristin, are you asleep? (KRISTIN *mumbles in her sleep.*) Kristin! Goodness, how she sleeps!

KRISTIN (*in her sleep*). The Count's boots are cleaned—put the coffee on—yes, yes, at once . . . (*Mumbles incoherently.*)

JULIE (*tweaking her nose*). Wake up, can't you!
JEAN (*sharply*). Let her sleep.
JULIE. What?
JEAN. When you've been standing at the stove all day you're likely to be tired at night. And sleep should be respected.
JULIE (*changing her tone*). What a nice idea. It does you credit. Thank you for it. (*Holds out her hand to him.*) Now come out and pick some lilac for me.

(*During the following* KRISTIN *goes sleepily in to her bedroom.*)

JEAN. Out with you, Miss Julie?
JULIE. Yes.
JEAN. It wouldn't do. It really wouldn't.
JULIE. I don't know what you mean. You can't possibly imagine that . . .
JEAN. I don't, but others do.
JULIE. What? That I'm in love with the valet?
JEAN. I'm not a conceited man, but such a thing's been known to happen, and to these rustics nothing's sacred.
JULIE. You, I take it, are an aristocrat.
JEAN. Yes, I am.
JULIE. And I am coming down in the world.
JEAN. Don't come down, Miss Julie. Take my advice. No one will believe you came down of your own acccord. They'll all say you fell.
JULIE. I have a higher opinion of our people than you. Come and put it to the test. Come on. (*Gazes into his eyes.*)
JEAN. You're very strange, you know.
JULIE. Perhaps I am, but so are you. For that matter everything is strange. Life, human beings, everything, just scum drifting about on the water until it sinks—down and down. That reminds me of a dream I sometimes have, in which I'm on top of a pillar and can't see any way of getting down. When I look down I'm dizzy; I have to get down but I haven't the courage to jump. I can't stay there and I long to fall, but I don't fall. There's no respite. There can't be any peace at all for me until I'm down, right down on the ground. And if I did get to the ground I'd want to be under the ground . . . Have you ever felt like that?

JEAN. No. In my dream I'm lying under a great tree in a dark wood. I want to get up, up to the top of it, and look out over the bright landscape where the sun is shining and rob that high nest of its golden eggs. And I climb and climb, but the trunk is so thick and smooth and it's so far to the first branch. But I know if I can once reach that first branch I'll go to the top just as if I'm on a ladder. I haven't reached it yet, but I shall get there, even if only in my dreams.

JULIE. Here I am chattering about dreams with you. Come on. Only into the park. (*She takes his arm and they go towards the door.*)

JEAN. We must sleep on nine midsummer flowers tonight; then our dreams will come true, Miss Julie. (*They turn at the door. He has a hand to his eye.*)

JULIE. Have you got something in your eye? Let me see.

JEAN. Oh, it's nothing. Just a speck of dust. It'll be gone in a minute.

JULIE. My sleeve must have rubbed against you. Sit down and let me see to it. (*Takes him by the arm and makes him sit down, bends his head back and tries to get the speck out with the corner of her handkerchief.*) Keep still now, quite still. (*Slaps his hand.*) Do as I tell you. Why, I believe you're trembling, big, strong man though you are! (*Feels his biceps.*) What muscles!

JEAN (*warning*). Miss Julie!

JULIE. Yes, Monsieur Jean?

JEAN. Attention. Je ne suis qu'un homme.

JULIE. Will you stay still! There now. It's out. Kiss my hand and say thank you.

JEAN (*rising*). Miss Julie, listen. Kristin's gone to bed now. Will you listen?

JULIE. Kiss my hand first.

JEAN. Very well, but you'll have only yourself to blame.

JULIE. For what?

JEAN. For what! Are you still a child at twenty-five? Don't you know it's dangerous to play with fire?

JULIE. Not for me. I'm insured.

JEAN (*bluntly*). No, you're not. And even if you are, there's still stuff here to kindle a flame.

JULIE. Meaning yourself?

JEAN. Yes. Not because I'm me, but because I'm a man and young and . . .

JULIE. And good-looking? What incredible conceit! A Don Juan perhaps? Or a Joseph? Good Lord, I do believe you are a Joseph!

JEAN. Do you?

JULIE. I'm rather afraid so. (JEAN *goes boldly up and tries to put his arms round her and kiss her. She boxes his ears.*) How dare you!

JEAN. Was that in earnest or a joke?

JULIE. In earnest.

JEAN. Then what went before was in earnest too. You take your games too seriously and that's dangerous. Anyhow I'm tired of playing now and beg leave to return to my work. The Count will want his boots first thing and it's past midnight now.

JULIE. Put those boots down.

JEAN. No. This is my work, which it's my duty to do. But I never undertook to be your playfellow and I never will be. I consider myself too good for that.

JULIE. You're proud.

JEAN. In some ways—not all.

JULIE. Have you even been in love?

JEAN. We don't put it that way, but I've been gone on quite a few girls. And once I went sick because I couldn't have the one I wanted. Sick, I mean, like those princes in the Arabian Nights who couldn't eat or drink for love.

JULIE. Who was she? (*No answer.*) Who was she?

JEAN. You can't force me to tell you that.

JULIE. If I ask as an equal, ask as a—friend? Who was she?

JEAN. You.

JULIE (*sitting*). How absurd!

JEAN. Yes, ludicrous if you like. That's the story I wouldn't tell you before, see, but now I will . . . Do you know what the world looks like from below? No, you don't. No more than the hawks and falcons do whose backs one hardly ever sees because they're always soaring up aloft. I lived in a labourer's hovel with seven other children and a pig, out in the grey fields where there isn't a single tree. But from the window I could see the wall round the Count's park with apple-trees above it. That was the Garden of Eden, guarded by many terrible angels with flaming swords. All the same I and the other boys managed to get to the tree of life. Does all this make you despise me?

JULIE. Goodness, all boy steal apples!

JEAN. You say that now, but all the same you do despise me. However, one time I went into the Garden of Eden with my mother to weed the onion beds. Close to the kitchen garden there was a Turkish pavilion hung all over with jasmine and honeysuckle. I hadn't any idea what it was used for, but I'd never seen such a beautiful building. People used to go in and then come out again, and one day the door was left open. I crept up and saw the walls covered with pictures of kings and emperors, and the windows had red curtains with fringes—you know now what the place was, don't you? I . . . (*Breaks off a piece of lilac and holds it for* JULIE *to smell. As he talks, she takes it from him.*) I had never been inside the manor, never seen anything but the church, and this was more beautiful. No matter where my thoughts went, they always came back—to that place. The longing went on growing in me to enjoy it fully, just once. Enfin, I sneaked in, gazed and admired. Then I heard someone coming. There was only one way out for the gentry, but for me there was another and I had no choice but to take it. (JULIE *drops the lilac on the table.*) Then I took to my heels, plunged through the raspberry canes, dashed across the strawberry beds and found myself on the rose terrace. There I saw a pink dress and a pair of white stockings—it was you. I crawled into a weed pile and lay there right under it among prickly thistles and damp rank earth. I watched you walking among the roses and said to myself: "If it's true that a thief can get to heaven and be with the angels, it's pretty strange that a labourer's child here on God's earth mayn't come in the park and play with the Count's daughter."

JULIE (*sentimentally*). Do you think all poor children feel the way you did?

JEAN (*taken aback, then rallying*). *All* poor children? . . . Yes, of course they do. Of course.

JULIE. It must be terrible to be poor.

JEAN (*with exaggerated distress*). Oh yes, Miss Julie, yes. A dog may lie on the Countess's sofa, a horse may have his nose stroked by a young lady, but a servant . . . (*change of tone*) well, yes, now and then you meet one with guts enough to rise in the world, but how often? Anyhow, do you know what I did? Jumped in the millstream with my clothes on, was pulled out and got a hiding. But the next Sunday, when Father and all the rest went to Granny's, I managed to get left behind. Then I washed with soap and hot water, put my best clothes on and went to church so as to see you. I did see you and went home determined to die. But I wanted to die beautifully and peacefully, without any pain. Then I remembered it was dangerous to sleep under an elder bush. We had a big one in full bloom, so I stripped it and climbed into the oats-bin with the flowers. Have you ever noticed how smooth oats are? Soft to touch as human skin . . . Well, I closed the lid and shut my eyes, fell asleep, and when they woke me I was very ill. But I didn't die, as you see. What I mean by all that I don't know. There was no hope of winning you—you were simply a symbol of the hopelessness of ever getting out of the class I was born in.

JULIE. You put things very well, you know. Did you go to school?

JEAN. For a while. But I've read a lot of novels and been to the theatre. Besides, I've heard educated folk talking—that's what's taught me most.

JULIE. Do you stand round listening to what we're saying?

JEAN. Yes, of course. And I've heard quite a bit too! On the carriage box or rowing the boat. Once I heard you, Miss Julie, and one of your young lady friends . . .

JULIE. Oh! Whatever did you hear?

JEAN. Well, it wouldn't be nice to repeat it. And I must say I was pretty startled. I couldn't think where you had learnt such words. Perhaps, at bottom, there isn't as much difference between people as one's led to believe.

JULIE. How dare you! We don't behave as you do when we're engaged.

JEAN. (*looking hard at her*). Are you sure? It's no use making out so innocent to me.

JULIE. The man I gave my love to was a rotter.

JEAN. That's what you always say—afterwards.

JULIE. Always?

JEAN. I think it must be always. I've heard the expression several times in similar circumstances.

JULIE. What circumstances?

JEAN. Like those in question. The last time . . .

JULIE (*rising*). Stop. I don't want to hear any more.

JEAN. Nor did she—curiously enough. May I go to bed now please?

JULIE (*gently*). Go to bed on Midsummer Eve?

JEAN. Yes. Dancing with that crowd doesn't really amuse me.

JULIE. Get the key of the boathouse and row me out on the lake. I want to see the sun rise.

JEAN. Would that be wise?

JULIE. You sound as though you're frightened for your reputation.

JEAN. Why not? I don't want to be made a fool of, nor to be sent packing without a character when I'm trying to better myself. Besides, I have Kristin to consider.

JULIE. So now it's Kristin.

JEAN. Yes, but it's you I'm thinking about too. Take my advice and go to bed.

JULIE. Am I to take orders from you?

JEAN. Just this one, for your own sake. Please. It's very late and sleepiness goes to one's head and makes one rash. Go to bed. What's more, if my ears don't deceive me, I hear people coming this way. They'll be looking for me, and if they find us here, you're done for.

(*The* CHORUS *approaches, singing. During the following dialogue the song is heard in snatches, and in full when the peasants enter.*)

> Out of the wood two women came,
> Tridiri-ralla, tridiri-ra.
> The feet of one were bare and cold,
> Tridiri-ralla-la.
>
> The other talked of bags of gold,
> Tridiri-ralla, tridiri-ra.
> But neither had a sou to her name,
> Tridiri-ralla-la

> The bridal wreath I give to you,
> Tridiri-ralla, tridiri-ra.
> But to another I'll be true,
> Tridiri-ralla-la

JULIE. I know our people and I love them, just as they do me. Let them come. You'll see.

JEAN. No, Miss Julie, they don't love you. They take your food, then spit at it. You must believe me. Listen to them, just listen to what they're singing . . . No, don't listen.

JULIE (*listening*). What are they singing?

JEAN. They're mocking—you and me.

JULIE. Oh no! How horrible! What cowards!

JEAN. A pack like that's always cowardly. But against such odds there's nothing we can do but run away.

JULIE. Run away? Where to? We can't get out and we can't go into Kristin's room.

JEAN. Into mine then. Necessity knows no rules. And you can trust me. I really am your true and devoted friend.

JULIE. But supposing . . . supposing they were to look for you in there?

JEAN. I'll bolt the door, and if they try to break in I'll shoot. Come on. (*Pleading.*) Please come.

JULIE (*tensely*). Do you promise . . . ?

JEAN. I swear!

(JULIE *goes quickly into his room and he excitedly follows her.*)

(*Led by the fiddler, the peasants enter in festive attire with flowers in their hats. They put a barrel of beer and a keg of spirits, garlanded with leaves, on the table, fetch glasses and begin to carouse. The scene becomes a ballet. They form a ring and dance and sing and mime:* "Out of the wood two women came." *Finally they go out, still singing.*)

(JULIE *comes in alone. She looks at the havoc in the kitchen, wrings her hands, then takes out her powder puff and powders her face.*)

(JEAN *enters in high spirits.*)

JEAN. Now you see! And you heard, didn't you? Do you still think it's possible for us to stay here?

JULIE. No, I don't. But what can we do?

JEAN. Run away. Far away. Take a journey.

JULIE. Journey? But where to?

JEAN. Switzerland. The Italian lakes. Ever been there?

JULIE. No. Is it nice?

JEAN. Ah! Eternal summer, oranges, evergreens ... ah!
JULIE. But what would we do there?
JEAN. I'll start a hotel. First-class accommodation and first-class customers.
JULIE. Hotel?
JEAN. There's life for you. New faces all the time, new languages—no time for nerves or worries, no need to look for something to do—work rolling up of its own accord. Bells ringing night and day, trains whistling, buses coming and going, and all the time gold pieces rolling on to the counter. There's life for you!
JULIE. For *you*. And I?
JEAN. Mistress of the house, ornament of the firm. With your looks, and your style ... oh, it's bound to be a success! Terrific! You'll sit like a queen in the office and set your slaves in motion by pressing an electric button. The guests will file past your throne and nervously lay their treasure on your table. You've no idea the way people tremble when they get their bills. I'll salt the bills and you'll sugar them with your sweetest smiles. Ah, let's get away from here! (*Produces a time-table.*) At once, by the next train. We shall be at Malmö at six-thirty, Hamburg eight-forty next morning, Frankfurt-Basle the following day, and Como by the St. Gothard pass in—let's see—three days. Three days!
JULIE. That's all very well. But Jean, you must give me courage. Tell me you love me. Come and take me in your arms.
JEAN (*reluctantly*). I'd like to, but I daren't. Not again in this house. I love you—that goes without saying. You can't doubt that, Miss Julie, can you?
JULIE (*shyly, very feminine*). Miss? Call me Julie. There aren't any barriers between us now. Call me Julie.
JEAN (*uneasily*). I can't. As long as we're in this house, there *are* barriers between us. There's the past and there's the Count. I've never been so servile to anyone as I am to him. I've only got to see his gloves on a chair to feel small. I've only to hear his bell and I shy like a horse. Even now, when I look at his boots, standing there so proud and stiff, I feel my back beginning to bend. (*Kicks the boots.*) It's those old, narrow-minded notions drummed into us as children ... but they can soon be forgotten. You've only got to get to another country, a republic, and people will bend themselves double before my porter's livery. Yes, double they'll bend themselves, but I shan't. I wasn't born to bend. I've got guts, I've got character, and once I reach that first branch, you'll watch me climb. Today I'm valet, next year I'll be proprietor, in ten years I'll have made a fortune, and then I'll go to Roumania, get myself decorated and I may, I only say *may*, mind you, end up as a Count.

JULIE (*sadly*). That would be very nice.

JEAN. You see in Roumania one can buy a title, and then you'll be a Countess after all. My Countess.

JULIE. What do I care about all that? I'm putting those things behind me. Tell me you love me, because if you don't . . . if you don't, what am I?

JEAN. I'll tell you a thousand times over—later. But not here. No sentimentality now or everything will be lost. We must consider this thing calmly like reasonable people. (*Takes a cigar, cuts and lights it.*) You sit down there and I'll sit here and we'll talk as if nothing has happened.

JULIE. My God, have you no feelings at all?

JEAN. Nobody has more. But I know how to control them.

JULIE. A short time ago you were kissing my shoe. And now . . .

JEAN (*harshly*). Yes, that was then. Now we have something else to think about.

JULIE. Don't speak to me so brutally.

JEAN. I'm not. Just sensibly. One folly's been committed, don't let's have more. The Count will be back at any moment and we've got to settle our future before that. Now, what do you think of my plans? Do you approve?

JULIE. It seems a very good idea—but just one thing. Such a big undertaking would need a lot of capital. Have you got any?

JEAN (*chewing his cigar*). I certainly have. I've got my professional skill, my wide experience and my knowledge of foreign languages. That's capital worth having, it seems to me.

JULIE. But it won't buy even one railway ticket.

JEAN. Quite true. That's why I need a backer to advance some ready cash.

JULIE. How could you get that at a moment's notice?

JEAN. You must get it, if you want to be my partner.

JULIE. I can't. I haven't any money of my own.

(*Pause.*)

JEAN. Then the whole thing's off.

JULIE. And . . . ?

JEAN. We go on as we are.

JULIE. Do you think I'm going to stay under this roof as your mistress? With everyone pointing at me. Do you think I can face my father after this? No. Take me away from here, away from this shame, this humiliation. Oh my God, what have I done? My God, my God! (*Weeps.*)

JEAN. So that's the tune now, is it? What have you done? Same as many before you.

JULIE (*hysterically*). And now you despise me. I'm falling, I'm falling.

JEAN. Fall as far as me and I'll lift you up again.

JULIE. Why was I so terribly attracted to you? The weak to the strong, the falling to the rising? Or was it love? Is that love? Do you know what love is?

JEAN. Do I? You bet I do. Do you think I never had a girl before?

JULIE. The things you say, the things you think!

JEAN. That's what life's taught me, and that's what I am. It's no good getting hysterical or giving yourself airs. We're both in the same boat now. Here, my dear girl, let me give you a glass of something special. (*Opens the drawer, takes out the bottle of wine and fills two used glasses.*)

JULIE. Where did you get that wine?

JEAN. From the cellar.

JULIE. My father's burgundy.

JEAN. Why not, for his son-in-law?

JULIE. And I drink beer.

JEAN. That only shows your taste's not so good as mine.

JULIE. Thief!

JEAN. Are you going to tell on me?

JULIE. Oh God! The accomplice of a petty thief! Was I blind drunk? Have I dreamt this whole night? Midsummer Eve, the night for innocent merrymaking.

JEAN. Innocent, eh?

JULIE. Is anyone on earth as wretched as I am now?

JEAN. Why should *you* be? After such a conquest. What about Kristin in there? Don't you think she has any feelings?

JULIE. I did think so, but I don't any longer. No. A menial is a menial...

JEAN. And a whore is a whore.

JULIE (*falling to her knees, her hands clasped*). O God in heaven, put an end to my miserable life! Lift me out of this filth in which I'm sinking. Save me! Save me!

JEAN. I must admit I'm sorry for you. When I was in the onion bed and saw you up there among the roses, I... yes, I'll tell you now... I had the same dirty thoughts as all boys.

JULIE. You, who wanted to die because of me?

JEAN. In the oats-bin? That was just talk.

JULIE. Lies, you mean.

JEAN (*getting sleepy*). More or less. I think I read a story in some paper about a chimney-sweep who shut himself up in a chest full of lilac because he'd been summonsed for not supporting some brat...

JULIE. So this is what you're like.

JEAN. I had to think up something. It's always the fancy stuff that catches the women.

JULIE. Beast!

JEAN. Merde!
JULIE. Now you have seen the falcon's back.
JEAN. Not exactly its *back*.
JULIE. I was to be the first branch.
JEAN. But the branch was rotten.
JULIE. I was to be a hotel sign.
JEAN. And I the hotel.
JULIE. Sit at your counter, attract your clients and cook their accounts.
JEAN. I'd have done that myself.
JULIE. That any human being can be so steeped in filth!
JEAN. Clean it up then.
JULIE. Menial! Lackey! Stand up when I speak to you.
JEAN. Menial's whore, lackey's harlot, shut your mouth and get out of here! Are you the one to lecture me for being coarse? Nobody of my kind would ever be as coarse as you were tonight. Do you think any servant girl would throw herself at a man that way? Have you ever seen a girl of my class asking for it like that? I haven't. Only animals and prostitutes.

JULIE (*broken*). Go on. Hit me, trample on me—it's all I deserve. I'm rotten. But help me! If there's any way out at all, help me.

JEAN (*more gently*). I'm not denying myself a share in the honour of seducing you, but do you think anybody in my place would have dared look in your direction if you yourself hadn't asked for it? I'm still amazed...

JULIE. And proud.

JEAN. Why not? Though I must admit the victory was too easy to make me lose my head.

JULIE. Go on hitting me.

JEAN (*rising*). No. On the contrary I apologise for what I've said. I don't hit a person who's down—least of all a woman. I can't deny there's a certain satisfaction in finding that what dazzled one below was just moonshine, that that falcon's back is grey after all, that there's powder on the lovely cheek, that polished nails can have black tips, that the handkerchief is dirty although it smells of scent. On the other hand it hurts to find that what I was struggling to reach wasn't high and isn't real. It hurts to see you fallen so low you're far lower than your own cook. Hurts like when you see the last flowers of summer lashed to pieces by rain and turned to mud.

JULIE. You're talking as if you're already my superior.

JEAN. I am. I might make you a Countess, but you could never make me a Count, you know.

JULIE. But I am the child of a Count, and you could never be that.

JEAN. True, but I might be the father of Counts if...

JULIE. You're a thief. I'm not.

JEAN. There are worse things than being a thief—much lower. Besides, when I'm in a place I regard myself as a member of the family to some extent, as one of the children. You don't call it stealing when children pinch a berry from overladen bushes. (*His passion is roused again.*) Miss Julie, you're a glorious woman, far too good for a man like me. You were carried away by some kind of madness, and now you're trying to cover up your mistake by persuading yourself you're in love with me. You're not, although you may find me physically attractive, which means your love's no better than mine. But I wouldn't be satisfied with being nothing but an animal for you, and I could never make you love me.

JULIE. Are you sure?

JEAN. You think there's a chance? Of my loving you, yes, of course. You're beautiful, refined—(*takes her hand*)—educated, and you can be nice when you want to be. The fire you kindle in a man isn't likely to go out. (*Puts his arm round her.*) You're like mulled wine, full of spices, and your kisses . . . (*He tries to pull her to him, but she breaks away.*)

JULIE. Let go of me! You won't win me that way.

JEAN. Not that way, how then? Not by kisses and fine speeches, not by planning the future and saving you from shame? How then?

JULIE. How? How? I don't know. There isn't any way. I loathe you—loathe you as I loathe rats, but I can't escape from you.

JEAN. Escape with me.

JULIE (*pulling herself together*). Escape? Yes, we must escape. But I'm so tired. Give me a glass of wine. (*He pours it out. She looks at her watch.*) First we must talk. We still have a little time. (*Empties the glass and holds it out for more.*)

JEAN. Don't drink like that. You'll get tipsy.

JULIE. What's that matter?

JEAN. What's it matter? It's vulgar to get drunk. Well, what have you got to say?

JULIE. We've got to run away, but we must talk first—or rather, I must, for so far you've done all the talking. You've told me about your life, now I want to tell you about mine, so that we really know each other before we begin this journey together.

JEAN. Wait. Excuse my saying so, but don't you think you may be sorry afterwards if you give away your secrets to me?

JULIE. Aren't you my friend?

JEAN. On the whole. But don't rely on me.

JULIE. You can't mean that. But anyway everyone knows my secrets. Listen. My mother wasn't well-born; she came of quite humble people, and was brought up with all those new ideas of sex-equality and women's rights and so on. She thought marriage was quite wrong. So when my father proposed to her, she said she would never become his *wife* . . . but in the end she did. I came into the world, as far as I can make out, against my mother's will, and I was left to run wild, but I had to do all the things a boy does—

to prove women are as good as men. I had to wear boys' clothes; I was taught to handle horses—and I wasn't allowed in the dairy. She made me groom and harness and go out hunting; I even had to try to plough. All the men on the estate were given the women's jobs, and the women the men's, until the whole place went to rack and ruin and we were the laughing-stock of the neighbourhood. At last my father seems to have come to his senses and rebelled. He changed everything and ran the place his own way. My mother got ill—I don't know what was the matter with her, but she used to have strange attacks and hide herself in the attic or the garden. Sometimes she stayed out all night. Then came the great fire which you have heard people talking about. The house and the stables and the barns—the whole place burnt to the ground. In very suspicious circumstances. Because the accident happened the very day the insurance had to be renewed, and my father had sent the new premium, but through some carelessness of the messenger it arrived too late. (*Refills her glass and drinks.*)

JEAN. Don't drink any more.

JULIE. Oh, what does it matter? We were destitute and had to sleep in the carriages. My father didn't know how to get money to rebuild, and then my mother suggested he should borrow from an old friend of hers, a local brick manufacturer. My father got the loan and, to his surprise, without having to pay interest. So the place was rebuilt. (*Drinks.*) Do you know who set fire to it?

JEAN. Your lady mother.

JULIE. Do you know who the brick manufacturer was?

JEAN. Your mother's lover?

JULIE. Do you know whose the money was?

JEAN. Wait . . . no, I don't know that.

JULIE. It was my mother's.

JEAN. In other words the Count's, unless there was a settlement.

JULIE. There wasn't any settlement. My mother had a little money of her own which she didn't want my father to control, so she invested it with her—friend.

JEAN. Who grabbed it.

JULIE. Exactly. He appropriated it. My father came to know all this. He couldn't bring an action, couldn't pay his wife's lover, nor prove it was his wife's money. That was my mother's revenge because he made himself master in his own house. He nearly shot himself then—at least there's a rumour he tried and didn't bring it off. So he went on living, and my mother had to pay dearly for what she'd done. Imagine what those five years were like for me. My natural sympathies were with my father, yet I took my mother's side, because I didn't know the facts. I'd learnt from her to hate and distrust men—you know how she loathed the whole male sex. And I swore to her I'd never become the slave of any man.

AUGUST STRINDBERG   243

JEAN. And so you got engaged to that attorney.
JULIE. So that he should be my slave.
JEAN. But he wouldn't be.
JULIE. Oh yes, he wanted to be, but he didn't have the chance. I got bored with him.
JEAN. Is that what I saw—in the stable-yard?
JULIE. What did you see?
JEAN. What I saw was him breaking off the engagement.
JULIE. That's a lie. It was I who broke it off. Did he say it was him? The cad.
JEAN. He's not a cad. Do you hate men, Miss Julie?
JULIE. Yes . . . most of the time. But when that weakness comes, oh . . . the shame!
JEAN. Then do you hate me?
JULIE. Beyond words. I'd gladly have you killed like an animal.
JEAN. Quick as you'd shoot a mad dog, eh?
JULIE. Yes.
JEAN. But there's nothing here to shoot with—and there isn't a dog. So what do we do now?
JULIE. Go abroad.
JEAN. To make each other miserable for the rest of our lives?
JULIE. No, to enjoy ourselves for a day or two, for a week, for as long as enjoyment lasts, and then—to die . . .
JEAN. Die? How silly! I think it would be far better to start a hotel.
JULIE (*without listening*). . . . die on the shores of Lake Como, where the sun always shines and at Christmas time there are green trees and glowing oranges.
JEAN. Lake Como's a rainy hole and I didn't see any oranges outside the shops. But it's a good place for tourists. Plenty of villas to be rented by—er—honeymoon couples. Profitable business that. Know why? Because they all sign a lease for six months and all leave after three weeks.
JULIE (*naïvely*). After three weeks? Why?
JEAN. They quarrel, of course. But the rent has to be paid just the same. And then it's let again. So it goes on and on, for there's plenty of love although it doesn't last long.
JULIE. You don't want to die with me?
JEAN. I don't want to die at all. For one thing I like living and for another I consider suicide's a sin against the Creator who gave us life.
JULIE. You believe in God—*you?*
JEAN. Yes, of course. And I go to church every Sunday. Look here, I'm tired of all this. I'm going to bed.
JULIE. Indeed! And do you think I'm going to leave things like this? Don't you know what you owe the woman you've ruined?

JEAN (*taking out his purse and throwing a silver coin on the table*). There you are. I don't want to be in anybody's debt.

JULIE (*pretending not to notice the insult*). Don't you know what the law is?

JEAN. There's no law unfortunately that punishes a woman for seducing a man.

JULIE. But can you see anything for it but to go abroad, get married and then divorce?

JEAN. What if I refuse this mésalliance?

JULIE. Mésalliance?

JEAN. Yes, for me. I'm better bred than you, see! Nobody in my family committed arson.

JULIE. How do you know?

JEAN. Well, you can't prove otherwise, because we haven't any family records outside the Registrar's office. But I've seen your family tree in that book on the drawing-room table. Do you know who the founder of your family was? A miller who let his wife sleep with the King one night during the Danish war. I haven't any ancestors like that. I haven't any ancestors at all, but I might become one.

JULIE. This is what I get for confiding in someone so low, for sacrificing my family honour . . .

JEAN. Dishonour! Well, I told you so. One shouldn't drink, because then one talks. And one shouldn't talk.

JULIE. Oh, how ashamed I am, how bitterly ashamed! If at least you loved me!

JEAN. Look here—for the last time—what do you want? Am I to burst into tears? Am I to jump over your riding whip? Shall I kiss you and carry you off to Lake Como for three weeks, after which . . . What am I to do? What do you want? This is getting unbearable, but that's what comes of playing around with women. Miss Julie, I can see how miserable you are; I know you're going through hell, but I don't understand you. We don't have scenes like this; we don't go in for hating each other. We make love for fun in our spare time, but we haven't all day and all night for it like you. I think you must be ill. I'm sure you're ill.

JULIE. Then you must be kind to me. You sound almost human now.

JEAN. Well, be human yourself. You spit at me, then won't let me wipe it off—on you.

JULIE. Help me, help me! Tell me what to do, where to go.

JEAN. Jesus, as if I knew!

JULIE. I've been mad, raving mad, but there must be a way out.

JEAN. Stay here and keep quiet. Nobody knows anything.

JULIE. I can't. People do know. Kristin knows.

JEAN. They don't know and they wouldn't believe such a thing.

JULIE (*hesitating*). But—it might happen again.

JEAN. That's true.

JULIE. And there might be—consequences.

JEAN (*in panic*). Consequences! Fool that I am I never thought of that. Yes, there's nothing for it but to go. At once. I can't come with you. That would be a complete giveaway. You must go alone—abroad—anywhere.

JULIE. Alone? Where to? I can't.

JEAN. You must. And before the Count gets back. If you stay, we know what will happen. Once you've sinned you feel you might as well go on, as the harm's done. Then you get more and more reckless and in the end you're found out. No. You must go abroad. Then write to the Count and tell him everything, except that it was me. He'll never guess that—and I don't think he'll want to.

JULIE. I'll go if you come with me.

JEAN. Are you crazy, woman? "Miss Julie elopes with valet." Next day it would be in the headlines, and the Count would never live it down.

JULIE. I can't go. I can't stay. I'm so tired, so completely worn out. Give me orders. Set me going. I can't think any more, can't act . . .

JEAN. You see what weaklings you are. Why do you give yourselves airs and turn up your noses as if you're the lords of creation? Very well, I'll give you your orders. Go upstairs and dress. Get money for the journey and come down here again.

JULIE (*softly*). Come up with me.

JEAN. To your room? Now you've gone crazy again. (*Hesitates a moment.*) No! Go along at once. (*Takes her hand and pulls her to the door.*)

JULIE (*as she goes*). Speak kindly to me, Jean.

JEAN. Orders always sound unkind. Now you know. Now you know.

(*Left alone,* JEAN *sighs with relief, sits down at the table, takes out a note-book and pencil and adds up figures, now and then aloud. Dawn begins to break.* KRISTIN *enters dressed for church, carrying his white dickey and tie.*)

KRISTIN. Lord Jesus, look at the state the place is in! What have you been up to? (*Turns out the lamp.*)

JEAN. Oh, Miss Julie invited the crowd in. Did you sleep through it? Didn't you hear anything?

KRISTIN. I slept like a log.

JEAN. And dressed for church already.

KRISTIN. Yes, you promised to come to Communion with me today.

JEAN. Why, so I did. And you've got my bib and tucker, I see. Come on then. (*Sits.* KRISTIN *begins to put his things on. Pause. Sleepily.*) What's the lesson today?

KRISTIN. It's about the beheading of John the Baptist, I think.

JEAN. That's sure to be horribly long. Hi, you're choking me! Oh Lord, I'm so sleepy, so sleepy!

KRISTIN. Yes, what have you been doing up all night? You look absolutely green.

JEAN. Just sitting here talking with Miss Julie.

KRISTIN. She doesn't know what's proper, that one.

(*Pause.*)

JEAN. I say, Kristin.

KRISTIN. What?

JEAN. It's queer really, isn't it, when you come to think of it? Her.

KRISTIN. What's queer?

JEAN. The whole thing.

(*Pause.*)

KRISTIN (*looking at the half-filled glasses on the table*). Have you been drinking together too?

JEAN. Yes.

KRISTIN. More shame you. Look me straight in the face.

JEAN. Yes.

KRISTIN. Is it possible? Is it possible?

JEAN (*after a moment*). Yes, it is.

KRISTIN. Oh! This I would never have believed. How low!

JEAN. You're not jealous of her, surely?

KRISTIN. No, I'm not. If it had been Clara or Sophie I'd have scratched your eyes out. But not of her. I don't know why; that's how it is though. But it's disgusting.

JEAN. You're angry with her then.

KRISTIN. No. With you. It was wicked of you, very wicked. Poor girl. And, mark my words, I won't stay here any longer now—in a place where one can't respect one's employers.

JEAN. Why should one respect them?

KRISTIN. You should know since you're so smart. But you don't want to stay in the service of people who aren't respectable, do you? I wouldn't demean myself.

JEAN. But it's rather a comfort to find out they're no better than us.

KRISTIN. I don't think so. If they're no better there's nothing for us to live up to. Oh and think of the Count! Think of him. He's been through so much already. No, I won't stay in the place any longer. A fellow like you too! If it had been that attorney now or somebody of her own class...

JEAN. Why, what's wrong with...

KRISTIN. Oh, you're all right in your own way, but when all's said and done there is a difference between one class and another. No, this is something I'll never be able to stomach. That our young lady who was so proud and so down on men you'd never believe she'd let one come near her should go and give herself to one like you. She who wanted to have poor Diana shot for running after the lodge-keeper's pug. No, I must say . . . ! Well, I won't stay here any longer. On the twenty-fourth of October I quit.

JEAN. And then?

KRISTIN. Well, since you mention it, it's about time you began to look around, if we're ever going to get married.

JEAN. But what am I to look for? I shan't get a place like this when I'm married.

KRISTIN. I know you won't. But you might get a job as porter or caretaker in some public institution. Government rations are small but sure, and there's a pension for the widow and children.

JEAN. That's all very fine, but it's not in my line to start thinking at once about dying for my wife and children. I must say I had rather bigger ideas.

KRISTIN. You and your ideas! You've got obligations too, and you'd better start thinking about them.

JEAN. Don't *you* start pestering me about obligations. I've had enough of that. (*Listens to a sound upstairs.*) Anyway we've plenty of time to work things out. Go and get ready now and we'll be off to church.

KRISTIN. Who's that walking about upstairs?

JEAN. Don't know—unless it's Clara.

KRISTIN (*going*). You don't think the Count could have come back without our hearing him.

JEAN (*scared*). The Count? No, he can't have. He'd have rung for me.

KRISTIN. God help us! I've never known such goings on. (*Exit.*)

(*The sun has now risen and is shining on the treetops. The light gradually changes until it slants in through the windows.* JEAN *goes to the door and beckons.* JULIE *enters in travelling clothes, carrying a small bird-cage covered with a cloth which she puts on a chair.*)

JULIE. I'm ready.

JEAN. Hush! Kristin's up.

JULIE (*in a very nervous state*). Does she suspect anything?

JEAN. Not a thing. But, my God, what a sight you are!

JULIE. Sight? What do you mean?

JEAN. You're white as a corpse and—pardon me—your face is dirty.

JULIE. Let me wash then. (*Goes to the sink and washes her face and hands.*) There. Give me a towel. Oh! The sun is rising!

JEAN. And that breaks the spell.

JULIE. Yes. The spell of Midsummer Eve . . . But listen, Jean. Come with me. I've got the money.

JEAN (*sceptically*). Enough?

JULIE. Enough to start with. Come with me. I can't travel alone today. It's Midsummer Day, remember. I'd be packed into a suffocating train among crowds of people who'd all stare at me. And it would stop at every station while I yearned for wings. No, I can't do that, I simply can't. There will be memories too; memories of Midsummer Days when I was little. The leafy church—birch and lilac—the gaily spread dinner table, relatives, friends—evening in the park—dancing and music and flowers and fun. Oh, however far you run away—there'll always be memories in the baggage car—and remorse and guilt.

JEAN. I will come with you, but quickly now then, before it's too late. At once.

JULIE. Put on your things. (*Picks up the cage.*)

JEAN. No luggage mind. That would give us away.

JULIE. No, only what we can take with us in the carriage.

JEAN (*fetching his hat*). What on earth have you got there? What is it?

JULIE. Only my greenfinch. I don't want to leave it behind.

JEAN. Well, I'll be damned! We're to take a bird-cage along, are we? You're crazy. Put that cage down.

JULIE. It's the only thing I'm taking from my home. The only living creature who cares for me since Diana went off like that. Don't be cruel. Let me take it.

JEAN. Put that cage down, I tell you—and don't talk so loud. Kristin will hear.

JULIE. No, I won't leave it in strange hands. I'd rather you killed it.

JEAN. Give the little beast here then and I'll wring its neck.

JULIE. But don't hurt it, don't . . . no, I can't.

JEAN. Give it here. I *can*.

JULIE (*taking the bird out of the cage and kissing it*). Dear little Serena, must you die and leave your mistress?

JEAN. Please don't make a scene. It's *your* life and future we're worrying about. Come on, quick now! (*He snatches the bird from her, puts it on a board and picks up a chopper.* JULIE *turns away*.) You should have learnt how to kill chickens instead of target-shooting. Then you wouldn't faint at a drop of blood.

JULIE (*screaming*). Kill me too! Kill me! You who can butcher an innocent creature without a quiver. Oh, how I hate you, how I loathe you! There is blood between us now. I curse the hour I first saw you. I curse the hour I was conceived in my mother's womb.

JEAN. What's the use of cursing. Let's go.

JULIE (*going to the chopping-block as if drawn against her will*). No, I won't go yet. I can't . . . I must look. Listen! There's a carriage. (*Listens without taking her eyes off the board and chopper.*) You don't think I can bear the sight of blood. You think I'm so weak. Oh, how I should like to see your blood and your brains on a chopping-block! I'd like to see the whole of your sex swimming like that in a sea of blood. I think I could drink out of your skull, bathe my feet in your broken breast and eat your heart roasted whole. You think I'm weak. You think I love you, that my womb yearned for your seed and I want to carry your offspring under my heart and nourish it with my blood. You think I want to bear your child and take your name. By the way, what is your name? I've never heard your surname. I don't suppose you've got one. I should be "Mrs. Hovel" or "Madam Dunghill." You dog wearing my collar, you lackey with my crest on your buttons! I share you with my cook; I'm my own servant's rival! Oh! Oh! Oh! . . . You think I'm a coward and will run away. No, now I'm going to stay—and let the storm break. My father will come back . . . find his desk broken open . . . his money gone. Then he'll ring that bell—twice for the valet—and then he'll send for the police . . . and I shall tell everything. Everything. Oh how wonderful to make an end of it all—a real end! He has a stroke and dies and that's the end of all of us. Just peace and quietness . . . eternal rest. The coat of arms broken on the coffin and the Count's line extinct . . . But the valet's line goes on in an orphanage, wins laurels in the gutter and ends in jail.

JEAN. There speaks the noble blood! Bravo, Miss Julie. But now, don't let the cat out of the bag.

(KRISTIN *enters dressed for church, carrying a prayer-book.* JULIE *rushes to her and flings herself into her arms for protection.*)

JULIE. Help me, Kristin! Protect me from this man!

KRISTIN (*unmoved and cold*). What goings-on for a feast day morning! (*Sees the board.*) And what a filthy mess. What's it all about? Why are you screaming and carrying on so?

JULIE. Kristin, you're a woman and my friend. Beware of that scoundrel!

JEAN (*embarrassed*). While you ladies are talking things over, I'll go and shave. (*Slips into his room.*)

JULIE. You must understand. You must listen to me.

KRISTIN. I certainly don't understand such loose ways. Where are you off to in those travelling clothes? And he had his hat on, didn't he, eh?

JULIE. Listen, Kristin. Listen, I'll tell you everything.

KRISTIN. I don't want to know anything.

JULIE. You must listen.

KRISTIN. What to? Your nonsense with Jean? I don't care a rap about that; it's nothing to do with me. But if you're thinking of getting him to run off with you, we'll soon put a stop to that.

JULIE (*very nervously*). Please try to be calm, Kristin, and listen. I can't stay here, nor can Jean—so we must go abroad.

KRISTIN. Hm, hm!

JULIE (*brightening*). But you see, I've had an idea. Supposing we all three go—abroad—to Switzerland and start a hotel together . . . I've got some money, you see . . . and Jean and I could run the whole thing—and I thought you would take charge of the kitchen. Wouldn't that be splendid? Say yes, do. If you come with us everything will be fine. Oh do say yes! (*Puts her arms round* KRISTIN.)

KRISTIN (*coolly thinking*). Hm, hm.

JULIE (*presto tempo*). You've never travelled, Kristin. You should go abroad and see the world. You've no idea how nice it is travelling by train—new faces all the time and new countries. On our way through Hamburg we'll go to the zoo—you'll love that—and we'll go to the theatre and the opera too . . . and when we get to Munich there'll be the museums, dear, and pictures by Rubens and Raphael—the great painters, you know . . . You've heard of Munich, haven't you? Where King Ludwig lived—you know, the king who went mad. . . . We'll see his castles—some of his castles are still just like in fairy-tales . . . and from there it's not far to Switzerland—and the Alps. Think of the Alps, Kristin dear, covered with snow in the middle of summer . . . and there are oranges there and trees that are green the whole year round . . . (JEAN *is seen in the door of his room, sharpening his razor on a strop which he holds with his teeth and his left hand. He listens to the talk with satisfaction and now and then nods approval.* JULIE *continues, tempo prestissimo.*) And then we'll get a hotel . . . and I'll sit at the desk, while Jean receives the guests and goes out marketing and writes letters . . . There's life for you! Trains whistling, buses driving up, bells ringing upstairs and downstairs . . . and I shall make out the bills—and I shall cook them too . . . you've no idea how nervous travellers are when it comes to paying their bills. And you—you'll sit like a queen in the kitchen . . . of course there won't be any standing at the stove for you. You'll always have to be nicely dressed and ready to be seen, and with your looks—no, I'm not flattering you—one fine day you'll catch yourself a husband . . . some rich Englishman, I shouldn't wonder—they're the ones who are easy—(*slowing down*)—to catch . . . and then we'll get rich and build ourselves a villa on Lake Como . . . of course it rains there a little now and then—but—(*dully*)—the sun must shine there too sometimes—even though it seems gloomy—and if not—then we can come home again—come back—(*pause*)—here—or somewhere else . . .

KRISTIN. Look here, Miss Julie, do you believe all that yourself?

JULIE (*exhausted*). Do I believe it?

KRISTIN. Yes.

JULIE (*wearily*). I don't know. I don't believe anything any more. (*Sinks down on the bench; her head in her arms on the table.*) Nothing. Nothing at all.

KRISTIN (*turning to* JEAN). So you meant to beat it, did you?

JEAN (*disconcerted, putting the razor on the table*). Beat it? What are you talking about? You've heard Miss Julie's plan, and though she's tired now with being up all night, it's a perfectly sound plan.

KRISTIN. Oh, is it? If you thought I'd work for that . . .

JEAN (*interrupting*). Kindly use decent language in front of your mistress. Do you hear?

KRISTIN. Mistress?

JEAN. Yes.

KRISTIN. Well, well, just listen to that!

JEAN. Yes, it would be a good thing if you did listen and talked less. Miss Julie is your mistress and what's made you lose your respect for her now ought to make you feel the same about yourself.

KRISTIN. I've always had enough self-respect—

JEAN. To despise other people.

KRISTIN. —not to go below my own station. Has the Count's cook ever gone with the groom or the swineherd? Tell me that.

JEAN. No, you were lucky enough to have a high-class chap for your beau.

KRISTIN. High-class all right—selling the oats out of the Count's stable.

JEAN. You're a fine one to talk—taking a commission on the groceries and bribes from the butcher.

KRISTIN. What the devil . . . ?

JEAN. And now you can't feel any respect for your employers. You, you!

KRISTIN. Are you coming to church with me? I should think you need a good sermon after your fine deeds.

JEAN. No, I'm not going to church today. You can go alone and confess your own sins.

KRISTIN. Yes, I'll do that and bring back enough forgiveness to cover yours too. The Saviour suffered and died on the cross for all our sins, and if we go to Him with faith and a penitent heart, He takes all our sins upon Himself.

JEAN. Even grocery thefts?

JULIE. Do you believe that, Kristin?

KRISTIN. That is my living faith, as sure as I stand here. The faith I learnt as a child and have kept ever since, Miss Julie. "But where sin abounded, grace did much more abound."

JULIE. Oh, if I had your faith! Oh, if . . .

KRISTIN. But you see you can't have it without God's special grace, and it's not given to all to have that.

JULIE. Who is it given to then?

KRISTIN. That's the great secret of the workings of grace, Miss Julie. God is no respecter of persons, and with Him the last shall be first . . .

JULIE. Then I suppose He does respect the last.

KRISTIN (*continuing*). . . . and it is easier for a camel to go through the eye of a needle than for a rich man to enter into the kingdom of God. That's how it is, Miss Julie. Now I'm going—alone, and on my way I shall tell the groom not to let any of the horses out, in case anyone should want to leave before the Count gets back. Goodbye. (*Exit.*)

JEAN. What a devil! And all on account of a greenfinch.

JULIE (*wearily*). Never mind the greenfinch. Do you see any way out of this, any end to it?

JEAN (*pondering*). No.

JULIE. If you were in my place, what would you do?

JEAN. In your place? Wait a bit. If I was a woman—a lady of rank who had—fallen. I don't know. Yes, I do know now.

JULIE (*picking up the razor and making a gesture*). This?

JEAN. Yes. But *I* wouldn't do it, you know. There's a difference between us.

JULIE. Because you're a man and I'm a woman? What is the difference?

JEAN. The usual difference—between man and woman.

JULIE (*holding the razor*). I'd like to. But I can't. My father couldn't either, that time he wanted to.

JEAN. No, he didn't want to. He had to be revenged first.

JULIE. And now my mother is revenged again, through me.

JEAN. Didn't you ever love your father, Miss Julie?

JULIE. Deeply, but I must have hated him too—unconsciously. And he let me be brought up to despise my own sex, to be half woman, half man. Whose fault is what's happened? My father's, my mother's or my own? I haven't anything that's my own. I haven't one single thought that I didn't get from my father, one emotion that didn't come from my mother, and as for this last idea—about all people being equal—I got that from him, my fiancé—that's why I call him a cad. How can it be my fault? Push the responsibility on to Jesus, like Kristin does? No, I'm too proud and—thanks to my father's teaching—too intelligent. As for all that about a rich person not being able to get into heaven, it's just a lie, but Kristin, who has money in the savings-bank, will certainly not get in. Whose fault is it? What does it matter whose fault it is? In any case I must take the blame and bear the consequences.

JEAN. Yes, but . . . (*There are two sharp rings on the bell.* JULIE *jumps to her feet.* JEAN *changes into his livery.*) The Count is back. Supposing Kristin . . . (*Goes to the speaking-tube, presses it and listens.*)

JULIE. Has he been to his desk yet?

JEAN. This is Jean, sir. (*Listens.*) Yes, sir. (*Listens.*) Yes, sir, very good, sir. (*Listens.*) At once, sir? (*Listens.*) Very good, sir. In half an hour.

JULIE (*in panic*). What did he say? My God, what did he say?

JEAN. He ordered his boots and his coffee in half an hour.

JULIE. Then there's half an hour . . . Oh, I'm so tired! I can't do anything. Can't be sorry, can't run away, can't stay, can't live—can't die. Help me. Order me, and I'll obey like a dog. Do me this last service—save my honour, save his name. You know what I ought to do, but haven't the strength to do. Use your strength and order me to do it.

JEAN. I don't know why—I can't now—I don't understand . . . It's just as if this coat made me—I can't give you orders—and now that the Count has spoken to me—I can't quite explain, but . . . well, that devil of a lackey is bending my back again. I believe if the Count came down now and ordered me to cut my throat, I'd do it on the spot.

JULIE. Then pretend you're him and I'm you. You did some fine acting before, when you knelt to me and played the aristocrat. Or . . . Have you ever seen a hypnotist at the theatre? (*He nods.*) He says to the person "Take the broom," and he takes it. He says "Sweep," and he sweeps . . .

JEAN. But the person has to be asleep.

JULIE (*as if in a trance*). I am asleep already . . . the whole room has turned to smoke—and you look like a stove—a stove like a man in black with a tall hat—your eyes are glowing like coals when the fire is low—and your face is a white patch of ashes. (*The sunlight has now reached the floor and lights up* JEAN.) How nice and warm it is! (*She holds out her hands as though warming them at a fire.*) And so light—and so peaceful.

JEAN (*putting the razor in her hand*). Here is the broom. Go now while it's light—out to the barn—and . . . (*Whispers in her ear.*)

JULIE (*waking*). Thank you. I am going now—to rest. But just tell me that even the first can receive the gift of grace.

JEAN. The first? No, I can't tell you that. But wait . . . Miss Julie, I've got it! You aren't one of the first any longer. You're one of the last.

JULIE. That's true. I'm one of the very last. I *am* the last. Oh! . . . But now I can't go. Tell me again to go.

JEAN. No, I can't now either. I can't.

JULIE. And the first shall be last.

JEAN. Don't think, don't think. You're taking my strength away too and making me a coward. What's that? I thought I saw the bell move . . . To be so frightened of a bell! Yes, but it's not just a bell. There's somebody behind it—a hand moving it—and something else moving the hand—and if you stop your ears—if you stop your ears—yes, then it rings louder than ever. Rings and rings until you answer—and then it's too late. Then the police come and . . . and . . . (*The bell rings twice loudly.* JEAN *flinches, then straightens himself up.*) It's horrible. But there's no other way to end it . . . Go!

(JULIE *walks firmly out through the door.*)

Miss Julie,
A Foreword

Theatre has long seemed to me—in common with much other art—a *Biblia Pauperum*, a Bible in pictures for those who cannot read what is written or printed; and I see the playwright as a lay preacher peddling the ideas of his time in popular form, popular enough for the middle-classes, mainstay of theatre audiences, to grasp the gist of the matter without troubling their brains too much. For this reason theatre has always been an elementary school for the young, the semi-educated and for women who still have a primitive capacity for deceiving themselves and letting themselves be deceived—who, that is to say, are susceptible to illusion and to suggestion from the author. I have therefore thought it not unlikely that in these days, when that rudimentary and immature thought-process operating through fantasy appears to be developing into reflection, research and analysis, that theatre, like religion, might be discarded as an outworn form for whose appreciation we lack the necessary conditions. This opinion is confirmed by the major crisis still prevailing in the theatres of Europe, and still more by the fact that in those countries of culture, producing the greatest thinkers of the age, namely England and Germany, drama—like other fine arts—is dead.

Some countries, it is true, have attempted to create a new drama by using the old forms with up-to-date contents, but not only has there been insufficient time for these new ideas to be popularized, so that the audience can grasp them, but also people have been so wrought up by the taking of sides that pure, disinterested appreciation has become impossible. One's deepest impressions are upset when an applauding or a hissing majority dominates as forcefully and openly as it can in the theatre. Moreover, as no new form has been devised for these new contents, the new wine has burst the old bottles.

In this play I have not tried to do anything new, for this cannot be done, but only to modernize the form to meet the demands which may, I think, be made on this art today. To this end I chose—or surrendered myself to—a theme which claims to be outside the controversial issues of today, since questions of social climbing or falling, of higher or lower, better or worse, of man and woman, are, have been and will be of lasting interest. When I took this theme from a true story told me some years ago, which made a deep impression, I saw it as a subject for tragedy, for as yet it is tragic to see one favoured by fortune go under, and still more to see a family heritage die out, although a time may come when we have grown so developed and enlightened that we shall view with indifference life's spectacle, now seeming so brutal, cynical and heartless. Then we shall have dispensed with those inferior, unreliable instruments of thought called feelings, which become harmful and superfluous as reasoning develops.

The fact that my heroine rouses pity is solely due to weakness: we cannot resist fear of the same fate overtaking us. The hyper-sensitive spectator may, it is true, go beyond this kind of pity, while the man with belief in the future may actually demand some suggestion for remedying the evil—in other words some kind of policy. But, to begin with, there is no such thing as absolute evil; the downfall of one family is the good fortune of another, which thereby gets a chance to rise, and, fortune being only comparative, the alternation of rising and falling is one of life's principal charms. Also, to the man of policy, who wants to remedy the painful fact that the bird of prey devours the dove, and lice the bird of prey, I should like to put the question: why should it be remedied? Life is not so mathematically idiotic as only to permit the big to eat the small, it happens just as often that the bee kills the lion or at least drives it mad.

That my tragedy depresses many people is their own fault. When we have grown strong as the pioneers of the French revolution, we shall be happy and relieved to see the national parks cleared of ancient rotting trees which have stood too long in the way of others equally entitled to a period of growth—as relieved as we are when an incurable invalid dies.

My tragedy "The Father" was recently criticised for being too sad—as if one wants cheerful tragedies! Everybody is clamouring for this supposed "joy of life," and theatre managers demand farces, as if the joy of life consisted in being ridiculous and portraying all human beings as suffering from St. Vitus's dance or total idiocy. I myself find the joy of life in its strong and cruel struggles, and my pleasure in learning, in adding to my knowledge. For this reason I have chosen for this play an unusual situation, but an instructive one—an exception, that is to say, but a great exception, one proving the rule, which will no doubt annoy all lovers of the commonplace. What will offend simple minds is that my plot is not simple, nor its point of view single. In real life an action— this, by the way, is a somewhat new discovery—is generally caused by a whole series of motives, more or less fundamental, but as a rule the spectator chooses just one of these—the one which his mind can most easily grasp or that does most credit to his intelligence. A suicide is committed. Business troubles, says the man of affairs. Unrequited love, say the women. Sickness, says the invalid. Despair, says the down-and-out. But it is possible that the motive lay in all or none of these directions, or that the dead man concealed his actual motive by revealing quite another, likely to reflect more to his glory.

I see Miss Julie's tragic fate to be the result of many circumstances: the mother's character, the father's mistaken upbringing of the girl, her own nature, and the influence of her fiancé on a weak, degenerate mind. Also, more directly, the festive mood of Midsummer Eve, her father's absence, her monthly indisposition, her pre-occupation with animals, the excitement of dancing, the magic of dusk, the strongly aphrodisiac influence of flowers, and finally the chance that drives the couple into a room alone—to which must be added the urgency of the excited man.

My treatment of the theme, moreover, is neither exclusively physiological nor psychological. I have not put the blame wholly on the inheritance from her mother, nor on her physical condition at the time, nor on immorality. I have not even preached a moral sermon; in the absence of a priest I leave this to the cook.

I congratulate myself on this multiplicity of motives as being up-to-date, and if others have done the same thing before me, then I congratulate myself on not being alone in my "paradoxes," as all innovations are called.

In regard to the drawing of the characters, I have made my people somewhat "characterless" for the following reasons. In the course of time the word character has assumed manifold meanings. It must have originally signified the dominating trait of the soul-complex, and this was confused with temperament. Later it became the middle-class term for the automaton, one whose nature had become fixed or who had adapted himself to a particular rôle in life. In fact a person who had ceased to grow was called a character, while one continuing to develop—the skilful navigator of life's river, sailing not with sheets set fast, but veering before the wind to luff again—was called characterless, in a derogatory sense, of course, because he was so hard to catch, classify and keep track of. This middle-class conception of the immobility of the soul was transferred to the stage where the middle-class has always ruled. A character came to signify a man fixed and finished: one who invariably appeared either drunk or jocular or melancholy, and characterization required nothing more than a physical defect such as a club-foot, a wooden leg, a red nose; or the fellow might be made to repeat some such phrase as: "That's capital!" or: "Barkis is willin'!" This simple way of regarding human beings still survives in the great Molière. Harpagon is nothing but a miser, although Harpagon might have been not only a miser, but also a first-rate financier, an excellent father and a good citizen. Worse still, his "failing" is a distinct advantage to his son-in-law and his daughter, who are his heirs, and who therefore cannot criticise him, even if they have to wait a while to get to bed. I do not believe, therefore, in simple stage character; and the summary judgments of authors—this man is stupid, that one brutal, this jealous, that stingy, and so forth—should be challenged by the Naturalists who know the richness of the soul-complex and realise that vice has a reverse side very much like virtue.

Because they are modern characters, living in a period of transition more feverishly hysterical than its predecessor at least, I have drawn my figures vacillating, disintegrated, a blend of old and new. Nor does it seem to me unlikely that, through newspapers and conversations, modern ideas may have filtered down to the level of the domestic servant.

My souls (characters) are conglomerations of past and present stages of civilization, bits from books and newspapers, scraps of humanity, rags and tatters of fine clothing, patched together as is the human soul. And I have added a little evolutionary history by making the weaker steal and repeat the words of the stronger, and by making the characters borrow ideas or "suggestions" from one another.

Miss Julie is a modern character, not that the half-woman, the man-hater, has not existed always, but because now that she has been discovered she has stepped to the front and begun to make a noise. The half-woman is a type who thrusts herself forward, selling herself nowadays for power, decorations, distinctions, diplomas, as formerly for money. The type implies degeneration; it is not a good type and it does not endure; but it can unfortunately transmit its misery, and degenerate men seem instinctively to choose their mates from among such women, and so they breed, producing offspring of indeterminate sex to whom life is torture. But fortunately they perish, either because they cannot come to terms with reality, or because their repressed instincts break out uncontrollably, or again because their hopes of catching up with men are shattered. The type is tragic, revealing a desperate fight against nature, tragic too in its Romantic inheritance now dissipated by Naturalism, which wants nothing but happiness—and for happiness strong and sound species are required.

But Miss Julie is also a relic of the old warrior nobility now giving way to the new nobility of nerve and brain. She is a victim of the discord which a mother's "crime" has produced in a family, a victim too of the day's complaisance, of circumstances, of her own defective constitution, all of which are equivalent to the Fate or Universal Law of former days. The Naturalist has abolished guilt with God, but the consequences of the action—punishment, imprisonment or the fear of it—he cannot abolish, for the simple reason that they remain whether he is acquitted or not. An injured fellow-being is not so complacent as outsiders, who have not been injured, can afford to be. Even if the father had felt impelled to take no vengeance, the daughter would have taken vengeance on herself, as she does here, from that innate or acquired sense of honour which the upper-classes inherit—whether from Barbarism or Aryan forebears, or from the chivalry of the Middle Ages, who knows? It is a very beautiful thing, but it has become a danger nowadays to the preservation of the race. It is the nobleman's *hara-kiri*, the Japanese law of inner conscience which compels him to cut his own stomach open at the insult of another, and which survives in modified form in the duel, a privilege of the nobility. And so the valet Jean lives on, but Miss Julie cannot live without honour. This is the thrall's advantage over the nobleman, that he lacks this fatal preoccupation with honour. And in all of us Aryans there is something of the nobleman, or the Don Quixote, which makes us sympathize with the man who commits suicide because he has done something ignoble and lost his honour. And we are noblemen enough to suffer at the sight of fallen greatness littering the earth like a corpse—yes, even if the fallen rise again and make restitution by honourable deeds. Jean, the valet, is a race-builder, a man of marked characteristics. He was a labourer's son who has educated himself towards becoming a gentleman. He has learnt easily, through his well-developed senses (smell, taste, vision)—and he also has a sense of beauty. He has already bettered himself, and is thick-skinned enough to have no scruples about using other people's services. He is already foreign to his associates, despising them as part of the life he has turned his back on, yet also fearing and fleeing from them because they know his secrets, pry into his plans, watch his rise with envy, and look forward with pleasure to his fall. Hence his dual, indeterminate character, vacillating between love of the heights and hatred of those who have already achieved them. He is, he says himself, an aristocrat; he has learned the secrets of good society. He is polished, but vulgar within; he already wears his tails with taste, but there is no guarantee of his personal cleanliness.

He has some respect for his young lady, but he is frightened of Kristin, who knows his dangerous secrets, and he is sufficiently callous not to allow the night's events to wreck his plans for the future. Having both the slave's brutality and the master's lack of squeamishness, he can see blood without fainting and take disaster by the horns. Consequently he emerges from the battle unscathed, and probably ends his days as a hotel-keeper. And even if *he* does not become a Roumanian Count, his son will doubtless go to the university and perhaps become a county attorney.

The light which Jean sheds on a lower-class conception of life, life seen from below, is on the whole illuminating—when he speaks the truth, which is not often, for he says what is favourable to himself rather than what is true. When Miss Julie suggests that the lower-classes must be oppressed by the attitude of their superiors, Jean naturally agrees, as his object is to gain her sympathy; but when he perceives the advantage of separating himself from the common herd, he at once takes back his words.

It is not because Jean is now rising that he has the upper hand of Miss Julie, but because he is a man. Sexually he is the aristocrat because of his virility, his keener senses and his capacity for taking the initiative. His inferiority is mainly due to the social environment in which he lives, and he can probably shed it with his valet's livery.

The slave mentality expresses itself in his worship of the Count (the boots), and his religious superstition; but he worships the Count chiefly because he holds that higher position for which Jean himself is striving. And this worship remains even when he has won the daughter of the house and seen how empty is that lovely shell.

I do not believe that a love relationship in the "higher" sense could exist between two individuals of such different quality, but I have made Miss Julie imagine that she is in love, so as to lessen her sense of guilt, and I let Jean suppose that if his social position were altered he would truly love her. I think love is like the hyacinth which has to strike roots in darkness *before* it can produce a vigorous flower. In this case it shoots up quickly, blossoms and goes to seed all at the same time, which is why the plant dies so soon.

As for Kristin, she is a female slave, full of servility and sluggishness acquired in front of the kitchen fire, and stuffed full of morality and religion, which are her cloak and scape-goat. She goes to church as a quick and easy way of unloading her household thefts on to Jesus and taking on a fresh cargo of guiltlessness. For the rest she is a minor character, and I have therefore sketched her in the same manner as the Pastor and the Doctor in "The Father," where I wanted ordinary human beings, as are most country pastors and provincial doctors. If these minor characters seem abstract to some people this is due to the fact that ordinary people are to a certain extent abstract in pursuit of their work; that is to say, they are without individuality, showing, while working, only one side of themselves. And as long as the spectator does not feel a need to see them from other sides, there is nothing wrong with my abstract presentation.

In regard to the dialogue, I have departed somewhat from tradition by not making my characters catechists who ask stupid questions in order to elicit a smart reply. I have avoided the symmetrical, mathematical construction of French dialogue, and let people's minds work irregularly, as they do in real life where, during a conversation, no topic is drained to the dregs, and one mind finds in another a chance cog to engage in. So too the dialogue wanders, gathering in the opening scenes material which is later picked up, worked over, repeated, expounded and developed like the theme in a musical composition.

The plot speaks for itself, and as it really only concerns two people, I have concentrated on these, introducing only one minor character, the cook, and keeping the unhappy spirit of the father above and behind the action. I have done this because it seems to me that the psychological process is what interests people most today. Our inquisitive souls are no longer satisfied with seeing a thing happen; we must also know how it happens. We want to see the wires themselves, to watch the machinery, to examine the box with the false bottom, to take hold of the magic ring in order to find the join, and look at the cards to see how they are marked.

In this connection I have had in view the documentary novels of the brothers de Goncourt, which appeal to me more than any other modern literature.

As far as the technical side of the work is concerned I have made the experiment of abolishing the division into acts. This is because I have come to the conclusion that our capacity for illusion is disturbed by the intervals, during which the audience has time to reflect and escape from the suggestive influence of the author-hypnotist. My play will probably take an hour and a half, and as one can listen to a lecture, a sermon or a parliamentary debate for as long as that or longer, I do not think a theatrical performance will be fatiguing in the same length of time. As early as 1872, in one of my first dramatic attempts, "The Outlaw," I tried this concentrated form, although with scant success. The play was written in five acts, and only when finished did I become aware of the restless, disjointed effect that it produced. The script was burnt and from the ashes rose a single well-knit act—fifty pages of print, playable in one hour. The form of the present play is, therefore, not new, but it appears to be my own, and changing tastes may make it timely. My hope is one day to have an audience educated enough to sit through a whole evening's entertainment in one act, but one would have to try this out to see. Meanwhile, in order to provide respite for the audience and the players, without allowing the audience to escape from the illusion, I have introduced three art forms: monologue, mime and ballet. These are all part of drama, having their origins in classic tragedy, monody having become monologue and the chorus, ballet.

Monologue is now condemned by our realists as unnatural, but if one provides motives for it one makes it natural, and then can use it to advantage. It is, surely, natural for a public speaker to walk up and down the room practicing his speech, natural for an actor to read his part aloud, for a servant girl to talk to her cat, a mother to prattle to her child, an old maid to chatter to her parrot, and a sleeper to talk in his sleep. And in order that the actor may have a chance, for once, of working independently, free from the author's direction, it is better that the monologue should not be written, but only indicated. For since it is of small importance what is said in one's sleep or to the parrot or to the cat—none of it influences the action—a talented actor, identifying himself with the atmosphere and the situation, may improvise better than the author, who cannot calculate ahead how much may be said or how long taken without waking the audience from the illusion.

Some Italian theatres have, as we know, returned to improvisation, thereby producing actors who are creative, although within the bounds set by the author. This may well be a step forward, or even the beginning of a new art-form worthy to be called *productive*.

In places where monologue would be unnatural I have used mime, leaving here an even wider scope for the actor's imagination, and more chance for him to win independent laurels. But so as not to try the audience beyond endurance, I have introduced music—fully justified by the Midsummer Eve dance—to exercise its power of persuasion during the dumb show. But I beg the music director to consider carefully his choice of compositions, so that conflicting moods are not induced by selections from the current operetta or dance show, or by folk-tunes of too local a character.

The ballet I have introduced cannot be replaced by the usual kind of "crowd-scene," for such scenes are too badly played—a lot of grinning idiots seizing the opportunity to show off and thus destroying the illusion. And as peasants cannot improvise their taunts, but use ready-made phrases with a double meaning, I have not composed their lampoon, but taken a little-known song and dance which I myself noted down in the Stockholm district. The words are not quite to the point, but this too is intentional, for the cunning, i.e. weakness, of the slave prevents him from direct attack. Nor can there be clowning in a serious action, or coarse joking in a situation which nails the lid on a family coffin.

As regards the scenery, I have borrowed from impressionist painting its asymmetry and its economy; thus, I think, strengthening the illusion. For the fact that one does not see the whole room and all the furniture leaves scope for conjecture—that is to say imagination is roused and complements what is seen. I have succeeded too in getting rid of those tiresome exits through doors, since scenery doors are made of canvas, and rock at the slightest touch. They cannot even express the wrath of an irate head of the family who, after a bad dinner, goes out slamming the door behind him, "so that the whole house shakes." On the stage it rocks. I have also kept to a single set, both in order to let the characters develop in their métier and to break away from over-decoration. When one has only one set, one may expect it to be realistic; but as a matter of fact nothing is harder than to get a stage room that looks something like a room, however easily the scene painter can produce flaming volcanoes and waterfalls. Presumably the walls must be of canvas; but it seems about time to dispense with painted shelves and cooking utensils. We are asked to accept so many stage conventions that we might at least be spared the pain of painted pots and pans.

I have set the back wall and the table diagonally so that the actors may play full-face and in half-profile when they are sitting opposite one another at the table. In the opera AÏDA I saw a diagonal background, which led the eye to unfamiliar perspectives and did not look like mere reaction against boring straight lines.

Another much needed innovation is the abolition of foot-lights. This lighting from below is said to have the purpose of making the actors' faces fatter. But why, I ask, should all actors have fat faces? Does not this underlighting flatten out all the subtlety of the lower part of the face, specially the jaw, falsify the shape of the nose and throw shadows up over the eyes? Even if this were not so, one thing is certain: that the lights hurt the performers' eyes, so that the full play of their expression is lost. The foot-lights strike part of the retina usually protected—except in sailors who have to watch sunlight on the water—and therefore one seldom sees anything other than a crude rolling of the eyes, either sideways or up towards the gallery, showing their whites. Perhaps this too causes that tiresome blinking of the eyelashes, especially by actresses. And when anyone on the stage wants to speak with his eyes, the only thing he can do is to look straight at the audience, with whom he or she then gets into direct communication, outside the framework of the set—a habit called, rightly or wrongly, "greeting one's friends."

Would not sufficiently strong side-lighting, with some kind of reflectors, add to the actor's powers of expression by allowing him to use the face's greatest asset:—the play of the eyes?

I have few illusions about getting the actors to play *to* the audience instead of *with* it, although this is what I want. That I shall see an actor's back throughout a critical scene is beyond my dreams, but I do wish crucial scenes could be played, not in front of the prompter's box, like duets expecting applause, but in the place required by the action. So, no revolutions, but just some small modifications, for to make the stage into a real room with the fourth wall missing would be too upsetting altogether.

I dare not hope that the actresses will listen to what I have to say about make-up, for they would rather be beautiful than life-like, but the actor might consider whether it is to his advantage to create an abstract character with grease-paints, and cover his face with it like a mask. Take the case of a man who draws a choleric charcoal line between his eyes and then, in this fixed state of wrath, has to smile at some repartee. What a frightful grimace the result is! And equally, how is that false forehead, smooth as a billiard ball, to wrinkle when the old man loses his temper?

In a modern psychological drama, where the subtlest reactions of a character need to be mirrored in the face rather than expressed by sound and gesture, it would be worth while experimenting with powerful side-lighting on a small stage and a cast without make-up, or at least with the minimum.

If, in addition, we could abolish the visible orchestra, with its distracting lamps and its faces turned toward the audience; if we could have the stalls raised so that the spectators' eyes were higher than the players' knees; if we could get rid of the boxes (the centre of my target), with their tittering diners and supper-parties, and have total darkness in the auditorium during the performance; and if, first and foremost, we could have a *small* stage and a *small* house, then perhaps a new dramatic art might arise, and theatre once more become a place of entertainment for educated people. While waiting for such a theatre it is as well for us to go on writing so as to stock that repertory of the future.

I have made an attempt. If it has failed, there is time enough to try again.

DISCUSSION

If all the plays written in the last hundred years were placed on a horizontal scale with the most objective on the left and the most subjective on the right, where would you expect to find *Miss Julie,* toward the left or toward the right? Most critics consider this Strindberg play naturalistic and thus would place it clearly on the left side of the imaginary scale. They see it as comparable to Ibsen's *A Doll's House* in its concern for preserving the illusion of reality, the appearance of photographic objectivity. Such critics would agree that, in the somewhat hypnotic trance into which she lapses near the end of the play, Julie expresses her dazed and bruised subjective state rather than her objective situation—for example, she sees Jean as an "iron stove" with "eyes like coals" and "a white smear" like ash for a face—but they would probably contend that the trance itself represents a kind of psychological realism. Having been abused and degraded by Jean to the point of losing every spark of willpower, every sense of identity, Julie has retreated into what might be called a state of shock. Strindberg is merely presenting one more clinical detail among a multitude of realistic details to show the destruction of Julie's personality.

While there is some truth to this interpretation of the play, it is also seriously misleading. If we look closely at the play's action, we can see that it is generally much more concerned with the inner states of mind of the characters, with their primitive drives to destroy one another, than with any objective, scientific description of their situation or any rational analyses of their motives for acting as they do. True, Julie dreams of descending from her aristocratic perch to the level of the community, and Jean dreams of attaining the kind of status she would reject. But why, then, do they play a cat-and-mouse game that becomes an all-out struggle for dominance? Why must Jean destroy Julie to make his way up in the world? And why does Julie fight so hard to dominate others that she drives her fiancé away by degrading him beyond endurance, just as Jean is about to do to her?

Perhaps a closer look at the language of the play will help to answer these questions. Even the most naturalistic language in *Miss Julie* is subjective. Usually representing the gut reactions of Julie and Jean toward one another and the world, the language of the play is a form of instinctual violence and animality rather than the sort of logical debate and analysis found in most naturalistic plays. Ibsen's naturalistic protagonists, for example, such as Nora in *A Doll's House* or Mrs. Alving in *Ghosts,* talk more to discover the truth than to engage in a tooth and claw confrontation with anyone. Strindberg's protagonists, however, even those in his most naturalistic plays, are gut fighters no matter how aristocratic they are by birth or experience. The couples in *The Father* and *Dance of Death* are aristocrats, members of the military elite. They try to cut each other to ribbons no less decisively than Jean and Julie do. Their civility resides in the fact that they use words rather than knives to do their hacking, but the result is much the same.

Why is Strindberg addicted to writing about such subjective characters, even in his most objective plays? How does this tendency affect the ways in which *Miss Julie* expresses the search for self? We must realize that the period in which Strindberg wrote was on the verge of an historical change in consciousness that included a change in the concept of character and the idea of the self. As he explains in his foreword to *Miss Julie*, Strindberg conceived of Julie as a person who is not limited to one consistent point of view or to one set of consistent characteristics. She is torn in a great many directions, many of which either have no logical connection with the others or contradict them. She wants to be both an aristocrat and a member of the community; to have power over others and to be liked by them as an equal; to enjoy the beauty of nature without recognizing its harsh aspects. We could go on ferreting out her contradictory desires at great length; for as Strindberg's foreword explains, she is a multiple-faceted character rather than another of the single-faceted ones found in most naturalistic plays.

To Strindberg the world was fast becoming a place in which inherited absolute values and hierarchical schemes and structures no longer worked, leaving people without a function or the rules of conduct that allow them to develop an identity and a sense of self. There is nothing in the world around her that Julie can hang onto to gain a sense of security, purpose, and direction. At the end of the play, she turns inward into a dream state, because the world, most insistently in the form of Jean, offers her no dignity, significance, or shelter from what seem the indifferent or even hostile pressures of reality. The world is too harsh for her; it is not a place of comfort or solace but a meaningless chaos in which she can find no place for herself. She has no place to turn but inward. For her life is a living hell, just as it is for the protagonists in Strindberg's later dream plays. It is a place where external relationships are, for the most part, destructive and degrading, where even those who by tradition should love one another— the husbands and wives whose ferocity Strindberg depicts again and again —can do nothing to stay afloat in a sea of chaos.

In his portrayal of these desperate men and women, Strindberg comes close to creating a kind of drama in many ways like the avant-garde drama of recent decades. His late dream plays are often called "expressionistic" because, like the avant-garde movement in the arts of his own time—the movement we call "expressionism"—they are concerned with directly expressing the subjective states of mind of those caught in the nightmarish reality of a world fast losing its human meaning. The absurdist plays of Ionesco and Beckett in our own time extend this situation to its logical conclusion. They portray a world all but devoid of vitality and human purpose, a world in which trivia and chance prevail, in which the arbitrary is all there is. In such a world, the struggle for mere survival at the animal level becomes the primary one. Man struggles for his very existence; he can no longer struggle for a self. As Strindberg says in his foreword, by making Julie a patchwork of many motivations, he is not making a moral judgment on her character but merely presenting her as a modern character "living in an age of transition more urgently hysterical . . . than the age which preceded it." With the example of our own expressionistic writers before us, that statement seems even more apt for us than it was for Strindberg.

THEME AND DISCUSSION QUESTIONS

1. The opening scene in which Jean tells Kristin about Julie's "crazy" behavior at the dance seems at first to be straight exposition, mere information for the audience. In what ways is it also dramatic?
2. Why did Julie treat her fiancé so harshly that he had to break off their engagement? How does her treatment of him relate to her predicament in the play?
3. Why does Julie act coquettishly toward Jean when she first comes into the kitchen?
4. How does the atmosphere of the Midsummer's Eve dance—the natural setting of the yard and trees showing through the windows, and the singing peasants—help to express the meaning and conflict of the play?
5. In the psychological struggle between Jean and Julie in the first half of the play, there are a great many small victories and defeats for each character. Discuss two or three sequences in which the dominance of one character by the other is reversed and then reversed again.
6. Why does the play continue for such a relatively long time after Jean has seduced Julie and is apparently the victor in their battle for domination?
7. Why does Strindberg make Jean so afraid of Julie's father, the Count?
8. Why is *Miss Julie* more than a mere melodrama? How do the particular events, like Julie's account of her mother's hatred for her father, gain general significance?
9. How well does the play reflect the concept of character presented by Strindberg in his foreword?
10. How does Christine's presence in the play help to express its main conflict?

11. In what ways and to what extent is Julie's problem a matter of finding the self? How is it similar to the predicament of many young people today?
12. Both Julie and Jean have recurrent dreams, which they relate to one another. How does Strindberg make their accounts of their dreams expressive of the play's main conflict rather than mere statements of information?

The Madwoman of Chaillot: Motion picture directed by Bryan Forbes (1969), starring Katherine Hepburn. Photograph courtesy of Museum of Modern Art Film Stills Archive.

JEAN GIRAUDOUX

The Madwoman of Chaillot

Jean Giraudoux, a diplomat and playwright, was born in Bellac, France, in 1882 and died in 1944. *The Madwoman of Chaillot*, the Giraudoux play in this collection, was first produced in the year following his death. It had been written during the Nazi occupation of Paris and was undoubtedly influenced by Giraudoux's experience of the Nazi military machine and wartime dehumanization. One of Giraudoux's best-known plays, *The Madwoman of Chaillot* is a fantasy of modern life, in which, according to Giraudoux, dehumanization is the greatest problem for humanity. However, his fantastic, fragmentary treatment of the problem implies that he did not believe it to be an insoluble

THE MADWOMAN OF CHAILLOT   Reprinted by permission of International Famous Agency. Copyright © 1947 by Maurice Valency, under the title *La Folle de Chaillot* by Jean Giraudoux. English version by Maurice Valency.

CAUTION: Professionals and amateurs are hereby warned that *The Madwoman of Chaillot*, being fully protected under the copyright laws of the United States, the British Empire including the Dominion of Canada, and all other countries of the Copyright Union, is subject to royalty. All rights, including professional, amateur, motion picture, recitation, lecturing, public reading, radio and television broadcasting, and the rights of translation into foreign languages, are strictly reserved. Particular emphasis is laid on the question of readings, permission for which must be obtained in writing from the author's agent. All inquiries should be addressed to the authors in care of the Publisher.

The amateur acting rights of *The Madwoman of Chaillot* are controlled exclusively by the Dramatists Play Service, Inc., 440 Park Avenue South, New York, New York, 10016. No amateur performance of the play may be given without obtaining in advance the written permission of the Dramatists Play Service, Inc., and paying the requisite fee.

Incidental Music. All the music mentioned in this manuscript may be secured from the Play Service in the shape of ten photostat pages. This is sold at $4.00, postage included, for all the music named. All nonprofessional groups having purchased the music, and having secured a clearance for the production rights of the play itself through the Play Service, will be permitted to use the music in question, without payment of a special fee.

one. By treating his characters unrealistically, by allowing us to laugh at their absurd, restrictive behavior, Giraudoux implies that we are capable of broader, more fully human perceptions than his characters; that, more perceptive and imaginative than his creations, we can opt for humanity.

CHARACTERS

The Waiter
The Little Man
The Prospector
The President
The Baron
Therese
The Street Singer
The Professor
The Flower Girl
The Ragpicker
Paulette
The Deaf-Mute
Irma
The Shoe-Lace Peddler
The Broker
The Street Juggler
Dr. Jadin

Countess Aurelia,
   The Madwoman of Chaillot
The Doorman
The Policeman
Pierre
The Sergeant
The Sewer-Man
Constance, *The Madwoman
   of Passy*
Gabrielle, *The Madwoman
   of St. Sulpice*
Josephine, *The Madwoman
   of La Concorde*
The Presidents
The Prospectors
The Press Agents
The Ladies
The Adolphe Bertauts

ACT ONE

Scene. *The café terrace at* Chez Francis, *on the Place de l'Alma in Paris. The Alma is in the stately quarter of Paris known as Chaillot, between the Champs Élysées and the Seine, across the river from the Eiffel Tower.*

Chez Francis *has several rows of tables set out under its awning, and, as it is lunch time, a good many of them are occupied. At a table, downstage, a somewhat obvious* blonde *with ravishing legs is sipping a vermouth-cassis and trying hard to engage the attention of the* Prospector, *who sits at an adjacent table taking little sips of water and rolling them over his tongue with the air of a connoisseur. Downstage right, in front of the tables on the sidewalk, is the usual Paris bench, a stout and uncomfortable affair provided by the municipality for the benefit of those who prefer to sit without drinking. A* Policeman *lounges about, keeping the peace without unnecessary exertion.*

TIME. *It is a little before noon in the Spring of next year.*

AT RISE. *The* PRESIDENT *and the* BARON *enter with importance, and are ushered to a front table by the* WAITER.

THE PRESIDENT. Baron, sit down. This is a historic occasion. It must be properly celebrated. The waiter is going to bring out my special port.
THE BARON. Splendid.
THE PRESIDENT (*offers his cigar case*). Cigar? My private brand.
THE BARON. Thank you. You know, this all gives me the feeling of one of those enchanted mornings in the *Arabian Nights* when thieves foregather in the market place. Thieves—pashas . . . (*He sniffs the cigar judiciously, and begins lighting it.*)
THE PRESIDENT (*chuckles*). Tell me about yourself.
THE BARON. Well, where shall I begin?

(*The* STREET SINGER *enters. He takes off a battered black felt with a flourish and begins singing an ancient mazurka.*)

STREET SINGER (*sings*).

    Do you hear, Mademoiselle,
    Those musicians of hell?

THE PRESIDENT. Waiter! Get rid of that man.
WAITER. He is singing *La Belle Polonaise*.
THE PRESIDENT. I didn't ask for the program. I asked you to get rid of him. (*The* WAITER *doesn't budge. The* SINGER *goes by himself.*) As you were saying, Baron . . . ?
THE BARON. Well, until I was fifty . . . (*The* FLOWER GIRL *enters through the café door, center*) my life was relatively uncomplicated. It consisted of selling off one by one the various estates left me by my father. Three years ago, I parted with my last farm. Two years ago, I lost my last mistress. And now—all that is left me is . . .
THE FLOWER GIRL (*to the* BARON). Violets, sir?
THE PRESIDENT. Run along. (*The* FLOWER GIRL *moves on.*)
THE BARON (*staring after her*). So, that, in short, all I have left now is my name.
THE PRESIDENT. Your name is precisely the name we need on our board of directors.
THE BARON (*with an inclination of his head*). Very flattering.
THE PRESIDENT. You will understand when I tell you that mine has been a very different experience. I came up from the bottom. My mother spent most of her life bent over a washtub in order to send me to school. I'm eternally grateful to her, of course, but I must confess that I no longer

remember her face. It was no doubt beautiful—but when I try to recall it, I see only the part she invariably showed—her rear.

The Baron. Very touching.

The President. When I was thrown out of school for the fifth and last time, I decided to find out for myself what makes the world go round. I ran errands for an editor, a movie star, a financier. . . . I began to understand a little what life is. Then, one day, in the subway, I saw a face. . . . My rise in life dates from that day.

The Baron. Really?

The President. One look at that face, and I knew. One look at mine, and he knew. And so I made my first thousand—passing a boxful of counterfeit notes. A year later, I saw another such face. It got me a nice berth in the narcotics business. Since then, all I do is to look out for such faces. And now here I am—president of eleven corporations, director of fifty-two companies, and, beginning today, chairman of the board of the international combine in which you have been so good as to accept a post. (*The* Ragpicker *passes, sees something under the* President's *table, and stoops to pick it up.*) Looking for something?

The Ragpicker. Did you drop this?

The President. I never drop anything.

The Ragpicker. Then this hundred-franc note isn't yours?

The President. Give it here.

(*The* Ragpicker *gives him the note, and goes out.*)

The Baron. Are you sure it's yours?

The President. All hundred-franc notes, Baron, are mine.

The Baron. Mr. President, there's something I've been wanting to ask you. What exactly is the purpsoe of our new company? Or is that an indiscreet question . . . ?

The President. Indiscreet? Not a bit. Merely unusual. As far as I know, you're the first member of a board of directors ever to ask such a question.

The Baron. Do we plan to exploit a commodity? A utility?

The President. My dear sir, I haven't the faintest idea.

The Baron. But if you don't know—who does?

The President. Nobody. And at the moment, it's becoming just a trifle embarrassing. Yes, my dear Baron, since we are now close business associates, I must confess that for the time being we're in a little trouble.

The Baron. I was afraid of that. The stock issue isn't going well?

The President. No, no—on the contrary. The stock issue is going beautifully. Yesterday morning at ten o'clock we offered 500,000 shares to the general public. By 10:05 they were all snapped up at par. By 10:20, when the police finally arrived, our offices were a shambles. . . . Windows smashed—doors torn off their hinges—you never saw anything so beautiful in your life! And this morning our stock is being quoted over the counter at 124 with no sellers, and the orders are still pouring in.

THE BARON. But in that case—what is the trouble?

THE PRESIDENT. The trouble is we have a tremendous capital, and not the slightest idea of what to do with it.

THE BARON. You mean all those people are fighting to buy stock in a company that has no object?

THE PRESIDENT. My dear Baron, do you imagine that when a subscriber buys a share of stock, he has any idea of getting behind a counter or digging a ditch? A stock certificate is not a tool, like a shovel or a commodity, like a pound of cheese. What we sell a customer is not a share in a business, but a view of the Elysian Fields. A financier is a creative artist. Our function is to stimulate the imagination. We are poets!

THE BARON. But in order to stimulate the imagination, don't you need some field of activity?

THE PRESIDENT. Not at all. What you need for that is a name. A name that will stir the pulse like a trumpet call, set the brain awhirl like a movie star, inspire reverence like a cathedral. *United General International Consolidated!* Of course that's been used. That's what a corporation needs.

THE BARON. And do we have such a name?

THE PRESIDENT. So far we have only a blank space. In that blank space a name must be printed. This name must be a masterpiece. And if I seem a little nervous today, it's because—somehow—I've racked my brains, but it hasn't come to me. Oho! Look at that! Just like the answer to a prayer . . . ! (*The* BARON *turns and stares in the direction of the* PROSPECTOR.) You see? There's one. And what a beauty!

THE BARON. You mean that girl?

THE PRESIDENT. No, no, not the girl. That face. You see . . . ? The one that's drinking water.

THE BARON. You call that a face? That's a tombstone.

THE PRESIDENT. It's a milestone. It's a signpost. But is it pointing the way to steel, or wheat, or phosphates? That's what we have to find out. Ah! He sees me. He understands. He will be over.

THE BARON. And when he comes . . . ?

THE PRESIDENT. He will tell me what to do.

THE BARON. You mean business is done this way? You mean, you would trust a stranger with a matter of this importance?

THE PRESIDENT. Baron, I trust neither my wife, nor my daughter, nor my closest friend. My confidential secretary has no idea where I live. But a face like that I would trust with my inmost secrets. Though we have never laid eyes on each other before, that man and I know each other to the depths of our souls. He's no stranger—he's my brother, he's myself. You'll see. He'll be over in a minute. (*The* DEAF-MUTE *enters and passes slowly among the tables, placing a small envelope before each customer. He comes to the* PRESIDENT's *table.*) What is this anyway? A conspiracy? We don't want your envelopes. Take them away. (*The* DEAF-MUTE *makes a short but pointed speech in sign language.*) Waiter, what the devil's he saying?

WAITER. Only Irma understands him.
THE PRESIDENT. Irma? Who's Irma?
WAITER (*calls*). Irma! It's the waitress inside, sir. Irma!

(IRMA *comes out. She is twenty. She has the face and figure of an angel.*)

IRMA. Yes?
WAITER. These gentlemen would . . .
THE PRESIDENT. Tell this fellow to get out of here, for God's sake! (*The* DEAF-MUTE *makes another manual oration.*) What's he trying to say, anyway?
IRMA. He says it's an exceptionally beautiful morning, sir. . . .
THE PRESIDENT. Who asked him?
IRMA. But, he says, it was nicer before the gentleman stuck his face in it.
THE PRESIDENT. Call the manager!

(IRMA *shrugs. She goes back into the restaurant. The* DEAF-MUTE *walks off, left. Meanwhile a* SHOELACE PEDDLER *has arrived.*)

PEDDLER. Shoelaces? Postcards?
THE BARON. I think I could use a shoelace.
THE PRESIDENT. No, no . . .
PEDDLER. Black? Tan?
THE BARON (*showing his shoes*). What would you recommend?
PEDDLER. Anybody's guess.
THE BARON. Well, give me one of each.
THE PRESIDENT (*putting a hand on the* BARON's *arm*). Baron, although I am your chairman, I have no authority over your personal life—none, that is, except to fix the amount of your director's fees, and eventually to assign a motor car for your use. Therefore, I am asking you, as a personal favor to me, not to purchase anything from this fellow.
THE BARON. How can I resist so gracious a request? (*The* PEDDLER *shrugs, and passes on.*) But I really don't understand . . . What difference would it make?
THE PRESIDENT. Look here, Baron. Now that you're with us, you must understand that between this irresponsible riff-raff and us there is an impenetrable barrier. *We* have no dealings whatever with *them.*
THE BARON. But without us, the poor devil will starve.
THE PRESIDENT. No, he won't. He expects nothing from us. He has

a clientele of his own. He sells shoelaces exclusively to those who have no shoes. Just as the necktie peddler sells only to those who wear no shirts. And that's why these street hawkers can afford to be insolent, disrespectful, and independent. They don't need us. They have a world of their own. Ah! My broker. Splendid. He's beaming.

(*The* BROKER *walks up and grasps the* PRESIDENT's *hand with enthusiasm.*)

BROKER. Mr. President! My heartiest congratulations! What a day! What a day!

(*The* STREET JUGGLER *appears, right. He removes his coat, folds it carefully, and puts it on the bench. Then he opens a suitcase, from which he extracts a number of colored clubs.*)

THE PRESIDENT (*presenting the* BROKER). Baron Tommard, of our Board of Directors. My broker. (*The* BROKER *bows. So does the* JUGGLER. *The* BROKER *sits down and signals for a drink. The* JUGGLER *prepares to juggle.*) What's happened?

BROKER. Listen to this. Ten o'clock this morning. The market opens. (*As he speaks, the* JUGGLER *provides a visual counterpart to the* BROKER's *lines, his clubs rising and falling in rhythm to the* BROKER's *words.*) Half million shares issued at par, par value a hundred, quoted on the curb at 124 and we start buying at 126, 127, 129—and it's going up—up—up—(*the* JUGGLER's *clubs rise higher and higher*)—132—133—138—141—141—141—141 . . .

THE BARON. May I ask . . . ?

THE PRESIDENT. No, no—any explanation would only confuse you.

BROKER. Ten forty-five we start selling short on rumors of a Communist plot, market bearish. . . . 141—138—133—132—and it's down—down—down—102—and we start buying back at 93. Eleven o'clock, rumors denied —95—98—101—106—124—141—and by 11:30 we've got it all back— net profit three and a half million francs.

THE PRESIDENT. Classical. Pure. (*The* JUGGLER *bows again. A* LITTLE MAN *leans over from a near-by table, listening intently, and trembling with excitement.*) And how many shares do we reserve to each member of the board?

BROKER. Fifty, as agreed.

THE PRESIDENT. Bit stingy, don't you think?

BROKER. All right—three thousand.

THE PRESIDENT. That's a little better. (*To the* BARON.) You get the idea?

THE BARON. I'm beginning to get it.

BROKER. And now we come to the exciting part . . . (*The* JUGGLER *prepares to juggle with balls of fire.*) Listen carefully: With 35 percent of our funded capital under Section 32 I buy 50,000 United at 36 which I immediately reconvert into 32,000 National Amalgamated two's preferred which I set up as collateral on 150,000 General Consols which I deposit against a credit of fifteen billion to buy Eastern Hennequin which I immediately turn into Argentine wheat realizing 136 percent of the original investment which naturally accrues as capital gain and not as corporate income thus saving twelve millions in taxes, and at once convert the 25 percent cotton reserve into lignite, and as our people swing into action in London and New York, I beat up the price on greige goods from 26 to 92—114—203—306—(*The* JUGGLER *by now is juggling his fire-balls in the sky. The balls no longer return to his hands.*) 404 . . . (*The* LITTLE MAN *can stand no more. He rushes over and dumps a sackful of money on the table.*)

LITTLE MAN. Here—take it—please, take it!

BROKER (*frigidly*). Who is this man? What is this money?

LITTLE MAN. It's my life's savings. Every cent. I put it all in your hands.

BROKER. Can't you see we're busy?

LITTLE MAN. But I beg you . . . It's my only chance . . . Please don't turn me away.

BROKER. Oh, all right. (*He sweeps the money into his pocket.*) Well?

LITTLE MAN. I thought—perhaps you'd give me a little receipt . . .

THE PRESIDENT. My dear man, people like us don't give receipts for money. We take them.

LITTLE MAN. Oh, pardon. Of course. I was confused. Here it is. (*Scribbles a receipt.*) Thank you—thank you—thank you. (*He rushes off joyfully. The* STREET SINGER *reappears.*)

STREET SINGER (*sings*).

> Do you hear, Mademoiselle,
> Those musicians of hell?

THE PRESIDENT. What, again? Why does he keep repeating those two lines like a parrot?

WAITER. What else can he do? He doesn't know any more and the song's been out of print for years.

THE BARON. Couldn't he sing a song he knows?

WAITER. He likes this one. He hopes if he keeps singing the beginning someone will turn up to teach him the end.

THE PRESIDENT. Tell him to move on. We don't know the song.

(*The* PROFESSOR *strolls by, swinging his cane. He overhears.*)

PROFESSOR (*stops and addresses the* PRESIDENT *politely*). Nor do I, my dear sir. Nor do I. And yet, I'm in exactly the same predicament. I remember just two lines of my favorite song, as a child. A mazurka also, in case you're interested. . . .

The President. I'm not.

Professor. Why is it, I wonder, that one always forgets the words of a mazurka? I suppose they just get lost in that damnable rhythm. All I remember is: (*He sings*)

> From England to Spain
> I have drunk, it was bliss. . . .

Street Singer (*walks over, and picks up the tune*).

> Red wine and champagne
> And many a kiss.

Professor. Oh, God! It all comes back to me . . . ! (*He sings.*)

> Red lips and white hands I have known
> Where the nightingales dwell. . . .

The President (*holding his hands to his ears*). Please—please . . .
Street Singer.

> And to each one I've whispered, "My own,"
> And to each one, I've murmured: "Farewell."

The President. Farewell. Farewell.
Street Singer, Professor (*Duo*).

> But there's one I shall never forget. . . .

The President. This isn't a café. It's a circus!

(*The two go off, still singing: "There is one that's engraved in my heart." The* Prospector *gets up slowly and walks toward the* President's *table. He looks down without a word. There is a tense silence.*)

Prospector. Well?
The President. I need a name.
Prospector (*nods, with complete comprehension*). I need fifty thousand.
The President. For a corporation.
Prospector. For a woman.
The President. Immediately.
Prospector. Before evening.
The President. Something . . .
Prospector. Unusual?
The President. Something . . .

JEAN GIRAUDOUX

Prospector. Provocative?
The President. Something...
Prospector. Practical.
The President. Yes.
Prospector. Fifty thousand. Cash.
The President. I'm listening.
Prospector. *International Substrate of Paris, Inc.*

The President (*snaps his fingers*). That's it! (*To the* Broker.) Pay him off. (*The* Broker *pays with the* Little Man's *money.*) Now—what does it mean?

Prospector. It means what it says. I'm a prospector.

The President (*rises*). A prospector! Allow me to shake your hand. Baron. You are in the presence of one of nature's noblemen. Shake his hand. This is Baron Tommard. (*They shake hands.*) It is this man, my dear Baron, who smells out in the bowels of the earth those deposits of metal or liquid on which can be founded the only social unit of which our age is capable—the corporation. Sit down, please. (*They all sit.*) And now that we have a name...

Prospector. You need a property.
The President. Precisely.
Prospector. I have one.
The President. A claim?
Prospector. Terrific.
The President. Foreign?
Prospector. French.
The Baron. In Indo-China?
Broker. Morocco?
The President. In France?
Prospector (*matter of fact*). In Paris.
The President. In Paris? You've been prospecting in Paris?
The Baron. For women, no doubt.
The President. For art?
Broker. For gold?
Prospector. Oil.
Broker. He's crazy.
The President. Sh! He's inspired.
Prospector. You think I'm crazy. Well, they thought Columbus was crazy.
The Baron. Oil in Paris?
Broker. But how is it possible?
Prospector. It's not only possible. It's certain.
The President. Tell us.
Prospector. You don't know, my dear sir, what treasures Paris con-

ceals. Paris is the least prospected place in the world. We've gone over the rest of the planet with a fine-tooth comb. But has anyone ever thought of looking for oil in Paris? Nobody. Before me, that is.

The President. Genius!

Prospector. No. Just a practical man. I use my head.

The Baron. But why has nobody ever thought of this before?

Prospector. The treasures of the earth, my dear sir, are not easy to find nor to get at. They are invariably guarded by dragons. Doubtless there is some reason for this. For once we've dug out and consumed the internal ballast of the planet, the chances are it will shoot off on some irresponsible tangent and smash itself up in the sky. Well, that's the risk we take. Anyway, that's not my business. A prospector has enough to worry about.

The Baron. I know—snakes—tarantulas—fleas . . .

Prospector. Worse than that, sir. Civilization.

The President. Does that annoy you?

Prospector. Civilization gets in our way all the time. In the first place, it covers the earth with cities and towns which are damned awkward to dig up when you want to see what's underneath. It's not only the real-estate people—you can always do business with them—it's human sentimentality. How do you do business with that?

The President. I see what you mean.

Prospector. They say that where we pass, nothing ever grows again. What of it? Is a park any better than a coal mine? What's a mountain got that a slag pile hasn't? What would you rather have in your garden—an almond tree or an oil well?

The President. Well . . .

Prospector. Exactly. But what's the use of arguing with these fools? Imagine the choicest place you ever saw for an excavation, and what do they put there? A playground for children! Civilization!

The President. Just show us the point where you want to start digging. We'll do the rest. Even if it's in the middle of the Louvre. Where's the oil?

Prospector. Perhaps you think it's easy to make an accurate fix in an area like Paris where everything conspires to put you off the scent? Women —perfume—flowers—history. You can talk all you like about geology, but an oil deposit, gentlemen, has to be smelled out. I have a good nose. I go further. I have a phenomenal nose. But the minute I get the right whiff— the minute I'm on the scent—a fragrance rises from what I take to be the spiritual deposits of the past—and I'm completely at sea. Now take this very point, for example, this very spot.

The Baron. You mean—right here in Chaillot?

Prospector. Right under here.

The President. Good heavens! (*He looks under his chair.*)

PROSPECTOR. It's taken me months to locate this spot.
THE BARON. But what in the world makes you think . . . ?
PROSPECTOR. Do you know this place, Baron?
THE BARON. Well, I've been sitting here for thirty years.
PROSPECTOR. Did you ever taste the water?
THE BARON. The water? Good God, no!
PROSPECTOR. It's plain to see that you are no prospector! A prospector, Baron, is addicted to water as a drunkard to wine. Water, gentlemen, is the one substance from which the earth can conceal nothing. It sucks out its innermost secrets and brings them to our very lips. Well—beginning at Notre Dame, where I first caught the scent of oil three months ago, I worked my way across Paris, glassful by glassful, sampling the water, until at least I came to this café. And here—just two days ago—I took a sip. My heart began to thump. Was it possible that I was deceived? I took another, a third, a fourth, a fifth. I was trembling like a leaf. But there was no mistake. Each time that I drank, my taste-buds thrilled to the most exquisite flavor known to a prospector—the flavor of— (*With utmost lyricism.*) Petroleum!

THE PRESIDENT. Waiter! Some water and four glasses. Hurry. This round, gentlemen, is on me. And as a toast—I shall propose International Substrate of Paris, Incorporated. (*The* WAITER *brings a decanter and the glasses. The* PRESIDENT *pours out the water amid profound silence. They taste it with the air of connoisseurs savoring something that has never before passed human lips. Then they look at each other doubtfully. The* PROSPECTOR *pours himself a second glass and drinks it off.*) Well . . .

BROKER. Ye-es . . .
THE BARON. Mm . . .
PROSPECTOR. Get it?
THE BARON. Tastes queer.
PROSPECTOR. That's it. To the unpracticed palate it tastes queer. But to the taste-buds of the expert—ah!
THE BARON. Still, there's one thing I don't quite understand . . .
PROSPECTOR. Yes?
THE BARON. This café doesn't have its own well, does it?
PROSPECTOR. Of course not. This is Paris water.
BROKER. Then why should it taste different here than anywhere else?
PROSPECTOR. Because, my dear sir, the pipes that carry this water pass deep through the earth, and the earth just here is soaked with oil, and this oil permeates the pores of the iron and flavors the water it carries. Ever so little, yes—but quite enough to betray its presence to the sensitive tongue of the specialist.

THE BARON. I see.
PROSPECTOR. I don't say everyone is capable of tasting it. No. But I—I

can detect the presence of oil in water that has passed within fifteen miles of a deposit. Under special circumstances, twenty.

THE PRESIDENT. Phenomenal!

PROSPECTOR. And so here I am with the greatest discovery of the age on my hands—but the blasted authorities won't let me drill a single well unless I show them the oil! Now how can I show them the oil unless they let me dig? Completely stymied! Eh?

THE PRESIDENT. What? A man like you?

PROSPECTOR. That's what they think. That's what they want. Have you noticed the strange glamour of the women this morning? And the quality of the sunshine? And this extraordinary convocation of vagabonds buzzing about protectively like bees around a hive? Do you know why it is? Because they know. It's a plot to distract us, to turn us from our purpose. Well, let them try. I know there's oil here. And I'm going to dig it up, even if I ... (*He smiles.*) Shall I tell you my little plan?

THE PRESIDENT. By all means.

PROSPECTOR. Well ... For heaven's sake, what's that?

(*At this point, the* MADWOMAN *enters. She is dressed in the grand fashion of 1885, a taffeta skirt with an immense train—which she has gathered up by means of a clothespin—ancient button shoes, and a hat in the style of Marie Antoinette. She wears a lorgnette on a chain, and an enormous cameo pin at her throat. In her hand she carries a small basket. She walks in with great dignity, extracts a dinner bell from the bosom of her dress, and rings it sharply.* IRMA *appears.*)

COUNTESS. Are my bones ready, Irma?

IRMA. There won't be much today, Countess. We had broilers. Can you wait? While the gentleman inside finishes eating?

COUNTESS. And my gizzard?

IRMA. I'll try to get it away from him.

COUNTESS. If he eats my gizzard, save me the giblets. They will do for the tomcat that lives under the bridge. He likes a few giblets now and again.

IRMA. Yes, Countess. (IRMA *goes back into the café. The* COUNTESS *takes a few steps and stops in front of the* PRESIDENT's *table. She examines him with undisguised disapproval.*)

THE PRESIDENT. Waiter. Ask that woman to move on.

WAITER. Sorry, sir. This is her café.

THE PRESIDENT. Is she the manager of the café?

WAITER. She's the Madwoman of Chaillot.

THE PRESIDENT. A Madwoman? She's mad?

WAITER. Who says she's mad?

THE PRESIDENT. You just said so yourself.

WAITER. Look, sir. You asked me who she was. And I told you. What's mad about her? She's the Madwoman of Chaillot.

THE PRESIDENT. Call a policeman.

(*The* COUNTESS *whistles through her fingers. At once, the* DOORMAN *runs out of the café. He has three scarves in his hands.*)

COUNTESS. Have you found it? My feather boa?

DOORMAN. Not yet, Countess. Three scarves. But no boa.

COUNTESS. It's five years since I lost it. Surely you've had time to find it.

DOORMAN. Take one of these, Countess. Nobody's claimed them.

COUNTESS. A boa like that doesn't vanish, you know. A feather boa nine feet long!

DOORMAN. How about this blue one?

COUNTESS. With my pink ruffle and my green veil? You're joking! Let me see the yellow. (*She tries it on.*) How does it look?

DOORMAN. Terrific.

(*With a magnificent gesture, she flings the scarf about her, upsetting the* PRESIDENT's *glass and drenching his trousers with water. She stalks off without a glance at him.*)

THE PRESIDENT. Waiter! I'm making a complaint.

WAITER. Against whom?

THE PRESIDENT. Against her! Against you! The whole gang of you! That singer! That shoelace peddler! That female lunatic? Or whatever you call her!

THE BARON. Calm yourself, Mr. President. . . .

THE PRESIDENT. I'll do nothing of the sort! Baron, the first thing we have to do is get rid of these people! Good heavens, look at them! Every size, shape, color and period of history imaginable. It's utter anarchy! I tell you, sir, the only safeguard of order and discipline in the modern world is a standardized worker with interchangeable parts. That would solve the entire problem of management. Here, the manager . . . And there—one composite drudge grunting and sweating all over the world. Just we two. Ah, how beautiful! How easy on the eyes! How restful for the conscience!

THE BARON. Yes, yes—of course.

THE PRESIDENT. Order. Symmetry. Balance. But instead of that, what? Here in Chaillot, the very citadel of management, these insolent phantoms of the past come to beard us with their raffish individualism—with the right of the voiceless to sing, of the dumb to make speeches, of trousers to have no seats and bosoms to have dinner bells!

THE BARON. But, after all, do these people matter?

THE PRESIDENT. My dear sir, wherever the poor are happy, and the servants are proud, and the mad are respected, our power is at an end. Look at that! That waiter! That madwoman! That flower girl! Do I get that sort of service? And suppose that I—president of twelve corporations and ten times a millionaire—were to stick a gladiolus in my buttonhole and start yelling— (*He tinkles his spoon in a glass violently, yelling.*) Are my bones ready, Irma?

THE BARON (*reprovingly*). Mr. President...

(*People at the adjoining tables turn and stare with raised eyebrows. The* WAITER *starts to come over.*)

THE PRESIDENT. You see? Now.
PROSPECTOR. We were discussing my plan.
THE PRESIDENT. Ah, yes, your plan. (*He glances in the direction of the* MADWOMAN's *table.*) Careful—she's looking at us.
PROSPECTOR. Do you know what a bomb is?
THE PRESIDENT. I'm told they explode.
PROSPECTOR. Exactly. You see that white building across the river. Do you happen to know what that is?
THE PRESIDENT. I do not.
PROSPECTOR. That's the office of the City Architect. That man has stubbornly refused to give me a permit to drill for oil anywhere within the limits of the city of Paris. I've tried everything with him—influence, bribes, threats. He says I'm crazy. And now...
THE PRESIDENT. Oh, my God! What is this one trying to sell us?

(*A little* OLD MAN *enters left, and doffs his hat politely. He is somewhat ostentatiously respectable—gloved, pomaded, and carefully dressed, with a white handkerchief peeping out of his breast pocket.*)

DR. JADIN. Nothing but health, sir. Or rather the health of the feet. But remember—as the foot goes, so goes the man. May I present myself...? Dr. Gaspard Jadin, French Navy, retired. Former specialist in the extraction of ticks and chiggers. At present specializing in the extraction of bunions and corns. In case of sudden emergency, Martial the waiter will furnish my home address. My office is here, second row, third table, week days, twelve to five. Thank you very much. (*He sits at his table.*)
WAITER. Your vermouth, Doctor?
DR. JADIN. My vermouth. My vermouths. How are your gallstones today, Martial?
WAITER. Fine. Fine. They rattle like anything.
DR. JADIN. Splendid. (*He spies the* COUNTESS.) Good morning, Countess. How's the floating kidney? Still afloat? (*She nods graciously.*) Splendid. Splendid. So long as it floats, it can't sink.
THE PRESIDENT. This is impossible! Let's go somewhere else.

PROSPECTOR. No. It's nearly noon.
THE PRESIDENT. Yes. It is. Five to twelve.
PROSPECTOR. In five minutes' time you're going to see that City Architect blown up, building and all—boom!
BROKER. Are you serious?
PROSPECTOR. That imbecile has no one to blame but himself. Yesterday noon, he got my ultimatum—he's had twenty-four hours to think it over. No permit? All right. Within two minutes my agent is going to drop a little package in his coal bin. And three minutes after that, precisely at noon ...
THE BARON. You prospectors certainly use modern methods.
PROSPECTOR. The method may be modern. But the idea is old. To get at the treasure, it has always been necessary to slay the dragon. I guarantee that after this, the City Architect will be more reasonable. The new one, I mean.
THE PRESIDENT. Don't you think we're sitting a little close for comfort?
PROSPECTOR. Oh no, no. Don't worry. And, above all, don't stare. We may be watched. (*A clock strikes.*) Why, that's noon. Something's wrong! Good God! What's this? (*A* POLICEMAN *staggers in bearing a lifeless body on his shoulders in the manner prescribed as "The Fireman's Lift."*) It's Pierre! My agent! (*He walks over with affected nonchalance.*) I say, Officer, what's that you've got?
POLICEMAN. Drowned man. (*He puts him down on the bench.*)
WAITER. He's not drowned. His clothes are dry. He's been slugged.
POLICEMAN. Slugged is also correct. He was just jumping off the bridge when I came along and pulled him back. I slugged him, naturally, so he wouldn't drag me under. Life Saving Manual, Rule 5: "In cases where there is danger of being dragged under, it is necessary to render the subject unconscious by means of a sharp blow." He's had that. (*He loosens the clothes and begins applying artificial respiration.*)
PROSPECTOR. The stupid idiot! What the devil did he do with the bomb? That's what comes of employing amateurs!
THE PRESIDENT. You don't think he'll give you away?
PROSPECTOR. Don't worry. (*He walks over to the* POLICEMAN.) Say, what do you think you're doing?
POLICEMAN. Lifesaving. Artificial respiration. First aid to the drowning.
PROSPECTOR. But he's not drowning.
POLICEMAN. But he thinks he is.
PROSPECTOR. You'll never bring him round that way, my friend. That's meant for people who drown in water. It's no good at all for those who drown without water.
POLICEMAN. What am I supposed to do? I've just been sworn in. It's

my first day on the beat. I can't afford to get in trouble. I've got to go by the book.

Prospector.   Perfectly simple. Take him back to the bridge where you found him and throw him in. Then you can save his life and you'll get a medal. This way, you'll only get fined for slugging an innocent man.

Policeman.   What do you mean, innocent? He was just going to jump when I grabbed him.

Prospector.   Have you any proof of that?

Policeman.   Well, I saw him.

Prospector.   Written proof? Witnesses?

Policeman.   No, but...

Prospector.   Then don't waste time arguing. You're in trouble. Quick—before anybody notices—throw him in and dive after him. It's the only way out.

Policeman.   But I don't swim.

The President.   You'll learn how on the way down. Before you were born, did you know how to breathe?

Policeman (*convinced*).   All right. Here we go. (*He starts lifting the body.*)

Dr. Jadin.   One moment, please. I don't like to interfere, but it's my professional duty to point out that medical science has definitely established the fact of intra-uterine respiration. Consequently, this policeman, even before he was born, knew not only how to breathe but also how to cough, hiccup, and belch.

The President.   Suppose he did—how does it concern you?

Dr. Jadin.   On the other hand, medical science has never established the fact of intra-uterine swimming or diving. Under the circumstances, we are forced to the opinion, Officer, that if you dive in you will probably drown.

Policeman.   You think so?

Prospector.   Who asked you for an opinion?

The President.   Pay no attention to that quack, Officer.

Dr. Jadin.   Quack, sir?

Prospector.   This is not a medical matter. It's a legal problem. The officer has made a grave error. He's new. We're trying to help him.

Broker.   He's probably afraid of the water.

Policeman.   Nothing of the sort. Officially, I'm afraid of nothing. But I always follow doctor's orders.

Dr. Jadin.   You see, Officer, when a child is born...

Prospector.   Now, what does he care about when a child is born? He's got a dying man on his hands.... Officer, if you want my advice...

Policeman.   It so happens, I care a lot about when a child is born. It's part of my duty to aid and assist any woman in childbirth or labor.

THE PRESIDENT. Can you imagine!

POLICEMAN. Is it true, Doctor, what they say, that when you have twins, the first born is considered to be the youngest?

DR. JADIN. Quite correct. And what's more, if the twins happen to be born at midnight on December 31st, the older is a whole year younger. He does his military service a year later. That's why you have to keep your eyes open. And that's the reason why a queen always gives birth before witnesses. . . .

POLICEMAN. God! The things a policeman is supposed to know! Doctor, what does it mean if, when I get up in the morning sometimes . . .

PROSPECTOR (*nudging the* PRESIDENT *meaningfully*). The old woman . . .

BROKER. Come on, Baron.

THE PRESIDENT. I think we'd better all run along.

PROSPECTOR. Leave him to me.

THE PRESIDENT. I'll see you later. (*The* PRESIDENT *steals off with the* BROKER *and the* BARON.)

POLICEMAN (*still in conference with* DR. JADIN). But what's really worrying me, Doctor, is this—don't you think it's a bit risky for a man to marry after forty-five?

(*The* BROKER *runs in breathlessly.*)

BROKER. Officer! Officer!

POLICEMAN. What's the trouble?

BROKER. Quick! Two women are calling for help—on the sidewalk—Avenue Wilson!

POLICEMAN. Two women at once? Standing up or lying down?

BROKER. You'd better go and see. Quick!

PROSPECTOR. You'd better take the Doctor with you.

POLICEMAN. Come along, Doctor, come along. . . . (*Pointing to* PIERRE.) Tell him to wait till I get back. Come along, Doctor. (*He runs out, the* DOCTOR *following. The* PROSPECTOR *moves over toward* PIERRE, *but* IRMA *crosses in front of him and takes the boy's hand.*)

IRMA. How beautiful he is! Is he dead, Martial?

WAITER. (*handing her a pocket mirror*). Hold this mirror to his mouth. If it clouds over . . .

IRMA. It clouds over.

WAITER. He's alive. (*He holds out his hand for the mirror.*)

IRMA. Just a sec— (*She rubs it clean and looks at herself intently. Before handing it back, she fixes her hair and applies her lipstick. Meanwhile the* PROSPECTOR *tries to get around the other side, but the* COUNTESS' *eagle eye drives him off. He shrugs his shoulders and exits with the* BARON.) Oh, look—he's opened his eyes!

(PIERRE *opens his eyes, stares intently at* IRMA *and closes them again with the expression of a man who is among the angels.*)

PIERRE (*murmurs*). Oh! How beautiful!
VOICE (*from within the café*). Irma!
IRMA. Coming. Coming. (*She goes in, not without a certain reluctance. The* COUNTESS *at once takes her place on the bench, and also the young man's hand.* PIERRE *sits up suddenly, and finds himself staring, not at* IRMA, *but into the very peculiar face of the* COUNTESS. *His expression changes.*)
COUNTESS. You're looking at my iris? Isn't it beautiful?
PIERRE. Very. (*He drops back, exhausted.*)
COUNTESS. The Sergeant was good enough to say it becomes me. But I no longer trust his taste. Yesterday, the flower girl gave me a lily, and he said it didn't suit me.
PIERRE (*weakly*). It's beautiful.
COUNTESS. He'll be very happy to know that you agree with him. He's really quite sensitive. (*She calls.*) Sergeant!
PIERRE. No, please—don't call the police.
COUNTESS. But I must. I think I hurt his feelings.
PIERRE. Let me go, Madame.
COUNTESS. No, no. Stay where you are. Sergeant! (PIERRE *struggles weakly to get up.*)
PIERRE. Please let me go.
COUNTESS. I'll do nothing of the sort. When you let someone go, you never see him again. I let Charlotte Mazumet go. I never saw her again.
PIERRE. Oh, my head.
COUNTESS. I let Adolphe Bertaut go. And I was holding him. And I never saw him again.
PIERRE. Oh, God!
COUNTESS. Except once. Thirty years later. In the market. He had changed a great deal—he didn't know me. He sneaked a melon from right under my nose, the only good one of the year. Ah, here we are. Sergeant! (*The* POLICE SERGEANT *comes in with importance.*)
SERGEANT. I'm in a hurry, Countess.
COUNTESS. With regard to the iris. This young man agrees with you. He says it suits me.
SERGEANT (*going*). There's a man drowning in the Seine.
COUNTESS. He's not drowning in the Seine. He's drowning here. Because I'm holding him tight—as I should have held Adolphe Bertaut. But if I let him go, I'm sure he will go and drown in the Seine. He's a lot better looking than Adolphe Bertaut, wouldn't you say?

(PIERRE *sighs deeply.*)

JEAN GIRAUDOUX

SERGEANT. How would I know?
COUNTESS. I've shown you his photograph. The one with the bicycle.
SERGEANT. Oh, yes. The one with the harelip.
COUNTESS. I've told you a hundred times! Adolphe Bertaut had no harelip. That was a scratch in the negative. (*The* SERGEANT *takes out his notebook and pencil.*) What are you doing?
SERGEANT. I am taking down the drowned man's name, given name, and date of birth.
COUNTESS. You think that's going to stop him from jumping in the river? Don't be silly, Sergeant. Put that book away and try to console him.
SERGEANT. I should try and console him?
COUNTESS. When people want to die, it is your job as a guardian of the state to speak out in praise of life. Not mine.
SERGEANT. I should speak out in praise of life?
COUNTESS. I assume you have some motive for interfering with people's attempts to kill each other, and rob each other, and run each other over? If you believe that life has some value, tell him what it is. Go on.
SERGEANT. Well, all right. Now look, young man ...
COUNTESS. His name is Roderick.
PIERRE. My name is not Roderick.
COUNTESS. Yes, it is. It's noon. At noon all men become Roderick.
SERGEANT. Except Adolphe Bertaut.
COUNTESS. In the days of Adolphe Bertaut, we were forced to change the men when we got tired of their names. Nowadays, we're more practical—each hour on the hour all names are automatically changed. The men remain the same. But you're not here to discuss Adolphe Bertaut, Sergeant. You're here to convince the young man that life is worth living.
PIERRE. It isn't.
SERGEANT. Quiet. Now then—what was the idea of jumping off the bridge, anyway?
COUNTESS. The idea was to land in the river. Roderick doesn't seem to be at all confused about that.
SERGEANT. Now how can I convince anybody that life is worth living if you keep interrupting all the time?
COUNTESS. I'll be quiet.
SERGEANT. First of all, Mr. Roderick, you have to realize that suicide is a crime against the state. And why is it a crime against the state? Because every time anybody commits suicide, that means one soldier less for the army, one taxpayer less for the ...
COUNTESS. Sergeant, isn't there something about life that you *really* enjoy?
SERGEANT. That I enjoy?
COUNTESS. Well, surely, in all these years, you must have found some-

thing worth living for. Some secret pleasure, or passion. Don't blush. Tell him about it.

SERGEANT. Who's blushing? Well, naturally, yes—I have my passions—like everybody else. The fact is, since you ask me—I love—to play—casino. And if the gentleman would like to join me, by and by when I go off duty, we can sit down to a nice little game in the back room with a nice cold glass of beer. If he wants to kill an hour, that is.

COUNTESS. He doesn't want to kill an hour. He wants to kill himself. Well? Is that all the police force has to offer by way of earthly bliss?

SERGEANT. Huh? You mean— (*He jerks a thumb in the direction of the pretty* BLONDE, *who has just been joined by a* BRUNETTE *of the same stamp.*) Paulette? (*The young man groans.*)

COUNTESS. You're not earning your salary, Sergeant. I defy anybody to stop dying on your account.

SERGEANT. Go ahead, if you can do any better. But you won't find it easy.

COUNTESS. Oh, this is not a desperate case at all. A young man who has just fallen in love with someone who has fallen in love with him!

PIERRE. She hasn't How could she?

COUNTESS. Oh, yes, she has. She was holding your hand, just as I'm holding it, when all of a sudden . . . Did you ever know Marshal Canrobert's niece?

SERGEANT. How could he know Marshal Canrobert's niece?

COUNTESS. Lots of people knew her—when she was alive. (PIERRE *begins to struggle energetically.*) No, no, Roderick—stop—stop!

SERGEANT. You see? You won't do any better than I did.

COUNTESS. No? Let's bet. I'll bet my iris against one of your gold buttons. Right?—Roderick, I know very well why you tried to drown yourself in the river.

PIERRE. You don't at all.

COUNTESS. It's because that Prospector wanted you to commit a horrible crime.

PIERRE. How did you know that?

COUNTESS. He stole my boa, and now he wants you to kill me.

PIERRE. Not exactly.

COUNTESS. It wouldn't be the first time they've tried it. But I'm not so easy to get rid of, my boy, oh, no . . . Because . . .

(*The* DOORMAN *rides in on his bicycle. He winks at the* SERGEANT, *who has now seated himself—while the* WAITER *serves him a beer.*)

DOORMAN. Take it easy, Sergeant.
SERGEANT. I'm busy saving a drowning man.
COUNTESS. They can't kill me because—I have no desire to die.

PIERRE. You're fortunate.

COUNTESS. To be alive is to be fortunate, Roderick. Of course, in the morning, when you first awake, it does not always seem so very gay. When you take your hair out of the drawer, and your teeth out of the glass, you are apt to feel a little out of place in this world. Especially if you've just been dreaming that you're a little girl on a pony looking for strawberries in the woods. But all you need to feel the call of life once more is a letter in your mail giving you your schedule for the day—your mending, your shopping, that letter to your grandmother that you never seem to get around to. And so, when you've washed your face in rosewater, and powdered it—not with this awful rice-powder they sell nowadays, which does nothing for the skin, but with a cake of pure white starch—and put on your pins, your rings, your brooches, bracelets, earrings, and pearls—in short, when you are dressed for your morning coffee—and have had a good look at yourself—not in the glass, naturally—it lies—but in the side of the brass gong that once belonged to Admiral Courbet—then, Roderick, then you're armed, you're strong, you're ready—you can begin again.

(PIERRE *is listening now intently. There are tears in his eyes.*)

PIERRE. Oh, Madame . . . ! Oh, Madame . . . !

COUNTESS. After that, everything is pure delight. First the morning paper. Not, of course, these current sheets full of lies and vulgarity. I always read the *Gaulois,* the issue of March 22, 1903. It's by far the best. It has some delightful scandal, some excellent fashion notes, and, of course, the last-minute bulletin on the death of Leonide Leblanc. She used to live next door, poor woman, and when I learn of her death every morning, it gives me quite a shock. I'd gladly lend you my copy but it's in tatters.

SERGEANT. Couldn't we find him a copy in some library?

COUNTESS. I doubt it, And so, when you've taken your fruit salts—not in water, naturally—no matter what they say, it's water that gives you gas—but with a bit of spiced cake—then in sunlight or rain, Chaillot calls. It is time to dress for your your morning walk. This takes much longer, of course—without a maid, impossible to do it under an hour, what with your corset, corset-cover, and drawers all of which lace or button in the back. I asked Madame Lanvin, a while ago, to fit the drawers with zippers. She was quite charming, but she declined. She thought it would spoil the style.

(*The* DEAF-MUTE *comes in.*)

WAITER. I know a place where they put zippers on anything.

(*The* RAGPICKER *enters.*)

COUNTESS. I think Lanvin knows best. But I really manage very well, Martial. What I do now is, I lace them up in front, then twist them around to the back. It's quite simple really. Then you choose a lorgnette, and then the usual fruitless search for the feather boa that the prospector stole—I know it was he: he didn't dare look me in the eye—and then all you need is a rubber band to slip around your parasol—I lost the catch the day I struck the cat that was stalking the pigeon—it was worth it—ah, that day I earned my wages!

THE RAGPICKER. Countess, if you can use it, I found a nice umbrella catch the other day with a cat's eye in it.

COUNTESS. Thank you, Ragpicker. They say these eyes sometimes come to life and fill with tears. I'd be afraid . . .

PIERRE. What a fool I've been!

COUNTESS. Ah! So life is beginning to interest you, is it? You see how beautiful it is?

PIERRE. What a fool I've been!

COUNTESS. Then, Roderick, I begin my rounds. I have my cats to feed, my dogs to pet, my plants to water. I have to see what the evil ones are up to in the district—those who hate people, those who hate plants, those who hate animals. I watch them sneaking off in the morning to put on their disguises—to the baths, to the beauty parlors, to the barbers. But they can't deceive me. And when they come out again with blonde hair and false whiskers, to pull up my flowers and poison my dogs, I'm there, and I'm ready. All you have to do to break their power is to cut across their path from the left. That isn't always easy. Vice moves swiftly. But I have a good long stride and I generally manage . . . Right, my friends? (*The* WAITER *and the* RAGPICKER *nod their heads with evident approval.*) Yes, the flowers have been marvelous this year. And the butcher's dog on the Rue Bizet, in spite of that wretch that tried to poison him, is friskier than ever. . . .

SERGEANT. That dog had better look out. He has no license.

COUNTESS. He doesn't seem to feel the need for one.

THE RAGPICKER. The Duchess de la Rochefoucauld's whippet is getting awfully thin. . . .

COUNTESS. What can I do? She bought that dog full grown from a kennel where they didn't know his right name. A dog without his right name is bound to get thin.

THE RAGPICKER. I've got a friend who knows a lot about dogs—an Arab . . .

COUNTESS. Ask him to call on the Duchess. She receives Thursdays, five to seven. You see, then, Roderick. That's life. Does it appeal to you now?

PIERRE. It seems marvelous.

COUNTESS. Ah! Sergeant. My button. (*The* SERGEANT *gives her his button and goes off. At this point the* PROSPECTOR *enters.*) That's only the morning. Wait till I tell you about the afternoon!

PROSPECTOR. All right, Pierre. Come along now.

PIERRE. I'm perfectly all right here.
PROSPECTOR. I said, come along now.
PIERRE (*to the* COUNTESS). I'd better go, Madame.
COUNTESS. No.
PIERRE. It's no use. Please let go my hand.
PROSPECTOR. Madame, will you oblige me by letting my friend go?
COUNTESS. I will not oblige you in any way.
PROSPECTOR. All right. Then I'll oblige you . . . ! (*He tries to push her away. She catches up a soda water siphon and squirts it in his face.*)
PIERRE. Countess . . .
COUNTESS. Stay where you are. This man isn't going to take you away. In the first place, I shall need you in a few minutes to take me home. I'm all alone here and I'm very easily frightened.

(*The* PROSPECTOR *makes a second attempt to drag* PIERRE *away. The* COUNTESS *cracks him over the skull with the siphon. They join battle. The* COUNTESS *whistles. The* DOORMAN *comes, then the other* VAGABONDS, *and lastly the* POLICE SERGEANT.)

PROSPECTOR. Officer! Arrest this woman!
SERGEANT. What's the trouble here?
PROSPECTOR. She refuses to let this man go.
SERGEANT. Why should she?
PROSPECTOR. It's against the law for a woman to detain a man on the street.
IRMA. Suppose it's her son whom she's found again after twenty years?
THE RAGPICKER (*gallantly*). Or her long-lost brother? The Countess is not so old.
PROSPECTOR. Officer, this is a clear case of disorderly conduct.

(*The* DEAF-MUTE *interrupts with frantic signals.*)

COUNTESS. Irma, what is the Deaf-Mute saying?
IRMA (*interpreting*). The young man is in danger of his life. He mustn't go with him.
PROSPECTOR. What does he know?
IRMA. He knows everything.
PROSPECTOR. Officer, I'll have to take your number.
COUNTESS. Take his number. It's 2133. It adds up to nine. It will bring you luck.
SERGEANT. Countess, between ourselves, what are you holding him for, anyway?
COUNTESS. I'm holding him because it's very pleasant to hold him.

I've never really held anybody before, and I'm making the most of it. And because so long as *I* hold him, he's free.

PROSPECTOR. Pierre, I'm giving you fair warning. . . .

COUNTESS. And I'm holding him because Irma wants me to hold him. Because if I let him go, it will break her heart.

IRMA. Oh, Countess!

SERGEANT (*to the* PROSPECTOR). All right, you—move on. Nobody's holding you. You're blocking traffic. Move on.

PROSPECTOR (*menacingly*). I have your number. (*And murderously, to* PIERRE.) You'll regret this, Pierre. (*Exit* PROSPECTOR.)

PIERRE. Thank you, Countess.

COUNTESS. They're blackmailing you, are they? (PIERRE *nods*.) What have you done? Murdered sombeody?

PIERRE. No.

COUNTESS. Stolen something?

PIERRE. No.

COUNTESS. What then?

PIERRE. I forged a signature.

COUNTESS. Whose signature?

PIERRE. My father's. To a note.

COUNTESS. And this man has the paper, I suppose?

PIERRE. He promised to tear it up, if I did what he wanted. But I couldn't do it.

COUNTESS. But the man is mad? Does he really want to destroy the whole neighborhood?

PIERRE. He wants to destroy the whole city.

COUNTESS (*laughs*). Fantastic.

PIERRE. It's not funny, Countess. He can do it. He's mad, but he's powerful, and he has friends. Their machines are already drawn up and waiting. In three months' time you may see the city covered by a forest of derricks and drills.

COUNTESS. But what are they looking for? Have they lost something?

PIERRE. They're looking for oil. They're convinced that Paris is sitting on a lake of oil.

COUNTESS. Suppose it is. What harm does it do?

PIERRE. They want to bring the oil to the surface, Countess.

COUNTESS (*laughs*). How silly! Is that a reason to destroy a city? What do they want with this oil?

PIERRE. They want to make war, Countess.

COUNTESS. Oh, dear, let's forget about these horrible men. The world is beautiful. It's happy. That's how God made it. No man can change it.

WAITER. Ah, Countess, if you only knew . . .

COUNTESS. If I only knew what?

WAITER. Shall we tell her now? Shall we tell her?

COUNTESS. What is it you are hiding from me?

THE RAGPICKER. Nothing, Countess. It's you who are hiding.

WAITER. You tell her. You've been a pitchman. You can talk.

ALL. Tell her. Tell her. Tell her.

COUNTESS. You're frightening me, my friends. Go on. I'm listening.

THE RAGPICKER. Countess. there was a time when old clothes were as good as new—in fact, they were better. Because when people wore clothes, they gave something to them. You may not believe it, but right this minute, the highest-priced shops in Paris are selling clothes that were thrown away thirty years ago. They're selling them for new. That's how good they were.

COUNTESS. Well?

THE RAGPICKER. Countess, there was a time when garbage was a pleasure. A garbage can was not what it is now. If it smelled a little strange, it was because it was a little confused—there was everything there—sardines, cologne, iodine, roses. An amateur might jump to a wrong conclusion. But to a professional—it was the smell of God's plenty.

COUNTESS. Well?

THE RAGPICKER. Countess, the world has changed.

COUNTESS. Nonsense. How could it change? People are the same, I hope.

THE RAGPICKER. No, Countess. The people are not the same. The people are different. There's been an invasion. An infiltration. From another planet. The world is not beautiful any more. It's not happy.

COUNTESS. Not happy? Is that true? Why didn't you tell me this before?

THE RAGPICKER. Because you live in a dream, Countess. And we don't like to disturb you.

COUNTESS. But how could it have happened?

THE RAGPICKER. Countess, there was a time when you could walk around Paris, and all the people you met were just like yourself. A little cleaner, maybe, or dirtier, perhaps, or angry, or smiling—but you knew them. They were you. Well, Countess, twenty years ago, one day, on the street, I saw a face in the crowd. A face, you might say, without a face. The eyes—empty. The expression—not human. Not a human face. It saw me staring, and when it looked back at me with its gelatine eyes, I shuddered. Because I knew that to make room for this one, one of us must have left the earth. A while later, I saw another. And another. And since then, I've seen hundreds come in—yes—thousands.

COUNTESS. Describe them to me.

THE RAGPICKER. You've seen them yourself, Countess. Their clothes don't wrinkle. Their hats don't come off. When they talk, they don't look at you. They don't perspire.

COUNTESS. Have they wives? Have they children?

THE RAGPICKER. They buy the models out of shop windows, furs and all. They animate them by a secret process. Then they marry them. Naturally, they don't have children.

COUNTESS. What work do they do?

THE RAGPICKER. They don't do any work. Whenever they meet, they whisper, and then they pass each other thousand-franc notes. You see them standing on the corner by the Stock Exchange. You see them at auctions—in the back. They never raise a finger—they just stand there. In theater lobbies, by the box office—they never go inside. They don't do anything, but wherever you see them, things are not the same. I remember well the time when a cabbage could sell itself just by being a cabbage. Nowadays it's no good being a cabbage—unless you have an agent and pay him a commission. Nothing is free any more to sell itself or give itself away. These days, Countess, every cabbage has its pimp.

COUNTESS. I can't believe that.

THE RAGPICKER. Countess, little by little, the pimps have taken over the world. They don't do anything, they don't make anything—they just stand there and take their cut. It makes a difference. Look at the shopkeepers. Do you ever see one smiling at a customer any more? Certainly not. Their smiles are strictly for the pimps. The butcher has to smile at the meat-pimp, the florist at the rose-pimp, the grocer at the fresh-fruit-and-vegetable pimp. It's all organized down to the slightest detail. A pimp for bird-seed. A pimp for fishfood. That's why the cost of living keeps going up all the time. You buy a glass of beer—it costs twice as much as it used to. Why? 10 percent for the glass-pimp, 10 percent for the beer-pimp, 20 percent for the glass-of-beer-pimp—that's where our money goes. Personally, I prefer the old-fashioned type. Some of those men at least were loved by the women they sold. But what feelings can a pimp arouse in a leg of lamb? Pardon my language, Irma.

COUNTESS. It's all right. She doesn't understand it.

THE RAGPICKER. So now you know, Countess, why the world is no longer happy. We are the last of the free people of the earth. You saw them looking us over today. Tomorrow, the street-singer will start paying the song-pimp, and the garbage-pimp will be after me. I tell you, Countess, we're finished. It's the end of free enterprise in this world!

COUNTESS. Is this true, Roderick?

PIERRE. I'm afraid it's true.

COUNTESS. Did you know about this, Irma?

IRMA. All I know is the doorman says that faith is dead.

DOORMAN. I've stopped taking bets over the phone.

JUGGLER. The very air is different, Countess. You can't trust it any more. If I throw my torches up too high, they go out.

JEAN GIRAUDOUX

The Ragpicker. The sky-pimp puts them out.
Flower Girl. My flowers don't last over night now. They wilt.
Juggler. Have you noticed, the pigeons don't fly any more?
The Ragpicker. They can't afford to. They walk.
Countess. They're a lot of fools and so are you! You should have told me at once! How can you bear to live in a world where there is unhappiness? Where a man is not his own master? Are you cowards? All we have to do is to get rid of these men.
Pierre. How can we get rid of them? They're too strong.

(*The* Sergeant *walks up again.*)

Countess (*smiling*). The Sergeant will help us.
Sergeant. Who? Me?
Irma. There are a great many of them, Countess. The Deaf-Mute knows them all. They employed him once, years ago, because he was deaf. (*The* Deaf-Mute *wigwags a short speech.*) They fired him because he wasn't blind. (*Another flash of sign language.*) They're all connected like the parts of a machine.
Countess. So much the better. We shall drive the whole machine into a ditch.
Sergeant. It's not that easy, Countess. You never catch these birds napping. They change before your very eyes. I remember when I was in the detectives... You catch a president, pfft! He turns into a trustee. You catch him as trustee, and pfft! he's not a trustee—he's an honorary vice-chairman. You catch a Senator dead to rights: he becomes Minister of Justice. You get after the Minister of Justice—he is Chief of Police. And there you are—no longer in the detectives.
Pierre. He's right Countess. They have all the power. And all the money. And they're greedy for more.
Countess. They're greedy? Ah, then, my friends, they're lost. If they're greedy, they're stupid. If they're greedy—don't worry, I know exactly what to do. Roderick, by tonight you will be an honest man. And, Juggler, your torches will stay lit. And your beer will flow freely again, Martial. And the world will be saved. Let's get to work.
The Ragpicker. What are you going to do?
Countess. Have you any kerosene in the house, Irma?
Irma. Yes. Would you like some?
Countess. I want just a little. In a dirty bottle. With a little mud. And some mange-cure, if you have it. (*To the* Deaf-Mute.) Deaf-Mute! Take a letter. (Irma *interprets in sign language. To the* Singer.) Singer, go and find Madame Constance.

(Irma *and the* Waiter *go into the café.*)

SINGER. Yes, Countess.

COUNTESS. Ask her to be at my house by two o'clock. I'll be waiting for her in the cellar. You may tell her we have to discuss the future of humanity. That's sure to bring her.

SINGER. Yes, Countess.

COUNTESS. And ask her to bring Mademoiselle Gabrielle and Madame Josephine with her. Do you know how to get in to speak to Madame Constance? You ring twice, and then meow three times like a cat. Do you know how to meow?

SINGER. I'm better at barking.

COUNTESS. Better practice meowing on the way. Incidentally, I think Madame Constance knows all the verses of your mazurka. Remind me to ask her.

SINGER. Yes, Countess. (*Exit.*)

(IRMA *comes in. She is shaking the oily concoction in a little perfume vial, which she now hands the* COUNTESS.)

IRMA. Here you are, Countess.

COUNTESS. Thanks, Irma. (*She assumes a presidential manner.*) Deaf-Mute! Ready?

(IRMA *interprets in sign language. The* WAITER *has brought out a portfolio of letter paper and placed it on a table. The* DEAF-MUTE *sits down before it, and prepares to write.*)

IRMA (*speaking for the* DEAF-MUTE). I'm ready.

COUNTESS. My dear Mr.— What's his name?

(IRMA *wigwags the question to the* DEAF-MUTE, *who answers in the same manner. It is all done so deftly that it is as if the* DEAF-MUTE *were actually speaking.*)

IRMA. They are all called Mr. President.

COUNTESS. My dear Mr. President: I have personally verified the existence of a spontaneous outcrop of oil in the cellar of Number 21 Rue de Chaillot, which is at present occupied by a dignified person of unstable mentality. (*The* COUNTESS *grins knowingly.*) This explains why, fortunately for us, the discovery has so long been kept secret. If you should wish to verify the existence of this outcrop for yourself, you may call at the above address at three P.M. today. I am herewith enclosing a sample so that you may judge the quality and consistency of the crude. Yours very truly. Roderick, can you sign the prospector's name?

PIERRE. You wish me to?

COUNTESS. One forgery wipes out the other.

JEAN GIRAUDOUX

(PIERRE *signs the letter. The* DEAF-MUTE *types the address on an envelope.*)

IRMA. Who is to deliver this?
COUNTESS. The Doorman, of course. On his bicycle. And as soon as you have delivered it, run over to the prospector's office. Leave word that the President expects to see him at my house at three.
DOORMAN. Yes, Countess.
COUNTESS. I shall leave you now. I have many pressing things to do. Among others, I must press my red gown.
RAGPICKER. But this only takes care of two of them, Countess.
COUNTESS. Didn't the Deaf-Mute say they are all connected like the works of a machine?
IRMA. Yes.
COUNTESS. Then, if one comes, the rest will follow. And we shall have them all. My boa, please.
DOORMAN. The one that's stolen, Countess?
COUNTESS. Naturally. The one the prospector stole.
DOORMAN. It hasn't turned up yet, Countess. But someone has left an ermine collar.
COUNTESS. Real ermine?
DOORMAN. Looks like it.
COUNTESS. Ermine and iris were made for each other. Let me see it.
DOORMAN. Yes, Countess. (*Exit* DOORMAN.)
COUNTESS. Roderick, you shall escort me. You still look pale. I have some old Chartreuse at home. I always take a glass each year. Last year I forgot. You shall have it.
PIERRE. If there is anything I can do, Countess . . . ?
COUNTESS. There is a great deal you can do. There are all the things that need to be done in a room that no man has been in for twenty years. You can untwist the cord on the blind and let in a little sunshine for a change. You can take the mirror off the wardrobe door, and deliver me once and for all from the old harpy that lives in the mirror. You can let the mouse out of the trap. I'm tired of feeding it. (*To her friends.*) Each man to his post. See you later, my friends. (*The* DOORMAN *puts the ermine collar around her shoulders.*) Thank you, my boy, It's rabbit. (*One o'clock strikes.*) Your arm, Valentine.
PIERRE. Valentine?
COUNTESS. It's struck one. At one, all men become Valentine.
PIERRE (*he offers his arm*). Permit me.
COUNTESS. Or Valentino. It's obviously far from the same, isn't it, Irma? But they have that much choice. (*She sweeps out majestically with* PIERRE. *The others disperse. All but* IRMA.)

IRMA (*clearing off the table*). I hate ugliness. I love beauty. I hate meanness. I adore kindness. It may not seem so grand to some to be a waitress in Paris. I love it. A waitress meets all sorts of people. She observes life. I hate to be alone. I love people. But I have never said I love you to a man. Men try to make me say it. They put their arms around me—I pretend I don't see it. They pinch me—I pretend I don't feel it. They kiss me—I pretend I don't know it. They take me out in the evening and make me drink—but I'm careful, I never say it. If they don't like it, they can leave me alone. Because when I say I love you to Him, He will know just by looking in my eyes that many have held me and pinched me and kissed me, but I have never said I love you to anyone in the world before. Never. No. (*Looking off in the direction in which* PIERRE *has gone, she whispers softly:*) I love you.

VOICE (*from within the café*). Irma!

IRMA. Coming. (*Exits.*)

Curtain.

ACT TWO

SCENE. *The cellar of the* COUNTESS' *house. An ancient vault set deep in the ground, with walls of solid masonry, part brick and part great ashlars, mossy and sweating. A staircase of medieval pattern is built into the thickness of the wall, and leads up to the street level from a landing halfway down. In the corners of the cellar are piled casks, packing cases, birdcages, and other odds and ends—the accumulation of centuries—the whole effect utterly fantastic.*

In the center of the vast underground room, some furniture has been arranged to give an impression of a sitting room of the 1890's. There is a venerable chaise-lounge piled with cushions that once were gay, three armchairs, a table with an oil lamp and a bowl of flowers, a shaggy rug. It is two P.M., *the same day.*

AT RISE. *The* COUNTESS *is sitting over a bit of mending, in one of the armchairs.* IRMA *appears on the landing and calls down.*

IRMA. Countess! The Sewer Man is here.

COUNTESS. Thank goodness, Irma. Send him down. (*The* SEWER MAN *enters. He carries his hip-boots in his hand.*) How do you do Mr. Sewer Man? (*The* SEWER MAN *bows.*) But why do you have your boots in your hand instead of on your feet?

SEWER MAN. Etiquette, Countess. Etiquette.

COUNTESS. How very American! I'm told that Americans nowadays apologize for their gloves if they happen to take one's hand. As if the skin of a human were nicer to touch than the skin of a sheep! And particularly if they have sweaty hands . . . !

SEWER MAN. My feet never sweat, Countess.

COUNTESS. How very nice! But please don't stand on ceremony here. Put your boots on. Put them on.

SEWER MAN (*complying*). Thanks very much, Countess.

COUNTESS (*while he draws on his boots*). I'm sure you must have a very poor opinion of the upper world, from what you see of it. The way people throw their filth into your territory is absolutely scandalous! I burn all my refuse, and I scatter the ashes. All I ever throw in the drain is flowers. Did you happen to see a lily float by this morning? Mine. But perhaps you didn't notice?

SEWER MAN. We notice a lot more down there, Countess, than you might think. You'd be surprised the things we notice. There's lots of things come along that were obviously intended for us—little gifts, you might call them—sometimes a brand-new shaving brush—sometimes, *The Brothers Karamavoz* . . . Thanks for the lily, Countess. A very sweet thought.

COUNTESS. Tomorrow you shall have this iris. But now, let's come to the point. I have two questions to ask you.

SEWER MAN. Yes, Countess?

COUNTESS. First—and this has nothing to do with your problem—it's just something that has been troubling me. . . . Tell me, is it true that the sewer men of Paris have a king?

SEWER MAN. Oh, now Countess, that's another of those fairy tales out of the Sunday supplements. It just seems those writers can't keep their minds off the sewers! It fascinates them. They keep thinking of us moving around in our underground canals like gondoliers in Venice, and it sends them into a fever of romance! The things they say about us! They say we have a race of girls down there who never see the light of day! It's completely fantastic! The girls naturally come out—every Christmas and Easter. And orgies by torchlight with gondolas and guitars! With troops of rats that dance as they follow the piper! What nonsense! The rats are not allowed to dance. No, no, no. Of course we have no king. Down in the sewers, you'll find nothing but good Republicans.

COUNTESS. And no queen?

SEWER MAN. No. We may run a beauty contest down there once in a while. Or crown a mermaid Queen of the May. But no queen what you'd call a queen. And, as for these swimming races they talk so much about . . . possibly once in a while—in the summer—in the dog days . . .

COUNTESS. I believe you. I believe you. And now tell me. Do you remember that night I found you here in my cellar—looking very pale and strange—you were half-dead as a matter of fact—and I gave you some brandy . . .

SEWER MAN. Yes, Countess.

COUNTESS. That night you promised if ever I should need it—you would tell me the secret of this room.

SEWER MAN. The secret of the moving stone?

COUNTESS. I need it now.

SEWER MAN. Only the King of the Sewer Men knows this secret.

COUNTESS. I'm sure of it. I know most secrets, of course. As a matter of fact, I have three magic words that will open any door that words can open. I have tried them all—in various tones of voice. They don't seem to work. And this is a matter of life and death.

SEWER MAN. Look, Countess. (*He locates a brick in the masonry, and pushes it. A huge block of stone slowly pivots and uncovers a trap from which a circular staircase winds into the bowels of the earth.*)

COUNTESS. Good heavens! Where do those stairs lead?

SEWER MAN. Nowhere.

COUNTESS. But they must go somewhere.

SEWER MAN. They just go down.

COUNTESS. Let's go and see.

SEWER MAN. No, Countess. Never again. That time you found me, I had a pretty close shave. I kept going down and around, and down and around for an hour, a year—I don't know. There's no end to it, Countess. Once you start you can't stop . . . Your head begins to turn—you're lost. No—once you start down, there's no coming up.

COUNTESS. You came up.

SEWER MAN. I—I am a special case. Besides, I had my tools, my ropes. And I stopped in time.

COUNTESS. You could have screamed—shouted.

SEWER MAN. You could fire off a cannon.

COUNTESS. Who could have built a thing like this?

SEWER MAN. Paris is old, you know. Paris is very old.

COUNTESS. You don't suppose, by any chance, there is oil down there?

SEWER MAN. There's only death down there.

COUNTESS. I should have preferred a little oil too—or a vein of gold—or emeralds. You're quite sure there is nothing?

SEWER MAN. Not even rats.

COUNTESS. How does one lower this stone?

SEWER MAN. Simple. To open, you press here. And to close it, you push there. (*He presses the brick. The stone descends.*) Now there's two of us in the world that knows it.

COUNTESS. I won't remember long. Is it all right if I repeat my magic words while I press it?

SEWER MAN. It's bound to help.

(IRMA *enters.*)

IRMA.   Countess, Madame Constance and Mademoiselle Gabrielle are here.

COUNTESS.   Show them down, Irma. Thank you very much, Mr. Sewer Man.

SEWER MAN.   Like that story about the steam laundry that's supposed to be running day and night in my sewer . . . I can assure you . . .

COUNTESS (*edging him toward the door*).   Thank you very much.

SEWER MAN.   Pure imagination! They never work nights. (*He goes off, bowing graciously.*)

(CONSTANCE, *the Madwoman of Passy, and* GABRIELLE, *the Madwoman of St. Sulpice, come down daintily.* CONSTANCE *is all in white. She wears an enormous hat graced with ostrich plumes, and a lavender veil.* GABRIELLE *is costumed with the affected simplicity of the 1880's. She is atrociously made up in a remorseless parody of blushing innocence, and she minces down the stairs with macabre coyness.*)

CONSTANCE.   Aurelia! Don't tell us they've found your feather boa?

GABRIELLE.   You don't mean Adolphe Bertaut has proposed at last! I knew he would.

COUNTESS.   How are you, Constance? (*She shouts.*) How are you, Gabrielle?

GABRIELLE.   You needn't shout today, my dear. It's Wednesday. Wednesdays, I hear perfectly.

CONSTANCE.   It's Thursday.

GABRIELLE.   Oh, dear. Well, never mind. I'm going to make an exception just this once.

CONSTANCE (*to an imaginary dog who has stopped on the landing*). Come along, Dickie. Come along. And stop barking. What a racket you're making! Come on, darling—we've come to see the longest boa and the handsomest man in Paris. Come on.

COUNTESS.   Constance, it's not a question of my boa today. Nor of poor Adolphe. It's a question of the future of the human race.

CONSTANCE.   You think it has a future?

COUNTESS.   Please don't make silly jokes. Sit down and listen to me. Today we must make a decision which may alter the fate of the world.

CONSTANCE.   Couldn't we do it tomorrow? I want to wash my slippers. Now, Dickie—please!

COUNTESS.   We haven't a moment to waste. Where is Josephine? Well, we'd best have our tea, and the moment Josephine comes . . .

GABRIELLE.   Josephine is sitting on her bench in front of the palace waiting for President Wilson to come out. She says she's sorry, but she positively must see him today.

CONSTANCE. Dickie!

COUNTESS. What a pity! (*She gets the tea things from the side table, pours tea and serves cake and honey.*) I wish she were here to help us. She has a first-class brain.

CONSTANCE. Go ahead, dear. We're listening. (*To* DICKIE.) What is it, Dickie? You want to sit in Aunt Aurelia's lap. All right, darling. Go on. Jump, Dickie.

COUNTESS. Constance, we love you, as you know. And we love Dickie. But this is a serious matter. So let's stop being childish for once.

CONSTANCE. And what does that mean, if you please?

COUNTESS. It means Dickie. You know perfectly well that we love him and fuss over him just as if he were still alive. He's a sacred memory and we wouldn't hurt his feelings for the world. But please don't plump him in my lap when I'm settling the future of mankind. His basket is in the corner—he knows where it is, and he can just go and sit in it.

CONSTANCE. So you're against Dickie too! You too!

COUNTESS. Constance! I'm not in the least against Dickie! I adore Dickie. But you know as well as I that Dickie is only a convention with us. It's a beautiful convention—but it doesn't have to bark all the time. Besides, it's you that spoil him. The time you went to visit your niece and left him with me, we got on marvelously together. He didn't bark, he didn't tear things, he didn't even eat. But when you're with him, one can pay attention to nothing else. I'm not going to take Dickie in my lap at a solemn moment like this, no, not for anything in the world. And that's that!

GABRIELLE (*very sweetly*). Constance, dear, I don't mind taking him in my lap. He loves to sit in my lap, don't you, darling?

CONSTANCE. Kindly stop putting on angelic airs, Gabrielle. I know you very well. You're much too sweet to be sincere. There's plenty of times that I make believe that Dickie is here, when really I've left him home, and you cuddle and pet him just the same.

GABRIELLE. I adore animals.

CONSTANCE. If you adore animals, you shouldn't pet them when they're not there. It's a form of hypocrisy.

COUNTESS. Now, Constance, Gabrielle has as much right as you ...

CONSTANCE. Gabrielle has no right to do what she does. Do you know what she does? She invites *people* to come to tea with us. *People* whom we know nothing about. *People* who exist only in her imagination.

COUNTESS. You think that's not an existence?

GABRIELLE. I don't invite them at all. They come by themselves. What can I do?

CONSTANCE. You might introduce us.

COUNTESS. If you think they're only imaginary, there's no point in your meeting them, is there?

CONSTANCE. Of course they're imaginary. But who likes to have imaginary people staring at one? Especially strangers.
GABRIELLE. Oh, they're really very nice. . . .
CONSTANCE. Tell me just one thing, Gabrielle—are they here now?
COUNTESS. Am I to be allowed to speak? Or is this going to be the same as the argument about inoculating Josephine's cat, when we didn't get to the subject at all?
CONSTANCE. Never! Never! Never! I'll never give my consent to that. (*To* DICKIE.) I'd never do a thing like that to you, Dickie sweet. . . . Oh, no! Oh, no! (*She begins to weep softly.*)
COUNTESS. Good heavens! Now we have her in tears. What an impossible creature! With the fate of humanity hanging in the balance! All right, all right, stop crying. I'll take him in my lap. Come, Dickie, Dickie.
CONSTANCE. No. He won't go now. Oh, how can you be so cruel? Don't you suppose I know about Dickie? Don't you think I'd rather have him here alive and woolly and frisking around the way he used to? You have your Adolphe. Gabrielle has her birds. But I have only Dickie. Do you think I'd be so silly about him if it wasn't that it's only by pretending that he's here all the time that I get him to come sometimes, really? Next time I won't bring him!
COUNTESS. Now let's not get ourselves worked up over nothing. Come here, Dickie. . . . Irma is going to take you for a nice walk. (*She rings her bell.*) Irma!

(IRMA *appears on the landing.*)

CONSTANCE. No. He doesn't want to go. Besides, I didn't bring him today. So there!
COUNTESS. Very well, then. Irma, make sure the door is locked.
IRMA. Yes, Countess. (IRMA *exits.*)
CONSTANCE. What do you mean? Why locked? Who's coming?
COUNTESS. If you'd let me get a word in, you'd know by now. A terrible thing has happened. This morning, this very morning, exactly at noon . . .
CONSTANCE (*thrilled*). Oh, how exciting!
COUNTESS. Be quiet. This morning, exactly at noon, thanks to a young man who drowned himself in the Seine . . . Oh, yes, while I think of it—do you know a mazurka called *La Belle Polonaise?*
CONSTANCE. Yes, Aurelia.
COUNTESS. Could you sing it now? This very minute?
CONSTANCE. Yes, Aurelia.
COUNTESS. All of it?
CONSTANCE. Yes, Aurelia. But who's interrupting now, Aurelia?

Countess. You're right. Well, this morning, exactly at noon, I discovered a horrible plot. There is a group of men who intend to tear down the whole city!

Constance. Is that all?

Gabrielle. But I don't understand, Aurelia. Why should men want to tear down the city? It was they themselves who put it up.

Countess. You are so innocent, my poor Gabrielle. There are people in the world who want to destroy everything. They have the fever of destruction. Even when they pretend that they're building, it is only in order to destroy. When they put up a new building, they quietly knock down two old ones. They build cities so that they can destroy the countryside. They destroy space with telephones and time with airplanes. Humanity is now dedicated to the task of universal destruction. I am speaking, of course, primarily of the male sex.

Gabrielle (*shocked*). Oh . . . !

Constance. Aurelia! Must you talk sex in front of Gabrielle?

Countess. There *are* two sexes.

Constance. Gabrielle is a virgin, Aurelia!

Countess. Oh, she can't be as innocent as all that. She keeps canaries.

Gabrielle. I think you're being very cruel about men, Aurelia. Men are big and beautiful, and as loyal as dogs. I preferred not to marry, it's true. But I hear excellent reports from friends who have had an opportunity to observe them closely.

Countess. My poor darling! You are still living in a dream. But one day, you will wake up as I have, and then you will see what is happening in the world. The tide has turned, my dear. Men are changing back into beasts. They know it. They no longer try to hide it. There was once such a thing as manners. I remember a time when the hungriest was the one who took the longest to pick up his fork. The one with the broadest grin was the one who needed most to go to the . . . It was such fun to keep them grinning like that for hours. But now they no longer pretend. Just look at them—snuffling their soup like pigs, tearing their meat like tigers, crunching their lettuce like crocodiles! A man doesn't take your hand nowadays. He gives you his paw.

Constance. Would that trouble you so much if they turned into animals? Personally, I think it's a good idea.

Gabrielle. Oh, I'd love to see them like that. They'd be sweet.

Constance. It might be the salvation of the human race.

Countess (*to* Constance). You'd make a fine rabbit, wouldn't you?

Constance. I?

Countess. Naturally. You don't think it's only the men who are changing? You change along with them. Husbands and wives together. We're all one race, you know.

CONSTANCE. You think so? And why would my poor husband have to be a rabbit if he were alive?

COUNTESS. Remember his front teeth? When he nibbled his celery?

CONSTANCE. I'm happy to say, I remember absolutely nothing about him. All I remember on that subject is the time that Father Lacordaire tried to kiss me in the park.

COUNTESS. Yes, yes, of course.

CONSTANCE. And what does that mean, if you please, "Yes, yes, of course"?

COUNTESS. Constance, just this once, look us in the eye and tell us truly—did that really happen or did you read about it in a book?

CONSTANCE. Now I'm being insulted!

COUNTESS. We promise you faithfully that we'll believe it all over again afterwards, won't we, Gabrielle? But tell us the truth this once.

CONSTANCE. How dare you question my memories? Suppose I said your pearls were false!

COUNTESS. They were.

CONSTANCE. I'm not asking what they were. I'm asking what they are. Are they false or are they real?

COUNTESS. Everyone knows that little by little, as one wears pearls, they become real.

CONSTANCE. And isn't it exactly the same with memories?

COUNTESS. Now do not let us waste time. I must go on.

CONSTANCE. I think Gabrielle is perfectly right about men. There are still plenty who haven't changed a bit. There's an old Senator who bows to Gabrielle every day when he passes her in front of the palace. And he takes off his hat each time.

GABRIELLE. That's perfectly true, Aurelia. He's always pushing an empty baby carriage, and he always stops and bows.

COUNTESS. Don't be taken in, Gabrielle. It's all make-believe. And all we can expect from these make-believe men is itself make-believe. They give us facepowder made of stones, sausages made of sawdust, shirts made of glass, stockings made of milk. It's all a vulgar pretence. And if that is the case, imagine what passes, these days, for virtue, sincerity, generosity, and love! I warn you, Gabrielle, don't let this Senator with the empty baby carriage pull the wool over your eyes.

GABRIELLE. He's really the soul of courtesy. He seems very correct.

COUNTESS. Those are the worst. Gabrielle, beware! He'll make you put on black riding boots, while he dances the can-can around you, singing God knows what filth at the top of his voice. The very thought makes one's blood run cold!

GABRIELLE. You think that's what he has in mind?

COUNTESS. Of course. Men have lost all sense of decency. They are all equally disgusting. Just look at them in the evening, sitting at their tables in the café, working away in unison with their toothpicks, hour after hour, digging up roast beef, veal, onion . . .

CONSTANCE. They don't harm anyone that way.

COUNTESS. Then why do you barricade your door, and make your friends meow before you let them come up? Incidentally, we must make an interesting sight, Gabrielle and I, yowling together on your doorstep like a couple of tomcats!

CONSTANCE. There's no need at all for you to yowl together. One would be quite enough. And you know perfectly well why I have to do it. It's because there are murderers.

COUNTESS. I don't quite see what prevents murderers from meowing like anybody else. But why are there murderers?

CONSTANCE. Why? Because there are thieves.

COUNTESS. And why are there thieves? Why is there almost nothing but thieves?

CONSTANCE. Because they worship money. Because money is king.

COUNTESS. Ah—now we've come to it. Because we live in the reign of the Golden Calf. Did you realize that, Gabrielle? Men now publicly worship the Golden Calf!

GABRIELLE. How awful! Have the authorities been notified?

COUNTESS. The authorities do it themselves, Gabrielle.

GABRIELLE. Oh! Has anyone talked to the bishop?

COUNTESS. Nowadays only money talks to the bishop. And so you see why I asked you to come here today. The world has gone out of its mind. Unless we do something, humanity is doomed! Constance, have you any suggestions?

CONSTANCE. I know what I always do in a case like this. . . .

COUNTESS. You write to the Prime Minister.

CONSTANCE. He always does what I tell him.

COUNTESS. Does he ever answer your letters?

CONSTANCE. He knows I prefer him not to. It might excite gossip. Besides, I don't always write. Sometimes I wire. The time I told him about the Archbishop's frigidaire, it was by wire. And they sent a new one the very next day.

COUNTESS. There was probably a commission in it for someone. And what do you suggest, Gabrielle?

CONSTANCE. Now, how can she tell you until she's consulted her voices?

GABRIELLE. I could go right home and consult them, and we could meet again after dinner.

COUNTESS. There's no time for that. Besides, your voices are not real voices.

GABRIELLE (*furious*). How dare you say a thing like that?

COUNTESS. Where do your voices come from? Still from your sewing-machine?

GABRIELLE. Not at all. They've passed into my hot-water bottle. And it's much nicer that way. They don't chatter any more. They gurgle. But they haven't been a bit nice to me lately. Last night they kept telling me to let my canaries out. "Let them out. Let them out. Let them out."

CONSTANCE. Did you?

GABRIELLE. I opened the cage. They wouldn't go.

COUNTESS. I don't call that *voices*. Objects talk—everyone knows that. It's the principle of the phonograph. But to ask a hot-water bottle for advice is silly. What does a hot-water bottle know? No, all we have to consult here is our own judgment.

CONSTANCE. Very well then, tell us what you have decided. Since you're asking our opinion, you've doubtless made up your mind.

COUNTESS. Yes, I've thought the whole thing out. All I really needed to discover was the source of the infection. Today I found it.

CONSTANCE. Where?

COUNTESS. You'll see soon enough. I've baited a trap. In just a few minutes, the rats will be here.

GABRIELLE (*in alarm*). Rats!

COUNTESS. Don't be alarmed. They're still in human form.

GABRIELLE. Heavens! What are you going to do with them?

COUNTESS. That's just the question. Suppose I get these wicked men all here at once—in my cellar—have I the right to exterminate them?

GABRIELLE. To kill them?

(COUNTESS *nods*.)

CONSTANCE. That's not a question for us. You'll have to ask Father Bridet.

COUNTESS. I have asked him. Yes. One day, in confession, I told him frankly that I had a secret desire to destroy all wicked people. He said: "By all means, my child. And when you're ready to go into action, I'll lend you the jawbone of an ass."

CONSTANCE. That's just talk. You get him to put that in writing.

GABRIELLE. What's your scheme, Aurelia?

COUNTESS. That's a secret.

CONSTANCE. It's not so easy to kill them. Let's say you had a tank full of vitriol all ready for them. You could never get them to walk into it. There's nothing so stubborn as a man when you want him to do something.

COUNTESS. Leave that to me.

CONSTANCE. But if they're killed, they're bound to be missed, and then we'll be fined. They fine you for every little thing these days.

COUNTESS. They won't be missed.
GABRIELLE. I wish Josephine were here. Her sister's husband was a lawyer. She knows all about these things.
COUNTESS. Do you miss a cold when it's gone? Or the germs that caused it? When the world feels well again, do you think it will regret its illness? No, it will stretch itself joyfully, and it will smile—that's all.
CONSTANCE. Just a moment! Gabrielle, are they here now? Yes or no?
COUNTESS. What's the matter with you now?
CONSTANCE. I'm simply asking Gabrielle if her friends are in the room or not. I have a right to know.
GABRIELLE. I'm not allowed to say.
CONSTANCE. I know very well they are. I'm sure of it. Otherwise you wouldn't be making faces.
COUNTESS. May I ask what difference it makes to you if her friends are in the room?
CONSTANCE. Just this: If they're here, I'm not going to say another word! I'm certainly not going to commit myself in a matter involving the death sentence in the presence of third parties, whether they exist or not.
GABRIELLE. That's not being very nice to my guests, is it?
COUNTESS. Constance, you must be mad! Or are you so stupid as to think that just because we're alone, there's nobody with us? Do you consider us so boring or repulsive that of all the millions of beings, imaginary or otherwise, who are prowling about in space, there's not one who might possibly enjoy spending a little time with us? On the contrary, my dear—my house is full of guests always. They know that here they have a place in the universe where they can come when they're lonely and be sure of a welcome. For my part, I'm delighted to have them.
GABRIELLE. Thank you, Aurelia.
CONSTANCE. You know perfectly well, Aurelia...
COUNTESS. I know perfectly well at this moment the whole universe is listening to us—and that every word we say echoes to the remotest star. To pretend otherwise is the sheerest hypocrisy.
CONSTANCE. Then why do you insult me in front of everybody? I'm not mean. I'm shy. I feel timid about giving an opinion in front of such a crowd. Furthermore, if you think I'm so bad and so stupid, why did you invite me, in the first place?
COUNTESS. I'll tell you. And I'll tell you why, disagreeable as you are, I always give you the biggest piece of cake and my best honey. It's because when you come there's always someone with you—and I don't mean Dickie—I mean someone who resembles you like a sister, only she's young and lovely, and she sits modestly to one side and smiles at me tenderly all the time you're bickering and quarreling, and never says a word. That's the Constance to whom I give the cake that you gobble, and it's because of her that

you're here today, and it's her vote that I'm asking you to cast in this critical moment. And not yours, which is of no importance whatever.

CONSTANCE. I'm leaving.

COUNTESS. Be so good as to sit down. I can't let her go yet.

CONSTANCE (*crossing toward the stairs*). No. This is too much. I'm taking her with me.

(IRMA *enters.*)

IRMA. Madame Josephine.

COUNTESS. Thank heaven!

GABRIELLE. We're saved. (JOSEPHINE, *the Madwoman of La Concorde, sweeps in majestically in a get-up somewhere between the regal and the priestly.*)

JOSEPHINE. My dear friends, today once again, I waited for President Wilson—but he didn't come out.

COUNTESS. You'll have to wait quite a while longer before he does. He's been dead since 1924.

JOSEPHINE. I have plenty of time.

COUNTESS. In anyone else, Josephine, these extravagances might seem a little childish. But a person of your judgment doubtless has her reasons for wanting to talk to a man to whom no one would listen when he was alive. We have a legal problem for you. Suppose you had all the world's criminals here in this room. And suppose you had a way of getting rid of them forever. Would you have the right to do it?

JOSEPHINE. Why not?

COUNTESS. Exactly my point.

GABRIELLE. But, Josephine, so many people!

JOSEPHINE. *De minimis non curat lex.* The more there are, the more legal it is. It's impersonal. It's even military. It's the cardinal principle of battle—you get all your enemies in one place, and you kill them all together at one time. Because if you had to track them down one by one in their houses and offices, you'd get tired, and sooner or later you'd stop. I believe your idea is very practical, Aurelia. I can't imagine why we never thought of it before.

GABRIELLE. Well, if you think it's all right to do it. . . .

JOSEPHINE. By all means. Your criminals have had a fair trial, I suppose?

COUNTESS. Trial?

JOSEPHINE. Certainly. You can't kill anybody without a trial. That's elementary. "No man shall be deprived of his life, liberty, and property without due process of law."

COUNTESS. They deprive us of ours.

JOSEPHINE. That's not the point. You're not accused of anything. Every accused—man, woman, or child—has the right to defend himself at the bar of justice. Even animals. Before the Deluge, you will recall, the Lord permittted Noah to speak in defense of his fellow mortals. He evidently stuttered. You know the result. On the other hand, Captain Dreyfus was not only innocent—he was defended by a marvelous orator. The result was precisely the same. So you see, in having a trial, you run no risk whatever.

COUNTESS. But if I give them the slightest cause for suspicion—I'll lose them.

JOSEPHINE. There's a simple procedure prescribed in such cases. You can summon the defendants by calling them three times—mentally, if you like. If they don't appear, the court may designate an attorney who will represent them. This attorney can then argue their case to the court, *in absentia*, and a judgment can then be rendered, *in contumacio*.

COUNTESS. But I don't know any attorneys. And we have only ten minutes.

GABRIELLE. Hurry, Josephine, hurry!

JOSEPHINE. In case of emergency, it is permissible for the court to order the first passer-by to act as attorney for the defense. A defense is like a baptism. Absolutely indispensable, but you don't have to know anything to do it. Ask Irma to get you somebody. Anybody.

COUNTESS. The Deaf-Mute?

JOSEPHINE. Well—that's getting it down a bit fine. That might be questionable on appeal.

COUNTESS (*calls*). Irma! What about the Police Sergeant?

JOSEPHINE. He won't do. He's under oath to the state.

(IRMA *appears*.)

IRMA. Yes, Countess?

COUNTESS. Who's out there, Irma?

IRMA. All our friends, Countess. There's the Ragpicker and . . .

COUNTESS. Send down the Ragpicker.

CONSTANCE. Do you think it's wise to have all those millionaires represented by a ragpicker?

JOSEPHINE. It's a first-rate choice. Criminals are always represented by their opposites. Murderers, by someone who obviously wouldn't hurt a fly. Rapists, by a member of the League for Decency. Experience shows it's the only way to get an acquittal.

COUNTESS. But we must not have an acquittal. That would mean the end of the world!

JOSEPHINE. Justice is justice, my dear.

(*The* RAGPICKER *comes down, with a stately air. Behind him, on the landing, appear the other* VAGABONDS.)

THE RAGPICKER. Greetings, Countess. Greetings, ladies. My most sincere compliments.

COUNTESS. Has Irma told you . . . ?

THE RAGPICKER. She said something about a trial.

COUNTESS. You have been appointed attorney for the defense.

THE RAGPICKER. Terribly flattered, I'm sure.

COUNTESS. You realize, don't you, how much depends on the outcome of this trial?

JOSEPHINE. Do you know the defendants well enough to undertake the case?

THE RAGPICKER. I know them to the bottom of their souls. I go through their garbage every day.

CONSTANCE. And what do you find there?

THE RAGPICKER. Mostly flowers.

GABRIELLE. It's true, you know, the rich are always surrounded with flowers.

CONSTANCE. How beautiful!

COUNTESS. Are you trying to prejudice the court?

THE RAGPICKER. Oh no, Countess, no.

COUNTESS. We want a completely impartial defense.

THE RAGPICKER. Of course, Countess, of course. Permit me to make a suggestion.

COUNTESS. Will you preside, Josephine?

THE RAGPICKER. Instead of speaking as attorney, suppose you let me speak directly as defendant. It will be more convincing, and I can get into it more.

JOSEPHINE. Excellent idea. Motion granted.

COUNTESS. We don't want you to be too convincing, remember.

THE RAGPICKER. Impartial, Countess, impartial.

JOSEPHINE. Well? Have you prepared your case?

THE RAGPICKER. How rich am I?

JOSEPHINE. Millions. Billions.

THE RAGPICKER. How did I get them? Theft? Murder? Embezzlement?

COUNTESS. Most likely.

THE RAGPICKER. Do I have a wife? A mistress?

COUNTESS. Everything.

THE RAGPICKER. All right. I'm ready.

GABRIELLE. Will you have some tea?

THE RAGPICKER. Is that good?

CONSTANCE. Very good for the voice. The Russians drink nothing but tea. And they talk like anything.

THE RAGPICKER. All right. Tea.

JOSEPHINE (*to the* VAGABONDS). Come in. Come in. All of you. You may take places. The trial is public. (*The* VAGABONDS *dispose themselves on the steps and elsewhere.*) Your bell, if you please, Aurelia.

COUNTESS. But what if I should need to ring for Irma?

JOSEPHINE. Irma will sit here, next to me. If you need her, she can ring for herself. (*To the* POLICE SERGEANT *and the* POLICEMAN.) Conduct the accused to the bar. (*The officers conduct the* RAGPICKER *to a bar improvised with a rocking chair and a packing case marked FRAGILE. The* RAGPICKER *mounts the box. She rings the bell.*) The court is now in session. (*All sit.*) Counsel for the defense, you may take the oath.

THE RAGPICKER. I swear to tell the truth, the whole truth, and nothing but the truth, so help me God.

JOSEPHINE. Nonsense! You're a witness. You're an attorney. It's your duty to lie, conceal, and distort everything, and slander everybody.

THE RAGPICKER. All right. I swear to lie, conceal, and distort everything, and slander everybody.

(JOSEPHINE *rings stridently.*)

JOSEPHINE. Quiet! Begin.

THE RAGPICKER. May it please the honorable, august and elegant Court . . .

JOSEPHINE. Flattery will get you nowhere. That will do. The defense has been heard. Cross-examination.

COUNTESS. Mr. President . . .

THE RAGPICKER (*bowing with dignity*). Madame.

COUNTESS. Do you know what you are charged with?

THE RAGPICKER. I can't for the life of me imagine. My life is an open book. My ways are known to all. I am a pillar of the church and the sole support of the Opera. My hands are spotless.

COUNTESS. What an atrocious lie! Just look at them!

CONSTANCE. You don't have to insult the man. He's only lying to please you.

COUNTESS. Be quiet, Constance! You don't get the idea at all. (*To the* RAGPICKER.) You are charged with the crime of worshipping money.

THE RAGPICKER. Worshipping money? Me?

JOSEPHINE. Do you plead guilty or not guilty? Which is it?

THE RAGPICKER. Why, Your Honor . . .

JOSEPHINE. Yes or no?

THE RAGPICKER. Yes or no? No! I don't worship money, Countess. Heavens, no! Money worships me. It adores me. It won't let me alone. It's damned embarrassing, I can tell you.

JOSEPHINE. Kindly watch your language.

COUNTESS. Defendant, tell the Court how you came by your money.

THE RAGPICKER. The first time money came to me, I was a mere boy, a little golden-haired child in the bosom of my dear family. It came to me suddenly in the guise of a gold brick which, in my innocence, I picked out of a garbage can one day while playing. I was horrified, as you can imagine. I immediately tried to get rid of it by swapping it for a little rundown one-track railroad which, to my consternation, at once sold itself for a hundred times its value. In a desperate effort to get rid of this money, I began to buy things. I bought the Northern Refineries, the Galeries Lafayette, and the Schneider-Creusot Munition Works. And now I'm stuck with them. It's a horrible fate—but I'm resigned to it. I don't ask for your sympathy, I don't ask for your pity—all I ask for is a little common human understanding. . . . (*He begins to cry.*)

COUNTESS. I object. This wretch is trying to play on the emotions of the Court.

JOSEPHINE. The Court has no emotions.

THE RAGPICKER. Everyone knows that the poor have no one but themselves to blame for their poverty. It's only just that they should suffer the consequences. But how is it the fault of the rich if they're rich?

COUNTESS. Dry your tears. You're deceiving nobody. If, as you say, you're ashamed of your money, why is it you hold onto it with such a death-grip?

THE RAGPICKER. Me?

STREET PEDDLER. You never part with a franc!

JUGGLER. You wouldn't even give the poor Deaf-Mute a sou!

THE RAGPICKER. Me, hold onto money? What slander! What injustice! What a thing to say to me in the presence of this honorable, august, and elegant Court! I spend all my time trying to spend my money. If I have tan shoes, I buy black ones. If I have a bicycle, I buy a motor car. If I have a wife, I buy . . .

JOSEPHINE (*rings*). Order!

THE RAGPICKER. I dispatch a plane to Java for a bouquet of flowers. I send a steamer to Egypt for a basket of figs. I send a special representative to New York to fetch me an ice-cream cone. And if it's not just exactly right, back it goes. But no matter what I do, I can't get rid of my money! If I play a hundred to one shot, the horse comes in by twenty lengths. If I throw a diamond in the Seine, it turns up in the trout they serve me for lunch. Ten diamonds—ten trout. Well, now, do you suppose I can get rid of forty millions by giving a sou to a deaf-mute? Is it even worth the effort?

CONSTANCE. He's right.

THE RAGPICKER. Ah! You see, my dear? At last, there is somebody who understands me! Somebody who is not only beautiful, but extraordinarily sensitive and intelligent.

COUNTESS. I object!

JOSEPHINE. Overruled!

THE RAGPICKER. I should be delighted to send you some flowers, Miss—directly I'm acquitted. What flowers do you prefer?
CONSTANCE. Roses.
THE RAGPICKER. You shall have a bale every morning for the next five years. Money means nothing to me.
CONSTANCE. And amaryllis.
THE RAGPICKER. I'll make a note of the name. (*In his best lyrical style.*) The lady understands, ladies and gentlemen. The lady is no fool. She's been around and she knows what's what. If I gave the Deaf-Mute a franc, twenty francs, twenty million francs—I still wouldn't make a dent in the forty times a thousand million francs that I'm afflicted with! Right, little lady?
CONSTANCE. Right.
JOSEPHINE. Proceed.
THE RAGPICKER. Like on the Stock Exchange. If *you* buy a stock, it sinks at once like a plummet. But if *I* buy a stock, it turns around and soars like an eagle. If I buy it at 33 . . .
PEDDLER. It goes up to a thousand.
THE RAGPICKER. It goes to twenty thousand! That's how I bought my twelve chateaux, my twenty villas, my 234 farms. That's how I endow the Opera and keep my twelve ballerinas.
FLOWER GIRL. I hope every one of them deceives you every moment of the day!
THE RAGPICKER. How can they deceive me? Suppose they try to deceive me with the male chorus, the general director, the assistant electrician, or the English horn—I own them all, body and soul. It would be like deceiving me with my big toe.
CONSTANCE. Don't listen, Gabrielle.
GABRIELLE. Listen to what?
THE RAGPICKER. No. I am incapable of jealousy. I have all the women—or I can have them, which is the same thing. I get the thin ones with caviar—the fat ones with pearls . . .
COUNTESS. So you think there are no women with morals?
THE RAGPICKER. I mix morals with mink—delicious combination. I drip pearls into protests. I adorn resistance with rubies. My touch is jeweled; my smile, a motor car. What woman can withstand me? I lift my little finger—and do they fall?— Like leaves in autumn—like tin cans from a second-story window.
CONSTANCE. That's going a little too far!
COUNTESS. You see where money leads.
THE RAGPICKER. Of course. When you have no money, nobody trusts you, nobody believes you, nobody likes you. Because to have money is to be virtuous, honest, beautiful, and witty. And to be without is to be ugly and boring and stupid and useless.

COUNTESS. One last question. Suppose you find this oil you're looking for. What do you propose to do with it?

THE RAGPICKER. I propose to make war! I propose to conquer the world!

COUNTESS. You have heard the defense, such as it is. I demand a verdict of guilty.

THE RAGPICKER. What are you talking about? Guilty? I? I am never guilty!

JOSEPHINE. I order you to keep quiet.

THE RAGPICKER. I am never quiet!

JOSEPHINE. Quiet, in the name of the law!

THE RAGPICKER. I am the law. When I speak, that is the law. When I present my backside, it is etiquette to smile and to apply the lips respectfully. It is more than etiquette—it is a cherished national privilege, guaranteed by the Constitution.

JOSEPHINE. That's contempt of court. The trial is over.

COUNTESS. And the verdict?

ALL. Guilty!

JOSEPHINE. Guilty as charged.

COUNTESS. Then I have full authority to carry out the sentence?

ALL. Yes!

COUNTESS. I can do what I like with them?

ALL. Yes!

COUNTESS. I have the right to exterminate them?

ALL. Yes!

JOSEPHINE. Court adjourned!

COUNTESS (*to the* RAGPICKER). Congratulations, Ragpicker. A marvelous defense. Absolutely impartial.

THE RAGPICKER. Had I known a little before, I could have done better. I could have prepared a little speech, like the time I used to sell the Miracle Spot Remover. . . .

JOSEPHINE. No need for that. You did very well, extempore. The likeness was striking and the style reminiscent of Clemenceau. I predict a brilliant future for you. Good-bye, Aurelia. I'll take our little Gabrielle home.

CONSTANCE. I'm going to walk along the river. (*To* DICKIE.) Oh! So here you are. And your ear all bloody! Dickie! Have you been fighting again? Oh, dear . . . !

COUNTESS (*to the* RAGPICKER). See that she gets home all right, won't you? She loses everything on the way. And in the queerest places. Her prayer book in the butcher shop. And her corset in church.

THE RAGPICKER (*bowing and offering his arm*). Permit me, Madame.

STREET SINGER. Oh, Countess—my mazurka. Remember?

COUNTESS. Oh, yes. Constance, wait a moment. (*To the* SINGER.) Well? Begin.

SINGER (*sings*).

> Do you hear, Mademoiselle,
> Those musicians of hell?

CONSTANCE. Why, of course, it's *La Belle Polonaise*. . . . (*She sings.*)

> From Poland to France
> Comes this marvelous dance,
>   So gracious,
>   Audacious,
> Will you foot it, perchance?

SINGER. I'm saved!
JOSEPHINE (*reappearing at the head of the stairs*).

> Now my arm I entwine
> Round these contours divine,
> So pure, so impassioned,
> Which Cupid has fashioned. . . .

GABRIELLE (*reappearing also, she sings a quartet with the others*).

> Come, let's dance the mazurka, that devilish measure,
> 'Tis a joy that's reserved to the gods for their pleasure—
>   Let's gallop, let's hop,
>   With never a stop,
>   My blond Polish miss,
> Let our heads spin and turn
> As the dance-floor we spurn—
> There was never such pleasure as this!

(*They all exit, dancing.*)

IRMA. It's time for your afternoon nap.
COUNTESS. But suppose they come, Irma!
IRMA. I'll watch out for them.
COUNTESS. Thank you, Irma. I *am* tired. (*She smiles.*) Did you ever see a trial end more happily in your life?
IRMA. Lie down and close your eyes a moment.

(*The* COUNTESS *stretches out on the chaise-longue and shuts her eyes.* IRMA *tiptoes out. In a moment,* PIERRE *comes down softly, the feather boa in his hands. He stands over the chaise-lounge, looking tenderly down at the sleeping woman, then kneels beside her and takes her hand.*)

COUNTESS (*without opening her eyes*). Is it you, Adolphe Bertaut?
PIERRE. It's only Pierre.

JEAN GIRAUDOUX   319

COUNTESS. Don't lie to me, Adolphe Bertaut. These are your hands. Why do you complicate things always? Say that it's you.

PIERRE. Yes. It is I.

COUNTESS. Would it cost you so much to call me Aurelia?

PIERRE. It's I, Aurelia.

COUNTESS. Why did you leave me, Adolphe Bertaut? Was she so very lovely, this Georgette of yours?

PIERRE. No. You are a thousand times lovelier.

COUNTESS. But she was clever.

PIERRE. She was stupid.

COUNTESS. It was her soul, then, that drew you? When you looked into her eyes, you saw a vision of heaven, perhaps?

PIERRE. I saw nothing.

COUNTESS. That's how it is with men. They love you because you are beautiful and clever and soulful—and at the first opportunity they leave you for someone who is plain and dull and soulless. But why does it have to be like that, Adolphe Bertaut? Why?

PIERRE. Why, Aurelia?

COUNTESS. I know very well she wasn't rich. Because when I saw you that time at the grocer's, and you snatched the only good melon from right under my nose, your cuffs, my poor friend, were badly frayed. . . .

PIERRE. Yes. She was poor.

COUNTESS. "Was" poor. Is she dead then? If it's because she's dead that you've come back to me—then no. Go away. I will not take their leavings from the dead. I refuse to inherit you. . . .

PIERRE. She's quite well.

COUNTESS. Your hands are still the same, Adolphe Bertaut. Your touch is young and firm. Because it's the only part of you that has stayed with me. The rest of you is pretty far gone, I'm afraid. I can see why you'd rather not come near me when my eyes are open. It's thoughtful of you.

PIERRE. Yes. I've aged.

COUNTESS. Not I. I am young because I haven't had to live down my youth, like you. I have it with me still, as fresh and beautiful as ever. But when you walk now in the park at Colombes with Georgette, I'm sure . . .

PIERRE. There is no longer a park at Colombes.

COUNTESS. Is there a park still at St. Cloud? Is there a park at Versailles? I've never gone back to see. But I think, if they could move, those trees would have walked away in disgust the day you went there with Georgette. . . .

PIERRE. They did. Not many are left.

COUNTESS. You take her also, I suppose, to hear *Denise*?

PIERRE. No one hears *Denise* any more.

COUNTESS. It was on the way home from *Denise*, Adolphe Bertaut, that I first took your arm. Because it was windy and it was late. I have never set foot in that street again. I go the other way round. It's not easy, in the winter, when there's ice. One is quite apt to fall. I often do.

PIERRE. Oh, my darling—forgive me.

COUNTESS. No, never. I will never forgive you. It was very bad taste to take her to the very places where we'd been together.

PIERRE. All the same, I swear, Aurelia . . .

COUNTESS. Don't swear. I know what you did. You gave her the same flowers. You bought her the same chocolates. But has she any left? No. I have all your flowers still. I have twelve chocolates. No, I will never forgive you as long as I live.

PIERRE. I always loved you, Aurelia.

COUNTESS. You "loved" me? Then you too are dead, Adolphe Bertaut?

PIERRE. No. I love you. I shall always love you, Aurelia.

COUNTESS. Yes. I know. That much I've always known. I knew it the moment you went away, Adolphe, and I knew that nothing could ever change it. Georgette is in his arms now—yes. But he loves me. Tonight he's taken Georgette to hear *Denise*—yes. But he loves me. . . . I know it. You never loved her. Do you think I believed for one moment that absurd story about her running off with the osteopath? Of course not. Since you didn't love her, obviously she stayed with you. And, after that, when she came back, and I heard about her going off with the surveyor—I knew that couldn't be true, either. You'll never get rid of her, Adolphe Bertaut—never. Because you don't love her.

PIERRE. I need your pity, Aurelia. I need your love. Don't forget me. . . .

COUNTESS. Farewell, Adolphe Bertaut. Farewell. Let go my hand, and give it to little Pierre. (PIERRE *lets go her hand, and after a moment takes it again. The* COUNTESS *opens her eyes.*) Pierre? Ah, it's you. Has he gone?

PIERRE. Yes, Countess.

COUNTESS. I didn't hear him go. Oh, he knows how to make a quick exit, that one. (*She sees the boa.*) Good heavens! Wherever did you find it!

PIERRE. In the wardrobe, Countess. When I took off the mirror.

COUNTESS. Was there a purple felt shopping bag with it?

PIERRE. Yes, Countess.

COUNTESS. And a little child's sewing box?

PIERRE. No, Countess.

COUNTESS. Oh, they're frightened now. They're trembling for their lives. You see what they're up to? They're putting back all the things they have stolen. I never open that wardrobe, of course, on account of the old woman in the mirror. But I have sharp eyes. I don't need to open it to see what's in it. Up to this morning, that wardrobe was empty. And now— you see? But, dear me, how stupid they are! The one thing I really miss is

JEAN GIRAUDOUX   321

my little sewing box. It's something they stole from me when I was a child. They haven't put it back? You're quite sure?

PIERRE. What was it like?

COUNTESS. Green cardboard with paper lace and gold stamping. I got it for Christtmas when I was seven. They stole it the very next day. I cried my eyes out every time I thought of it—until I was eight.

PIERRE. It's not there, Countess.

COUNTESS. The thimble was gilt. I swore I'd never use any other. Look at my poor fingers. . . .

PIERRE. They've kept the thimble too.

COUNTESS. Splendid! Then I'm under no obligation to be merciful. Put the boa around my neck, Pierre. I want them to see me wearing it. They'll think it's a real boa.

(IRMA *runs in excitedly.*)

IRMA. Here they come, Countess! You were right—it's a procession. The street is full of limousines and taxis!

COUNTESS. I will receive them. (As PIERRE *hesitates to leave her.*) Don't worry. There's nothing to be frightened of. (PIERRE *goes out.*) Irma, did you remember to stir the kerosene into the water?

IRMA. Yes, Countess. Here it is.

COUNTESS (*looking critically at the bottle*). You might as well pour in what's left of the tea. (IRMA *shakes up the liquid.*) Don't forget, I'm supposed to be deaf. I want to hear what they're thinking.

IRMA. Yes, Countess.

COUNTESS (*putting the finishing touches to her make-up*). I don't have to be merciful—but, after all, I do want to be just. . . .

(IRMA *goes up to the landing and exits. As soon as she is alone, the* COUNTESS *presses the brick, and the trap door opens. There is a confused sound of auto horns in the street above, and the noise of an approaching crowd.*)

IRMA (*offstage*). Yes, Mr. President. Come in, Mr. President. You're expected, Mr. President. This way, Mr. President. (*The* PRESIDENTS *come down, led by the* PRESIDENT. *They all look alike, are dressed alike, and all have long cigars.*) The Countess is quite deaf, gentlemen. You'll have to shout. (*She announces.*) The presidents of the boards of directors!

THE PRESIDENT. I had a premonition, Madame, when I saw you this morning, that we should meet again. (*The* COUNTESS *smiles vaguely. He continues, a tone louder.*) I want to thank you for your trust. You may place yourself in our hands with complete confidence.

SECOND PRESIDENT. Louder. The old trot can't hear you.

THE PRESIDENT. I have a letter here, Madame, in which . . .

SECOND PRESIDENT. Louder. Louder.

THIRD PRESIDENT (*shouting*). Is it true that you've located . . . ? (*The* COUNTESS *stares at him blankly. He shouts at the top of his voice.*) Oil? (*The* COUNTESS *nods with a smile, and points down. The* PRESIDENT *produces a legal paper and a fountain pen.*) Sign here.

COUNTESS. What is it? I haven't my glasses.

THE PRESIDENT. Your contract. (*He offers the pen.*)

COUNTESS. Thank you.

SECOND PRESIDENT (*normal voice*). What is it?

THIRD PRESIDENT. Waiver of all rights. (*He takes it back signed.*) Thank you. (*He hands it to the* SECOND PRESIDENT.) Witness. (*The* SECOND PRESIDENT *witnesses it. The* PRESIDENT *passes it on to the* THIRD PRESIDENT.) Notarize. (*The paper is notarized. The* PRESIDENT *turns to the* COUNTESS *and shouts.*) My congratulations. And now, Madame—(*He produces a gold brick wrapped in tissue paper.*) If you'll show us the well, this package is yours.

COUNTESS. What is it?

THE PRESIDENT. Pure gold. Twenty-four karat. For you.

COUNTESS. Thank you very much. (*She takes it.*) It's heavy.

SECOND PRESIDENT. Are you going to give her that?

THE PRESIDENT. Don't worry. We'll pick it up again on the way out. (*He shouts at the* COUNTESS, *pointing at the trap door.*) Is this the way?

COUNTESS. That's the way.

(*The* SECOND PRESIDENT *tries to slip in first. The* PRESIDENT *pulls him back.*)

THE PRESIDENT. Just a minute, Mr. President. After me, if you don't mind. And watch those cigars. It's oil, you know.

(*But as he is about to descend, the* COUNTESS *steps forward.*)

COUNTESS. Just one moment . . .

THE PRESIDENT. Yes?

COUNTESS. Did any of you happen to bring along a little sewing box?

THE PRESIDENT. Sewing box? (*He pulls back another impatient* PRESIDENT.) Take it easy.

COUNTESS. Or a little gold thimble?

THE PRESIDENT. Not me.

THE PRESIDENTS. Not us.

COUNTESS. What a pity!

THE PRESIDENT. Can we go down now?

COUNTESS. Yes. You may go down now. Watch your step.

(*They hurry down eagerly. When they have quite disappeared,* IRMA *appears on the landing and announces the next echelon.*)

IRMA. Countess, the Prospectors.
COUNTESS. Heavens! Are there more than one?
IRMA. There's a whole delegation.
COUNTESS. Send them down.

(*The* PROSPECTOR *comes in, following his nose.*)

IRMA. Come in, please.
THE PROSPECTOR (*sniffing the air like a bloodhound*). I smell something. . . . Who's that?
IRMA. The Countess. She is very deaf.
THE PROSPECTOR. Good.

(*The* PROSPECTORS *also look alike. Sharp clothes, Western hats, and long noses. They crowd down the stairs after the* PROSPECTOR, *sniffing in unison. The* PROSPECTOR *is especially talented. He casts about on the scent until it leads him to the decanter on the table. He pours himself a glass, drinks it off, and belches with much satisfaction. The others join him at once, and follow his example. They all belch in unison.*)

THE PROSPECTORS. Oil?
THE PROSPECTOR. Oil!
COUNTESS. Oil.
THE PROSPECTOR. Traces? Puddles?
COUNTESS. Pools. Gushers.
SECOND PROSPECTOR. Characteristic odor? (*He sniffs.*)
THE PROSPECTOR. Chanel Number 5. Nectar! Undoubtedly—the finest—rarest! (*He drinks.*) Sixty gravity crude: straight gasoline! (*To the* COUNTESS.) How found? By blast? Drill?
COUNTESS. By finger.
THE PROSPECTOR (*whipping out a document*). Sign here, please.
COUNTESS. What is it?
THE PROSPECTOR. Agreement for dividing the profits . . .

(*The* COUNTESS *signs.*)

SECOND PROSPECTOR (*to* FIRST PROSPECTOR). What is it?
THE PROSPECTOR (*pocketing the paper*). Application to enter a lunatic asylum. Down there?
COUNTESS. Down there. (*The* PROSPECTORS *go down, sniffing.*)

(IRMA *enters.*)

IRMA. The gentlemen of the press are here.
COUNTESS. The rest of the machine! Show them in.
IRMA. The Public Relations Counselors! (*They enter, all shapes and*

sizes, all in blue pin-striped suits and black homburg hats.) The Countess is very deaf, gentlemen. You'll have to shout!

FIRST PRESS AGENT.   You don't say— Delighted to make the acquaintance of so charming and beautiful a lady....

SECOND PRESS AGENT.   Louder. She can't hear you.

FIRST PRESS AGENT.   What a face! (*Shouts.*) Madame, we are the press. You know our power. We fix all values. We set all standards. Your entire future depends on us.

COUNTESS.   How do you do?

FIRST PRESS AGENT.   What will we charge the old trull? The usual thirty?

SECOND PRESS AGENT.   Forty.

THIRD PRESS AGENT.   Sixty.

FIRST PRESS AGENT.   All right—seventy-five. (*He fills in a form and offers it to the* COUNTESS.) Sign here, Countess. This contract really gives you a break.

COUNTESS.   That is the entrance.

FIRST PRESS AGENT.   Entrance to what?

COUNTESS.   The oil well.

FIRST PRESS AGENT.   Oh, we don't need to see that, Madame.

COUNTESS.   Don't need to see it?

FIRST PRESS AGENT.   No, no—we don't have to see it to write about it. We can imagine it. An oil well is an oil well. "That's oil we know on earth, and oil we need to know." (*He bows.*)

COUNTESS.   But if you don't see it, how can you be sure the oil is there?

FIRST PRESS AGENT.   If it's there, well and good. If it's not, by the time we get through, it will be. You underestimate the creative aspect of our profession, Madame. (*The* COUNTESS *shakes her head, handing back the papers.*) I warn you, if you insist on rubbing our noses in this oil, it will cost you 10 percent extra.

COUNTESS.   It's worth it. (*She signs. They cross toward the trapdoor.*)

SECOND PRESS AGENT (*descending*).   You see, Madame, we of the press can refuse a lady nothing.

THIRD PRESS AGENT.   Especially, such a lady. (THIRD PRESS AGENT *starts going down.*)

SECOND PRESS AGENT (*going down. Gallantly*).   It's plain to see, Madame, that even fountains of oil have their nymphs.... I can use that somewhere. That's copy!

(*The* PRESS AGENTS *go down. As he disappears, the* FIRST PRESS AGENT *steals the gold brick and blows a kiss gallantly to the* COUNTESS, *who blows one back.*)

(*There is a high-pitched chatter offstage, and* IRMA *comes in, trying hard to hold back* Three Women *who pay no attention to her whatever. These* Women *are tall, slender, and as soulless as if they were molded of wax. They march down the steps, erect and abstracted like animated window models, but chattering incessantly.*)

Irma. But, ladies, please—you have no business here—you are not expected. (*To the* Countess.) There are some strange ladies coming....

Countess. Show them in, Irma. (*The* Women *come down, without taking the slightest interest in their surroundings.*) Who are you?

First Woman. Madame, we are the most powerful pressure group in the world.

Second Woman. We are the ultimate dynamic.

Third Woman. The mainspring of all combinations.

First Woman. Nothing succeeds without our assistance. Is that the well, Madame?

Countess. That is the well.

First Woman. Put out your cigarettes, girls. We don't want any explosions. Not with my brand-new eyelashes.

(*They go down, still chattering. The* Countess *crosses to the wall to close the trap. As she does so, there is a commotion on the landing.*)

Irma. Countess ... (*A* Man *rushes in breathlessly.*)

Man. Just a minute! Just a minute! (*He rushes for the trap door.*)

Countess. Wait! Who are you?

Man. I'm in a hurry. Excuse me. It's my only chance! (*He rushes down.*)

Countess. But ... (*But he is gone. She shrugs her shoulders, and presses the brick. The trap closes. She rings the bell for* Irma.) My gold brick! Why, they've stolen my gold brick! (*She moves toward the trap. It is now closed.*) Well, let them take their god with them.

(Irma *enters and sees with astonishment that the stage is empty of all but the* Countess. *Little by little, the scene is suffused with light, faint at first, but increasing as if the very walls were glowing with the quiet radiance of universal joy. Only around the closed trap a shadow lingers.*)

Irma. But what's happened? They've gone! They've vanished!

Countess. They've evaporated, Irma. They were wicked. Wickedness evaporates.

(Pierre *enters. He is followed by the* Vagabonds, *all of them. The new radiance of the world is now very perceptible. It glows from their faces.*)

Pierre. Oh, Countess...!

WAITER. Countess, everything's changed. Now you can breathe again. Now you can see.

PIERRE. The air is pure! The sky is clear!

IRMA. Life is beautiful again.

THE RAGPICKER (*rushes in*). Countess—the pigeons! The pigeons are flying!

FLOWER GIRL. They don't have to walk any more.

THE RAGPICKER. They're flying. . . . The air is like crystal. And young grass is sprouting on the pavements.

COUNTESS. Is it possible?

IRMA (*interpreting for the* DEAF-MUTE). Now, Juggler, you can throw your fireballs up as high as you please—they won't go out.

SERGEANT. On the street, utter strangers are shaking hands, they don't know why, and offering each other almond bars!

COUNTESS. Oh, my friends . . .

WAITER. Countess, we thank you. . . .

(*They go on talking with happy and animated gestures, but we no longer hear them, for their words blend into a strain of unearthly music which seems to thrill from the uttermost confines of the universe. And out of this music comes a voice.*)

FIRST VOICE. Countess . . . (*Only the* COUNTESS *hears it. She turns from the group of* VAGABONDS *in wonder.*)

SECOND VOICE. Countess . . .

THIRD VOICE. Countess . . .

(*As she looks up in rapture, the* FIRST VOICE *speaks again.*)

FIRST VOICE. Countess, we thank you. We are the friends of animals.

SECOND VOICE. We are the friends of people.

THIRD VOICE. We are the friends of friendship.

FIRST VOICE. You have freed us!

SECOND VOICE. From now on, there will be no hungry cats. . . .

THIRD VOICE. And we shall tell the Duchess her dog's right name!

(*The* VOICES *fade off. And now another group of voices is heard.*)

FIRST VOICE. Countess, we thank you. We are the friends of flowers.

SECOND VOICE. From now on, every plant in Paris will be watered. . . .

THIRD VOICE. And the sewers will be fragrant with jasmine!

(*These voices, too, are silent. For an instant, the stage is vibrant with music. Then the* DEAF-MUTE *speaks, and his voice is the most beautiful of all.*)

DEAF-MUTE. Sadness flies on the wings of the morning, and out of the heart of darkness comes the light.

(*Suddenly a group of figures detaches itself from the shadows. These are exactly similar in face and figure and in dress. They are shabby in the fashion of 1900 and their cuffs are badly frayed. Each bears in his hand a ripe melon.*)

FIRST ADOLPHE BERTAUT. Countess, we thank you. We, too, are freed at last. We are the Adolphe Bertauts of the world.

SECOND ADOLPHE BERTAUT. We are no longer timid.

THIRD ADOLPHE BERTAUT. We are no longer weak.

FIRST ADOLPHE BERTAUT. From this day on, we shall hold fast to what we love. For your sake, henceforth, we shall be handsome, and our cuffs forever immaculate and new. Countess, we bring you this melon and with it our hearts...! (*They all kneel.*) Will you do us the honor to be our wife?

COUNTESS (*sadly*). Too late! Too late! (*She waves them aside. They take up their melons sadly and vanish. The voices of the* VAGABONDS *are heard again, and the music dies.*) Too late! Too late!

PIERRE. Too late, Countess?

IRMA. Too late for what?

COUNTESS. I say that it's too late for them. On the twenty-fourth of May, 1881, the most beautiful Easter in the memory of man, it was not too late. And on the fifth of September, 1887, the day they caught the trout and broiled it on the open fire by the brook at Villeneuve, it was not too late. And it was even not too late for them on the twenty-first of August, 1897, the day the Czar visited Paris with his guard. But they did nothing and they said nothing, and now—kiss each other, you two, this very instant!

IRMA. You mean...?

PIERRE. You mean...?

IRMA. But, Countess....

COUNTESS. It's three hours since you've met and known and loved each other. Kiss each other quickly. (PIERRE *hesitates.*) Look at him. He hesitates. He trembles. Happiness frightens him.... How like a man! Oh, Irma, kiss him, kiss him! If two people who love each other let a single instant wedge itself between them, it grows—it becomes a month, a year, a century; it becomes too late. Kiss him, Irma, kiss him while there is time, or in a moment his hair will be white and there will be another madwoman in Paris! Oh, make her kiss him, all of you! (*They kiss.*) Bravo! Oh, if only you'd had the courage to do that thirty years ago, how different I would be today! Dear Deaf-Mute, be still—your words dazzle our eyes! And Irma is too busy to translate for you. (*They kiss once more.*) Well, there we are. The world is saved. And you see how simple it all was? Nothing is ever so wrong in this world that a sensible woman can't set it right in the course of an afternoon. Only, the next time, don't wait until things begin to look black. The minute you notice anything, tell me at once.

THE RAGPICKER. We will, Countess. We will.

COUNTESS (*puts on her hat. Her tone becomes business-like*). Irma. My bones. My gizzard.

IRMA. I have them ready, Countess.

COUNTESS. Good. (*She puts the bones into her basket and starts for the stairs.*) Well, let's get on to more important things. Four o'clock. My poor cats must be starved. What a bore for them if humanity had to be saved every afternoon. They don't think much of it, as it is.

Curtain

DISCUSSION

The hysteria of the age to which Strindberg refers in his foreword to *Miss Julie* is full blown and the center of attention in Giraudoux's *The Madwoman of Chaillot*. Just as Julie has had to retreat into herself, so have the madwomen who are among the protagonists of this play. But, whereas Strindberg shows us a character in the process of turning away from the world, Giraudoux's women have turned from it long since. Whereas *Miss Julie* maintains at least the appearance of objective realism until its end, *The Madwoman of Chaillot* is subjective fantasy from start to finish. Paradoxically, Giraudoux tells us, the real world, the world of physical, external reality, is so insane that it takes the madwomen to make sense of it. Those who are humane, who seek love and beauty, are deemed mad in a world dedicated to genuine madness, to the inhuman, the mechanical, the gratification of greed. The fantastical nature of the play is especially appropriate to what Giraudoux seems to be trying to express. Everyone in the play, whether among those the world takes as sane or those whom it thinks mad, lives in a fantasy of his own making. The difference between the groups is that those who control the world—the corporation presidents, the prospectors, the public relations men, the politicians—create a fantasy devoid of love and humanity, while those who oppose them—the madwomen who lead the cripples, beggars, and workers—fight for a fantasy that is humane and filled with beauty and love.

Almost immediately, we are shown how arbitrary, abstract, and insane the world of the manipulators is. Nothing concrete counts in that world—not the faces or the suffering or the hopes of individual people, not even concrete objects. All that counts are numbers, questions of profit and loss, ways of manipulating the market. The Baron's personal history and present situation mean nothing; all that matters is his name. He may be bankrupt, but his name will look good on a listing of the members of the Board of Directors. The President cannot remember his mother's face; the only faces he remembers vividly are those that inspired him to make profitable investments. And those faces are not really the faces of others but extensions of himself, mirror images of his own ego. He places trust in nothing other than those faces—that is, in nothing other than himself.

The President's discussion with the Baron and the Broker of the problems connected with the new international combine he heads shows the insanity and abstractness of his relationship to the real world of objects and to other people. All that concerns him is the name of the new combine. Neither he nor any of the financiers who direct it has any idea of its specific purpose. Will it manufacture something? Will it provide a service? What will it do? All this is beside the point, says the chairman of this combine, a man who is also director of fifty-two companies and president of eleven corporations. What he and his new associates need is a name, not a product. Their function is "to stimulate the imagination"; they are creative artists, poets of a new world dedicated to making money. With an inspiring name, they can sweep the stock market. That is their purpose: to manipulate the market, to make a killing.

What Giraudoux presents in this play is a picture of two types of imagination—the poetic and the abstract. The President's imagination is of the latter type. What he and those who follow his lead want is a world devoid of genuine poetry and humanity. They think they are the real poets, but everything they stand for is abstract, anonymous, or mechanical. They require wives who are activated mannikins; followers who are mirror images of themselves; prospectors who will serve their desires for greed, even to the point of destroying civilization itself; and public relations men who will manipulate the truth without regard to reality. Above everything, they want order, standardization, and anonymity. As the President says to the Baron, "the first thing we have to do is get rid of these people! Good Heavens, look at them! Every size, shape, color and period of history imaginable. It's utter anarchy! I tell you sir, the only safeguard of order and discipline in the modern world is a standardized worker with interchangeable parts. That would solve the entire problem of management."

Against these managers, perpetrators of the abstract imagination, Giraudoux pits genuinely poetic souls who represent the vitality and uniqueness of the individual. They are the mad, the crippled, the lonely—all those who resist manipulation and standardization in a search for love and beauty. The Madwoman and her friends are out to save civilization itself; they seek to restore music to life, while the managers cannot even tolerate songs. The managers manipulate everything and everyone for profit; the madwomen seek to restore nature to its plenitude and variety. They want the birds to fly again, people to like and love one another again, a world in which even the cats and dogs count. They want a world imbued with human significance again, a world in which the self, each individual, and each thing in its uniqueness, is once again what matters most.

In treating both the managers and the madwomen as fantasy makers, Giraudoux opens up an avenue that a great many recent dramatists have since explored. Is it true, they ask, that we all live by fictions or fantasies? If so, why? Does the reason have something to do with the breakdown of traditions? Are we so disillusioned by the mass slaughter of millions in the wars of this century that we no longer believe that there is meaning and purpose in the world, that whatever structure or meaning we find there is something we imposed on it? Science today also seems to say that we participate in whatever we discover in nature, that we can no longer consider ourselves only observers. Does this, too, mean that we all play games all the time, create fictions to live by? Are we all essentially subjective, living out our own fantasies or those imposed on us by society, as if they were reality? If everyone is living a fiction, how do we know which fictions are creative and which are destructive? How do we justify one fiction over another? These are some of the questions many recent plays and films have asked; and in doing so, many have made use of play-within-the-play techniques. Pirandello's *Six Characters in Search of an Author* is the prototype of such plays, but there are many others as well. Jean Genêt's plays, for example, are all centrally concerned with how such techniques reveal contemporary man's plight. Through such devices, the playwright reminds us that we are watching a play, something man-made, not reality. When a play that seems real in some sense suddenly reminds us that it is, after all, a play and not life, it prompts us to reconsider other phenomena we accept as real. Everything we call reality may actually be a play, too. The implications of such ideas are exciting and staggering. One thing they convey to us is that if life is a play, then a play may tell us a great deal about life. *The Madwoman of Chaillot* helps us to understand this idea; for in showing us that fantasy can reveal both the destructive and the creative forces at work in our time, Giraudoux has helped us to understand, in modern terms, how fiction can be truer than fact.

THEME AND DISCUSSION QUESTIONS

1. What is Giraudoux trying to accomplish by having the Singer and the Professor try to sing in front of the President?
2. What truths about the President and his followers does the Ragpicker reveal in his impassioned defense of their values during the "trial"?
3. Why is there so much talk about animals—mostly imaginary—in the play?
4. Why have the old women in the play all become mad?
5. Why do the workers and beggars join forces with the madwomen? What do they all have in common?
6. What is the purpose of having the sewer man first deny that the tall tales about life in the sewers are true and then reveal that for the most part they are true?
7. Why do all of the Presidents who go down the stairs at the end of the play look alike in every detail?
8. Why does Giraudoux introduce public relations men at the end of the play? What do they add to the play's meaning?
9. At one point toward the end of Act I, Irma says that all of those who

are bringing unhappiness to the world are "all connected like the parts of a machine," to which the Countess responds, "So much the better. We shall drive the whole machine into a ditch." The Sergeant then says that that's not easy, "You catch a President, pfft! He turns into a trustee. You catch him as trustee, and pfft! He's not a trustee . . ." Examine these passages and explain how they express the playwright's conception of what prevents self-realization in the world today.

10. To some critics, *The Madwoman of Chaillot* seems essentially a simple melodrama—the good guys (or rather girls) against the bad guys. What evidence is there to support this interpretation? What aspects of the play make it a richer melodrama than the average television or movie western or detective story?
11. In what ways are the characters in *The Madwoman of Chaillot* unrealistic? In what ways are they credible despite these unrealistic features?
12. Why do the values of men like the President and the Prospector keep others from discovering a sense of self?
13. In what specific ways are the Madwoman and her followers more sane than the President and his followers?
14. What comparisons can be made between the events of the play and current national or international events?

Death of a Salesman: Production directed by Elia Kazan, at Morosco Theatre, New York (1949); starring Lee J. Cobb, Mildred Dunnock, Arthur Kennedy, and Cameron Mitchell. Photograph courtesy of Graphic House.

ARTHUR MILLER

Death of a Salesman

Arthur Miller, born in 1915 and raised in New York City, is best known for plays that attempt to dramatize the social and psychological tragedies of the common man. The recipient of a Pulitzer Prize for his *Death of a Salesman* (1949), he has also earned respect as a dramatist through the writing of such plays as *The Crucible* (1953) and *A View from the Bridge* (1955). Greatly influenced by Ibsen's social-problem plays—in 1950 Miller wrote an adaptation of Ibsen's *An Enemy of the People*—Miller's plays generally deal with the ways in which social values and taboos prevent the lone individual from achieving selfhood. One example, *The Crucible,* a play about the irrationality of political persecution, was undoubtedly inspired by Miller's own appearance before Senator Joseph McCarthy's investigating committee in the early 1950s. *Death of a Salesman,* the Miller play in this collection, is a more psychological view of the denial of individual freedom and fulfillment. Its protagonist, Willy Loman, is a product of modern society; and to many people, he has become synonymous with the misguided faith in money and business that developed in America in the 1930s and 40s.

DEATH OF A SALESMAN by Arthur Miller. Copyright 1949 by Arthur Miller. All rights reserved. Reprinted by permission of the Viking Press.

CAUTION: This play in its printed form is designed for the reading public only. All dramatic rights in it are fully protected by copyright, and no public or private performance—professional or amateur—may be given without the written permission of the author and the payment of royalty. As the courts have also ruled that the public reading of a play constitutes a public performance, no such reading may be given except under the conditions stated above. Communication should be addressed to the author's representative, International Famous Agency, Inc., 1301 Avenue of the Americas, New York, N.Y. 10019.

CHARACTERS

Willy Loman	Howard Wagner
Linda	Jenny
Biff	Stanley
Happy	Miss Forsythe
Bernard	Letta
The Woman	Charley

Uncle Ben

The Place. Willy Loman's *house and yard and various places he visits in the New York and Boston of today.*

Throughout the play, in the stage directions, left and right mean stage left and stage right.

ACT I

A melody is heard, played upon a flute. It is small and fine, telling of grass and trees and the horizon. The curtain rises.

Before us is the Salesman's house. We are aware of towering, angular shapes behind it, surrounding it on all sides. Only the blue light of the sky falls upon the house and forestage; the surrounding area shows an angry glow of orange. As more light appears, we see a solid vault of apartment houses around the small, fragile-seeming home. An air of the dream clings to the place, a dream rising out of reality. The kitchen at center seems actual enough, for there is a kitchen table with three chairs, and a refrigerator. But no other fixtures are seen. At the back of the kitchen there is a draped entrance, which leads to the living-room. To the right of the kitchen, on a level raised two feet, is a bedroom furnished only with a brass bedstead and a straight chair. On a shelf over the bed a silver athletic trophy stands. A window opens onto the apartment house at the side.

Behind the kitchen, on a level raised six and a half feet, is the boys' bedroom, at present barely visible. Two beds are dimly seen, and at the back of the room a dormer window. (This bedroom is above the unseen living-room.) At the left a stairway curves up to it from the kitchen.

The entire setting is wholly or, in some places, partially transparent. The roof-line of the house is one-dimensional; under and over it we see the apartment buildings. Before the house lies an apron, curving beyond the forestage into the orchestra. This forward area serves as the back yard as well as the locale of all Willy's *imaginings and of his city scenes. Whenever the action is in the present the actors observe the imaginary wall-lines, entering the house only through its door at the left. But in the scenes of the past these boundaries are broken, and characters enter or leave a room by stepping "through" a wall onto the forestage.*

From the right, WILLY LOMAN, *the Salesman, enters, carrying two large sample cases. The flute plays on. He hears but is not aware of it. He is past sixty years of age, dressed quietly. Even as he crosses the stage to the doorway of the house, his exhaustion is apparent. He unlocks the door, comes into the kitchen, and thankfully lets his burden down, feeling the soreness of his palms. A word-sigh escapes his lips—it might be "Oh, boy, oh, boy." He closes the door, then carries his cases out into the living-room, through the draped kitchen doorway.*

LINDA, *his wife, has stirred in her bed at the right. She gets out and puts on a robe, listening. Most often jovial, she has developed an iron repression of her exceptions to* WILLY'S *behavior—she more than loves him, she admires him, as though his mercurial nature, his temper, his massive dreams and little cruelties, served her only as sharp reminders of the turbulent longings within him, longings which she shares but lacks the temperament to utter and follow to their end.*

LINDA (*hearing* WILLY *outside the bedroom, calls with some trepidation*). Willy!

WILLY. It's all right. I came back.

LINDA. Why? What happened? (*Slight pause*) Did something happen, Willy?

WILLY. No, nothing happened.

LINDA. You didn't smash the car, did you?

WILLY (*with casual irritation*). I said nothing happened. Didn't you hear me?

LINDA. Don't you feel well?

WILLY. I'm tired to the death. (*The flute has faded away. He sits on the bed beside her, a little numb.*) I couldn't make it. I just couldn't make it, Linda.

LINDA (*very carefully, delicately*). Where were you all day? You look terrible.

WILLY. I got as far as a little above Yonkers. I stopped for a cup of coffee. Maybe it was the coffee.

LINDA. What?

WILLY (*after a pause*). I suddenly couldn't drive any more. The car kept going off onto the shoulder, y'know?

LINDA (*helpfully*). Oh. Maybe it was the steering again. I don't think Angelo knows the Studebaker.

WILLY. No, it's me, it's me. Suddenly I realize I'm goin' sixty miles an hour and I don't remember the last five minutes. I'm—I can't seem to—keep my mind to it.

LINDA. Maybe it's your glasses. You never went for your new glasses.

WILLY. No, I see everything. I came back ten miles an hour. It took me nearly four hours from Yonkers.

LINDA (*resigned*). Well, you'll just have to take a rest, Willy, you can't continue this way.

WILLY. I just got back from Florida.

LINDA. But you didn't rest your mind. Your mind is overactive, and the mind is what counts, dear.

WILLY. I'll start out in the morning. Maybe I'll feel better in the morning. (*She is taking off his shoes.*) These goddam arch supports are killing me.

LINDA. Take an aspirin. Should I get you an aspirin? It'll soothe you.

WILLY (*with wonder*). I was driving along, you understand? And I was fine. I was even observing the scenery. You can imagine, me looking at scenery, on the road every week of my life. But it's so beautiful up there, Linda, the trees are so thick, and the sun is warm. I opened the windshield and just let the warm air bathe over me. And then all of a sudden I'm goin' off the road! I'm tellin' ya, I absolutely forgot I was driving. If I'd've gone the other way over the white line I might've killed somebody. So I went on again—and five minutes later I'm dreamin' again, and I nearly—(*He presses two fingers against his eyes.*) I have such thoughts, I have such strange thoughts.

LINDA. Willy, dear. Talk to them again. There's no reason why you can't work in New York.

WILLY. They don't need me in New York. I'm the New England man. I'm vital in New England.

LINDA. But you're sixty years old. They can't expect you to keep traveling every week.

WILLY. I'll have to send a wire to Portland. I'm supposed to see Brown and Morrison tomorrow morning at ten o'clock to show the line. Goddammit, I could sell them! (*He starts putting on his jacket.*)

LINDA (*taking the jacket from him*). Why don't you go down to the place tomorrow and tell Howard you've simply got to work in New York? You're too accommodating, dear.

WILLY. If old man Wagner was alive I'd a been in charge of New York now! That man was a prince, he was a masterful man. But that boy of his, that Howard, he don't appreciate. When I went north the first time, the Wagner Company didn't know where New England was!

LINDA. Why don't you tell those things to Howard, dear?

WILLY (*encouraged*). I will, I definitely will. Is there any cheese?

LINDA. I'll make you a sandwich.

WILLY. No, go to sleep. I'll take some milk. I'll be up right away. The boys in?

LINDA. They're sleeping. Happy took Biff on a date tonight.

WILLY (*interested*). That so?

LINDA. It was so nice to see them shaving together, one behind the other, in the bathroom. And going out together. You notice? The whole house smells of shaving lotion.

WILLY. Figure it out. Work a lifetime to pay off a house. You finally own it, and there's nobody to live in it.

LINDA. Well, dear, life is a casting off. It's always that way.

WILLY. No, no, some people—some people accomplish something. Did Biff say anything after I went this morning?

LINDA. You shouldn't have criticized him, Willy, especially after he just got off the train. You mustn't lose your temper with him.

WILLY. When the hell did I lose my temper? I simply asked him if he was making any money. Is that a criticism?

LINDA. But, dear, how could he make any money?

WILLY (*worried and angered*). There's such an undercurrent in him. He became a moody man. Did he apologize when I left this morning?

LINDA. He was crestfallen, Willy. You know how he admires you. I think if he finds himself, then you'll both be happier and not fight any more.

WILLY. How can he find himself on a farm? Is that a life? A farmhand? In the beginning, when he was young, I thought, well, a young man, it's good for him to tramp around, take a lot of different jobs. But it's more than ten years now and he has yet to make thirty-five dollars a week!

LINDA. He's finding himself, Willy.

WILLY. Not finding yourself at the age of thirty-four is a disgrace!

LINDA. Shh!

WILLY. The trouble is he's lazy, goddammit!

LINDA. Willy, please!

WILLY. Biff is a lazy bum!

LINDA. They're sleeping. Get something to eat. Go on down.

WILLY. Why did he come home? I would like to know what brought him home.

LINDA. I don't know. I think he's still lost, Willy. I think he's very lost.

WILLY. Biff Loman is lost. In the greatest country in the world a young man with such—personal attractiveness, gets lost. And such a hard worker. There's one thing about Biff—he's not lazy.

LINDA. Never.

WILLY (*with pity and resolve*). I'll see him in the morning; I'll have a nice talk with him. I'll get him a job selling. He could be big in no time. My God! Remember how they used to follow him around in high school?

When he smiled at one of them their faces lit up. When he walked down the street . . . (*He loses himself in reminiscences.*)

LINDA (*trying to bring him out of it*). Willy, dear, I got a new kind of American-type cheese today. It's whipped.

WILLY. Why do you get American when I like Swiss?

LINDA. I just thought you'd like a change—

WILLY. I don't want a change! I want Swiss cheese. Why am I always being contradicted?

LINDA (*with a covering laugh*). I thought it would be a surprise.

WILLY. Why don't you open a window in here, for God's sake?

LINDA (*with infinite patience*). They're all open, dear.

WILLY. The way they boxed us in here. Bricks and windows, windows and bricks.

LINDA. We should've bought the land next door.

WILLY. The street is lined with cars. There's not a breath of fresh air in the neighborhood. The grass don't grow any more, you can't raise a carrot in the back yard. They should've had a law against apartment houses. Remember those two beautiful elm trees out there? When I and Biff hung the swing between them?

LINDA. Yeah, like being a million miles from the city.

WILLY. They should've arrested the builder for cutting those down. They massacred the neighborhood. (*Lost*) More and more I think of those days, Linda. This time of year it was lilac and wisteria. And then the peonies would come out, and the daffodils. What fragrance in this room!

LINDA. Well, after all, people had to move somewhere.

WILLY. No, there's more people now.

LINDA. I don't think there's more people. I think—

WILLY. There's more people! That's what's ruining this country! Population is getting out of control. The competition is maddening! Smell the stink from that apartment house! And another one on the other side . . . How can they whip cheese?

(*On* WILLY's *last line,* BIFF *and* HAPPY *raise themselves up in their beds, listening.*)

LINDA. Go down, try it. And be quiet.

WILLY (*turning to* LINDA, *guiltily*). You're not worried about me, are you, sweetheart?

BIFF. What's the matter?

HAPPY. Listen!

LINDA. You've got too much on the ball to worry about.

WILLY. You're my foundation and my support, Linda.

LINDA. Just try to relax, dear. You make mountains out of molehills.

WILLY. I won't fight with him any more. If he wants to go back to Texas, let him go.

LINDA. He'll find his way.

WILLY. Sure. Certain men just don't get started till later in life. Like

Thomas Edison, I think. Or B. F. Goodrich. One of them was deaf. (*He starts for the bedroom doorway.*) I'll put my money on Biff.

LINDA. And Willy—if it's warm Sunday we'll drive in the country. And we'll open the windshield, and take lunch.

WILLY. No, the windshields don't open on the new cars.

LINDA. But you opened it today.

WILLY. Me? I didn't. (*He stops.*) Now isn't that peculiar! Isn't that a remarkable—(*He breaks off in amazement and fright as the flute is heard distantly.*)

LINDA. What, darling?

WILLY. That is the most remarkable thing.

LINDA. What, dear?

WILLY. I was thinking of the Chevvy. (*Slight pause*) Nineteen twenty-eight . . . when I had that red Chevvy—(*Breaks off*) That's funny? I coulda sworn I was driving that Chevvy today.

LINDA. Well, that's nothing. Something must've reminded you.

WILLY. Remarkable. Ts. Remember those days? The way Biff used to simonize that car? The dealer refused to believe there was eighty thousand miles on it. (*He shakes his head.*) Heh! (*To* LINDA) Close your eyes, I'll be right up. (*He walks out of the bedroom.*)

HAPPY (*to* BIFF). Jesus, maybe he smashed up the car again!

LINDA (*calling after* WILLY). Be careful on the stairs, dear! The cheese is on the middle shelf! (*She turns, goes over to the bed, takes his jacket, and goes out of the bedroom.*)

(*Light has risen on the boys' room. Unseen,* WILLY *is heard talking to himself, "Eighty thousand miles," and a little laugh.* BIFF *gets out of bed, comes downstage a bit, and stands attentively.* BIFF *is two years older than his brother* HAPPY, *well built, but in these days bears a worn air and seems less self-assured. He has succeeded less, and his dreams are stronger and less acceptable than* HAPPY'S. HAPPY *is tall, powerfully made. Sexuality is like a visible color on him, or a scent that many women have discovered. He, like his brother, is lost, but in a different way, for he has never allowed himself to turn his face toward defeat and is thus more confused and hard-skinned, although seemingly more content.*)

HAPPY (*getting out of bed*). He's going to get his license taken away if he keeps that up. I'm getting nervous about him, y'know, Biff?

BIFF. His eyes are going.

HAPPY. No, I've driven with him. He sees all right. He just doesn't keep his mind on it. I drove into the city with him last week. He stops at a green light and then it turns red and he goes. (*He laughs.*)

BIFF. Maybe he's color-blind.

HAPPY. Pop? Why he's got the finest eye for color in the business. You know that.

BIFF (*sitting down on his bed*). I'm going to sleep.

HAPPY. You're not still sour on Dad, are you, Biff?

BIFF. He's all right, I guess.

WILLY (*underneath them, in the living-room*). Yes, sir, eighty thousand miles—eighty-two thousand!

BIFF. You smoking?

HAPPY (*holding out a pack of cigarettes*). Want one?

BIFF (*taking a cigarette*). I can never sleep when I smell it.

WILLY. What a simonizing job, heh!

HAPPY (*with deep sentiment*). Funny, Biff, y'know? Us sleeping in here again? The old beds. (*He pats his bed affectionately.*) All the talk that went across those two beds, huh? Our whole lives.

BIFF. Yeah. Lotta dreams and plans.

HAPPY (*with a deep and masculine laugh*). About five hundred women would like to know what was said in this room.

(*They share a soft laugh.*)

BIFF. Remember that big Betsy something—what the hell was her name—over on Bushwick Avenue?

HAPPY (*combing his hair*). With the collie dog!

BIFF. That's the one. I got you in there, remember?

HAPPY. Yeah, that was my first time—I think. Boy, there was a pig! (*They laugh, almost crudely.*) You taught me everything I know about women. Don't forget that.

BIFF. I bet you forgot how bashful you used to be. Especially with girls.

HAPPY. Oh, I still am, Biff.

BIFF. Oh, go on.

HAPPY. I just control it, that's all. I think I got less bashful and you got more so. What happened, Biff? Where's the old humor, the old confidence? (*He shakes* BIFF's *knee.* BIFF *gets up and moves restlessly about the room.*) What's the matter?

BIFF. Why does Dad mock me all the time?

HAPPY. He's not mocking you, he—

BIFF. Everything I say there's a twist of mockery on his face. I can't get near him.

HAPPY. He just wants you to make good, that's all. I wanted to talk to you about Dad for a long time, Biff. Something's—happening to him. He—talks to himself.

BIFF. I noticed that this morning. But he always mumbled.

HAPPY. But not so noticeable. It got so embarrassing I sent him to Florida. And you know something? Most of the time he's talking to you.

BIFF. What's he say about me?

HAPPY. I can't make it out.

BIFF. What's he say about me?

HAPPY. I think the fact that you're not settled, that you're still kind of up in the air...

BIFF. There's one or two other things depressing him, Happy.

HAPPY. What do you mean?

BIFF. Never mind. Just don't lay it all to me.

HAPPY. But I think if you just got started—I mean—is there any future for you out there?

BIFF. I tell ya, Hap, I don't know what the future is. I don't know—what I'm supposed to want.

HAPPY. What do you mean?

BIFF. Well, I spent six or seven years after high school trying to work myself up. Shipping clerk, salesman, business of one kind or another. And it's a measly manner of existence. To get on that subway on the hot mornings in summer. To devote your whole life to keeping stock, or making phone calls, or selling or buying. To suffer fifty weeks of the year for the sake of a two-week vacation, when all you really desire is to be outdoors, with your shirt off. And always to have to get ahead of the next fella. And still—that's how you build a future.

HAPPY. Well, you really enjoy it on a farm? Are you content out there?

BIFF (*with rising agitation*). Hap, I've had twenty or thirty different kinds of jobs since I left home before the war, and it always turns out the same. I just realized it lately. In Nebraska when I herded cattle, and the Dakotas, and Arizona, and now in Texas. It's why I came home now, I guess, because I realized it. This farm I work on, it's spring there now, see? And they've got about fifteen new colts. There's nothing more inspiring or—beautiful than the sight of a mare and a new colt. And it's cool there now, see? Texas is cool now, and it's spring. And whenever spring comes to where I am, I suddenly get the feeling, my God, I'm not gettin' anywhere! What the hell am I doing, playing around with horses, twenty-eight dollars a week! I'm thirty-four years old, I oughta be makin' my future. That's when I come running home. And now, I get here, and I don't know what to do with myself. (*After a pause*) I've always made a point of not wasting my life, and everytime I come back here I know that all I've done is to waste my life.

HAPPY. You're a poet, you know that, Biff? You're a—you're an idealist!

BIFF. No, I'm mixed up very bad. Maybe I oughta get married. Maybe I oughta get stuck into something. Maybe that's my trouble. I'm like a boy. I'm not married, I'm not in business, I just—I'm like a boy. Are you content, Hap? You're a success, aren't you? Are you content?

HAPPY. Hell, no!

BIFF. Why? You're making money, aren't you?

HAPPY (*moving about with energy, expressiveness*). All I can do now is wait for the merchandise manager to die. And suppose I get to be merchandise manager? He's a good friend of mine, and he just built a terrific estate on Long Island. And he lived there about two months and sold it, and now he's building another one. He can't enjoy it once it's finished. And I know that's just what I would do. I don't know what the hell I'm workin' for. Sometimes I sit in my apartment—all alone. And I think of the rent I'm paying. And it's crazy. But then, it's what I always wanted. My own apartment, a car, and plenty of women. And still, goddammit, I'm lonely.

BIFF (*with enthusiasm*). Listen, why don't you come out West with me?

HAPPY. You and I, heh?

BIFF. Sure, maybe we could buy a ranch. Raise cattle, use our muscles. Men built like we are should be working out in the open.

HAPPY (*avidly*). The Loman Brothers, heh?

BIFF (*with vast affection*). Sure, we'd be known all over the counties!

HAPPY (*enthralled*). That's what I dream about, Biff. Sometimes I want to just rip my clothes off in the middle of the store and outbox that goddam merchandise manager. I mean I can outbox, outrun, and outlift anybody in that store, and I have to take orders from those common, petty sons-of-bitches till I can't stand it any more.

BIFF. I'm tellin' you, kid, if you were with me I'd be happy out there.

HAPPY (*enthused*). See, Biff, everybody around me is so false that I'm constantly lowering my ideals . . .

BIFF. Baby, together we'd stand up for one another, we'd have someone to trust.

HAPPY. If I were around you—

BIFF. Hap, the trouble is we weren't brought up to grub for money. I don't know how to do it.

HAPPY. Neither can I!

BIFF. Then let's go!

HAPPY. The only thing is—what can you make out there?

BIFF. But look at your friend. Builds an estate and then hasn't the peace of mind to live in it.

HAPPY. Yeah, but when he walks into the store the waves part in front of him. That's fifty-two thousand dollars a year coming through the revolving door, and I got more in my pinky finger than he's got in his head.

BIFF. Yeah, but you just said—

HAPPY. I gotta show some of those pompous, self-important executives over there that Hap Loman can make the grade. I want to walk into the store the way he walks in. Then I'll go with you, Biff. We'll be together yet, I swear. But take those two we had tonight. Now weren't they gorgeous creatures?

BIFF. Yeah, yeah, most gorgeous I've had in years.

HAPPY. I get that any time I want, Biff. Whenever I feel disgusted. The only trouble is, it gets like bowling or something. I just keep knockin' them over and it doesn't mean anything. You still run around a lot?

BIFF. Naa. I'd like to find a girl—steady, somebody with substance.

HAPPY. That's what I long for.

BIFF. Go on! You'd never come home.

HAPPY. I would! Somebody with character, with resistance! Like Mom, y'know? You're gonna call me a bastard when I tell you this. That girl Charlotte I was with tonight is engaged to be married in five weeks. (*He tries on his new hat.*)

BIFF. No kiddin'!

HAPPY. Sure, the guy's in line for the vice-presidency of the store. I don't know what gets into me, maybe I just have an overdeveloped sense of competition or something, but I went and ruined her, and furthermore I can't get rid of her. And he's the third executive I've done that to. Isn't that a crummy characteristic? And to top it all, I go to their weddings! (*Indignantly, but laughing*) Like I'm not supposed to take bribes. Manufacturers offer me a hundred-dollar bill now and then to throw an order their way. You know how honest I am, but it's like this girl, see. I hate myself for it. Because I don't want the girl, and, still, I take it and—I love it!

BIFF. Let's go to sleep.

HAPPY. I guess we didn't settle anything, heh?

BIFF. I just got one idea that I think I'm going to try.

HAPPY. What's that?

BIFF. Remember Bill Oliver?

HAPPY. Sure, Oliver is very big now. You want to work for him again?

BIFF. No, but when I quit he said something to me. He put his arm on my shoulder, and he said, "Biff, if you ever need anything, come to me."

HAPPY. I remember that. That sounds good.

BIFF. I think I'll go to see him. If I could get ten thousand or even seven or eight thousand dollars I could buy a beautiful ranch.

HAPPY. I bet he'd back you. 'Cause he thought highly of you, Biff. I mean, they all do. You're well liked, Biff. That's why I say to come back here, and we both have the apartment. And I'm tellin' you, Biff, any babe you want . . .

BIFF. No, with a ranch I could do the work I like and still be something. I just wonder though. I wonder if Oliver still thinks I stole that carton of basketballs.

HAPPY. Oh, he probably forgot that long ago. It's almost ten years. You're too sensitive. Anyway, he didn't really fire you.

BIFF. Well, I think he was going to. I think that's why I quit. I was never sure whether he knew or not. I know he thought the world of me, though. I was the only one he'd let lock up the place.

WILLY (*below*). You gonna wash the engine, Biff?

HAPPY. Shh!

(BIFF *looks at* HAPPY, *who is gazing down, listening.* WILLY *is mumbling in the parlor.*)

HAPPY. You hear that?

(*They listen.* WILLY *laughs warmly.*)

BIFF (*growing angry*). Doesn't he know Mom can hear that?
WILLY. Don't get your sweater dirty, Biff!

(*A look of pain crosses* BIFF's *face.*)

HAPPY. Isn't that terrible? Don't leave again, will you? You'll find a job here. You gotta stick around. I don't know what to do about him, it's getting embarrassing.
WILLY. What a simonizing job!
BIFF. Mom's hearing that!
WILLY. No kiddin', Biff, you got a date? Wonderful!
HAPPY. Go on to sleep. But talk to him in the morning, will you?
BIFF (*reluctantly getting into bed*). With her in the house. Brother!
HAPPY (*getting into bed*). I wish you'd have a good talk with him.

(*The light on their room begins to fade.*)

BIFF (*to himself in bed*). That selfish, stupid . . .
HAPPY. Sh . . . Sleep, Biff.

(*Their light is out. Well before they have finished speaking,* WILLY's *form is dimly seen below in the darkened kitchen. He opens the refrigerator, searches in there, and takes out a bottle of milk. The apartment houses are fading out, and the entire house and surroundings become covered with leaves. Music insinuates itself as the leaves appear.*)

WILLY. Just wanna be careful with those girls, Biff, that's all. Don't make any promises. No promises of any kind. Because a girl, y'know, they always believe what you tell 'em, and you're very young, Biff, you're too young to be talking seriously to girls.

(*Light rises on the kitchen.* WILLY, *talking, shuts the refrigerator door and comes downstage to the kitchen table. He pours milk into a glass. He is totally immersed in himself, smiling faintly.*)

WILLY. Too young entirely, Biff. You want to watch your schooling first. Then when you're all set, there'll be plenty of girls for a boy like you. (*He smiles broadly at a kitchen chair.*) That so? The girls pay for you? (*He laughs.*) Boy, you must really be makin' a hit.

(WILLY *is gradually addressing—physically—a point offstage, speaking through the wall of the kitchen, and his voice has been rising in volume to that of a normal conversation.*)

WILLY. I been wondering why you polish the car so careful. Ha! Don't leave the hubcaps, boys. Get the chamois to the hubcaps. Happy, use newspaper on the windows, it's the easiest thing. Show him how to do it, Biff! You see, Happy? Pad it up, use it like a pad. That's it, that's it, good work. You're doin' all right, Hap. (*He pauses, then nods in approbation for a few seconds, then looks upward.*) Biff, first thing we gotta do when we get time is clip that big branch over the house. Afraid it's gonna fall in a storm and hit the roof. Tell you what. We get a rope and sling her around, and then we climb up there with a couple of saws and take her down. Soon as you finish the car, boys, I wanna see ya. I got a surprise for you, boys.

BIFF (*offstage*). Whatta ya got, Dad?

WILLY. No, you finish first. Never leave a job till you're finished—remember that. (*Looking toward the "big trees"*) Biff, up in Albany I saw a beautiful hammock. I think I'll buy it next trip, and we'll hang it right between those two elms. Wouldn't that be something? Just swingin' there under those branches. Boy, that would be . . .

(YOUNG BIFF *and* YOUNG HAPPY *appear from the direction* WILLY *was addressing.* HAPPY *carries rags and a pail of water.* BIFF, *wearing a sweater with a block "S," carries a football.*)

BIFF (*pointing in the direction of the car offstage*). How's that, Pop, professional?

WILLY. Terrific. Terrific job, boys. Good work, Biff.

HAPPY. Where's the surprise, Pop?

WILLY. In the back seat of the car.

HAPPY. Boy! (*He runs off.*)

BIFF. What is it, Dad? Tell me, what'd you buy?

WILLY (*laughing, cuffs him*). Never mind, something I want you to have.

BIFF (*turns and starts off*). What is it, Hap?

HAPPY (*offstage*). It's a punching bag!

BIFF. Oh, Pop!

WILLY. It's got Gene Tunney's signature on it!

(HAPPY *runs onstage with a punching bag.*)

BIFF. Gee, how'd you know we wanted a punching bag?

WILLY. Well, it's the finest thing for the timing.

HAPPY (*lies down on his back and pedals with his feet*). I'm losing weight, you notice, Pop?

WILLY (*to* HAPPY). Jumping rope is good too.

BIFF. Did you see the new football I got?

WILLY (*examining the ball*). Where'd you get a new ball?

BIFF. The coach told me to practice my passing.

WILLY. That so? And he gave you the ball, heh?

BIFF. Well, I borrowed it from the locker room. (*He laughs confidentially.*)

WILLY (*laughing with him at the theft*). I want you to return that.

HAPPY. I told you he wouldn't like it!

BIFF (*angrily*). Well, I'm bringing it back!

WILLY (*stopping the incipient argument, to* HAPPY). Sure, he's gotta practice with a regulation ball, doesn't he? (*To* BIFF) Coach'll probably congratulate you on your initiative!

BIFF. Oh, he keeps congratulating my initiative all the time, Pop.

WILLY. That's because he likes you. If somebody else took that ball there'd be an uproar. So what's the report, boys, what's the report?

BIFF. Where'd you go this time, Dad? Gee, we were lonesome for you.

WILLY (*pleased, puts an arm around each boy and they come down to the apron*). Lonesome, heh?

BIFF. Missed you every minute.

WILLY. Don't say? Tell you a secret, boys. Don't breathe it to a soul. Someday I'll have my own business, and I'll never have to leave home any more.

HAPPY. Like Uncle Charley, heh?

WILLY. Bigger than Uncle Charley! Because Charley is not—liked. He's liked, but he's not—well liked.

BIFF. Where'd you go this time, Dad?

WILLY. Well, I got on the road, and I went north to Providence. Met the Mayor.

BIFF. The Mayor of Providence!

WILLY. He was sitting in the hotel lobby.

BIFF. What'd he say?

WILLY. He said, "Morning!" And I said, "You got a fine city here, Mayor." And then he had coffee with me. And then I went to Waterbury. Waterbury is a fine city. Big clock city, the famous Waterbury clock. Sold a nice bill there. And then Boston—Boston is the cradle of the Revolution. A fine city. And a couple of other towns in Mass., and on to Portland and Bangor and straight home!

BIFF. Gee, I'd love to go with you sometime, Dad.

WILLY. Soon as summer comes.

HAPPY. Promise?

WILLY. You and Hap and I, and I'll show you all the towns. America is full of beautiful towns and fine, upstanding people. And they know me, boys, they know me up and down New England. The finest people. And when I bring you fellas up, there'll be open sesame for all of us, 'cause one thing, boys: I have friends. I can park my car in any street in New England, and the cops protect it like their own. This summer, heh?

BIFF *and* HAPPY (*together*). Yeah! You bet!

WILLY. We'll take our bathing suits.

HAPPY. We'll carry your bags, Pop!

WILLY. Oh, won't that be something! Me comin' into the Boston stores with you boys carryin' my bags. What a sensation!

(BIFF *is prancing around, practicing passing the ball.*)

WILLY. You nervous, Biff, about the game?

BIFF. Not if you're gonna be there.

WILLY. What do they say about you in school, now that they made you captain?

HAPPY. There's a crowd of girls behind him everytime the classes change.

BIFF (*taking* WILLY's *hand*). This Saturday, Pop, this Saturday—just for you, I'm going to break through for a touchdown.

HAPPY. You're supposed to pass.

BIFF. I'm takin' one play for Pop. You watch me, Pop, and when I take off my helmet, that means I'm breakin' out. Then you watch me crash through that line!

WILLY (*kisses* BIFF). Oh, wait'll I tell this in Boston!

(BERNARD *enters in knickers. He is younger than* BIFF, *earnest and loyal, a worried boy.*)

BERNARD. Biff, where are you? You're supposed to study with me today.

WILLY. Hey, looka Bernard. What're you lookin' so anemic about, Bernard?

BERNARD. He's gotta study, Uncle Willy. He's got Regents next week.

HAPPY (*tauntingly, spinning* BERNARD *around*). Let's box, Bernard!

BERNARD. Biff! (*He gets away from* HAPPY.) Listen, Biff, I heard Mr. Birnbaum say that if you don't start studyin' math he's gonna flunk you, and you won't graduate. I heard him!

WILLY. You better study with him, Biff. Go ahead now.

BERNARD. I heard him!

BIFF. Oh, Pop, you didn't see my sneakers! (*He holds up a foot for* WILLY *to look at.*)

WILLY. Hey, that's a beautiful job of printing!

BERNARD (*wiping his glasses*). Just because he printed University of Virginia on his sneakers doesn't mean they've got to graduate him. Uncle Willy!

WILLY (*angrily*). What're you talking about? With scholarships to three universities they're gonna flunk him?

BERNARD. But I heard Mr. Birnbaum say—

WILLY. Don't be a pest, Bernard! (*To his boys*) What an **anemic**!

BERNARD. Okay, I'm waiting for you in my house, Biff.

(BERNARD *goes off.* THE LOMANS *laugh.*)

WILLY. Bernard is not well liked, is he?

BIFF. He's liked, but he's not well liked.

HAPPY. That's right, Pop.

WILLY. That's just what I mean. Bernard can get the best marks in school, y'understand, but when he gets out in the business world, y'understand, you are going to be five times ahead of him. That's why I thank Almighty God you're both built like Adonises. Because the man who makes an appearance in the business world, the man who creates personal interest, is the man who gets ahead. Be liked and you will never want. You take me, for instance. I never have to wait in line to see a buyer. "Willy Loman is here!" That's all they have to know, and I go right through.

BIFF. Did you knock them dead, Pop?

WILLY. Knocked 'em cold in Providence, slaughtered 'em in Boston.

HAPPY (*on his back, pedaling again*). I'm losing weight, you notice, Pop?

(LINDA *enters, as of old, a ribbon in her hair, carrying a basket of washing.*)

LINDA (*with youthful energy*). Hello, dear!

WILLY. Sweetheart!

LINDA. How'd the Chevvy run?

WILLY. Chevrolet, Linda, is the greatest car ever built. (*To the* BOYS) Since when do you let your mother carry wash up the stairs?

BIFF. Grab hold there, boy!

HAPPY. Where to, Mom?

LINDA. Hang them up on the line. And you better go down to your friends, Biff. The cellar is full of boys. They don't know what to do with themselves.

BIFF. Ah, when Pop comes home they can wait!

WILLY (*laughs appreciatively*). You better go down and tell them what to do, Biff.

BIFF. I think I'll have them sweep out the furnace room.

WILLY. Good work, Biff.

BIFF (*goes through wall-line of kitchen to doorway at back and calls down*). Fellas! Everybody sweep out the furnace room! I'll be right down!

VOICES. All right! Okay, Biff.

BIFF. George and Sam and Frank, come out back! We're hangin' up the wash! Come on, Hap, on the double! (*He and* HAPPY *carry out the basket.*)

LINDA. The way they obey him!

WILLY. Well, that's training, the training. I'm tellin' you, I was sellin' thousands and thousands, but I had to come home.

LINDA. Oh, the whole block'll be at that game. Did you sell anything?

WILLY. I did five hundred gross in Providence and seven hundred gross in Boston.

LINDA. No! Wait a minute, I've got a pencil. (*She pulls pencil and paper out of her apron pocket.*) That makes your commission . . . Two hundred—my God! Two hundred and twelve dollars!

WILLY. Well, I didn't figure it yet, but . . .

LINDA. How much did you do?

WILLY. Well, I—I did—about a hundred and eighty gross in Providence. Well, no—it came to—roughly two hundred gross on the whole trip.

LINDA (*without hesitation*). Two hundred gross. That's . . . (*She figures.*)

WILLY. The trouble was that three of the stores were half closed for inventory in Boston. Otherwise I woulda broke records.

LINDA. Well, it makes seventy dollars and some pennies. That's very good.

WILLY. What do we owe?

LINDA. Well, on the first there's sixteen dollars on the refrigerator—

WILLY. Why sixteen?

LINDA. Well, the fan belt broke, so it was a dollar eighty.

WILLY. But it's brand new.

LINDA. Well, the man said that's the way it is. Till they work themselves in, y'know.

(*They move through the wall-line into the kitchen.*)

WILLY. I hope we didn't get stuck on that machine.

LINDA. They got the biggest ads of any of them!

WILLY. I know, it's a fine machine. What else?

LINDA. Well, there's nine-sixty for the washing machine. And for the vacuum cleaner there's three and a half due on the fifteenth. Then the roof, you got twenty-one dollars remaining.

WILLY. It don't leak, does it?

LINDA. No, they did a wonderful job. Then you owe Frank for the carburetor.

WILLY. I'm not going to pay that man! That goddam Chevrolet, they ought to prohibit the manufacture of that car!

LINDA. Well, you owe him three and a half. And odds and ends, comes to around a hundred and twenty dollars by the fifteenth.

WILLY. A hundred and twenty dollars! My God, if business don't pick up I don't know what I'm gonna do!

LINDA. Well, next week you'll do better.

WILLY. Oh, I'll knock 'em dead next week. I'll go to Hartford. I'm very well liked in Hartford. You know, the trouble is, Linda, people don't seem to take to me.

(*They move onto the forestage.*)

LINDA. Oh, don't be foolish.

WILLY. I know it when I walk in. They seem to laugh at me.

LINDA. Why? Why would they laugh at you? Don't talk that way, Willy.

(WILLY *moves to the edge of the stage.* LINDA *goes into the kitchen and starts to darn stockings.*)

WILLY. I don't know the reason for it, but they just pass me by. I'm not noticed.

LINDA. But you're doing wonderful, dear. You're making seventy to a hundred dollars a week.

WILLY. But I gotta be at it ten, twelve hours a day. Other men—I don't know—they do it easier. I don't know why—I can't stop myself—I talk too much. A man oughta come in with a few words. One thing about Charley. He's a man of few words, and they respect him.

LINDA. You don't talk too much, you're just lively.

WILLY (*smiling*). Well, I figure, what the hell, life is short, a couple of jokes. (*To himself*) I joke too much! (*The smile goes.*)

LINDA. Why? You're—

WILLY. I'm fat. I'm very—foolish to look at, Linda. I didn't tell you, but Christmas time I happened to be calling on F. H. Stewarts, and a salesman I know, as I was going in to see the buyer I heard him say something about—walrus. And I—I cracked him right across the face. I won't take that. I simply will not take that. But they do laugh at me. I know that.

LINDA. Darling . . .

WILLY. I gotta overcome it. I know I gotta overcome it. I'm not dressing to advantage, maybe.

LINDA. Willy, darling, you're the handsomest man in the world—

WILLY. Oh, no, Linda.

LINDA. To me you are. (*Slight pause*) The handsomest.

(*From the darkness is heard the laughter of a woman.* WILLY *doesn't turn to it, but it continues through* LINDA's *lines.*)

LINDA. And the boys, Willy. Few men are idolized by their children the way you are.

(*Music is heard as behind a scrim, to the left of the house,* THE WOMAN, *dimly seen, is dressing.*)

WILLY (*with great feeling*). You're the best there is, Linda, you're a pal, you know that? On the road—on the road I want to grab you sometimes and just kiss the life outa you.

(*The laughter is loud now, and he moves into a brightening area at the left, where* THE WOMAN *has come from behind the scrim and is standing, putting on her hat, looking into a "mirror" and laughing.*)

WILLY. 'Cause I get so lonely—especially when business is bad and there's nobody to talk to. I get the feeling that I'll never sell anything again, that I won't make a living for you, or a business, a business for the boys. (*He talks through* THE WOMAN's *subsiding laughter;* THE WOMAN *primps at the "mirror."*) There's so much I want to make for—

THE WOMAN. Me? You didn't make me, Willy. I picked you.

WILLY (*pleased*). You picked me?

THE WOMAN (*who is quite proper-looking, WILLY's age*). I did. I've been sitting at that desk watching all the salesmen go by, day in, day out. But you've got such a sense of humor, and we do have such a good time together, don't we?

WILLY. Sure, sure. (*He takes her in his arms.*) Why do you have to go now?

THE WOMAN. It's two o'clock . . .

WILLY. No, come on in! (*He pulls her.*)

THE WOMAN. . . . my sisters'll be scandalized. When'll you be back?

WILLY. Oh, two weeks about. Will you come up again?

THE WOMAN. Sure thing. You do make me laugh. It's good for me. (*She squeezes his arm, kisses him.*) And I think you're a wonderful man.

WILLY. You picked me, heh?

THE WOMAN. Sure. Because you're so sweet. And such a kidder.

WILLY. Well, I'll see you next time I'm in Boston.

THE WOMAN. I'll put you right through to the buyers.

WILLY (*slapping her bottom*). Right. Well, bottoms up!

THE WOMAN (*slaps him gently and laughs*). You just kill me, Willy. (*He suddenly grabs her and kisses her roughly.*) You kill me. And thanks for the stockings. I love a lot of stockings. Well, good night.

WILLY. Good night. And keep your pores open!

THE WOMAN. Oh, Willy!

(THE WOMAN *bursts out laughing, and* LINDA's *laughter blends in.* THE WOMAN *disappears into the dark. Now the area at the kitchen table brightens.* LINDA *is sitting where she was at the kitchen table, but now is mending a pair of her silk stockings.*)

LINDA. You are, Willy. The handsomest man. You've got no reason to feel that—

WILLY (*coming out of* THE WOMAN's *dimming area and going over to* LINDA). I'll make it all up to you, Linda, I'll—

LINDA. There's nothing to make up, dear. You're doing fine, better than—

WILLY (*noticing her mending*). What's that?

LINDA. Just mending my stockings. They're so expensive—

WILLY (*angrily, taking them from her*). I won't have you mending stockings in this house! Now throw them out!

(LINDA *puts the stockings in her pocket.*)

BERNARD (*entering on the run*). Where is he? If he doesn't study!

WILLY (*moving to the forestage, with great agitation*). You'll give him the answers!

BERNARD. I do, but I can't on a Regents! That's a state exam! They're liable to arrest me!

WILLY. Where is he? I'll whip him, I'll whip him!

LINDA. And he'd better give back that football, Willy, it's not nice.
WILLY. Biff! Where is he? Why is he taking everything?
LINDA. He's too rough with the girls, Willy. All the mothers are afraid of him!
WILLY. I'll whip him!
BERNARD. He's driving the car without a license!

(THE WOMAN's *laugh is heard.*)

WILLY. Shut up!
LINDA. All the mothers—
WILLY. Shut up!
BERNARD (*backing quietly away and out*). Mr. Birnbaum says he's stuck up.
WILLY. Get outa here!
BERNARD. If he doesn't buckle down he'll flunk math! (*He goes off.*)
LINDA. He's right, Willy, you've gotta—
WILLY (*exploding at her*). There's nothing the matter with him! You want him to be a worm like Bernard? He's got spirit, personality . . .

(*As he speaks,* LINDA, *almost in tears, exits into the living-room.* WILLY *is alone in the kitchen, wilting and staring. The leaves are gone. It is night again, and the apartment houses look down from behind.*)

WILLY. Loaded with it. Loaded! What is he stealing? He's giving it back, isn't he? Why is he stealing? What did I tell him? I never in my life told him anything but decent things.

(HAPPY *in pajamas has come down the stairs;* WILLY *suddenly becomes aware of* HAPPY's *presence.*)

HAPPY. Let's go now, come on.
WILLY (*sitting down at the kitchen table*). Huh! Why did she have to wax the floors herself? Everytime she waxes the floors she keels over. She knows that!
HAPPY. Shh! Take it easy. What brought you back tonight?
WILLY. I got an awful scare. Nearly hit a kid in Yonkers. God! Why didn't I go to Alaska with my brother Ben that time! Ben! That man was a genius, that man was success incarnate! What a mistake! He begged me to go.
HAPPY. Well, there's no use in—
WILLY. You guys! There was a man started with the clothes on his back and ended up with diamond mines!
HAPPY. Boy, someday I'd like to know how he did it.
WILLY. What's the mystery? The man knew what he wanted and went out and got it! Walked into a jungle, and comes out, the age of twenty-one, and he's rich! The world is an oyster, but you don't crack it open on a mattress.

HAPPY. Pop, I told you I'm gonna retire you for life.

WILLY. You'll retire me for life on seventy goddam dollars a week? And your women and your car and your apartment, and you'll retire me for life! Christ's sake, I couldn't get past Yonkers today! Where are you guys, where are you? The woods are burning! I can't drive a car!

(CHARLEY *has appeared in the doorway. He is a large man, slow of speech, laconic, immovable. In all he says, despite what he says, there is pity, and, now, trepidation. He has a robe over pajamas, slippers on his feet. He enters the kitchen.*)

CHARLEY. Everything all right?

HAPPY. Yeah, Charley, everything's . . .

WILLY. What's the matter?

CHARLEY. I heard some noise. I thought something happened. Can't we do something about the walls? You sneeze in here, and in my house hats blow off.

HAPPY. Let's go to bed, Dad. Come on.

(CHARLEY *signals to* HAPPY *to go.*)

WILLY. You go ahead, I'm not tired at the moment.

HAPPY (*to* WILLY). Take it easy, huh? (*He exits.*)

WILLY. What're you doin' up?

CHARLEY (*sitting down at the kitchen table opposite* WILLY). Couldn't sleep good. I had a heartburn.

WILLY. Well, you don't know how to eat.

CHARLEY. I eat with my mouth.

WILLY. No, you're ignorant. You gotta know about vitamins and things like that.

CHARLEY. Come on, let's shoot. Tire you out a little.

WILLY (*hesitantly*). All right. You got cards?

CHARLEY (*taking a deck from his pocket*). Yeah, I got them. Someplace. What is it with those vitamins?

WILLY (*dealing*). They build up your bones. Chemistry.

CHARLEY. Yeah, but there's no bones in a heartburn.

WILLY. What are you talkin' about? Do you know the first thing about it?

CHARLEY. Don't get insulted.

WILLY. Don't talk about something you don't know anything about.

(*They are playing. Pause.*)

CHARLEY. What're you doin' home?

WILLY. A little trouble with the car.

CHARLEY. Oh. (*Pause*) I'd like to take a trip to California.

WILLY. Don't say.

CHARLEY. You want a job?

WILLY. I got a job, I told you that. (*After a slight pause*) What the hell are you offering me a job for?

CHARLEY. Don't get insulted.

WILLY. Don't insult me.

CHARLEY. I don't see no sense in it. You don't have to go on this way.

WILLY. I got a good job. (*Slight pause*) What do you keep comin' in here for?

CHARLEY. You want me to go?

WILLY (*after a pause, withering*). I can't understand it. He's going back to Texas again. What the hell is that?

CHARLEY. Let him go.

WILLY. I got nothin' to give him, Charley, I'm clean, I'm clean.

CHARLEY. He won't starve. None a them starve. Forget about him.

WILLY. Then what have I got to remember?

CHARLEY. You take it too hard. To hell with it. When a deposit bottle is broken you don't get your nickel back.

WILLY. That's easy enough for you to say.

CHARLEY. That ain't easy for me to say.

WILLY. Did you see the ceiling I put up in the living-room?

CHARLEY. Yeah, that's a piece of work. To put up a ceiling is a mystery to me. How do you do it?

WILLY. What's the difference?

CHARLEY. Well, talk about it.

WILLY. You gonna put up a ceiling?

CHARLEY. How could I put up a ceiling?

WILLY. Then what the hell are you bothering me for?

CHARLEY. You're insulted again.

WILLY. A man who can't handle tools is not a man. You're disgusting.

CHARLEY. Don't call me disgusting, Willy.

(UNCLE BEN, *carrying a valise and an umbrella, enters the forestage from around the right corner of the house. He is a stolid man, in his sixties, with a mustache and an authoritative air. He is utterly certain of his destiny, and there is an aura of far places about him. He enters exactly as* WILLY *speaks.*)

WILLY. I'm getting awfully tired, Ben.

(BEN's *music is heard.* BEN *looks around at everything.*)

CHARLEY. Good, keep playing; you'll sleep better. Did you call me Ben?

(BEN *looks at his watch.*)

WILLY. That's funny. For a second there you reminded me of my brother Ben.

BEN. I only have a few minutes.

(*He strolls, inspecting the place.* WILLY *and* CHARLEY *continue playing.*)

CHARLEY. You never heard from him again, heh? Since that time?
WILLY. Didn't Linda tell you? Couple of weeks ago we got a letter from his wife in Africa. He died.
CHARLEY. That so.
BEN (*chuckling*). So this is Brooklyn, eh?
CHARLEY. Maybe you're in for some of his money.
WILLY. Naa, he had seven sons. There's just one opportunity I had with that man . . .
BEN. I must make a train, William. There are several properties I'm looking at in Alaska.
WILLY. Sure, sure! If I'd gone with him to Alaska that time, everything would've been totally different.
CHARLEY. Go on, you'd froze to death up there.
WILLY. What're you talking about?
BEN. Opportunity is tremendous in Alaska, William. Surprised you're not up there.
WILLY. Sure, tremendous.
CHARLEY. Heh?
WILLY. There was the only man I ever met who knew the answers.
CHARLEY. Who?
BEN. How are you all?
WILLY (*taking a pot, smiling*). Fine, fine.
CHARLEY. Pretty sharp tonight.
BEN. Is Mother living with you?
WILLY. No, she died a long time ago.
CHARLEY. Who?
BEN. That's too bad. Fine specimen of a lady, Mother.
WILLY (*to* CHARLEY). Heh?
BEN. I'd hoped to see the old girl.
CHARLEY. Who died?
BEN. Heard anything from Father, have you?
WILLY (*unnerved*). What do you mean, who died?
CHARLEY (*taking a pot*). What're you talkin' about?
BEN (*looking at his watch*). William, it's half-past eight!
WILLY (*as though to dispel his confusion he angrily stops* CHARLEY's *hand*). That's my build!
CHARLEY. I put the ace—
WILLY. If you don't know how to play the game I'm not gonna throw my money away on you!
CHARLEY (*rising*). It was my ace, for God's sake!
WILLY. I'm through, I'm through!

BEN. When did Mother die?

WILLY. Long ago. Since the beginning you never knew how to play cards.

CHARLEY (*picks up the cards and goes to the door*). All right! Next time I'll bring a deck with five aces.

WILLY. I don't play that kind of game!

CHARLEY (*turning to him*). You ought to be ashamed of yourself!

WILLY. Yeah?

CHARLEY. Yeah! (*He goes out.*)

WILLY (*slamming the door after him*). Ignoramus!

BEN (*as* WILLY *comes toward him through the wall-line of the kitchen*). So you're William.

WILLY (*shaking* BEN'*s hand*). Ben! I've been waiting for you so long! What's the answer? How did you do it?

BEN. Oh, there's a story in that.

(LINDA *enters the forestage, as of old, carrying the wash basket.*)

LINDA. Is this Ben?

BEN (*gallantly*). How do you do, my dear.

LINDA. Where've you been all these years? Willy's always wondered why you—

WILLY (*pulling* BEN *away from her impatiently*). Where is Dad? Didn't you follow him? How did you get started?

BEN. Well, I don't know how much you remember.

WILLY. Well, I was just a baby, of course, only three or four years old—

BEN. Three years and eleven months.

WILLY. What a memory, Ben!

BEN. I have many enterprises, William, and I have never kept books.

WILLY. I remember I was sitting under the wagon in—was it Nebraska?

BEN. It was South Dakota, and I gave you a bunch of wild flowers.

WILLY. I remember you walking away down some open road.

BEN (*laughing*). I was going to find Father in Alaska.

WILLY. Where is he?

BEN. At that age I had a very faulty view of geography, William. I discovered after a few days that I was heading due south, so instead of Alaska, I ended up in Africa.

LINDA. Africa!

WILLY. The Gold Coast!

BEN. Principally diamond mines.

LINDA. Diamond mines!

BEN. Yes, my dear. But I've only a few minutes—

WILLY. No! Boys! Boys! (YOUNG BIFF and HAPPY *appear*.) Listen to this. This is your Uncle Ben, a great man! Tell my boys, Ben!

BEN. Why, boys, when I was seventeen I walked into the jungle, and when I was twenty-one I walked out. (*He laughs.*) And by God I was rich.

WILLY (*to the boys*). You see what I been talking about? The greatest things can happen!

BEN (*glancing at his watch*). I have an appointment in Ketchikan Tuesday week.

WILLY. No, Ben! Please tell about Dad. I want my boys to hear. I want them to know the kind of stock they spring from. All I remember is a man with a big beard, and I was in Mamma's lap, sitting around a fire, and some kind of high music.

BEN. His flute. He played the flute.

WILLY. Sure, the flute, that's right!

(*New music is heard, a high, rollicking tune.*)

BEN. Father was a very great and a very wild-hearted man. We would start in Boston, and he'd toss the whole family into the wagon, and then he'd drive the team right across the country; through Ohio, and Indiana, Michigan, Illinois, and all the Western states. And we'd stop in the towns and sell the flutes that he'd made on the way. Great inventor, Father. With one gadget he made more in a week than a man like you could make in a lifetime.

WILLY. That's just the way I'm bringing them up, Ben—rugged, well liked, all-around.

BEN. Yeah? (*To* BIFF) Hit that, boy—hard as you can. (*He pounds his stomach.*)

BIFF. Oh, no, sir!

BEN (*taking boxing stance*). Come on, get to me! (*He laughs.*)

WILLY. Go to it, Biff! Go ahead, show him!

BIFF. Okay! (*He cocks his fists and starts in.*)

LINDA (*to* WILLY). Why must he fight, dear?

BEN (*sparring with* BIFF). Good boy! Good boy!

WILLY. How's that, Ben, heh?

HAPPY. Give him the left, Biff!

LINDA. Why are you fighting?

BEN. Good boy! (*Suddenly comes in, trips* BIFF, *and stands over him, the point of his umbrella poised over* BIFF'S *eye.*)

LINDA. Look out, Biff!

BIFF. Gee!

BEN (*patting* BIFF'S *knee*). Never fight fair with a stranger, boy. You'll never get out of the jungle that way. (*Taking* LINDA'S *hand and bowing*) It was an honor and a pleasure to meet you, Linda.

LINDA (*withdrawing her hand coldly, frightened*). Have a nice—trip.

BEN (*to* WILLY). And good luck with your—what do you do?
WILLY. Selling.
BEN. Yes. Well . . . (*He raises his hand in farewell to all.*)
WILLY. No, Ben, I don't want you to think . . . (*He takes* BEN's *arm to show him.*) It's Brooklyn, I know, but we hunt too.
BEN. Really, now.
WILLY. Oh, sure, there's snakes and rabbits and—that's why I moved out here. Why, Biff can fell any one of these trees in no time! Boys! Go right over to where they're building the apartment house and get some sand. We're gonna rebuild the entire front stoop right now! Watch this, Ben!
BIFF. Yes, sir! On the double, Hap!
HAPPY (*as he and* BIFF *run off*). I lost weight, Pop, you notice?

(CHARLEY *enters in knickers, even before the boys are gone.*)

CHARLEY. Listen, if they steal any more from that building the watchman'll put the cops on them!
LINDA (*to* WILLY). Don't let Biff . . .

(BEN *laughs lustily.*)

WILLY. You shoulda seen the lumber they brought home last week. At least a dozen six-by-tens worth all kinds a money.
CHARLEY. Listen, if that watchman—
WILLY. I gave them hell, understand. But I got a couple of fearless characters there.
CHARLEY. Willy, the jails are full of fearless characters.
BEN (*clapping* WILLY *on the back, with a laugh at* CHARLEY). And the stock exchange, friend!
WILLY (*joining in* BEN's *laughter*). Where are the rest of your pants?
CHARLEY. My wife bought them.
WILLY. Now all you need is a golf club and you can go upstairs and go to sleep. (*To* BEN) Great athlete! Between him and his son Bernard they can't hammer a nail!
BERNARD (*rushing in*). The watchman's chasing Biff!
WILLY (*angrily*). Shut up! He's not stealing anything!
LINDA (*alarmed, hurrying off left*). Where is he? Biff, dear! (*She exits.*)
WILLY (*moving toward the left, away from* BEN). There's nothing wrong. What's the matter with you?
BEN. Nervy boy. Good!
WILLY (*laughing*). Oh, nerves of iron, that Biff!
CHARLEY. Don't know what it is. My New England man comes back and he's bleedin', they murdered him up there.
WILLY. It's contacts, Charley, I got important contacts!
CHARLEY (*sarcastically*). Glad to hear it, Willy. Come in later, we'll

shoot a little casino. I'll take some of your Portland money. (*He laughs at* WILLY *and exits.*)

WILLY (*turning to* BEN).   Business is bad, it's murderous. But not for me, of course.

BEN.   I'll stop by on my way back to Africa.

WILLY (*longingly*).   Can't you stay a few days? You're just what I need, Ben, because I—I have a fine position here, but I—well, Dad left when I was such a baby and I never had a chance to talk to him and I still feel—kind of temporary about myself.

BEN.   I'll be late for my train.

(*They are at opposite ends of the stage.*)

WILLY.   Ben, my boys—can't we talk? They'd go into the jaws of hell for me, but I—

BEN.   William, you're being first-rate with your boys. Outstanding, manly chaps!

WILLY (*hanging on to his words*).   Oh, Ben, that's good to hear! Because sometimes I'm afraid that I'm not teaching them the right kind of— Ben, how should I teach them?

BEN (*giving great weight to each word, and with a certain vicious audacity*).   William, when I walked into the jungle, I was seventeen. When I walked out I was twenty-one. And, by God, I was rich! (*He goes off into darkness around the right corner of the house.*)

WILLY.   . . . was rich! That's just the spirit I want to imbue them with! To walk into a jungle! I was right! I was right! I was right!

(BEN *is gone, but* WILLY *is still speaking to him as* LINDA, *in nightgown and robe, enters the kitchen, glances around for* WILLY, *then goes to the door of the house, looks out and sees him. Comes down to his left. He looks at her.*)

LINDA.   Willy, dear? Willy?

WILLY.   I was right!

LINDA.   Did you have some cheese? (*He can't answer.*) It's very late, darling. Come to bed, heh?

WILLY (*looking straight up*).   Gotta break your neck to see a star in this yard.

LINDA.   You coming in?

WILLY.   Whatever happened to that diamond watch fob? Remember? When Ben came from Africa that time? Didn't he give me a watch fob with a diamond in it?

LINDA.   You pawned it, dear. Twelve, thirteen years ago. For Biff's radio correspondence course.

WILLY.   Gee, that was a beautiful thing. I'll take a walk.

LINDA. But you're in your slippers.

WILLY (*starting to go around the house at the left*). I was right! I was! (*Half to* LINDA, *as he goes, shaking his head*) What a man! There was a man worth talking to. I was right!

LINDA (*calling after* WILLY). But in your slippers, Willy!

(WILLY *is almost gone when* BIFF, *in his pajamas, comes down the stairs and enters the kitchen.*)

BIFF. What is he doing out there?
LINDA. Sh!
BIFF. God Almighty, Mom, how long has he been doing this?
LINDA. Don't, he'll hear you.
BIFF. What the hell is the matter with him?
LINDA. It'll pass by morning.
BIFF. Shouldn't we do anything?
LINDA. Oh, my dear, you should do a lot of things, but there's nothing to do, so go to sleep.

(HAPPY *comes down the stairs and sits on the steps.*)

HAPPY. I never heard him so loud, Mom.
LINDA. Well, come around more often; you'll hear him. (*She sits down at the table and mends the lining of* WILLY's *jacket.*)
BIFF. Why didn't you ever write me about this, Mom?
LINDA. How would I write to you? For over three months you had no address.
BIFF. I was on the move. But you know I thought of you all the time. You know that, don't you, pal?
LINDA. I know, dear, I know. But he likes to have a letter. Just to know that there's still a possibility for better things.
BIFF. He's not like this all the time, is he?
LINDA. It's when you come home he's always the worst.
BIFF. When I come home?
LINDA. When you write you're coming, he's all smiles, and talks about the future, and—he's just wonderful. And then the closer you seem to come, the more shaky he gets, and then, by the time you get here, he's arguing, and he seems angry at you. I think it's just that maybe he can't bring himself to—to open up to you. Why are you so hateful to each other? Why is that?
BIFF (*evasively*). I'm not hateful, Mom.
LINDA. But you no sooner come in the door than you're fighting!
BIFF. I don't know why. I mean to change. I'm tryin', Mom, you understand?
LINDA. Are you home to stay now?
BIFF. I don't know. I want to look around, see what's doin'.

LINDA. Biff, you can't look around all your life, can you?

BIFF. I just can't take hold, Mom. I can't take hold of some kind of a life.

LINDA. Biff, a man is not a bird, to come and go with the springtime.

BIFF. Your hair . . . (*He touches her hair.*) Your hair got so gray.

LINDA. Oh, it's been gray since you were in high school. I just stopped dyeing it, that's all.

BIFF. Dye it again, will ya? I don't want my pal looking old. (*He smiles.*)

LINDA. You're such a boy! You think you can go away for a year and . . . You've got to get it into your head now that one day you'll knock on this door and there'll be strange people here—

BIFF. What are you talking about? You're not even sixty, Mom.

LINDA. But what about your father?

BIFF (*lamely*). Well, I meant him too.

HAPPY. He admires Pop.

LINDA. Biff, dear, if you don't have any feeling for him, then you can't have any feeling for me.

BIFF. Sure I can, Mom.

LINDA. No. You can't just come to see me, because I love him. (*With a threat, but only a threat, of tears*) He's the dearest man in the world to me, and I won't have anyone making him feel unwanted and low and blue. You've got to make up your mind now, darling, there's no leeway any more. Either he's your father and you pay him that respect, or else you're not to come here. I know he's not easy to get along with—nobody knows that better than me—but . . .

WILLY (*from the left, with a laugh*). Hey, hey, Biffo!

BIFF (*starting to go out after* WILLY). What the hell is the matter with him?

(HAPPY *stops him.*)

LINDA. Don't—don't go near him!

BIFF. Stop making excuses for him! He always, always wiped the floor with you. Never had an ounce of respect for you.

HAPPY. He's always had respect for—

BIFF. What the hell do you know about it?

HAPPY (*surlily*). Just don't call him crazy!

BIFF. He's got no character—Charley wouldn't do this. Not in his own house—spewing out that vomit from his mind.

HAPPY. Charley never had to cope with what he's got to.

BIFF. People are worse off than Willy Loman. Believe me, I've seen them.

LINDA. Then make Charley your father, Biff. You can't do that, can you? I don't say he's a great man. Willy Loman never made a lot of money.

His name was never in the paper. He's not the finest character that ever lived. But he's a human being, and a terrible thing is happening to him. So attention must be paid. He's not to be allowed to fall into his grave like an old dog. Attention, attention must be finally paid to such a person. You called him crazy—

BIFF. I didn't mean—

LINDA. No, a lot of people think he's lost his—balance. But you don't have to be very smart to know what his trouble is. The man is exhausted.

HAPPY. Sure!

LINDA. A small man can be just as exhausted as a great man. He works for a company thirty-six years this March, opens up unheard-of territories to their trademark, and now in his old age they take his salary away.

HAPPY (*indignantly*). I didn't know that, Mom.

LINDA. You never asked, my dear! Now that you get your spending money someplace else you don't trouble your mind with him.

HAPPY. But I gave you money last—

LINDA. Christmas time, fifty dollars! To fix the hot water it cost ninety-seven fifty! For five weeks he's been on straight commission, like a beginner, an unknown!

BIFF. Those ungrateful bastards!

LINDA. Are they any worse than his sons? When he brought them business, when he was young, they were glad to see him. But now his old friends, the old buyers that loved him so and always found some order to hand him in a pinch—they're all dead, retired. He used to be able to make six, seven calls a day in Boston. Now he takes his valises out of the car and puts them back and takes them out again and he's exhausted. Instead of walking he talks now. He drives seven hundred miles, and when he gets there no one knows him any more, no one welcomes him. And what goes through a man's mind, driving seven hundred miles home without having earned a cent? Why shouldn't he talk to himself? Why? When he has to go to Charley and borrow fifty dollars a week and pretend to me that it's his pay? How long can that go on? How long? You see what I'm sitting here and waiting for? And you tell me he has no character? The man who never worked a day but for your benefit? When does he get the medal for that? Is this his reward—to turn around at the age of sixty-three and find his sons, who he loved better than his life, one aphilandering bum—

HAPPY. Mom!

LINDA. That's all you are, my baby! (*To* BIFF) And you! What happened to the love you had for him? You were such pals! How you used to talk to him on the phone every night! How lonely he was till he could come home to you!

BIFF. All right, Mom. I'll live here in my room, and I'll get a job.

I'll keep away from him, that's all.

LINDA. No, Biff. You can't stay here and fight all the time.

BIFF. He threw me out of this house, remember that.

LINDA. Why did he do that? I never knew why.

BIFF. Because I know he's a fake and he doesn't like anybody around who knows!

LINDA. Why a fake? In what way? What do you mean?

BIFF. Just don't lay it all at my feet. It's between me and him—that's all I have to say. I'll chip in from now on. He'll settle for half my pay check. He'll be all right. I'm going to bed. (*He starts for the stairs.*)

LINDA. He won't be all right.

BIFF (*turning on the stairs, furiously*). I hate this city and I'll stay here. Now what do you want?

LINDA. He's dying, Biff.

(HAPPY *turns quickly to her, shocked.*)

BIFF (*after a pause*). Why is he dying?

LINDA. He's been trying to kill himself.

BIFF (*with great horror*). How?

LINDA. I live from day to day.

BIFF. What're you talking about?

LINDA. Remember I wrote you that he smashed up the car again? In February?

BIFF. Well?

LINDA. The insurance inspector came. He said that they have evidence. That all these accidents in the last year—weren't—weren't—accidents.

HAPPY. How can they tell that? That's a lie.

⎰ LINDA. It seems there's a woman . . . (*She takes a breath as*)
⎱ BIFF (*sharply but contained*). What woman?

LINDA (*simultaneously*). . . . and this woman . . .

LINDA. What?

BIFF. Nothing. Go ahead.

LINDA. What did you say?

BIFF. Nothing. I just said what woman?

HAPPY. What about her?

LINDA. Well, it seems she was walking down the road and saw his car. She says that he wasn't driving fast at all, and that he didn't skid. She says he came to that little bridge, and then deliberately smashed into the railing, and it was only the shallowness of the water that saved him.

BIFF. Oh, no, he probably just fell asleep again.

LINDA. I don't think he fell asleep.

BIFF. Why not?

LINDA. Last month . . . (*With great difficulty*) Oh, boys, it's so hard to say a thing like this! He's just a big stupid man to you, but I tell you there's more good in him than in many other people. (*She chokes, wipes her eyes.*) I was looking for a fuse. The lights blew out, and I went down the cellar. And behind the fuse box—it happened to fall out—was a length of rubber pipe—just short.

HAPPY. No kidding?

LINDA. There's a little attachment on the end of it. I knew right away. And sure enough, on the bottom of the water heater there's a new little nipple on the gas pipe.

HAPPY (*angrily*). That—jerk.

BIFF. Did you have it taken off?

LINDA. I'm—I'm ashamed to. How can I mention it to him? Every day I go down and take away that little rubber pipe. But, when he comes home, I put it back where it was. How can I insult him that way? I don't know what to do. I live from day to day, boys. I tell you, I know every thought in his mind. It sounds so old-fashioned and silly, but I tell you he put his whole life into you and you've turned your backs on him. (*She is bent over in the chair, weeping, her face in her hands.*) Biff, I swear to God! Biff, his life is in your hands!

HAPPY (*to* BIFF). How do you like that damned fool!

BIFF (*kissing her*). All right, pal, all right. It's all settled now. I've been remiss. I know that, Mom. But now I'll stay, and I swear to you, I'll apply myself. (*Kneeling in front of her, in a fever of self-reproach*) It's just—you see, Mom, I don't fit in business. Not that I won't try. I'll try, and I'll make good.

HAPPY. Sure you will. The trouble with you in business was you never tried to please people.

BIFF. I know, I—

HAPPY. Like when you worked for Harrison's. Bob Harrison said you were tops, and then you go and do some damn fool thing like whistling whole songs in the elevator like a comedian.

BIFF (*against* HAPPY). So what? I like to whistle sometimes.

HAPPY. You don't raise a guy to a responsible job who whistles in the elevator!

LINDA. Well, don't argue about it now.

HAPPY. Like when you'd go off and swim in the middle of the day instead of taking the line around.

BIFF (*his resentment rising*). Well, don't you run off? You take off sometimes, don't you? On a nice summer day?

HAPPY. Yeah, but I cover myself!

LINDA. Boys!

HAPPY. If I'm going to take a fade the boss can call any number where I'm supposed to be and they'll swear to him that I just left. I'll tell you something that I hate to say, Biff, but in the business world some of them think you're crazy.

BIFF (*angered*). Screw the business world!

HAPPY. All right, screw it! Great, but cover yourself!

LINDA. Hap, Hap!

BIFF. I don't care what they think! They've laughed at Dad for years, and you know why? Because we don't belong in this nuthouse of a city! We should be mixing cement on some open plain, or—or carpenters. A carpenter is allowed to whistle!

(WILLY *walks in from the entrance of the house, at left.*)

WILLY. Even your grandfather was better than a carpenter. (*Pause. They watch him.*) You never grew up. Bernard does not whistle in the elevator, I assure you.

BIFF (*as though to laugh* WILLY *out of it*). Yeah, but you do, Pop.

WILLY. I never in my life whistled in an elevator! And who in the business world thinks I'm crazy?

BIFF. I didn't mean it like that, Pop. Now don't make a whole thing out of it, will ya?

WILLY. Go back to the West! Be a carpenter, a cowboy, enjoy yourself!

LINDA. Willy, he was just saying—

WILLY. I heard what he said!

HAPPY (*trying to quiet* WILLY). Hey, Pop, come on now . . .

WILLY (*continuing over* HAPPY'S *line*). They laugh at me, heh? Go to Filene's, go to the Hub, go to Slattery's, Boston. Call out the name Willy Loman and see what happens! Big shot!

BIFF. All right, Pop.

WILLY. Big!

BIFF. All right!

WILLY. Why do you always insult me?

BIFF. I didn't say a word. (*To* LINDA) Did I say a word?

LINDA. He didn't say anything, Willy.

WILLY (*going to the doorway of the living-room*). All right, good night, good night.

LINDA. Willy, dear, he just decided . . .

WILLY (*to* BIFF). If you get tired hanging around tomorrow, paint the ceiling I put up in the living-room.

BIFF. I'm leaving early tomorrow.

HAPPY. He's going to see Bill Oliver, Pop.

WILLY (*interestedly*). Oliver? For what?

BIFF (*with reserve, but trying, trying*). He always said he'd stake me. I'd like to go into business, so maybe I can take him up on it.

LINDA. Isn't that wonderful?

WILLY. Don't interrupt. What's wonderful about it? There's fifty men in the City of New York who'd stake him. (*To* BIFF) Sporting goods?

BIFF. I guess so. I know something about it and—

WILLY. He knows something about it! You know sporting goods better than Spalding, for God's sake! How much is he giving you?

BIFF. I don't know, I didn't even see him yet, but—

WILLY. Then what're you talkin' about?

BIFF (*getting angry*). Well, all I said was I'm gonna see him, that's all!

WILLY (*turning away*). Ah, you're counting your chickens again.

BIFF (*starting left for the stairs*). Oh, Jesus, I'm going to sleep!

WILLY (*calling after him*). Don't curse in this house!

BIFF (*turning*). Since when did you get so clean?

HAPPY (*trying to stop them*). Wait a . . .

WILLY. Don't use that language to me! I won't have it!

HAPPY (*grabbing* BIFF, *shouts*). Wait a minute! I got an idea. I got a feasible idea. Come here, Biff, let's talk this over now, let's talk some sense here. When I was down in Florida last time, I thought of a great idea to sell sporting goods. It just came back to me. You and I, Biff—we have a line, the Loman Line. We train a couple of weeks, and put on a couple of exhibitions, see?

WILLY. That's an idea!

HAPPY. Wait! We form two basketball teams, see? Two water-polo teams. We play each other. It's a million dollars' worth of publicity. Two brothers, see? The Loman Brothers. Displays in the Royal Palms—all the hotels. And banners over the ring and the basketball court: "Loman Brothers." Baby, we could sell sporting goods!

WILLY. That is a one-million-dollar idea!

LINDA. Marvelous!

BIFF. I'm in great shape as far as that's concerned.

HAPPY. And the beauty of it is, Biff, it wouldn't be like a business. We'd be out playin' ball again . . .

BIFF (*enthused*). Yeah, that's . . .

WILLY. Million-dollar . . .

HAPPY. And you wouldn't get fed up with it, Biff. It'd be the family again. There'd be the old honor, and comradeship, and if you wanted to go off for a swim or somethin'—well, you'd do it! Without some smart cooky gettin' up ahead of you!

WILLY. Lick the world! You guys together could absolutely lick the civilized world.

BIFF. I'll see Oliver tomorrow. Hap, if we could work that out . . .

LINDA. Maybe things are beginning to—

WILLY (*wildly enthused, to* LINDA). Stop interrupting! (*To* BIFF) But don't wear sport jacket and slacks when you see Oliver.

BIFF. No, I'll—
WILLY. A business suit, and talk as little as possible, and don't crack any jokes.
BIFF. He did like me. Always liked me.
LINDA. He loved you!
WILLY (*to* LINDA). Will you stop! (*To* BIFF) Walk in very serious. You are not applying for a boy's job. Money is to pass. Be quiet, fine, and serious. Everybody likes a kidder, but nobody lends him money.
HAPPY. I'll try to get some myself, Biff. I'm sure I can.
WILLY. I see great things for you kids, I think your troubles are over. But remember, start big and you'll end big. Ask for fifteen. How much you gonna ask for?
BIFF. Gee, I don't know—
WILLY. And don't say "Gee." "Gee" is a boy's word. A man walking in for fifteen thousand dollars does not say "Gee!"
BIFF. Ten, I think, would be top though.
WILLY. Don't be so modest. You always started too low. Walk in with a big laugh. Don't look worried. Start off with a couple of your good stories to lighten things up. It's not what you say, it's how you say it—because personality always wins the day.
LINDA. Oliver always thought the highest of him—
WILLY. Will you let me talk?
BIFF. Don't yell at her, Pop, will ya?
WILLY (*angrily*). I was talking, wasn't I?
BIFF. I don't like you yelling at her all the time, and I'm tellin' you, that's all.
WILLY. What're you, takin' over this house?
LINDA. Willy—
WILLY (*turning on her*). Don't take his side all the time, goddammit!
BIFF (*furiously*). Stop yelling at her!
WILLY (*suddenly pulling on his cheek, beaten down, guilt ridden*). Give my best to Bill Oliver—he may remember me. (*He exits through the living-room doorway.*)
LINDA (*her voice subdued*). What'd you have to start that for? (BIFF *turns away.*) You see how sweet he was as soon as you talked hopefully? (*She goes over to* BIFF.) Come up and say good night to him. Don't let him go to bed that way.
HAPPY. Come on, Biff, let's buck him up.
LINDA. Please, dear. Just say good night. It takes so little to make him happy. Come. (*She goes through the living-room doorway, calling upstairs from within the living-room.*) Your pajamas are hanging in the bathroom, Willy!
HAPPY (*looking toward where* LINDA *went out*). What a woman! They broke the mold when they made her. You know that, Biff?

BIFF. He's off salary. My God, working on commission!

HAPPY. Well, let's face it: he's no hot-shot selling man. Except that sometimes, you have to admit, he's a sweet personality.

BIFF (*deciding*). Lend me ten bucks, will ya? I want to buy some new ties.

HAPPY. I'll take you to a place I know. Beautiful stuff. Wear one of my striped shirts tomorrow.

BIFF. She got gray. Mom got awful old. Gee, I'm gonna go in to Oliver tomorrow and knock him for a—

HAPPY. Come on up. Tell that to Dad. Let's give him a whirl. Come on.

BIFF (*steamed up*). You know, with ten thousand bucks, boy!

HAPPY (*as they go into the living-room*). That's the talk, Biff, that's the first time I've heard the old confidence out of you! (*From within the living-room, fading off*) You're gonna live with me, kid, and any babe you want just say the word . . . (*The last lines are hardly heard. They are mounting the stairs to their parents' bedroom.*)

LINDA (*entering her bedroom and addressing* WILLY, *who is in the bathroom. She is straightening the bed for him*). Can you do anything about the shower? It drips.

WILLY (*from the bathroom*). All of a sudden everything falls to pieces! Goddam plumbing, oughta be sued, those people. I hardly finished putting it in and the thing . . . (*His words rumble off.*)

LINDA. I'm just wondering if Oliver will remember him. You think he might?

WILLY (*coming out of the bathroom in his pajamas*). Remember him? What's the matter with you, you crazy? If he'd've stayed with Oliver he'd be on top by now! Wait'll Oliver gets a look at him. You don't know the average caliber any more. The average young man today—(*he is getting into bed*)—is got a caliber of zero. Greatest thing in the world for him was to bum around.

(BIFF *and* HAPPY *enter the bedroom. Slight pause.*)

WILLY (*stops short, looking at* BIFF). Glad to hear it, boy.

HAPPY. He wanted to say good night to you, sport.

WILLY (*to* BIFF). Yeah. Knock him dead, boy. What'd you want to tell me?

BIFF. Just take it easy, Pop. Good night. (*He turns to go.*)

WILLY (*unable to resist*). And if anything falls off the desk while you're talking to him—like a package or something—don't you pick it up. They have office boys for that.

LINDA. I'll make a big breakfast—

WILLY. Will you let me finish? (*To* BIFF) Tell him you were in the business in the West. Not farm work.

BIFF. All right, Dad.

LINDA. I think everything—
WILLY (*going right through her speech*). And don't undersell yourself. No less than fifteen thousand dollars.
BIFF (*unable to bear him*). Okay. Good night, Mom. (*He starts moving.*)
WILLY. Because you got a greatness in you, Biff, remember that. You got all kinds of greatness . . .

(*He lies back, exhausted.* BIFF *walks out.*)

LINDA (*calling after* BIFF). Sleep well, darling!
HAPPY. I'm gonna get married, Mom. I wanted to tell you.
LINDA. Go to sleep, dear.
HAPPY (*going*). I just wanted to tell you.
WILLY. Keep up the good work. (HAPPY *exits.*) God . . . remember that Ebbets Field game? The championship of the city?
LINDA. Just rest. Should I sing to you?
WILLY. Yeah. Sing to me. (LINDA *hums a soft lullaby.*) When that team came out—he was the tallest, remember?
LINDA. Oh, yes. And in gold.

(BIFF *enters the darkened kitchen, takes a cigarette, and leaves the house. He comes downstage into a golden pool of light. He smokes, staring at the night.*)

WILLY. Like a young god. Hercules—something like that. And the sun, the sun all around him. Remember how he waved to me? Right up from the field, with the representatives of three colleges standing by? And the buyers I brought, and the cheers when he came out—Loman, Loman, Loman! God Almighty, he'll be great yet. A star like that, magnificent, can never really fade away!

(*The light on* WILLY *is fading. The gas heater begins to glow through the kitchen wall, near the stairs, a blue flame beneath red coils.*)

LINDA (*timidly*). Willy dear, what has he got against you?
WILLY. I'm so tired. Don't talk anymore.

(BIFF *slowly returns to the kitchen. He stops, stares toward the heater.*)

LINDA. Will you ask Howard to let you work in New York?
WILLY. First thing in the morning. Everything'll be all right.

(BIFF *reaches behind the heater and draws out a length of rubber tubing. He is horrified and turns his head toward* WILLY'S *room, still dimly lit, from which the strains of* LINDA'S *desperate but monotonous humming rise.*)

WILLY (*staring through the window into the moonlight*). Gee, look at the moon moving between the buildings!

(BIFF *wraps the tubing around his hand and quickly goes up the stairs.*)

ACT II

Music is heard, gay and bright. The curtain rises as the music fades away. WILLY, *in shirt sleeves, is sitting at the kitchen table, sipping coffee, his hat in his lap.* LINDA *is filling his cup when she can.*

WILLY. Wonderful coffee. Meal in itself.
LINDA. Can I make you some eggs?
WILLY. No. Take a breath.
LINDA. You look so rested, dear.
WILLY. I slept like a dead one. First time in months. Imagine, sleeping till ten on a Tuesday morning. Boys left nice and early, heh?
LINDA. They were out of here by eight o'clock.
WILLY. Good work!
LINDA. It was so thrilling to see them leaving together. I can't get over the shaving lotion in this house!
WILLY (*smiling*). Mmm—
LINDA. Biff was very changed this morning. His whole attitude seemed to be hopeful. He couldn't wait to get downtown to see Oliver.
WILLY. He's heading for a change. There's no question, there simply are certain men that take longer to get—solidified. How did he dress?
LINDA. His blue suit. He's so handsome in that suit. He could be a—anything in that suit!

(WILLY *gets up from the table.* LINDA *holds his jacket for him.*)

WILLY. There's no question, no question at all. Gee, on the way home tonight I'd like to buy some seeds.
LINDA (*laughing*). That'd be wonderful. But not enough sun gets back there. Nothing'll grow any more.
WILLY. You wait, kid, before it's all over we're gonna get a little place out in the country, and I'll raise some vegetables, a couple of chickens . . .
LINDA. You'll do it yet, dear.

(WILLY *walks out of his jacket.* LINDA *follows him.*)

WILLY. And they'll get married, and come for a weekend. I'd build a little guest house. 'Cause I got so many fine tools, all I'd need would be a little lumber and some peace of mind.
LINDA (*joyfully*). I sewed the lining . . .
WILLY. I would build two guest houses, so they'd both come. Did he decide how much he's going to ask Oliver for?
LINDA (*getting him into the jacket*). He didn't mention it, but I imagine ten or fifteen thousand. You going to talk to Howard today?
WILLY. Yeah. I'll put it to him straight and simple. He'll just have to

take me off the road.

LINDA. And, Willy, don't forget to ask for a little advance, because we've got the insurance premium. It's the grace period now.

WILLY. That's a hundred . . .?

LINDA. A hundred and eight, sixty-eight. Because we're a little short again.

WILLY. Why are we short?

LINDA. Well, you had the motor job on the car . . .

WILLY. That goddam Studebaker!

LINDA. And you got one more payment on the refrigerator . . .

WILLY. But it just broke again!

LINDA. Well, it's old, dear.

WILLY. I told you we should've bought a well-advertised machine. Charley bought a General Electric and it's twenty years old and it's still good, that son-of-a-bitch.

LINDA. But, Willy—

WILLY. Whoever heard of a Hastings refrigerator? Once in my life I would like to own something outright before it's broken! I'm always in a race with the junkyard! I just finished paying for the car and it's on its last legs. The refrigerator consumes belts like a goddam maniac. They time those things. They time them so when you finally paid for them, they're used up.

LINDA (*buttoning up his jacket as he unbuttons it*). All told, about two hundred dollars would carry us, dear. But that includes the last payment on the mortgage. After this payment, Willy, the house belongs to us.

WILLY. It's twenty-five years!

LINDA. Biff was nine years old when we bought it.

WILLY. Well, that's a great thing. To weather a twenty-five year mortgage is—

LINDA. It's an accomplishment.

WILLY. All the cement, the lumber, the reconstruction I put in this house! There ain't a crack to be found in it any more.

LINDA. Well, it served its purpose.

WILLY. What purpose? Some stranger'll come along, move in, and that's that. If only Biff would take this house, and raise a family . . . (*He starts to go.*) Good-by, I'm late.

LINDA (*suddenly remembering*). Oh, I forgot! You're supposed to meet them for dinner.

WILLY. Me?

LINDA. At Frank's Chop House on Forty-eighth near Sixth Avenue.

WILLY. Is that so! How about you?

LINDA. No, just the three of you. They're gonna blow you to a big meal!

WILLY. Don't say! Who thought of that?

LINDA. Biff came to me this morning, Willy, and he said, "Tell Dad, we want to blow him to a big meal." Be there six o'clock. You and your two boys are going to have dinner.

WILLY. Gee whiz! That's really somethin'. I'm gonna knock Howard for a loop, kid. I'll get an advance, and I'll come home with a New York job. Goddammit, now I'm gonna do it!

LINDA. Oh, that's the spirit, Willy!

WILLY. I will never get behind a wheel the rest of my life!

LINDA. It's changing, Willy, I can feel it changing!

WILLY. Beyond a question. G'by, I'm late. (*He starts to go again.*)

LINDA (*calling after him as she runs to the kitchen table for a handkerchief*). You got your glasses?

WILLY (*feels for them, then comes back in*). Yeah, yeah, got my glasses.

LINDA (*giving him the handkerchief*). And a handkerchief.

WILLY. Yeah, handkerchief.

LINDA. And your saccharine?

WILLY. Yeah, my saccharine.

LINDA. Be careful on the subway stairs.

(*She kisses him, and a silk stocking is seen hanging from her hand.* WILLY *notices it.*)

WILLY. Will you stop mending stockings? At least while I'm in the house. It gets me nervous. I can't tell you. Please.

(LINDA *hides the stocking in her hand as she follows* WILLY *across the forestage in front of the house.*)

LINDA. Remember, Frank's Chop House.

WILLY (*passing the apron*). Maybe beets would grow out there.

LINDA (*laughing*). But you tried so many times.

WILLY. Yeah. Well, don't work hard today. (*He disappears around the right corner of the house.*)

LINDA. Be careful!

(As WILLY *vanishes,* LINDA *waves to him. Suddenly the phone rings. She runs across the stage and into the kitchen and lifts it.*)

LINDA. Hello? Oh, Biff! I'm so glad you called, I just . . . Yes, sure, I just told him. Yes, he'll be there for dinner at six o'clock, I didn't forget. Listen, I was just dying to tell you. You know that little rubber pipe I told you about? That he connected to the gas heater? I finally decided to go down the cellar this morning and take it away and destroy it. But it's gone! Imagine? He took it away himself, it isn't there! (*She listens.*) When? Oh, then you took it. Oh—nothing, it's just that I'd hoped he'd taken it away himself. Oh, I'm not worried, darling, because this morning he left in such high spirits, it was like the old days! I'm not afraid any more. Did Mr. Oliver see you? . . . Well, you wait there then. And make a nice impression on him, darling. Just don't perspire too much before you see him. And have a nice time with Dad. He may have big news too! . . . That's right, a New York job. And be sweet to him tonight, dear. Be loving to him. Because he's only a little boat looking for a harbor. (*She is trembling with sorrow and joy.*) Oh, that's wonderful, Biff, you'll save his life. Thanks, darling. Just put your arm around him when he comes into the restaurant. Give him a smile. That's the boy . . . Good-by, dear . . . You got your comb? . . . That's fine. Good-by, Biff dear.

(*In the middle of her speech,* HOWARD WAGNER, *thirty-six, wheels on a small typewriter table on which is a wire-recording machine and proceeds to plug it in. This is on the left forestage. Light slowly fades on* LINDA *as it rises on* HOWARD. HOWARD *is intent on threading the machine and only glances over his shoulder as* WILLY *appears.*)

WILLY. Pst! Pst!
HOWARD. Hello, Willy, come in.
WILLY. Like to have a little talk with you, Howard.
HOWARD. Sorry to keep you waiting. I'll be with you in a minute.
WILLY. What's that, Howard?
HOWARD. Didn't you ever see one of these? Wire recorder.
WILLY. Oh. Can we talk a minute?
HOWARD. Records things. Just got delivery yesterday. Been driving me crazy, the most terrific machine I ever saw in my life. I was up all night with it.
WILLY. What do you do with it?
HOWARD. I bought it for dictation, but you can do anything with it. Listen to this. I had it home last night. Listen to what I picked up. The first one is my daughter. Get this. (*He flicks the switch and "Roll Out the Barrel" is heard being whistled.*) Listen to that kid whistle.
WILLY. That is lifelike, isn't it?
HOWARD. Seven years old. Get that tone.
WILLY. Ts, ts. Like to ask a little favor if you . . .

(*The whistling breaks off, and the voice of* HOWARD's *daughter is heard.*)

HIS DAUGHTER. "Now you, Daddy."
HOWARD. She's crazy for me! (*Again the same song is whistled.*) That's me! Ha! (*He winks.*)
WILLY. You're very good!

(*The whistling breaks off again. The machine runs silent for a moment.*)

HOWARD. Sh! Get this now, this is my son.
HIS SON. "The capital of Alabama is Montgomery; the capital of

Arizona is Phoenix; the capital of Arkansas is Little Rock; the capital of California is Sacramento . . ." (*and on, and on*).

HOWARD (*holding up five fingers.*)   Five years old, Willy!

WILLY.   He'll make an announcer some day!

HIS SON (*continuing*).   "The capital . . ."

HOWARD.   Get that—alphabetical order! (*The machine breaks off suddenly.*) Wait a minute. The maid kicked the plug out.

WILLY.   It certainly is a—

HOWARD.   Sh, for God's sake!

HIS SON.   "It's nine o'clock, Bulova watch time. So I have to go to sleep."

WILLY.   That really is—

HOWARD.   Wait a minute! The next is my wife.

(*They wait.*)

HOWARD'S VOICE.   "Go on, say something." (*Pause*) "Well, you gonna talk?"

HIS WIFE.   "I can't think of anything."

HOWARD'S VOICE.   "Well, talk—it's turning."

HIS WIFE (*shyly, beaten*).   "Hello." (*Silence*) "Oh, Howard, I can't talk into this . . ."

HOWARD (*snapping the machine off*).   That was my wife.

WILLY.   That is a wonderful machine. Can we—

HOWARD.   I tell you, Willy, I'm gonna take my camera, and my bandsaw, and all my hobbies, and out they go. This is the most fascinating relaxation I ever found.

WILLY.   I think I'll get one myself.

HOWARD.   Sure, they're only a hundred and a half. You can't do without it. Supposing you wanna hear Jack Benny, see? But you can't be at home at that hour. So you tell the maid to turn the radio on when Jack Benny comes on, and this automatically goes on with the radio . . .

WILLY.   And when you come home you . . .

HOWARD.   You can come home twelve o'clock, one o'clock, any time you like, and you get yourself a Coke and sit yourself down, throw the switch, and there's Jack Benny's program in the middle of the night!

WILLY.   I'm definitely going to get one. Because lots of time I'm on the road, and I think to myself, what I must be missing on the radio!

HOWARD.   Don't you have a radio in the car?

WILLY.   Well, yeah, but who ever thinks of turning it on?

HOWARD.   Say, aren't you supposed to be in Boston?

WILLY.   That's what I want to talk to you about, Howard. You got a minute? (*He draws a chair in from the wing.*)

HOWARD.   What happened? What're you doing here?

WILLY.   Well . . .

HOWARD. You didn't crack up again, did you?
WILLY. Oh, no. No . . .
HOWARD. Geez, you had me worried there for a minute. What's the trouble?
WILLY. Well, tell you the truth, Howard. I've come to the decision that I'd rather not travel any more.
HOWARD. Not travel! Well, what'll you do?
WILLY. Remember, Christmas time, when you had the party here? You said you'd try to think of some spot for me here in town.
HOWARD. With us?
WILLY. Well, sure.
HOWARD. Oh, yeah, yeah. I remember. Well, I couldn't think of anything for you, Willy.
WILLY. I tell ya, Howard. The kids are all grown up, y'know. I don't need much any more. If I could take home—well, sixty-five dollars a week, I could swing it.
HOWARD. Yeah, but Willy, see I—
WILLY. I tell ya why, Howard. Speaking frankly and between the two of us, y'know—I'm just a little tired.
HOWARD. Oh, I could understand that, Willy. But you're a road man, Willy, and we do a road business. We've only got a half-dozen salesmen on the floor here.
WILLY. God knows, Howard, I never asked a favor of any man. But I was with the firm when your father used to carry you in here in his arms.
HOWARD. I know that, Willy, but—
WILLY. Your father came to me the day you were born and asked me what I thought of the name of Howard, may he rest in peace.
HOWARD. I appreciate that, Willy, but there just is no spot here for you. If I had a spot I'd slam you right in, but I just don't have a single solitary spot.

(*He looks for his lighter.* WILLY *has picked it up and gives it to him. Pause.*)

WILLY (*with increasing anger*). Howard, all I need to set my table is fifty dollars a week.
HOWARD. But where am I going to put you, kid?
WILLY. Look, it isn't a question of whether I can sell merchandise, is it?
HOWARD. No, but it's a business, kid, and everybody, gotta pull his own weight.
WILLY (*desperately*). Just let me tell you a story, Howard—
HOWARD. 'Cause you gotta admit, business is business.
WILLY (*angrily*). Business is definitely business, but just listen for a minute. You don't understand this. When I was a boy—eighteen, nineteen—

I was already on the road. And there was a question in my mind as to whether selling had a future for me. Because in those days I had a yearning to go to Alaska. See, there were three gold strikes in one month in Alaska, and I felt like going out. Just for the ride, you might say.

HOWARD (*barely interested*). Don't say.

WILLY. Oh, yeah, my father lived many years in Alaska. He was an adventurous man. We've got quite a little streak of self-reliance in our family. I thought I'd go out with my older brother and try to locate him, and maybe settle in the North with the old man. And I was almost decided to go, when I met a salesman in the Parker House. His name was Dave Singleman. And he was eighty-four years old, and he'd drummed merchandise in thirty-one states. And old Dave, he'd go up to his room, y'understand, put on his green velvet slippers—I'll never forget—and pick up his phone and call the buyers, and without ever leaving his room, at the age of eighty-four, he made his living. And when I saw that, I realized that selling was the greatest career a man could want. 'Cause what could be more satisfying than to be able to go, at the age of eighty-four, into twenty or thirty different cities, and pick up a phone, and be remembered and loved and helped by so many different people? Do you know? when he died—and by the way he died the death of a salesman, in his green velvet slippers in the smoker of the New York, New Haven and Hartford, going into Boston—when he died, hundreds of salesmen and buyers were at his funeral. Things were sad on a lotta trains for months after that. (*He stands up.* HOWARD *has not looked at him.*) In those days there was personality in it, Howard. There was respect, and comradeship, and gratitude in it. Today, it's all cut and dried, and there's no chance for bringing friendship to bear—or personality. You see what I mean? They don't know me any more.

HOWARD (*moving away, to the right*). That's just the thing, Willy.

WILLY. If I had forty dollars a week—that's all I'd need. Forty dollars, Howard.

HOWARD. Kid, I can't take blood from a stone, I—

WILLY (*desperation is on him now*). Howard, the year Al Smith was nominated, your father came to me and—

HOWARD (*starting to go off*). I've got to see some people, kid.

WILLY (*stopping him*). I'm talking about your father! There were promises made across this desk! You mustn't tell me you've got people to see —I put thirty-four years into this firm, Howard, and now I can't pay my insurance! You can't eat the orange and throw the peel away—a man is not a piece of fruit! (*After a pause*) Now pay attention. Your father—in 1928 I had a big year. I averaged a hundred and seventy dollars a week in commissions.

HOWARD (*impatiently*). Now, Willy, you never averaged—

WILLY (*banging his hand on the desk*). I averaged a hundred and seventy dollars a week in the year of 1928! And your father came to me—

or rather, I was in the office here—it was right over this desk—and he put his hand on my shoulder—

HOWARD (*getting up*).   You'll have to excuse me, Willy, I gotta see some people. Pull yourself together. (*Going out*) I'll be back in a little while.

(*On* HOWARD'S *exit, the light on his chair grows very bright and strange.*)

WILLY.   Pull myself together! What the hell did I say to him? My God, I was yelling at him! How could I! (WILLY *breaks off, staring at the light, which occupies the chair, animating it. He approaches this chair, standing across the desk from it.*) Frank, Frank, don't you remember what you told me that time? How you put your hand on my shoulder, and Frank . . . (*He leans on the desk and as he speaks the dead man's name he accidentally switches on the recorder, and instantly*)

HOWARD'S SON.   ". . . of New York is Albany. The capital of Ohio is Cincinnati, the capital of Rhode Island is . . ." (*The recitation continues.*)

WILLY (*leaping away with fright, shouting*).   Ha! Howard! Howard! Howard!

HOWARD (*rushing in*).   What happened?

WILLY (*pointing at the machine, which continues nasally, childishly, with the capital cities*).   Shut it off! Shut it off!

HOWARD (*pulling the plug out*).   Look, Willy . . .

WILLY (*pressing his hands to his eyes*).   I gotta get myself some coffee. I'll get some coffee . . .

(WILLY *starts to walk out.* HOWARD *stops him.*)

HOWARD (*rolling up the cord*).   Willy, look . . .

WILLY.   I'll go to Boston.

HOWARD.   Willy, you can't go to Boston for us.

WILLY.   Why can't I go?

HOWARD.   I don't want you to represent us. I've been meaning to tell you for a long time now.

WILLY.   Howard, are you firing me?

HOWARD.   I think you need a good long rest, Willy.

WILLY.   Howard—

HOWARD.   And when you feel better, come back, and we'll see if we can work something out.

WILLY.   But I gotta earn money, Howard. I'm in no position to—

HOWARD.   Where are your sons? Why don't your sons give you a hand?

WILLY.   They're working on a very big deal.

HOWARD.   This is no time for false pride, Willy. You go to your sons and you tell them that you're tired. You've got two great boys, haven't you?

WILLY.   Oh, no question, no question, but in the meantime . . .

HOWARD.   Then that's that, heh?

WILLY.   All right, I'll go to Boston tomorrow.

HOWARD. No, no.
WILLY. I can't throw myself on my sons. I'm not a cripple!
HOWARD. Look, kid, I'm busy this morning.
WILLY (*grasping* HOWARD's *arm*). Howard, you've got to let me go to Boston!
HOWARD (*hard, keeping himself under control*). I've got a line of people to see this morning. Sit down, take five minutes, and pull yourself together, and then go home, will ya? I need the office, Willy. (*He starts to go, turns, remembering the recorder, starts to push off the table holding the recorder.*) Oh, yeah. Whenever you can this week, stop by and drop off the samples. You'll feel better, Willy, and then come back and we'll talk. Pull yourself together, kid, there's people outside.

(HOWARD *exits, pushing the table off left.* WILLY *stares into space, exhausted. Now the music is heard*—BEN's *music—first distantly, then closer, closer. As* WILLY *speaks,* BEN *enters from the right. He carries valise and umbrella.*)

WILLY. Oh, Ben, how did you do it? What is the answer? Did you wind up the Alaska deal already?
BEN. Doesn't take much time if you know what you're doing. Just a short business trip. Boarding ship in an hour. Wanted to say good-by.
WILLY. Ben, I've got to talk to you.
BEN (*glancing at his watch*). Haven't the time, William.
WILLY (*crossing the apron to* BEN). Ben, nothing's working out. I don't know what to do.
BEN. Now, look here, William. I've bought timberland in Alaska and I need a man to look after things for me.
WILLY. God, timberland! Me and my boys in those grand outdoors!
BEN. You've a new continent at your doorstep, William. Get out of these cities, they're full of talk and time payments and courts of law. Screw on your fists and you can fight for a fortune up there.
WILLY. Yes, yes! Linda, Linda!

(LINDA *enters as of old, with the wash.*)

LINDA. Oh, you're back?
BEN. I haven't much time.
WILLY. No, wait! Linda, he's got a proposition for me in Alaska.
LINDA. But you've got—(*To* BEN) He's got a beautiful job here.
WILLY. But in Alaska, kid, I could—
LINDA. You're doing well enough, Willy!
BEN (*to* LINDA). Enough for what, my dear?
LINDA (*frightened of* BEN *and angry at him*). Don't say those things to him! Enough to be happy right here, right now. (*To* WILLY, *while* BEN *laughs*) Why must everybody conquer the world? You're well liked, and the boys love you, and someday—(*to* BEN)—why, old man Wagner told him

just the other day that if he keeps it up he'll be a member of the firm, didn't he, Willy?

WILLY. Sure, sure. I am building something with this firm, Ben, and if a man is building something he must be on the right track, mustn't he?

BEN. What are you building? Lay your hand on it. Where is it?

WILLY (*hesitantly*). That's true, Linda, there's nothing.

LINDA. Why? (*To* BEN) There's a man eighty-four years old—

WILLY. That's right, Ben, that's right. When I look at that man I say, what is there to worry about?

BEN. Bah!

WILLY. It's true, Ben. All he has to do is go into any city, pick up the phone, and he's making his living and you know why?

BEN (*picking up his valise*). I've got to go.

WILLY (*holding* BEN *back*). Look at this boy!

(BIFF, *in his high school sweater, enters carrying suitcase.* HAPPY *carries* BIFF's *shoulder guards, gold helmet, and football pants.*)

WILLY. Without a penny to his name, three great universities are begging for him, and from there the sky's the limit, because it's not what you do, Ben. It's who you know and the smile on your face! It's contacts, Ben, contacts! The whole wealth of Alaska passes over the lunch table at the Commodore Hotel, and that's the wonder, the wonder of this country, that a man can end with diamonds here on the basis of being liked! (*He turns to* BIFF) And that's why when you get out on that field today, it's important. Because thousands of people will be rooting for you and loving you. (*To* BEN, *who has again begun to leave*) And Ben! when he walks into a business office his name will sound out like a bell and all the doors will open to him! I've seen it, Ben, I've seen it a thousand times! You can't feel it with your hand like timber, but it's there!

BEN. Good-by, William.

WILLY. Ben, am I right? Don't you think I'm right? I value your advice.

BEN. There's a new continent at your doorstep, William. You could walk out rich. Rich! (*He is gone.*)

WILLY. We'll do it here, Ben! You hear me? We're gonna do it hear!

(YOUNG BERNARD *rushes in. The gay music of the boys is heard.*)

BERNARD. Oh, gee, I was afraid you left already!

WILLY. Why? What time is it?

BERNARD. It's half-past one!

WILLY. Well, come on, everybody! Ebbets Field next stop! Where's the pennants? (*He rushes through the wall-line of the kitchen and out into the living-room.*)

LINDA (*to* BIFF). Did you pack fresh underwear?

BIFF (*who has been limbering up*). I want to go!

BERNARD. Biff, I'm carrying your helmet, ain't I?
HAPPY. No, I'm carrying the helmet.
BERNARD. Oh, Biff, you promised me.
HAPPY. I'm carrying the helmet.
BERNARD. How am I going to get in the locker room?
LINDA. Let him carry the shoulder guards. (*She puts her coat and hat on in the kitchen.*)
BERNARD. Can I, Biff? 'Cause I told everybody I'm going to be in the locker room.
HAPPY. In Ebbets Field it's the clubhouse.
BERNARD. I meant the clubhouse, Biff!
HAPPY. Biff!
BIFF (*grandly, after a slight pause*). Let him carry the shoulder guards.
HAPPY (*as he gives* BERNARD *the shoulder guards*). Stay close to us now.

(WILLY *rushes in with the pennants.*)

WILLY (*handing them out*). Everybody wave when Biff comes out on the field. (HAPPY *and* BERNARD *run off.*) You set now, boy?

(*The music has died away.*)

BIFF. Ready to go, Pop. Every muscle is ready.
WILLY (*at the edge of the apron*). You realize what this means?
BIFF. That's right, Pop.
WILLY (*feeling* BIFF's *muscles*). You're comin' home this afternoon captain of the All-Scholastic Championship Team of the City of New York.
BIFF. I got it, Pop. And remember, pal, when I take off my helmet, that touchdown is for you.
WILLY. Let's go! (*He is starting out, with his arm around* BIFF, *when* CHARLEY *enters, as of old, in knickers.*) I got no room for you, Charley.
CHARLEY. Room? For what?
WILLY. In the car.
CHARLEY. You goin' for a ride? I wanted to shoot some casino.
WILLY (*furiously*). Casino! (*Incredulously*) Don't you realize what today is?
LINDA. Oh, he knows, Willy. He's just kidding you.
WILLY. That's nothing to kid about!
CHARLEY. No, Linda, what's goin' on?
LINDA. He's playing in Ebbets Field.
CHARLEY. Baseball in this weather?
WILLY. Don't talk to him. Come on, come on! (*He is pushing them out.*)
CHARLEY. What a minute, didn't you hear the news?
WILLY. What?

CHARLEY. Don't you listen to the radio? Ebbets Field just blew up.

WILLY. You go to hell! (CHARLEY *laughs. Pushing them out*) Come on, come on! We're late.

CHARLEY (*as they go*). Knock a homer, Biff, knock a homer!

WILLY (*the last to leave, turning to* CHARLEY). I don't think that was funny, Charley. This is the greatest day of his life.

CHARLEY. Willy, when are you going to grow up?

WILLY. Yeah, heh? When this game is over, Charley, you'll be laughing out of the other side of your face. They'll be calling him another Red Grange. Twenty-five thousand a year.

CHARLEY (*kidding*). Is that so?

WILLY. Yeah, that's so.

CHARLEY. Well, then, I'm sorry, Willy. But tell me something.

WILLY. What?

CHARLEY. Who is Red Grange?

WILLY. Put up your hands. Goddam you, put up your hands!

(CHARLEY, *chuckling, shakes his head and walks away, around the left corner of the stage.* WILLY *follows him. The music rises to a mocking frenzy.*)

WILLY. Who the hell do you think you are, better than everybody else? You don't know everything, you big, ignorant, stupid . . . Put up your hands!

(*Light rises, on the right side of the forestage, on a small table in the reception room of* CHARLEY's *office. Traffic sounds are heard.* BERNARD, *now mature, sits whistling to himself. A pair of tennis rackets and an overnight bag are on the floor beside him.*)

WILLY (*offstage*). What are you walking away for? Don't walk away! If you're going to say something say it to my face! I know you laugh at me behind my back. You'll laugh out of the other side of your goddam face after this game. Touchdown! Touchdown! Eighty thousand people! Touchdown! Right between the goal posts.

(BERNARD *is a quiet, earnest, but self-assured young man.* WILLY's *voice is coming from right upstage now.* BERNARD *lowers his feet off the table and listens.* JENNY, *his father's secretary, enters.*)

JENNY (*distressed*). Say, Bernard, will you go out in the hall?

BERNARD. What is that noise? Who is it?

JENNY. Mr. Loman. He just got off the elevator.

BERNARD (*getting up*). Who's he arguing with?

JENNY. Nobody. There's nobody with him. I can't deal with him any more, and your father gets all upset everytime he comes. I've got a lot of typing to do, and your father's waiting to sign it. Will you see him?

WILLY (*entering*). Touchdown! Touch—(*He sees* JENNY.) Jenny, Jenny, good to see you. How're ya? Workin'? Or still honest?

JENNY. Fine. How've you been feeling?

WILLY. Not much any more, Jenny. Ha, Ha! (*He is surprised to see the rackets.*)

BERNARD. Hello, Uncle Willy.

WILLY (*almost shocked*). Bernard! Well, look who's here! (*He comes quickly, guiltily, to* BERNARD *and warmly shakes his hand.*)

BERNARD. How are you? Good to see you.

WILLY. What are you doing here?

BERNARD. Oh, just stopped by to see Pop. Get off my feet till my train leaves. I'm going to Washington in a few minutes.

WILLY. Is he in?

BERNARD. Yes, he's in his office with the accountant. Sit down.

WILLY (*sitting down*). What're you going to do in Washington?

BERNARD. Oh, just a case I've got there, Willy.

WILLY. That so? (*Indicating the rackets*) You going to play tennis there?

BERNARD. I'm staying with a friend who's got a court.

WILLY. Don't say. His own tennis court. Must be fine people, I bet.

BERNARD. They are, very nice. Dad tells me Biff's in town.

WILLY (*with a big smile*). Yeah, Biff's in. Working on a very big deal, Bernard.

BERNARD. What's Biff doing?

WILLY. Well, he's been doing very big things in the West. But he decided to establish himself here. Very big. We're having dinner. Did I hear your wife had a boy?

BERNARD. That's right. Our second.

WILLY. Two boys! What do you know!

BERNARD. What kind of a deal has Biff got?

WILLY. Well, Bill Oliver—very big sporting goods man—he wants Biff very badly. Called him in from the West. Long distance, carte blanche, special deliveries. Your friends have their own private tennis court?

BERNARD. You still with the old firm, Willy?

WILLY (*after a pause*). I'm—I'm overjoyed to see how you made the grade, Bernard, overjoyed. It's an encouraging thing to see a young man really—really—Looks very good for Biff—very—(*He breaks off, then*) Bernard—(*He is so full of emotion, he breaks off again.*)

BERNARD. What is it, Willy?

WILLY (*small and alone*). What—what's the secret?

BERNARD. What secret?

WILLY. How—how did you? Why didn't he ever catch on?

BERNARD. I wouldn't know that, Willy.

WILLY (*confidentially, desperately*). You were his friend, his boyhood friend. There's something I don't understand about it. His life ended after that Ebbets Field game. From the age of seventeen nothing good ever happened to him.

BERNARD. He never trained himself for anything.

WILLY. But he did, he did. After high school he took so many correspondence courses. Radio mechanics; television; God knows what, and never made the slightest mark.

BERNARD (*taking off his glasses*). Willy, do you want to talk candidly?

WILLY (*rising, faces* BERNARD). I regard you as a very brilliant man, Bernard. I value your advice.

BERNARD. Oh, the hell with the advice, Willy. I couldn't advise you. There's just one thing I've always wanted to ask you. When he was supposed to graduate, and the math teacher flunked him—

WILLY. Oh, that son-of-a-bitch ruined his life.

BERNARD. Yeah, but, Willy, all he had to do was go to summer school and make up that subject.

WILLY. That's right, that's right.

BERNARD. Did you tell him not to go to summer school?

WILLY. Me? I begged him to go. I ordered him to go!

BERNARD. Then why wouldn't he go?

WILLY. Why? Why! Bernard, that question has been trailing me like a ghost for the last fifteen years. He flunked the subject, and laid down and died like a hammer hit him!

BERNARD. Take it easy, kid.

WILLY. Let me talk to you—I got nobody to talk to. Bernard, Bernard, was it my fault? Y'see? It keeps going around in my mind, maybe I did something to him. I got nothing to give him.

BERNARD. Don't take it so hard.

WILLY. Why did he lay down? What is the story there? You were his friend!

BERNARD. Willy, I remember, it was June, and our grades came out. And he'd flunked math.

WILLY. That son-of-a-bitch!

BERNARD. No, it wasn't right then. Biff just got very angry, I remember, and he was ready to enroll in summer school.

WILLY (*surprised*). He was?

BERNARD. He wasn't beaten by it at all. But then, Willy, he disappeared from the block for almost a month. And I got the idea that he'd gone up to New England to see you. Did he have a talk with you then?

(WILLY *stares in silence.*)

BERNARD. Willy?

WILLY (*with a strong edge of resentment in his voice*). Yeah, he came to Boston. What about it?

BERNARD. Well, just that when he came back—I'll never forget this, it always mystifies me. Because I thought so well of Biff, even though he'd always taken advantage of me. I loved him, Willy, y'know? And he came back after that month and took his sneakers—remember those sneakers with "University of Virginia" printed on them? He was so proud of those, wore them every day. And he took them down in the cellar, and burned them up in the furnace. We had a fist fight. It lasted at least half an hour. Just the two of us, punching each other down the cellar, and crying right through it. I've often thought of how strange it was that I knew he'd given up his life. What happened in Boston, Willy?

(WILLY *looks at him as at an intruder.*)

BERNARD. I just bring it up because you asked me.

WILLY (*angrily*). Nothing. What do you mean, "What happened?" What's that go to do with anything?

BERNARD. Well, don't get sore.

WILLY. What are you trying to do, blame it on me? If a boy lays down is that my fault?

BERNARD. Now, Willy, don't get—

WILLY. Well, don't—don't talk to me that way! What does that mean, "What happened?"

(CHARLEY *enters. He is in his vest, and he carries a bottle of bourbon.*)

CHARLEY. Hey, you're going to miss that train. (*He waves the bottle.*)

BERNARD. Yeah, I'm going. (*He takes the bottle.*) Thanks, Pop. (*He picks up his rackets and bag.*) Good-by, Willy, and don't worry about it. You know, "If at first you don't succeed . . ."

WILLY. Yes, I believe in that.

BERNARD. But sometimes, Willy, it's better for a man just to walk away.

WILLY. Walk away?

BERNARD. That's right.

WILLY. But if you can't walk away?

BERNARD (*after a slight pause*). I guess that's when it's tough. (*Extending his hand*) Good-by, Willy.

WILLY (*shaking* BERNARD's *hand*). Good-by, boy.

CHARLEY (*an arm on* BERNARD's *shoulder*). How do you like this kid? Gonna argue a case in front of the Supreme Court.

BERNARD (*protesting*). Pop!

WILLY (*genuinely shocked, pained, and happy*). No! The Supreme Court!

BERNARD. I gotta run. 'By, Dad!

CHARLEY. Knock 'em dead, Bernard!

(BERNARD *goes off.*)

WILLY (*as* CHARLEY *takes out his wallet*). The Supreme Court! And he didn't even mention it!

CHARLEY (*counting out money on the desk*). He don't have to—he's gonna do it.
WILLY. And you never told him what to do, did you? You never took any interest in him.
CHARLEY. My salvation is that I never took any interest in anything. There's some money—fifty dollars. I got an accountant inside.
WILLY. Charley, look . . . (*With difficulty*) I got my insurance to pay. If you can manage it—I need a hundred and ten dollars.

(CHARLEY *doesn't reply for a moment; merely stops moving.*)

WILLY. I'd draw it from my bank but Linda would know, and I . . .
CHARLEY. Sit down, Willy.
WILLY (*moving toward the chair*). I'm keeping an account of everything, remember. I'll pay every penny back. (*He sits.*)
CHARLEY. Now listen to me, Willy.
WILLY. I want you to know I appreciate . . .
CHARLEY (*sitting down on the table*). Willy, what're you doin'? What the hell is goin' on in your head?
WILLY. Why? I'm simply . . .
CHARLEY. I offered you a job. You can make fifty dollars a week. And I won't send you on the road.
WILLY. I've got a job.
CHARLEY. Without pay? What kind of a job is a job without pay? (*He rises.*) Now, look, kid, enough is enough. I'm no genius but I know when I'm being insulted.
WILLY. Insulted!
CHARLEY. Why don't you want to work for me?
WILLY. What's the matter with you? I've got a job.
CHARLEY. Then what're you walkin' in here every week for?
WILLY (*getting up*). Well, if you don't want me to walk in here—
CHARLEY. I am offering you a job.
WILLY. I don't want your goddam job!
CHARLEY. When the hell are you going to grow up?
WILLY (*furiously*). You big ignoramus, if you say that to me again I'll rap you one! I don't care how big you are! (*He's ready to fight.*)

(*Pause.*)

CHARLEY (*kindly, going to him*). How much do you need, Willy?
WILLY. Charley, I'm strapped. I'm strapped. I don't know what to do. I was just fired.
CHARLEY. Howard fired you?
WILLY. That snotnose. Imagine that? I named him. I named him Howard.
CHARLEY. Willy, when're you gonna realize that them things don't

mean anything? You named him Howard, but you can't sell that. The only thing you got in this world is what you can sell. And the funny thing is that you're a salesman, and you don't know that.

WILLY. I've always tried to think otherwise, I guess. I always felt that if a man was impressive, and well liked, that nothing—

CHARLEY. Why must everybody like you? Who liked J. P. Morgan? Was he impressive? In a Turkish bath he'd look like a butcher. But with his pockets on he was very well liked. Now listen, Willy, I know you don't like me, and nobody can say I'm in love with you, but I'll give you a job because—just for the hell of it, put it that way. Now what do you say?

WILLY. I—I just can't work for you, Charley.

CHARLEY. What're you, jealous of me?

WILLY. I can't work for you, that's all, don't ask me why.

CHARLEY (*angered, takes out more bills*). You been jealous of me all your life, you damned fool! Here, pay your insurance. (*He puts the money in* WILLY's *hand.*)

WILLY. I'm keeping strict accounts.

CHARLEY. I've got some work to do. Take care of yourself. And pay your insurance.

WILLY (*moving to the right*). Funny, y'know? After all the highways, and the trains, and the appointments, and the years, you end up worth more dead than alive.

CHARLEY. Willy, nobody's worth nothin' dead. (*After a slight pause*) Did you hear what I said? (WILLY *stands still, dreaming.*) Willy!

WILLY. Apologize to Bernard for me when you see him. I didn't mean to argue with him. He's a fine boy. They're all fine boys, and they'll end up big—all of them. Someday they'll all play tennis together. Wish me luck, Charley. He saw Bill Oliver today.

CHARLEY. Good luck.

WILLY (*on the verge of tears*). Charley, you're the only friend I got. Isn't that a remarkable thing? (*He goes out.*)

CHARLEY. Jesus!

(CHARLEY *stares after him a moment and follows. All light blacks out. Suddenly raucous music is heard, and a red glow rises behind the screen at right.* STANLEY, *a young waiter, appears, carrying a table, followed by* HAPPY, *who is carrying two chairs.*)

STANLEY (*putting the table down*). That's all right, Mr. Loman, I can handle it myself. (*He turns and takes the chairs from* HAPPY *and places them at the table.*)

HAPPY (*glancing around*). Oh, this is better.

STANLEY. Sure, in the front there you're in the middle of all kinds a noise. Whenever you got a party, Mr. Loman, you just tell me and I'll put you back here. Y'know, there's a lotta people they don't like it private, because when they go out they like to see a lotta action around them because they're sick and tired to stay in the house by theirself. But I know you, you ain't from Hackensack. You know what I mean?

HAPPY (*sitting down*). So how's it coming, Stanley?

STANLEY. Ah, it's a dog's life. I only wish during the war they'd a took me in the Army. I coulda been dead by now.

HAPPY. My brother's back, Stanley.

STANLEY. Oh, he come back, heh? From the Far West.

HAPPY. Yeah, big cattle man, my brother, so treat him right. And my father's coming too.

STANLEY. Oh, your father too!

HAPPY. You got a couple of nice lobsters?

STANLEY. Hundred per cent, big.

HAPPY. I want them with the claws.

STANLEY. Don't worry, I don't give you no mice. (HAPPY *laughs.*) How about some wine? It'll put a head on the meal.

HAPPY. No. You remember, Stanley, that recipe I brought you from overseas? With the champagne in it?

STANLEY. Oh, yeah, sure. I still got it tacked up yet in the kitchen. But that'll have to cost a buck apiece anyways.

HAPPY. That's all right.

STANLEY. What'd you, hit a number or somethin'?

HAPPY. No, it's a little celebration. My brother is—I think he pulled off a big deal today. I think we're going into business together.

STANLEY. Great! That's the best for you. Because a family business, you know what I mean?—that's the best.

HAPPY. That's what I think.

STANLEY. 'Cause what's the difference? Somebody steals? It's in the family. Know what I mean? (*Sotto voce*) Like this bartender here. The boss is goin' crazy what kinda leak he's got in the cash register. You put it in but it don't come out.

HAPPY (*raising his head*). Sh!

STANLEY. What?

HAPPY. You notice I wasn't lookin' right or left, was I?

STANLEY. No.

HAPPY. And my eyes are closed.

STANLEY. So what's the—?

HAPPY. Strudel's comin'.

STANLEY (*catching on, looks around*). Ah, no, there's no—

(*He breaks off as a furred, lavishly dressed girl enters and sits at the next table. Both follow her with their eyes.*)

STANLEY. Geez, how'd ya know?

HAPPY. I got radar or something. (*Staring directly at her profile*) Oooooooo . . . Stanley.

STANLEY. I think that's for you, Mr. Loman.

HAPPY. Look at that mouth. Oh, God. And the binoculars.

STANLEY. Geez, you got a life, Mr. Loman.

HAPPY. Wait on her.

STANLEY (*going to the* GIRL'*s table*). Would you like a menu, ma'am?

GIRL. I'm expecting someone, but I'd like a—

HAPPY. Why don't you bring her—excuse me, miss, do you mind? I sell champagne, and I'd like you to try my brand. Bring her a champagne, Stanley.

GIRL. That's awfully nice of you.

HAPPY. Don't mention it. It's all company money. (*He laughs.*)

GIRL. That's a charming product to be selling, isn't it?

HAPPY. Oh, gets to be like everything else. Selling is selling, y'know.

GIRL. I suppose.

HAPPY. You don't happen to sell, do you?

GIRL. No, I don't sell.

HAPPY. Would you object to a compliment from a stranger? You ought to be on a magazine cover.

GIRL (*looking at him a little archly*). I have been.

(STANLEY *comes in with a glass of champagne.*)

HAPPY. What'd I say before, Stanley? You see? She's a cover girl.

STANLEY. Oh, I could see, I could see.

HAPPY (*to the* GIRL). What magazine?

GIRL. Oh, a lot of them. (*She takes the drink.*) Thank you.

HAPPY. You know what they say in France, don't you? "Champagne is the drink of the complexion"—Hya, Biff!

(BIFF *has entered and sits with* HAPPY.)

BIFF. Hello, kid. Sorry I'm late.

HAPPY. I just got here. Uh, Miss—?

GIRL. Forsythe.

HAPPY. Miss Forsythe, this is my brother.

BIFF. Is Dad here?

HAPPY. His name is Biff. You might've heard of him. Great football player.

GIRL. Really? What team?

HAPPY. Are you familiar with football?

GIRL. No, I'm afraid I'm not.

HAPPY. Biff is quarterback with the New York Giants.

GIRL. Well, that is nice, isn't it? (*She drinks.*)

HAPPY. Good health.

GIRL. I'm happy to meet you.

HAPPY. That's my name. Hap. It's really Harold, but at West Point they called me Happy.

GIRL (*now really impressed*). Oh, I see. How do you do? (*She turns her profile.*)

BIFF. Isn't Dad coming?

HAPPY. You want her?

BIFF. Oh, I could never make that.

HAPPY. I remember the time that idea would never come into your head. Where's the old confidence, Biff?

BIFF. I just saw Oliver—

HAPPY. Wait a minute. I've got to see that old confidence again. Do you want her? She's on call.

BIFF. Oh, no. (*He turns to look at the* GIRL.)

HAPPY. I'm telling you. Watch this. (*Turning to the* GIRL) Honey? (*She turns to him.*) Are you busy?

GIRL. Well, I am . . . but I could make a phone call.

HAPPY. Do that, will you, honey? And see if you can get a friend. We'll be here for a while. Biff is one of the greatest football players in the country.

GIRL (*standing up*). Well, I'm certainly happy to meet you.

HAPPY. Come back soon.

GIRL. I'll try.

HAPPY. Don't try, honey, try hard.

(*The* GIRL *exits.* STANLEY *follows, shaking his head in bewildered admiration.*)

HAPPY. Isn't that a shame now? A beautiful girl like that? That's why I can't get married. There's not a good woman in a thousand. New York is loaded with them, kid!

BIFF. Hap, look—

HAPPY. I told you she was on call!

BIFF (*strangely unnerved*). Cut it out, will ya? I want to say something to you.

HAPPY. Did you see Oliver?

BIFF. I saw him all right. Now look, I want to tell Dad a couple of things and I want you to help me.

HAPPY. What? Is he going to back you?

BIFF. Are you crazy? You're out of your goddam head, you know that?

HAPPY. Why? What happened?

BIFF (*breathlessly*). I did a terrible thing today, Hap. It's been the strangest day I ever went through. I'm all numb, I swear.

HAPPY. You mean he wouldn't see you?

ARTHUR MILLER

BIFF. Well, I waited six hours for him, see? All day. Kept sending my name in. Even tried to date his secretary so she'd get me to him, but no soap.

HAPPY. Because you're not showin' the old confidence, Biff. He remembered you, didn't he?

BIFF (*stopping* HAPPY *with a gesture*). Finally, about five o'clock, he comes out. Didn't remember who I was or anything. I felt like such an idiot, Hap.

HAPPY. Did you tell him my Florida idea?

BIFF. He walked away. I saw him for one minute. I got so mad I could've torn the walls down! How the hell did I ever get the idea I was a salesman there? I even believed myself that I'd been a salesman for him! And then he gave me one look and—I realized what a ridiculous lie my whole life has been! We've been talking in a dream for fifteen years. I was a shipping clerk.

HAPPY. What'd you do?

BIFF (*with great tension and wonder*). Well, he left, see. And the secretary went out. I was all alone in the waiting-room. I don't know what came over me, Hap. The next thing I know I'm in his office—paneled walls, everything. I can't explain it. I—Hap, I took his fountain pen.

HAPPY. Geez, did he catch you?

BIFF. I ran out. I ran down all eleven flights. I ran and ran and ran.

HAPPY. That was an awful dumb—what'd you do that for?

BIFF (*agonized*). I don't know, I just—wanted to take something, I don't know. You gotta help me, Hap, I'm gonna tell Pop.

HAPPY. You crazy? What for?

BIFF. Hap, he's got to understand that I'm not the man somebody lends that kind of money to. He thinks I've been spiting him all these years and it's eating him up.

HAPPY. That's just it. You tell him something nice.

BIFF. I can't.

HAPPY. Say you got a lunch date with Oliver tomorrow.

BIFF. So what do I do tomorrow?

HAPPY. You leave the house tomorrow and come back at night and say Oliver is thinking it over. And he thinks it over for a couple of weeks, and gradually it fades away and nobody's the worse.

BIFF. But it'll go on forever!

HAPPY. Dad is never so happy as when he's looking forward to something!

(WILLY *enters.*)

HAPPY. Hello, scout!

WILLY. Gee, I haven't been here in years!

(STANLEY *has followed* WILLY *in and sets a chair for him.* STANLEY *starts off but* HAPPY *stops him.*)

HAPPY. Stanley!

(STANLEY *stands by, waiting for an order.*)

BIFF (*going to* WILLY *with guilt, as to an invalid*). Sit down, Pop. You want a drink?
WILLY. Sure, I don't mind.
BIFF. Let's get a load on.
WILLY. You look worried.
BIFF. N-no. (*To* STANLEY) Scotch all around. Make it doubles.
STANLEY. Doubles, right. (*He goes.*)
WILLY. You had a couple already, didn't you?
BIFF. Just a couple, yeah.
WILLY. Well, what happened, boy? (*Nodding affirmatively, with a smile*) Everything go all right?
BIFF (*takes a breath, then reaches out and grasps* WILLY'*s hand*). Pal ... (*He is smiling bravely, and* WILLY *is smiling too.*) I had an experience today.
HAPPY. Terrific, Pop.
WILLY. That so? What happened?
BIFF (*high, slightly alcoholic, above the earth*). I'm going to tell you everything from first to last. It's been a strange day. (*Silence. He looks around, composes himself as best he can, but his breath keeps breaking the rhythm of his voice.*) I had to wait quite a while for him, and—
WILLY. Oliver?
BIFF. Yeah, Oliver. All day, as a matter of cold fact. And a lot of— instances—facts, Pop, facts about my life came back to me. Who was it, Pop? Who ever said I was a salesman with Oliver?
WILLY. Well, you were.
BIFF. No, Dad, I was a shipping clerk.
WILLY. But you were practically—
BIFF (*with determination*). Dad, I don't know who said it first, but I was never a salesman for Bill Oliver.
WILLY. What're you talking about?
BIFF. Let's hold on to the facts tonight, Pop. We're not going to get anywhere bullin' around. I was a shipping clerk.
WILLY (*angrily*). All right, now listen to me—
BIFF. Why don't you let me finish?
WILLY. I'm not interested in stories about the past or any crap of that kind because the woods are burning, boys, you understand? There's a big blaze going on all around. I was fired today.
BIFF (*shocked*). How could you be?
WILLY. I was fired, and I'm looking for a little good news to tell your mother, because the woman has waited and the woman has suffered. The gist of it is that I haven't got a story left in my head, Biff. So don't give me a

lecture about facts and aspects. I am not interested. Now what've you got to say to me?

(STANLEY *enters with three drinks. They wait until he leaves.*)

WILLY. Did you see Oliver?
BIFF. Jesus, Dad!
WILLY. You mean you didn't go up there?
HAPPY. Sure he went up there.
BIFF. I did. I—saw him. How could they fire you?
WILLY (*on the edge of his chair*). What kind of a welcome did he give you?
BIFF. He won't even let you work on commission?
WILLY. I'm out! (*Driving*) So tell me, he gave you a warm welcome?
HAPPY. Sure, Pop, sure!
BIFF (*driven*). Well, it was kind of—
WILLY. I was wondering if he'd remember you. (*To* HAPPY) Imagine, man doesn't see him for ten, twelve years and gives him that kind of a welcome!
HAPPY. Damn right!
BIFF (*trying to return to the offensive*). Pop look—
WILLY. You know why he remembered you, don't you? Because you impressed him in those days.
BIFF. Let's talk quietly and get this down to the facts, huh?
WILLY (*as though* BIFF *had been interrupting*). Well, what happened? It's great news, Biff. Did he take you into his office or'd you talk in the waiting-room?
BIFF. Well, he came in, see, and—
WILLY (*with a big smile*). What'd he say? Betcha he threw his arm around you.
BIFF. Well, he kinda—
WILLY. He's a fine man. (*To* HAPPY) Very hard man to see, y'know.
HAPPY (*agreeing*). Oh, I know.
WILLY (*to* BIFF). Is that where you had the drinks?
BIFF. Yeah, he gave me a couple of—no, no!
HAPPY (*cutting in*). He told him my Florida idea.
WILLY. Don't interrupt. (*To* BIFF) How'd he react to the Florida idea?
BIFF. Dad, will you give me a minute to explain?
WILLY. I've been waiting for you to explain since I sat down here! What happened? He took you into his office and what?
BIFF. Well—I talked. And—and he listened, see.
WILLY. Famous for the way he listens, y'know. What was his answer?
BIFF. His answer was—(*He breaks off, suddenly angry.*)Dad, you're not letting me tell you what I want to tell you!
WILLY (*accusing, angered*). You didn't see him, did you?

BIFF. I did see him!
WILLY. What'd you insult him or something? You insulted him, didn't you?
BIFF. Listen, will you let me out of it, will you just let me out of it!
HAPPY. What the hell!
WILLY. Tell me what happened!
BIFF (*to* HAPPY). I can't talk to him!

(*A single trumpet note jars the ear. The light of green leaves stains the house, which holds the air of night and a dream.* YOUNG BERNARD *enters and knocks on the door of the house.*)

YOUNG BERNARD (*frantically*). Mrs. Loman, Mrs. Loman!
HAPPY. Tell him what happened!
BIFF (*to* HAPPY). Shut up and leave me alone!
WILLY. No, no! You had to go and flunk math!
BIFF. What math? What're you talking about?
YOUNG BERNARD. Mrs. Loman, Mrs. Loman!

(LINDA *appears in the house, as of old.*)

WILLY (*wildly*). Math, math, math!
BIFF. Take it easy, Pop!
YOUNG BERNARD. Mrs. Loman!
WILLY (*furiously*). If you hadn't flunked you'd've been set by now!
BIFF. Now, look, I'm gonna tell you what happened, and you're going to listen to me.
YOUNG BERNARD. Mrs. Loman!
BIFF. I waited six hours—
HAPPY. What the hell are you saying?
BIFF. I kept sending in my name but he wouldn't see me. So finally he . . . (*He continues unheard as light fades low on the restaurant.*)
YOUNG BERNARD. Biff flunked math!
LINDA. No!
YOUNG BERNARD. Birnbaum flunked him! They won't graduate him!
LINDA. But they have to. He's gotta go to the university. Where is he? Biff! Biff!
YOUNG BERNARD. No, he left. He went to Grand Central.
LINDA. Grand—You mean he went to Boston!
YOUNG BERNARD. Is Uncle Willy in Boston?
LINDA. Oh, maybe Willy can talk to the teacher. Oh, the poor, poor boy!

(*Light on house area snaps out.*)

BIFF (*at the table, now audible, holding up a gold fountain pen*). . . . so I'm washed up with Oliver, you understand? Are you listening to me?

WILLY (*at a loss*). Yeah, sure. If you hadn't flunked—
BIFF. Flunked what? What're you talking about?
WILLY. Don't blame everything on me! I didn't flunk math—you did! What pen?
HAPPY. That was awful dumb, Biff, a pen like that is worth—
WILLY (*seeing the pen for the first time*). You took Oliver's pen?
BIFF (*weakening*). Dad, I just explained it to you.
WILLY. You stole Bill Oliver's fountain pen!
BIFF. I didn't exactly steal it! That's just what I've been explaining to you!
HAPPY. He had it in his hand and just then Oliver walked in, so he got nervous and stuck it in his pocket!
WILLY. My God, Biff!
BIFF. I never intended to do it, Dad!
OPERATOR'S VOICE. Standish Arms, good evening!
WILLY (*shouting*). I'm not in my room!
BIFF (*frightened*). Dad, what's the matter? (*He and* HAPPY *stand up.*)
OPERATOR. Ringing Mr. Loman for you!
WILLY. I'm not there, stop it!
BIFF (*horrified, gets down on one knee before* WILLY). Dad, I'll make good, I'll make good. (WILLY *tries to get to his feet.* BIFF *holds him down.*) Sit down now.
WILLY. No, you're no good, you're no good for anything.
BIFF. I am, Dad, I'll find something else, you understand? Now don't worry about anything. (*He holds up* WILLY'S *face.*) Talk to me, Dad.
OPERATOR. Mr. Loman does not answer. Shall I page him?
WILLY (*attempting to stand, as though to rush and silence the* OPERATOR). No, no, no!
HAPPY. He'll strike something, Pop.
WILLY. No, no . . .
BIFF (*desperately, standing over* WILLY). Pop, listen! Listen to me! I'm telling you something good. Oliver talked to his partner about the Florida idea. You listening? He—he talked to his partner, and he came to me . . . I'm going to be all right, you hear? Dad, listen to me, he said it was just a question of the amount!
WILLY. Then you . . . got it?
HAPPY. He's gonna be terrific, Pop!
WILLY (*trying to stand*). Then you got it, haven't you? You got it! You got it!
BIFF (*agonized, holds* WILLY *down*). No, no. Look, Pop. I'm supposed to have lunch with them tomorrow. I'm just telling you this so you'll know that I can still make an impression, Pop. And I'll make good somewhere, but I can't go tomorrow, see?

WILLY. Why not? You simply—
BIFF. But the pen, Pop!
WILLY. You give it to him and tell him it was an oversight!
HAPPY. Sure, have lunch tomorrow!
BIFF. I can't say that—
WILLY. You were doing a crossword puzzle and accidentally used his pen!
BIFF. Listen, kid, I took those balls years ago, now I walk in with his fountain pen? That clinches it, don't you see? I can't face him like that! I'll try elsewhere.
PAGE'S VOICE. Paging Mr. Loman!
WILLY. Don't you want to be anything?
BIFF. Pop, how can I go back?
WILLY. You don't want to be anything, is that what's behind it?
BIFF (*now angry at* WILLY *for not crediting his sympathy*). Don't take it that way! You think it was easy walking into that office after what I'd done to him? A team of horses couldn't have dragged me back to Bill Oliver!
WILLY. Then why'd you go?
BIFF. Why did I go? Why did I go! Look at you! Look at what's become of you!

(*Off left,* THE WOMAN *laughs.*)

WILLY. Biff, you're going to go to that lunch tomorrow, or—
BIFF. I can't go. I've got no appointment!
HAPPY. Biff, for . . . !
WILLY. Are you spiting me?
BIFF. Don't take it that way! Goddammit!
WILLY (*strikes* BIFF *and falters away from the table*). You rotten little louse! Are you spiting me?
THE WOMAN. Someone's at the door, Willy!
BIFF. I'm no good, can't you see what I am?
HAPPY (*separating them*). Hey, you're in a restaurant! Now cut it out, both of you! (*The* GIRLS *enter.*) Hello, girls, sit down.

(THE WOMAN *laughs, off left.*)

MISS FORSYTHE. I guess we might as well. This is Letta.
THE WOMAN. Willy, are you going to wake up?
BIFF (*ignoring* WILLY). How're ya, miss, sit down. What do you drink?
MISS FORSYTHE. Letta might not be able to stay long.
LETTA. I gotta get up very early tomorrow. I got jury duty. I'm so excited! Were you fellows ever on a jury?

BIFF. No, but I been in front of them! (*The* GIRLS *laugh.*) This is my father.

LETTA. Isn't he cute? Sit down with us, Pop.

HAPPY. Sit him down, Biff!

BIFF (*going to him*). Come on, slugger, drink us under the table. To hell with it! Come on, sit down, pal.

(*On* BIFF's *last insistence,* WILLY *is about to sit.*)

THE WOMAN (*now urgently*). Willy, are you going to answer the door!

(THE WOMAN's *call pulls* WILLY *back. He starts right, befuddled.*)

BIFF. Hey, where are you going?
WILLY. Open the door.
BIFF. The door?
WILLY. The washroom . . . the door . . . where's the door?
BIFF (*leading* WILLY *to the left*). Just go straight down.

(WILLY *moves left.*)

THE WOMAN. Willy, Willy, are you going to get up, get up, get up, get up?

(WILLY *exits left.*)

LETTA. I think it's sweet you bring your daddy along.

MISS FORSYTHE. Oh, he isn't really your father!

BIFF (*at left, turning to her resentfully*). Miss Forsythe, you've just seen a prince walk by. A fine, troubled prince. A hard-working, unappreciated prince. A pal, you understand? A good companion. Always for his boys.

LETTA. That's so sweet.

HAPPY. Well, girls, what's the program? We're wasting time. Come on, Biff. Gather round. Where would you like to go?

BIFF. Why don't you do something for him?

HAPPY. Me!

BIFF. Don't you give a damn for him, Hap?

HAPPY. What're you talking about? I'm the one who—

BIFF. I sense it, you don't give a good goddam about him. (*He takes the rolled-up hose from his pocket and puts it on the table in front of* HAPPY.) Look what I found in the cellar, for Christ's sake. How can you bear to let it go on?

HAPPY. Me? Who goes away? Who runs off and—

BIFF. Yeah, but he doesn't mean anything to you. You could help him—I can't! Don't you understand what I'm talking about? He's going to kill himself, don't you know that?

HAPPY. Don't I know it! Me!

BIFF. Hap, help him! Jesus . . . help him . . . Help me, help me, I can't bear to look at his face! (*Ready to weep, he hurries out, up right.*)

HAPPY (*starting after him*). Where are you going?

MISS FORSYTHE. What's he so mad about?

HAPPY. Come on, girls, we'll catch up with him.

MISS FORSYTHE (*as* HAPPY *pushes her out*). Say, I don't like that temper of his!

HAPPY. He's just a little overstrung, he'll be all right!

WILLY (*off left, as* THE WOMAN *laughs*). Don't answer! Don't answer!

LETTA. Don't you want to tell your father—

HAPPY. No, that's not my father. He's just a guy. Come on, we'll catch Biff, and, honey, we're going to paint this town! Stanley, where's the check! Hey, Stanley!

(*They exit.* STANLEY *looks toward left.*)

STANLEY (*calling to* HAPPY *indignantly*). Mr. Loman! Mr. Loman!

(STANLEY *picks up a chair and follows them off. Knocking is heard off left.* THE WOMAN *enters, laughing.* WILLY *follows her. She is in a black slip; he is buttoning his shirt. Raw, sensuous music accompanies their speech.*)

WILLY. Will you stop laughing? Will you stop?

THE WOMAN. Aren't you going to answer the door? He'll wake the whole hotel.

WILLY. I'm not expecting anybody.

THE WOMAN. Whyn't you have another drink, honey, and stop being so damn self-centered?

WILLY. I'm so lonely.

THE WOMAN. You know you ruined me, Willy? From now on, whenever you come to the office, I'll see that you go right through to the buyers. No waiting at my desk any more, Willy. You ruined me.

WILLY. That's nice of you to say that.

THE WOMAN. Gee, you are self-centered! Why so sad? You are the saddest, self-centeredest soul I ever did see-saw. (*She laughs. He kisses her.*) Come on inside, drummer boy. It's silly to be dressing in the middle of the night. (*As knocking is heard*) Aren't you going to answer the door?

WILLY. They're knocking on the wrong door.

THE WOMAN. But I felt the knocking. And he heard us talking in here. Maybe the hotel's on fire!

WILLY (*his terror rising*). It's a mistake.

THE WOMAN. Then tell him to go away!

WILLY. There's nobody there.

THE WOMAN. It's getting on my nerves, Willy. There's somebody

ARTHUR MILLER   399

standing out there and it's getting on my nerves!

WILLY (*pushing her away from him*). All right, stay in the bathroom here, and don't come out. I think there's a law in Massachusetts about it, so don't come out. It may be that new room clerk. He looked very mean. So don't come out. It's a mistake, there's no fire.

(*The knocking is heard again. He takes a few steps away from her, and she vanishes into the wing. The light follows him, and now he is facing* YOUNG BIFF, *who carries a suitcase.* BIFF *steps toward him. The music is gone.*)

BIFF. Why didn't you answer?

WILLY. Biff! What are you doing in Boston?

BIFF. Why didn't you answer? I've been knocking for five minutes, I called you on the phone—

WILLY. I just heard you. I was in the bathroom and had the door shut. Did anything happen home?

BIFF. Dad—I let you down.

WILLY. What do you mean?

BIFF. Dad . . .

WILLY. Biffo, what's this about? (*Putting his arm around* BIFF) Come on, let's go downstairs and get you a malted.

BIFF. Dad, I flunked math.

WILLY. Not for the term?

BIFF. The term. I haven't got enough credits to graduate.

WILLY. You mean to say Bernard wouldn't give you the answers?

BIFF. He did, he tried, but I only got a sixty-one.

WILLY. And they wouldn't give you four points.

BIFF. Birnbaum refused absolutely. I begged him, Pop, but he won't give me those points. You gotta talk to him before they close the school. Because if he saw the kind of man you are, and you just talked to him in your way, I'm sure he'd come through for me. The class came right before practice, see, and I didn't go enough. Would you talk to him? He'd like you, Pop. You know the way you could talk.

WILLY. You're on. We'll drive right back.

BIFF. Oh, Dad, good work! I'm sure he'll change it for you!

WILLY. Go downstairs and tell the clerk I'm checkin' out. Go right down.

BIFF. Yes, sir! See, the reason he hates me, Pop—one day he was late for class so I got up at the blackboard and imitated him. I crossed my eyes and talked with a lithp.

WILLY (*laughing*). You did? The kids like it?

BIFF. They nearly died laughing!

WILLY. Yeah? What'd you do?

BIFF. The thquare root of thixthy twee is . . . (WILLY *bursts out laughing;* BIFF *joins him.*) And in the middle of it he walked in!

(WILLY *laughs and* THE WOMAN *joins in offstage.*)

WILLY (*without hesitation*).   Hurry downstairs and—
BIFF.   Somebody in there?
WILLY.   No, that was next door.

(THE WOMAN *laughs offstage.*)

BIFF.   Somebody got in your bathroom!
WILLY.   No, it's the next room, there's a party—
THE WOMAN (*enters, laughing. She lisps this*).   Can I come in? There's something in the bathtub, Willy, and it's moving!

(WILLY *looks at* BIFF, *who is staring open-mouthed and horrified at* THE WOMAN.)

WILLY.   Ah—you better go back to your room. They must be finished painting by now. They're painting her room so I let her take a shower here. Go back, go back . . . (*He pushes her.*)
THE WOMAN (*resisting*).   But I've got to get dressed, Willy, I can't—
WILLY.   Get out of here! Go back, go back . . . (*Suddenly striving for the ordinary*) This is Miss Francis, Biff, she's a buyer. They're painting her room. Go back, Miss Francis, go back . . .
THE WOMAN.   But my clothes, I can't go out naked in the hall!
WILLY (*pushing her offstage*).   Get outa here! Go back, go back!

(BIFF *slowly sits down on his suitcase as the argument continues offstage.*)

THE WOMAN.   Where's my stockings? You promised me stockings, Willy!
WILLY.   I have no stockings here!
THE WOMAN.   You had two boxes of size nine sheers for me, and I want them!
WILLY.   Here, for God's sake, will you get outa here!
THE WOMAN (*enters holding a box of stockings*).   I just hope there's nobody in the hall. That's all I hope. (*To* BIFF) Are you football or baseball?
BIFF.   Football.
THE WOMAN (*angry, humiliated*).   That's me too. G'night. (*She snatches her clothes from* WILLY *and walks out.*)
WILLY (*after a pause*).   Well, better get going. I want to get to the school first thing in the morning. Get my suits out of the closet. I'll get my valise. (BIFF *doesn't move.*) What's the matter? (BIFF *remains motionless, tears falling.*) She's a buyer. Buys for J. H. Simmons. She lives down the hall—they're painting. You don't imagine—(*He breaks off. After a pause*) Now listen, pal, she's just a buyer. She sees merchandise in her room and

they have to keep it looking just so . . . (*Pause. Assuming command*) All right, get my suits. (BIFF *doesn't move.*) Now stop crying and do as I say. I gave you an order. Biff, I gave you an order! Is that what you do when I give you an order? How dare you cry! (*Putting his arm around* BIFF) Now look, Biff, when you grow up you'll understand about these things. You mustn't—you mustn't overemphasize a thing like this. I'll see Birnbaum first thing in the morning.

BIFF. Never mind.

WILLY (*getting down beside* BIFF). Never mind! He's going to give you those points. I'll see to it.

BIFF. He wouldn't listen to you.

WILLY. He certainly will listen to me. You need those points for the U. of Virginia.

BIFF. I'm not going there.

WILLY. Heh? If I can't get him to change that mark you'll make it up in summer school. You've got all summer to—

BIFF (*his weeping breaking from him*). Dad . . .

WILLY (*infected by it*). Oh, my boy . . .

BIFF. Dad . . .

WILLY. She's nothing to me, Biff. I was lonely, I was terribly lonely.

BIFF. You—you gave her Mama's stockings! (*His tears break through and he rises to go.*)

WILLY (*grabbing for* BIFF). I gave you an order!

BIFF. Don't touch me, you—liar!

WILLY. Apologize for that!

BIFF. You fake! You phony little fake! You fake! (*Overcome, he turns quickly and weeping fully goes out with his suitcase.* WILLY *is left on the floor on his knees.*)

WILLY. I gave you an order! Biff, come back here or I'll beat you! Come back here! I'll whip you!

(STANLEY *comes quickly in from the right and stands in front of* WILLY.)

WILLY (*shouts at* STANLEY). I gave you an order . . .

STANLEY. Hey, let's pick it up, pick it up, Mr. Loman. (*He helps* WILLY *to his feet.*) Your boys left with the chippies. They said they'll see you home.

(*A second waiter watches some distance away.*)

WILLY. But we were supposed to have dinner together.

(*Music is heard,* WILLY'S *theme.*)

STANLEY. Can you make it?

WILLY. I'll—sure, I can make it. (*Suddenly concerned about his clothes*) Do I—I look all right?

STANLEY. Sure, you look all right. (*He flicks a speck off* WILLY's *lapel.*)
WILLY. Here—here's a dollar.
STANLEY. Oh, your son paid me. It's all right.
WILLY (*putting it in* STANLEY's *hand*). No, take it. You're a good boy.
STANLEY. Oh, no, you don't have to . . .
WILLY. Here's some more, I don't need it any more. (*After a slight pause*) Tell me—is there a seed store in the neighborhood?
STANLEY. Seeds? You mean like to plant?

(*As* WILLY *turns*, STANLEY *slips the money back into his jacket pocket.*)

WILLY. Yes. Carrots, peas . . .
STANLEY. Well, there's hardware stores on Sixth Avenue, but it may be too late now.
WILLY (*anxiously*). Oh, I'd better hurry. I've got to get some seeds. (*He starts off to the right.*) I've got to get some seeds, right away. Nothing's planted. I don't have a thing in the ground.

(WILLY *hurries out as the light goes down.* STANLEY *moves over to the right after him, watches him off. The other waiter has been staring at* WILLY.)

STANLEY (*to the waiter*). Well, whatta you looking at?

(*The waiter picks up the chairs and moves off right.* STANLEY *takes the table and follows him. The light fades on this area. There is a long pause, the sound of the flute coming over. The light gradually rises on the kitchen, which is empty.* HAPPY *appears at the door of the house, followed by* BIFF. HAPPY *is carrying a large bunch of long-stemmed roses. He enters the kitchen, looks around for* LINDA. *Not seeing her, he turns to* BIFF, *who is just outside the house door, and makes a gesture with his hands, indicating "Not here, I guess." He looks into the living-room and freezes. Inside,* LINDA, *unseen, is seated,* WILLY's *coat on her lap. She rises ominously and quietly and moves toward* HAPPY, *who backs up into the kitchen, afraid.*)

HAPPY. Hey, what're you doing up? (LINDA *says nothing but moves toward him implacably.*) Where's Pop? (*He keeps backing to the right, and now* LINDA *is in full view in the doorway to the living-room.*) Is he sleeping?
LINDA. Where were you?
HAPPY (*trying to laugh it off*). We met two girls, Mom, very fine types. Here, we brought you some flowers. (*Offering them to her*) Put them in your room, Ma.

(*She knocks them to the floor at* BIFF's *feet. He has now come inside and closed the door behind him. She stares at* BIFF, *silent.*)

HAPPY. Now what'd you do that for? Mom, I want you to have some flowers—

LINDA (*cutting* HAPPY *off, violently to* BIFF). Don't you care whether he lives or dies?
HAPPY (*going to the stairs*). Come upstairs, Biff.
BIFF (*with a flare of disgust, to* HAPPY). Go away from me! (*To* LINDA) What do you mean, lives or dies? Nobody's dying around here, pal.
LINDA. Get out of my sight! Get out of here!
BIFF. I wanna see the boss.
LINDA. You're not going near him!
BIFF. Where is he? (*He moves into the living-room and* LINDA *follows*.)
LINDA (*shouting after* BIFF). You invite him for dinner. He looks forward to it all day—(BIFF *appears in his parents' bedroom, looks around, and exits*)—and then you desert him there. There's no stranger you'd do that to!
HAPPY. Why? He had a swell time with us. Listen, when I—(LINDA *comes back into the kitchen*)—desert him I hope I don't outlive the day!
LINDA. Get out of here!
HAPPY. Now look, Mom . . .
LINDA. Did you have to go to women tonight? You and your lousy rotten whores!

(BIFF *re-enters the kitchen*.)

HAPPY. Mom, all we did was follow Biff around trying to cheer him up! (*To* BIFF) Boy, what a night you gave me!
LINDA. Get out of here, both of you, and don't come back! I don't want you tormenting him any more. Go on now, get your things together! (*To* BIFF) You can sleep in his apartment. (*She starts to pick up the flowers and stops herself*.) Pick up this stuff, I'm not your maid any more. Pick it up, you bum, you!

(HAPPY *turns his back to her in refusal*. BIFF *slowly moves over and gets down on his knees, picking up the flowers*.)

LINDA. You're a pair of animals! Not one, not another living soul would have had the cruelty to walk out on that man in a restaurant!
BIFF (*not looking at her*). Is that what he said?
LINDA. He didn't have to say anything. He was so humiliated he nearly limped when he came in.
HAPPY. But, Mom, he had a great time with us—
BIFF (*cutting him off violently*). Shut up!

(*Without another word,* HAPPY *goes upstairs*.)

LINDA. You! You didn't even go in to see if he was all right!
BIFF (*still on the floor in front of* LINDA, *the flowers in his hand; with self-loathing*). No. Didn't. Didn't do a damned thing. How do you like that, heh? Left him babbling in a toilet.

LINDA. You louse. You . . .

BIFF. Now you hit it on the nose! (*He gets up, throws the flowers in the wastebasket.*) The scum of the earth, and you're looking at him!

LINDA. Get out of here!

BIFF. I gotta talk to the boss, Mom. Where is he?

LINDA. You're not going near him. Get out of this house!

BIFF (*with absolute assurance, determination*). No. We're gonna have an abrupt conversation, him and me.

LINDA. You're not talking to him!

(*Hammering is heard from outside the house, off right.* BIFF *turns toward the noise.*)

LINDA (*suddenly pleading*). Will you please leave him alone?

BIFF. What's he doing out there?

LINDA. He's planting the garden!

BIFF (*quietly*). Now? Oh, my God!

(BIFF *moves outside,* LINDA *following. The light dies down on them and comes up on the center of the apron as* WILLY *walks into it. He is carrying a flashlight, a hoe, and a handful of seed packets. He raps the top of the hoe sharply to fix it firmly, and then moves to the left, measuring off the distance with his foot. He holds the flashlight to look at the seed packets, reading off the instructions. He is in the blue of night.*)

WILLY. Carrots . . . quarter-inch apart. Rows . . . one-foot rows. (*He measures it off.*) One foot. (*He puts down a package and measures off.*) Beets. (*He puts down another package and measures again.*) Lettuce. (*He reads the package, puts it down.*) One foot—(*He breaks off as* BEN *appears at the right and moves slowly down to him.*) What a proposition, ts, ts. Terrific, terrific. 'Cause she's suffered, Ben, the woman has suffered. You understand me? A man can't go out the way he came in. Ben, a man has got to add up to something. You can't, you can't—(BEN *moves toward him as though to interrupt.*) You gotta consider, now. Don't answer so quick. Remember, it's a guaranteed twenty-thousand-dollar proposition. Now look, Ben, I want you to go through the ins and outs of this thing with me. I've got nobody to talk to, Ben, and the woman has suffered, you hear me?

BEN (*standing still, considering*). What's the proposition?

WILLY. It's twenty thousand dollars on the barrelhead. Guaranteed, gilt-edged, you understand?

BEN. You don't want to make a fool of yourself. They might not honor the policy.

WILLY. How can they dare refuse? Didn't I work like a coolie to meet every premium on the nose? And now they don't pay off? Impossible!

BEN. It's called a cowardly thing, William.

WILLY. Why? Does it take more guts to stand here the rest of my life ringing up a zero?

BEN (*yielding*). That's a point, William. (*He moves, thinking, turns.*) And twenty thousand—that *is* something one can feel with the hand, it is there.

WILLY (*now assured, with rising power*). Oh, Ben, that's the whole beauty of it! I see it like a diamond, shining in the dark, hard and rough, that I can pick up and touch in my hand. Not like—like an appointment! This would not be another damned-fool appointment, Ben, and it changes all the aspects. Because he thinks I'm nothing, see, and so he spites me. But the funeral—(*Straightening up*) Ben, that funeral will be massive! They'll come from Maine, Massachusetts, Vermont, New Hampshire! All the old-timers with the strange license plates—that boy will be thunder-struck, Ben, because he never realized—I am known! Rhode Island, New York, New Jersey—I am known, Ben, and he'll see it with his eyes once and for all. He'll see what I am, Ben! He's in for a shock, that boy!

BEN (*coming down to the edge of the garden*). He'll call you a coward.

WILLY (*suddenly fearful*). No, that would be terrible.

BEN. Yes. And a damned fool.

WILLY. No, no, he mustn't, I won't have that! (*He is broken and desperate.*)

BEN. He'll hate you, William.

(*The gay music of the boys is heard.*)

WILLY. Oh, Ben, how do we get back to all the great times? Used to be so full of light, and comradeship, the sleigh-riding in winter and the ruddiness on his cheeks. And always some kind of good news coming up, always something nice coming up ahead. And never even let me carry the valises in the house, and simonizing, simonizing that little red car! Why, why can't I give him something and not have him hate me?

BEN. Let me think about it. (*He glances at his watch.*) I still have a little time. Remarkable proposition, but you've got to be sure you're not making a fool of yourself.

(BEN *drifts off upstage and goes out of sight.* BIFF *comes down from the left.*)

WILLY (*suddenly conscious of* BIFF, *turns and looks up at him, then begins picking up the packages of seeds in confusion*). Where the hell is that seed? (*Indignantly*) You can't see nothing out here! They boxed in the whole goddam neighborhood!

BIFF. There are people all around here. Don't you realize that?

WILLY. I'm busy. Don't bother me.

BIFF (*taking the hoe from* WILLY). I'm saying good-by to you, Pop. (WILLY *looks at him, silent, unable to move.*) I'm not coming back any more.

WILLY. You're not going to see Oliver tomorrow?

BIFF. I've got no appointment, Dad.

WILLY. He put his arms around you, and you've got no appointment?

BIFF. Pop, get this now, will you? Every time I've left it's been a fight that sent me out of here. Today I realized something about myself and I tried to explain it to you and I—I think I'm just not smart enough to make any sense out of it for you. To hell with whose fault it is or anything like that. (*He takes* WILLY's *arm.*) Let's just wrap it up, heh? Come on in, we'll tell Mom. (*He gently tries to pull* WILLY *to left.*)

WILLY (*frozen, immobile, with guilt in his voice*). No, I don't want to see her.

BIFF. Come on!

(*He pulls again, and* WILLY *tries to pull away.*)

WILLY (*highly nervous*). No, no, I don't want to see her.

BIFF (*tries to look into* WILLY's *face, as if to find the answer there.*) Why don't you want to see her?

WILLY (*more harshly now*). Don't bother me, will you?

BIFF. What do you mean, you don't want to see her? You don't want them calling you yellow do you? This isn't your fault; it's me, I'm a bum. Now come inside! (WILLY *strains to get away.*) Did you hear what I said to you?

(WILLY *pulls away and quickly goes by himself into the house.* BIFF *follows.*)

LINDA (*to* WILLY). Did you plant, dear?

BIFF (*at the door, to* LINDA). All right, we had it out. I'm going and I'm not writing any more.

LINDA (*going to* WILLY *in the kitchen*). I think that's the best way, dear. 'Cause there's no use drawing it out, you'll just never get along.

(WILLY *doesn't respond.*)

BIFF. People ask where I am and what I'm doing, you don't know, and you don't care. That way it'll be off your mind and you can start brightening up again. All right? That clears it, doesn't it? (WILLY *is silent, and* BIFF *goes to him.*) You gonna wish me luck, scout? (*He extends his hand.*) What do you say?

LINDA. Shake his hand, Willy.

WILLY (*turning to her, seething with hurt*). There's no necessity to mention the pen at all, y'know.

BIFF (*gently*). I've got no appointment, Dad.

WILLY (*erupting fiercely*). He put his arm around . . . ?

BIFF. Dad, you're never going to see what I am, so what's the use of arguing? If I strike oil I'll send you a check. Meantime forget I'm alive.

WILLY (*to* LINDA). Spite, see?

BIFF. Shake hands, Dad.
WILLY. Not my hand.
BIFF. I was hoping not to go this way.
WILLY. Well, this is the way you're going. Good-by.

(BIFF *looks at him a moment, then turns sharply and goes to the stairs.*)

WILLY (*stops him with:*) May you rot in hell if you leave this house!
BIFF (*turning*). Exactly what is it that you want from me?
WILLY. I want you to know, on the train, in the mountains, in the valleys, wherever you go, that you cut down your life for spite!
BIFF. No, no.
WILLY. Spite, spite, is the word of your undoing! And when you're down and out, remember what did it. When you're rotting somewhere beside the railroad tracks, remember, and don't you dare blame it on me!
BIFF. I'm not blaming it on you!
WILLY. I won't take the rap for this, you hear?

(HAPPY *comes down the stairs and stands on the bottom step, watching.*)

BIFF. That's just what I'm telling you!
WILLY (*sinking into a chair at the table, with full accusation*). You're trying to put a knife in me—don't think I don't know what you're doing!
BIFF. All right, phony! Then let's lay it on the line. (*He whips the rubber tube out of his pocket and puts it on the table.*)
HAPPY. You crazy—
LINDA. Biff! (*She moves to grab the hose, but* BIFF *holds it down with his hand.*)
BIFF. Leave it there! Don't move it!
WILLY (*not looking at it*). What is that?
BIFF. You know goddam well what that is.
WILLY (*caged, wanting to escape*). I never saw that.
BIFF. You saw it. The mice didn't bring it into the cellar! What is this supposed to do, make a hero out of you? This supposed to make me sorry for you?
WILLY. Never heard of it.
BIFF. There'll be no pity for you, you hear it? No pity!
WILLY (*to* LINDA). You hear the spite!
BIFF. No, you're going to hear the truth—what you are and what I am!
LINDA. Stop it!
WILLY. Spite!
HAPPY (*coming down toward* BIFF). You cut it now!
BIFF (*to* HAPPY). The man don't know who we are! The man is gonna know! (*To* WILLY) We never told the truth for ten minutes in this house!
HAPPY. We always told the truth!
BIFF (*turning on him*). You big blow, are you the assistant buyer?

You're one of the two assistants to the assistant, aren't you?

HAPPY. Well, I'm practically—

BIFF. You're practically full of it! We all are! And I'm through with it. (*To* WILLY) Now hear this, Willy, this is me.

WILLY. I know you!

BIFF. You know why I had no address for three months? I stole a suit in Kansas City and I was in jail. (*To* LINDA, *who is sobbing*) Stop crying. I'm through with it.

(LINDA *turns away from them, her hands covering her face.*)

WILLY. I suppose that's my fault!

BIFF. I stole myself out of every good job since high school!

WILLY. And whose fault is that?

BIFF. And I never got anywhere because you blew me so full of hot air I could never stand taking orders from anybody! That's whose fault it is!

WILLY. I hear that!

LINDA. Don't, Biff!

BIFF. It's goddam time you heard that! I had to be boss big shot in two weeks, and I'm through with it!

WILLY. Then hang yourself! For spite, hang yourself!

BIFF. No! Nobody's hanging himself, Willy! I ran down eleven flights with a pen in my hand today. And suddenly I stopped, you hear me? And in the middle of that office building, do you hear this? I stopped in the middle of that building and I saw—the sky. I saw the things that I love in this world. The work and the food and time to sit and smoke. And I looked at the pen and said to myself, what the hell am I grabbing this for? Why am I trying to become what I don't want to be? What am I doing in an office, making a contemptuous, begging fool of myself, when all I want is out there, waiting for me the minute I say I know who I am! Why can't I say that, Willy?

(*He tries to make* WILLY *face him, but* WILLY *pulls away and moves to the left.*)

WILLY (*with hatred, threateningly*). The door of your life is wide open!

BIFF. Pop! I'm a dime a dozen, and so are you!

WILLY (*turning on him now in an uncontrolled outburst*). I am not a dime a dozen! I am Willy Loman, and you are Biff Loman!

(BIFF *starts for* WILLY, *but is blocked by* HAPPY. *In his fury,* BIFF *seems on the verge of attacking his father.*)

BIFF. I am not a leader of men, Willy, and neither are you. You were never anything but a hard-working drummer who landed in the ash can like all the rest of them! I'm one dollar an hour, Willy! I tried seven states and couldn't raise it. A buck an hour! Do you gather my meaning? I'm not bringing home any prizes any more, and you're going to stop waiting for me to bring them home!

WILLY (*directly to* BIFF). You vengeful, spiteful mutt!

(BIFF *breaks from* HAPPY. WILLY, *in fright, starts up the stairs.* BIFF *grabs him.*)

BIFF (*at the peak of his fury*). Pop, I'm nothing! I'm nothing, Pop. Can't you understand that? There's no spite in it any more. I'm just what I am, that's all.

(BIFF's *fury has spent itself, and he breaks down, sobbing, holding on to* WILLY, *who dumbly fumbles for* BIFF's *face.*)

WILLY (*astonished*). What're you doing? What're you doing? (*To* LINDA) Why is he crying?

BIFF (*crying, broken*). Will you let me go, for Christ's sake? Will you take that phony dream and burn it before something happens? (*Struggling to contain himself, he pulls away and moves to the stairs.*) I'll go in the morning. Put him—put him to bed. (*Exhausted,* BIFF *moves up the stairs to his room.*)

WILLY (*after a long pause, astonished, elevated*). Isn't that—isn't that remarkable? Biff—he likes me!

LINDA. He loves you, Willy!

HAPPY (*deeply moved*). Always did, Pop.

WILLY. Oh, Biff! (*Staring wildly*) He cried! Cried to me. (*He is choking with his love, and now cries out his promise.*) That boy—that boy is going to be magnificent!

(BEN *appears in the light just outside the kitchen.*)

BEN. Yes, outstanding, with twenty thousand behind him.

LINDA (*sensing the racing of his mind, fearfully, carefully*). Now come to bed, Willy. It's all settled now.

WILLY (*finding it difficult not to rush out of the house*). Yes, we'll sleep. Come on. Go to sleep, Hap.

BEN. And it does take a great kind of a man to crack the jungle.

(*In accents of dread,* BEN's *idyllic music starts up.*)

HAPPY (*his arm around* LINDA). I'm getting married, Pop, don't forget it. I'm changing everything. I'm gonna run that department before the year is up. You'll see, Mom. (*He kisses her.*)

BEN. The jungle is dark but full of diamonds, Willy.

(WILLY *turns, moves, listening to* BEN.)

LINDA. Be good. You're both good boys, just act that way, that's all.

HAPPY. 'Night, Pop. (*He goes upstairs.*)

LINDA (*to* WILLY). Come, dear.

BEN (*with greater force*). One must go in to fetch a diamond out.
WILLY (*to* LINDA, *as he moves slowly along the edge of the kitchen, toward the door*). I just want to get settled down, Linda. Let me sit alone for a little.
LINDA (*almost uttering her fear*). I want you upstairs.
WILLY (*taking her in his arms*). In a few minutes, Linda. I couldn't sleep right now. Go on, you look awful tired. (*He kisses her.*)
BEN. Not like an appointment at all. A diamond is rough and hard to the touch.
WILLY. Go on now. I'll be right up.
LINDA. I think this is the only way, Willy.
WILLY. Sure, it's the best thing.
BEN. Best thing!
WILLY. The only way. Everything is gonna be—go on, kid, get to bed. You look so tired.
LINDA. Come right up.
WILLY. Two minutes.

(LINDA *goes into the living-room, then reappears in her bedroom.* WILLY *moves just outside the kitchen door.*)

WILLY. Loves me. (*Wonderingly*) Always loved me. Isn't that a remarkable thing? Ben, he'll worship me for it!
BEN (*with promise*). It's dark there, but full of diamonds.
WILLY. Can you imagine that magnificence with twenty thousand dollars in his pocket?
LINDA (*calling from her room*). Willy! Come up!
WILLY (*calling into the kitchen*). Yes! Yes. Coming! It's very smart, you realize that, don't you, sweetheart? Even Ben sees it. I gotta go, baby. 'By! 'By! (*Going over to* BEN, *almost dancing*) Imagine? When the mail comes he'll be ahead of Bernard again!
BEN. A perfect proposition all around.
WILLY. Did you see how he cried to me? Oh, if I could kiss him, Ben!
BEN. Time, William, time!
WILLY. Oh, Ben, I always knew one way or another we were gonna make it, Biff and I!
BEN (*looking at his watch*). The boat. We'll be late. (*He moves slowly off into the darkness.*)
WILLY (*elegiacally, turning to the house*). Now when you kick off, boy, I want a seventy-yard boot, and get right down the field under the ball, and when you hit, hit low and hit hard, because it's important, boy. (*He swings around and faces the audience.*) There's all kinds of important people in the stands, and the first thing you know . . . (*Suddenly realizing he is alone*) Ben! Ben, where do I . . . ? (*He makes a sudden movement of search.*) Ben, how do I . . . ?

LINDA (*calling*). Willy, you coming up?

WILLY (*uttering a gasp of fear, whirling about as if to quiet her*). Sh! (*He turns around as if to find his way; sounds, faces, voices, seem to be swarming in upon him and he flicks at them, crying*) Sh! Sh! (*Suddenly music, faint and high, stops him. It rises in intensity, almost to an unbearable scream. He goes up and down on his toes, and rushes off around the house.*) Shhh!

LINDA. Willy?

(*There is no answer.* LINDA *waits.* BIFF *gets up off his bed. He is still in his clothes.* HAPPY *sits up.* BIFF *stands listening.*)

LINDA (*with real fear*). Willy, answer me! Willy!

(*There is the sound of a car starting and moving away at full speed.*)

LINDA. No!

BIFF (*rushing down the stairs*). Pop!

(*As the car speeds off, the music crashes down in a frenzy of sound, which becomes the soft pulsation of a single cello string.* BIFF *slowly returns to his bedroom. He and* HAPPY *gravely don their jackets.* LINDA *slowly walks out of her room. The music has developed into a dead march. The leaves of day are appearing over everything.* CHARLEY *and* BERNARD, *somberly dressed, appear and knock on the kitchen door.* BIFF *and* HAPPY *slowly descend the stairs to the kitchen as* CHARLEY *and* BERNARD *enter. All stop a moment when* LINDA, *in clothes of mourning, bearing a little bunch of roses, comes through the draped doorway into the kitchen. She goes to* CHARLEY *and takes his arm. Now all move toward the audience, through the wall-line of the kitchen. At the limit of the apron,* LINDA *lays down the flowers, kneels, and sits back on her heels. All stare down at the grave.*)

REQUIEM

CHARLEY. It's getting dark, Linda.

(LINDA *doesn't react. She stares at the grave.*)

BIFF. How about it, Mom? Better get some rest, heh? They'll be closing the gate soon.

(LINDA *makes no move. Pause.*)

HAPPY (*deeply angered*). He had no right to do that. There was no necessity for it. We would've helped him.

CHARLEY (*grunting*). Hmmm.

BIFF. Come along, Mom.

LINDA. Why didn't anybody come?

CHARLEY. It was a very nice funeral.

LINDA. But where are all the people he knew? Maybe they blame him.

CHARLEY. Naa. It's a rough world, Linda. They wouldn't blame him.

LINDA. I can't understand it. At this time especially. First time in thirty-five years we were just about free and clear. He only needed a little salary. He was even finished with the dentist.

CHARLEY. No man only needs a little salary.

LINDA. I can't understand it.

BIFF. There were a lot of nice days. When he'd come home from a trip; or on Sundays, making the stoop; finishing the cellar; putting on the new porch; when he built the extra bathroom; and put up the garage. You know something, Charley, there's more of him in that front stoop than in all the sales he ever made.

CHARLEY. Yeah. He was a happy man with a batch of cement.

LINDA. He was so wonderful with his hands.

BIFF. He had the wrong dreams. All, all, wrong.

HAPPY (*almost ready to fight* BIFF). Don't say that!

BIFF. He never knew who he was.

CHARLEY (*stopping* HAPPY's *movement and reply. To* BIFF). Nobody dast blame this man. You don't understand: Willy was a salesman. And for a salesman, there is no rock bottom to the life. He don't put a bolt to a nut, he don't tell you the law or give you medicine. He's a man way out there in the blue, riding on a smile and a shoeshine. And when they start not smiling back—that's an earthquake. And then you get yourself a couple of spots on your hat, and you're finished. Nobody dast blame this man. A salesman is got to dream, boy. It comes with the territory.

BIFF. Charley, the man didn't know who he was.

HAPPY (*infuriated*). Don't say that!

BIFF. Why don't you come with me, Happy?

HAPPY. I'm not licked that easily. I'm staying right in this city, and I'm gonna beat this racket! (*He looks at* BIFF, *his chin set.*) The Loman Brothers!

BIFF. I know who I am, kid.

HAPPY. All right, boy. I'm gonna show you and everybody else that Willy Loman did not die in vain. He had a good dream. It's the only dream you can have—to come out number-one man. He fought it out here, and this is where I'm gonna win it for him.

BIFF (*with a hopeless glance at* HAPPY, *bends toward his mother*). Let's go, Mom.

LINDA. I'll be with you in a minute. Go on, Charley. (*He hesitates.*) I want to, just for a minute. I never had a chance to say good-by.

(CHARLEY *moves away, followed by* HAPPY. BIFF *remains a slight distance up and left of* LINDA. *She sits there, summoning herself. The flute begins, not far away, playing behind her speech.*)

LINDA. Forgive me, dear. I can't cry. I don't know what it is, but I can't cry. I don't understand it. Why did you ever do that? Help me, Willy,

I can't cry. It seems to me that you're just on another trip. I keep expecting you. Willy, dear, I can't cry. Why did you do it? I search and search and I search, and I can't understand it, Willy. I made the last payment on the house today. Today, dear. And there'll be nobody home. (*A sob rises in her throat.*) We're free and clear. (*Sobbing more fully, released*) We're free. (BIFF *comes slowly toward her.*) We're free . . . We're free . . .

(BIFF *lifts her to her feet and moves out up right with her in his arms.* LINDA *sobs quietly.* BERNARD *and* CHARLEY *come together and follow them, followed by* HAPPY. *Only the music of the flute is left on the darkening stage as over the house the hard towers of the apartment buildings rise into sharp focus, and the curtain falls.*)

DISCUSSION

Death of a Salesman is one of the best-known literary expressions of the disillusionment that beset Americans in the 1930s and 40s. Originally produced in 1949, the play reflects the painful discovery made by many Americans in those decades that the "American Dream" was at best illusory, at worst, destructive. Just prior to this period, from the turn of the century until the Depression, Americans indulged in an unbridled optimism. The United States won two wars—the Spanish American and First World wars —and became a global power; and, as the country's industries thrived, success through salesmanship, investment, and hard work seemed almost automatic. Among the nation's most popular writers was Horatio Alger, whose novels were dedicated to the proposition that an industrious and virtuous young man could become wealthy and powerful without losing his virtue. The stock market was giddy proof of the virtues of buying and selling. With the oversimplification of the Puritan work ethic through the centuries, many Americans now believed that *money* and *success* were synonymous, and that a man's identity and the measure of his worth resided in his success in business.

But with the stock market crash and the Depression, many Americans discovered that hard work could not guarantee financial success. How could one "succeed" when there were no jobs available, even for the most industrious and virtuous of men? Without work and money as sources of identity and measures of worth, and unable to find alternative ways of defining themselves, many Americans suffered a profound depression psychologically as well as economically. Some discovered that even the traditional refuges, one's family and friends, could be affected by material concerns. A man was successful because he was "liked," but, conversely, he was "liked" because he was successful.

Willy Loman is a symbol and a victim of all these beliefs and dislocations. His disillusionment and eventual self-destruction are symbolic of the experience of many Americans in the 1930s and 40s. From the outset of the play, Arthur Miller suggests Willy's symbolic rather than his literal quality. The setting he specifies features the skeleton of the Loman house, its inner areas unlit save for whichever one is the site of the action. The exterior of the house is actually a series of light projections, and like the surrounding office buildings, seems a suggestion painted in light rather than a literal construction. Willy is himself a skeleton of a man, concerned only with his business identity and his escape into a happier past. We know little about his wife, Linda, except that she loves Willy. Their son Biff is a high-school football hero gone sour, and his younger brother, Happy, is a typical salesman-operator of the post-Second World War society. The minor characters, too, are stereotypes of certain facets of society: Charlie is the neighborhood friend, Howard is the "compleat" businessman, Bernard, the success through intellect. We also discover very quickly that the structure of the play is nonrealistic. Willy's inchoate ramblings keep "materializing" on stage; his brother, his past on the road, his memories of Biff and Happy as teen-agers, all take on concrete form and shape as we watch. But the form is that of memory. Happy and Biff are seen at their present ages and are merely translated back in costume to an earlier period. His brother Ben is always the older man Willy last saw, regardless of the date of his recollections. The play does not represent the reality of the present, but the fabric of Willy's mind.

This nonrealistic structure is an important part of what Miller is saying about Willy; for what creates Willy's final crisis and suicide is not only his inability to find a place in the present but his inability to understand the past as well. It is part of Willy's blindness, his obsession with success, that although he remembers the facts of the past, he cultivates only those that support his present illusions. For example, he remembers Bernard's warnings about Biff's math grades, but he chooses to sublimate those details in his dream of Biff. He recalls the penchant for brutality that marks his brother Ben, but he chooses to incorporate only Ben's high-sounding phrases when picturing him as a successful businessman. It is not so much what has happened to Willy as what he has chosen to make of those events that pushes him toward self-destruction.

Willy's problem, then, resides in his own mind and his own values, and the nonrealistic structure of the play is designed to explore the interior, subjective aspects of Willy that make him so desperate. The nonrealistic, symbolic quality of the supporting characters is also designed to help us understand some of the conflicts inherent in American social values. The characters, through their flat and fragmentary presentation, emerge for us as symbols of values rather than as real people. We look at the play as an exploration of social values more than as the particular experience of a particular character.

Our recognition of the symbolic nature of Willy and his family and friends is important in our final evaluation of the play. Through his fragmentary characters, his nonrealistic settings, and his "memory" structure, Miller is telling us that his play covers only a single aspect of the American experience. However, even if one recognizes Miller's own integrity in limiting his criticism to a single aspect of American values, some questions remain. How should we feel about Willy? Is his suicide inevitable, or is it merely a result of his own obsessive allegiance to materialistic values? If the suicide is inevitable, then is Willy a tragic figure or merely pathetically misguided? And if Willy is merely pathetically misguided, is Miller justified in treating him with such seriousness? If not, is Miller himself guilty of sentimentality? The answers to these questions are neither easy nor absolute. But in trying to answer them, the student of drama may learn a great deal about the aspects of a drama that give it continuing validity over the years.

THEME AND DISCUSSION QUESTIONS

1. Flashbacks in movies are often annoying because they do not occur under pressure, that is, they are not a form of motivated action, but merely a way of getting information across to the audience. How well do Miller's flashbacks work? Are they dramatic or static?
2. How does their dedication to the dream of success drive Willy and Biff away from discovering their true selves? What hints do we get as to what Willy really wants out of life?
3. How, specifically, does Miller try to avoid writing a simple propagandist play in which capitalism is the villain and the poor protagonist is completely victimized by society? How successful is he in this effort?
4. Willy is presented as a negative figure; tired and incapable of coping with the world, he finally elects to commit suicide. Does Willy's negativism limit the dramatic effectiveness of the play in any way? Explain.
5. Miller has suggested that his play represents the tragedy of the common man. How great does Willy's tragedy seem compared with those of Oedipus and Othello?
6. At the end of the play, Biff says that he knows who he is, and Happy vows to show everybody that Willy did not die in vain. How believable are these remarks? Are they meant to give the play a final positive note? How well do they fulfill this function?
7. How does Willy's perception of himself color his perception of his sons?

8. Why is the scene in which Willy tries to get a raise so dramatically effective?
9. In what ways might young people today meet the same fate as Willy? In what ways might they avoid his fate?

A Son, Come Home: Production directed by Robert MacBeth, at American Palace Theatre, New York (1968); starring Estelle Evans, Wayne Grice, Kelly-Marie Berry, and Gary Bolling. Photograph courtesy of Martha Holmes.

ED BULLINS

A Son, Come Home

Ed Bullins, born in 1935, and raised and educated in Philadelphia, has written most of his plays either on the West Coast or in New York. After Imamu Baraka (LeRoi Jones), with whom he worked in California, Bullins is the most prolific and influential of the black dramatists; and like Baraka, he writes from a militantly black perspective. However, both playwrights see in the contemporary black experience an intense expression of the problems of contemporary man in general. Bullins' *A Son, Come Home* is not only about a young black man who is trying to set his past in order, but about all young people who feel cut off from the past because they can neither understand nor accept its codes and conventions. Bullins and Baraka both see the black experience in America today as an intensification of the crisis suffered by all who want, in this age of rapid and great change, to be individuals. Change threatens to cut people off from their heritage; and without a heritage one loses part of himself. How, Bullins asks, is it possible to avoid that loss in an age which seems to demand it? How can a person gain wholeness when his own values and those of his society seem to deny an important part of what he is?

A SON, COME HOME from *Five Plays* by Ed Bullins. Copyright © 1968 by Ed Bullins. Reprinted by permission of the author.

CAUTION: This play is fully protected, in whole, in part, or in any form under the copyright laws of the United States of America, the British Empire including the Dominion of Canada, and all other countries of the copyright union, and is subject to royalty. All rights including professional, amateur, motion picture, radio, television, recitation, and public reading, are strictly reserved. All inquiries for performance rights should be sent to Mr. Bullins' attorney, Donald C. Farber, 800 Third Avenue, New York, New York 10017.

MOTHER, *early 50's*
SON, *30 years old*
THE GIRL
THE BOY

The BOY and the GIRL wear black tights and shirts. They move the action of the play and express the MOTHER's and the SON's moods and tensions. They become various embodiments recalled from memory and history: they enact a number of personalities and move from mood to mood.

The players are Black.

SCENE. Bare stage but for two chairs positioned so as not to interfere with the actions of the BOY and the GIRL.

The MOTHER enters, sits in chair and begins to use imaginary iron and board. She hums a spiritual as she works.

MOTHER. You came three times ... Michael? It took you three times to find me at home?

(*The GIRL enters, turns and peers through the cracked, imaginary door.*)

SON'S VOICE (*offstage*). Is Mrs. Brown home?
GIRL (*an old woman*). What?
MOTHER. It shouldn't have taken you three times. I told you that I would be here by two and you should wait, Michael.

(*The SON enters, passes the GIRL and takes his seat upon the other chair.*)
(*The BOY enters, stops on other side of the imaginary door and looks through at the GIRL.*)

BOY. Is Mrs. Brown in?
GIRL. Miss Brown ain't come in yet. Come back later ... She'll be in before dark.
MOTHER. It shouldn't have taken you three times . . . You should listen to me, Michael. Standin' all that time in the cold.
SON. It wasn't cold, Mother.
MOTHER. I told you that I would be here by two and you should wait, Michael.
BOY. Please tell Mrs. Brown that her son's in town to visit her.
GIRL. You little Miss Brown's son? Well, bless the Lord. (*Calls over her shoulder.*) Hey, Mandy, do you hear that? Little Miss Brown upstairs got a son ... a great big boy ... He's come to visit her.
BOY. You'll tell her, won't you?
GIRL. Sure, I'll tell her. (*Grins and shows gums.*) I'll tell her soon she gets in.

420   A SON, COME HOME

MOTHER. Did you get cold, Michael?
SON. No, Mother. I walked around some . . . sightseeing.
BOY. I walked up Twenty-third Street toward South. I had phoned that I was coming.
MOTHER. Sightseeing? But this is your home, Michael . . . always has been.
BOY. Just before I left New York I phoned that I was taking the bus. Two hours by bus, that's all. That's all it takes. Two hours.
SON. This town seems so strange. Different than how I remember it.
MOTHER. Yes, you have been away for a good while . . . How long has it been, Michael?
BOY. Two hours down the Jersey Turnpike, the trip beginning at the New York Port Authority Terminal . . .
SON. . . . and then straight down through New Jersey to Philadelphia . . .
GIRL. . . . and home . . . Just imagine . . . little Miss Brown's got a son who's come home.
SON. Yes, home . . . an anachronism.
MOTHER. What did you say, Michael?
BOY. He said . . .
GIRL (*late teens*). What's an anachronism, Mike?
SON. Anachronism: 1: an error in chronology; *esp*: a chronological misplacing of persons, events, objects, or customs in regard to each other 2: a person or a thing that is chronologically out of place—anachronistic/*also* anachronic/*or* anachronous—anachronistically/*also* anachronously.
MOTHER. I was so glad to hear you were going to school in California.
BOY. College.
GIRL. Yes, I understand.
MOTHER. How long have you been gone, Michael?
SON. Nine years.
BOY. Nine years it's been. I wonder if she'll know me . . .
MOTHER. You've put on so much weight, son. You know that's not healthy.
GIRL (*20 years old*). And that silly beard . . . how . . .
SON. Oh . . . I'll take it off. I'm going on a diet tomorrow.
BOY. I wonder if I'll know her.
SON. You've put on some yourself, Mother.
MOTHER. Yes, the years pass. Thank the Lord.
BOY. I wonder if we've changed much.
GIRL. Yes, thank the Lord.
SON. The streets here seem so small.
MOTHER. Yes, it seems like that when you spend a little time in Los Angeles.

GIRL. I spent eighteen months there with your aunt when she was sick. She had nobody else to help her . . . she was so lonely. And you were in the service . . . away. You've always been away.

BOY. In Los Angeles the boulevards, the avenues, the streets . . .

SON. . . . are wide. Yes, they have some wide ones out West. Here, they're so small and narrow. I wonder how cars get through on both sides.

MOTHER. Why, you know how . . . we lived on Derby Street for over ten years, didn't we?

SON. Yeah, that was almost an alley.

MOTHER. Did you see much of your aunt before you left Los Angeles?

SON. What?

GIRL (*middle-aged woman*) (*to Boy*). Have you found a job yet, Michael?

MOTHER. Your aunt. My sister.

BOY. Nawh, not yet . . . Today I just walked downtown . . . quite a ways . . . this place is plenty big, ain't it?

SON. I don't see too much of Aunt Sophie.

MOTHER. But you're so much alike.

GIRL. Well, your bags are packed and are sitting outside the door.

BOY. My bags?

MOTHER. You shouldn't be that way, Michael. You shouldn't get too far away from your family.

SON. Yes, Mother.

BOY. But I don't have any money. I had to walk downtown today. That's how much money I have. I've only been here a week.

GIRL. I packed your bags, Michael.

MOTHER. You never can tell when you'll need or want your family, Michael.

SON. That's right, Mother.

MOTHER. You and she are so much alike.

BOY. Well, goodbye, Aunt Sophie.

GIRL.

(*Silence.*)

MOTHER. All that time in California and you hardly saw your aunt. My baby sister.

BOY. Tsk tsk tsk.

SON. I'm sorry, Mother.

MOTHER. In the letters I'd get from both of you there'd be no mention of the other. All these years. Did you see her again?

SON. Yes.

GIRL (*on telephone*). Michael? Michael who? . . . Ohhh . . . Bernice's boy.

MOTHER. You didn't tell me about this, did you?
SON. No, I didn't.
BOY. Hello, Aunt Sophie. How are you?
GIRL. I'm fine, Michael. How are you? You're looking well.
BOY. I'm getting on okay.
MOTHER. I prayed for you.
SON. Thank you.
MOTHER. Thank the Lord, Michael.
BOY. Got me a job working for the city.
GIRL. You did now.
BOY. Yes, I've brought you something.
GIRL. What's this, Michael . . . ohhh . . . it's money.
BOY. It's for the week I stayed with you.
GIRL. Fifty dollars. But, Michael, you didn't have to.
MOTHER. Are you still writing that radical stuff, Michael?
SON. Radical?
MOTHER. Yes . . . that stuff you write and send me all the time in those little books.
SON. My poetry, Mother?
MOTHER. Yes, that's what I'm talking about.
SON. No.
MOTHER. Praise the Lord, son. Praise the Lord. Didn't seem like anything I had read in school.
BOY (*on telephone*). Aunt Sophie? . . . Aunt Sophie? . . . It's me, Michael . . .
GIRL. Michael
BOY. Yes . . . Michael . . .
GIRL. Oh . . . Michael . . . yes . . .
BOY. I'm in jail, Aunt Sophie . . . I got picked up for drunk driving.
GIRL. You did . . . how awful . . .
MOTHER. When are you going to get your hair cut, Michael?
BOY. Aunt Sophie . . . will you please come down and sign my bail. I've got the money . . . I just got paid yesterday . . . They're holding more than enough for me . . . but the law says that someone has to sign for it.
MOTHER. You look almost like a hoodlum, Michael.
BOY. All you need to do is come down and sign . . . and I can get out.
MOTHER. What you tryin' to be . . . a savage or something. Are you keeping out of trouble, Michael?
GIRL. Ohhh . . . Michael . . . I'm sorry but I can't do nothin' like that . . .
BOY. But all you have to do is sign . . . I've got the money and everything.
GIRL. I'm sorry . . . I can't stick my neck out.

Boy. But, Aunt Sophie . . . if I don't get back to work I'll lose my job and everything . . . please . . .

Girl. I'm sorry, Michael . . . I can't stick my neck out . . . I have to go now . . . Is there anyone I can call?

Boy. No.

Girl. I could call your mother. She wouldn't mind if I reversed the charges on her, would she? I don't like to run my bills up.

Boy. No, thanks.

Mother. You and your aunt are so much alike.

Son. Yes, Mother. Our birthdays are in the same month.

Mother. Yes, that year was so hot . . . so hot and I was carrying you . . . (*as the* Mother *speaks the* Boy *comes over and takes her by the hand and leads her from the chair, and they stroll around the stage, arm in arm. The* Girl *accompanies them and she and the* Boy *enact scenes from the* Mother's *mind.*) . . . carrying you, Michael . . . and you were such a big baby . . . kicked all the time. But I was happy. Happy that I was having a baby of my own . . . I worked as long as I could and bought you everything you might need . . . diapers . . . and bottles . . . and your own spoon . . . and even toys . . . and even books . . . And it was so hot in Philadelphia that year . . . Your Aunt Sophie used to come over and we'd go for walks . . . sometimes up on the avenue . . . I was living in West Philly then . . . in that old terrible section they called "The Bottom." That's where I met your father.

Girl. You're such a fool, Bernice. No nigger . . . man or boy's . . . ever going to do a thing to me like that.

Mother. Everything's going to be all right, Sophia.

Girl. But what is he going to do? How are you going to take care of a baby by yourself?

Mother. Everything's going to all right, Sophia. I'll manage.

Girl. You'll manage? How? Have you talked about marriage?

Mother. Oh, please, Sophia!

Girl. What do you mean "please"? Have you?

Mother. I just can't. He might think . . .

Girl. Think! That dirty nigger better think. He better think before he really messes up. And you better too. You got his baby comin' on. What are you going to do?

Mother. I don't know . . . I don't know what I can do.

Girl. Is he still tellin' you those lies about . . .

Mother. They're not lies.

Girl. Haaaa . . .

Mother. They're not.

Girl. Some smooth-talkin' nigger comes up from Georgia and tell you he escaped from the chain gang and had to change his name so he can't get married 'cause they might find out . . . What kinda shit is that, Bernice?

MOTHER. Please, Sophia. Try and understand. He loves me. I can't hurt him.

GIRL. Loves you . . . and puts you through this?

MOTHER. Please . . . I'll talk to him . . . Give me a chance.

GIRL. It's just a good thing you got a family, Bernice. It's just a good thing. You know that, don't cha?

MOTHER. Yes . . . yes, I do . . . but please don't say anything to him.

SON. I've only seen my father about a half dozen times that I remember, Mother. What was he like?

MOTHER. Down in The Bottom . . . that's where I met your father. I was young and hinkty then. Had big pretty brown legs and a small waist. Everybody used to call me Bernie . . . and me and my sister would go to Atlantic City on the weekends and work as waitresses in the evenings and sit all afternoon on the black part of the beach at Boardwalk and Atlantic . . . getting blacker . . . and having the times of our lives. Your father probably still lives down in The Bottom . . . perched over some bar down there . . . drunk to the world . . . I can see him now . . . He had good white teeth then . . . not how they turned later when he started in drinkin' that wine and wouldn't stop . . . he was so nice then.

BOY. Awwww, listen, kid. I got my problems too.

GIRL. But Andy . . . I'm six months gone . . . and you ain't done nothin'.

BOY. Well, what can I do?

GIRL. Don't talk like that . . . What can you do? . . . You know what you can do.

BOY. You mean marry you? Now lissen, sweetheart . . .

GIRL. But what about our baby?

BOY. Your baby.

GIRL. Don't talk like that! It took more than me to get him.

BOY. Well . . . look . . . I'll talk to you later, kid. I got to go to work now.

GIRL. That's what I got to talk to you about too, Andy. I need some money.

BOY. Money! Is somethin' wrong with your head, woman? I ain't got no money.

GIRL. But I can't work much longer, Andy. You got to give me some money. Andy . . . you just gotta.

BOY. Woman . . . all I got to *ever* do is die and go to hell.

GIRL. Well, you gonna do that, Andy. You sho are . . . you know that, don't you? . . . You know that.

MOTHER. . . . Yes, you are, man. Praise the Lord. We all are . . . All of us . . . even though he ain't come for you yet to make you pay. Maybe he's waitin' for us to go together so I can be a witness to the retribution that's handed down. A witness to all that He'll bestow upon your sinner's head . . . A witness! . . . That's what I am, Andy! Do you hear me? . . . A witness!

SON. Mother . . . what's wrong? What's the matter?

MOTHER. Thank the Lord that I am not blinded and will see the fulfillment of divine . . .

SON. Mother!

MOTHER. Oh! . . . is something wrong, Michael?

SON. You're shouting and walking around . . .

MOTHER. Oh . . . it's nothing, son. I'm just feeling the power of the Lord.

SON. Oh . . . is there anything I can get you, Mother?

MOTHER. No, nothing at all. (*She sits again and irons.*)

SON. Where's your kitchen? . . . I'll get you some coffee . . . the way you like it. I bet I still remember how to fix it.

MOTHER. Michael . . . I don't drink anything like that no more.

SON. No?

MOTHER. Not since I joined the service of the Lord.

SON. Yeah? . . . Well, do you mind if I get myself a cup?

MOTHER. Why, I don't have a kitchen. All my meals are prepared for me.

SON. Oh . . . I thought I was having dinner with you.

MOTHER. No. There's nothing like that here.

SON. Well, could I take you out to a restaurant? . . . Remember how we used to go out all the time and eat? I've never lost my habit of liking to eat out. Remember . . . we used to come down to this part of town and go to restaurants. They used to call it home cooking then . . . now, at least where I been out West and up in Harlem . . . we call it soul food. I bet we could find a nice little restaurant not four blocks from here, Mother. Remember that old man's place we used to go to on Nineteenth and South? I bet he's dead now . . . but . . .

MOTHER. I don't even eat out no more, Michael.

SON. No?

MOTHER. Sometimes I take a piece of holy bread to work . . . or some fruit . . . if it's been blessed by my Spiritual Mother.

SON. I see.

MOTHER. Besides . . . we have a prayer meeting tonight.

SON. On Friday?

MOTHER. Every night. You'll have to be going soon.

SON. Oh.

MOTHER. You're looking well.

SON. Thank you.

MOTHER. But you look tired.
SON. Do I?
MOTHER. Yes, those rings around your eyes might never leave. Your father had them.
SON. Did he?
MOTHER. Yes... and cowlicks... deep cowlicks on each side of his head.
SON. Yes... I remember.
MOTHER. Do you?

(*The* BOY *and the* GIRL *take crouching positions behind and in front of them. They are in a streetcar. The* BOY *behind the* MOTHER *and* SON, *the* GIRL *across the aisle, a passenger.*)

MOTHER (*young woman*) (*to the* BOY). Keep your damn hands off him, Andy!
BOY (*chuckles*). Awww, c'mon... Bernie. I ain't seen him since he was in the crib.
MOTHER. And you wouldn't have seen neither of us... if I had anything to do with it... Ohhh... why did I get on this trolley?
BOY. C'mon... Bernie... don't be so stuckup.
MOTHER. Don't even talk to us... and stop reaching after him.
BOY. Awww... c'mon... Bernie. Let me look at him.
MOTHER. Leave us alone. Look... people are looking at us.

(*The* GIRL *across the aisle has been peeking at the trio but looks toward front at the mention of herself.*)

BOY. Hey, big boy... do you know who I am?
MOTHER. Stop it, Andy! Stop it, I say... Mikie... don't pay any attention to him... you hear?
BOY. Hey, big boy... know who I am?... I'm your daddy. Hey, there...
MOTHER. Shut up... shut up, Andy... you nothin' to us.
BOY. Where you livin' at... Bernie? Let me come on by and see the little guy, huh?
MOTHER. No! You're not comin' near us... ever... you hear?
BOY. But I'm his father... look... Bernie... I've been an ass the way I've acted but...
MOTHER. He ain't got no father.
BOY. Oh, come off that nonsense, woman.
MOTHER. Mikie ain't got no father... his father's dead... you hear?
BOY. Dead?
MOTHER. Yes, dead. My son's father's dead.
BOY. What you talkin' about?... He's the spittin' image of me.

MOTHER. Go away . . . leave us alone, Andrew.

BOY. See there . . . he's got the same name as me. His first name is Michael after your father . . . and Andrew after me.

MOTHER. No, stop that, you hear?

BOY. Michael Andrew . . .

MOTHER. You never gave him no name . . . his name is Brown . . . Brown. The same as mine . . . and my sister's . . . and my daddy . . . You never gave him nothin' . . . and you're dead . . . go away and get buried.

BOY. You know that trouble I'm in . . . I got a wife down there, Bernie. I don't care about her . . . what could I do?

MOTHER (*rises, pulling up the* SON). We're leavin' . . . don't you try and follow us . . . you hear, Andy? C'mon . . . Mikie . . . watch your step now.

BOY. Well . . . bring him around my job . . . you know where I work. That's all . . . bring him around on payday.

MOTHER (*leaving*). We don't need anything from you . . . I'm working . . . just leave us alone.

(*The* BOY *turns to the* GIRL.)

BOY (*shrugs*). That's the way it goes . . . I guess. Ships passing on the trolley car . . . Hey . . . don't I know you from up around 40th and Market?

(*The* GIRL *turns away*.)

SON. Yeah . . . I remember him. He always had liquor on his breath.

MOTHER. Yes . . . he did. I'm glad that stuff ain't got me no more . . . Thank the Lord.

GIRL (*35 years old*). You want to pour me another drink, Michael?

BOY (*15 years old*). You drink too much, Mother.

GIRL. Not as much as some other people I know.

BOY. Well, me and the guys just get short snorts, Mother. But you really hide some port.

GIRL. Don't forget you talkin' to your mother. You gettin' more like your father every day.

BOY. Is that why you like me so much?

GIRL (*grins drunkenly*). Oh, hush up now, boy . . . and pour me a drink.

BOY. There's enough here for me too.

GIRL. That's okay . . . when Will comes in he'll bring something.

SON. How is Will, Mother?

MOTHER. I don't know . . . haven't seen Will in years.

SON. Mother.

MOTHER. Yes, Michael.

Son. Why you and Will never got married? . . . You stayed together for over ten years.
Mother. Oh, don't ask me questions like that, Michael.
Son. But why not?
Mother. It's just none of your business.
Son. But you could be married now . . . not alone in this room . . .
Mother. Will had a wife and child in Chester . . . you know that.
Son. He could have gotten a divorce, Mother . . . Why . . .
Mother. Because he just didn't . . . that's why.
Son. You never hear from him?
Mother. Last I heard . . . Will had cancer.
Son. Oh, he did.
Mother. Yes.
Son. Why didn't you tell me? . . . You could have written.
Mother. Why?
Son. So I could have known.
Mother. So you could have known? Why?
Son. Because Will was like a father to me . . . the only one I've really known.
Mother. A father? And you chased him away as soon as you got big enough.
Son. Don't say that, Mother.
Mother. You made me choose between you and Will.
Son. Mother.
Mother. The quarrels you had with him . . . the mean tricks you used to play . . . the lies you told to your friends about Will . . . He wasn't much . . . when I thought I had a sense of humor I us'ta call him just plain Will. But we was his family.
Son. Mother, listen.
Mother. And you drove him away . . . and he didn't lift a hand to stop you.
Son. Listen, Mother.
Mother. As soon as you were big enough you did all that you could to get me and Will separated.
Son. Listen.
Mother. All right, Michael . . . I'm listening.

(*Pause.*)

Son. Nothing. (*Pause. Lifts an imaginary object.*) Is this your tambourine?
Mother. Yes.
Son. Do you play it?

ED BULLINS

MOTHER. Yes.
SON. Well?
MOTHER. Everything I do in the service of the Lord I do as well as He allows.
SON. You play it at your meetings.
MOTHER. Yes, I do. We celebrate the life He has bestowed upon us.
SON. I guess that's where I get it from.
MOTHER. Did you say something, Michael?
SON. Yes. My musical ability.
MOTHER. Oh . . . you've begun taking your piano lessons again?
SON. No . . . I was never any good at that.
MOTHER. Yes, three different teachers and you never got past the tenth lesson.
SON. You have a good memory, Mother.
MOTHER. Sometimes, son. Sometimes.
SON. I play an electric guitar in a combo.
MOTHER. You do? That's nice.
SON. That's why I'm in New York. We got a good break and came East.
MOTHER. That's nice, Michael.
SON. I was thinking that Sunday I could rent a car and come down to get you and drive you up to see our show. You'll get back in plenty of time to rest for work Monday.
MOTHER. No, I'm sorry. I can't do that.
SON. But you would like it, Mother. We could have dinner up in Harlem, then go down and . . .
MOTHER. I don't do anything like that any more, Michael.
SON. You mean you wouldn't come to see me play even if I were appearing here in Philly?
MOTHER. That's right, Michael. I wouldn't come. I'm past all that.
SON. Oh, I see.
MOTHER. Yes, thank the Lord.
SON. But it's my life, Mother.
MOTHER. Good . . . then you have something to live for.
SON. Yes.
MOTHER. Well, you're a man now, Michael . . . I can no longer live it for you. Do the best with what you have.
SON. Yes . . . I will, Mother.
GIRL'S VOICE (*off stage*). Sister Brown . . . Sister Brown . . . hello.
MOTHER (*uneasy; peers at watch*). Oh . . . it's Mother Ellen . . . I didn't know it was so late.
GIRL (*enters*). Sister Brown . . . how are you this evening?
MOTHER. Oh, just fine, Mother.
GIRL. Good. It's nearly time for dinner.

MOTHER. Oh, yes, I know.
GIRL. We don't want to keep the others waiting at meeting ... do we?
MOTHER. No, we don't.
GIRL (*self-assured*). Hello, son.
SON. Hello.
MOTHER. Oh, Mother ... Mother ...
GIRL. Yes, Sister Brown, what is it?
MOTHER. Mother ... Mother ... this is ... this is ... (*pause*) ... this is ...
SON. Hello, I'm Michael. How are you?
MOTHER (*relieved*). Yes, Mother ... This is Michael ... my son.
GIRL. Why, hello, Michael. I've heard so much about you from your mother. She prays for you daily.
SON (*embarrassed*). Oh ... good.
GIRL (*briskly*). Well ... I have to be off to see about the others.
MOTHER. Yes, Mother Ellen.
GIRL (*as she exits; chuckles*). Have to tell everyone that you won't be keeping us waiting Bernice.

(*Silence.*)

SON. Well, I guess I better be going, Mother.
MOTHER. Yes.
SON. I'll write.
MOTHER. Please do.
SON. I will.
MOTHER. You're looking well ... Thank the Lord.
SON. Thank you, so are you, Mother. (*He moves toward her and hesitates.*)
MOTHER. You're so much like your aunt. Give her my best ... won't you?
SON. Yes, I will, Mother.
MOTHER. Take care of yourself, son.
SON. Yes, Mother. I will. (*The* SON *exits. The* MOTHER *stands looking after him as the lights go slowly down to ...*)

Blackness

DISCUSSION

For the members of some contemporary groups, the problem of finding an identity, a sense of self, has become crucial. Many young people, many women, and many members of ethnic minorities have found themselves profoundly torn by the discrepancies between their image of themselves and the image dictated for them by society. Young blacks are finding this conflict to be particularly intense. They sense that their own identities cannot be adequately defined by either the standards of the white world or those of their parents. White standards are considered inadequate because they are foreign to the black culture and because they do not take into account the continuing effects of racial discrimination. The standards of the older generation of blacks are also often considered inadequate because of the extent to which they reflect white codes and values. Faced with this situation, many young blacks feel driven either to a militant assertion of their uniqueness or to a retreat into subjectivity, a refusal to communicate with an outside world that appears neither willing nor able to understand them.

The situation can be particularly difficult for the black writer. For, although he wishes to assert his uniqueness, he must do so using language, and language is an essentially traditional medium. Words mean not only what their writer wants them to mean but also what they have meant to other generations of readers and writers. This is especially true for a dramatist; he writes in a medium intended to reach and be understood by a fairly wide public. Poems can be written for a single reader, but plays are generally written for groups. The problem for the black playwright is finding a way to use traditional language without undermining the uniqueness of his vision. A number of black dramatists have made this problem the subject of their dramas. They have taken as their theme the exploration of the conflict between the public demand for conformity to traditional language and forms of drama and their private sense that their unique experience and identity does not yield to traditional forms of language and art. Ed Bullins' one-act play, *A Son, Come Home,* is such a drama. On a literal level, the play is about a son who returns home to visit his mother in the hope of establishing some kind of creative relationship with her. But everything she says evokes in him a recognition of how destructive his family relationships have always been; every time he tries to reach out to her, he discovers afresh how little she understands or cares about him. Their efforts at communication fail, and he again drifts into the darkness.

On this literal level, the play seems to concern the son's discovery that he cannot depend on his past for his identity. But the devices Bullins uses to dramatize this conflict show a situation far more complex than a simple case of alienation. When the play begins, the relationship between the son and the mother is already so troubled that language is no longer a means by which they can communicate. The son is bitterly resentful of his fatherless state, of his mother's failure to tell him of his surrogate father's illness, of his aunt's failure to grant him even common concern. But the conventions of mother–son conversation demand that he speak to his mother with respect, that he remain silent about her sister's crass selfishness, that he avoid overtly blaming his mother for his isolation. So on an overt level, he can only make polite small-talk with his mother, talk that leads nowhere and only serves to mask his resentment.

The mother finds the son's presence painful. It reminds her of a past she considers sinful, a past from which she is trying to escape by immersing herself in a fanatical spiritualism. She cannot talk with her son without destroying the fragile illusion of religious purity that allows her to avoid facing her past and its effect on her son. So she uses pious excuses to avoid her son's overtures. Instead of talking with him, she joins her spiritualist group and prays for him. The literal discussions in this play do not serve, like those in Ibsen, to uncover truth, nor, like those in Strindberg, to expose primitive conflicts, nor even, like those in Giraudoux, to give fantastic form to painful realities. The literal discussions here serve merely to stifle further conversation. The polite conversation contradicts the intense responses buried in the consciousnesses of both mother and son.

It is this contradiction that Bullins wants to explore. In order to get at the double nature of the conversation—what is said versus what is felt—he includes on stage two actors who represent the alter egos of the two main characters. These two actors, shifting from one role to another, act out the inner conflicts of the main characters, their unspoken memories, the contradictions between the surface of good manners and the underlying realities of hurt and destruction. By allowing the memories to be acted out as the conversations take place, Bullins lets us experience the conflicts of the characters and allows us to feel the pressures that force both mother and son toward silence and escape. The problem, as we come to understand it, is not that the two characters want to remain isolated, but rather that there are no civilized language conventions that will permit either of them to speak without destroying the other. Without language, neither of them can discover a way to make the past a creative part of the present. Because both are shut off from exploring a crucial part of their past, neither of them will ever achieve a full sense of self.

A Son, Come Home, then, is a study of the relationship between honest communication and a full sense of identity. Moreover, although his characters cannot communicate, by resorting to fresh, nonrealistic conventions,

Bullins bridges the gap between his unique vision and the audience's need for publicly understandable language.

THEME AND DISCUSSION QUESTIONS

1. What does "coming home" mean to the son?
2. How does the attitude of each character he encounters serve to alienate the son more from his past?
3. The son is trying to communicate with his mother. But does he really have an imaginative understanding of her feelings? Cite as many details as you can to explain your answer.
4. In what ways does Bullins count on his audience's familiarity with film conventions to help them interpret the stage action?
5. Why does Bullins use a bare stage for his play? How would a conventional stage set change the play's effectiveness?
6. Like a great many other experimental writers today, Bullins presents us with a paradox: he tells us and seems to firmly believe that language is incapable of communicating at the deepest levels, and yet he uses language to communicate precisely what he says it cannot. How, specifically, does Bullins use language to overcome the corruption of language itself? You may wish to compare his approach to this problem with those taken by Imamu Baraka in *Dutchman* and Eugène Ionesco in *The Bald Soprano*.
7. Some plays by black writers seem to be a means of expressing outrage at the treatment blacks have received at the hands of whites. In what ways does this Bullins play seem to have a more universal message?
8. Select one important experimental technique that Bullins uses and show how it functions to express the play's main conflict.
9. How is the son's problem like those of sons (and daughters) you know?

STEPHEN CRANE

"The Bride Comes to Yellow Sky"

Stephen Crane was born in 1871 in Newark, New Jersey, the youngest of fourteen children. He spent his childhood in New Jersey and briefly attended two Eastern universities (Lafayette and Syracuse) before deciding, in 1891, to leave school and become a professional writer. In his short life, Crane published two major novels—*Maggie, A Girl of the Streets* (1893) and *The Red Badge of Courage* (1895)—two volumes of short stories, and two volumes of poetry; he died of tuberculosis in 1900. Crane's writing is suffused with the sense that what a human being wants is always controlled and conditioned by forces outside of him, such forces as nature, government, and society. *The Red Badge of Courage*, for example, is the story of a young Civil War soldier who comes of age at the Battle of Chancelorsville, when he realizes that, personally insignificant, he is caught in impersonal forces that may destroy him. "The Bride Comes to Yellow Sky," the Crane story reprinted in this collection, also deals with the encroachment of social forces on the individual—but in a humorous way. Indeed, it is widely recognized as one of the greatest humorous short stories in American literature.

THE BRIDE COMES TO YELLOW SKY From *Stephen Crane: An Omnibus,* edited by R. W. Stallman (New York: Alfred A. Knopf, Inc., 1952).

I

The great pullman was whirling onward with such dignity of motion that a glance from the window seemed simply to prove that the plains of Texas were pouring eastward. Vast flats of green grass, dull-hued spaces of mesquit and cactus, little groups of frame houses, woods of light and tender trees, all were sweeping into the east, sweeping over the horizon, a precipice.

A newly married pair had boarded this coach at San Antonio. The man's face was reddened from many days in the wind and sun, and a direct result of his new black clothes was that his brick-colored hands were constantly performing in a most conscious fashion. From time to time he looked down respectfully at his attire. He sat with a hand on each knee, like a man waiting in a barber's shop. The glances he devoted to other passengers were furtive and shy.

The bride was not pretty, nor was she very young. She wore a dress of blue cashmere, with small reservations of velvet here and there, and with steel buttons abounding. She continually twisted her head to regard her puff sleeves, very stiff, straight, and high. They embarrassed her. It was quite apparent that she had cooked, and that she expected to cook, dutifully. The blushes caused by the careless scrutiny of some passengers as she had entered the car were strange to see upon this plain, under-class countenance, which was drawn in placid, almost emotionless lines.

They were evidently very happy. "Ever been in a parlor car before?" he asked, smiling with delight.

"No," she answered; "I never was. It's fine, ain't it?"

"Great! And then after a while we'll go forward to the diner, and get a big lay-out. Finest meal in the world. Charge a dollar."

"Oh, do they?" cried the bride. "Charge a dollar? Why, that's too much—for us—ain't it Jack?"

"Not this trip, anyhow," he answered bravely. "We're going to go the whole thing."

Later he explained to her about the trains. "You see, it's a thousand miles from one end of Texas to the other; and this train runs right across it, and never stops but four times." He had the pride of an owner. He pointed out to her the dazzling fittings of the coach; and in truth her eyes opened wider as she contemplated the sea-green figured velvet, the shining brass, silver, and glass, the wood that gleamd as darkly brilliant as the surface of a pool of oil. At one end a bronze figure sturdily held a support for a separated chamber, and at convenient places on the ceiling were frescoes in olive and silver.

To the minds of the pair, their surroundings reflected the glory of their marriage that morning in San Antonio; this was the environment of their new estate; and the man's face in particular beamed with an elation that made him appear ridiculous to the Negro porter. This individual at times surveyed them from afar with an amused and superior grin. On other occasions he bullied them with skill in ways that did not make it exactly plain to them that they were being bullied. He subtly used all the manners of the most unconquerable kind of snobbery. He oppressed them; but of this oppression they had small knowledge, and they speedily forgot that infrequently a number of travelers covered them with stares of derisive enjoyment. Historically there was supposed to be something infinitely humorous in their situation.

"We are due in Yellow Sky at 3:42," he said, looking tenderly into her eyes.

"Oh, are we?" she said, as if she had not been aware of it. To evince surprise at her husband's statement was part of her wifely amiability. She took from a pocket a little silver watch; and as she held it before her, and stared at it with a frown of attention, the new husband's face shone.

"I bought it in San Anton' from a friend of mine," he told her gleefully.

"It's seventeen minutes past twelve," she said, looking up at him with a kind of shy and clumsy coquetry. A passenger, noting this play, grew excessively sardonic, and winked at himself in one of the numerous mirrors.

At last they went to the dining car. Two rows of Negro waiters, in glowing white suits, surveyed their entrance with the interest, and also the equanimity, of men who have been forewarned. The pair fell to the lot of a waiter who happened to feel pleasure in steering them through their meal. He viewed them with the manner of a fatherly pilot, his countenance radiant with benevolence. The patronage, entwined with the ordinary deference, was not plain to them. And yet, as they returned to their coach, they showed in their faces a sense of escape.

To the left, miles down a long purple slope, was a little ribbon of mist where moved the keening Rio Grande. The train was approaching it at an angle, and the apex was Yellow Sky. Presently it was apparent that, as the distance from Yellow Sky grew shorter, the husband became commensurately restless. His brick-red hands were more insistent in their prominence. Occasionally he was even rather absent-minded and faraway when the bride leaned forward and addressed him.

As a matter of truth, Jack Potter was beginning to find the shadow of a deed weigh upon him like a leaden slab. He, the town marshal of Yellow Sky, a man known, liked, and feared in his corner, a prominent person, had gone to San Antonio to meet a girl he believed he loved, and there, after the usual prayers, had actually induced her to marry him, without consulting Yellow Sky for any part of the transaction. He was now bringing his bride before an innocent and unsuspecting community.

Of course people in Yellow Sky married as it pleased them, in accordance with a general custom; but such was Potter's thought of his duty to his friends, or of their idea of his duty, or of an unspoken form which does not control men in these matters, that he felt he was heinous. He had committed an extraordinary crime. Face to face with this girl in San Antonio, and spurred by his sharp impulse, he had gone headlong over all the social hedges. At San Antonio he was like a man hidden in the dark. A knife to sever any friendly duty, any form, was easy to his hand in that remote sky. But the hour of Yellow Sky—the hour of daylight—was approaching.

He knew full well that his marriage was an important thing to his town. It could only be exceeded by the burning of the new hotel. His friends could not forgive him. Frequently he had reflected on the advisability of telling them by telegraph, but a new cowardice had been upon him. He feared to do it. And now the train was hurrying him toward a scene of amazement, glee, and reproach. He glanced out of the window at the line of haze swinging slowly in toward the train.

Yellow Sky had a kind of brass band, which played painfully, to the delight of the populace. He laughed without heart as he thought of it. If the citizens could dream of his prospective arrival with his bride, they would parade the band at the station and escort them, amid cheers and laughing congratulations, to his adobe home.

He resolved that he would use all the devices of speed and plainscraft in making the journey from the station to his house. Once within that safe citadel, he could issue some sort of vocal bulletin, and then not go among the citizens until they had time to wear off a little of their enthusiasm.

The bride looked anxiously at him. "What's worrying you, Jack?"

He laughed again. "I'm not worrying, girl; I'm only thinking of Yellow Sky."

She flushed in comprehension.

A sense of mutual guilt invaded their minds and developed a finer tenderness. They looked at each other with eyes softly aglow. But Potter often laughed the same nervous laugh; the flush upon the bride's face seemed quite permanent.

The traitor to the feelings of Yellow Sky narrowly watched the speeding landscape. "We're nearly there," he said.

Presently the porter came and announced the proximity of Potter's home. He held a brush in his hand, and, with all his airy superiority gone, he brushed Potter's new clothes as the latter slowly turned this way and that way. Potter fumbled out a coin and gave it to the porter, as he had seen others do. It was a heavy and muscle-bound business, as that of a man shoeing his first horse.

The porter took their bag, and as the train began to slow they moved forward to the hooded platform of the car. Presently the two engines and their long string of coaches rushed into the station of Yellow Sky.

"They have to take water here," said Potter, from a constricted throat and in mournful cadence, as one announcing death. Before the train stopped his eye had swept the length of the platform, and he was glad and astonished to see there was none upon it but the station agent, who, with a slightly hurried and anxious air, was walking toward the water tanks. When the train had halted, the porter alighted first, and placed in position a little temporary step.

"Come on, girl," said Potter hoarsely. As he helped her down they each laughed on a false note. He took the bag from the Negro, and bade his wife cling to his arm. As they slunk rapidly away, his hangdog glance perceived that they were unloading two trunks, and also that the station agent, far ahead near the baggage car, had turned and was running toward him, making gestures. He laughed, and groaned as he laughed, when he noted the first effect of his marital bliss upon Yellow Sky. He gripped his wife's arm firmly to his side, and they fled. Behind them the porter stood, chuckling fatuously.

II

The California express on the Southern Railway was due at Yellow Sky in twenty-one minutes. There were six men at the bar of the Weary Gentleman saloon. One was a drummer who talked a great deal and rapidly; three were Texans who did not care to talk at that time; and two were Mexican sheep-herders, who did not talk as a general practice in the Weary Gentleman saloon. The barkeeper's dog lay on the boardwalk that crossed in front of the door. His head was on his paws, and he glanced drowsily here and there with the constant vigilance of a dog that is kicked on occasion. Across the sandy street were some vivid green grass-plots, so wonderful in appearance, amid the sands that burned near them in a blazing sun, that they caused a doubt in the mind. They exactly resembled the grass mats used to represent lawns on the stage. At the cooler end of the railway station, a man without a coat sat in a tilted chair and smoked his pipe. The fresh-cut bank of the Rio Grande circled near the town, and there could be seen beyond it a great plum-colored plain of mesquit.

Save for the busy drummer and his companions in the saloon, Yellow Sky was dozing. The newcomer leaned gracefully upon the bar, and recited many tales with the confidence of a bard who has come upon a new field.

"—and at the moment that the old man fell downstairs with the bureau in his arms, the old woman was coming up with two scuttles of coal, and of course—"

The drummer's tale was interrupted by a young man who suddenly appeared in the open door. He cried: "Scratchy Wilson's drunk, and has turned loose with both hands." The two Mexicans at once set down their glasses and faded out of the rear entrance of the saloon.

The drummer, innocent and jocular, answered: "All right, old man. S'pose he has? Come in and have a drink, anyhow."

But the information had made such an obvious cleft in every skull in the room that the drummer was obliged to see its importance. All had become instantly solemn. "Say," said he, mystified, "what is this?" His three companions made the introductory gesture of eloquent speech; but the young man at the door forestalled them.

"It means, my friend," he answered, as he came into the saloon, "that for the next two hours this town won't be a health resort."

The barkeeper went to the door, and locked and barred it; reaching out of the window, he pulled in heavy wooden shutters, and barred them. Immediately a solemn, chapel-like gloom was upon the place. The drummer was looking from one to another.

"But say," he cried out, "what is this, anyhow? You don't mean there is going to be a gun fight?"

"Don't know whether there'll be a fight or not," answered one man, grimly, "but there'll be some shootin'—some good shootin'."

The young man who had warned them waved his hand. "Oh, there'll be a fight fast enough, if any one wants it. Anybody can get a fight out there in the street. There's a fight just waiting."

The drummer seemed to be swayed between the interest of a foreigner and a perception of personal danger.

"What did you say his name was?" he asked.

"Scratchy Wilson," they answered in chorus.

"And will he kill anybody? What are you going to do? Does this happen often? Does he rampage around like this once a week or so? Can he break in that door?"

"No; he can't break down that door," replied the barkeeper. "He's tried it three times. But when he comes you'd better lay down on the floor, stranger. He's dead sure to shoot at it, and a bullet may come through."

Thereafter the drummer kept a strict eye upon the door. The time had not yet been called for him to hug the floor, but, as a minor precaution, he sidled near to the wall. "Will he kill anybody?" he said again.

The men laughed low and scornfully at the question.

"He's out to shoot, and he's out for trouble. Don't see any good in experimentin' with him."

"But what do you do in a case like this? What do you do?"

A man responded: "Why, he and Jack Potter—"

"But," in chorus the other men interrupted, "Jack Potter's in San Anton'."

"Well, who is he? What's he got to do with it?"

"Oh, he's the town marshal. He goes out and fights Scratchy when he gets on one of these tears."

"Wow!" said the drummer, mopping his brow. "Nice job he's got."

The voices had toned away to mere whisperings. The drummer wished to ask further questions, which were born of an increasing anxiety and bewilderment; but when he attempted them, the men merely looked at him in irritation and motioned him to remain silent. A tense waiting hush was upon them. In the deep shadows of the room their eyes shone as they listened for sounds from the street. One man made three gestures at the barkeeper; and the latter, moving like a ghost, handed him a glass and a bottle. The man poured a full glass of whisky, and set down the bottle noiselessly. He gulped the whisky in a swallow, and turned again toward the door in immovable silence. The drummer saw that the barkeeper, without a sound, had taken a Winchester from beneath the bar. Later he saw this individual beckoning to him, so he tiptoed across the room.

"You better come with me back of the bar."

"No, thanks," said the drummer, perspiring; "I'd rather be where I can make a break for the back door."

Whereupon the man of bottles made a kindly but peremptory gesture. The drummer obeyed it, and, finding himself seated on a box with his head below the level of the bar, calm was laid upon his soul at sight of various zinc and copper fittings that bore a resemblance to armor plate. The barkeeper took a seat comfortably upon an adjacent box.

"You see," he whispered, "this here Scratchy Wilson is a wonder with a gun—a perfect wonder; and when he goes on the war-trail, we hunt our holes—naturally. He's about the last one of the old gang that used to hang out along the river here. He's a terror when he's drunk. When he's sober he's all right—kind of simple—wouldn't hurt a fly—nicest fellow in town. But when he's drunk—whoo!"

There were periods of stillness. "I wish Jack Potter was back from San Anton'," said the barkeeper. "He shot Wilson up once—in the leg—and he would sail in and pull out the kinks in this thing."

Presently they heard from a distance the sound of a shot, followed by three wild yowls. It instantly removed a bond from the men in the darkened saloon. There was a shuffling of feet. They looked at each other. "Here he comes," they said.

III

A man in a maroon-colored flannel shirt, which had been purchased for purposes of decoration, and made principally by some Jewish women on the East Side of New York, rounded a corner and walked into the middle of the main street of Yellow Sky. In either hand the man held a long, heavy, blue-black revolver. Often he yelled, and these cries rang through a semblance of a deserted village, shrilly flying over the roofs in a volume that seemed to have no relation to the ordinary vocal strength of a man. It was as if the surrounding stillness formed the arch of a tomb over him. These cries of ferocious challenge rang against walls of silence. And his boots had red tops with gilded imprints, of the kind beloved in winter by little sledding boys on the hillsides of New England.

The man's face flamed in a rage begot of whisky. His eyes, rolling, and yet keen for ambush, hunted the still doorways and windows. He walked with the creeping movement of the midnight cat. As it occurred to him, he roared menacing information. The long revolvers in his hands were as easy as straws; they were moved with an electric swiftness. The little fingers of each hand played sometimes in a musician's way. Plain from the low collar of the shirt, the cords of his neck straightened and sank, straightened and sank, as passion moved him. The only sounds were his terrible invitations. The calm adobes preserved their demeanor at the passing of this small thing in the middle of the street.

There was no offer of fight—no offer of fight. The man called to the sky. There were no attractions. He bellowed and fumed and swayed his revolvers here and everywhere.

The dog of the barkeeper of the Weary Gentleman saloon had not appreciated the advance of events. He yet lay dozing in front of his master's door. At sight of the dog, the man paused and raised his revolver humorously. At sight of the man, the dog sprang up and walked diagonally away, with a sullen head, and growling. The man yelled, and the dog broke into a gallop. As it was about to enter an alley, there was a loud noise, a whistling, and something spat the ground directly before it. The dog screamed, and, wheeling in terror, galloped headlong in a new direction. Again there was a noise, a whistling, and sand was kicked viciously before it. Fear-stricken, the dog turned and flurried like an animal in a pen. The man stood laughing, his weapons at his hips.

Ultimately the man was attracted by the closed door of the Weary Gentleman saloon. He went to it and, hammering with a revolver, demanded drink.

The door remaining imperturbable, he picked a bit of paper from the walk, and nailed it to the framework with a knife. He then turned his back contemptuously upon this popular resort and, walking to the opposite side of the street and spinning there on his heel quickly and lithely, fired at the bit of paper. He missed it by a half-inch. He swore at himself, and went away. Later he comfortably fusilladed the windows of his most intimate friend. The man was playing with this town; it was a toy for him.

But still there was no offer of fight. The name of Jack Potter, his ancient antagonist, entered his mind, and he concluded that it would be a glad thing if he should go to Potter's house, and by bombardment induce him to come out and fight. He moved in the direction of his desire, chanting Apache scalp-music.

When he arrived at it, Potter's house presented the same still front as had the other adobes. Taking up a strategic position, the man howled a challenge. But this house regarded him as might a great stone god. It gave no sign. After a decent wait, the man howled further challenges, mingling with them wonderful epithets.

Presently there came the spectacle of a man churning himself into deepest rage over the immobility of a house. He fumed at it as the winter wind attacks a prairie cabin in the North. To the distance there should have gone the sound of a tumult like the fighting of two hundred Mexicans. As necessity bade him, he paused for breath or to reload his revolvers.

IV

Potter and his bride walked sheepishly and with speed. Sometimes they laughed together shamefacedly and low.

"Next corner, dear," he said finally.

They put forth the efforts of a pair walking bowed against a strong wind. Potter was about to raise a finger to point the first appearance of the new home when, as they circled the corner, they came face to face with a man in a maroon-colored shirt, who was feverishly pushing cartridges into a large revolver. Upon the instant the man dropped his revolver to the ground and, like lightning, whipped another from its holster. The second weapon was aimed at the bridegroom's chest.

There was a silence. Potter's mouth seemed to be merely a grave for his tongue. He exhibited an instinct to at once loosen his arm from the woman's grip, and he dropped the bag to the sand. As for the bride, her face had gone as yellow as old cloth. She was a slave to hideous rites, gazing at the apparitional snake.

The two men faced each other at a distance of three paces. He of the revolver smiled with a new and quiet ferocity.

"Tried to sneak up on me," he said. "Tried to sneak up on me!" His eyes grew more baleful. As Potter made a slight movement, the man thrust his revolver venomously forward. "No; don't you do it, Jack Potter. Don't you move a finger toward a gun just yet. Don't you move an eyelash. The time has come for me to settle with you, and I'm goin' to do it my own way, and loaf along with no interferin'. So if you don't want a gun bent on you, just mind what I tell you."

Potter looked at his enemy. "I ain't got a gun on me, Scratchy," he said. "Honest, I ain't." He was stiffening and steadying, but yet somewhere at the back of his mind a vision of the Pullman floated: the sea-green figured velvet, the shining brass, silver, and glass, the wood that gleamed as darkly brilliant as the surface of a pool of oil—all the glory of the marriage, the environment of the new estate. "You know I fight when it comes to fighting, Scratchy Wilson; but I ain't got a gun on me. You'll have to do all the shootin' yourself."

His enemy's face went livid. He stepped forward, and lashed his weapon to and fro before Potter's chest. "Don't you tell me you ain't got no gun on you, you whelp. Don't tell me no lie like that. There ain't a man in Texas ever seen you without no gun. Don't take me for no kid." His eyes blazed with light, and his throat worked like a pump.

"I ain't takin' you for no kid," answered Potter. His heels had not moved an inch backward. "I'm takin' you for a damn fool. I tell you I ain't got a gun, and I ain't. If you're goin' to shoot me up, you better begin now; you'll never get a chance like this again."

So much enforced reasoning had told on Wilson's rage; he was calmer. "If you ain't got a gun, why ain't you got a gun?" he sneered. "Been to Sunday school?"

"I ain't got a gun because I've just come from San Anton' with my wife. I'm married," said Potter. "And if I'd thought there was going to be any galoots like you prowling around when I brought my wife home, I'd had a gun, and don't you forget it."

"Married!" said Scratchy, not at all comprehending.

"Yes, married. I'm married," said Potter, distinctly.

"Married?" said Scratchy. Seemingly for the first time, he saw the drooping, drowning woman at the other man's side. "No!" he said. He was like a creature allowed a glimpse of another world. He moved a pace backward, and his arm, with the revolver, dropped to his side. "Is this the lady?" he asked.

"Yes; this is the lady," answered Potter.

There was another period of silence.

"Well," said Wilson at last slowly, "I s'pose it's all off now."

"It's all off if you say so, Scratchy. You know I didn't make the trouble." Potter lifted his valise.

"Well, I 'low it's off, Jack," said Wilson. He was looking at the ground. "Married!" He was not a student of chivalry; it was merely that in the presence of this foreign condition he was a simple child of the earlier plains. He picked up his starboard revolver, and, placing both weapons in their holsters, he went away. His feet made funnel-shaped tracks in the heavy sand.

The Bride Comes to Yellow Sky: Motion picture released as part of *Face to Face* (1952), starring Robert Preston. Photograph courtesy of Harbrace Collection.

JAMES AGEE

The Bride Comes to Yellow Sky

James Agee, who was born 1910 in Knoxville, Tennessee, was a novelist, film writer, and literary critic. Throughout most of his career, he was also associated with Time, Inc., doing occasional in-depth reporting and film reviews for *Time* magazine. His greatest piece of film criticism may be his essay on silent-film comedy, "Comedy's Greatest Era," which first appeared in *Life* magazine and helped to generate the current appreciation of silent-film comedians. In 1948 Agee went to Hollywood, where he wrote the scripts for several important films, among them John Huston's *The African Queen* (1951) and Charles Laughton's *The Night of the Hunter* (1955). He also wrote the narration for *The Quiet One,* a study of a troubled child that is considered one of the great American film documentaries. Agee died of a heart attack in 1955; his novel *A Death in the Family* was published posthumously in late 1957 and in 1958 was awarded the Pulitzer Prize. It was later adapted for the stage under the title *All the Way Home.* The Agee script for *The Bride Comes to Yellow Sky* is a product of his Hollywood years and illustrates his sensitivity to the differences between fiction and film.

THE BRIDE COMES TO YELLOW SKY From *Agee on Film: Vol. II* by James Agee, "The Bride Comes to Yellow Sky" by James Agee. Copyright © 1958 by Theasquare Productions, Inc. Reprinted by permission of the publisher, Grosset & Dunlap, Inc., New York.

GLOSSARY OF FILM TERMS USED IN AGEE'S THE BRIDE COMES TO YELLOW SKY.

FADE-IN: the gradual emergence of a picture on a previously darkened screen. When it occurs in the middle of a film, the fade-in is generally preceded by a—

FADE-OUT: the gradual fading of the picture into darkness. When fade-out and fade-in are used together, they generally signal a lapse in time, a change of place, or both. Fade-out is also used to signal the end of a film.

DISSOLVE: the fading out of one image as another comes into focus. Since it avoids black-outs, this technique allows for smooth transitions between scenes; and it generally implies that the two scenes involved are closely related in content. Ideally, the scene fading out has a geometrical resemblance to the scene fading in, but such resemblances are not always possible to achieve. Sometimes the disharmony between the shapes of two scenes can express a conflict between one situation and the other.

PULL-DOWN: not a common term in film scripts, but Agee uses it frequently to indicate that the camera is moving at an angle and focusing down on a particular person or object.

DOLLY SHOT: a view of the action through a camera that has been placed on a cart so as to follow the movements of characters or objects.

CUT: the direct splicing together of two different film shots.

VIEWPOINT SHOT: a camera view of the action from the angle of vision (and therefore the attitude) of a particular character.

CLOSE SHOT: a head and shoulders shot of a character; a close view of an object is generally called a *detail shot*. The purpose of a close shot (close-up) is to record the element that best expresses the moment.

MEDIUM SHOT: a view of the character from roughly the knees up; sometimes called "the American shot." More distant than the close shot, it is used when the director wishes to show how two or more characters relate to each other, or how a character relates to an object or to his immediate environment.

LONG SHOT: a view of a character or object from a distance that allows the inclusion of much of its physical context. A long shot at the beginning of a film that shows the general setting in which the action is to take place is called an *establishing shot*.

PAN SHOT: the rotation of the camera, either horizontally or vertically, to show more area than a long shot could encompass. It is often used to emphasize movement, as when a camera panning from the right films a train rushing on from the left.

TWO-SHOT or THREE-SHOT: a close shot of two or three people in which the heads and shoulders of the characters fill the frame of the picture. The British call this a "portrait" shot.

FREEZE SHOT: a sequence in which the motions of the camera and its subject are suddenly halted, producing a still shot.

REVERSE ANGLE SHOT: the camera first picks up a character or object coming toward it, and then, from precisely the same angle, catches it going away. The viewer's experience of this shot is similar to that of a by-stander as he watches a passing parade.

* * *

Fade in.

Exterior Main Street of Yellow Sky—Dusk.

Late summer dusk; sound of church bells (off screen). Pull down onto POTTER's *little home, of which the second story is a jail—barred windows.* JACK POTTER *comes out his door, dressed for travel, carrying a bag. He walks a few steps, then glances back around at his house.*

PRISONER (*in upper window*).   So long, Marshal. Don't do nothing I wouldn't do.
POTTER.   Don't you do nothing I wouldn't, s'more like it. You lock yourself in right after mealtimes.
PRISONER.   You can trust me, Marshal.
POTTER.   I don't need to. I done told Laura Lee to keep an eye on you. (*Pause; shyly.*) Well, so long. I'll be back in a couple of days. (*He walks away.*)
PRISONER (*calling after*).   Give my howdy to the gals in San Antone!
POTTER.   You do that when you git out. I ain't no hand fer it.
PRISONER.   Oh, I doan know, Marshal. They tell me still waters run deep.

(POTTER *doesn't answer. He walks on away.*)

*Dolly Shot—*POTTER *and* DEACON SMEED.

(DEACON SMEED *falls in with him. Camera dollies along with them. The following dialogue interrupted two or three times by eminently respectable people converging on the church. All treat* POTTER *respectfully but a little remotely.*)

SMEED.   Evening, Mr. Potter.
POTTER.   Evening, Deacon.
SMEED.   Leaving town so soon again?
POTTER.   It's been most two months.
SMEED.   Oh *has* it indeed, indeed. Hm. And what's going to happen to your prisoner, if I may ask?

JAMES AGEE

POTTER.   Laura Lee's gonna take care of him.
SMEED.   Mrs. Bates? (POTTER *nods*.) She'll bring him his meals?
POTTER.   He'll let himself out for 'em.
SMEED.   Do you think that—ah—looks right?
POTTER (*quietly*).   Afraid I ain't worryin' *how* it looks, Deacon. It's the easiest way, and you know as well as I do, he ain't gonna make no trouble.
SMEED.   I'm afraid you don't care how *anything* looks, Mr. Potter.
POTTER.   Oh now, Deacon, don't start on that church business again!
SMEED.   I'm sorry, Marshal, but every respectable person in Yellow Sky agrees with me. If only for appearance' sake, you ought to come to church.
POTTER.   Looky here, Deacon. We never did get nowheres with that argument, and we never will. I ain't got nothin' against church-goin'; I just don't hold with it fer myself.
SMEED.   And then all these mysterious trips to San Antonio lately— (*They pause in front of church.*)
POTTER.   Now looky here, Deacon—if you mean light women and such, you know I ain't a man to fool around with them.
SMEED.   Oh, you *misconstrue me*, Marshal, *indeed* you do. But . . . Caesar's wife, you know . . .

(*The church bell stops ringing.*)

POTTER.   How's that?
SMEED.   She must be *above* suspicion.
POTTER.   Well, who's suspicious? You?
SMEED.   Of course not, Marshal. Perish the thought. Only you never *say why* you're going to San Antonio.
POTTER (*after a pause*).   Just business. Goodnight, Deacon.
SMEED.   Goodnight, Mr. Potter.

(POTTER *walks ahead; he blows out his cheeks; his eyes focus gratefully on:*)

Viewpoint Shot—"*The Weary Gentleman*" *Saloon.*　　　　　CUT TO

POTTER *As Before.*
(*He checks his watch and speeds up out of shot.*)　　　　　CUT TO

Medium Shot—DEACON.
(*He pauses at the church door, sees* POTTER *enter the "Weary Gentleman," and goes into church, over sound of first hymn.*)　　　CUT TO

Interior "Weary Gentleman"—*Dusk.*
(*There is a typical western bar, behind which* LAURA LEE, *a woman in her fifties, is presiding as bartender. Camera pans* POTTER *to bar. He leaves his bag on a table near the door.*)

POTTER. Evenin', Laura Lee.
LAURA LEE (*behind bar*). Hi, Jack.
JASPER. Jack.
ED. Howdy, Marshal.
POTTER. Jasper—Ed.
ED. Leavin' town again?
POTTER. That's right.
ED. San Antone?
POTTER (*nods; drinks*). Laura Lee, you tell Frank no drinks, no foolin' around. Just come right straight here and eat and get right back again. 'Cause it's got the Deacon bothered, him goin' out at all.
LAURA LEE. Aw, Smeed. I tell you, Jack, when you waded in here and cleaned the town up, it wasn't just a favor you done us. Everything's gettin' too blame respectable.
POTTER. It was my job.
LAURA LEE. I don't hold it agin you. But if things get too tame around here, you'll up an' quit town fer good.
POTTER. Uh, uh. I aim to be buried here. Besides, long as ole Scratchy busts loose now an' then, things won't never get *too* tame.

(*Over mention of* SCRATCHY, LAURA LEE's *eyes focus on something off screen.*)

LAURA LEE (*a little absently*). Here's *to* 'im.

(POTTER's *eyes follow hers.*)

Medium Shot—Along Bar—From Their Angle.
(*A half-finished glass of beer, no customer.*)

Close Shot—POTTER.
(*A glance from the beer to* LAURA LEE, *a look of slightly concerned inquiry, meaning, "Is that* SCRATCHY's?")

Close Shot—LAURA LEE.
(*Nodding.*)

LAURA LEE. It don't work holding him to nothing, Jack. I figured maybe beer, on 'lowance . . .
POTTER. Don't hear me hollerin', do you? It's worth tryin'. Only thing bothers me is if I'm out of town.
LAURA LEE. He ain't due for another tear yet.
POTTER. Ain't sure we can count on him hittin' 'em regular, no more. He's gettin' rouncier all the time.
JASPER (*breaking a pause*). What ye doin' in San Antone, Jack?

(LAURA LEE *gives him a cold glance.*)

JAMES AGEE

POTTER. Just a business trip.

(*Over this last,* SCRATCHY *comes in through a side door and up to bar, to a half-finished glass of beer.*)

POTTER. Howdy, Scratchy.

(SCRATCHY *doesn't answer.* POTTER *and others are quietly amused.*)

LAURA LEE. What's wrong with ye, Scratchy? Cat got yer tongue?

(SCRATCHY *drinks glass down.*)

LAURA LEE (*continuing*). Yer last one tonight. Rather wait fer it?
SCRATCHY. Just draw me my beer.
POTTTER. Ain't still sore, are ye, Scratchy?
SCRATCHY. You know it was all in fun. What d'ye go an' plug me fer?
POTTER. 'Tain't fun, Scratchy. Not skeerin' the daylights out o' folks that ain't used to gun-play.
SCRATCHY. You're a fine one to talk about gun-play. Mean, sneakin' skunk!
POTTER. Sneakin'? It was fair and above board, like it always is.
LAURA LEE. He just beat ye to the draw, an' you know it.
SCRATCHY. That don't make my leg no happier.
POTTER. Mendin' a'right, Scratchy?
SCRATCHY. Oh, *I* git around.
POTTER. Just mind where ye git *to*, that's all I ask.
SCRATCHY. Next time, I'll make *you* dance.
POTTER. Better not be no next time. 'Cause next time, instead o' the meat o' the leg, I might have to pop you in the kneecap.
SCRATCHY. You wouldn't do that.
POTTER. I wouldn't want to. But I might have to, Scratchy, just to learn you. You don't know it but you're gettin' dangersome when you drink, lately.
SCRATCHY. Me—dangersome? A good man with a gun's a safe man with a gun, an' I'm the best they is.
LAURA LEE. When you're in yer likker, yeah. But you don't drink fer fun no more, Scratchy. You kinda go out o' yer head.
POTTER. That's right, Scratchy. One o' these days you're gonna shoot to kill, an' swing fer it, an' then all of us'll be sorry.
SCRATCHY. I don't need to kill nobody more—I got my notches, an' to spare—(*he pats his gun*).
POTTER. That was all right, agin the kind o' varmints that used to be around here in the old days—You come in right handy. Sort of a scavenger, like a turkey-buzzard. But you can't go shootin' up law-abidin' citizens an' git away with it.

SCRATCHY (*with extreme contempt*). Who wants to shoot a law-abidin' citizen!

(*Under the above,* POTTER *finishes his drink, pays, starts out.*)

POTTER. Well ...
SCRATCHY. You leavin' town again?
POTTER. 'Bye, Laura Lee. See you day after tomorrow. (*To* SCRATCHY) You watch yer drinkin' while I'm gone.
SCRATCHY. I'll save it all up fer you, Jack. 'Tain't nobody else is wuth the hangover.

(POTTER *exits*.)

JASPER. Reckon what he's up to, all these trips to San Antone?
LAURA LEE. Never mind, it's his business.
ED. You ain't sweet on Jack, are ye, Laura Lee?
LAURA LEE (*a cold look at him*). Only man I ever was, he's in his grave ten year. (*She hears the train draw out, pours and drinks.*) (*Continuing.*) But if I was, that's the only one *man* enough since. CUT TO

*Interior Day Coach—Close Shot—*POTTER*—Night.*
(*He finishes rolling a cigarette, lights it and, elbow on windowsill, settles into the tired posture of night travel, gazing out of window. Camera slowly pans, losing his face, then his reflected face, squaring on the dark land flooding past.*) FADE OUT

Fade in.
Interior Parlor Car.
(*Camera looks squarely through window at fast-moving daylit land, reversing direction of preceding shot; then in a slow pan picks up the reflection of* BRIDE*'s face in window; then the face itself, then pulls away into:*)

*Two-Shot—*POTTER *and* BRIDE.
(*For a few moments we merely hold on them, as though this were a provincial wedding portrait of the period [circa 1895].*) *He has an outdoor clumsiness in his new suit, which is a shade tight and small for him. Her very new-looking hat and dress are in touchingly ambitious, naive taste.*)

(*Between their heads, in the seat just behind theirs, the head of a "*SO-PHISTICATED*"* MAN *turns slowly, slyly watching, filled with patronizing amusement.* POTTER, *gradually aware, turns and looks him in the eye; the guy shrivels and turns away fast.*)

Hold on BRIDE *and* POTTER *a moment.* BRIDE *looks at something off screen.*

*Medium Shot—*TWO WOMEN.
(*Watch her, whispering and giggling.*)

Medium Shot—Centering POTTER *and* BRIDE—*From Viewpoint of* WOMEN.

(*The* BRIDE *smiles very sweetly, looking straight into the camera, and we hear off screen a more intense giggling and whispering and a few inaudible words.*)

(*The* BRIDE *looks a little puzzled, her smile fading; then she smiles again, sure there can be no malice toward her; then looks straight ahead of her. Both are glowing and intensely shy. His large, spread hands englobe his knees; hers are discreet in her lap. He stares straight ahead, his eyes a little unfocused. She keeps looking around. With almost the manner of a little girl, she draws a deep breath and utters a quiet sigh of joy, at the same time slightly raising, then relaxing, the hands on her lap. He hears her happy sigh; he looks at her; he watches her shyly and with a certain awe. He slowly shakes his head in the manner of one who can scarcely believe his good fortune. He lifts his own hands from his knees; decides they were where they belong; carefully replaces them. When he finally speaks he tries to be light and tender and it is clear that the loudness of his voice startles and embarrasses him, and in the background heads flinch slightly.*)

POTTER. WELL, MRS. POTTER!
BRIDE (*by reflex*). Shh!

(*Both are terribly embarrassed.*)

POTTER (*quick and low*). Sorry! Frog in my throat.
BRIDE (*ditto*). I'm sorry, I didn't mean to shush you. It just made me jump's all.
POTTER. You shush me any time yer a mind to.
BRIDE (*after a pause; with shy daring*). You *call* me that, any time yer a mind to. 'Cause I like to hear you say it. Only not so loud.
POTTER (*after a pause, whispering it, very shy*). Mrs. Potter . . . (*Overwhelmed by his daring, he blushes and looks away. She shivers with quiet delight; she glances up at him, then all around, with shy pride; then, as delicately as if it were asleep, she moves her hands in her lap as to uncover her wedding ring, and slowly, almost unbelievingly, lowers her eyes and looks at it. Then she looks around again, speculatively.*)
BRIDE. Think they can tell we just got m—— (*she speaks the word almost sacredly*) married?
POTTER. Don't see how they would. We ain't treatin' 'em to no lovey dovey stuff or none o' that monkey business.
BRIDE (*whisper*). Jack!
POTTER. 'Scuse me.
BRIDE. It's all right.
POTTER. No it ain't neither. It ain't fitting I talk to you like that.
BRIDE. Yes it is, Jack. I reckon it just kinda crep up on me from behind.

(*Silent, they look out the window. They have run out of talk. They have plenty to think about, but soon he feels he has to make conversation.*)

POTTER. This yer-train sure does gobble up the miles, don't it?
BRIDE. My yes. Just goes like the wind.
POTTER. It's a thousand mile from one end o' Texas to the other, and it don't only stop but four times.
BRIDE. My land!
POTTER. It only stops for water at Yaller Sky.
BRIDE. Oh.
POTTER. Hope you ain't gonna mind. What I mean, it's a good town, but it might look awful puny, side o' San Antone.
BRIDE. Oh *no*. I never did like a big town. I like it where ever'body *knows* ever'body else.
POTTER. You'll like it there then.

(*They run out of talk again. She looks around with more and more appreciation of the opulence and splendor of the car. Camera pans around Pullman car.*)

BRIDE'S VOICE (*off screen*). I just can't get over it! (*Pause.*) It's all so handsome and rich-lookin'!
POTTER'S VOICE (*off screen*). Yeah. They do it in style, sure enough, don't they?
BRIDE'S VOICE (*off screen*). It's just like it was a palace or sumpin'. Even the ceilin'!

Medium Shot—A Fancy Ceiling Oil Painting—Cupids, etc.

POTTER'S VOICE (*off screen*). You sure do notice things. I never even seen it.

*Close Shot—*POTTER.
(*Who has been looking up.*)

POTTER (*continuing*). Ever rode a parlor car before?
BRIDE. No.
POTTER. Me neither. One of these days we'll go on a trip overnight.

(*Both are quietly aghast with embarrassment.*)

POTTER (*struggling*). I mean, I always did have a hankerin' to see what them Pullman berths are like.
BRIDE (*helping him*). This is wonderful enough.
POTTER. Shucks. This ain't *nothing*. After a while we'll go forward to the diner and get a big layout. Ever et in a diner?
BRIDE. No. I always took me along some lunch.

POTTER. Finest meal in the world. Charge a dollar.

Close Three Shot—POTTER, BRIDE *and* SOPHISTICATED MAN.
(SOPHISTICATED MAN *registers,* "God, what rubes!")

BRIDE. A dollar? Why that's too much—for us—ain't it, Jack?
POTTER. Not this trip, anyhow. We're gonna do the whole thing.

(*He swells up, a little like a nabob, and looks away so she can look at him admiringly.*) DISSOLVE TO

Insert.
Interior SCRATCHY's *House* (*Adobe*)—*Day.*

Extreme Close Shot.
(*Sighting above the bore of a long-barreled, blue-black revolver, against a raggedly-curtained window.*)

Insert.
(*The smoothly spinning cylinder of a revolver.* SCRATCHY's *other hand, with a rag, wipes the weapon clear of cleaning oil; the weapon is turned this way and that, lovingly, catching the light; then is sighted along, aiming it at Indians on a calendar, and is dry fired, with a click of the tongue and a whispered,* "Got ye that time, ye dog!"; *then it is laid delicately down on a patchwork quilt. Camera pans with* SCRATCHY's *hand to a pint whiskey bottle on the floor by the bed.* [*Next to it is another bottle, empty.*] *Hand and bottle move out of shot; sound of drinking; bottle is returned, a good inch lower; hand unwraps a second revolver from a worn, fine old napkin. Then a rag, then a little can of cleaning oil and a little rod. The hands start cleaning revolver.*)

(*Over this entire scene,* SCRATCHY WILSON's *voice is heard, deeply and still tranquilly drunk, humming as much as singing,* "Brighten The Corner." *The singing is of course interrupted; by his muttered line; by occasional shortness of breath; by his drinking and a sharp cough afterward; and just as it resumes after the drinking, the voice is raw. But in overall mood it is as happy and innocent as a baby talking to itself in its crib. Over hand cleaning revolver,*) CUT TO

Interior Parlor Car—*Day.*
Medium Shot—*Centering* POTTER *and* BRIDE.
(*The* DINING STEWARD *walks through shot fast, hitting chimes.*)

STEWARD. Fust call for dinnah! Fust call!

(*Only* POTTER *and* BRIDE *react. A quick exchange of glances and they get up and follow* STEWARD *out of shot.*)

Interior Dining Car—Day.
Medium Shot.
(*Shooting past waiters ranked ready beside empty tables as* POTTER *and* BRIDE *enter the car, registering abrupt dismay at all the service, whiteness, glitter and loneliness.*)

*Viewpoint Shot—*THREE WAITERS.
(*Solicit them, with knowing glances.*)

Medium Shot—Dolly.
(*The* WAITER *nearest them tries to steer them toward a two-some table.* POTTER, *in a replying spasm of independence, steers* BRIDE *to a 4-chair table opposite. The two sit down side by side as camera dollies sidelong into a Two Shot.*)

POTTER (*low*). Looks like we're the only customers.

(*Instantly a hand plants a large menu in* POTTER'S *hand, blocking off his face, and then the same to the* BRIDE.)

WAITER'S VOICE (*juicy, off screen*). There you are, sir! An' how're *you*-all today!

(POTTER *slowly lowers menu, looks to waiter.* BRIDE, *ditto, looks to* POTTER.)

POTTER. Gone up on yer prices, ain't ye?
WAITER'S VOICE (*off screen*). Things are costin' more all ovah, these days. (*Oily.*) Matter o' fact, though, we can 'commodate folks of more moderate means. (*His finger reaches down and points out on menu.*) There's a nice gumbo, good sandwiches . . .
POTTER (*across him*). We'll have the dollar and a quarter dinner.

(*The* BRIDE *watches him with admiration.*)

WAITER. Yes indeed, sir. The chicken or the ham, sir. The ham is *mighty* delicious today, sir.
POTTER. Chicken.
WAITER. Yes, sir!

(*They unfold their napkins.* POTTER *glances about.*)

Viewpoint Up-Shot.
(*Several waiters pretend not to watch.*)

BRIDE *and* POTTER *As Before.*
(*As* BRIDE *settles her napkin in lap, he starts tucking his high into his vest.*)
DISSOLVE TO

Exterior "Weary Gentleman" Saloon—Day.
Dolly Shot.
(*Following the nattily dressed* DRUMMER *through swinging doors into interior "Weary Gentleman" Saloon, we pause and shoot past him as he hesitates and looks around at* JASPER, LAURA LEE *and* FRANK. *All glance at him casually and resume talking.*)

FRANK. Not even a small beer?

LAURA LEE (*sliding a tall one toward* JASPER). Not even that, Frank. What's more, it's high time you locked yourself back in. 'Cause Jack Potter's treatin' you white, an' it's up to you to treat him the same. Now git along with ye.

*Close Shot—*DRUMMER.
(*Over "lock yourself back in," he registers sharp interest, glancing keenly back and forth between* FRANK *and* LAURA LEE.)

FRANK'S VOICE (*off screen*). He'd treat me a whole lot whiter if he'd get back when he said he would.

LAURA LEE'S VOICE (*off screen*). He ain't but a day late.

FRANK'S VOICE (*off screen*). A day's a long time when you spend it in jail.

(DRUMMER *registers curiosity and consternation and looks exclusively at* FRANK.)

*New Angle—*LAURA LEE *and* FRANK.

LAURA LEE. Read them magazines he give ye.

(*Camera pans with* FRANK *as he starts toward door, holding on* DRUMMER.)

FRANK. Done read 'em four or five times. Git tired of it, all that bang-bang stuff. (*To* DRUMMER.) Howdy stranger. (*He walks on out.*)

DRUMMER (*belated and odd*). Howdy.

(*Camera pans with his walk up to the bar.*)

DRUMMER (*to* LAURA LEE). Did I hear that man correrctly, ma'am? Is he a *jail-bird*?

LAURA LEE. If you want to put it that way.

DRUMMER (*looks to* JASPER *who is wholly neutral*). Well! (*He looks to both; both are neutral.*) Well!

LAURA LEE. What'll ye have, mister?

DRUMMER. Beer, please, a big head on it.

(LAURA LEE *draws and hands it to him, sizing him up.*)

Laura Lee. Big head.
Drummer. Nice little town.
Laura Lee. It'll pass.
Drummer. Oh, I've had quite a profitable morning's work. (*He sips.*)
Laura Lee. That'll be a nickel, mister.

(*He pays and sips again.*)

Drummer. Matter of fact, I'm a Drummer.
Laura Lee. I can see that.
Drummer. That's right. I travel in stockings. "Exquisite" stockings. (*Hustling his sample case to bar.*) Paris to your doorstep, that's our slogan. Now if you're willing to spare a moment of your time, I can *promise* you, a lady of your taste and refinement, you just won't be able to *resist!*
Laura Lee (*across him*). Don't trouble yourself, mister, I don't—

(*But the* Drummer *is already lifting the lid of the case. She leans her arms on it, nipping his fingers.*)

Laura Lee (*continuing*).—Now, looky here, young feller; I ain't even a'goin' to *look* at them fool stockin's, let alone *resist* 'em.

(*Over this, two* Mexican Sheepherders *enter quietly by the rear door and sit at a table.*)

Laura Lee (*to* Mexicans). What's yours, Narciso Gulliermo Diorisio Mario?
1st Mexican. Cervezas.

(*The second* Mexican *nods.*)

Drummer (*sucking his fingers*). That hurt, ma'am.
Laura Lee (*drawing beer*). Wouldn't be surprised.
Jasper. Seen Scratchy around, Laura Lee?
Laura Lee. Not since t'other night.
Jasper. Gittin' so ye can't count on him fer nothin'. He was 'sposed to clair out my cess-pool yesterday. Never showed up.
Laura Lee (*pause—quietly*). Can't say as I blame him, Jasper; that's a job ye do yourself—and nobody ought to have to do it for him.
Jasper. Well—sometimes ye gotta take what ye can get. (*She is silent.*) (*Continuing.*) All I hope is, he ain't a-tyin' one on.

Close Shot—Laura Lee.

Laura Lee. If I had to do a job like that fer you, I might tie on a few myself.

(*Camera pans as she takes beer to end of bar.* First Mexican *pays and takes them. She sits on her stool, looking at nobody.*)

A New Angle—JASPER.
(*He watches her, nettled, and a little malicious.*)

JASPER. Hey, Laura Lee.
LAURA LEE. Yeah.
JASPER. Reckon what Jack Potter's *up* to in San Antone.
LAURA LEE. Reckon what business 'tis o' yourn.
JASPER. Just figured he might of *told you*.
LAURA LEE (*quiet and stern*). Jack Potter ain't tied to *my* apron strings, nor nobody's. FAST WIPE TO

Interior Dining Car—*Day.*
(POTTER *and* BRIDE *are finishing their desserts opposite a wooden, middle-aged married couple [the car is now full of people].*)

(*We inter-cut close shot as* POTTER *and the* MAN *meet glances;* BRIDE *and* WOMAN *do same.* POTTER *glances secretively down at his lapel and, privately as he can, scratches with his thumb-nail at a food stain.*)

(*Their voices are low:*)

BRIDE. Don't worry. I can get that off in a jiffy.
POTTER. Ain't likely I'll wear it much, nohow.
BRIDE. Why, you'll wear it a-Sundays, church an' all.
POTTER (*uneasy*). I ain't never been much of a hand for church.
BRIDE. You don't ever go?

(POTTER *uneasily shakes his head.*)

BRIDE (*continuing; uneasy*). I don't know what I'd do, for lonesomeness, without no church to go to.
WAITER'S VOICE (*off screen*). Look at what I done brung yah both! An extra pot of nice fresh coffee.

Viewpoint Up-Shot Cuts Into His Line.
(*He leans out, setting down pot, beaming, proprietary, working for a big tip.*)

New Angle—POTTER *and* BRIDE.
(*Mild embarrassment reactions; they murmur appreciations ad lib.*)

BRIDE. Want some more?
POTTER. No thanks.

(*She pours for herself. The sugar is not in easy reach.*)

POTTER (*formally, to other* MAN). Pass the sugar, please.
MAN (*glumly*). Certainly.

POTTER. Thank you.
MAN. Certainly.
POTTER (*to* BRIDE). Sugar?
BRIDE. Sure you won't have some more coffee?
POTTER. All right. Thanks. Thank you.
BRIDE. Certainly. (*She leans to pour for him, much enjoying serving him, and knocks her napkin from the edge of the table to the floor between them. Both quickly stoop to reach for it.*)

Insert.
(*Their hands touch accidentally and fly apart as if they had struck a spark.*)

BOTH. 'Scuse me!

Two Shot—POTTER *and* BRIDE *As Before.*
(*As they straighten up quickly,* POTTER *bumps the table making a clatter and the* BRIDE *slops a little of the coffee from the pot in her other hand onto their clothes.*)

TOGETHER: POTTER (*to everyone*). 'Scuse me. BRIDE (*to him*). Gee, I'm sorry.

Reverse Angle.
(*The two older people exchange unsmiling glances and pretend nothing is happening.*)

POTTER *and* BRIDE *As Before.*
(*He with his handkerchief, she with her napkin, they gently dab coffee off each other; they are embarrassed but not at all at odds.*)

(*As the* WAITER's *arm presents the check to* POTTER, *the camera lifts and tilts, dollying gently in to center his right hand near his trousers pocket. The hand makes the odd, helpless gesture of putting aside a holster which isn't there.*)

BRIDE'S VOICE (*off screen*). What's the matter?
POTTER'S VOICE (*off screen*). Just habit I reckon. Fust time in years I ain't totin' a gun.

Camera Zooms, Centering.   FAST DISSOLVE TO

Interior SCRATCHY's—*Day*—*Close Viewpoint Shot.*
(SCRATCHY's *loaded cartridge belt lies heavy and lethal across his knees. He thumbs in the last cartridge and lays aside the belt. The camera, as* SCRATCHY *rises to his feet, goes into a short spinning blur in and out of focus.*)

SCRATCHY'S VOICE (*off screen*). Whoa there.

(*Camera proceeds into a slow, wobbly dollying pan, past window and bureau to pegs where* SCRATCHY's *hand fumbles among his few clothes. Most of them are old and poor but his hands select and get off the hook a violently fancy pseudowestern shirt on which camera comes into ultra sharp focus. Then one hand, as camera creeps in, focus ditto, reaches for a real shocker of a necktie, muffs it, and as camera comes into extreme close shot, drags it drunkenly, snakily, slithering from its hook. All this time* SCRATCHY *is muttering and humming. Over the slithering tie we*)   IRIS OUT

Iris In.
Interior Parlor Car—Day.
   (*Center camera on* POTTER's *more conservative tie. Tense and uneasy, he adjusts it.*)

Two Shot—POTTER *and* BRIDE.
   (*He is tense; she is content. He takes out and looks at a thick hunter watch. Watching him, she realizes his uneasiness. She checks her own watch with his.*)

   BRIDE. Mine's slow.
   POTTER. Nope: I trust yourn. She's a seventeen jeweller.

   (*Behind them, the* "SOPHISTICATED" MAN *slopes an amused eye.*)

   BRIDE. Gracious.

   (POTTER *corrects his watch, pockets it and avoids her eyes. She watches him. An uneasy silence. He looks at his watch again.*)

   BRIDE (*continuing*).   Jack.
   POTTER. Hmm.
   BRIDE. Somethin's eatin' at you.
   POTTER. Me?

   (*She nods—a pause.*)

   POTTER. Nuthin' much. Only I wisht I'd sent a telegram.
   BRIDE. Thought you did, there at the depot.
   POTTER. I just tore it up.

   (*Silence.*)

   BRIDE (*shyly*).   Was it—about us—gittin' married this morning?
   POTTER. I oughta told 'um, back in Yaller Sky. That's all. You see, they're so used to me being a bachelor an' all. They ain't gonna take it no way good, me never tellin' 'em—an' all of a sudden I come home married—(*an inarticulate pause; ashamed*)—Reckon I'm just plain bashful.
   BRIDE (*very shy*).   Reckon I feel the same.

(*He looks at her, unbelieving. She corroborates her statement with a little nod. They are so relieved they awkwardly resist an impulse to join hands and both face rigidly front, their tension growing.*) FAST DISSOLVE TO

Interior Scratchy's House—Day.
(*A lurching close pan to a broken, distorting mirror. The camera is on* Scratchy, *and the reflection is his. He is wearing a fancy shirt, both revolvers and the cartridge belt and he has to stoop to see himself. He is in a reeling slouch, glaring, stinking drunk. He draws closer, making savage faces which are still more savagely distorted in the mirror. He becomes momentarily fascinated by these distortions. He draws both guns and lurches into extreme closeup, growling low:*)

Scratchy. All right, Jack Potter. Yore time has come!

(*Camera pulls back centering hands getting, from his dresser drawer, a newish hat as phony as the shirt. The hands lift this through the shot as valuably as the Holy Grail and camera again leans for mirror reflection as he preens the hat on his head.*) DISSOLVE TO

Interior—"Weary Gentleman"—Day.
Close Shot—The Drummer.
(*His eyes fixed almost on the lens in the cold manner of a snake charming a bird. Camera pulls away along his fully extended, shirt-sleeved, and fancily sleeve-gartered arm. It is clothed to the armpit in a super-sheer, elaborately clocked dark stocking.*)

Drummer (*soft and almost lascivious*). Speaks louder than words, doesn't it! (*He shifts his eye off screen.*) *You* tell her, gentlemen; in *all your experience*, did you ever meet a lady that wouldn't *swoon* just to look at it? (*Eyes back to center.*) Sheer as twilight air. And just look at that clocking! (*He points it out, then his subtle hand impersonates a demi-mondaine foot.*) Nothing like it ever contrived before, by the most inspired continental designers, to give style to the ankle and moulding to the calf. (*He runs fingers up his arm to the armpit, his eyes follow.*) And they run all the way up—opera length. (*He casts his eyes down, then returns to off-center and gives his eyes all he's got. With a trace of hoarseness, almost whispering.*) How about it, madam? (*He gives her an homme-fatale smile. A grand pause.*)

Two Shot—Jasper *and* Ed.
(*They look toward him with quiet disgust.*)

Two Shot—Two Mexicans.
(*They glance at each other and toward* Laura Lee.)

Close Shot—Laura Lee.

(*She gives the merchandise one more cold, fascinated once-over, then looks the* DRUMMER *in the eye.*)

LAURA LEE.   All right son. I'm still resistin'. So, fork over that dollar.
DRUMMER.   But madam, you haven't given the Exquizzit—
LAURA LEE (*across him*).   Save yer breath young feller. Why, if my husband had caught me in a pair o' them things, he'd a' broke my jaw. You're in the *wrong territory*, son. 'Cause this is a man's country. It's hard country.

(*A* YOUNG MAN *comes in quickly.*)

YOUNG MAN.   Scratchy Wilson's drunk an' he's turned loose with both hands.

(*Both* MEXICANS *set down their unfinished beers and fade out the rear door. The* DRUMMER *views with mystification; nobody pays any attention to him. They're as quick and efficient as a well-rehearsed fire-drill.* JASPER *and* ED *go out the front door and close the window shutters. The* YOUNG MAN *bolts the rear door.* LAURA LEE *bars the window on her side and goes center, swinging shut one leaf of the plank door. As* JASPER *and* ED *return,* JASPER *swings the other shut and bars his window and* ED *brings from the corner the bar for the main door and helps* LAURA LEE *put it in place.* LAURA LEE *returns to her place behind the bar. In the sudden, solemn, chapel-like gloom, the* DRUMMER *is transfixed; his eyes glitter.*)

DRUMMER.   Say, what *is* this? (*A silent reaction from the men.*)
DRUMMER (*continuing*).   Is there going to be a gun-fight?
JASPER (*grimly*).   Dunno if there'll be a fight or not, but there'll be some shootin'—some good shootin'.
YOUNG MAN.   Oh, there's a fight just *waitin'* out there in the street, if anyone wants it.

(JASPER *and* ED *nod solemnly.*)

DRUMMER (*to* YOUNG MAN).   What'd ye say his name was?
ALL.   Scratchy Wilson.

(*The* DRUMMER *does a fast multiple take, person-to-person.*)

DRUMMER.   What're you goin' to do? (*Grim silence.*)
DRUMMER (*continuing*).   Does he do this often? (*More silence.*)
DRUMMER (*continuing*).   Can he break down that door?
LAURA LEE.   No: he's give that up. But when he comes you'd better lay down on the floor, stranger. He's dead sure to *shoot* at that door, an' there's no tellin' what a stray bullet might do.

(*The* DRUMMER, *keeping a strict eye on the door, begins carefully removing the stocking from his arm.*)

DRUMMER. Will he kill anybody?

(*The men laugh low and scornfully.*)

JASPER. He's out to shoot, an' he's out fer trouble. Don't see no good experimentin' with him.
DRUMMER. But what do you *do* in a case like this? What do you do?
YOUNG MAN. Why, he an' Jack Potter—
JASPER AND ED (*across him*). Jack ain't back yet.
YOUNG MAN (*suddenly frightened*). Lordy!
DRUMMER. Well who's he? What's *he* got to do with it?
YOUNG MAN. He's Marshal.
LAURA LEE. Comes to shoootin', he's the only one in town can go up agin him.

(*Far off, off screen, we hear a wild Texas yell, a shot, another yell. Everyone becomes very still and tense.*)

DRUMMER (*half whispered*). That must be him comin', hey?

(*The men look at him in irritation and look away again. They wait, their eyes shining in the gloom.* JASPER *holds up three fingers. Moving like a ghost,* LAURA LEE *gets out three glasses and the bottle. The* DRUMMER *lifts one forlorn finger; she adds another glass. They pour. In unison they snap the drinks down at a gulp and walk to windows to look through chinks. The* DRUMMER *quietly puts a coin on the bar.* LAURA LEE *just looks at it, at him, and away. He shamefacedly takes back his coin. She silently takes a Winchester from beneath the bar and breaks it.*)

DRUMMER (*whispered*). You goin' to shoot him?

(*Silence; everyone looks at him bleakly.*)

LAURA LEE (*low*). Not if I can help it. I ain't a good enough shot. Might kill him.
DRUMMER. Well it'd be pure self defense if you did, wouldn't it?

(*No answer.*)

DRUMMER (*continuing*). Well, *wouldn't* it? Good riddance *too, I'd* say.

(LAURA LEE *closes the breech.*)

LAURA LEE (*low*). Mister, Scratchy Wilson's an old friend. Nobody'd harm a hair of his head if they's any way out—let alone kill him. You see, trouble is, he's a wonder with a gun. Just a wonder. An' he's a terror when he's drunk. So when he goes on the war trail, we hunt our holes—naturally.
DRUMMER. But—why do they allow him—what's he doin' in a town like this?

Laura Lee.   He's the last of the old gang that used to hang out along the river here.

(*A silence. Then nearer, but distant, a howl is heard. The* Drummer *reacts, jittery.*)

Laura Lee (*continuing*).   You better come back o' the bar. I kinda fixed it up.

Drummer (*ashamed*).   No thanks, I'll—

Laura Lee (*with a peremptory gesture*).   Come on.

(*He does. He squats low in the front angle of the bar and examines, with some relief, the various plates of scrap metal with which she has armored it. Off screen, nearer, we hear another shot and three yowls. There's a shuffling of feet. They look at each other.*)

Men (*quietly*).   Here he comes!

Pan Shot.

(*We dolly with* Laura Lee, *carrying her gun, to look through a chink in the shutter, and through the chink see* Scratchy *round the corner at the far end of the empty street, yelling, a long heavy blue-black revolver in either hand. We hear his words, distant, but preternaturally powerful, as he strides to the middle of the street and stops dead, both guns alert, threatening and at bay.*)

Scratchy.   Yaller Sky, hyar I come!

Medium Shot—Scratchy.

(*He holsters a revolver, extracts a pint bottle from his belt, cocks it vertically and drains it, and tosses it high and glittering into the sunlight, in mid-air; then shoots it into splinters, left-handed, and does a quick 360-degree whirl, drawing both guns, as if against enemies ambushing him from the rear. He raises a small tornado of dust. Cut to a head closeup into which he finishes his pivot, glaring. His eyes are glittering, drunk, mad, frightening. He is eaten up with some kind of interior bitter wildness.*)

Scratchy (*a low growl*).   Got ye, ye yaller-bellies!

(*Pull down and away. He gives a lonely Texas yowl; the echoes die. He glares all about him; his eyes, focusing on something off screen, take on sudden purpose.*)

Scratchy (*loud*).   Jack Potter!

Medium Shot—*With Still Camera*—Potter's *House*—*Freeze Closer Shot*—
   Scratchy.
      (*Trying to adjust his eyes to this oddity.*)

SCRATCHY (*louder*).   Jack Potter!

Medium Shot—POTTER's *House*—*As Before.*

SCRATCHY'S VOICE (*off screen*).   You heared me, Jack Potter. Come on out an' face the music. Caze it's time to dance.

Close Shot—SCRATCHY.
(*Dead silence.*)

(*He is puzzled.*)

SCRATCHY.   'Tain't no ways like you Potter, asullin' there in yer house. You ain't no possum. I treated ye fair an' square. I saved it all up for ye, like I told ye. Now you play square with me.
FRANK'S VOICE (*off screen, scared*).   Hey, Scratchy.
SCRATCHY (*puzzled, looking around*).   How's that? Who *is* that?

POTTER's *House*—*Past* SCRATCHY.

FRANK'S VOICE.   Hit's me. Frank.
SCRATCHY.   Why don't ye say so. Whar ye at?
FRANK'S VOICE.   I'm up yere in the jail.
SCRATCHY.   Well *show* yerself! What ye skeered of?
FRANK'S VOICE.   You.
SCRATCHY.   Me? Shucks. Only man needs to be skeered o' me is Jack Potter, the yaller hound.
FRANK'S VOICE.   Jack ain't here, Scratchy.
SCRATCHY.   What ye mean he ain't here?
FRANK'S VOICE.   He ain't got back yet, that's what I mean. That's what I was tryin' to tell you.
SCRATCHY.   Ain't back! Don't gimme none o' that. He come back yesterday when he promised he would.
FRANK'S VOICE.   No he didn't.
SCRATCHY.   You lie to *me*. Frank Gudger, I'll give ye what *fer*.

(*He shoots, striking a bar and ringing a musical note.*)

FRANK'S VOICE.   Scratchy! Don't do that! Hit's dangersome.
SCRATCHY.   Not if ye keep yer head low it ain't.
FRANK'S VOICE.   'Tis too. Ye can't tell *whar* them bullets'll *re*bound.
SCRATCHY.   Don't you dast tell me how to shoot, ye pore wall-eyed woods colt. *Is* Jack Potter back or *ain't* he?
FRANK'S VOICE.   No he ain't and that's the honest truth.
SCRATCHY.   Don't you *sass me*.

Close Shot.

(SCRATCHY *shoots another bar, ringing a different musical note, which is followed by a shattering of glass.*)

SCRATCHY (*continuing*). Is he back?
FRANK'S VOICE. Quit it, Scratchy. Ye done busted my lamp chimbley.
SCRATCHY. *Is* he back or *ain't* he?
FRANK'S VOICE. All right, have it yer own way. He's back if you say so.
SCRATCHY. Well, why didn't you tell me so straight off?

(*No answer.*)

SCRATCHY (*continuing*). Why don't he come on out then?
FRANK'S VOICE. Reckon he would if he was inside.
SCRATCHY. Oh, he ain't inside, huh?
FRANK'S VOICE. Not that I know of.
SCRATCHY. Well, that leaves just one other place for him to be.

(*He turns toward the "Weary Gentleman," hikes his trousers, reaches for the bottle which is no longer there.*)

SCRATCHY (*growling and starting.*) Dad burn it. Never seed it yet I didn't run out just at the wrong time!

(*He walks fast past the respectable houses, the churches and so on, and dollying, shooting past him, we see they all have an unearthly quietness. As he walks, he talks, now to himself, now shouting.*)

SCRATCHY (*continuing*). But that's all right. Just lay low. 'Caze quick as I wet my whistle, I'm gonna show ye some shootin'!

(*He stops in front of* MORGAN's *house.*)

SCRATCHY (*continuing*). You, Jasper Morgan. Yeah, and that snivellin' woman o' yourn, too! Too dainty to do like ordinary folks. Too high an' mighty! Git yerself a lot o' fancy plumbing, an' ye ain't man enough to clean out yer own cess-pool. "Let Scratchy do it." Ain't nuthin' so low but Scratchy'll do it for the price of a pint.

(*He glares around for a target. He spies a potted fern suspended from the porch ceiling. He shoots the suspension chain and the whole thing drops to the porch floor with a foomp. There! Clean that up! He turns,* DEACON's *house is opposite.*)

SCRATCHY (*continuing; a horrible travesty of a sissy voice*). Deacon! Oh *Deacon* Smee-eed! (*He makes two syllables of* Smeed.) You home, Deacon? Kin I pay ye a little call? *Most* places in town, ye just *knock* an' walk *in,* but that ain't *good* enough for a *good* man, *is* it, Deacon? Oh *no!* No— *no!* Pay a little call on the Deacon, ye got to shove a 'lectric bell, real special.

(*A hard shift of tone.*) All right, Smeed, start singin' them psalms o' yourn. You'll be whangin' 'em on a harp, few mo' minutes, you an' yer missuz, too. Can't stop in right now, I'm a mite too thirsty. But I'll be back, Deacon. Oh, I'll be back. (*He studies the house.*) Here's my callin' card.

(*He takes careful aim, and*)

Insert.
(*Hits the doorbell, so fusing it that it rings continuously. We hear a woman scream hysterically.*)

Close Shot of SCRATCHY.

SCRATCHY. Ah, quit it. Don't holler 'til yer hurt.

Interior DEACON's House—DEACON and WIFE.
(*Past DEACON and his WIFE, through the curtained window, we see SCRATCHY pass.*)

(*The DEACON has an arm around his WIFE. He is trying pathetically to resemble an intrepid doomed frontiersman in an Indian fight.*)

DEACON. He'll pay for this. By the Almighty, he'll pay dearly. I'm not going to stand for it, I'm simply not going—
MRS. SMEED. Oh hush. For goodness sake, stop that horrid *bell!*

(*He looks at her, goes into the hallway with wounded dignity, and jerks a wire loose. Just as the bell stops, there is a shot and the stinging sound off screen of the church bell being shot at. The DEACON reacts to this latest outrage.*)

Medium Shot—Upward—Church Bell—From SCRATCHY's Viewpoint.

Close Shot—Shooting Down—SCRATCHY.
(*Looking up at bell, both pleased and angry, and shooting again at the church bell.*)

SCRATCHY (*he bellows*). Come on out and fight if you dast—only you don't dast.

(*He starts glancing all around; the revolvers in each hand are as sensitive as snakes; the little fingers play in a musician-like way; inter-cut with still facades of details of greater stillness; a motionless curtain of machine-made lace with a head dimly silhouetted behind; a drawn shade, with an eye and fingertips visible at the edge.*)

SCRATCHY (*continuing*). O no! You know who's *boss* in *this* town. Marcellus T. Wilson, that's who. He ain't fittin' to wipe yer boots on, nosirree, he's the lowest of the low, but he's boss all the same. 'Caze *this* is a boss, (*gesturing with a revolver*) an' *this* is a boss, (*another*) an' this is the feller that can boss the both of 'em better'n any other man that's left in this wore-out womanizin' country. An' there ain't hardly a man of ye dast *touch* a gun, let alone come up agin a *man* with one. Oh no! Got lil' ole honey-bunch to worry about, lil' ole wifey-pifey, all the young 'uns, make ye some easy money runnin' a store, doctorin', psalm-singing, fix ye a purty lawn so Scratchy kin cut it for ye, if ye can't get a Mex cheap enough. Oh, I— (*he searches helplessly, then half-says*)—hate—I could wipe every one of ye offen the face o' the earth, a-hidin' behind yore women's skirts, ever' respectable last one of ye! Come out an' fight! Come on! Come on! Dad *blast* ye!

(*He glares all around again. There is no kind of response at all. His attention shifts; his eyes focus on something off screen, he becomes purposeful.*)

Exterior "Weary Gentleman" Saloon—Barricaded—Day.
Dolly Shot Over SCRATCHY'*s Shoulder As He Advances on Door.*   CUT TO

Medium Close Shot—SCRATCHY.
(*He comes to door and hammers on it with gun butt.*)

SCRATCHY. Laura Lee. (*Pause.*) Laura Lee. (*Pause.*) (*Now he hammers with both revolvers.*) (*Continuing; yelling.*) Laura Lee! (*No answer.*) You can't fool me. I know you're there. Open up. I want a drink. (*No answer.*) All I want's a little drink.

(*Now he hammers harder than ever. Over sound of hammering, cut inside.*)

To Close Shots in This Order.

Close Shot—LAURA LEE.
(*Low behind bar, her rifle ready if need be, thumb on safety.*)

Close Shot—THREE LOCAL MEN.
(*On floor, watching the door fixedly.*)

Close Shot—The DRUMMER.
(*Behind the bar, plenty scared.*)

Close Shot—*Back to* SCRATCHY.
(*Finishing his hammering. He is rather tired. He glares at the door a moment, then:*)

SCRATCHY. All right then. All right.

(*He looks around him, sore. He sights a scrap of paper in the dirt, picks it up, and with a vicious and cruel thrust, nails it to the door with a knife. Then he turns his back contemptuously on the saloon, walks to the far side of the street and, spinning quickly and lithely, fires at the sheet of paper.*)

Insert.
  (*The bullet misses by half an inch.*)

SCRATCHY *As Before.*

  SCRATCHY. Well, I, Gah . . . gittin' old in yer old age, Scratchy.

  (*He takes careful aim and fires.*)

Insert.
  (*The bullet splits the haft of the knife; the blade clatters down; the paper follows, fluttering; a hole appears in the door.*)

Close Shot—Interior "Weary Gentleman."
  (JASPER *is on floor, between a chair and a spittoon. Bullet flicks wood from chair, ricochets with appropriate sounds, puncturing spittoon from which dark liquid oozes.* JASPER, *with slow horror, looks at it.*)

From SCRATCHY's *Viewpoint.*
  (*The paper finishes settling.*)

*Close Shot—*SCRATCHY.
  (*He is satisfied; he turns and starts walking grandly away. Suddenly he cries out:*)

  SCRATCHY. Hey! (*and stops and faces the saloon again.*) Hey, tell Jack Potter to come on out o' there like a man!

Reverse Angle—Over SCRATCHY.
  (*No answer.*)

  SCRATCHY (*continuing; yelling*). Jack! JACK POTTER?

Close Shot—Interior Saloon.

  LAURA LEE. Jack Potter ain't here, Scratchy, an' *you know it!* 'Cause if he was, he'd be out thar arter ye.

*Close Shot—*SCRATCHY.
  (*He hesitates, thinks it over.*)

  SCRATCHY (*uncertainly*). You wouldn't fool me, would ye, Laura Lee?
  LAURA LEE's VOICE (*off screen*). I never did, did I?
  SCRATCHY. Well don't never you try it. 'Caze I ain't the man'll stand fer it. (*Suddenly sore.*) That lyin' no-count Frank! I'll fix *him!* I'll cook *his* goose!

  (*He starts out fast up the street—there is the sound of a distant train whistle off screen. Over it.*)   DISSOLVE TO

Interior Parlor Car—Day.
(*Sound of dying wail of whistle off screen. Throughout scene, sound of slowing train.*)

Two Shot—POTTER *and* BRIDE.
(*Tension and emotion increase in their faces.*)

POTTER (*with desperate finality*).   Well—

(*She looks to him anxiously—he meets her eyes briefly and both smile, then lower their eyes pathetically. He gratefully thinks of* **something** *to do.*)

POTTER (*continuing*).   Better git down our trunk. (*With day-coach reflex, he stands up, reaching for the non-existent baggage rack, realizes his mistake, and pretends he is only tidying his clothes.*)

PORTER'S VOICE (*off screen, loud and glad*).   Don't you bother, mister—
CUT TO

Close Shot—PORTER.
(*Grinning.*)

PORTER (*continuing*).—I got it all ready an' waitin'!

Full Shot.
(*Some amused heads turn.*)

BRIDE *and* POTTER *As Before.*
(*He sits down abashed. Train sound is much slower. Their time is short.*)

POTTER (*smiling and wretched*).   Home at last.
BRIDE (*uneasy*).   Mm-hmm.

(*A silence.*)

Close Shot—POTTER.
(*In real desperation. Off screen sound of train bell.*)

POTTER (*sweating; rapidly*).   Say listen. You ain't gonna like me fer this an' I don't blame ye, but I just can't face 'em if we can help it, not right yet. What I want, I want to sorta *sneak* in, if we can git away with it, an' make home without nobody seein' us, an' then study what to do about 'em. I figure we got a chance if we kinda skin along the hind side o' Main Street. We got cover 'til about sixty foot from my door. Would ye do it?

Camera Pulls and Pans into Two Shot—POTTER *and* BRIDE.

BRIDE (*fervent*).   Oh gee, if only they don't ketch us!
POTTER (*incredulously grateful*).   You don't hate me fer it?
BRIDE (*with all her heart*).   Hate you?

(*They look at each other with entirely new love. The train is stopping. They get up fast and leave the shot.*)
CUT TO

Exterior Station Yellow Sky—Day.
   (*As train pulls to a stop, pan and dolly into close up shot of train steps. The* PORTER *descends first and leaves the shot.* POTTER, *with* BRIDE *behind and above him, peers anxiously forward along the station platform.*)

Long Shot—His Viewpoint.
   (*The empty platform.*)

Medium Shot—Panning.

   POTTER (*over shoulder*).   Come on girl. Hurry.

   (*He steps to platform, she follows unassisted. He grabs up both bags and, looking back to her, collides with the untipped, dismayed* PORTER.)

   POTTER.   Oh.
   (*He sets down bags. A fumbling rush for change. He hands out a coin.*)
   POTTER (*continuing*).   Much obliged.
   (*He picks up bags and starts walking, the* BRIDE *alongside.*)
   POTTER.   Let's git outa here.
   PORTER (*across him*).   Much obliged to *you*, sir.

   (POTTER *walks away so fast that she has to hustle to keep alongside. Both are eagle-eyed—he with anxiety, she with that and with simple interest.*)

Reverse Angle Shot.
   (*We glimpse an empty segment of street.*)

   BRIDE'S VOICE (*off screen*).   Gee, I don't see *nobody*.

   BRIDE *and* POTTER *As Before.*

   POTTER.   Just the hot time o' day, let's not risk it.

   (*They walk still faster around rear corner of station and out of sight.*)

                                                                CUT TO

Close Shot—Cell Window in POTTER'S *House.*
   (*It is empty; very, very slowly a little mirror rises to eye level above the sill—and jerks down fast.*)

Close Shot.
   (*Between the rear of two buildings toward the vacant Main Street.* POTTER'S *head comes close into shot, then the* BRIDE'S.)

   POTTER (*whispering*).   All right.

   (*They dart noiselessly across the gap.*)

   POTTER (*continuing*).   Good girl.

   (*They laugh, low and sheepish, and steal ahead. Camera pans with them left to right.*)

POTTER (*still whispering*).   Next corner, dear, an' I can show you our home.
BRIDE (*same*).   Oh, Jack. (*She stops. Her eyes are damp. He stops.*)
POTTER (*whispering*).   Sumpin' the matter?

Very Close Shot—BRIDE.

BRIDE.   The way you said that!
POTTER'S VOICE (*off screen*).   Said what?
BRIDE (*moved*).   Our home! (*She smiles very shyly. He is moved and says, in a most embarrassed voice:*)
POTTER.   Come on then, girl—Let's get there.

Another Angle.
(*They start walking fast and quiet; we pan with them, approaching the frame corner of a house.*)

POTTER (*continuing*).   Now right the next second, you can see it!

(*They continue, we lead them slightly as they circle the corner and come face to face with a close shot of* SCRATCHY. *He is leaning against the wall, just around the corner, reloading. Instantly he drops his revolver, whips the other from its holster, and aims it at* POTTER's *chest.*)

(*A deadly silence.*)

Reverse Angle—Over SCRATCHY *Onto* POTTER *and* BRIDE.
(*The Bride grabs* POTTER's *right arm. He drops both bags and exhibits the desperate reflex of a man whose fighting arm has never before been encumbered. He reaches for the gun that is not there. He sweeps her behind him.*)

*Closeup—*SCRATCHY.

Close Shot—The BRIDE.
(*Her face looks crumpled with terror; she gazes at the gun as at an apparitional snake.*)

*Close Shot—*POTTER.
(*He looks up from the gun into* SCRATCHY's *eyes.*)

Close Shot—The Revolver.

Camera Rises Slowly to Bring in SCRATCHY *in Extreme Closeup.*
(*His eyes are cold and mad; his face is almost solemn.*)

SCRATCHY (*almost reproachfully*).   Tried to sneak up on me. Tried to sneak up on me!

Two Shot of the Men—The BRIDE *Behind* POTTER.
(POTTER *makes a slight movement;* SCRATCHY *thrusts his revolver venomously forward; camera lunges forward correspondingly.*)

Close Shot of SCRATCHY.

SCRATCHY (*he smiles with a new and quiet ferocity*). No' don't ye do it, Jack Potter. Don't you move a finger towards a gun just yet. Don't you bat an eyelash. The time has come fer me to settle with you, so I aim to do it my own way, an' loaf along without no interferin'. So if ye don't want a gun bent on ye, or a third eye right now, just mind what I tell ye. (*He slowly raises his revolver to eye level, so that it is pointing a little upward, dead into the lens.*)

*Close Shot—*POTTER*—Past Gun.*
(*He is looking directly down the barrel. He is not at all a cowardly man but he is looking directly into the eye of death. Sweat breaks out on his face.*)

Extreme Close Shot.
(*Looking down the pistol barrel.*)

*Extreme Close Shot—*POTTER.
(*Then,*)

The BRIDE*'s face, saying "our home"* (*without sound*) *and smiling.*

Return to POTTER.
(*His eyes, a little dizzily out of focus, restore to normal.*)

POTTER (*quietly*). I ain't got a gun, Scratchy. Honest I ain't. You'll have to do all the shootin' yerself.

*Close Shot—*SCRATCHY*—Past* POTTER.
(*He goes livid and steps forward and lashes his weapon to and fro.*)

SCRATCHY. Don't you tell me you ain't got no gun on you, you whelp. Don't tell me no lie like that. There ain't a man in Texas ever seen you without no gun. Don't take me fer no kid. (*His eyes blaze with light; his throat works like a pump.*)

*Close Shot—*POTTER*—Past* SCRATCHY.

POTTER. I ain't takin' you fer no kid. I'm takin' you fer a damned fool. I tell you I ain't got a gun an' I ain't. If you're gonna shoot me up, ya better do it now; you'll never get a chance like this again.

*Pull Away Into Two Shot—*SCRATCHY *Calms a Little.*

SCRATCHY (*sneering*). If you ain't got a gun, why ain't you got a gun? Been to Sunday school?

JAMES AGEE

POTTER. You know where I been. I been to San Antone. An' I ain't got a gun because I just got married. An' if I'd thought there was goin' to be any galoots like you prowlin' around, when I brought my wife home, I'd a had a gun, an' don't you fergit it.

SCRATCHY (*says the word with total, uncomprehending vacancy*). Married?

POTTER. Yes, married. I'm married.

SCRATCHY (*a little more comprehension*). Married? You mean *you*? (*He backs off a pace, the arm and pistol drop.*) No. (*He studies* POTTER *cagily and shakes his head.*) (*Then literally for the first time, he sees the* BRIDE.)

SCRATCHY (*continuing*). What's that ye got there? Is this the lady?

POTTER. Yes, this is the lady.

(*A silence.*)

SCRATCHY. Well, I 'spose it's all off now.

POTTER. It's all off if you say so, Scratchy. You know I didn't make the trouble.

(*He picks up both valises.*)

New Shot—SCRATCHY—*Over* POTTER.

(*He studies* POTTER *up and down, slowly, incredulously. Then he looks at the ground.*)

SCRATCHY. Well, I 'low it's off, Jack. (*He shakes his head.*) Married!

(*He looks up with infinite reproach, sadness and solitude. He picks up his fallen revolver. He hefts and turns both revolvers in his hands, looking at them, then puts them with finality into their holsters. Then he again meets* POTTER'S *eyes.*)

SCRATCHY (*continuing; almost inaudibly*). G'bye, Jack.

Close Shot—POTTER.

(*He begins to comprehend; he is moved.*)

POTTER. 'Bye, Scratchy.

Reverse Angle—SCRATCHY.

(*He looks at* POTTER *a moment, then turns around and walks heavily away.*)

Two Shot—POTTER *and* BRIDE.

(*She emerges from behind him, whimpering, glancing from man to man, hugging his arm. His eyes on* SCRATCHY *off screen, he is hardly aware of her.*)

Insert.
> (*A lace curtain is plucked aside and* DEACON's WIFE *looks out.*)

Close Shot.
> (*A front door opens cautiously, squeakily; and cautiously, a man we don't know emerges.*) CUT TO

Interior "Weary Gentleman"—Day.
> (*The doors open;* JASPER, ED, *the* YOUNG MAN, *and finally* LAURA LEE, *followed by the* DRUMMER, *emerge onto the porch, looking up the street.*)

Long Shot—POTTER, BRIDE *and* SCRATCHY.
> (*Through this group as a few people timidly venture into the space between.*)

Reverse Shot—Group Shot—Favoring LAURA LEE *and* DRUMMER.

DRUMMER (*smug*). You were saying, ma'am—this is a *hard* country?

> (*She gives him a look and looks again toward* SCRATCHY *and company.*)

Long Shot—Past ED *and* DRUMMER.
> (*The* DEACON *trots out to* POTTER, *frantically effusive.*)

Pantomime introductions.

ED. Drummer: looks like ye got ye a new customer.

> (DRUMMER *registers certainty and anticipation.*)

DRUMMER (*to* LAURA LEE). And how about you, ma'am?

*Close Shot—*LAURA LEE.
> (*She turns on him, colder than ever.*)

LAURA LEE (*in measured tones*). I wouldn't wear them things if it killed me.

> (*Then she realizes she is dead. Her eyes fall, tragic and defiant, to a neutral angle. In background,* JASPER, *watching her, realizes a little of the meaning. He is sympathetic.*)

ED'S VOICE (*off screen*). Well look at that!

Long Shot—Past All of Them.
> (POTTER *is walking toward home with* DEACON *and the* BRIDE *as if between custodians. The* DEACON, *extra effusive, peels off and toddles for home.*)

*Close Moving Shot—*POTTER *and* BRIDE *Walking.*
> (*She glances back toward the filling, watchful street, which we see past them.* POTTER *is looking toward* SCRATCHY *off screen.*)

BRIDE. Sure looks like the cat's outa the bag.
POTTER. More like a wild-cat.

(*He stops. So do* BRIDE *and camera.*)

POTTER (*continuing*). You know? There's somethin' I always wanted to do. (*He sets down the suitcases and looks her up and down, business-like. She is willing but mystified. He picks her up.*)
BRIDE (*surprised and grateful*). Oh, Jack . . .

(*As he carries her forward out of the shot, he looks sadly again toward* SCRATCHY *off screen while she, loving and puzzled, looks at him.*)

Medium Shot—FRANK.
(*At the window.*)

FRANK. Howdy Marshal! Proud to know ye Miz Potter! Welcome home!

(*With the attempted velocity of a fast baseball, he slams down handsful of improved confetti. Pull camera down.* POTTER *and* BRIDE *walk to door amid showering confetti.*)

(*Continue pulling down as* POTTER *shoves door open with his shoe, enters,* BRIDE *in arms, and shoves door shut.*)

Dolly in—Still Pulling Down to.
(*Close shot showing that* SCRATCHY *has shot the lock to pieces.*)

(*End pull down—vertical to the doorstep as last confetti flutters down. Salient are the torn pieces of the murderous faces and weapons of early western fiction.*)

Very Long Shot—SCRATCHY.
(*Very small, he walks heavily away toward a solitary, still more distant hovel; empty earth and sky all around. A long hold; then camera pulls down to.*)

(*Close shot—the funnel-shaped tracks of his feet in heavy sand.*)

(*The end.*)

DISCUSSION

"The Bride Comes to Yellow Sky" is a comic version of the fall of the Old West. It is the story of a confrontation between Jack Potter, a man who is adjusting, albeit reluctantly, to civilization, and Scratchy Wilson, a man who refuses to become "civilized." Both Stephen Crane's short story and James Agee's screenplay are structured to show the comedy and pathos of a man who continues to play "gunfighter" in a world where the game is no longer popular, and the comedy of another man who is adjusting very awkwardly to the new game of "law and order" and to the absurdity of a cow town that is "easternizing" its identity and mores. But, where Crane, the short story writer, accomplishes his purpose through details expressed in language, Agee, the film writer, has to find visual details to express the theme and conflict of the story.

The short story's opening description suggests the encroachment of civilization: a train is crossing Texas, making the landscape seem to travel "eastward." In fact, Yellow Sky's excuse for existing is that it is a watering and refueling stop for trains, and thus a center for shipping cattle and grain east. Jack Potter, the ex-gunslinger turned sheriff, is himself a victim of civilization; he has just been married—tamed and domesticated. Comically ill at ease in his new role, he wavers between timidity and braggadocio. He is eager to accept his newly acquired civilized status and to appear sophisticated in the eyes of his new wife, but his awkwardness earns him the scorn of the porter and the amused snobbery of his fellow passengers. Everything overwhelms him, from the decor of the railroad car to the process of ordering a meal, but he is determined to swagger his way through.

The town Jack Potter serves, Yellow Sky, is equally gauche. It is a sleepy cow town with unpaved and largely unused sidewalks and a mongrel dog sleeping comfortably in the undisturbed dust of its main street. But civilization is coming to Yellow Sky; a traveling salesman from the east is in the saloon, swapping stories and plying his wares. The town itself has given up vigilante law and now leaves Jack Potter to cope with the occasional miscreants, such as Scratchy Wilson. The town is so far from being able to defend itself that when Scratchy goes on a shooting spree during Jack's absence, no one is capable of confronting him. The townspeople close their shutters to keep out some of the stray bullets, but the shutters furnish only an illusion of security. When Scratchy starts shooting, everyone in the saloon gets down on the floor; and the quiet Mexican "bandidos" sneak out through the back door.

Even Scratchy himself, the hold-out against civilization, is already in some ways its victim; his flannel shirt comes from the New York garment district. Not a cold-blooded killer, he shoots toward the dog in the street but deliberately misses him and is willing to substitute shooting at a piece of paper on the saloon door for a face-to-face encounter with another gunfighter. He wants to play the gunfight game with Jack Potter, but it is obviously a game from which both will emerge unharmed, an empty, ritualistic survival of a once-vital and mortal confrontation. When he finally encounters Potter and discovers that the sheriff is now married, Scratchy understands immediately that even the make-believe gunfights are over. He staggers out of town, leaving only transitory, funnel-shaped footprints in the dust of the street. He no longer has a place in Yellow Sky.

It is worth noting that all of these details are significant in Crane's story because they are filtered through some specific point of view. We know the railroad car overwhelms Jack because of the awe and reverence in the description; it is apparent to the reader that only a naive person would be so impressed with the florid decor. Only the narrator of the story, the teller who knows the meaning of the details he selects, can get us to see the isolation and absurdity of the mongrel dog, the ludicrousness of Scratchy's machine-made shirt, the pathos of Scratchy's footprints. The meaning of these details emerges for us largely because of the words through which they are expressed. What seem to be "objective" details are, in fact, very subjective renderings of an event. Even the ordering of the story, shifting from the train to Yellow Sky and back to the train, is a subjective order intended to help us feel the inevitable onrush of civilization to this small town.

James Agee, a script writer and film critic, was also a Pulitzer Prize-winning novelist. In adapting Crane's story, he understood that he had to find visual details that would convey the feelings and attitudes Crane had expressed through narrative language. Agee's problem was all the more difficult because, although Crane is very subjective in his handling of details, his story is essentially realistic. The camera can attempt this kind of subjectivity by taking the attitude of a single character, but such distortion always tells the viewer that he is looking at a situation unrealistically. To treat Crane's story unrealistically would be to rob it of much of its comedy; a great deal of the reader's amusement at the story rests in the capacity to see the discrepancy between what really exists and what the characters believe. Jack Potter's response to the railroad car is comic only because we realize the gap between this worship of the Victorian decor and its genuine ostentation and ugliness. We laugh at the drummer in the saloon because we see the difference between his image of Scratchy and Scratchy's essential harmlessness.

Agee sought to find visual details that would convey the meaning of the action without destroying the necessary sense of realism. His selection of details from the short story is imaginative and sensitive. He heightens the reaction of the train passengers to Jack and his bride. We can see, from this heightening, both the comedy of Jack and the sympathy he deserves. For the male barkeeper, Agee substitutes a saloon-girl, thus providing another sign of the encroachment of civilization. Further, the drummer in the Agee script sells exotic silk stockings, affectations of civilization whose appearance in Yellow Sky conveys the same point Crane makes in connection with Scratchy's shirt.

Providing an accurate picture of Scratchy may have been Agee's most difficult problem. The story's details about the dog would not be successful on film, for although Crane's prose style makes us understand that Scratchy is not a villain who shoots at helpless animals, those same details treated objectively on film might be shocking and brutal rather than comic. Thus, Agee had to find other visual details to show how out of date, ineffectual, and pathetic Scratchy actually is. He solves the problem by including the long sequence in which Scratchy is dressing in his room, looking at himself in a small cracked mirror. His effort to see himself and his satisfaction with his distorted image tell us how much Scratchy is wrapped up in his illusion of heroic status. Moreover, the camera keeps focusing on his jeans. Scratchy is an old man. His shrunken rear will not fill the jeans. They droop pathetically on this old man who thinks of himself as a hero. When Scratchy finally finishes dressing, we know, although Scratchy does not, that he is ludicrous and ineffectual, no match for either Jack Potter or the town. Agee has found a way, through original visual images, to communicate to us the complex attitudes of comedy and pathos that are so important in Crane's original story.

THEME AND DISCUSSION QUESTIONS

1. Both Crane's story and Agee's film seem to tell the story of an external conflict between Jack and Scratchy. What details in each version suggest that each of the two characters also has internal conflicts? Crane uses language to suggest some of these subjective conflicts, but Agee has to depend more on pictures. How does he use pictures to suggest the kind of subjective problems that Crane suggests through words?
2. Why does Agee include a saloon-girl in the film version? What attitudes and values does she symbolize? Are all of these attitudes in the original story, or has Agee added an interpretation of his own?
3. Does Agee treat Scratchy the same way Crane does? Explain. What specific details reveal the similarities and differences in the two artists' attitudes toward Scratchy?
4. The film script written by Agee frequently calls for close-ups, two-shots, and three-shots. Apparently, he wants a great deal of emphasis placed on faces in the film. Why? In what way might this change the meaning of the story?
5. Why does Agee include the long sentence in which Scratchy is alone before his mirror? How does this sequence reveal Agee's attitude toward Scratchy?
6. Toward the end of Agee's film, the townspeople come out and look at the bride. In having them do this, is Agee making a complimentary or uncomplimentary comment on the town?
7. The film *The Bride Comes to Yellow Sky* includes some important

changes in Agee's script. For instance, while the bride in the script is coarse and not very bright, the bride in the film is beautiful and refined. Is this change an improvement upon the script? If you can view the film, try to notice other important discrepancies between it and the script. Also try to explain the probable reasons for them and the resulting differences in the effects of the two versions.

8. How is *The Bride Comes to Yellow Sky* both similar to and different from other popular western stories and films?
9. The story concerns a time of great social change. How does social change affect each character's sense of his own identity?
10. How are Jack Potter and Scratchy Wilson like the heroes of such contemporary films as *Butch Cassidy and the Sundance Kid* and *M.A.S.H.?*
11. In both the story and the film script, how does the traveling salesman help to reveal and develop the main conflict?
12. If you were adapting Crane's story for a film, would you make any changes in Agee's script? If so, what and why?

Appendixes

Approaches to Writing about Drama and Film

Most college students eventually face the unwelcome prospect of writing themes about plays and films they have experienced and enjoyed. Usually, their problem with this task is not that they do not know how to write—most college freshmen have generally been taught a great deal about how to organize and document their ideas—but rather, that they do not know how to find specific subjects for their themes. Such students are not necessarily bereft of ideas, however; almost any student who has paid close attention to a given work and to the class discussion of it can cite details that were never mentioned in class or arrive at a defensible interpretation of a scene that differs from those expressed by his instructor and classmates. Rather than ideas, what the student who is uncertain about writing a theme usually needs is help in articulating his observations as aspects of a coherent subject, and assurance that his subject is a "proper" one for the composition.

The usual method of overcoming their uncertainties is to furnish students with a list of subjects that they may use either as actual bases for their themes or as models in developing their own subjects. But, for several reasons, this method can do great harm to the imagination and individuality of the student: first, it often imposes on students subjects they consider far removed from their own interests in drama and film; and second, it imposes on students approaches that may not be congenial with their own perspectives.

Thus, though we have furnished selected theme subjects for each play in this collection, it is our hope that student readers will use their own theme ideas instead of ours. Toward that end, this section of the volume will offer a list of questions students may ask themselves as an aid in developing themes based on their own observations and interpretations. These questions are, to some extent, an outgrowth of the analytical questions that follow the discussions of the major elements of drama—that is, many of the questions in this section are intended to help students summarize the conclusions they have reached using the analytical questions. Some of these upcoming questions are intended to help students relate their analyses of plays to their own experiences; and some are intended to help students discuss the broader social, psychological, and moral implications of the plays.

Many students will also find that writing themes that answer specific questions will help them deal with problems of organization. If they think of a theme as an answer to a question, they can quickly test their arguments and documentations by asking themselves the following five questions:

1) Does each major point of my composition help to answer my theme question?
2) Is the conclusion the only one I could reach?
3) Is my answer complete, or should it be amplified by facts I have not mentioned?
4) Have I illustrated each part of my answer with specific material from the play or film?
5) In order to prove my point, have I ignored some facts that seem to contradict my argument? If so, are those facts important, and should I qualify my argument to take them into account?

We hope that the following checklist of questions will help students to write about film and drama confidently and imaginatively.

QUESTIONS ABOUT THE CHARACTERS

1. Why does a certain character act as he does in a particular scene?
2. How does a character's behavior in a particular scene relate to his behavior in the rest of the play?
3. What is the purpose of a particular character in the play, in terms of either the theme or the conflict?
4. What does the character need to understand about himself before he can solve his problems? About others? About society?
5. Is a particular character realistic or flat? How well does his kind of character express the conflict of the play?
6. In a particular scene, how does a character reveal what seems to be conflicting aspects of himself?
7. Does a particular character seem capable of making the choices and performing the actions the playwright has assigned to him?

QUESTIONS ABOUT ACTION

1. What major goal unites the characters in the play?
2. What does a particular scene in the play show about the problems of achieving this major goal?

3. How does a particular scene show the playwright broadening or qualifying the meaning of the goal the characters are trying to achieve?
4. How does a scene that at first seems unnecessary actually move the total action of the play forward?
5. Are there some unnecessary scenes in the play? If so, why are they unnecessary?
6. Characters in a play often pretend to be something they are not. In the play being analyzed, how does the role-playing, or pretense, of a particular character help or hinder him in achieving his goal? How might it help him to resolve some of his internal conflicts?

QUESTIONS ABOUT PLOT

1. How does the initial scene suggest the conflicts that develop later in the play?
2. In which scenes of the play does a character make the final choices or commit the acts that determine whether he succeeds or fails?
3. Does the ending of the play seem to resolve the conflicts? Why or why not?
4. Does the play have a true ending, or does the action seem to be "open-ended," that is, capable of continuing past the closing dialogue or direction? What is it about the central conflict or the central characters that requires an "open" ending?
5. How does the plot itself suggest that the characters are struggling with major forces beyond the limited action on the stage?

QUESTIONS ABOUT DIALOGUE

1. What descriptive phrases or images are used recurrently by a particular character? What do these language patterns reveal about the character's internal conflicts?
2. In what ways is a speech in the play that seems merely philosophical actually an important expression of a character's main conflict?
3. In what ways is an apparently casual or playful conversation an expression of a major conflict?
4. In what ways do some speeches in the play seem to be mere "padding," unnecessary to the progress of the conflict?
5. How do the users of a particular word or phrase of dialogue change as the play progresses? How is the meaning of the term greater at the end of the play than at its beginning?
6. How do the words a character uses in moments of great crisis in the play reveal more about him than he intends to reveal or perhaps consciously knows?

QUESTIONS ABOUT THEME
 1. What seem to be the themes of the play?
 2. Which of the several possible themes best accommodates the whole play?
 3. How have other plays or movies approached similar themes?
 4. How might a different arrangement of events change the theme?
 5. How do the set, music, and other production features express the theme?
 6. How are the ideas presented by characters in the play or film distinct from the theme? How do they contribute to it?
 7. How do details of imagery, or the lack of it, in the speeches of specific characters help to express the theme?
 8. Does the theme have any special relevance to your own experience?

SOME LARGER CONSIDERATIONS
 1. How does the situation in which one of the major characters finds himself resemble a crisis common today?
 2. How is a particular character representative of contemporary society?
 3. How are the choices a particular character makes similar to choices you have had to make? Based on your own experience, do these choices seem valid or invalid?
 4. What problems do you have in discovering and expressing your identity that are like the problems faced by a particular character?
 5. Using examples from any two of the plays in this collection, explain how the society in which a person lives may, to some extent, control the way he sees himself.
 6. Using examples from any two of the plays in this collection, explain how a person may have great problems because he sees himself in a way that differs from the way society sees him.
 7. How does the language a major character uses indicate that he is a conformist, even when he believes he is not? How does it show that he is a nonconformist even when he or others believe he is a conformist?
 8. How do the words a character uses reveal that he thinks primarily in terms of how he can manipulate people? How do his manipulative uses of language compare with the ways in which politicians, advertising people, business executives, or educators use language today?
 9. Why are today's plays and films so concerned with role-playing?
 10. Why do so many contemporary movies find ways to remind their viewers that they are watching a movie?
 11. Comparing a recent play with one or more from another period, how would you say the idea of the self has changed?
 12. Comparing two plays from different periods, discuss the relationship between changes in the idea of the self and changes in the idea of freedom.

13. Comparing two or more plays from different periods, discuss the relationship between changes in the idea of the self and changes in the idea of drama.
14. Comparing two or more plays from different periods, discuss the ways in which changes in social customs and the structure of society are related to changes in the idea of the self.
15. Explain why it is probably more difficult for people in today's society to have any real sense of who they are than it was for the hero of either *Oedipus* or *Othello*.

Filmography

The following is a list of film versions of selections in this anthology. For information regarding rental of any of these films, contact the film's distributor.

OEDIPUS THE KING

Oedipus Rex (1957): starring Douglas Campbell; directed by Tyrone Guthrie. 88 minutes. Color. Distributor: McGraw-Hill Films, 1221 Ave. of the Americas, New York, New York 10020.

Oedipus Rex (1959): 90 minutes. Color. Distributor: Encyclopedia Britannica Films, 425 North Michigan Ave., Chicago, Ill. 60611.

Oedipus the King (1960): starring Christopher Plummer and Orson Welles; directed by Philip Saville. Adapted from the Paul Roche translation and filmed in a Greek theater. 97 minutes. Color. Distributor: Universal Pictures, 445 Park Ave., New York 10022.

OTHELLO

Othello (1955): Russian film directed by Sergei Youtkevich, for which he won the Cannes Film Festival prize for best direction. Dubbed in English. 108 minutes. Color. Distributor: Audio/Brandon Films, 1619 North Cherokee, Los Angeles, Calif. 90028.

Othello (1965): starring Laurence Olivier, Maggie Smith, and Frank Finlay; directed by Stuart Burg. 166 minutes. Color. Distributor: Warner Brothers Film Rental, 4000 Warner Blvd., Burbank, Calif. 91505.

A DOLL'S HOUSE

A Doll's House (1967): 61 minutes (in two parts). Color. Distributor: Encyclopedia Britannica Films, 425 North Michigan Ave., Chicago, Ill. 60611.

A Doll's House (1973): starring Claire Bloom, Anthony Hopkins, Ralph Richardson, and Denholm Elliot; directed by Patrick Garland. 95 minutes. Color. Distributor: Films Incorporated, 440 Park Ave. So., New York, New York 10016.

A Doll's House (1973): starring Jane Fonda, David Warner, Trevor Howard, and Delphine Seyrig; directed by Joseph Losey. 109 minutes. Color. Distributor: Learning Corporation of America, 1350 Ave. of the Americas, New York, New York 10019.

MISS JULIE

Miss Julie (1950): Swedish film starring Anita Bjork; directed by Alf Sjoberg. English subtitles. 90 minutes. Black and white. Distributor: Janus Films, 745 Fifth Ave., New York, New York 10022.

THE MADWOMAN OF CHAILLOT

The Madwoman of Chaillot (1969): starring Katherine Hepburn, Margaret Leighton, Edith Evans, Yul Brynner, Charles Boyer, Danny Kaye, Richard Chamberlain, and Donald Pleasance; directed by Bryan Forbes. 135 minutes. Color. Distributor: Audio/Brandon Films, 34 MacQuesten Pkwy. So., Mount Vernon, New York 10550.

DEATH OF A SALESMAN

Death of a Salesman (1951): starring Frederick March and Mildred Dunnock; directed by Laslow Benedict. 115 minutes. Black and white. Distributor: Columbia Pictures, 711 Fifth Ave., New York, New York 10022.

THE BRIDE COMES TO YELLOW SKY

Face to Face (1952): two-part film of Conrad's "The Secret Sharer," starring James Mason, and Agee's adaptation of Crane's "The Bride Comes to Yellow Sky," starring Robert Preston and Joanne Dru. 90 minutes. Black and white. Distributor: Willoughby-Peerless Film Library, 110 West 32 St., New York, New York 10001.